CUNEIFORM TEXTS FROM NIMRUD II

THE GOVERNOR'S PALACE ARCHIVE

By

J. N. POSTGATE

BRITISH SCHOOL OF ARCHAEOLOGY IN IRAQ
1973

ISBN 0 903472 01 5

PRINTED IN GREAT BRITAIN BY
STEPHEN AUSTIN AND SONS LIMITED, HERTFORD

PREFACE

This volume continues the work of publishing the epigraphical discoveries made at Nimrud by the British School of Archaeology in Iraq, under the direction of Professor Sir Max Mallowan and, latterly, of Professor David Oates. The editor was invited by Professor D. J. Wiseman in the autumn of 1968 to undertake the publication of legal and administrative texts from these excavations, and it is hoped that this volume will be the first of three which are planned to meet that objective. The tablets here edited are mainly divided between Baghdad and London, and since the preparation of the publication has taken a little over four years, it is only natural that I should find myself with the pleasant task of expressing my gratitude to many helpers over that period.

Without the co-operation of the staff of the museums where the tablets are stored, my work would have been impossible, but it is a pleasure to record that in all cases I was given assistance and welcomed in a manner which went far beyond the standard courtesies. In particular my thanks go to the Director-General of Antiquities in Iraq, Dr. Isa Salman, and to Dr. Fawzi Rashid, Director of the Iraq Museum, for permission to work in the Museum, as well as to all their staff who helped, especially Dr. Bahija Khalil Ismail and Dr. Abdul-Hadi al-Fouadi (in 1971). I am also indebted to the Director of the Mosul Museum, Sayyid Hazim Abdul-Hamid, for permission to collate inscriptions on display there. Most of my work in Iraq was made possible by the generosity of the School of Oriental and African Studies, University of London, which gave me study leave and financed my visit to Iraq in the academic year 1969–70, and also gave financial help in 1971 on the occasion of my second visit, which was chiefly supported by the Central Research Fund of the University of London. On behalf of the British School of Archaeology in Iraq I must also record our gratitude to the Master and Fellows of Trinity College, Cambridge, for their most generous grant towards the cost of printing this volume.

For permission to study the texts in the British Museum I am indebted to the Keeper of the Department of Western Asiatic Antiquities, and I am also most grateful to the members of that Department for all their willing help. Thanks are also due to Professor Sir Max Mallowan, for his kind permission to use the plan of the Governor's Palace; to Professor O. R. Gurney, for lending me excellent photographs of the "Practical Vocabulary of Assur"; to D. A. Kennedy and Professor W. G. Lambert, for their help with the neo-Babylonian and "literary" texts respectively; to J. V. Kinnier-Wilson, for generously putting at my disposal proofs of part of *The Nimrud Wine Lists* (Cuneiform Texts from Nimrud I), and answering my questions about his texts; to Professor A. J. Sachs, for his patient advice; for various services, to Messrs. C. B. F. Walker, J. D. Hawkins, and J. J. Orchard; and to Professor E. E. D. M. Oates and Miss B. Parker for their general advice and encouragement.

Special thanks must go to Professor Karlheinz Deller and Dr. Simo Parpola, who read through a draft of the text, and thus contributed many invaluable additions and corrections: I only regret that shortage of time prevents me from giving due weight to all their suggestions, some of which raise problems too considerable to be broached here, to which I hope they will return elsewhere. Finally, Professor D. J. Wiseman has earned my gratitude in a variety of ways: apart from entrusting me with the publication of the texts in the first place, he has put at my disposal his field notes and catalogues of the texts, together with many copies, which has much lightened my work and supplied me with invaluable information. He also collated for me the tablets assigned to the Australian Institute of Archaeology, and I must further acknowledge the time he has devoted to the editing of this volume.

For their excellent photographs, and for the care given to them, I am very grateful to Messrs. Paul Fox (in London) and Michael Haggerty (in Baghdad). My greatest single debt, however, is to my wife Carolyn, who has not only given much time and patience to the tedious preparation of the Plates, but, consciously and unconsciously, has eased the work in a multitude of ways.

J. N. P.

Baghdad
January 1972

CONTENTS

	PAGE
Preface	v
Abbreviations	ix
Note on Copies and Transcriptions	xi
Foreword, by Sir Max Mallowan	xiii
Introduction	1
Arrangement	1
Provenances	3
The Governor's Palace Archive	8
The palace personnel	8
The texts	16
Conclusions	23
Note on Aramaean names and currency	24
Transliterations and Translations	27
Appendix: Seal Impressions	247
Catalogue of Texts (by Excavation Number)	253
Indexes	
Index of Personal Names	265
Index of Place Names	275
Index of Professions	277
Index of Words	282
Plates	
Text copies	1–90
Photographs of texts and seals	91–98

ABBREVIATIONS

Bibliographical (for further details see *HKL* I)

ABL	R. F. Harper, Assyrian and Babylonian letters . . .
ADB	C. H. W. Johns, An Assyrian doomsday book . . .
ADD	C. H. W. Johns, Assyrian deeds and documents . . .
AfO	Archiv für Orientforschung (with *Beihefts*)
AHw.	W. von Soden, Akkadisches Handwörterbuch
AJSL	American journal of Semitic languages and literatures
AKA	E. A. W. Budge and L. W. King, Annals of the kings of Assyria, I
AOAT	Alter Orient und Altes Testament (*AOAT* 6 = S. Parpola, Neo-Assyrian Toponyms)
An.Or.	Analecta Orientalia (*An.Or.* 43 = J. A. Brinkman, A political history of Post-Kassite Babylonia)
An.St.	Anatolian Studies
APN	K. L. Tallqvist, Assyrian personal names
ARU	J. Kohler and A. Ungnad, Assyrische Rechtsurkunden
AS[2]	W. von Soden and W. Röllig, Das Akkadische Syllabar, 2. Auflage (= *An.Or.* 42)
Asarhaddon	R. Borger, Die Inschriften Asarhaddons . . . (= *AfO Beiheft* 9)
BASOR	Bulletin of the American Schools of Oriental Research
BBR	H. Zimmern, Beiträge zur Kenntnis der Babylonischen Religion
Billa	(Tablets from Tell Billa, published in *JCS* 7)
Bi.Or.	Bibliotheca Orientalis
BM	Siglum for tablets in British Museum
BSOAS	Bulletin of the School of Oriental and African Studies
BT	Siglum for tablets excavated at Balawat (published in *Iraq* 25)
CAD	The Assyrian Dictionary of the University of Chicago
DAB	R. C. Thompson, A dictionary of Assyrian botany
GAG	W. von Soden, Grundriss der akkadischen Grammatik (= *An.Or.* 33) (*GAG Erg.* = Ergänzungsheft = *An.Or.* 47)
HKL	R. Borger, Handbuch der Keilschriftliteratur I
Hwb.	F. Delitzsch, Assyrisches Handwörterbuch
ICC	A. H. Layard, Inscriptions in the cuneiform character
IM	Siglum for tablets in the Iraq Museum
JCS	Journal of cuneiform studies
KAJ	E. Ebeling, Keilschrifttexte aus Assur juristischen Inhalts
KAV	O. Schroeder, Keilschrifttexte aus Assur verschiedenen Inhalts
Landfahrzeuge	A. Salonen, Die Landfahrzeuge des alten Mesopotamien
LAS	S. Parpola, Letters from Assyrian scholars . . . (= *AOAT* 5/1)
Métal	H. Limet, Le travail du métal au pays de Sumer . . .
MSL	B. Landsberger *et al.*, Materialien zum sumerischen Lexikon
ND	Siglum for tablets excavated at Nimrud, 1949–63
NL	Nimrud Letter (H. W. F. Saggs, *Iraq* 17 *et seq.*)
N&R	M.E.L. Mallowan, Nimrud and its Remains
OLZ	Orientalistische Literaturzeitung
OrNS	Orientalia Nova Series
Provinzeinteilung	E. O. Forrer, Die Provinzeinteilung des assyrischen Reiches
PVA	The practical vocabulary of Assur (B. Landsberger and O. R. Gurney, *AfO* 18 (1957–8), 328 ff. (quoted by line number))
R	H. C. Rawlinson *et al.*, The cuneiform inscriptions of Western Asia, I–V
RCAE	L. Waterman, Royal correspondence of the Assyrian Empire

RGD	J. N. Postgate, Neo-assyrian royal grants and decrees (Studia Pohl, Series Maior I)
RLA	E. Ebeling *et al.*, Reallexikon der Assyriologie
ŠL	A. Deimel, Šumerisches Lexikon, II (quoted by sign number)
STT	O. R. Gurney *et al.*, The Sultantepe Tablets I and II
SVAT	E. Ebeling, Stiftungen und Vorschriften für assyrische Tempel
Tell Halaf	(Tablets from Tell Halaf, published in *AfO Beiheft* 6 = J. Friedrich *et al.*, Die Inschriften vom Tell Halaf)
TR	Siglum for tablets excavated at Tell al-Rimaḥ
VAT	Siglum for tablets in the Berlin Museum
WZKM	Wiener Zeitschrift für die Kunde des Morgenlandes
ZA	Zeitschrift für Assyriologie . . .

Non-bibliographical (normal English abbreviations not given but note the following)

App.	Appendix
B.E.	Bottom Edge
br.	brother
Col.	Column
coll.	collated
d.	daughter
DN	divine name
f.	father
FPN	female personal name
Gen.	genitive
GN	geographical name
gov.	governor
h.	homer
inscr.	inscribed/inscription
L.E.	Left Edge
lit.	literally
m.	mother; mina
mA	middle Assyrian (dialect/period)
nA	neo-Assyrian (dialect/period)
No.	Number of text in this edition
obv.	obverse
ow.	owner
pl.	plate; plural
PN	personal name
r.	= rev.
rev.	reverse
s.	son; sūtu
scr.	scribe
s.i.	seal inscription
sing.	singular
sl.	slave
sup.ras.	over erasure
t.	talent
T.E.	Top Edge
uninscr.	uninscribed
unn.	unnumbered
w.	witness
wr.	written

NOTE ON COPIES AND TRANSCRIPTIONS

Copies

These were made at different times and under different conditions and vary accordingly. They are not to any one scale, nor are individual tablets drawn to scale, since one dimension or the other may be exaggerated. On the other hand it has been my concern to reproduce the ductus and the spacing of the signs as accurately as possible without actual measurement. All copies are my own except for Plates 18 and 90, which I owe to the kindness of Professor D. J. Wiseman.

Transcription

For the problems of transcribing neo-Assyrian texts in the present state of our knowledge, see S. Parpola, *LAS*, pp. xv–xvii, and for his conventions in transcription, ibid., p. xx. In general I have used the same conventions, with these exceptions: I have not distinguished the two different LÚ and KÁM signs, but I have used the transcription *ṭiḫi** for the so-called SUḪUR; an exclamation mark (!) means that my transcription emends the sign on tablet (or copy); space in broken passages is indicated with one or more *x* signs, each such *x* standing for " space for a sign "; round brackets imply " optional ", e.g. [(*x x*) *x x*] = " space for two to four signs ", and it must be stressed that all such estimates are only of the roughest. Other deviations are unimportant.

At the head of each text are shown, on the right, the ND (excavation) number, the museum number or place of storage, and, where possible, the date of the text; on the left are given the dimensions and provenance. For further details on the provenance and museum numbers the reader is referred to the Catalogue of Texts (pp. 253 ff.). The dimensions, given in centimetres, are, in order, the tablet's width (i.e. maximum dimension parallel to the line of writing), maximum height, and maximum thickness (this last being omitted occasionally where not measured). Dimensions enclosed in round brackets, e.g. (9·8), indicate that the tablet is broken and the measurement in question consequently incomplete.

FOREWORD

By Sir Max Mallowan

The exhaustive publication of the Archive from the Governor's Palace brings back memories of the first season's excavations under the auspices of the British School of Archaeology in Iraq at Nimrud, Assyrian Kalḫu. Our small expedition, the first of a long series was working under difficulties in an exceptionally rainy season and we were fortunate to discover in a sector of the mound hardly touched by Layard and his successors an administrative building, the ancient seat of the Governors of the city throughout the eighth century B.C. This "Palace", as it may justly be termed, was built on the vast and grandiose scale which the rulers of Assyria deemed appropriate to their authority. What we recovered was the nucleus of a much larger complex; it measured no less than 50×50 metres, embracing an area of $2\frac{1}{2}$ hectares or a fraction over 6 acres of ground. We may attribute the main structure to the reign of Adad-nērārī III (810–782 B.C.) who made use of a large quantity of bricks of an ancestor (Shalmaneser III), apparently left over from what was required for the ziggurat. These pavement bricks were beautifully laid and firmly embedded in bitumen and lent a cachet to the building which otherwise was constructed mostly of mud-brick, with burnt-brick skins for some of the walls.

The Palace was gaily decorated with mural paintings originally described by me as frescoes, although as we now know from expert advice the paint was not applied *à frais* as true fresco should be. These paintings consisted of simple geometric designs [1] in black, red, white and a brilliant cobalt blue—the latter colour was a vivid feature of the great halls at the northern end of the building where doubtless the governor himself sat in state, in convenient proximity to various record offices concerned with his administration. Separated from these offices by a vast courtyard there was at the opposite, southern end of the building, another great hall or reception room with access to a lustral chamber or ritual bathroom which contained on the floor two ablution slabs against opposite walls. The adjoining chamber B at the SW angle yielded a beautifully engraved cylinder seal of pale mauve translucent chalcedony illustrating three shaggy heroes holding the heavens aloft.[2] So fine a gem must have belonged to the governor himself, possibly therefore to the first of a long line, Bēl-tarṣi-iluma, who was appointed by Adad-nērārī and dedicated statues to the god Nabu for the life of the young king and his mother Sammuramat.[3] We know that this high officer was a court eunuch, and the statues which he dedicated to the god illustrate a rotund figure with fleshy, flabby cheeks and hands, and a beard which we may guess concealed a heavy jowl. Perhaps it was not exaggerated to see this figure as a mirror of the highly placed royal eunuchs who wielded great power at the time. These relics of the governor help us in a personal vision of what went on in this great building, and as it were stand at the head of a wonderful archive of more than 200 tablets or rather fragments of tablets discovered within its precincts. Although these inscribed

[1] Illustrated in *Iraq* 12 (1950), Pl. XXX, where the preliminary account of these excavations was published. The design consisted of framed concentric arches and rosettes approximately at eye level.

[2] Mallowan, *N & R, I*, Pl. 12, p. 48. The seal could have been made at any time between *c.* 800 and 750 B.C.

[3] S. Smith, *Assyrian Sculptures in the British Museum from Shalmaneser III to Sennacherib* (1938), Pls. III, IV.

clay fragments are but a pitiful remnant of a once vast record, they enable us to reconstruct a picture crowded with the everyday life in ancient Assyria; and they inform us of the problems which confronted the hierarchy responsible for its fortunes. Mr. Postgate, through his patient and scholarly examination of the whole collection, has re-animated for us the architectural remains and invested them with the breath of life.

Thus twenty-four years after the discovery we have before us as full a presentation of the evidence as its fragmentation allows. In this achievement we should not forget the pioneer work of D. J. Wiseman, now professor, who was in the field from 1950, 1951, and again in 1953. His work, often done under pressure, and in difficult conditions in the field was frequently provisional, but in issuing the first catalogue with exemplary promptness he not only smoothed the path for the archaeologists who pressed and sometimes overtaxed him for information, but he was equally helpful to the epigraphists who were presented with a manual of orderly information which was at their disposal when they came to penetrate the records more thoroughly. This method of presenting the evidence has inevitably meant that some of our first reflections on these discoveries need modification [4]; but in all archaeological research the process of attaining a firm position is bound to be long drawn. In these early labours J. V. Kinnier Wilson also deserves our thanks for his share.[5]

The result of all these labours has been to give us an animated picture of the Governor's Palace as a hive of human activity where thousands of busy persons in the course of the eighth century played their parts in order to clear up their business affairs.

The history of the building revealed through the archaeological sequences has been adequately summarized by Mr. Postgate and it is clear that the secretariat was most active from the last decade of the ninth century for about one hundred years thereafter. Moreover since the excavation of the building at the very outset of our campaigns, it became clear that the sequences revealed on this site were similar to those detected in other parts of the acropolis. As in the Burnt Palace and Ezida the final destructions occurred in about 614 and 612 B.C. and thereafter there was evidence of squatters' occupation. The great courtyard eventually became a burial ground, which apparently ceased to be used shortly before the beginning of the Parthian occupation of Mesopotamia in about 140 B.C. In the seventh century a part of the building may already have been derelict, for example in chamber E at the southern end of the building nineteen successive layers of mud, beaten down by the tramp of human feet, were interpreted as the twice yearly accumulation from the spring and autumn rains. This evidence may imply a lapse of about ten years during which the great hall remained open to the sky. A reconstruction occurred thereafter and the original floor level was raised by about a metre.[6] This evidence accords with observations concerning the Burnt Palace and Ezida at the end of the seventh century.[7] Some chambers were, however, still in use, and the discovery in room S of a mud-brick pedestal against the NW corner of the room was striking proof that the administration was still active in the late seventh century. Here in the NW corner of the room, on top of the

[4] Thus Mallowan, *N & R, I*, 47, was not justified in the statement that the tablet ND 462 concerned Cilicia, although the Assyrians were in touch with that country at the time. See now Postgate, No. 195, who reads Da'unāni and rightly surmises that this refers to an unknown place probably situated within the province of Kalḫu.

[5] See now also *Cuneiform Texts from Nimrud I, The Nimrud Wine Lists* (1972).

[6] *Iraq* 12 (1950), 167.

[7] Mallowan, *N & R, I*, 287, under phase H, level 3.

pedestal, some fine palace-ware vases had been stacked. We call them the governor's dinner service, and some of the vessels were of the same fine quality as another set discovered in the administrative wing of the North-west Palace. I had the impression that these vases were deposited on the table either in baskets or in bales of straw, of which a few traces remained.[8]

There is no need to dilate on the nature of the activities with which the officers housed in this building were concerned for Mr. Postgate has described them with exemplary clarity, but we may pause to make a few comments on this Comédie humaine in which the Assyrians present themselves as feeling and acting much as we would under the impact of the problems of daily life. A concern with basic justice, and an understanding of the balance of power in human affairs, the attempts to stem the insolence of office, to redress wrongs and to buttress the authority of an orderly administration aıe to theiı credit. These mundane matters in no way reflect the cruel side of the Assyrian *imperium* manifest in the deliberate propaganda of their imperial inscriptions which have tended, no doubt unfairly, to suggest that the Assyrians were more brutal than their neighbours. We know that they were also endowed with the quality of mercy, for they were obviously an intelligent people with a humane as well as a cruel streak.

However that may be their administrative, business and legal texts reveal in detail both the competence and the conscientiousness of the Assyrian civil service in dealing with the inevitable complexities which arose out of a host of avocations. Land and taxation, problems involving sales and exchanges of estates, sales of slaves, troop movements, the distribution of rations, inventories of state property including elaborate furniture, buckets, pails, braziers and the like are of absorbing interest and as the evidence accrues will broaden our understanding of the sociology and economy of ancient Assyria. The basic evidence is now beginning to be available for an estimate of crop yields per acre and the return of sustenance in varying conditions to the Assyrian farmer.

It is evident that the governor's office played an important part as an agricultural credit bank in a largely illiterate society to which the currency of coinage was as yet unknown: here copper and silver as well perhaps as the highly prized tin and gold served as the principal standards of value. Here the governor acted as intermediary between debtor and creditor and kept the economy solvent by discharging debts through loans.

In the background we visualize through these texts the activities of cereal farmers and stockbreeders, wine growers, smiths, carpenters, weavers, a host of persons engaged in the textile trade, clothiers, leather workers, chariot makers and the like. A large proportion of Arameans, a most important element in Assyrian society, and doubtless some Hurrians were involved. It is interesting that one tablet mentions the import of the valuable hardwood *Dalbergia sissoo* which was imported from Makkan in Iran and became highly prized by the later Achaemenians for the building of their palaces: the stocking of the royal gardens with fruit trees and saplings also received due attention. It is interesting that one tablet, No. 207, refers to the cultivation of *ŠE kurangu* which was interpreted by the late R. Campbell Thompson as rice because of its apparent correspondence with the Iranian name for this plant. The Assyrians, who were able irrigators, may well have

[8] Mr. Postgate, on reading the plan, rightly deduced that this pedestal stood at the NW corner of room S. There is a misprint in *N & R II*, 51, where NE should read NW. See also thereunder for further archaeological information and *op. cit.*, Pls. 13–17, for illustrations of the pottery. Tablets might once have been stored in boxes in this chamber, but not as has been suggested under the pedestal.

cultivated it, but as yet, so far as I know, rice has never been identified as a plant on any excavation in Assyria.

The administration of the law and its execution is also a subject of paramount interest. We note that eleven tribesmen, mostly Arameans in the district of Assur, were caught red-handed stealing seventy sheep, No. 119.

There is also much other information of absorbing interest to be extracted from a close study of these texts. We may note in the contracts the curious, and doubtless archaic and obsolete, penalty clauses which involve occasionally the reduction of man to the animal whereby he was to be compelled in default of his obligations or repudiation of them to eat cress (?) all the way from the city gate of Kalḫu to the inner gate of Assur. Other penalties are even more drastic and remind us that within living memory, in the country no contract was considered respectable unless it contained some clauses impossible of fulfilment. Another interesting custom which still survives is the inclusion in the sale of house property of the specific mention of the wooden beams and the door. In our early negotiations for the purchase of a house from a watchman at Nimrud we suffered from our ignorance of the fact that specific mention had to be made of these fittings, even in a verbal contract, and the owner, within his rights, carted them away.

Altercations and complaints were liable to arise between one governor and another. Assur complains that tribesmen subject to Kalḫu are extensively burning the steppe in his district. A delegate of the governor of Kalḫu is unable to obtain from the *Turtānu* the quota of prisoners after the Assyrian victory at Rapīqu. There is also an amusing passage in which the insolent household staff of the *Turtānu*, a cook, a victualler and a baker refuse the transport which, no doubt at much trouble, has been provided for them. Behind all these texts lies as we have said a basic concept of justice well exemplified by a request, No. 196, sent to the governor of Kalḫu that he should pay taxes on property owned by him in Arzuḫina, remote from his own province. Every official kept a watchful eye on domains subject to his authority and in this way a check was kept by one official on another against rapacity, nepotism and the abuse of power. There is also a human touch on the advent of a delegation from Ialuna, one suspects of wine growers, who sought the privilege of an interview with the governor of Kalḫu who doubtless had special interests in that domain, as we know from his titles.

It is thus apparent that the office of an Assyrian governor was no sinecure; the threat of famine was never far off; there were plagues of locusts that infested the land from the Upper Zab, Kasappa (modern Tell Keshef), and far afield; there were runaway harvesters who refused to cultivate the land.

In this same volume Mr. Postgate has for good measure systematically examined other texts or fragments of texts from the Burnt Palace and from the briefly conducted excavations in two other administrative buildings known as A.50 and B.50 north of the Governor's Palace also in the eastern sector of the citadel.[9] Here we find treatment of such varied subjects as marriage dowries, issues of wool, and lists of flocks. In the Throne Room of the Burnt Palace we find a note on an official of King Sargon seeking to dissipate malicious rumours concerning his person, and in the same reign we learn of anxiety about the growing aggression of the Cimmerians, No. 243, in the north.

A few texts from the domestic wing of the North-west Palace leave us in no doubt that

[9] Position marked as 1950 building in Map Folder No. 1 of *Nimrud and its Remains*.

in Sargon's reign, though that burning was no longer the residence of the king, it still housed wealthy members of the royal house who owned flocks, and herds of camels as well as extensive and valuable property. One of the rooms, F, contained an incantation and ritual text and a duplicate of the Marduk ordeal composition.

Finally Mr. Postgate has rewarded us by a re-examination of the famous stele of Aššur-naṣir-pal II, the *editio princeps* of which was achieved by D. J. Wiseman based on his field copy and published in little more than a year of its discovery,[10] a remarkable feat comparable with that of the late Père Scheil who gave the world the first edition of the " Code " of Hammurabi shortly after its discovery at Susa. Inevitably some important emendations and improvements to these texts have followed. In the case of the Aššur-naṣir-pal II stele Mr. Postgate has been able to apply himself to the monument, working under good conditions in the Mosul Museum where it now stands and, in addition to several fresh observations, No. 266, has been able to decipher a number of lines at the bottom of the obverse of the stele hitherto barely legible, including a delectable passage which wafts us back to the scent of fruit and flowers in the garden of Aššur-naṣir-pal.

[10] Discovery in April 1951, first published by D. J. Wiseman in *Iraq* 14 (1952), 24 f.

INTRODUCTION

The main purpose of this publication is to make available in its entirety the archive discovered at Nimrud in the building referred to as the " Governor's Palace ", during the years 1949 to 1951.[1] However, while preparing this work it seemed sensible to study other texts of the same type found during those seasons, and also to copy or at least collate texts of other genres since they were available. In the proposed scheme for the edition of the texts from Nimrud these various inscriptions go best with the others from their seasons, and hence this volume contains not only the Governor's Palace archive, but also all the texts found in the Burnt Palace, and all other tablets of an administrative or legal nature from the seasons 1949–51; in addition various " literary " texts from those years are here published or re-edited, and I have included one or two of the historical inscriptions where this seemed profitable.[2] In general, I have not collated or edited the brick inscriptions, but a list of excavation numbers provides a complete catalogue of the epigraphical finds belonging to the first three seasons at Nimrud, gives the present location of the objects, and will enable the reader to identify texts published previously under their ND numbers. The remainder of the introduction describes the arrangement of the texts and their archaeological provenances, and then gives a more detailed description of the Governor's Palace archive.

Arrangement

In accordance with the main aim of the edition, which is to present the texts as an archive, they are grouped under their broad provenances, viz.

Governor's Palace	Nos. 1–217
A 49, A 50, B 50	Nos. 218–230
Burnt Palace	Nos. 231–246
North-west Palace	Nos. 247–272

Within these groups, the texts are arranged by type: legal (broadly in the order sales—sales or loans—loans—uncertain), administrative, letters, and uncertain type, with " literary " at the end. So as to compensate for the resulting separation of texts of the same kind from one another, I give here a classification of the texts by type, in which texts not from the Governor's Palace are indicated by italics.

[1] When in 1967 Professor D. J. Wiseman and Miss B. Parker suggested to me that I should undertake the publication of legal and administrative texts from the Nimrud excavations I was based in London, and it seemed sensible to begin work on the texts available to me there, which happened to be those from the first three seasons. These texts had been catalogued, and some of them published, by Professor D. J. Wiseman (in *Iraq*, volumes 12 to 14), in advance of a final publication. Professor Wiseman also made available to me many copies of the texts from the second season of excavations which had not been published in *Iraq* 13, and which he had been prevented from preparing for final publication by the pressure of more remarkable epigraphical finds from later seasons.

[2] The edition includes many small fragments which may be thought not worth publication, but the copying of such fragments does at least save others the fruitless task of hunting them down in the future, and it has occasionally been possible to join some, and further such joins are obviously conceivable, especially where the fragments are in different museums. Moreover, while small pieces are of course useless out of context, as part of an archive they may at least have statistical interest.

LEGAL

Marriage: Nos. 1; *247*; cf. also No. *219*
Sales: of daughter: Nos. 4; 5; 11; 13(?); *219*
of single slave: Nos. 2; 3 (brother); 7; 8; 10; *220*(?); cf. also No. 67
of several persons: Nos. 9; 12; *248*

of land: Nos. 17; 18(?); 20; 23 (+49); 24; 25; 26; 27; 31; 32; 33; 34; 35; 36(?); 42(?); 43; 46(?); 47; 48; 50; 74(?); cf. also Nos. 69; 70; 72
of land with orchard and/or house, threshing-floor, etc.: Nos. 15; 16(?); 21; 30; 37
of orchard: No. 19
of *tabriu*: No. 45
of ground (*qaqqerē*): Nos. 29; 38; 41; 44
of house: Nos. 14; 22 (*bēt qāti*); 28; 39; 40; cf. No. 177
of object unknown: Nos. 51–63
Sales with more than one seller: Nos. 15; 16; 30; 32; 35; [36(?)]; 45; 46; 47
Sales with more than one buyer: No. 22
Exchange (of land): Nos. 64; 65
(of metals ?): No. 100
Grant (*of land*) (?): No. 66
Gift of slave (?): No. 67
Herding contract (?): No. 68
Receipts: Nos. 98 (wages); 99; cf. also No. 73
(for payment of debt by third party) Nos. 90; 91; 93; 94(?); 97(?); cf. also Nos. 69; 70
(for payment of fine by third party) Nos. 92; 95(?); 96; cf. also No. 75
Loans: of bronze: No. 101(?)
of silver: Nos. 106; 107
of corn: No. 105 (with harvesters); cf. No. 110
item uncertain: No. 102; cf. also No. 76 (+124)
Debt-notes: Nos. 103 (men + bronze); 104 (copper; purchase price); 109 (bronze; purchase price); 108 (metals; work contract ?)
Type uncertain: Nos. 71–5; 76 (+124); 77; cf. also Nos. 158; 176–9
(witnesses): Nos. 78–89
(dates): Nos. 174; 175

ADMINISTRATIVE

Memoranda: Nos. 111; 112
Lists and notes:
people: Nos. 113–24; *233–9*
animals: Nos. 125–34; *232*; *250*; *256*; *257*
corn + other comestibles: Nos. 135–41; *251*
metals: Nos. 142–51; *225*; *255*
textiles: Nos. 152; 153; *223*; *224*; *252–4*
various items ("census"): 154; 155; *222*

land: Nos. 156; 157(?)
uncertain: Nos. 158–69; *218*; *226–8*; *257–62*

Sealings ("*dockets*"): Nos. 132; 133; 170–3; *233–9*; *256–63*
Clay strips with seal impressions: Nos. *229*; *264*
Type uncertain (perhaps mainly legal): Nos. 176–9

LETTERS

Nos. 180–211: *230*; *240–5*; cf. also Nos. 166; 167

OTHER GENRES

Nos. 212; 213; 214 (prayer); 215 (ritual); 216 (lexical ?); 217 (historical); *231*; *246* (ritual); *266–7* (historical); *268–9* (literary); *270* (incantation + ritual); *271–2* (lexical)

* * *

Provenances

While the provenance of each text is given briefly with the transliteration, and further details, where known, are included with the Catalogue of Texts (pp. 253 ff.), it may be helpful to give here a short description of the find-spots of the tablets edited in the volume, and in particular of those from the Governor's Palace, making use of the information contained in the preliminary reports in Iraq, and in M. E. L. Mallowan, Nimrud and its Remains (hereafter abbreviated *N&R*). It is of course impossible for one who was not present at the excavation to present an account of the various provenances comparable to that of the excavator, but the particular circumstances of the archive from the Governor's Palace justify the inclusion here of a discussion of the light thrown on the building by the archive, and vice versa.

The Governor's Palace [3]

This large and obviously important building was excavated during the first two seasons at Nimrud, 1949 and 1950, and it is described in *N&R, I*, 38–51, as well as in the preliminary reports in *Iraq*, in particular *Iraq* 12 (1950), 163 ff. The building (marked on the site plan, *Iraq* 12 (1950), Pl. XXVI, as the "1949 building"), lies towards the centre of the acropolis mound, just north of a deep ravine marking the line of an Assyrian street which ran between the Governor's Palace and the Nabû temple and Burnt Palace to its south.

The palace was arranged on the usual plan round a central courtyard, flanked to the

[3] This designation, coined by the excavator, may profitably be adopted. Although there is no absolute proof that the building housed the governor's administration, the archives from it make it practically certain. The term "palace" is justified by the building's architectural character, although it is clear that the Assyrians themselves referred to it as the governor's "house" (cf. No. 3, 4).

north and south by long " audience rooms ", and the great size of these rooms, together with the frescoes which still survived on many of the walls, would have been sufficient to identify the building as one of some importance, even without the archives discovered in it. Almost all the tablets were in fact found in three rooms only on the north side of the building, Rooms K, M, and S. With these I shall deal first, and then list more briefly the other find-spots. The location of the rooms may be determined by reference to the plan of the Governor's Palace reproduced here by the kind permission of Professor Sir Max Mallowan.

Room K: This is a relatively small room (*c.* 5·00 × 6·00 m.),[4] situated in the north-west corner of the palace, against the west wall. It originally had two doors, but the subsequent blocking of that in the north wall [5] left the room accessible only from Room M to the east, through a doorway with a raised stone threshold (visible in the photograph published in *Iraq* 12 (1950), Pl. XXIX.1, and again in *N&R, I*, p. 42, fig. 9; note the stone door socket as well). Room K was consequently well situated to serve as a storage room, and it may indeed have been used to house the archive which was mostly found within its walls. These tablets, according to the excavator's description, began to appear some 2·40 m. below the ground surface, under a thin line of black ash. " They were in no sort of order, but were lying in confusion, some flat, some upright, some aslant in soft thrown debris, part clay, part ash, part broken mud-brick; most of them lay in the southern half of the room through a depth of 80 centimetres (about 2 ft.). A few of them were actually wedged between the partly torn up burnt-brick pavement of Shalmaneser III. Although there were, in places, signs of a trodden mud floor a foot above the level of the original one, this can only have been short-lived, and I suspect that it represented a period of abandonment when mud was falling in from the tops of the ruined walls." [6]

The exact dating of the strata poses problems: the floor of Room K was of burnt bricks of Shalmaneser III, but although these bricks were used in other rooms as well, the inscriptions on them tell us that they were intended originally for the ziqqurat, and the excavator is no doubt right to question their validity as evidence that the building belongs to that king. In the absence of other clear evidence, the archives serve as a guide, and although it cannot of course be shown that the tablets were not transferred to the Governor's Palace at a later date, the considerable number of texts dating to the reign of Adad-nirari III does make it probable that the palace was already being used by the governors then; whether it was in fact erected in the early part of Adad-nirari's reign (as initially assumed by M. E. L. Mallowan),[7] or rather already in the time of Shalmaneser III, seems to me uncertain, and the same uncertainty is voiced by the excavator in his cautious statement in *N&R, I*, p. 50.

The date of the later phases of occupation in Room K is also subject to some uncertainties. The latest tablet among those from the room is dated to the end of 710 B.C. (No. 146), and the 80 cm. of deposit (see quote above) must clearly represent the passing of 100 years or more from the erection of the building; but whether it was a single deposit of rubbish,

[4] So in *N&R, I*, 42; from the plan it seems nearer 5·00 × 4·00 m.

[5] This doorway is not marked on the plan, and the date of the blocking is not entirely certain (see below, p. 5, n. 10).

[6] *N&R, I*, 43.

[7] e.g. *Iraq* 12 (1950), 166; note that the archive now appears to include a text dated to 830 B.C.

including tablets, intended to raise the level of the floor, or a more gradual accumulation in two or more stages, seems less clear.[8] At some point, probably not long after 710 B.C., the room was re-used, and remained in use thereafter probably until the sack of the city in 612 B.C.[9] After its abandonment the northern end of the palace was used to accommodate burials, including one in Room K which was dug parallel to the east wall and sunk down to the level of the original floor, dislodging the bricks (cf. the photograph, *N&R, I*, p. 43, fig. 10).[10] During the seventh century no documents were deposited in the Governor's Palace as far as we know, and other parts of the building were already deserted,[11] suggesting that it may no longer have served as the governor's residence. It seems quite likely that after Sargon's transference of the capital to Dūr-šarrukēn, the governor of Kalhu moved across to the North-west Palace or to another of the more recent buildings left free by the removal of the royal court.[12]

In conclusion we may say that Room K may well have been the archive room for at least one department of the Governor's Palace, and that the tablets found there and in Room M (see below) were actually stored there before the disuse and/or reconstruction of the room (some time after 710 B.C.), in the course of which the tablets we have were discarded and allowed to form part of the fill below the new floor level.

Room M: This is one of the great "audience chambers", with Room K to its west, two doorways through its south wall into the central courtyard (see photograph, *Iraq* 12 (1950), Pl. XXIX.2 = *N&R, I*, p. 44, fig. 11, looking south-east), and to its east Room S. Along the north side there was evidently a parallel room of equal size, but the access between the two is not clearly indicated on the plan.

The tablets from Room M are not attributed any precise provenance, but evidently the level in which they were found was identical with that in Room K where the major part

[8] In favour of the assumption of a single-period deposit is the fact that the tablets were found throughout a depth of *c.* 80 cm., which corresponds with the difference of level between the original brick floor and the "post-710" floor (cf. *N&R, I*, 44). On the other hand, there was a "trodden mud floor" some 30–40 cm. above the first floor (see passage quoted above, p. 4), which implies that not all the fill between the two floors can have been deposited in one go. The same conclusion follows from the fact that many of the tablets must have lain exposed to the weather for a time, since one face of each is well preserved, while the other is entirely destroyed and pitted as though from rain. This would not have happened if the tablets had been included in fill and immediately covered by a floor, and it strengthens Professor Sir Max Mallowan's suggestion that the room underwent a phase when it was entirely abandoned and mud was falling in from the tops of the ruined walls (quoted above).

[9] The date of the new beaten-mud floor rather depends on the status of the layer of ash discovered in Room K. From *Iraq* 12 (1950), 167, it seems certain that the beaten-mud floor lay above this layer of ash, which was associated with burnt levels in the rest of the palace. Since then, however, the destruction layer in the other rooms has proved to belong to the final sack of the city (612 B.C., cf. *N&R, I*, 49). Therefore either our floor is subsequent to the final sack, or the layer of ash beneath it should not be equated with that in the rest of the building (for which see *N&R, I*, 43). I would favour the second of these alternatives, in view of the sequence of events referred to in note 10, and the floor could then, as before, be dated to shortly after 710 B.C.

[10] In *N&R, I*, 43, the beaten floor is associated with the re-plastering of the walls, and with the sealing of the doorway in the north wall. Obviously the doorway will have been plastered over when the rest of the room was done, and it does not seem impossible that the actual blocking of the door was completed earlier in the room's history. The burial (indicated on the plan) will evidently not have been made immediately after the room had been repaired, and is more likely to have been placed there only after the roof had fallen in, so that it should strictly be assigned to a third phase, probably after the final sack of the city, as suggested in *N&R, I*, 49.

[11] Cf. *Iraq* 12 (1950), 167.

[12] Cf. below, p. 7, on B50.

of the archive came from, since it lay directly above the original floor.[13] There is no obvious difference in the character or date of the Room M and Room K tablets, and it is certain that those from Room M belong to the same archive as those found in Room K, but were scattered further from their place of origin. It is likely that they all belong to the west end of the room, off which Room K gives, but this is not specified in the reports.

Room S: As may be seen from the plan, Room S adjoined Room M, the audience chamber, on the east side, and like Room K it seems only to have given on to Room M. The excavation of Room S was undertaken during the second season (1950), and the details are not included in the preliminary report for that year, which is devoted to the remarkable achievements on the main site of excavation, the North-west Palace. Details of the find-spot of the tablets are however given in Professor D. J. Wiseman's notebooks as follows: " Room S, under brick mastaba over m(ud)-b(rick) floor level in SW corner, 1 m. to left of door in S wall." A glance at the plan will show that the only doorway marked is in the wall usually described as west, and if this difference is carried through logically, we find that a brick feature is shown in the north-west corner of the room which can be plausibly identified with the " mastaba ".[14] In *N&R, I*, 51, another important find in Room S is described, which consisted of nearly 100 palace-ware vessels, lying in a heap on a mud-brick " table " or " pedestal " at the north-eastern end of the room. However, the plan shows no such feature at the room's north-eastern end or corner, and we are led to wonder whether this is not the same feature once more, and hence identical with the " mastaba " in which the tablets were discovered. Whether this is so or not, the discovery of a large collection of tablets within a square mud-brick construction reminds us of the arrangements in the North-west Palace's administrative wing (Zigurrat Terrace), where the letters and administrative archives had been accommodated in rows of brick boxes.[15] It is perhaps not too rash to suggest that in Room S too there was a single such " filing cabinet ", which was later filled in and re-used as a table.

Other rooms: in Room U, lying on the east side of the courtyard, adjoining Room S, were found the historical text of Tiglath-pileser III (ND 400), an early legal text (No. 14), and a fragment of a letter (No. 209). No. 131, a note of animals, was found in Room B; this lay in the opposite corner of the building, and was a small entrance chamber leading into the " ablution room ".[16] This is hardly intended as a depository for tablets, and I have suggested in the commentary to No. 232 that No. 131 may not belong to the Governor's Palace at all, but have strayed from the Burnt Palace where the very similar No. 232 was found. The remaining rooms named as provenance of inscribed material (mainly bricks), are Rooms C, H, and I (ND 277–8 and 283), none of which are indicated

[13] For the stratigraphy of Room M see the photograph in *Iraq* 12 (1950), Pl. XXIX.2 (= *N&R, I*, 44, fig. 11), with commentary, ibid., p. 182; this shows that the tablets belonged to Level IV (which is equivalent to the layer of fill directly above the floor in Room K), and that three levels (III–I) were distinguished for the seventh century, before the area was made to serve as a burial-site. This Level IV in Room M is presumably identical with the layer called Level II in both Room K and Room M in the epigraphical catalogue (cf. *Catalogue of Texts*, pp. 253 ff.).

[14] As is clear from the plan (*Iraq* 12 (1950), Pl. XXVI), the Governor's Palace was not on an exact N–S axis, the " N " being more accurately described as NNW. (The rough indication of N on the plan published here (Fig. 1) is taken from the overall site plan.) This may account for the apparent discrepancy between this description and the plans.

[15] See *Iraq* 15 (1953), 33, with Pl. IV.1.

[16] For Room B cf. photograph, *Iraq* 12 (1950), Pl. XXX.3; a cylinder seal from this room is illustrated in *N&R, I*, 48, fig. 12.

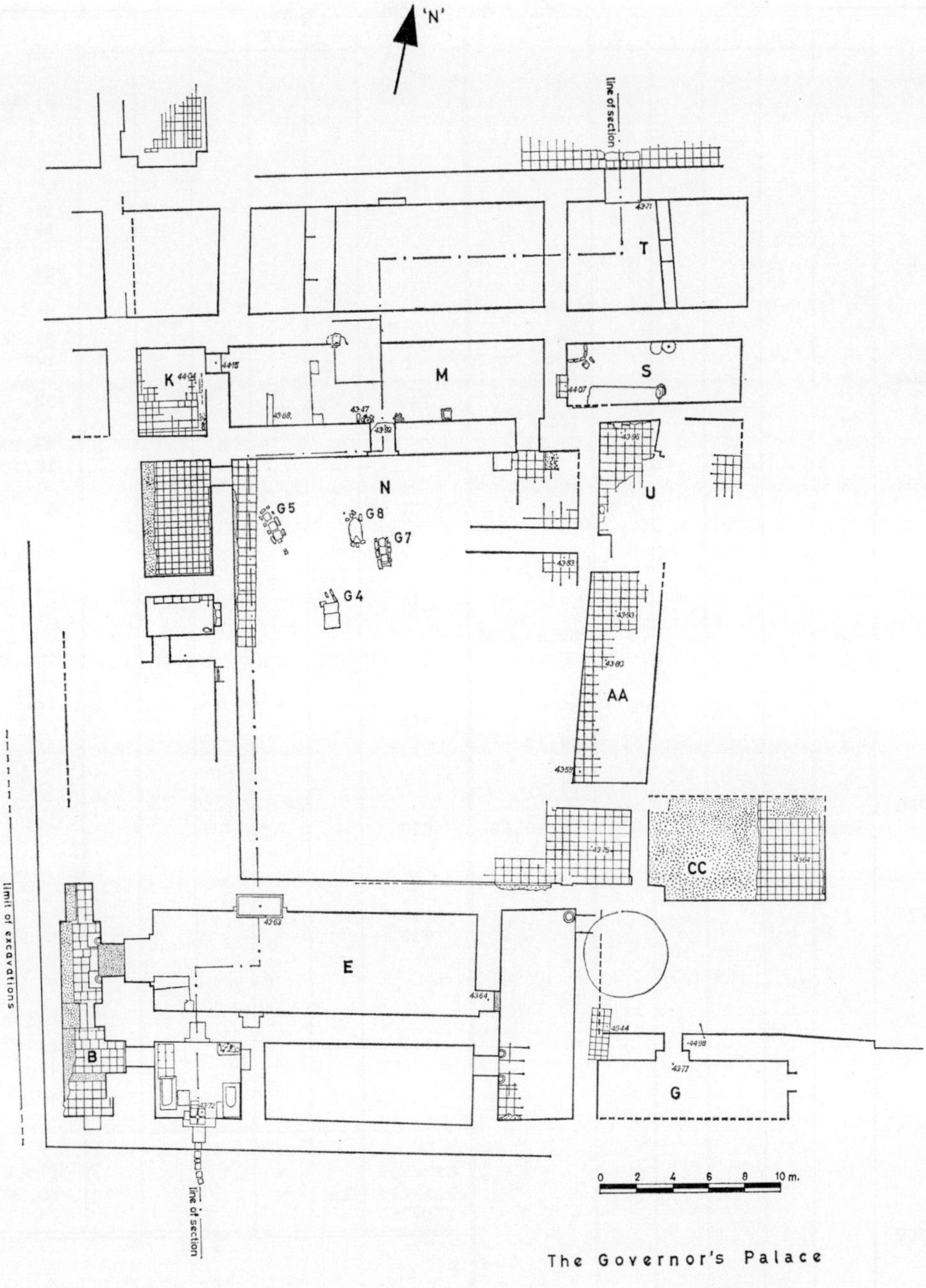
'N'
line of section
T
K
M
S
N
U
G5
G8
G7
G4
AA
CC
limit of excavations
E
B
G
0 2 4 6 8 10 m.
The Governor's Palace
Nimrud 1949-50

Fig. 1

B.C.	K	K/M	M	S	U	Nos.
835			x			100
805						
					x	14
800	x					74?
	x					101
	xx					51,91
795	x		x			102,92
	x					93
	xxx					3,15,16
790						
	xxx					52,94,103
785						
	x		x			79,17
	x					18
780						
	xxx					19,20,68
	x					53
775						
	x					54
770						
	x					4
765						
760						
			x			22
755						

B.C.	K	K/M	M	S	U	Nos.
755						
	xxx					5,23,81
750						
	x					104
	x					24
745						
	x					25
	xxx					26,27,28
			x			105
740	x					95
	x		x			98,106
	x		x			96,107
735			x			6
	x		x			134,174
730						
				x		108
			x			29
		x				175
725						
720						
715						
	x					144
710	xxx					145-7
817/808		x	x			170,2
803/775	xx	x				80,90,21
792/766						78

Fig. 2 Chart to show occurrence of datable tablets from the Governor's Palace

on the plan; they may all be in the southern part of the building, and Room C certainly is, as it gave access to Room E, the long room flanking the courtyard on the south. Room P, leading off Room H, is also unidentified.

A 49, A 50, and B 50

These are trenches dug during the first two seasons, which were not pursued for a variety of reasons. According to D. J. Wiseman, Trench A 50 was " situated in squares F 3, 4, and the B 50 building in F 5, 6 ", and the latter is marked as " 1950 building " on the contour map (*Iraq* 13 (1951), 105, note 2).[17] A 50 is described in the text (*Iraq* 13 (1951), 105), as " a private house built against the citadel wall ", and its position, as shown on the contour map (*Iraq* 12 (1950), Pl. XXVI), shows that the " private house " must have been an integral part of the buildings known later as TW 53, and described in *N&R, I*, 184–97. The exact position of the A 50 trench in relation to the 1953 excavations is shown in *Iraq* 16 (1954), Pl. XXVIII, where an earlier trench labelled Trench A 1949 joins the more recent excavations from the south-west. It is clear from the compass-alignment that this must in fact be the same trench as that shown in squares F 3–4 on *Iraq* 12 (1950), Pl. XXVI, and is therefore identical with A 50. It is therefore no coincidence that the purchaser in No. 219 (from A 50) is called Mannu-kī-ninurta, and that a man of the same name is found among the regular witnesses of the TW 53 archive, once being described as " the entrance-supervisor ".[18] One find made in this trench is referred to in *Iraq* 14 (1952), 4, where it is described as " component parts of a . . . stool leg in bronze ", discovered in Sq. F 4 in 1950; this is no doubt the " cache of small objects " which was found together with Nos. 219–21 (ND 407–9), according to the epigraphist's field notes (see *Catalogue of Texts*, p. 259).[19]

A 49 was a similar undertaking to A 50, but since it produced only one useless fragment, its location is of no great importance to us here. It is probably the trench marked on the plan (*Iraq* 12 (1950), Pl. XXVI) in squares E 5 and F 5, and referred to (ibid., p. 162) with the comment that " our efforts in E 5 . . . were similarly curtailed ".

B 50, marked as the " 1950 building " on *Iraq* 12 (1950), Pl. XXVI (cf. above), was evidently an important structure, but efforts here too were overtaken by the weather and more urgent tasks elsewhere. The only evidence as to the building's identity therefore comes from the few texts discovered in it, and as most of these are clearly administrative, we are no doubt justified in concluding that it was the home of some branch of the administration. Unfortunately there was no dated text, but it is conceivable that it was to this part of the mound that the provincial government moved after leaving the Governor's Palace, since No. 230 (found here) is actually addressed to the governor. The plan and scale of the building would support this—note that its walls were *c.* 2·50 m. thick, noticeably thicker than those of the Governor's Palace.

The Burnt Palace

The few texts found in this building are mostly republished here for the sake of complete-

[17] The excavation of A 50 was probably begun in 1949, and it must be mentioned in *Iraq* 12 (1950), 161–2, as " a broad trench in squares F 3, 4 ".

[18] *ša pān nēribi*; see *Iraq* 15 (1953), 156b, and Pl. XII ND 3426, 45.

[19] At least one of these pieces of bronze is probably located in the Institute of Archaeology, London, according to information kindly given me by J. E. Curtis.

ness, though little is added to the previous editions.[20] The excavation of the Burnt Palace is described in *N&R, I*, 200 ff. (plan, p. 201), and in *Iraq* 15 (1953), 5 ff. and especially 11 ff., and 16 (1954), 63–4 with Pl. XI. Our tablets were mostly found in Room viii (the throne room, occasionally referred to as the "Long Room"), and in Room vii, a small chamber leading off the north-eastern end of Room viii (see *N&R, I*, 203 ff.; *Iraq* 15 (1953), 9–10; 16 (1954), 71–2). The tablets themselves provide a *terminus post quem* for the burning of the palace, and the circumstances of their discovery are described e.g. in *Iraq* 15 (1953), 16, or 14 (1952), 61.

The North-west Palace

The major finds of epigraphical material in the North-west Palace (built by Assur-nāṣir-apli and refurbished by Sargon) were made during the 1952 season, and the texts included here are only those stray pieces which were recovered in the rooms lying to the south-east of the main courtyard (see the convenient summary of D. J. Wiseman, *Iraq* 13 (1951), 104–5). Reports on this part of the North-west Palace may be consulted in *N&R, I*, 93 ff., especially 119 ff., and in *Iraq* 14 (1952), 6 ff.

* * *

The Governor's Palace Archive

Both by their find-spots and by their contents the texts from the Governor's Palace fall into two major groups: the tablets from Rooms K and M, which are mainly legal documents, and those from Room S which include all the correspondence and most of the administrative texts. As can be seen from the accompanying calibrated chart of the datable texts (Fig. 2), the legal documents belong chiefly to the first half of the eighth century, whereas in general the Room S texts, although undated, seem to belong to the second half of that century. The ensuing discussion of the archive deals first with the prosopography, then with various salient characteristics of the texts themselves, and concludes with an assessment of the archive as a whole.

The Palace personnel

1. *The governor*

There are five persons mentioned in our texts as governors (*šaknu* or *bēl pāḫiti*) [21] of Kalhu, viz. Mušēzib-ninurta, Bēl-tarṣi-iluma, Bēl-dān, Marduk-rēmāni, and Šarru-dūrī

[20] Although excavation did continue here in later seasons, inscribed finds were scant. Known to me are the ND numbers 2052 (cf. *Iraq* 15 (1953), 13), 2063 (*Iraq* 16 (1954), 32), 3481 (cf. D. J. Wiseman, *Iraq* 15 (1953), 148), and 2053–2060 (unpublished). None of these belonged in the same context as the texts edited here, from 1951.

[21] I consider that the evidence of our archive proves conclusively that in the eighth century the Assyrian terms *šaknu* and *bēl-pāḫiti* were two descriptions of the same office: Šarru-dūrī and Bēl-dān are each referred to as both LÚ.EN.NAM and *šakin Kalḫi*. I do not deny, of course, that the word *šaknu* had many other usages, and it seems likely that it was the ambiguity occasioned by the title's wide application which was responsible for the increased use of the term *bēl-pāḫiti*. *Šaknu* is rarely used in letters or administrative texts to refer to a governor, but where his office is described in formal contexts—such as in *limmu* lists, or datings, or inscriptions on seal or stele—he is called *šakin* GN, where the term *šaknu* is, of course, quite unambiguous. I cannot accept the theory of R. A. Henshawe that the *šaknu* and *bēl piḫati* (*sic*) were different officials (*JAOS* 87 (1967), 517–25; 88 (1968), 461–83), and consequently in what follows no distinction is made between the two titles.

(for references see *Index of Personal Names*). When the evidence of these texts is combined with what is already known from elsewhere, we may construct the following list of governors for the period which concerns us—the late ninth and eighth centuries B.C.[22]

Šamaš-bēlu-uṣur	851	*limmu*
	844	(s. *Iraq* 25, p. 67 (bottom))
Mušēzib-ninurta	817/808	No. 2
Bēl-tarṣi-iluma	808	No. 170
	803/775	No. 90
	797	*limmu*
	793	No. 93
[ ]*x x*	791	No. 15
Aššur-bēlu-uṣur	772	*limmu*
Bēl-dān	744	*limmu*
	734	*limmu*
Marduk-rēmāni	728	No. 108
Aššur-bāni	713	*limmu*
Šarru-dūrī	—	

Taking these names in order, we may say that with the possible exception of No. 100 none of our texts belongs under the governorship of Šamaš-bēlu-uṣur, and only No. 2 under Mušēzib-ninurta. So far as I know, this Mušēzib-ninurta is not otherwise attested, unless he is to be identified with the priest of Šadikanni, grandson of Samanuha-šar-ilāni, for whom see E. Unger, *BASOR* 130 (1953), 15 ff.[23]

Bēl-tarṣi-iluma is of course well known already, in particular from his Nabû temple statue inscriptions where he is described as governor of Kalhu, Hamedi (not = Amedu), Sirgāna, *māt* Temeni, and Ialuna. His own seal, as far as reconstructed (see on No. 171), mentions at least *māt* Temeni and Ialuna, as well as Kalhu.[24] As pointed out in the commentary to No. 171, it may be significant that Hamedi and Sirgāna appear not to be mentioned, since the sealing dates from 808 B.C., whereas the statue inscriptions could easily belong to some time after 808.[25] If No. 2 is also to be dated to 808 B.C., then Bēl-tarṣi-iluma was created governor of Kalhu in that very year; but since No. 2 could equally well belong to 817 B.C., this cannot of course be proved. The lower limit to his period as governor

[22] The list does not include mentions of governors where the name is not given or not preserved; for these see the *Index of Professions* under the respective words.

[23] There is no direct evidence to support this identification, which may at first sight seem improbable. However, it is clear that Mušēzib-ninurta of Šadikanni had some political standing, since he was able to inscribe the winged bulls of 'Arbān (= Šadikanni) with his own name alone (cf. A. H. Layard, *Nineveh and Babylon* 276), and he kept the title priest held by his grandfather who was an independent ruler. Moreover, a single governorship of Kalhu on the one hand, and districts in the northwest (e.g. Ialuna) on the other, is attested for Šamaš-bēlu-uṣur and Bēl-tarṣi-iluma, and is therefore probable for any intervening governor. Admittedly, Šadikanni seems more logically to fall under the governor of Raṣappa at this date, but provincial boundaries in the ninth century are very illogical in any case. The identity must therefore be treated as a possibility, though no more.

[24] That is in fact all, if the restoration of l. 4 of the seal is right.

[25] Although not too long after, in view of the reference to Sammuramat.

is at present 793 B.C., which might have to be brought down to 791 if his name were to be restored in No. 15; but the text is so badly damaged that this is very uncertain.[26]

The governorship of Bēl-tarṣi-iluma, and perhaps also that of his successor, is the time during which the main part of the Room K and M texts must have been written. Admittedly only nine numbers can be certainly attributed to his term of office (see the table of dated texts, Fig. 2), with some sixteen more certainly before 772, the one year for which Aššur-bēlu-uṣur is attested as governor, but similarities of script, and to a certain extent the prosopography, make it likely that the majority of the legal texts from these rooms belong in the period *c.* 800–770 B.C. This fact is of considerable interest, since we are thus able to trace the form of neo-Assyrian sale texts (in particular) back almost a century further, and in matters of script and language our texts constitute a very welcome addition to the early eighth century archive from Tell Halaf.[27]

Finally we should perhaps observe that the Governor's Palace archive does not seem to include the private archives of Bēl-tarṣi-iluma himself. Those texts which do refer to him as a principal are of different kinds: the sealings with his seal impression are of course public administrative matters, and a possible grant with his seal impression (No. 66) should belong to the archive of the beneficiary. On the other hand the debt clearance texts (for which see below, p. 17) would have been retained by Bēl-tarṣi-iluma, but since these are the only texts where he is virtually "creditor" it is quite likely that the payments are of a public nature, which agrees well with the conclusion reached below, on other grounds. Consequently we have no texts which must have formed part of Bēl-tarṣi-iluma's personal archives, which is not surprising, as he doubtless had a private residence apart from his rooms in the Governor's Palace. Note in conclusion that we have a mention of Bēl-tarṣi-iluma's brother (No. 64), and that like Šarru-dūrī and perhaps other governors of Kalḫu, he was a eunuch.

Aššur-bēlu-uṣur is only attested as an eponym. He could of course be identical with the eponym for 796 B.C. (governor of Kirruri), or, perhaps more likely, with the man of this name who was an official under Palil-ēreš, governor of Raṣappa.[28]

Bēl-dān, eponym for 744 and 734, was clearly governor during the most active years of Tiglath-pileser III. He is attested in our archive chiefly as recipient of letters, including some from the king and two from his son in Babylonia, but these can only be dated by relative criteria such as the script, which does not at least conflict with a date in Tiglath-pileser's reign.[29]

[26] Other references to Bēl-tarṣi-iluma (besides his occurrence in *limmu* datings) are *RGD* No. 2 and a cylinder seal, first correctly interpreted by F. E. Peiser, *OLZ* 3 (1900), 434, which has been described as his although it in fact belonged to a eunuch of his. The text reads: ^{1} *šá* ^{m}*rém-ma-ni*-DINGIR ^{2} LÚ.SAG ^{3} *šá* ^{m}EN.LÁ.DINGIR-*ma* ^{4} ^{lú}*šá-kìn* ^{uru}*kal-ḫi*. This Rēmāni-ilu does not figure in our texts; note that since he is a eunuch, he is represented on the seal as unbearded.

[27] The most obvious characteristic of the script is the use of slanting wedges where horizontals were used later. Most frequent in the sign *ša* (e.g. No. 1, 5′), it is also encountered in *qi* (e.g. No. 14, 6) which thus tends to resemble SIG × ḪI and in the Tell Halaf texts was often mistaken for DAR (e.g. in the place-names given as *Qa-tar-i-ni* and *Bu-ru-dar-*[*r*]*i*, *AfO Beiheft* 6, 82). Note also the absence of the later *ba* with horizontal wedges. On the other hand, both *bu* and *na* may be written with horizontals where slanting wedges would later have been *de rigueur* (for *bu* cf. No. 17, 10; for *na*, No. 9, 3).

[28] His seal, published in L. Delaporte, *Catalogue des cylindres . . . de la Bibliothèque Nationale*, No. 354, must be restored thus: ^{1} NA_4.KIŠIB ^{m}[*aš-š*]*ur*-U.PAP ^{2} LÚ.[SAG *šá* $^{\text{m.d}}$]⌜IGI.DU⌝.KAM ^{3} ^{lú}*šá-kìn* KUR *ra-ṣa-p*[*a*]; the restoration of his title as LÚ.SAG (= eunuch) is assured by similar seal inscriptions, and by the fact that the human figure on the seal is beardless (cf. note 26).

[29] This Bēl-dān should not of course be confused with the eponym for the year 750 B.C., who bore the same name.

Marduk-rēmāni, attested as governor in 728 at the end of Tiglath-pileser III's reign, is not certainly found anywhere else.[29a]

Aššur-bāni does not occur among the Governor's Palace texts, although he is author of No. 241, from the Burnt Palace, and of other letters from the Kouyunjik collection (cf. *APN*, p. 37).

Šarru-dūrī, identified as a governor of Kalhu both by his cylinder seal (see No. 172) and by a reference to him in a letter probably written by the king (No. 203), has not been encountered elsewhere. He did not hold the *limmu* office, and none of the texts in which he is mentioned can be accurately dated. Hence only the most general considerations are available to fix his dates. Script and phraseology preclude dating the letters in which he is found earlier than *c.* the middle of the eighth century, and the find-spot of the texts—associated with the correspondence of Bēl-dān, and with No. 108 (dated to 728 B.C. during the tenure of Marduk-rēmāni)—must place him before Aššur-bāni (713 B.C.). We are therefore left with three choices: between Aššur-bēlu-uṣur and Bēl-dān (i.e. limits of 772–744), between Bēl-dān and Marduk-rēmāni (734–728), or after Marduk-rēmāni (728–713). A possible indication in favour of the earliest of these may be sought in Šarru-dūrī's cylinder seal, which is noticeably similar to that of Bēl-tarṣi-iluma, and in the use of a similar stamp seal on the sealings of these two governors (see *Appendix*, on Nos. 132 and 173); note further that the sealings of Šarru-dūrī (Nos. 132, 172–3) come from Rooms K and M like those of Bēl-tarṣi-iluma. On the other hand, the information from No. 188 that *māt* Sūhi and Hadallu were under Assyrian control suggests a time of Assyrian strength, and strongly favours a date after the accession of Tiglath-pileser III.[30] A further reason for placing him under Tiglath-pileser or later is Šarru-dūrī's seal inscription, which designates him simply "governor of Kalhu": Bēl-tarṣi-iluma's seal inscription gives a number of territories under his governorship, and if Šarru-dūrī also had such wide areas under him we should expect these to be mentioned on his seal too. It is perhaps not too bold, then, to suggest that this points to a date after the reorganization of the provinces by Tiglath-pileser.

When these various considerations are taken together, the easiest solution seems to be to place Šarru-dūrī after Bēl-dān. A date before Bēl-dān is initially attractive, but even though there is no reason why all our texts mentioning Šarru-dūrī should not date from a single year, it is hard to see how Tiglath-pileser could have carried through his reorganization of the provinces and have established control of the Sūhu region within the year between his accession and the *limmu* year of Bēl-dān, 744 B.C. As for the third choice, after 728, this seems to me difficult to reconcile with the cylinder seal.[29a]

[29a] Collation of NL 16 (*Iraq* 17 (1955), 134–5, Pl. XXXIII), 2, reveals that the author of this letter was Marduk-rēm[āni]. Since he is describing to the king the arrival of ambassadors in Kalhu, he is certainly the same man, holding the office of governor. The letter must be dated early in the reign of Sargon, probably around 716 B.C. (712 B.C., as proposed by H. W. F. Saggs, *Iraq* 17 (1955), 152, although otherwise plausible, is now excluded because Aššur-bāni is known to have been governor by then). The resulting extension of Marduk-rēmāni's tenure of office into the reign of Sargon makes it even less likely that Šarru-dūrī held the governorship after him.

[30] Campaigns of Tiglath-pileser III on the Euphrates towards Babylonia are not specifically attested, but Hadallu occurs among the list of Aramaean "tribes" subjected. The land of Sūhu is very sparsely attested in the late Assyrian period (cf. H. W. F. Saggs, *Iraq* 17 (1955), 153, on NL 17), but the inscription of Šamaš-rēš-uṣur makes it unlikely that *māt* Sūhi was under Assyrian control in the first half of the eighth century; see J. A. Brinkman, *An.Or.* 43, 183–4 with note 1127, 271 with note 1740.

2. *Bēl-issīya*

It was already observed by D. J. Wiseman (*Iraq* 12 (1950), 185) that several of the tablets from Room K make mention of Bēl-issīya. Altogether there are seven sale texts where he acts as purchaser (in Nos. 4 and 22 : owner of purchaser), and three other texts (Nos. 92, 94, and 103) in which he is a contracting party ; the dated texts range from 791 (No. 15) to 756 (No. 22). Since it is the purchaser who keeps a sale document as proof of his right to ownership, we are justified in concluding that our texts include the archives of Bēl-issīya.

From Nos. 7(?) ; 15 ; 22 ; 33 we learn that he was a " village-inspector " (*rab ālāni*).[31] In Nos. 33 ; 34, however, he is simply " eunuch of Bēl-tarṣi-iluma, governor of Kalhu " ; the name of the governor as whose " village-inspector " he served was given in No. 15 (791 B.C.), but is unfortunately too broken to read with certainty. Our Bēl-issīya therefore began his career as a eunuch of Bēl-tarṣi-iluma under Adad-nirari III, and remained in the palace until at least 756, long after Bēl-tarṣi-iluma's disappearance, and just before the accession of Tiglath-pileser III, some thirty-five years later.

During this time he purchased two individual slaves, a group of three men and a woman, and the following land :

Area	*Price*	*Location*	*Date*	*No.*
[large area]	[x+] 15 *m.* bronze	Kurbail	791	No. 15
[large area]	[ ]	[ ]	791	No. 16 (?)
8 homers	8 *m.* copper	? Kupruna	[—]	No. 33
2 homers	2 *m.* copper	? Kupruna	[—]	No. 34
[x+] 15 homers	1 *t.* copper	Kurbail	[—]	No. 35

Perhaps the most striking feature of this rather meagre list is that Nos. 15 and 35 deal with purchases of land in the region of Kurbail [32] ; it is moreover very likely that No. 16, which resembles No. 15 in more than just its date, also recorded a purchase of land by Bēl-issīya in the Kurbail district—hence its inclusion here. Similarly, No. 36, although later in date than Nos. 15 and 16, must have dealt with a land sale in the Kurbail region, and since it has a number of witnesses in common with No. 15 it is very likely that it too documented a purchase of land by Bēl-issīya.

Each of the Kurbail land purchases seems to have been made from a consortium of owners—five priests in No. 35, but in Nos. 15 and 16 a large number of persons not obviously having anything in common except presumably the location of their property. A similar tie probably linked the sellers in Nos. 33 and 34, where however separate documents were made out for the different owners, although the two tablets were obviously prepared simultaneously (cf. Nos. 24 and 25). As to the location of the land in Nos. 33 and 34, some doubt exists, but although the reference to the town Kupruna may be defining the measure used, and not indicating the location of the land, the only obvious reason for the use of such a measure (which is not elsewhere attested) would be that the transaction was in the region of Kupruna. Hence I think we may safely assume that these two plots of land also were some distance from Bēl-issīya's town of Kalhu.

[31] This is the usual reading of the title, but cf. note on No. 129, 3.

[32] For the town Kurbail see on No. 15, 24.

This leads us to wonder why these land transactions were initiated. From the point of view of the sellers the answer is no doubt simple necessity: I. M. Diakonoff has recently pointed out [33] that the sale of land in the ancient Orient was not a light matter, and must be assumed to have occurred only under considerable economic pressure, and I have also had occasion to make the same observation with regard to land sales in the middle Assyrian period.[34] In our present texts excellent confirmation is available for this assertion in Nos. 15 and 16, which are dated in a year of famine (see note on No. 15, 52), and the same could easily have applied to the other sales—note that No. 68 probably mentions famine, and that the years of Assyrian inactivity in the first half of the eighth century probably also saw economic instability.

However, if owners in Kurbail were prepared to sell their lands, it seems likely that conditions round Kalhu, well to the south, were equally bad if not worse, and why, in that case, should Bēl-issīya not have bought land nearer home? In the present state of our knowledge there seem to be two possible answers to this. One is that all the land round Kalhu was already in the hands of large land-owners who were not of course susceptible to such economic pressures, and the other explanation is that land in the region of Kurbail was preferred precisely because it lay so much further north than Kalhu, and was hence less liable to crop failures in bad years. In either case, the activities of Bēl-issīya have to be compared with those of Rēmāni-adad [35] in the seventh century under Aššur-bān-apli, and they show that not only the highest officials and provincial governors were able to acquire estates in separate provinces at the time of Adad-nirari III.

The foregoing paragraphs are written with the assumption that in all these transactions Bēl-issīya was acting as a private individual. However, this is by no means certain: in No. 92 and perhaps No. 94 (on these texts relating to fines see below, p. 18) he may well be involved in an official capacity, and have nothing to do personally with the transaction. He is however simply given his name, without any title, whereas in some of the sale texts he is accorded the title of "village-inspector" more than once. It has been observed elsewhere [36] that there is no formal way in which the private and public transactions of an Assyrian official can be distinguished, and hence only indirect means can be used to decide one way or the other. In this case Bēl-issīya's function as "village-inspector" would be entirely in accord with the theory that the governor used him as a representative to visit distant regions for the purpose of buying land, although how in that case the ownership of the land was later transferred from the "proxy-purchaser" Bēl-issīya, who is named as buyer on the tablet, to the true purchaser, is a problem which cannot be answered. The advantage of this explanation is that it accounts for the presence of these sale documents of Bēl-issīya among what should be a public archive (cf. above, p. 10, on Bēl-tarṣi-iluma). However, the same situation exists for all those people who appear among the Governor's Palace texts as purchasers or creditors, and in particular for Sîn-ēṭir and Šamaš-kumūa (see below), so that for the moment I feel that the simpler explanation is that Bēl-issīya's private archives are included with those of other private individuals and with texts of a more official kind.

[33] *Troisième conférence internationale d'histoire économique* (Munich, 1965), "Main features of the economy in the monarchies of ancient western Asia", p. 25.

[34] *BSOAS* 34 (1971), 520.

[35] Cf. G. van Driel, *Bi. Or.* 27 (1970), 170, for this man.

[36] J. N. Postgate, *Iraq* 32 (1970), 35.

3. *Sîn-ēṭir and Šamaš-kumūa*

Two other persons parts of whose archives seem to have found their way into Rooms K and M are a certain Sîn-ēṭir, a contemporary of Bēl-issīya, and Šamaš-kumūa, probably also active at the same time.

The only dated text of Sîn-ēṭir's is No. 20 (779 B.C.), but the script and size of the remaining pieces where he is or may be involved are sufficient to show that they too belong to the early eighth century. In No. 64, where Sîn-ēṭir is one party to an exchange of land, he is described as the brother of Bēl-tarṣi-iluma, and this description is also given on his seal which was impressed on the same tablet (see commentary to the text). Like his brother, Sîn-ēṭir was a eunuch: this is clear from No. 20, 15, where the phrase " and his sons . . .", etc. is absent, while in No. 47, 8 he is probably given the double title of [LÚ.S]AG LÚ.A.BA. If his name is correctly restored in this last text, he was accordingly a eunuch and a scribe, but his title is broken away in No. 65, and there is unfortunately nothing to indicate whether our Sîn-ēṭir is to be identified with the man of that name who was the house-overseer of the chief eunuch (No. 17, 36).

If we assume that Sîn-ēṭir's name is in fact correctly restored in all cases (only in Nos. 20, 64, and 65 is it certain), we may list the following transactions of his:

Area	*Price*	*Location*	*Date*	*No.*
24[+x] homers	1[+x] *t.* [copper?]	[ ]	779	No. 20
50 homers (incl. *adru*, etc.)	[x] *t.* [copper?]	[ ]	[ ]	No. 37
[ ]	[ ]	[ ]	[ ]	No. 42
[x] homers	160 *m.* bronze	Kapru-bēl[. .]	[ ]	No. 47
40 homers	30 homers	Halahhu	[ ]	No. 64
70 homers	[x homers]	[ ]	[ ]	No. 65

It seems from this that Sîn-ēṭir was, like Bēl-issīya, the owner of considerable areas of land, which did not always lie in the vicinity of Kalhu. In this case, however, we have no reason to suppose that Sîn-ēṭir was a village-inspector, or was in other ways likely to have acted as a representative of the governor in his acquisition of land. Indeed, this possibility is more or less entirely excluded by No. 64, where he exchanges land with Mušallim-ištar, since he could surely only be described in a legal document as having " given " away the land if he was indeed the owner of it, without any qualifications.

A similar conclusion may be drawn in the case of Šamaš-kumūa, who is the purchaser in Nos. 17, 31, and 57. He, in No. 17, is described as the " eunuch of Adad-nirari, king of Assyria " (year 783), and No. 57 also shows that he was a eunuch since only his brothers and no sons are mentioned as possible inheritors of the purchased property. In No. 31 his title is LÚ.A.BA LÚ.NIMGIR [É.GAL(?)], which probably means that he was the [palace] herald's scribe, rather than " scribe (and) herald ". In either case the fact that we have at least two other sale texts with Šamaš-kumūa as purchaser from the same archive is probably sufficient to permit us to identify this scribe with the eunuch of the other two (possibly earlier) texts. Whether the Šamaš-kumūa who acts as witness in No. 68 is the same man is of course uncertain, but since he is a scribe it is at least possible.

Details of two of Šamaš-kumūa's land purchases survive: in No. 17 he buys 60 (or more ?) homers in the village of Du'ūa which is perhaps in the neighbourhood of Nineveh, and in No. 31 the area bought is 40 homers. Hence, although the material is scarce, his known activities fall into the general pattern established in the cases of Bēl-issīya and Sîn-ēṭir.

4. *Other personnel*

There is quite a number of people who, like Bēl-issīya, Sîn-ēṭir, and Šamaš-kumūa, are represented in the archive by sale texts in which they are the purchasers: Dayānī (No. 3), Bēl-nūrka-lāmur (No. 5), Marduk-aplu-uṣur (No. 6), Aššur-taklak (No. 14), Rīb-marduk (No. 19), Ṣābu-damqu and Šamaš-šēzib (No. 22), Mannu-kī-māt-aššur (No. 23), Girītu (Nos. 24 and 25), Kurbānu (Nos. 26 and 27), a woman (Iutātu ?, No. 29), Ubru-ištar (No. 30), Šamaš-kēnu-uballiṭ (No. 32), Ṣil-aššur (No. 40), Aššur-dūru-uṣur (No. 43), Adi-māti-ili (No. 44), Qibīt-aššur (No. 45), and AD.BU.SI(?) (No. 48), not to mention those with lost or damaged names. To these people we should add those who appear in other kinds of text of which they would normally have been the holders: Bēl-ēṭir(?) (recipient of grant, No. 66), Aššur-dūru-uṣur (No. 104), Sami' (No. 105), Pān-ištar-lāmur (No. 106), and Bēl-šadūa (No. 107), all these being creditors in loan texts.

Unfortunately we do not know enough about any of these people to determine why their tablets should have been stored in these rooms of the Governor's Palace, and indeed in several cases the name is only found here among our texts. Sometimes, it is true, they have titles which could point to an official position within the palace: Aššur-taklak and Mannu-kī-māt-aššur were both "house-overseers" (GAL É), while Marduk-aplu-uṣur could well be the *rab kallāpi* of No. 81, and Aššur-dūru-uṣur is very likely the eunuch of Bēl-dān, the governor, in No. 99, since he is found both as a purchaser and as a creditor in the archive. However, in most cases the absence of such information makes it impossible to decide if the appearance of these people as purchasers or creditors among our archive is of itself sufficient reason to assume that they were at some time members of the governor's household or administrative circle. It is of course possible that all of them were so employed, even the woman, but in any case, since these are private documents which seem to have found their way into public archives, there can be no presumption that they were.

More light is thrown on the personnel of the Governor's Palace by the various professions associated with the governor in our texts. Besides Bēl-issīya, who was eunuch and subsequently "village-inspector" to the governors of Kalhu, we have a house-supervisor (*ša muḫḫi bēti*), who was probably a different official from the *rab bēti* (cf. Aššur-taklak and Mannu-kī-māt-aššur above),[37] a *rab kallāpi* (a military post), a eunuch (in addition to Aššur-dūru-uṣur, see above), an information-officer, and a singer, all described as "of" (*ša*) the governor; besides these, there are people described simply as "of the house of the governor". There can be little doubt that many of the other people named as witnesses or otherwise must have belonged to the governor's household too, and an indication of other professions which might have been at home there may be drawn from a comparison with the households of the chief eunuch and the *turtānu*. Thus in No. 17 one of the parties

[37] For the *rab bēti* cf. in particular *ABL* 242, 34; 282 r. 19; *ADD* 127 (*ša Gargamiš*); *ABL* 746 ([*ša*] *Laḫiri*); NL 28 (*Iraq* 18 (1956), 45); NL 75 (*Iraq* 27 (1965), 23); NL 89 (*Iraq* 28 (1966), Pl. LVI, ll. 26–9); and NL 92 (*Iraq* 28 (1966), 189). These examples make it clear that he was a provincial official, who functioned as the governor's deputy in military affairs. His original association with the household seems to have become secondary, at least by the reign of Tiglath-pileser III.

must have belonged to the chief eunuch's household, and among the witnesses we find a *rab bēti* (" house-overseer "), a doctor, scribe, messenger, and " third-rider " of the chief eunuch's household, while the seller himself, a eunuch, was probably also a member of the same household. Dependants of the *turtānu* appear on several occasions as witnesses, and they seem to come from two quite separate establishments of his. In the land-sale texts of Bēl-issīya the witnesses from Kurbail include a " chief of the female votaries of the house of the *turtānu* ", and a " house-supervisor " (*ša muḫḫi bēti*) and another man also from the *turtānu's* household in Kurbail. In other cases members of his household probably belong to his Kalhu establishment—Kalhu in the eighth century still being Assyria's political and military capital—and they consist of a " house-supervisor " (*ša muḫḫi bēti*) and two weavers (in No. 91), possibly a company-commander (LÚ.GAL 50), and two men in different texts described as " of the *turtānu's* household ".

* * *

The texts

Not all the various types of text are described here; my purpose is rather to give a general view of the contents of the archive, and to take up certain points which do not belong strictly in the commentary to individual texts since they emerge from the consideration of a group of documents. For a detailed list of the types of text the reader is referred to the list above, pp. 2–3.

1. *Sales*

In general the real estate sales are formulated like those of the seventh century known from the Kouyunjik archive; only the occasional formula is unusual, and even then it can often be found among the texts in *ADD.* There is, however, a change in the outward appearance of the tablets: in the early eighth century B.C. the normal script was large and bold, not to say coarse, and consequently a sale text would require quite a large tablet. An excellent example of this is No. 17, but several other land sales have the same characteristics (the largest being No. 15, 10·8 × 15·4 cm.), and they also share the same very flat surface, rare later (except of course for large or literary tablets), which gives a sharp angle where obverse and reverse meet the edges (cf. the photo of No. 18, Pl. 94a, not the best example). These observations may apply equally to slave sale tablets: a comparison of No. 6 (735 B.C.) with No. 9 (date lost, but certainly earlier) shows how the flat surface survived at least until the reign of Tiglath-pileser, while the reduction in the script size occasioned a reduction in the size of the tablet (see photos, Pls. 92b, 93b).

However, not all the slave sales were as carefully prepared as these two, and there does seem to be a difference in the earlier texts between the real estate and the slave sales, in the degree of formality required. The slave sales may be more casually written on smaller, less handsome tablets, while Nos. 2 and 4 (808 and 769 B.C.) are lacking most of the formulae usual later—No. 4 does not even have finger-nail impressions—and of all our slave sales only No. 11 has the *ṣibtu bennu* clause which is customary later, and that in the reverse order.

Perhaps because the cheaper stamp seal was not yet in common use, the seal impression is almost always replaced by finger-nail marks. Of all the sale texts, only one real estate sale (No. 18) has a seal impression. This is of course hardly surprising, since the richer families who could afford the luxury of a cylinder seal would not have needed to sell their property (or, in the case of a loan, to borrow money). In contrast, cylinder seals belonging to Bēl-tarṣi-iluma and his brother are found on Nos. 66 and 64 respectively, where the land is not being sold by them but either granted or exchanged. Later, however, we find a fine cylinder seal on No. 44 (*c.* Tiglath-pileser, but the cylinder seal does not belong to the seller), and on No. 13 a stamp seal, which itself points to a relatively late date.

2. *Receipts*

Some of the most interesting of the Governor's Palace texts are Nos. 90–9, which are receipt texts of various kinds. Nos. 90, 91, and 93 in particular hold our attention, since they all record the payment of debts by Bēl-tarṣi-iluma instead of the men who had incurred them. Thus in No. 90 he pays a total of more than 52½ minas of bronze (or copper) for two debtors, to nine or ten creditors; in No. 91 the sum is 53½ minas of bronze, and there are twenty-three creditors, the debtor, Urdu-ištar, being a weaver; and in No. 93 the total debts amount to 2 talents 20 minas (= 80 minas) of bronze, there are eleven creditors, and the debtor is ironically a merchant (LÚ.DAM.GÀR). It is interesting to note that the formulation of the documents is not consistent, although they serve an identical purpose, since this rather suggests that this type of text was either rare or an innovation, and hence unfamiliar to the scribes. Thus, while all three texts are validated with the creditors' finger-nail impressions, Nos. 91 and 93 have them at the top of the obverse, while on No. 90 they are relegated to the top edge, at the end of the text; and in No. 91 there is a heading which is lacking in No. 93. As suggested in the commentary to No. 91, these texts seem to fulfil two functions at once: while they strictly only testify that the creditors have no further claims on the debtor, they also give Bēl-tarṣi-iluma a document which transfers the entire credit to him, and obviously places the debtor very heavily in the governor's debt, although his consent to this situation is only legally attested by his seal or nail impressions on the original loan texts.

The background to these three transactions is not easy to establish. In the first place we must determine whether Bēl-tarṣi-iluma is acting privately or in his capacity as the governor—if such a distinction can usefully be made—and then we must try to define his reasons for intervening—was it on behalf of the debtor, or to ensure that the creditors received what was owed to them? In the case of the weaver (No. 91) we could suppose that he was a member of the governor's establishment,[38] and that the payment was made to prevent the governor from losing his services or else as part of the governor's traditional patronage *vis-à-vis* his subordinates, but there is no good reason to assign a merchant (No. 93) to Bēl-tarṣi-iluma's household, and instead it seems preferable to suppose that the governor might step in to satisfy creditors once a man's debts had become manifestly excessive. This would of course mean that Bēl-tarṣi-iluma was acting in his official capacity as governor, since it was hardly an example of private charity, and hence we seem to have the beginnings of a government policy to deal with bankruptcy, intended for the protection of creditors, and considerably more effective in this respect than most modern states. This solution also provides an explanation of why the texts were preserved in the Governor's Palace, rather than in Bēl-tarṣi-iluma's private residence (cf. above, p. 10). As to the

[38] Cf. the weavers belonging to the *turtānu's* household, No. 91, 35–6.

fate of the debtors, clearly the texts were retained in the palace until some sort of repayment had been made; it is quite possible that until this time the debtor was required to serve the governor (as a LÚ.ŠÀM, bought man ?), but this side of the picture remains dark.

Further debt receipts are No. 94 (payment by Bēl-issīya, details not very clear), and Nos. 92, 95, and 96, where the payment is for a fine. This is specified in Nos. 92 (*sartu*) and 96 (*šalluntu sarte*), and may be deduced in No. 95 where only the word *šalluntu* is used. From other neo-Assyrian texts where fines are mentioned, it seems that it was usual to pay the sum prescribed to the injured party (and not, e.g., to the authorities),[39] and this would obviously be the case in No. 95, where the payment is blood-money (see note to No. 95, 16). We might therefore expect that these texts would be receipts, validated by the seal or finger-nail impression of the injured party receiving the fine, and held by the payer as evidence of the payment. This, however, cannot be so, since none of these texts (including No. 94) has seal or finger-nail impressions (nor indeed a space for them): the texts are bare statements that the payment has been made, and in No. 95 indeed the injured party, who was presumably the recipient of the money, is only mentioned as a witness (l. 15).

I think we may reasonably conclude that in the case of a judicial fine—effectively an obligation between two parties determined by the courts—procedure demanded that the payment of the fine should take place before the authorities, probably those which had determined the case, and that on that occasion a record of the payment was made and deposited in the public archives. Hence in No. 95 we read that the payment was made " in the house of the palace scribe ", and doubtless that is where the document was housed thereafter. Whether a separate document would have been made out for the payer, as evidence that his obligation was fulfilled is a question which must await further texts.[40]

3. *Loans* (*and debt-notes*)

Unfortunately the archive contains relatively few loans, which makes it difficult to make comparisons with later ones, and dangerous to draw any very broad conclusions. What is said below is consonant with the evidence we possess, but it should be stressed that it is liable to revision on the basis of new evidence.

The most interesting characteristic of these early loan texts is their outward appearance: as is pointed out in the Commentary to No. 101, this early eighth-century text, which is certainly not a sale document, is not encased in an envelope on which the contents of the tablet are repeated together with a seal or finger-nail impression, which is the normal practice later. Instead the nail-marks are placed at the head of the tablet, just as on a contemporary sale text, and like a sale text too, the writing is along the short axis of the tablet. In contrast, No. 99 (a receipt, dating to the middle of the eighth century) is indeed encased in an envelope on which the text is repeated, and the writing is parallel to the short axis; as with the later texts too, the seal impression is on the envelope, but there is a difference in that it is not on the obverse of the envelope but on the uninscribed reverse.

[39] This emerges clearly from text No. 2, 10–13, in *Iraq* 32 (1970), 131–2, and is probably to be deduced from *ARU* No. 660 as well (fine payable to several persons).

[40] A comparable text from a much later period is No. 2 in *Iraq* 32 (1970), 131–2; it too has no seal or finger-nail impressions, and l. 13 probably recorded the fine's payment, as is shown by ll. 14 ff., which obviously contained a " Nichtanfechtungsklausel ". This tablet should therefore be categorized as a " record of payment of fine ".

Between the two extremes of Nos. 101 and 99, Nos. 106 and 107 constitute a half-way stage: in No. 106 (738 B.C.) the nail-marks are still made directly on to the tablet and there are no signs of an envelope, but it has lost the phrase *ṣupur* PN identifying the nail-marks (which was present in No. 101), and the marks themselves are not at the beginning of the text but on the reverse, between the witnesses' names and the date. Similarly in No. 107 (737 B.C.) the text begins at once by naming the item loaned, and the cylinder seal impression is to be found on the reverse, separating two lines of the date.

It seems easiest to summarize these changes in the outward appearance of the loan text by drawing up a list of the various features which were subject to change:

No.	*Envelope*	*Axis of writing*	*Nail/Seal (position)*	*Nail/Seal note*	*Date*
101	no	short	head	yes	798(?)
102[a]	no	short	[head]	[?]	795
106	no	long	Rev.	no	738
107	no	long	Rev.	no	737
108	no	long	T.E.(?)	yes	[ ]
99	yes	long	Rev. of env.	no	*c.* 745–730
ND 3488[b]	yes	long	Obv. + rev. of env.	[yes]	706
ND 2331[c]	yes	long	Obv. + rev. of env.	yes	679
ND 3437[d]	yes	long	Obv. of env.	yes	650

Notes:

a: The obverse of No. 102 is lost, but what remains of reverse indicates a loan; no nail-marks or seal impressions are present on the reverse, and they were therefore probably on the obverse.

b: *Iraq* 17 (1955), Pl. XXVIII.4, p. 122; *Iraq* 15 (1953), p. 148. It is not certain if there was a "seal-note" on obverse, but highly probable.

c: *Iraq* 17 (1955), Pl. XXVII.5, p. 121; *Iraq* 16 (1954), p. 43. Although described as a tablet with seal impression, in the photograph it appears to have all the characteristics of an unbroken envelope.

d: *Iraq* 17 (1955), Pl. XXIV.6, p. 117; *Iraq* 15 (1953), p. 142. The "seal-note" (NA_4.KIŠIB PN) is visible on photograph.

Despite the unfortunate gap between 795 and 738 B.C., this table shows a gradual process during the eighth century from a kind of document outwardly similar to a sale text, to the characteristic loan texts of the seventh century, pillow shaped and encased in a sealed envelope. For the sake of comparison three of such texts have been included in the table from other provenances at Nimrud: although they are generally very similar to one another, it may not be a coincidence that the two earlier examples have seal impressions on the reverse as well, although it should be stressed that the texts have been selected at random for their date, and that I have not compared all the available evidence on this point. Finally we may note how the introduction of the stamp seal led to a great increase in the number of seal owners, and a corresponding decrease in the frequency of finger-nail impressions.

As to the wording of the loan texts, there is no great difference from that of later texts.

True loans are characterized by the phrase *ina pūḫi* (Nos. 105–7; 742–737 B.C.), while in No. 105 (742 B.C.) we have an early instance of a corn-loan with "harvester clause".[41] On the other hand Nos. 103 and 104 are debt-notes, and hence do not have the phrase *ina pūḫi* (*ittiši*); No. 108 is not so much a debt-note as a delivery contract, and No. 109, despite its use of the word *ittiši* ("he has taken") which is normally used of incurring an obligation, is perhaps a receipt for the purchase(?) price of seven persons.

4. *Administrative texts*

In contrast to the legal texts, the bulk of the administrative texts comes from the Room S archive, and is presumably therefore like the letters (see 5. below) to be dated to the reign of Tiglath-pileser III. Like most neo-Assyrian administrative texts, however, they are undated, and some may indeed be later.[42]

Neither in phrasing, nor in their outward characteristics, do the various administrative texts show much of especial interest. There are no large account tablets, such as are known from Nineveh and the North-west Palace at Nimrud, and indeed the only tablet with more than one column is No. 155. For very brief notes the scribes used the "cigar-shaped" tablets (not "dockets", since they were not usually attached to anything else), on which the transition from obverse to reverse is practically imperceptible (e.g. Nos. 144 ff.); and for longer texts, e.g. lists, the tablets might be written across the shorter axis (e.g. the lists of PNs, Nos. 119–20) or on the long axis, when more detail was needed in each line, e.g. the horse texts (Nos. 125–7) or the corn and wood texts (Nos. 135–6, 139).

As to their content, the administrative texts reveal the expected preoccupations of a provincial administration, and have little to indicate that the province's capital was also the capital of the empire, and that the royal palace was only the other side of the acropolis. A comparison of our texts with those from the rather earlier Tell Halaf archive shows the same broad categories: they list persons, including law-breakers, horses, cattle, and sheep, corn and other edible commodities, and equipment of various kinds, including metal objects and textiles. Regrettably, their terse phraseology, and in particular our ignorance with regard to the prosopography, prevent us from using these texts to reconstruct in detail the methods of administration, but the individual texts do often convey interesting information, and No. 155, a long inventory, is particularly worthy of mention, despite the crucial broken passages at beginning and end.

Sealings (Nos. 132–3; 170–3): Although only these few inscribed sealings were found in the Governor's Palace, they are of some interest. It seems that in all cases the clay was sealed with the seal of the governor of the day, but unfortunately on most of them either the text is entirely broken away, or only the date survives. The only sealings where the subject is clear are Nos. 132–3, where there is mention of sheep. These two texts, obscure of themselves, should be compared with No. 257, from the North-west Palace, which mentions "x sheep, *ṣibtu*", and which may itself be restored after Nos. 132–3, to say that these sheep are "at the disposal of" (*ina pān*) the shepherds of Nabû-dūr-bēlīya. Correspondingly in No. 132 the sheep are *ina pān* a shepherd, and in No. 133 they are *ina pān* two persons, who may also be assumed to have been shepherds.

[41] See *CAD* E 350a for references to other such nA texts.

[42] e.g. No. 137, which mentions Ša-aššur-dubbu, very likely the same man as the governor of Tušhan under Sargon and Sennacherib.

These " sheep-sealings " seem to me to pose three main questions:

(1) Why were the sheep handed over to the shepherds ?
(2) Why was the governor's seal impressed ?
(3) To what were the sealings attached ?

A possible answer to the first of these questions is that the sheep, being the property of the provincial government (perhaps, in No. 257, as *ṣibtu* tax), were handed over to the shepherds for pasturing until they were required again by the government. It might of course be suggested instead, that the sheep were not in fact " issued " to the shepherds, but rather owed by them to the provincial governor so that these sealings would be effectively debt-notes; but this idea does not recommend itself because the sealings were definitely not legal documents, but administrative, and in any case if they recorded a debt the acknowledgement of the shepherds would be necessary, and not as here the seal of the governor, who would be the creditor. Hence it seems preferable to take *ina pān* in its administrative sense of " under ", " in the charge of ", rather than in the legal sense equivalent to " incumbent on (as a debt) ". Our sealings therefore must attest the system of " herding-contractors ", already well known in both ancient and modern Near East,[43] and they would harmonize well with other neo-Assyrian evidence for such practices in the administration, which will be discussed in the writer's study of taxation.

There remain the second and third problems listed above, which are closely bound to each other. Since, according to normal practice, the shepherds can have been only marginally members of the administration, if members at all, it is possible in a vague way to understand the use of the governor's seal in order to record his assent to the transaction, but undoubtedly a more precise explanation must depend on our reconstruction of the purpose of the sealing itself. Unfortunately the impressions on the reverse of these sealings do not help us much: No. 257 was probably applied to a small jar, like a larger group of sealings from the Burnt Palace (Nos. 233–7), and it is possible that No. 133 also comes from the neck of a jar, since it has the same cross-section as those sealings (cf. copy, Pl. 54). No. 132 on the other hand is sharply curved in two directions, and unfortunately the impression on the reverse is not clear, showing only the marks of a string-knot. Thus it is clear that the sealings were indeed attached to some larger object, but except for the fact that in two cases this object seems to have been a jar, I cannot make any useful suggestion as to what these objects might have been or what purpose they could have served.[44]

5. *Letters*

Like most of the administrative texts, the letters in the Governor's Palace archive come from Room S, and as they were found in a group together they genuinely constitute an

[43] Cf. recently J. J. Finkelstein, *JAOS* 88 (1968), 30–6.

[44] Only at first sight comparable are the old Babylonian " animal tags " published in C. E. Keiser, *Babylonian Records in the Library of J. Pierpont Morgan, III*, Nos. 57–70 (photographs on Pl. VI), which are edited in A. Ungnad and P. Koschaker, *Hammurabi's Gesetz, VI*, Nos. 1907–1923. Both Keiser (ibid., pp. 11 ff.), and Ungnad (*OLZ* 25 (1922), 255) assume that these clay labels were hung round the animals' necks. Since each mentions only one animal with its shepherd (NA.KAD), this is possible, and since they are not sealed the similarities with our sealings are very superficial. Dr. K. K. Riemschneider refers me to three further such tags from the same archive (S. Levy and P. Artzi, *'Atiqot* 4 (1965), Nos. 90–2); of these No. 91 is interesting since it concludes (l. 4): u_4? *ba-ug*$_6$*-a*, and suggests that the animals in question were dead.

archive.[45] Before discussing the date of the letters, it seems useful to give a list of the letters, showing their writers and receivers:

No.	*Writer*	*Recipient*
180	Hunānu	The king
181	The king	Scribe(?) of Kalhu
182	,,	Qāt-ili-gabbu
183	,,	Bēl-dān
184	,,	,,
185	,,	Šarru-dūrī
186	[,,]	[Šarru]-dūrī?
187	[,,]	Šarru-[dūrī]
188	*šakin māti*	Šarru-dūrī
189	,,	,,
190	The governor	Ṣil-šarri
191	*ša pān ēkalli*	The governor
192	*rab mūgi*	,,
193	Ninurta-ilāya	,,
194	Nergal-ēṭir	,,
195	Adad?-ēṭir	,,
196	Aššur-taklak	,,
197	Mār-ištar	,,
198	Ubru-nabû	,,
199	Adad-ahu-iddina	,,
200	[—]	,,
201	Mišarrum-nāṣir	Bēl-dān
202	,,	,,
203	[The king(?)]	[—]
204–6	[—]	[—]
207	[—]	[The governor(?)]
208–11	[—]	[—]

It is immediately apparent from this list that we have here part of the correspondence files of two governors of Kalhu, Bēl-dān and Šarru-dūrī (see above, p. 10 f.). Unfortunately only those letters written by the king, by the governor of Aššur, and by Bēl-dān's son are addressed to the governors by name; just as letters to the king never give his name, referring to him simply as "the king, my lord", so the majority of the letters to the governors begin "to the governor, my lord"—evidently it was customary for an inferior person to address letters to his superiors using only the title and not the name. As a result of this custom, in most cases we cannot decide whether Bēl-dān or Šarru-dūrī was the governor addressed.

The letters of Bēl-dān may be dated to the reign of Tiglath-pileser III, and reasons

[45] Twenty-two letters were found in the brick "mastaba" in Room S. No. 209 came from Room U, while the provenance of Nos. 180, 187, 200, 204–5, and 211 is not certain, although they probably also belong to Room S. No. 195 is from the bricked-in doorway in the west wall of Room S, and No. 197 from Room M.

are advanced above for placing Šarru-dūrī either directly before or directly after Bēl-dān; naturally one of the arguments in favour of this is the fact that the correspondence of the two governors was found together.

Excluding the two Babylonian letters from Mišarrum-nāṣir, Bēl-dān's son, the governors' letters may all be classed as administrative, and can easily be divided into two main groups: "external" and "internal" correspondence. Thus where the letter is from the king or the governor of Aššur, the Kalhu governor is receiving orders or requests from outside to take action with regard to his province, whereas most of the remaining letters are directed to the governor with reports or requests for advice from his subordinates in the provincial administration. Between these two categories are a letter from the "palace overseer" and one from the *rab mūgi*: unlike the others, these writers do not call themselves "servants" of the governor, and yet they do acknowledge his superior standing by addressing the letter by his title only, and by placing their own titles only after his in the introduction (cf. on No. 191, 1–2). Evidently both these officials were subordinate in rank to the governor, as we should have anticipated, but in both cases they are giving him instructions—albeit in the precative—and it is clear that they are writing directly to the governor as representatives of the royal establishments, instead of transmitting their requests through higher authorities as would probably have been done if the governor concerned had been in a separate provincial capital and not on the doorstep of the royal palace at Kalhu.

With regard to their physical characteristics our letters have no very special features; as normal, they are mostly written across the short axis of the tablet, sometimes ending high up the reverse, but sometimes carrying on round the top edge and on to the left side. An exception is No. 182, a letter from the king, which is written parallel to the tablet's long axis. The script of the letters is very variable, but as far as it is possible to generalize it stands closer to the letters from the reign of Sargon than to the script used in the early eighth century legal texts and the letters from Tell Halaf. On the whole the sign forms are indistinguishable from those of the Kouyunjik archive, and equally varied, and if there is one major difference from the letters of Sargon's reign it lies in the size of the script, which is larger in the earlier period, and somewhat coarser as a result. Whether this is entirely due to the slightly earlier date, or is in part caused by the less formal and important nature of the provincial correspondence, is hard to tell, since a similar difference seems to exist between the few "royal" letters of the reign of Tiglath-pileser III and those of Sargon that I have had the opportunity to examine. On the other hand, it is obvious that letters written *to* the king are likely to be more carefully prepared than the king's own messages, some of which we have in our texts, and it is perhaps no coincidence that the single letter which is indeed addressed to the king (No. 180) is noticeably better written than the remainder. Until we have more examples of non-royal correspondence from the seventh century, we have no excuse for disparaging the scribes of Tiglath-pileser's reign simply because of the very variable quality of the letters in our group.

Conclusions

The importance of the Governor's Palace archive has recently been pointed out by J. V. Kinnier-Wilson,[46] who stresses the value accorded to the tablets by their discovery

[46] *The Nimrud Wine Lists*, p. 12.

in days when find-spots are recorded. Apart from the smaller archive of Tell Halaf, and the (not unimportant) fragments from Tell Billa, our texts constitute the only neo-Assyrian provincial archive which can be identified as such. Consequently it is of particular importance to assess the value of the texts as a group, and to make use of the general picture thus obtained as a corrective to isolated scraps of information from individual tablets.

In conclusion, therefore, we must stress the incompleteness of the archive. Although the texts from Room S were mostly found together, in a relatively undisturbed context (see above, p. 6), those from Room K (and M) were found in very disturbed circumstances, and even if Room K was intended as their resting-place it is obvious that many tablets were lost by dispersion or destruction in the course of time. This is of course no more disruptive to our sources than we are used to expect, for, beyond perhaps the old Babylonian palace archive at Mari, what archives do we possess in their entirety ? None the less, these deficiencies must be borne in mind, and a glance at the chronological disparity of our texts, and at the wide gaps in our list of dated tablets, shows that an enormous amount is missing. While we cannot tell how many of the apparently " private " legal transactions have vanished, it is obvious that the great bulk of correspondence is lost, along with the most important of the provincial administrative records, such as account texts.

On the other hand, we must despite all have a fairly representative cross-section of the palace scribes' activities ; besides the letters, the administrative texts cover a wide range of subjects, as mentioned above (p. 20), and the same applies to the various types of legal texts. Curiously, therefore, we have a group of tablets which is not restricted in time or in character, and there seems to be no way of determining why those tablets which have reached us should have been preserved together, in preference to the many other equally plausible candidates. Although of course we can never know what was lost, we should perhaps be grateful for the very randomness of the material, since this does something to counteract its paucity.

* * *

Before presenting the texts themselves, there remain two specific points arising from our texts which could neither be dealt with above, nor be incorporated into the commentary on individual texts. Since they are both large subjects with wide reaching implications, no attempt is made here to deal with them exhaustively, and the ensuing notes are intended merely to call attention to the kind of new evidence our texts provide.

Aramaean names : Since the fusion of Assyrian with Aramaean culture is gradually emerging as one of the major components of the Assyrian empire, any new information on the progress of the Aramaeans or their language is historically interesting as well as of value to linguists. Outside Tell Halaf, where the position is complicated by the almost exclusively Aramaean population of the entire area, no large group of names has been recovered for the early eighth century B.C., and hence the names in our texts are of some interest. Note, for example, the names Šēr-ma'ādi and Šēr-hanāna in No. 93 (793 B.C.), carried by men sufficiently settled to be lending money to a merchant. In other texts of comparable date we meet a Bahiānu, a Silu/i who is actually described as an Aramaean (No. 90, 10–11), and a Bi-silu who is the mayor of Du'ūa, a village near Nineveh (No. 17, 41). These instances prove, if proof were needed, that some part of the population of the settled districts between the Upper Zab and Tigris rivers bore Aramaic names. It is, however, my impression that there is a higher proportion of true Assyrian names at this date than there was later, which would not of course be surprising in view of the extensive deportation of conquered populations into the Assyrian homeland, but this is an impression which would require careful and lengthy documentation to confirm it.[47]

Another side of the picture is given by the texts Nos. 113, 119, and 120, which clearly do not list settled population. In No. 113 the exact purpose of the list is lost, but the names are manifestly non-Assyrian, and lists of this kind—giving details of families including children—almost invariably refer to groups of prisoners or deportees being handled by the administration. In No. 119 the persons named, who had taken part in a razzia, are described either as Ruqahaean, or as being from Si'-altaru?; hence it is of interest to encounter the names Mudada and Harānu, a century or more after the Assyrian kings had encountered the same names among the rulers of the Aramaean states on the Habur. The only other occurrences of these two names, as far as I know, are at Tell Halaf (Nos. 42, 5; 28, 2), and it would seem therefore that they did not survive the eighth century, at least in Assyria proper. Other Aramaean names of equal antiquity, however, did not suffer the same fate, such as Bahiānu, attested now in the ninth, eighth, and seventh centuries B.C.

Currency: This subject equally belongs in a much larger investigation of the currency and prices of the neo-Assyrian empire. All I want to do here is to point out that, in contrast to the seventh century when silver is undoubtedly the standard medium of currency, although copper was still fairly commonly used, in the texts of the early eighth century copper is very much more common than silver. In our sale texts—which include some as late as 743 and even 727 B.C.—we have thirty-four instances of copper or bronze[48] as purchase price,[49] to three instances of silver,[50] and two texts with a mixed price of copper and silver (Nos. 17 and 18). Consequently we are justified in stating that in most of the eighth century copper was the standard medium of currency; silver is used in Nos. 30 and 31, where the area sold is considerable and the purchase price accordingly high, and the same reason probably applies to Nos. 17 and 18, where the bulk of the price was paid in silver, presumably for convenience, and the remaining small sum made up in the more accurate copper. The reasons for the (doubtless gradual) shift to silver are no doubt various, and it would be pointless to attempt to investigate them here when no study of prices for the later period has been made and other basic economic forces remain inadequately described.[51]

[47] Cf. the charts in J. Zabłocka, *Stosunki agrarne w państwie Sargonidow* (Uniwersytet im. Adama Mickiewicza w Poznaniu, Wydział filozoficzno-historyczny, Seria historica Nr. 47. Poznań, 1971), in particular those listing the deported populations between the kings Aššur-dān II and Aššur-nirārī V, and in the Sargonid period.

[48] For the suggestion that both " copper " (URUDU) and " bronze " (ZABAR) may be used for bronze at this date, cf. C. Zaccagnini, *Oriens Antiquus* 10 (1971), 123–44; his thesis seems to me to be supported by the parallel usage of the two logograms in our texts, and I do not therefore make a distinction between them here.

[49] " Bronze " in Nos. 2, 11, 15, 45, 47; " copper " in Nos. 3, 4, 6, 9, 10, 12, 14, 19, 21–7, 29, 32–5, 43, 44, 59. From the quantity mentioned we must have to do with copper or bronze in Nos. 5, 8, 16, 20, 37, 48.

[50] Silver is used in Nos. 30 and 31, and in view of the quantity of 1 mina must be restored in No. 13.

[51] To make a very rough comparison, we may quote the following figures extracted from the 100 texts of varying kinds edited in *ARU* 200–99; they date mostly if not all from the seventh century: silver: 72 texts; copper: 6; uncertain: 16; no metal involved: 6. In comparison with our texts, these figures speak for themselves, however much allowance is made for chance or non-random selection.

TRANSLITERATIONS AND TRANSLATIONS

No. 1 Plate 1 ND 267
IM 56834

9·4 × (11·0) × (3·2) [—]

Governor's Palace, Room K.

Obv. 1′ [ ]⌜*ša*?⌝[ ]
2′ [*i*]*š*? *pu x*[ ]
(stamp seal impressions)
3′ [(x) x *m*]*i*? ÍD-*la-te* 2 TÚG *dáp-pa-*⌞*áš*?⌟-[*te*]
4′ [x T]ÚG SI.LUḪ.MEŠ-*te* [( )]
5′ [x T]ÚG *ki-ṣip-te ša pu-uš-ka-a-a* [( )]
6′ [x]+½ TÚG *ša-ḫi-li ša* SÍG ḪÉ.ME.D[A]
7′ [x TÚ]G *ki-ṣip-*[*t*]*e ša* SÍG ZA.GÌN.DIR *a-di* TÚG *ša x*[ ]
8′ [x TÚG *k*]*i-ṣip-te ša* SÍG ZA.GÌN.DIR *a-di* [T]ÚG KIMIN
9′ [( )]*x x x ša* [lú]*ḫa-ti-ni*
10′ 6 TÚG.⌜GÚ⌝.È.MEŠ *sad-ra-te* 2 TÚG *ša-ḫi-la-t*[*e*]
11′ 2 TÚG *ḫ*[*ul*?]*-se*? 4 TÚG *gu-li-na-te*
12′ 2 TÚG *g*[*a-me*]*-da-te* PAP 32 TÚG.PA.MEŠ
13′ 3 *sal*?-⌜*x x* (*x*)⌝.MEŠ UTÚL UD.KA.B[AR] *sa-ap-lu* URUDU
14′ *ša* 4 MA.NA ḪAR URUDU NA$_4$.GIL NA$_4$ ME-*ṣi*?[( )]
15′ *ša* 5 GÍN *qu-da-si* GUŠKIN
16′ [*i*]*na* ŠÀ *šá* [uru]*gar-ga-miš*
B.E. 17′ [(*x*) *x x*]*kab* URUDU
(remainder broken)

Translation

3′: . . . . .; 2 cloth covers; [x] *S*. cloths; [x] pieces of *ša puškāyi* cloth; [x]+½ *š*. cloths of red wool; [x] pieces of purple wool, together with a [. . .] cloth; [x] pieces of purple wool together with a ditto cloth; a . . . . cloth(?) of the bridegroom; 10′: 6 ordinary coats; 2 *š*. garments; 2 *ḫ*. cloths; 4 coats(?); 2 *g*. garments; in all 32 textiles(?). 13′: 3 . . . . s; a cauldron of bronze; a bowl of copper; a copper arm-ring of 4 minas; a . . . . of . . . . stone; a gold (finger-)ring of 5 shekels, by (the mina) of Carchemish; [a . . .] . . of copper; (remainder broken).

Notes

4′: TÚG SI.LUḪ: this textile is presumably to be restored in *PVA* 256 (there: TÚK SI.G[A] !), and is also attested in *ADD* 959, 5: 1 TÚG SI.LUḪ, and *ADD* 957, 10: 4 SI.LUḪ ḪÉ.MED(!). Any connection with UDU SI.LUḪ (*RGD* No. 48, 3′) is uncertain. Also TÚG.SI.LUḪ SA$_5$ GI$_6$ (VAT 9849, 20) and TÚG.SI.LUḪ KUR *tab*(*a*)*-la-a-a* (ibid., 24), courtesy K. Deller.

5′: *kiṣiptu*, apparently hitherto unknown, must be a derivative from the verb **kaṣāb/pu*. This verb seems to be an nA by-form of *kasāpu*(*m*) I (*AHw* 453a), cf. *ka-*ZIB (*ADD* 676 rev. 11′, coll.); the meaning of the verb being " to cut off " or similar, we may suggest a translation of *kiṣiptu* as " cut-off piece ".

ša puškāyī (*sic* ?) recalls *PVA* 232: TÚG.GÚ.È *ša bu-u*[*š-x*]; collation from photograph indicates that there is just enough space to accommodate *pu-u*[*š-ka-a-a*]. K. Deller quotes me 3 TÚG.BAR.DUL *ša pu-uš-ka-a-a* (VAT 9849, 22).

6′: *šaḫili* also *PVA* 240(!) and Billa No. 71, 2–3 (*JCS* 7 (1953), 137); plural *šaḫilāte* probably first attested here (l. 10′). The word is derived, according to *AHw* 345b, from *ša ḫi-li*.

SÍG.ḪÉ.ME.DA (= *tabribu*), see *Iraq* 32 (1970), 158, on No. 26.iv.5.

7′: SÍG.ZA.GÌN.DIR: B. Landsberger, *JCS* 21 (1967), 161a, *et passim*.

9′: The mention here of a bridegroom indicates that the text lists items to do with a marriage; the first sign in the line could be TÚG, in which case it might refer to a special kind of garment appropriate to a bridegroom. Any other sort of reference to him at this point seems unlikely.

11′: *ḫulsē* is tentatively restored after *PVA* 242; however, as K. Deller points out to me, it is possible that the *PVA* entry is an error for *nik-se*, which would fit equally well here, and is (unlike *ḫulsē*) otherwise attested (also in VAT 9849, 10 and 31).

12′: TÚG.PA: this term, whose Akkadian reading is unknown to me, is elsewhere used to sum up certain types of textile: TÚG.KAD and *šadinnu* (ND 2672 (*Iraq* 23 (1961), 42), and, without TÚG, in *ADD* 1124 rev. 1–2).

14′: Possible restoration: *me-ṣi-*[*ra-nu*], cf. No. 125, 4.

14–15′: The word order in these lines is curious, but as indicated in the translation, it is clear that the mentions of weight apply to the following, and not the preceding, items.

17′: Sign *kab* confirmed by collation.

Commentary

Since the opening lines are lost, we can say little about this text, except that it lists items transferred as part of a marriage transaction. For such texts, cf. *par excellence* ND 2307 (*Iraq* 16 (1954), 37–8), which includes textiles and metal vessels as here, but is richer by far.

No. 2 Plate 3 ND 492

BM 132003

5·1 × 6·9 × 2·6 —.xii.808/817

Governor's Palace, Room M.

Obv. 1 *ṣu-pur* ^{m}EN-*a-ḫi*

2 DUMU ^{m}ḪAR-*ṭu*?-*na-a-a*

(finger-nail impressions)

3 ^{m}*x*[(*x*)]-*ta-'a*

4 Ì[R š]*a* ^{m}EN-*a-ḫi*

5 *ina* ŠÀ 20 MA.NA UD.KA.BAR.MEŠ

6 *i-zi-rip*

7 *a-na* ^{m}*mu-še-zib-*^{d}MAŠ

8 ^{lú}*šá-kìn* ^{uru}*kal-ḫi*

9 *i-ti-din*

Rev. 10 *kas-pu ga-mur*

11 *ta-din* LÚ *za-rip*

12 *la-qi*

13 IGI ^{m}ÌR.DINGIR.MEŠ-*ni*

14 DUMU [^{m}]DINGIR-*dà-ra-ni*

15 IGI ^{m}*ra-ši*-DINGIR
16 ^{lú}*mu-kil*-KUŠ.⌞PA⌟.MEŠ
17 IGI ^{m}MU.GIŠ DUMU ^{m}*ki-rib-te*
18 IGI ^{m}*ib-ni-i*
19 DUMU $^{m.d}$UTU.KAR-*ir*
20 IGI ^{m}*la-qi-pu*
21 ^{lú}*še-lap-pa-a-a*
T.E. 22 ^{iti}ŠE *li-me*
23 $^{m.d}$ŠEŠ.GAL.DINGIR-*a-a*

Translation

1: Nail of Bēl-ahi, son of HARṭunāyu. (Nail marks.) 3: [. .]ta'a, slave of Bēl-ahi, he (Bēl-ahi) has contracted and given to Mušēzib-ninurta, the governor of Kalhu, in exchange for 20 minas of bronze. 10: The price has been paid *in toto*, the man is legally acquired.

13: Before Urdu-ilāni, son of Ilu-darānu, before Raši-ilu, the rein-holder, before Šūmu-lēšir, son of Kiribtu, before Ibnī, son of Šamaš-ēṭir, before Laqīpu, the Shelappaean.

22: Month of Addāru (XII), *limmu* of Nergal-ilāya (817/808 B.C.).

Notes

2: ḪAR-*ku*- also possible but less likely.

6: *i-zi-rip* . . . . . *i-ti-din*: this rare combination is found elsewhere only in *ADD* 384, 7, although the phrase *za-rip ta-din* is found in an unpublished Assur text (Ass. Fd. Nr. 10805, see K. Deller, *OrNS* 33 (1964), 93). Here the phrase appears to replace the more usual *utappiš ittidin.* Deller has discussed the verb *zarāpu* (and its treatment in *CAD*, Vol. 16 (Ṣ), 105b) in his review of that volume in *OrNS* 33 (1964), 92–3. He is surely right in his reasons for taking the initial sibilant as *z*, not *ṣ*, and it is now quite clear that he was correct in rejecting *CAD*'s translation of the verb: " to buy, acquire ". It appears from our passage that *zarāpu* must have had a function very like that of *uppušu*; Deller tries to set up the two opposing pairs *uppušu* + *tadānu* (procedure of sale) and *zarāpu* + *laqā'u* (procedure of purchase), and there is no denying that the scribes habitually used the verbs in this way. But the occurrence here (and in *ADD* 384, wrongly emended by *CAD* and not explained by Deller) of *zarāpu* + *tadānu* shows (1) that *CAD*'s translation is wrong, and (2) that Deller has attempted to draw too fine a distinction.

In short, it seems that, theoretically, *zarāpu* and *uppušu* are interchangeable, and both mean approximately " entered into " (or " concluded ") " a legal contract ", although in practice *uppušu* tends to be used more with *tadānu, zarāpu* more with *laqā'u.* It is no chance that our text is so early: *ADD* 384 (date lost) also has the archaic formula *apil zaku,* and collation reveals that it is a characteristic early eighth-century sale tablet, being large, and having the coarse script found on the Nimrud tablets of this date.

22: Note the absence of a day date; this too could be due to the text's early period, although the omission does of course occur later as well.

Commentary

Whether the text dates to 808, or to 817, it is one of the earliest of our documents, and indeed (apart from a few from Tell Billa) of all nA legal texts. Two features which may be explained by this early date have already been noted above. The only other point worthy of comment is probably not to be attributed to this cause: the text completely lacks penalty clauses, even the invariable *tuāru* (*dēnu*) *dabābu laššu.* In this it agrees with No. 4 (769 B.C.), which is not particularly early within the context of this archive. In that case I have suggested that the informality of the document may be because the transaction is between two members of the administration; the same might be true here, but there can be no proof of this.

No. 3 | Plate 2 | ND 253
Inst. Arch. London

5·8 × 8·1 × 2·9 | 3.xi.791

Governor's Palace, Room K.

Obv.	1	*ku-mu* NA$_4$.KIŠIB-*šú ṣ[u-p]ur-šú [iš]-kun*
		(finger-nail impressions)
	2	*ṣ[u-p]ur* ^{m}SUḪUŠ.ŠEŠ.MEŠ
	3	LÚ.[Ì]R ⌞*ša*⌟ LÚ UGU É
	4	*ša* ^{lú}EN.NAM *ša* [^{u}]^{ru}*kal-ḫi*
	5	^{m}AD-*ul*-ZU ŠEŠ-*šú*
	6	*ina* ŠÀ 8 MA.NA URUDU.MEŠ
	7	*a-na* ^{m}DI.KUD-*i*
	8	*i-ti-din*
	9	^{m}DI.KUD-*i* TA IGI
	10	^{m}[SUḪ]UŠ.ŠEŠ.MEŠ *ú-tap-piš* TI-*qí*
	11	[Š]EŠ-*šú ša* ^{m}SUḪUŠ.ŠEŠ.MEŠ
B.E.	12	[*za-rip la*]-⌜*qi*⌝
	13	[*kas-pu*] *ga-mur ta-din*
	14	[ ] *x x x x*
Rev.	15	[ ]*x x*
	16	[MA].NA ⌜AN.NA⌝.MEŠ
	17	[ ]*x x* SUM-⌜*an*⌝
	18	[ ] GÚ.UN [UR]UDU.MEŠ
	19	[ ] *x*
	20	[ ]*i* [(*x x*)]
	21	[ ] *x x*
	22	[ ] *x x*
	23	[ ]*x x x*
	24	[IG]I ^{m}*ta*-⌜*x*⌝-*qa*? [(*x*)]
	25	[IGI] ^{m}*si-lim-aš*-⌞*šur*⌟ ^{lú}[*x*]-*pur*?
	26	[IGI] ^{m}SAR?-*a-a* IGI ^{m}*a-ri*?-*bu* LÚ.ŠÀM
	27	IGI ^{m}*ḫu*?-*la-a-a ša* ^{uru}EN-*li-bur*
	28	IGI ^{m}ÌR.^{d}15 DUMU ^{m}*nu-ra-a-ni*
	29	IGI ^{m}*qa-ru-ru* IGI ^{m}*di-di-i* LÚ.ŠÀM
	30	PAP 8 IGI.MEŠ ^{iti}ZÍZ UD.3.KÁM
T.E.	31	*lim-mu* ^{m}EN.GAR.BA-*a-ni*

Translation

1: Instead of his seal he impressed his nail. (Nail marks.) 2: Nail of Ubru-ahhē, slave of the house-supervisor of the governor of Kalhu. 5: He has given Abu-ūl-īdi, his brother, to Dayānī in exchange for 8 minas of copper. 9: Dayānī contracted and took (him) from Ubru-ahhē. 11: The brother of Ubru-ahhē [has been legally ac]quired, [the price] has been paid *in toto*.

(Long break; ll. 16–18 mention payment of fines in tin (16) and in copper (18).)

24: [before] Ta . . .[. ., before] Silim-aššur, a . . . . ., [before] Kiṣrāyu, before Aribu$^{?}$, a "bought man", before Hulāyu$^{?}$ of the village of Bēl-lību̅r, before Urdu-ištar, son of Nūrānu, before Qaruru, before Didī, a "bought man". In all, 8 witnesses.

30: Month of Šabāṭu (XI), 3rd day, *limmu* of Bēl-iqīšāni (791 B.C.).

Notes

7: Dayānī: DI.KUD alternates with *da-an* and Aramaic דין in the PN Dayān-kurbail (K. Tallqvist, *APN* 68a); our name DI.KUD-*i* is also found in a list of specimen names (*ADD* II, App. 1.x.29, p. 361), where Tallqvist (ibid.) reads Dayān-na'id, which seems less likely to me than Dayānī.

12: Note that the gap between the traces of *qi* is exaggerated wrongly in the copy.

25: No space for [DUG.QA].BUR; the last sign could also be PAD. If ^{lú}SIP.PUR (*RGD* No. 27.8 and *ADD* 952.7′, coll.) were a syllabic spelling, we could perhaps restore here [*si*], but the connection with sheep in *ADD* 952 suggests that SIP has to be taken as the sign for shepherd; cf. perhaps Billa No. 76, 6:]2 *ši pur* (*JCS* 7 (1953), 171)?

26: Or possibly *ḫu* (for *ri*).

Commentary

Ubru-ahhē sells his brother to Dayānī. Ubru-ahhē is himself described as the slave of an official of the provincial governor, and it is therefore likely that his brother is also a slave (there is no reason to suppose that LÚ.ÌR in l. 3 does not mean "slave" in its fullest sense). This does not however explain the nature of Ubru-ahhē's legal powers over his brother Abu-ūl-īdi. It might be that in the case of a slave-family the elder brother might exercise a father's authority over the rest of the family, but even if this were so, and there is no evidence to support it, he would surely not have the right of sale, which would lie with the slaves' owner. The same difficulty would affect the theory that Abu-ūl-īdi was in some way legally obliged to his brother, such as by debt.

Even if we choose to assume that the term "slave" as used in this text is only relative, and should be considered to mean rather "subordinate", we still have no obvious solution, or explanation, of why one brother might sell another. If the brother, as a free man, was being sold into slavery—a rare event in any case, at this date—we might expect a clause of release such as is found in No. 10, or better preserved in No. 248.

No. 4 Plate 3 ND 265
IM 56832
6·2 × 8·4 × 2·9 13.i.769

Governor's Palace, Room K.

Obv. 1 ^{m}PAP-*a*-SU
2 LÚ.ÌR *ša* ^{lú}AGRIG.GAL
3 DUMU.MÍ-*su*
4 *a-na* LÚ.ÌR *ša* ^{m}EN.KI-*a*

Obv. 5 *ina lìb-bi* 36 MA.NA URUDU.MEŠ
6 SUM-*in kás-[p]u gam-mur*
7 *ta-din* MÍ *za-ar-pat*
8 TI-*at šúm-ma* MÍ
9 *taḫ-ti-liq* AD-*šá*
10 *pu-tuḫ-šá na-ši*
Rev. 11 IGI ^{m}*šùl-mu*-PAP.MEŠ
12 IGI $^{m.d}$NA$_4$.ŠÚ.PAP.AŠ
13 LÚ.KA.ŠÈR *ša ša* IGI.É.GAL
14 IGI ^{m}*ḫu-ṭu-su* ^{lú} ''
15 IGI ^{m}*šùl-mu*-EN.IGI GAL *ši-ma-ni*
16 IGI ^{m}ERÍN.MEŠ.SIG LÚ.TIN.NA
17 IGI ^{m}*si-si-ia* LÚ.NINDA
18 IGI ^{m}*a-ḫu-a-nu* ^{lú}*ḫa-za-nu*
19 *ša* URU.ŠE ^{lú}*tar-ta-ni*
20 IGI ^{m}*gab-bu-a-na*-15 LÚ.TIN.NA
21 IGI ^{m}GIŠ.MI.15
T.E. 22 IGI $^{m.d}$MAŠ.I
23 *ṣa-bit* IM
L.E. 24 IGI ^{m}*ṣa-ṣi-i* [^{it}]^{i}BARAG UD.13
25 *lim-mu* ^{m}EN.DINGIR-*a-a*

Translation

1 : Ahua-(e)rība, slave of the chief steward, has given his daughter to the slave of Bēl-issīya in exchange for 36 minas of copper. 6 : The price has been paid *in toto*, the woman is legally acquired. 8 : If the woman flees, her father bears the responsibility.

11 : Before Šulmu-ahhē, before . . .-ahu-iddina, the tailor(?) of the palace supervisor, before Huṭusu, ditto, before Šulmu-bēli-lāmur, chief maltster(?), before Ṣābu-damqu, vintner, before Sisīya, baker(?), before Ahuānu, mayor of the village of the *turtānu*, before Gabbu-ana-ištar, vintner, before Ṣil-ištar, before Ninurta-na'id, writer of the tablet, before Ṣaṣī.

24 : Month of Nīsānu (I), 13th day, *limmu* of Bēl-ilāya (769 B.C.).

Notes

4 : It is not possible to turn Bēl-issīya into the purchaser by rendering this line " to (be) a slave of B.", because LÚ.ÌR cannot apply to a girl.

5 : 30 is written like KUR (collated).

12 : ^{d}NA$_4$.ŠÚ : no reading can be suggested ; collated.

13 : *sic* (*ša* repeated) ; this necessitates reading IGI É.GAL, and not AGRIG.GAL.

14 : The unusual *ditto* sign is written over an erased GAM (a common sign of repetition).

15 : *ši-ma-ni* must be the Assyrian form for the ingredient of beer called *isimmānû* (for which see the dictionaries) ; any doubt on this score is settled by the subsequent mention of two " vintners " (LÚ.TIN.NA).

16 : For reading SIG as *damqu* (i.e. for SIG$_5$), see the other instances of this name in the Index ; the reading of the first element of the name seems to be proved by the writing *ṣa-bu*-SIG (*APN* 204b).

22 : There is the possibility of reading the *-i* as a simple phonetic complement (cf. Deller's suggestion for reading ^{d}MAŠ.TI.I as Ni'urtī or similar, in *Iraq* 32 (1970), 143[9], and *OrNS* 34 (1965), 383).

Commentary

Ahua-(e)rība sells his daughter (un-named) to a slave of Bēl-issīya (who was presumably at this date the *rab ālāni* of the governor of Kalhu). Curiously, the name of the actual purchaser is not given, and the document lacks the usual penalty clauses, including the *ṣibtu bennu* clause, although there is a less usual condition, which lays the responsibility for the girl on the father should she run away.

Of the witnesses two belong to the establishment of the palace supervisor, while four others (Šulmu-bēli-lāmur, Ṣābu-damqu, Sisīya, and Gabbu-ana-ištar) have similar professions, and perhaps form a group under the *abarakku*, since it is in commodities of this sort that he is known to deal. It may be that the curious features of this document are to be explained by the fact that the transaction is between members of the administration (cf. commentary on No. 2); the absence of penalty clauses could be accepted by itself as insignificant, but when the text has no seal or nail impressions either, some explanation of its deviation from standard practice must be sought. There seems to be no good legal reason for it, and hence I can only suggest that the whole transaction was relatively informal because of continuing close contact between the parties concerned.

No. 5 Plate 1 ND 212
IM 56813
20.vii.754

6·2 × 8·1 × 2·4

Governor's Palace, Room K.

Obv. 1 [*ṣ*]*u-pur* ᵐ*na-ga-*[*a-a*]
2 EN MÍ (finger-nail impressions)
3 ᵐ[ⁱ]*x-na-ia* DUMU.M[Í(*-su*)]
4 *ina* ŠÀ ⌜1⌝ GÚ.UN MA.N[A]
5 ᵐ*na-ga-a-a* [( )]
6 *a-na* ᵐ·ᵈEN.ZALÁG-*ka-*⌜*la-mur*⌝
7 ⌜*ú*⌝*-tap-piš i-ti-din*
8 [*k*]*as-pu ga-mur ta-din*
9 MÍ *za-ár-pat la-qi-at*
10 *tu-a-ru da-ba-bu la-a-šú*
11 *ša* BAL*-u-ni*
Rev. 12 ⌜*kas*⌝*-pu a-na* 10.MEŠ*-te*
13 *a-na* [E]N.MEŠ*-šú ú-tar*
14 [I]G[I] ᵐ⌜*bi*?⌝*-bi-i*
15 [I]GI ᵐ⌜*x*⌝*-qi-i*
16 IGI ᵐ*pu-uš-ḫi-i*
17 IGI ᵐDU*-i* ⌞LÚ.A.BA!⌟
18 ⁱᵗⁱDUL UD.20.K[ÁM]
19 *lim-me* ᵐ·ᵈMAŠ*-še-zib-a-n*[*i*]

Translation

1: Nail of Nagāyu, owner of the woman. (Nail marks.) 3: [. .]nāya [(his)] daughter Nagāyu has contracted and given to Bēl-nūrka-lāmur in exchange for one talent of [copper/bronze]. 8: The price has been paid *in toto*, the woman is legally acquired. There is no (further) withdrawal (or) litigation. Whoever revokes shall return the price ten-fold to its owners.

14: Before Bibī(?), before [. .]qī, before Pušhī, before Kēnī, the scribe.

18: Month of Tašrītu (VII), 20th day, *limmu* of Ninurta-šēzibāni (754 B.C.).

Notes

17: BA! is written ZU, but the emendation and restoration is supported by the occurrence of a Kēnī as the scribe of No. 26 (ll. 29–30). That Kēnī is the correct reading of DU-*i* is shown by *ADD* 676, where in rev. 6′ we have ^{m}*ke-ni-i* and in rev. 10′ ^{m}DU-*i* (collated).

No. 6 Plate 4; Photo Plate 93b ND 251

5·2 × 8·1 × 2·1 Inst. Arch. London 28.[—].735

Governor's Palace, Room M.

Obv. 1 *ku-um* NA$_4$.KIŠIB-*šú ṣu-pu*[*r-šú iš-ku*]*n*

2 *ṣu-pur* $^{m.uru}$NINA-*a-a* ^{lú}TÚG.K[A.ŠÈ]R

(finger-nail impressions)

3 ^{m} *x* [(*x*) *x q*]*i* KA.ŠÈR ÌR *ša* ^{uru}NI[NA]-*a-a*

4 *up-p*[*iš-ma* ^{m}]$^{.d}$AMAR.UTU.A.PAP DUMU ^{m}EN.PAP-*ir*

5 *ina* ŠÀ[(-*bi*) *x* MA.N]A URUDU.MEŠ TI-*qí*

6 *kás-p*[*u ga*(*m*)-*mur* S]UM-*ni* LÚ-*u šu-a-tu*

7 *za-r*[*i-ip laqi tú-a*]-*ru de-e-nu*

8 KA.[KA *laššu*] *man-nu šá ina ur-kiš*

9 *i-na* [*matē-ma de-*]*e-nu* KA.KA

10 *ub-ta-'*[*u-ni* 1 M]A.NA KÙ.BABBAR LUḪ-*u*

11 1 MA.NA GUŠKIN *sag-ru ina bur-ki*

12 ^{d}15 *ša* ^{uru}NINA *i-šak-kan*

13 [*k*]*ás-pu a-na* 10.MEŠ-*te ana* EN-*š*[*ú*]

14 [*ú-t*]*a-ra ina de-ni-š*[*ú*] K[A.KA-*ma*]

15 [*la* T]I-*qí bi-lat*? AN!.NA [( )]

16 [*ana* L]Ú.EN.NAM URU-[*šú iddan*]

17 2 ANŠE.KUR.RA ⌜BABBAR⌝.M[EŠ]

Rev. 18 [ ]

19 [IGI ^{m}]-*aš-šur* LÚ [ ]

20 [IGI ^{m}]*x* LÚ *x*[ ]

21 [IGI ^{m}] L[Ú].⌞DIN?⌟ [( )]

22 [IGI $^{m.d}$I]M-*iq-bi* L[Ú] *x* [( )]

23 [IGI $^{m.d}$*ni*]*n*?-*urta*?-PAP.PAP [( )]

24 IGI [^{m} *x*] *x x* LÚ *x*

25 IGI [^{m}*é-s*]*ag-gíl*-A.PAP A[.BA] *ṣa-bit* IM
26 ^{iti}[*x* UD].28.KAM *lim-m*[*u*]
27 ^{m}*aš-šur-*[*ša*]*l-lim-an-ni* ^{l}[^{ú}*šá-kìn*(?)]
28 ^{uru}*ár-ba*$_6$(Ú)$^?$-[*x*]

Translation

1: Instead of his seal [he impressed his] nail. Nail of Ninuāyu, tailor. (Nail marks.) 3: [. . .]qi, tailor(?), slave of Ninuāyu, Marduk-aplu-uṣur, son of Bēl-nāṣir, has contracted and taken in exchange for [x] minas of copper. 6: The price has been paid [*in toto*], that man is legally [acquired; there is no (further) with]drawal, lawsuit, (or) litigation. Anyone who [at any time] in the future initiates lawsuit (or) litigation shall place [1] mina of purified silver (and) 1 mina of refined gold in the lap of Ishtar of Nineveh. [He shall] return the price ten-fold to its owners, [he shall plead] in his lawsuit, [but not] succeed. He shall [pay] 1 talent(?) of tin [to] the governor of [his] city, [he shall offer] 2 white horses [to DN].

19: [Before . . . .]-aššur, the [. . . ., before . . . . .], the [. . . ., before . . . . .], the builder(?), [before A]dad-iqbi, the [. . . ., before Nin]urta?-ahu-uṣur, [the . . . . .], before [. . . . .], the . . . . . Before [Es]aggil-aplu-uṣur, the scribe, writer of the tablet.

26: Month [of . . . .], 28th [day], *limmu* of Aššur-šallimanni, the [governor] of Ar[rapha] (735 B.C.).

Notes

6: Note the unusual writing LÚ-*u*.

17: There may be a faint ruling after this line on the Bottom Edge; the penalties in ll. 15–17 are obviously an afterthought of the scribe.

18: This line may not have been present at all.

28: The city name required is Arrapha; I can see no convincing reading for the second sign, the first part of which is quite clear.

Commentary

Sale of a slave by a man called Ninuāyu, or "the Ninevite". Since the text mentions Ishtar of Nineveh (l. 12), it seems likely that he was in fact a resident of that city, and indeed the omission of the PN determinative before his name in l. 3 suggests that it was perhaps not strictly his name, and that the scribe was conscious of this.

No. 7 Plate 5 ND 242
IM, for study

6·4 × (8·7) × (2·8) [—].ii.[—]

Governor's Palace, Room K.

Obv. 1 *k*[*u-um/mu*]
2 *ṣu-p*[*ur* PN]
3 ^{uru}[ ]

(finger-nail impressions)

Obv. 4 $^{m.d}$UTU.⌜AD⌝.[ÌR-*šú*]
5 *ša* ^{m}*mu*-D[I$^{?}$.^{d}UTU ( )]
6 *ú-piš-*[*m*]*a* [^{m}E]N.KI-*a*$^{?}$
7 LÚ.GAL.⌜URU$^{?}$.MEŠ$^{?}$⌝ *ina lìb-bi bi-la*[*t*$^{?}$ *x* (*x*)]
8 TA* IGI ^{m}*mu*-DI$^{?}$.^{d}UTU *i*[*l-qi*]
9 [*ka*]*s-pu* [*g*]*am-mur* [*t*]*a-d*[*in*]
10 L[Ú] *za-rip la-a-*[*qi*]
11 [*tú-a-ru*] *de-e-*[*nu d*]*a-*[*ba-bu*]
12 [(*x*) *x x*]⌞*x x*⌟[ ]
(remainder of obv. and all rev. broken)

L.E. 1′ [^{iti}]⌜GUD⌝[
2′ [*i*]*a*$^{?}$*-di* IGI ^{m}*x*[
3′ [ ] IGI ^{m}*ša*[*l*]*-lim*-DINGIR LÚ.SAG

Translation

1: In[stead of his seal he impressed his nail]. Nail [of Mušallim$^{?}$-šamaš of] the town [. . . . .]. (Nail marks.)

4: Šamaš-abu-[. . ., the slave] of Muša[llim$^{?}$-šamaš] Bēl-issīya has contracted and taken from Mušallim$^{?}$-šamaš in exchange for 1 talent [of . . .]. 9: The price has been paid *in toto*, the man is legally acquired. [There is no (further) withdrawal], lawsuit, (or) litigation [. . . . .]. (long gap).

L.E. 1′: [ ] Month of Ayāru (II) [. . . . .], [before . . i]adi, before [. . . . ., before . . . . .], before Šallim-ilu, eunuch.

No. 8 Plate 3 ND 478

Inst. Arch. London

(5·8) × 7·5 × (2·3) [—]

Governor's Palace, Room K.

Obv. 1 [*ku-um* NA$_{4}$].⌜KIŠIB-*šú ṣ*⌝[*u-pur-šú* (*iškun*)]
(finger-nail impressions)

2 [*ṣu-pur*] ^{m}DINGIR.SU KUR *ḫa-ma-t*[*a*$^{?}$*-a-a*]
3 [^{m}(*x*)]*x-du-lu* LÚ.ÌR-[*šu*]
4 [*ša*] ^{m}DINGIR.SU [( )]
5 [*ú-ta*]*p-piš ina* ŠÀ 21 MA.N[A
6 *a-na* ^{m}EN-*i-si-a i-t*[*i-din*]
7 *kás-pu gam-mur ta-din*
8 LÚ *za-rip la-a-q*[*i*]
9 *tu-a-ru* KA.KA ⌞*la*⌟-[*a*(*š*)-*šu* (*mannu*)]
10 *ša i-pa-r*[*i-ku-u-ni*]
11 ⌞1⌟ GÚ.UN AN.[NA
(remainder broken)

N.B.—The fragment shown in the copy together with ND 478 fills the gap in ll. 6–9; it is at present housed in Baghdad together with ND 479(b) (No. 37). It measures (2·5) × (2·2) × (0·9).

Translation

1: [Instead of] his seal [he impressed his nail]. (Nail marks.) [Nail] of Ilu-(e)rība, the [man of] Hamath.

3: [. .]dulu, [the] slave [of] Ilu-(e)rība he (Ilu-(e)rība) has contracted and giv[en] to Bēl-issīya in exchange for 21 minas [of copper/bronze]. 7: The price has been paid *in toto*, the man is legally acquired. [There is no (further)] withdrawal (or) litigation. [Anyone] who contravenes (the agreement) [shall pay] 1 talent of tin [. . . . .

No. 9 Plate 6; Photo Plate 92b ND 474
IM 56862

7·7 × 10·3 × (3·0) [—]

Governor's Palace, Room K.

Obv. 1 *ṣu-pur* ^{m}PAP-*la-mur* DUMU ^{m}*ki-si-i*

(finger-nail impressions)

2 3 LÚ.ERÍN.MEŠ 1 MÍ PAP 4 ZI.MEŠ
3 *a-na* ^{m}EN.KI-*ia ina* 1 *me* 50 MA.NA URUDU.MEŠ
4 TA* IGI ^{m}PAP-*la-mur* DUMU ^{m}*ki-si-ia*
5 *ú-tap-piš i-si-qi*
6 *kás-pu ga-mur ta-din*
7 UN.MEŠ *za-ar-pu la-qi-ú*
8 *tu-a-ru da-ba-bu la-a-šú*
9 *man-nu šá ina ur-kiš* TA* ^{m}EN.KI-*ia*
10 *de-nu da-ba-bu ub-ta-ú-ni*
11 1 MA.NA KÙ.BABBAR 1 MA.NA GUŠKIN
12 *ina bur-ki* ^{d}MAŠ *i-šá-kan*
13 *ina de-ni-šu i-da-bu-ub*
14 *la i-la-qi*

15 IGI ^{m}*i-ma-ri-i ša qur-bu-ti*
16 IGI ^{m}EN.URU GAL ^{lú}*kal-la-pi*
17 [I]GI ^{m}*aš-šur-rém-ni mu-tir-⟨ṭe⟩-mi*

B.E. (uninscribed)
(remainder broken)

Translation

1: Nail of Ahu-lāmur, son of Kisī. (Nail marks.)

2: 3 men and 1 woman, in all 4 persons, Bēl-issīya has contracted and taken from Ahu-lāmur, son of Kisīya, in (exchange for) 150 minas of copper. 6: The price has been paid *in toto*, the people are legally acquired. There is no (further) withdrawal (or) litigation. Anyone who in the future initiates a lawsuit or litigation against Bēl-issīya shall place 1 mina of silver (and) 1 mina of gold in the lap of Ninurta, (and) he shall plead in his lawsuit (but) not succeed.

15: Before Imārī, officer, before Bēl-āli, chief *kallāpu*, before Aššur-rēmāni, information officer, [. . . . .

Notes

1: The alternation *ki-si-i* : *ki-si-ia* shows that the distinction *-i* : *-ia* need not always be Ass : Bab (cf. M. Dietrich, *AOAT* 7, 50[2]).

3: It would in theory be possible to translate this line as it stands: "in all 4 persons (sold) to Bēl-issīya. He has contracted and taken . . .", but this phrasing would be most unusual. I think it is easier to assume that the *a-na* is a mistake, and that the scribe had intended to use the phrase *ana Bēl-issīya ittidin*, but lost the thread of his intentions. *Ina* in place of the usual *ina libbi* might also be a slip.

15: *ša qur-bu-ti* clearly shows that the profession normally read ^{lú}*qurbūtu* should (after the pattern of LÚ.SAG = *ša rēši*) be read *ša qurbūti* (lit. "he of closeness"). This at least seems to be the rule until the reign of Sargon. Besides the unequivocal instances in this volume (see glossary), we may compare the following passages (a sample only) where LÚ *qur-bu-ti/te* is plainly a Nom. or Acc. singular: *ABL* 99 rev. 17; 306, 2–4, 12 (both Sargon); 165 rev. 8; NL 44 (*Iraq* 20 (1958), 195–6), 14–20; NL 54 (*Iraq* 21 (1959), 163–5), 16 (but cf. 32); NL 62 (*Iraq* 21 (1959), 172–4), 20; NL 89 (*Iraq* 28 (1966), 185–7), 25; *ADD* 865, 2.

On the other hand, from Sargon's reign onwards, we find the writing LÚ *qur-bu-tú*, which cannot in every case be a misreading for *-te*: ND 2732 (*Iraq* 23 (1961), Pl. XXV) rev. 11′; ND 2803 (*Iraq* 23, Pl. XXIX–XXX) rev. i.1 (but cf. ibid. rev. i.8, 11, 33, 35, ii.14, 17—all *-te*); *ABL* 167, 20 (Sargon); 339 rev. 11 (Esarhaddon); 415 rev. 14; and many others. It is not clear whether these writings are for *ša-qurbūtu* or just *qurbūtu*; even the occasional omission of the LÚ is not decisive (e.g. *ABL* 415; *ADD* 993.iii.3; ND 2489 (*Iraq* 23 (1961), Pl. XVI, coll.), i.7: *qur-ub-tú*), since this could be an abbreviation like GAL.SAG for *rab ša rēši*.

Other instances are indecisive: (*ša*) *qurbūti* might be the Gen. sing. or the Plural of a **qurbūtu* or *ša-qurbūtu*, whilst the writing *qur*-ZAG leaves the final vowel in doubt. In my opinion the evidence suggests that towards the end of the eighth century B.C. the phrase *ša qurbūti* came to be treated as a single noun *ša-qurbūtu*, the period of transition falling chiefly within the reign of Sargon. A fuller investigation might permit us to define the position more accurately. A different explanation for the change of vowel is given by K. Deller and S. Parpola (*OrNS* 36 (1967), 338).

No. 10 Plate 5

ND 243
IM 56826
[—]

7·6 × (8·6) × (2·7)

Governor's Palace, Room K.

Obv. 1′ [-]⸢*ni*⸣

(trace of one stamp seal impression)

2′ [( ) ^{m}*la-ma*]*r*-⸢*ia-a*⸣-[*nu x* (*x*)]*x-šú* [( )]
3′ [*up-p*]*iš-ma* $^{m.d}$⸢*x x x x*⸣
4′ [*i*]*na* [*l*]*ìb-bi* 1 [G]Ú.UN ⸢MA.NA URUDU⸣.MEŠ
5′ TA* *pa-an* ^{m}MU.U.U *il*-[*q*]*i*
6′ [*k*]*as-pu ga-mur ta-ad-din*
7′ [L]Ú *šu-a-tu za-rip laq-qi*
8′ [*šúm-m*]*u* LUGAL(!) *an-du-ra-ru*
9′ [*i*-]⸤*ša-kan*⸥ ^{m}*la-mar-ia-a-nu*
10′ [ ]⸤*x x*⸥[L]Ú?.ÌR ⸤*ša*⸥ L[Ú *x* (*x*)]
(remainder broken)

Translation

[Seal of PN, owner of the man being sol]d. (Seal impressions.)

2′: [Lama]riānu, his [slave(?)] PN [contrac]ted and took from Šūm?-adad-milki in exchange for 1 talent of copper. 6′: The price has been paid *in toto*, that man has been legally acquired. 8′: If? the king creates an amnesty, Lamariānu [. . . . .] the slave of the [. . . . .

Notes

5′: The reading of the name MU.U.U is uncertain, although the second part (if it is to be taken thus) is fairly well established now (see K. Deller, *OrNS* 34 (1965), 382 f.). K. Deller suggests to me that the name be understood as Šumma/u-adad-milki, which is certainly attractive.

8′–9′: Although l. 8′ was collated, it does not tend to support the emendation of *in* to LUGAL. However, the suggested emendations seem to be the only means of giving sense to the passage, and may be justified by a comparison with No. 248, 13′–16′. In l. 9′ *ša* preferable to *šá* (coll.).

Commentary

This seems to be a slave sale, with an unusual clause which envisages the possibility that the man being sold might be released from his slavery as a result of an *(an)durāru* (" amnesty "), and that therefore the present purchaser might lose the benefit he is here acquiring. No. 248 is a similar text, and since it is better preserved, I have held back a brief discussion of the possible implications of these clauses to the commentary on that text.

No. 11 Plate 5 ND 246
IM 56827
[—]

5·8 × 7·8 × 3·0

Governor's Palace, Room K.

Obv. 1 [*ṣupur* ^{m} *x* *x* M]U?.A[PIN? EN MÍ (?)]
(finger-nail impressions)
2 [^{mí} *x* (*x*) *p*]*u?-šú* DUMU.M[Í-*su*]
3 [(*x*) *x*]*x* MEŠ *ú-piš-ma*
4 [^{m} (*x*) *x*]*x*.⌞MU⌟.APIN? *ina lìb-bi*
5 [UD.K]A.BAR.MEŠ
6 [*a-na* ^{m}(*x*) *x* *x*]-⌜*ib?*⌝-*ni*-PAP
7 [*id-din kas-pu*] *ga-mur*
8 [*ta-din* ( )] *be-en-nu ṣib-tu*
9 [*ana* 1 *me* UD.MEŠ] *sa-ar-tú*
(remainder of obv. broken; gap of 3–6 lines)
Rev. 1′ [IGI ^{m} *x* *x*]-*'a?-tú* *x* [(*x* *x*)]
2′ [( )] ^{lú}*mu-kil*-KUŠ.PA.ME
3′ [IGI] $^{m.d}$IM-*ṣa-a'-du*-⌜*i*⌝-*din*
4′ LÚ.3.U$_5$
5′ [I]GI ^{m}AD.DINGIR-*a-a* ^{lú}*ḫa-za-nu*
6′ IGI ^{m}UD.⌜5⌝.KÁM-*a-a* ŠEŠ.AD-*šú*
7′ IGI $^{m.d}$I[M].DÙ ^{uru}ḪAR-*ša-a-a*

Rev. 8′ IGI ^{m}*ḫar-ma-ku* DUMU ^{m}*aš-šur-l*[*e-i*(?)]
9′ IGI ^{m}*mu-mi-i* KIMIN
10′ IGI ^{m}*aš-šur*-PAP-*ir* LÚ.MU
11′ [I]GI ^{m}PAP-*lu*-TI ^{lú}*kar-ka-di-nu*
12′ [IG]I ^{m}*qa-na-si-i* LÚ.DUMU-*š*[*ú*?]
13′ [IGI] ^{m}*qur-di*-^{d}15 LÚ [*x x*]
14′ [IGI ^{m}*i*]*na*?-DI.PAP-*ir* L[Ú.A.BA]
T.E. 15′ [*ṣa-bit*] *ṭup*-[*pi* ( )]
(remainder broken)

Translation

1: [Nail of . . .]-šūmu-ēreš(?) [owner of the woman]. (Nail marks.)

2: [. . .p]ušu, [his] daughter ..... [. . .]-šūmu-ēreš(?) contracted and [gave to . . .]-ibni-ahu(?) in exchange for [. . . . of] bronze. 7: [The price has been paid] *in toto*, (she is guaranteed against) sickness and seizure [for 100 days] (and against) criminal charges [for ever . . . (break of 3–6 lines).

Rev. 1′: [Before . .]'atu[. . .], rein holder, [before] Adad-ṣa'du-iddin, third rider, before Abu-ilāya, mayor, before Ha(n)šāyu, his father's brother, before Adad-ibni, man of HARšu, before Harmaku, son of Aššur-le['i?], before Mumī, ditto, before Aššur-nāṣir, cook, before Ahu-luballiṭ, victualler, before Qanasī, his son, [before] Qurdi-ištar, [. . . . ., before I]na-šulmi-nāṣir(?), [the scribe, writer] of the tablet.

(Remainder, probably including the date, broken.)

Notes

4–6: The restoration of the first name (in l. 4) as the seller, and the second as the purchaser (by supplying *iddin*, not *ilqi*, etc.), is based on the observation that the *-su* which has to be restored at the end of l. 2 can only refer to the man mentioned in l. 4, who must therefore be the owner of the girl.

8: It may be that the unusual order of *bennu ṣibtu* (the reverse is the rule, though cf. *ADD* 310 rev. 13 (coll. *CAD* B 206b)) should be an indicator of early date, before the phrase was standard.

Rev. 9′: Before KIMIN an erased LÚ.

No. 12 Plate 7 ND 244
Inst. Arch. London
[—]

6·9 × (7·9) × 3·0

Governor's Palace, Room K.

Obv. (space for seal or finger-nail impressions)
1′–3′ (undeciphered; includes PNs)
4′ [*ina* Š]À 3? GÚ.UN ⸤URUDU⸥.[M]EŠ ⸢TA?⸣[IGI]
5′ ^{m}EN.DÙ-*uš x* [(*x*) *x*] *il*?-*q*[*i*?]
6′ *kás-pu ga-mur* [*ta-din*] ERÍN.MEŠ
7′ *za-a*[*r-p*]*u* [*l*]*a*-⸤*qí*⸥-*ú*
8′ *tú-a-ru* [*de-nu*(?)] *la*?-*áš-šú*
9′ *man-nu* ⸢*ša*⸣ *i*-⸤*par*?⸥-*ka*?-*ni*

10′ [1] MA.NA [K]Ù.[BABBAR] 1 M[A.NA KÙ.G]I
11′ *a-na* [(*x*) *x*] *x x*[(*x*)] *x* [( )]
12′ [D]UMU.M[Í-*su*(?)] *x x x x*[ ]
13′ [ ] GÌR^{II}(?) *x*[ ]
Rev. 14′–17′ (undeciphered ; 17′ is the first line of witnesses' names)

Translation

(2(+) PNs) 4′: [in] exchange for 3$^{?}$ talents of copper (PN contracted and] took(?) from Bēl-ēpuš. 6′: The price has been [paid] *in toto*, the people are legally acquired. There is no (further) withdrawal [(or) lawsuit]; anyone who contravenes(?) (the agreement) [shall pay 1] mina of silver (and) 1 mina of [gold] to [DN . . . . .] his daughter(?) [. . . . . at the] feet of [DN . . . . (remainder broken).

Notes

3′: This line should at least include the name of the purchaser.

9′: *man* is written over an erased *ma*. The verbal form restored would be acceptable if derived from the N stem of *parāku*, but that stem is not otherwise attested in this context.

Commentary

This multiple slave sale is unfortunately in piteous condition. That it involves more than one person is shown by the plurals of lines 6′–7′, and by the high purchase price.

No. 13 Plate 6; Photo Plate 92a ND 257
Inst. Arch. London
4·8 × 8·1 × 2·2 29.iv.?

Governor's Palace, Room M.

Obv. 1 NA$_4$.KIŠIB ^{m}*d*[*a*$^{?}$-]
2 EN M[Í]
(stamp seal impressions)
3 ^{mí}[ ]
4 DU[MU.MÍ(?)]
5 *ú*$^{?}$[-]
6 *ina lìb-*⌜*bi* 1 MA⌝.[NA KÙ.BABBAR]
7 *il-qí kas-pu g*[*a*$^{?}$*-mur*]
8 [*t*]*a-din tu-a-ru d*[*e-*(*e-*)*nu*]
9 [K]A.KA *la-a-*[*šú*]
Rev. 10 [ ]
11 [(*x*) *x x*] *na* [ ]
12 IGI ^{m}EN.GIŠ.*x* [ ]
13 IG[I] $^{m.d}$PA$^{?}$.⌜*x*⌝ [ ]
14 I[GI ^{m}]$^{.d}$UTU-*nu-r*[*u*$^{?}$( )]
15 [IGI] ^{m}SUḪUŠ.1[5$^{?}$ ( )]

Rev. 16 ⌜IGI⌝ ᵐ30.I? [( )]
17 ⁱᵗⁱŠU UD.29.KÁ[M]
18 *lim-mu* ᵐ *x x x x x*

Translation

1: Seal of Da[...], owner of the woman [(being sold)]. (Seal impressions.)

3: FPN, daughter(?) [of Da..., PN contracted and] took in exchange for 1 mina [(+x) of silver]. 7: The price has been paid *in* [*toto*], there is no (further) withdrawal, [lawsuit] (or) litigation. [........].

12: Before Bēl-...., before Nabû?-...., before Šamaš-nūr[ī?], before Ubru-i[štar?], before Sîn-nā'id?.

17: Month of Du'uzu (IV), 29th day, *limmu* of .....

Notes

1: ᵐ*i*[*d*- would also be possible.

18: Despite the considerable traces surviving, I have been unable to identify this *limmu's* name.

No. 14 Plate 8 ND 401 + 402
Inst. Arch. London
18.xii.802

7·0 × 10·4 × 2·6

Governor's Palace, Room U.

Obv. 1 *ku-um* NA_4.KIŠIB-*šú ṣu-pár-šú iš-ku*[*n*]
(space for finger-nail impressions)
2 ᵐ*me-ni-'i* É *ep-šú*
3 *a-di* GIŠ.ÙR.MEŠ-*šú*
4 ᵐ*aš-šur-tàk-lak* LÚ.GAL É
5 *ina* ŠÀ 40 M[A.N]A URUDU.MEŠ
6 *ú-tap-piš i-si-qi kás-pu*
7 *ga-mur ta-*⟨*din*⟩ É *za-rip*
8 *laq-qí tu-a-ru* KA.KA *la-šú*
9 *man-nu šá ina ur-kiš* TA ᵐ*aš-šur-tàk-lak*
10 *lu-u* ᵐ*me-ni-'i lu-u* DUMU.MEŠ-*šú*
11 [*l*]*u-u* ŠEŠ.MEŠ-*šú de-e-nu*
12 [KA].KA *u*[*b-t*]*a-'u-ni*
13 [*x x x*] GUŠKIN DIR *ina bur-ki* DINGIR
14 [(*x*) *x x*] *a-šib* ᵘʳᵘ*kal-ḫi* GAR-*an*
B.E. 15 [*x x x* K]Ù.BABBAR? *a-na*? LÚ.EN.NAM
16 [URU-*šú*] SUM-*an*
Rev. 17 [IGI ᵐ(*x*) *x x*]-*a*-DINGIR
18 [-]*si*?-*mu*
19 [IGI] ᵐ[*x x*]*x*.PAP
20 [LÚ].SAG *ša* LÚ.EN.NAM

21 [IGI] ^{m}*iš-me*-DINGIR
22 [IGI] $^{m.d}$UTU-*šal-lim*
23 ^{l}[^{ú}*m*]*u-kil-ap-pa-te*
24 IGI ^{m}*ḫar-ma-ku*
25 IGI $^{m.d(?)}$MAŠ?.ŠU$^{ii(?)}$.DIB
26 IGI ^{m}*si-si-ia* A.BA? URU?
27 ^{iti}ŠE UD.18.KÁM
28 *lim-me* ^{m}*aš-šur*-UR.É.KUR

Translation

1 : Instead of his seal he impressed his nail. (Unused space for nail marks.) (Nail of) Meni'i.

2 : A built house together with its beams Aššur-taklak, the major-domo, has contracted and taken in exchange for 40 minas of copper.

6 : The price has been paid *in toto*, the house is legally acquired ; there is no (further) withdrawal (or) litigation. Anyone who in the future initiates a lawsuit [(or) litigation] against Aššur-taklak—whether Meni'i, or his sons, or his brothers—shall place [x mina(s)] of red(?) gold in the lap of [DN] who dwells in Kalhu, (and) shall give [x mina(s)?] of silver? to the governor [of his city].

17 : [Before . . . .]a-ilu, [before . . . .]simu, [before . . . .]-uṣur(?), eunuch of the governor, [before] Išme-ilu, [before] Šamaš-šallim, the rein holder, before Harmaku, before Ninurta?-qātī?-ṣabat?, before Sisīya, the city scribe(?).

27 : Month of Addāru (XII), 18th day, *limmu* of Aššur-bašti-ēkurri (802 B.C.).

Notes

13 : The sign DIR is written, characteristically for nA, with a " missing " vertical (cf. on No. 24, 5), but the initial " SI " shows clearly that DIR and not KAL was intended. Here it is used where we are accustomed to expect *sagru*, which refers (like *mesû* used of *kaspu*) to a condition of the metal (refined, or the like), rather than to a colour. DIR is found describing gold in historical texts (see R. Borger, *Asarhaddon*, p. 83, on l. 30), but against Borger, and with *CAD* A Pt. 2, 500a, it must be *sāmu*, " red ", and not *utru* " extra-fine ", which belongs to old Assyrian.

28 : Aššur-bašti (read : bāsi ?)-ēkurri is the correct version of the name previously read Aššur-baltinišī (A. Ungnad, *RLA* II, 422–3, 442b), as was already shown by the Sultantepe *limmu* lists (see O. R. Gurney, *An.St.* 3 (1953), 17).

No. 15 Plates 9–10 ND 203
IM 56810
10·8 × 15·4 × 3·0 15.vii.791

Governor's Palace, Room K.

Obv. 1 [*ku-um* NA$_4$.KIŠIB-*šú-nu ṣ*]*u-pár-šú-nu iš-ku-nu*

(finger-nail impressions)

2 [*ṣupur*] ^{m}*qu-ni-ia*
3 [ ] $^{m.d}$UTU.ZU
4 [ ] $^{m.d}$IM.ŠEŠ.⌞PAP⌟

Obv. 5 [ ]$^{d(?)}$⌞INANNA?⌟.[*x* (*x*)]
6 [ ]⌜EN⌝.MEŠ
7 [*ina ma*]-*a*[*z*?]-*ru*?-*ti ina* GIŠ.BÁN *ša* 10 *qa*
8 [ ]*x e*? PÚ É *ad-ru*
9 [ ] *lìb-bi ud*? *x x bi ki*? *e ú-tap-pi-šú*
10 [*ina lìb-b*]*i* [(*x*+)] 15 MA.NA UD.KA.BAR.MEŠ
11 [*a-na* ^{m}]EN.KI-*ia* LÚ.GAL URU.MEŠ-*ni*
12 [*ša* ^{m} (*x x*)]*x x x* ^{lú}*šá-kìn* ^{uru}*kal-ḫi*
13 [*i*(*t*)?]-*tan*-[*nu*?] *kás-pu ga-mur ta-din*
14 [A.Š]À? *ša*⌞-*a-tú*⌟[( )] *za-rip laq-qi*
15 *tú-a-ru* [KA].KA [( )] *la-áš-šu*
16 ⌜*i-na*⌝ *ur*-[*kiš i-na m*]*a-ti-e-ma*
17 ⌞*lu*⌟-*u* LÚ.ERÍN.M[EŠ] *an*-[*nu-te*] EN A.ŠÀ.GA.MEŠ
18 [*lu-u* ŠEŠ.MEŠ-*šú-nu lu-u* DUMU].MEŠ-⌞*šú*⌟-*nu lu-u* DUMU.DUMU.MEŠ-*šú-nu*
19 [*lu*]-*u* LÚ.ERÍN.MEŠ EN.[MEŠ *il*]-*ki-šú-nu*
20 [*lu-u*] ^{l}[^{ú}]*šak-nu* [(*x x*)]⌞*lu*⌟-*u* ^{lú}*ḫa-za-nu*
21 [*l*]*u-u mám-ma-nu-šú-nu* ⌜*qur*⌝-*bu ša* [*i*]*l-la-an-ni*
22 TA* ^{m}EN.KI-*ia de-e-nu* KA.KA *ub-ta-'u-u-ni*
23 [5?] MA.NA KÙ.BABBAR ⌜5⌝ MA.NA GUŠKIN *a-na* ^{d}IM
24 *a-šib* ^{uru}⌞*kur*⌟-*ba-ìl* SUM-*an*

B.E. 25 7 LÚ.MAŠ.MEŠ 7 MÍ.MAŠ.MEŠ *a-na* ^{d}*ša-la*
26 *ḫi-rat* ^{d}IM *ú-maš-šar*

Rev. 27 2 ANŠE.KUR.RA.MEŠ BABBAR.MEŠ *ina* GÌR^{ii} *aš-šur i-ra-kas*
28 1 MA.NA SÍG *qer-du* KÚ *am-mar* ^{dug}*a-ga-ni*
29 *sad-ru* NAG 1-BÁN *saḫ-lé-e* TA* ⌜KÁ⌝.GAL *šá* ^{uru}*kur-ba-ìl*
30 *a-di* KÁ.GAL *ša* ^{uru}*kal-ḫi i-zar-ru-ni-šú*
31 *ina ap-pi* EME-*šú i-laq-qut* [(*x*)] KÁ GIŠ.BÁN-*šú-nu ú-mal-la*
32 *kas-pu a-na* 10.MEŠ-*ti a-na* EN.M[EŠ]-*šú ip-pal*
33 *a-na de-ni-šu i-da-bu-bu la i-laq-qi*

---

34 IGI $^{m.d}$EN.NUN!.DINGIR.MEŠ LÚ.SANGA *ša* ^{uru}*kur-ba-ìl*
35 IGI $^{m.d}$EN.A.SUM-*na* DUMU-*šú*
36 IGI $^{m.d}$EN.KI-*ia* ŠEŠ-*šú ša* $^{m.d}$EN.NUN.DINGIR.MEŠ
37 IGI ^{m}*si*-[*p*]*ár-ra-a-nu* GAL KUŠ.MEŠ *ša* ^{uru}*kur-ba-ìl*
38 IGI ^{m}DUMU.^{d}INANNA ^{lú}*ḫa-za-nu šá* ^{uru}*kur-ba-ìl*
39 IGI ^{m}[*s*]*a-ni-ni* IGI $^{m.d}$IM.ŠEŠ.AŠ
40 IGI ^{m}DUMU.^{d}INANNA GAL MÍ.MAŠ.MEŠ *ša* É ^{lú}*tur-ta-ni*
41 IGI ^{m}*ra-'u-ú-zu* A ^{m}*sa-ni-ni*
42 PAP 9 LÚ.I[G]I.MEŠ-*ti* ^{uru}*kur-ba-ìl-a-a*
43 IGI ^{m}*am-pa-a-r*[*u*?] LÚ.ÌR *ša* $^{mí.d}$*ṣar-pa-ni-tum-šar-rat*
44 IGI $^{m.d}$UTU.PAP.AŠ L[Ú].⌞ÌR⌟ *ša* ^{m}*aš-šur*-A.PAP
45 IGI ^{m}*ir-ni-ia* LÚ ⌜*x* (*x*) IGI?⌝ [^{m}(*x*)]*x-ḫi-su*
46 IGI $^{m.uru}$ḪI-*a-a* LÚ.DUMU-*ši-pír ša* GAL.LÚ.SAG.MEŠ
47 IGI ^{m}*iz-bu*-SI.SÁ ^{lú}*ša qur-bu-ti*
48 IGI ^{m}*nu-uq-sa-a ša* É ^{lú}*sar-ten-ni*
49 IGI ^{m}SUḪUŠ.^{d}UTU LÚ.ÌR *ša* ^{m}*mar-duk*-⌜*ia*?⌝
50 IGI $^{m.d}$U.GUR.MU.P[A]P *ṣa-bit* IM

51 ^{iti}DUL UD.15.KÁM [*lim*]-*mu* ^{m}EN.BA-*a-ni šá-kìn* ^{uru}*šib-ḫi-ni-iš*
52 *i-na* M[U.A]N.NA *uk-li la ba-ši-ti*

Translation

1: [Instead of their seals] they impressed their nails. (Nail marks.) [Nail of ..... (and) .....] (and) Qunia [(and) ..... (and) .....] (and) Šamaš-(i)le'i [(and) ..... (and) .....] (and) Adad-ahu-uṣur [(and) ..... (and) .....] (and) Ištar?-[..., in all x men], owners [of the land (being sold)].

7: [An estate of x homers of land in cult]ivation?, (measured) by the *sūtu* of 10 *qa*, [(and) ....]..., a well, a house, a threshing-floor, [.....].... (these men) have contracted [(and) in exchange] for [(x+)] 15 minas of bronze have [sold to] Bēl-issīya, the village inspector [of P]N, the governor of Kalhu. 13: The price has been paid *in toto*, that [la]nd is legally acquired. There is no (further) withdrawal (or) litigation. In the future at any [time] (anyone) either (one of) these men, the owners of the land, [or their brothers or] their [sons] or their grandsons, or the men responsible for their *ilku*-duties, or an officer or a mayor, or any relation of theirs, who comes up and initiates a lawsuit (or) litigation against Bēl-issīya, shall pay [5?] minas of silver (and) 5 minas of gold to Adad who dwells in Kurbail, and shall dedicate 7 male (and) 7 female votaries(?) to Šala, the first wife of Adad. He shall offer 2 white horses at the feet of Aššur. 28: He shall eat 1 mina of carded wool, (and) drink a standard *agannu*-bowl. They shall strew for him 1 *sūtu* of cress?-seed from the gate of Kurbail to the gate of Kalhu, and he shall gather it with the tip of his tongue, and fill their *sūtu* up (again to) the brim. 31: He shall repay the price to its owners ten-fold; he shall plead in his lawsuit (but) not succeed.

34: Before Bēl-rubā'-ilāni, the priest of Kurbail, before Bēl-aplu-iddina, his son, before Bēl-issīya, the brother of Bēl-rubā'-ilāni, before Siparrānu, the leather official of Kurbail, before Mār-ištar, the mayor of Kurbail, before Sanini, before Adad-ahu-iddina, before Mār-ištar, chief of the female votaries (?) of the house of the *turtānu*, before Ra'ūzu, son of Sanini, in all 9 witnesses of Kurbail.

43: Before Ampār[u?], slave of Ṣarpanītum-šarrat, before Šamaš-ahu-iddina, slave of Aššur-aplu-uṣur, before Irnīya, before? [...]hisu, before Hiāyu(?), messenger of the chief eunuch, before Izbu-lēšir, officer, before Nuqsā, of the house of the *sartennu*, before Ubru-šamaš, slave of Mardukia?, before Nergal-šūmu-uṣur, the writer of the tablet.

51: Month of Tašrītu (VII), 15th day, *limmu* of Bēl-iqīšāni, governor of Šibhiniš, in a non-.... year.

Notes

24: This is one of a small group of our texts which concerns land transactions in the vicinity of Kurbail, a city which certainly lay to the north of Nineveh. For the reading of the name, and for discussion of its location, see B. Parker, E. E. D. M. Oates, and J. V. Kinnier-Wilson in *Iraq* 23 (1961), 31; *Iraq* 24 (1962), 16[26] and 97–9 respectively.

25: LÚ.MAŠ and MÍ.MAŠ are also found in No. 17, 30, followed by LÚ./MÍ.SUḪUR.LÁ. For this sort of dedication in nA times, see K. Deller, *OrNS* 34 (1965), 384; for SUḪUR.LÁ see now *CAD* K, 314–15, making the reading *kazrutu* (pl. *kazrāte*) probable for nA. For LÚ.MAŠ *MSL* XII 236 viii 12 offers the nA gloss *ma-šu-ú*, but no reading for MÍ.MAŠ is known. Otherwise one might have seen in MÍ.MAŠ the logographic writing for *ḫarimtu*.

28–31: For the penalties described in these lines (and in No. 17, 27–9), see W. von Soden, *OrNS* 26 (1957), 135–6, and *Analecta Biblica* 12 (= *Studia Biblica et Orientalia III* (1959)), 365–6. The plant *saḫlû* is generally identified with a kind of cress (*Lepidium sativum*), which has similarities to mustard, and whose seed was used as food (R. C. Thompson, *DAB* 56).

32: Note the rare use of *apālu*.

34: NUN! emended after l. 36.

37: Is it mere coincidence that, of the people known with this name (*APN* 202b), one (*ADD* 75 rev. 9, 742 B.C.) is a *ṣa-rip duḫ-ši-e* (read so after *ARU* 652)?

42: The writing LÚ.IGI.MEŠ-*ti* seems to suggest reading this logogram used by the Assyrian scribes as *šībūti*, especially if we compare *ši-bu-ti* in Tell Halaf No. 20, 8 (*AfO Beiheft* 6, 23).

52: The interpretation of this line (and No. 16 rev. 8′) is made particularly difficult by its careless formulation. As it stands, it should mean " in a non-existent year of (the) *uklu* ", but " a non-existent year " is a meaningless concept, and one must suspect that the phrase is intended to convey rather that it was the *uklu* which did not exist. This obscurity is even worse in the only comparable passage (ND 3421, 15–17; a slave sale): *ina* MU.AN.NA *la ba-ši-ti a-ki* 1 *qa* ŠE.PAD.MEŠ 1½ MA.NA URUDU.MEŠ *ta-lak-u-ni* GEMÉ TI-*at*—" the slave-girl was bought in a ' non-existent year ' when 1 *qa* of corn went for 1½ minas of copper "; however, this passage does give us a clue to the correct understanding of the phrase, since it includes a note of the price of corn (" Getreidekursangabe ") similar to those discussed by K. Deller in *OrNS* 33 (1964), 257 ff. The price given in ND 3421—1 *qa* of corn for 1½ minas of copper—is extremely high, and this suggests that *ina šatti lā bašīti* means loosely " in a year of famine ". Following a suggestion of A. L. Oppenheim's, I would therefore take *uklu* here as " food ", and not, as I had previously conjectured, as (*waklu*=)*uklu*, the king's title in a legal context.

The phrase then means " in a non-existent food-year ", and describes economic conditions at the time of the sale. I can find no Assyrian parallel for this sort of remark, but it is perhaps worth referring to the third millennium phrases *mu-ḫé-gál(-la)* and *mu-nu-gál-la* (see D. O. Edzard, *Sumerische Rechtsurkunden des III. Jahrtausends*, p. 223 for references).

43: For the use of Ṣarpanītum in this name compare my note on *RGD* No. 28, 3′ (p. 57).

49: -⌜*ia*⌝ is probable, but LUGAL would perhaps also be possible; however, the syllabic writing of the first part of the name favours the suggested reading.

Commentary

This text is discussed above (pp. 12–13) along with the others which refer to Kurbail. This particular land sale records the purchase by Bēl-issīya of an area of land which includes a well, a house, and a threshing-floor, from at least 8, probably 12, owners. It is impossible to gauge the area of the land from the price of 15(+) minas of copper, since the economic conditions—which may have occasioned the sale in the first place—will have lowered the price. Another question which cannot be definitely answered, is whether Bēl-issīya is here acting on his own behalf, or as an official agent of the provincial governor of Kalhu.

No. 16 Plate 7

ND 247 and 275(m)
Inst. Arch. London
[—.—].791

(4·9) × (6·2) × 3·7 (ND 247)
(3·9) × (3·6) × 3·0 (ND 275(m))

Governor's Palace, Room K.

Obv. 1 [*ku-mu* NA_4.KIŠIB-*šú-nu ṣu-pár-šú-n*]*u iš-ku-nu*

(finger-nail impressions)

2 [*ṣupur* -]*iš*?-*tu-a* ^{m}[^{m}]$^{.d}$IM.A.SUM-*na*

3 [-*n*]*u*? ^{m}DINGIR-*ma*-[^{m}]SUḪUŠ.^{d}⌜IM?⌝

4 [ ]*x* ^{m}*k*[*a*?-]*x* [ ]
5 [ ]^{m}SUḪUŠ.ḪAL.[ ]
6 [^{d}]IM [ ]
7 [D]Ù [ ]
8 [ ]⌞*x x*⌟[ ]
(remainder of obv. broken)

Rev. 1′ [ ] *x* [ ]
2′ [ ] *x*[ ]
3′ [ ]*ni* [ ]⌜*x x*⌝[( )]
4′ [-]*ra-ia x*[ ]LÚ (*x*) M[U ( )]
5′ [ ]*ši* [(*x*) *x*] *x*[ ] *nu* [( )]
6′ [ ] *x x* [ ]$^{m.d}$U.GUR.MU.PA[P]
7′ [*lim-mu*] ^{m}EN.[BA-*a-ni*] ^{lú}*šá-kìn* ⌜^{uru}⌝*šib-ḫ*[*i-ni-iš*]
8′ [*i-n*]*a*? ⌞MU⌟.[AN.NA (*uk-li*) *la ba-š*]*i-ti*

N.B.—These two fragments do not join, but must be from the same tablet. The minimum width of the two fragments together is 8·3 cm., the minimum width of the gap between the inscribed surfaces as preserved is 1·5 cm.

Commentary

These two fragments come from a companion tablet to No. 15, and must have documented a very similar transaction, probably with Bēl-issīya as the purchaser. There must have been 12 or more sellers.

No. 17 Plates 11–12 ND 496
IM 56869
9·0 × 13·7 cm. (thickness not measured) 6.ii.783

Governor's Palace, Room M.

Obv. 1 ⌜*ku-um*⌝ NA_4.KIŠIB-*šú ṣu-pur-šú iš-kun*
(finger-nail impressions)
2 *ṣu-*⌜*pur*⌝ ^{m}DINGIR.DÙ-*áš* LÚ.SAG *ša* L[Ú?.GAL.SAG(?)]
3 ⌞É 60?⌟ ANŠE A.ŠÀ *ina ma-*[*za-r*]*u-ti*
4 *ina* ŠÀ GIŠ.BÁN *ša* 10 *qa ina* [GIŠ.BÁ]N? URUDU
5 *ina* ^{uru}*du-'u-ú-a ša* LÚ.UŠ ANŠE.MEŠ
6 *ú-piš-ma ina* ŠÀ 2 MA.NA 2 GÍN KÙ.BABBAR $2\frac{1}{2}$ MA.NA URUDU
7 *a-na* $^{m.d}$UTU-*ku-mu-a* LÚ.SAG *ša* ^{m}U.ERÍN.GAB
8 [LUGAL K]UR *aš-šur*^{ki} *id-din*
9 [*kas-pu ga*(*m*)]-⌞*mur*⌟ *ta-din* A.ŠÀ *za-rip la-qi*
10 [*t*]*u-a-*⌜*ru*⌝ *d*[*e-nu*] *da-ba-bu la-áš-šu*
11 [*ma*]*n-nu* [*ša*] *ina ur-kiš lu-u* ^{m}DINGIR.DÙ-*áš*
12 [*l*]*u-u* [ŠEŠ.M]EŠ-*šú lu-u* DUMU.ŠEŠ.MEŠ-*šú lu-u mám-ma-nu-šú qur-bu*
13 [*l*]*u-u* L[Ú].SAG EN *il-ki-šú lu-u* ^{lú}*ḫa-za-nu*

Obv. 14 *lu-u* ^{lú}*šak-nu lu-u* ^{lú}*qe-pu lu-u* LÚ.GA[L.UR]U.MEŠ
15 *lu-u* LÚ.EN.NAM *lu-u mám-ma zaq-pu ša e-*[*la*]*-ni*
16 *ina* UGU A.ŠÀ *šu-a-tu* ŠU-*su um-ma-du-*⟨*ni*⟩
17 TA* $^{m.d}$UTU-*ku-mu-a* ŠEŠ.MEŠ-*šú* DUMU.ŠEŠ.MEŠ-*šú*
18 *de-nu da-ba-bu ub-ta-'u-ni*
19 1 MA.NA KÙ.BABBAR 1 MA.NA GUŠKIN *ina bur-ki* ^{d}MAŠ
20 *a-šib* ^{uru}*kal-ḫi i-šá-kan*
Rev. 21 4 ANŠE.KUR.RA.MEŠ BABBAR.MEŠ *ina* [G]ÌR^{ii} *aš-šur i-ra-kas*
22 4 ANŠE.KUR.RA.MEŠ ḪUR-*ba-ka-ni ina* GÌR^{ii} ^{d}ŠEŠ.GAL *ú-še-rab*
23 1 MA.NA SÍG *qer-du* ⌜KÚ⌝?
24 *am-mar* ^{dug}*a-ga-ni sad-ru* ⌜NAG⌝
25 DUMU.UŠ-*šú* GAL-*ú ina pa-an* ^{d}30 [G]IBÍL
26 DUMU.MÍ-*su* GAL-*tu ina* IGI ^{d}*be*?-*x*[(*x*)] *i*-⌜*šar*⌝-*rap*
27 3-BÁN ^{ú}*saḫ-lé-e* TA* KÁ.[G]AL [*ša*] ^{uru}[*kal-ḫ*]*i*
28 *a-di* KÁ.GAL *ša* URU.ŠÀ.URU ⌜*i-za*⌝-*ru-ni-šú*
29 *ina ap-pi* EME-*šú i-la-qu-*[*u*]*t* GIŠ?.BÁN-*šú-nu ú-mal-la*
30 7 LÚ.MAŠ.MEŠ 7 MÍ.MAŠ.MEŠ *a-na* ^{d}IM *a-šib* ^{uru}*kur-b*[*a*]*-ìl ú-šar*
31 7 LÚ.SUḪUR.LÁ.MEŠ 7 MÍ.SUḪUR.LÁ.MEŠ
32 *a-na* ^{d}*iš-tar a-ši-bat* ^{uru}TAB.TAB.DINGIR *i-da-an*
33 *kás-pu a-na* 10-*a-ti a-na* EN-*šú ú-ta-ra*
34 *ina de-ni-šú i-da-bu-bu la i-la-qi*

---

35 IGI ^{m}ḪI.IM.BU LÚ.⌜SANGA⌝ *ša* ^{d}ŠEŠ.GAL
36 IGI $^{m.d}$30.KAR-*ir* LÚ.GAL É *ša* LÚ.GAL.SAG
37 IGI ^{m}*bir-ta-a-a* LÚ.A.ZU *ša* LÚ.GAL.SAG
38 IGI ^{m}*ub-ru*-^{d}AK LÚ.A.BA *ša* LÚ.GAL.SAG
39 IGI $^{m.d}$AK-*šal-lim* LÚ.A.BA IGI ^{m}*sa-mu-te* LÚ.ḪAL LUGAL
40 IGI ^{m}AD.GIŠ IGI ^{m}*i-tu-'a-a-a* DUMU ^{m}AD.GIŠ
41 IGI ^{m}*bi-si-lu* ^{lú}*ḫa-za-nu ša* ^{uru}*du-'u-ú-a*
42 IGI ^{m}KAB.PAP.IGI IGI ^{m}*rém-ni*-DINGIR IGI ^{m}*ṣi-id-qi*-DINGIR
43 PAP 4 LÚ.MEŠ *ša* ^{uru}*du-'u-ú-a*
44 [IG]I ^{m}*man-nu-ki*-PAP.MEŠ ^{uru}*kal-ḫa-a-a la-bi-ru*
45 [IG]I ^{m}*iq-bi*-DINGIR KIMIN I[GI] ^{m}GÌR^{ii}-*aš-šur-aṣ-bat* KIMIN
T.E. 46 [IGI $^{m.d}$]IM-*ba-nu* KIMIN I[GI $^{m.}$]^{d}PA.MU.PAP.MEŠ KIMIN
47 [IGI ^{m}D]Ù?-*a-a* LÚ.A.BA I[GI ^{m}]*šu-nu-qar-du* LÚ.NU(!).LUL MAN
48 [^{iti}G]UD UD.6.KÁM *lim-me* [^{m}]$^{.d}$MAŠ.PAP-*ir*
49 [IGI $^{m.}$]^{d}AK.DU-*d*[*u*?-*g*]*ul*? *ṣa-bit ṭup-pi*
L.E. 50 IGI ^{m}*mu-šal-lim*-^{d}AMAR.UTU LÚ.3.U$_5$ *ša* LÚ.GAL.SAG

Translation

1: [Instead of] his seal he impressed his nail. (Nail marks.) Nail of Ilu-eppaš, eunuch of the [chief eunuch(?)].

3: An estate of 60? homers of land in cultivation, (measured) by the *sūtu* of 10 *qa* in the [*sūtu*?] of copper, in the village of Du'ūa of the donkey-drivers, he (Ilu-eppaš) contracted and gave to Šamaš-kūmūa, eunuch of Adad-nērārī [king] of Assyria, in exchange for 2 minas 2 shekels of silver (and) 2½ minas of copper. 9: [The price] has been paid *in toto*, the land is legally acquired; there is no (further) withdrawal, [lawsuit] (or) litigation. Anyone [who] in the future—whether Ilu-eppaš, or his [brothers], or his brothers' sons, or any relative of his, [or] a eunuch responsible for his *ilku*-duties, or a mayor, or an officer, or an executive, or a village-inspector, or a governor, or anyone who comes forward—(who) lays his hand on that land (and) initiates a lawsuit (or) litigation against Šamaš-kūmūa, (or) his brothers, (or) his brothers' sons, shall place 1 mina of silver (and) 1 mina of gold in the lap of Ninurta who dwells in Kalhu. 21: He shall dedicate 4 white horses at the feet of Aššur, (and) introduce 4 ..... horses at the feet of Nergal. He shall eat 1 mina of carded wool, he shall drink a standard *agannu*-bowl. He shall burn his eldest son before Sîn, and he shall burn his eldest daughter before Bē[lat?-x]. They shall strew for him 3 *sūtu* of cress?(-seed) from the gate [of Kalhu(?)] as far as the gate of the inner city (Aššur), (and) he shall gather it with the tip of his tongue (and) fill up their *sūtu* (again). 30: He shall dedicate 7 male (and) 7 female votaries(?) to Adad who dwells in Kurbail, (and) give 7 male (and) 7 female hierodules(?) to Ishtar who dwells in Arbailu. He shall return the price ten-fold to its owner. He shall plead in his lawsuit (but) not succeed.

35: Before Himbu(?), priest of Nergal, before Sîn-ēṭir, the major-domo of the chief eunuch, before Birtāyu, the doctor of the chief eunuch, before Ubru-nabû, scribe of the chief eunuch, before Nabû-šallim, scribe, before Sāmūtu, the diviner of the king, before Abu-lēšir, before Itu'āyu, the son of Abu-lēšir, before Bisilu, mayor of the village of Du'ūa, before Kimir?-ahi-lāmur, before Rēmāni-ilu, before Ṣidqi-ilu, in all 4 witnesses of Du'ūa. 44: Before Mannu-kī-ahhē, a long-standing Kalhu man, before Iqbi-ilu, ditto, before Šēp-aššur-aṣbat, ditto, [before] Adad-banu, ditto, before Nabû-nādin-ahhē, ditto, [before B]ūnāya(?), scribe, before Šunu-qardu, the butler(?) of the king.

48: [Month of] Ayāru (II), 6th day, *limmu* of Ninurta-nāṣir (783 B.C.).

49: [Before] Nabû-kēnu-dugul?, writer of the tablet. Before Mušallim-marduk, the third rider of the chief eunuch.

Notes

2: The restoration at the end of the line takes account of the number of witnesses who belong to the household of the chief eunuch. This suggests that one of the participants in the transaction belongs to that household as well, and the buyer Šamaš-kūmūa does not, being a eunuch of the king's household.

3: The number of homers is not certain. It is unclear whether the DIŠ is preceded by a sign or merely by a break; as the space is restricted, the simplest solution is that given, but another possibility would be to read 71 (i.e. [60+1]0+1) homers.

4: A copper *sūtu* is known also from texts from the Nabû temple at Nimrud: ND 5451, 2; 5453, 3; 5460, 2; 5468, 3 (*Iraq* 19 (1957), 129–34).

5: Du'ūa also occurs in texts from Nineveh, see S. Parpola, *AOAT* 6, 106.

7: Šamaš-kūmūa is the purchaser also in Nos. 31 and 57.

12: For the restoration of [brothers] and not [sons], compare l. 17: both buyer and seller were eunuchs!

13: It appears from this line as though the "men responsible for *ilku* duties" were in the case of eunuchs other eunuchs; but it is difficult to know how rigorously to accept this.

15: The translation is literally "or anyone arisen who comes up".

16: The phrase "to lay hands upon" is unparalleled in nA legal texts, although it is used in old Babylonian.

23: KÚ, which does not agree with the traces, is nevertheless necessary (cf. No. 15, 28).

27–9: For this (and other clauses here) cf. No. 15, 29–31; in l. 29 read possibly rather KÁ! BÁN.

30: *ú-šar* replaces the form *umaššar* in No. 15, 26; the use of this verb is rare in nA and probably consciously literary; the use of these two forms of the present supports the idea that the verb was falling out of use (cf. K. Deller, *OrNS* 30 (1961), 347).

31: On SUḪUR.LÁ see note to No. 15, 25.

35: This line is squeezed in as an afterthought; presumably the scribe omitted to give the priest his proper place at the head of the list. As for the name, the reading Ṭāb-šār-x is tempting, and this would suggest taking the BU as *še-rù*, as suggested to me by K. Deller; however, the sign itself is clearly BU and not ŠE+RUM, which poses problems of transliteration if the suggestion is correct.

42: For the PN see on No. 42, 14.

44: For *Kalḫāyu labīru* K. Deller refers me to *ABL* 1103, 7′–8′, *qi-in-na-te ša* ^{uru}NINA *la-bi-ru-te*; our phrases probably should be taken as " member of a long-established Kalhu family ".

47: The reading Būnāya for DÙ-*a-a* is based on comparison with longer names with this component, e.g. the eponyms for the years 850, 844, 823, and 816 (*RLA* II, 420–1). In the translation NU.LUL is emended to KAŠ.LUL (not collated).

49: *d[u-g]ul* seems probable, but could not be collated.

Commentary

The unusual size and length of this text, together with its careful redaction, may be due to the importance of the transaction which involved a considerable area of land. Unfortunately we cannot define the location of the village in whose territory the land lay, but its mention in texts from Nineveh suggests that it was not in the near vicinity of Kalhu. However, we cannot use the mention of Adad of Kurbail (l. 30) to associate this text with those which are concerned with the Kurbail area, since the god was too well known to be only local; nor does the phrase in ll. 27–8 help us to decide where the land was situated.

No. 18 Plate 13; Photo Plate 94a ND 209

10·7 × 14·1 × 3·6 IM 56812

15.i.781

Governor's Palace, Room K.

Obv. 1 [NA$_4$KIŠ]IB ^{m}*aš-šur*-A.PAP DUMU ^{m} *x x -ni*

(cylinder seal impression)

2 [*t*]*i*? *a* [(*x*) *x*] *x x*

3 [ ]*x x ša*? LÚ.EN.NAM [( )]

4 [*ú-t*]*ap-piš* [(*x x*)] *ina lìb-bi* 10+⌞6?⌟ [M]A.NA ⌜KÙ.BABBAR⌝

5 [(*x*) *x*]*x* URUDU?.MEŠ *il-qi*

6 [ ]*x x*[(*x*) *tu-*]*a-ru*? *de-*[*e*?]*-nu*

7 [^{m}]*aš-šur*-A.⌜PAP *lu*⌝ DUMU.M[EŠ]-*šú*

8 [-*š*]*ú lu* ⌞LÚ *qur-ub-šú*⌟

9 [ ].MEŠ-*ni*

10 [ ] *x*[ ]-*ni*

11 [*x*] MA.NA K[Ù.BABBAR?] *x x* [(*x*) *x* G]AR-*an*

12 [ ]

Rev. 13 [ ]

14 IGI ^{m}*u*[*b*?-*x x x*] DUMU $^{m.d}$INANNA-*ta-ri-ba*

15 IGI ^{m}*bur-*⸢*ki* (*x*) *si*?⸣ *lim*? *si*? *x* (*x*) DUMU $^{m.d}$MAŠ.E
16 IGI ^{m}*šùl-mu-*LUGAL DUMU ^{m}ERÍN.MEŠ-*da-qu*
17 [IG]I ^{m}ÌR.^{d}INANNA ^{lú}*ḫa-za-nu*
18 ⸢*ša*⸣ ^{uru}*kal-ḫi*
19 IGI ^{m}*mu-šal-lim-*^{d}MAŠ ^{lú}*mu-tir-ṭe-me*
20 *ša* LÚ.EN.NAM *ša* ^{uru}*kal-ḫi*
21 IGI ^{m}⸤*sa-la*⸥*-ma-nu*
22 IGI ^{m}*pu-*[(*x*)]-⸢*ša*⸣*-a-a*
23 EN *x x me ša* ^{uru}*kap-ru da-lal*
24 [IG]I ^{m}*sa-la-*⸢*ma*⸣*-nu* LÚ.GAL KA.ŠÈR
25 *ša* ^{lú}*rak-su-te*
26 IGI $^{m.d}$PA.MU.AŠ DUMU ^{m}ḪI-*ba-ni*
27 [*ṣ*]*a-bit ṭup-pi*

---

28 ^{iti}BARAG ⟨UD⟩.15.KÁM *li-*[*m*]*u* ^{m}EN.SI.⸢SÁ⸣
29 [L]Ú.NIMGIR *ša* ^{m}*šùl-ma-nu-*MAŠ
30 [LUGA]L KUR *aš-šur*

Translation

1: [Seal] of Aššur-aplu-uṣur, son of . . .ni. (Seal impression.)

2: [. . . . . . . PN, the . . . .] of? the governor [( )] has contracted (and) taken in exchange for 16? minas of silver [(and) . . . .] of copper. 6: [. . . . . there is no (further) with]drawal?, lawsuit?, [(or) litigation. Anyone, whether] Aššur-aplu-uṣur, or his sons, or his [. . . . .] or any of his relatives, [. . . . . . .] shall put [x] minas of silver? [. . . . .].

14: Before U[bru?-. . .], son of Ištar-tarība, before Burki-. . ., son of Ninurta-iqbi, before Šulmu-šarri, son of Ṣābu-da(m)qu, [bef]ore Urdu-ištar, the mayor of Kalhu, before Mušallim-ninurta, information-officer of the governor of Kalhu, before Salamānu, before Pušāya?, the . . . . . of the village of Dalal, before Salamānu, chief tailor(?) of the *raksu* men, before Nabû-šūmu-iddina, son of HIbāni, writer of the tablet.

28: Month of Nīsānu (I), 15th, *limmu* of Bēl-lēšir, herald of Šulmānu-ašarēd, [king] of Assyria (781 B.C.).

Notes

15: The final E is written over an erased *iq* (from *iq-bi*).
22: The name is restored after that in No. 92, 9.
26: The name perhaps rather *ṭi-ba-ni*.

Commentary

Strictly there is no certainty that this is a property sale at all, as the crucial lines naming the purchaser and the thing sold are lost. However the tablet is superficially very similar, by its size and script, to Nos. 15 and 17, although it has a seal impression, not finger-nail impressions. Moreover the mention of both the mayor of Kalhu and a man from a village (l. 23) among the witnesses, does perhaps add to the statistical likelihood that this is a land sale.

No. 19 Plate 8 ND 207
IM 56911
4·8 × 7·0 × 2·5 20.xii.779

Governor's Palace, Room K.

Obv. 1 *ku-mu* NA$_4$.KIŠIB-*šú*
2 *ṣu-pár-šú iš-kun*
(finger-nail impressions)
3 *ṣu-pur* ^{m}*ku-ku-na-a-te*
4 DUMU ^{m}*ṣa-bu-ú-ia*
5 GIŠ.ŠAR Ú *ina* KÁ.MEŠ-*šú*
6 *ša* É ^{m}SU.^{d}AMAR.UTU
7 46 GÍD 30 DAGAL
8 ⸢*a-na*⸣ ^{m}SU.^{d}AMAR.UTU
9 *ina* ŠÀ ⸢5?⸣ MA.NA URUDU.MEŠ
10 ⸤*i*⸥-*ti-di*-⸤*ni*⸥
11 [*kas-pu g*]*a-m*[*ur ta-din*]
B.E. 12 [*tu-a*]-*ru* K[A.KA]
13 [*la-á*]*š-š*[*ú*]
Rev. 14 [ ]*x*[ ]
15 [*x* MA.N]A KÙ.BABBAR [ ]
16 [*ina bur-ki*(?) *š*]*a*? ^{d}IM *š*[*a*]
17 [*i-š*]*á-ka-an ina de-*[*ni-šú*]
18 [K]A.KA *la i-l*[*a-qi*]

19 [IGI] ^{m}KÁ.DINGIR-*a-a* PAP[ ]
20 I[GI] $^{m.d}$30.E [( )]
21 IGI ^{m}*gu-un-g*[*u-x*]
22 IGI ^{m}*ṭa-bu-s*[*u* ( )]
23 IGI ^{m}*ḫa-de-e*[( )]
24 IGI ^{mí}*su-ni-*[*x* ( )]
25 IGI $^{m.d}$PA.*x*[( )]
26 [*ṣ*]*a*-⟨*bit*⟩ *ṭup-pi* ^{iti}ŠE [(*x*)] *x*
T.E. 27 UD.20.KÁM *lim-mu* $^{m.d}$AMAR.UTU-⸢*rém*?⸣-*ni*

Translation

1: Instead of his seal he impressed his nail. (Nail marks.) Nail of Kukunātu, son of Ṣābūya.

5: A vegetable(?) garden within the gates of the house of Rīb-marduk, 46 (cubits) long, 30 (cubits) wide, he (Kukunātu) has sold to Rīb-marduk in exchange for 5? minas of copper. 11: [The price has been paid *in*] *toto*, [there is] no (further) [withdraw]al (or) liti[gation. Anyone who contravenes the agreement(?) shall] place [x minas] of silver [(and) x minas of gold(?) in the lap] of Adad of [. . . . .]. He shall plead in his law[suit (but)] not [succeed].

19: Before Bābilāyu, brother(?) [. . .], before Sîn-iqbi, before Gung[u . .], before

Ṭābūs[u(. . .)], before Hadē[. . .], before Suni[. . .], before Nabû-. .[. . .], writer of the tablet.

26: Month of Addāru (XII) [. . .], 20th day, *limmu* of Marduk-rēmāni (779 B.C.).

Notes

5: The translation "vegetable garden" assumes that GIŠ.ŠAR Ú.SAR (= *urqi*) was intended, but it is also possible that *ú* is a phonetic complement to GIŠ.ŠAR (*kirû*). The very small area in question makes the vegetable patch the more likely.

9: 4 MA.NA would also be possible (coll.).

14: This line should possibly read]*i-z*[*a*!-*qu-pa-*(*a-*)*ni*].

15: This line is written over erasures.

24: Note that this witness is a woman.

25: Not ᵈPA.M[U, as might have been conjectured by comparison with No. 18 (collated). B[A, Z[U, and S[U are all possibilities.

26: The traces after ŠE do not seem to favour DIRIG (collated), but it is hard to see what else could stand here.

Commentary

Sale of a small plot of ground to the man, Rīb-marduk, within whose "gates" (presumably implying an enclosure wall) the land lay. Note that the formula of sale does not include the usual *uppušu* or *zarāpu*, but uses *tadānu* by itself (cf. note to No. 2, 6).

No. 20 Plate 14 ND 230(a)
Inst. Arch. London

(6·0) × 12·0 × 2·6 11.[—].779

Governor's Palace, Room K.

Obv. 1 GIM NA₄.KIŠIB-*š*[*ú ṣu-pár-šú iškun*]
(finger-nail impressions)
2 *ṣu-pur* ᵐEN.[DÙ-*a-a* EN A.ŠÀ( )]
3 É 24? ANŠE [A.ŠÀ]
4 *i-se-ni-i*[*š*?]
5 ᵐ·ᵈ30.KAR-*ir*[ ]
6 *ina lìb-bi* 1 G[Ú.UN]
7 *ú-tap-piš* [T]A? [ ]
8 *i-si-q*[*i*] *kás-p*[*u ga*(*m*)*-mur ta-din*]
9 A.ŠÀ *za-r*[*ip*] *laq-q*[*i tu-a-ru* (*dēnu*)]
10 *da-ba-bu* [*la-áš-šu* ( )]
11 *ina ur-kiš im-ma-t*[*e*]-⌜*ma*⌝ [( )]
12 *lu-ú* ᵐEN.DÙ-*a-a lu-ú* [DUMU.MEŠ-*šú*]
13 *lu-ú* ŠEŠ.MEŠ-*šú lu-ú m*[*ám-ma-nu-šú*]
14 *lu-ú* LÚ.MEŠ-*e* ERÍN.MEŠ [ ]
15 *ša* TA* ᵐ·ᵈ3[0].KAR-*ir x* [ ]
16 *de-nu da-*⌜*ba-bu*⌝ [*ub-ta-'u-ni*]
17 5 MA.NA KÙ.BABBAR 2 MA.N[A GUŠKIN ( )]
18 *ina bur-ki* ᵈ*n*[*in-urta*]
19 *i-ša*[*k-kan*]

Rev. 20 4 AN[ŠE.KUR.RA.MEŠ]
21 *i*-[*rak-kas*]
22 *šá* [ ]
23 *ka*[*s-pu*]
24 *i*[-]
25 *x*[ ]
(remainder of rev. broken)

T.E. 1′ IGI [ ]
2′ IGI ᵐ[ ]
3′ IGI ᵐ·ᵈ[ ]
L.E. 4′ ⁱᵗⁱ[*x* U]D.11.KÁM *li-mu* [ᵐ]·ᵈAMAR.UTU⌜-*rém-ni*⌝

Translation

1: Instead of his seal [he impressed his nail]. (Nail marks.) Nail of Bēl-[būnāya, owner of the land (being sold)].

3: An estate of 24? homers of [land ....], together [with ....] Sîn-ēṭir [.....] in exchange for 1 talent [.......] has contracted and taken from? [Bēl-būnāya]. 8: The price [has been paid *in toto*], the land is legally acquired. [There is no (further) withdrawal, (lawsuit), (or)] litigation. (Anyone) at any time in the future, whether Bēl-būnāya, or [his sons], or his brothers, or any [relative of his], or men (who are?) people [.....], who [initiates] a lawsuit (or) litigation against Sîn-ēṭir (or) aga[inst his sons(?)] shall place 5 minas of silver (and) 2 minas [of gold] in the lap of Ni[nurta who dwells in Kalhu(?),] shall [dedicate] 4 [white] horses [to Aššur..... (remainder broken)].

T.E. 1′–3′: (3 witnesses).

L.E. 4′: Month of [...], 11th day, *limmu* of Marduk-rēmāni (779 B.C.).

Notes

1: For GIM = *kūm*(*u*) see K. Deller, *OrNS* 36 (1967), 81 (on NL 87).

4: For this usage of *issēniš* cf. *ARU* 342.

12: For the reading of the name cf. note on No. 17, 47.

15: In view of the restricted space, we should perhaps restore L[Ú.SAG] (cf. No. 33, 15) or T[A* ŠEŠ.MEŠ-*šú*], which would imply that Sîn-ēṭir was a eunuch.

No. 21 Plate 14 ND 252(h)
IM, for study
(3·5) × (3·6) × (1·8) [—.—].803/775

Governor's Palace, Room K or M.

Obv. 1 [*kūm*(*u*) NA_4.KIŠIB-*šú ṣ*]*u-pár-šú iš-kun*
(finger-nail impressions)
2 [*ṣupur* *g*]*a*? É 10 ANŠE A.ŠÀ
3 [ ]É? *ad-ru* GIŠ.ŠA[R]
4 [ ]*x*

5 [UR]UDU.MEŠ
(remainder of obv. and upper part of rev. broken)

Rev. 1′ [ ]x-⌜li⌝
2′ [ ]-⌞DINGIR?⌟.MEŠ
T.E. 3′ [LÚ?].MU *ša* GAL.SAG
4′ [ ] lú*ḫa-za-nu*
5′ [ ]EN
6′ [UD.x].KÁM *lim-mu* m.dIGI.DU.KAM

Translation

1 : [Instead of his seal] he impressed his nail. (Nail marks.) [Nail of P]N.

2 : An estate of 10 homers of land [. . . . . . .], a house, a threshing-floor, (and) orchard, [. . . . . in exchange for . . . . .]copper [. . . . .

Rev. 1′ : [before . . . .]li, [before . . . .]-ilāni?, [before . . . . ., the] cook of the chief eunuch, [before . . . . .], the mayor, [before . . . .]-bēl.

6′ : [Month of . . . . ., xth] day, *limmu* of Palil-ēreš (803/775 B.C.).

Notes

2 : The *g*]*a*? could be the final syllable of the seller's name, but a better restoration is probably [*ṣupur* PN EN A.ŠÀ.G]A. . . .

No. 22 Plate 15 ND 495
IM 56868
26.ii.756

6·0 × 8·5 × 3·1

Governor's Palace, Room M.

Obv. 1 *ṣu-pur* m*ki-qi-la-a-ni*
2 ÌR *ša* mEN.KI-*ia*
3 [L]Ú.GAL.URU.MEŠ-*ni*
(finger-nail impressions)
4 EN É ŠUii É *qa-ti*
5 *a-na gi-mir-ti-šú*
6 *ú-piš-šú* mERÍN.MEŠ.SIG!
7 m.dUTU-*še-zib i-na* 1 GÚ.UN URUDU.MEŠ
8 TA* IGI m*ki-qi-la-a-ni*
9 TI-*qi-ú kas-pu ga-mur*
10 SUM-*ni* É ŠUii *šu-a-tú*
11 *za-pa-at la-qi-at*
12 *tú-a-ru de-nu*
B.E. 13 KA.KA *la-áš-šú*
14 *man-nu šá ina ur-kiš*
Rev. 15 *ina* MAN-*ti-ma lu* m*ki-qi-la-nu*
16 *lu* DUMU-*šú lu* DUMU.DUMU-*šú*

Rev. 17 TA* mERÍN.MEŠ.SIG TA* m.dUTU-*še-zib*
18 *de-nu* KA.KA *ub-ta-'u-ni*
19 *kas-pu a-na* 10-*te a-na* EN-*šú*
20 GUR-*ár ina de-ni-šú*
21 KA.KA *la* TI-*qi*
22 [I]GI m⌜KUR⌝-*man-d*[*i*?]-*a-a*
23 IGI mUD.⌞SUM?.MU? DUMU⌟ m⌞*x*⌟.IGI.DU
24 IGI m*pa-na-a-a*
25 IGI mAPIN-*eš*-DINGIR
26 IGI mEN.BÀD lú*mu-kil*-⌜KUŠ.PA⌝.MEŠ
27 IGI mEN.A[Š] LÚ.GAL ⌞*x*⌟[(*x*)] *ša* MAN
T.E. 28 IGI m.dMAŠ.I? *ṣa-bit* [I]M
29 itiGUD UD.26.KAM
L.E. 30 *lim-mu* mEN.KUR-*ú-a* [l]ú*šá-kìn* uru*par-*ḪA-*na*
31 IGI mAD.GIŠ lú*š*[*e-l*]*a-pa-a-a*

Translation

1: Nail of Kiqilānu, slave of Bēl-issīya, the village-inspector, (nail marks), owner of the workshop.

4: A workshop in its entirety Ṣābu-da(m)qu (and) Šamaš-šēzib contracted (and) took from Kiqilānu in (exchange for) 1 talent of copper. 9: The price has been paid *in toto*, that workshop is legally acquired; there is no (further) withdrawal, lawsuit, (or) litigation. Anyone who at any time in the future, whether Kiqilānu, or his son, or his grandson, initiaties a lawsuit (or) litigation against Ṣābu-da(m)qu (or) against Šamaš-šēzib, shall return the price ten-fold to its owner. He shall plead in his lawsuit (but) not succeed.

22: Before (Māt)mandiāyu(?), before Šamaš-nādin-šūmi(??) son of . . .-ālik-pāni(?), before Pānāya, before Ēreš-ilu, before Bēl-dūrī, the rein-holder, before Bēl-iddina?, the chief . . . . of the king, before Ninurta-na'id, writer of the tablet.

29: Month of Ayāru (II), 26th day, *limmu* of Bēl-šadūa, governor of Parnunna (756 B.C.).

31: Before Abu-lēšir, the Šelappaean.

Notes

4: The scribe may have written *bēt qāti* syllabically the second time in order to make it clear that the repetition was not mistaken.

6: The text has *ḫu* for SIG (collated), but l. 17 makes it clear that SIG was in fact intended; for the name see No. 4, 16 (note).

11: *za*(*r*)*pat*: the loss of the *r* is attested elsewhere in the form *za-pat* (*ARU* 57; 463; and in a text from Sultantepe (*An.St.* 7 (1957), 138–9: SU 51/36, 11) collated). Cf. also *rš* becoming *šš* (note on No. 24, 5).

Note that *bēt qāti* is apparently feminine (though cf. ll. 5, 10 !), unlike *bētu* alone !

15: Error for *mat-ti-ma* ? MAN is written over an erasure.

19–20: As appears on the copy, the scribe at first jumped a phrase somewhere here, and these lines are consequently written over erasures; at the end of l. 20 TI-*qi* is still recognizable.

28: The correct reading of dMAŠ.I is open to doubt, cf. on No. 4, 22.

Commentary

An unusual feature of this sale is that we have two buyers, and it is unfortunate that the text gives us no clue as to why the two men co-operated in the purchase, or how their joint ownership was later regulated.

No. 23 Plate 16 ND 229
Inst. Arch. London
[—.—].754

7·1 × 10·3 × 2·6

Governor's Palace, Room K.

Obv. 1 [*kūm(u)* NA$_4$.KI]ŠIB-*šú* *ṣu-pur-šú* GAR-*un*
2 [*ṣu-pur* ^{m}*n*]*a-te-ia* EN A.[Š]À
(finger-nail impressions)
3 [É *x*] ANŠE ⌞3-BÁN?⌟ A.ŠÀ *ina mu-li-*⌜*e*⌝
4 [*x* ANŠE *x*-]BÁN ⌞*ina ú-šal-*⌟[*l*]*i* PAP 4 ANŠE A.ŠÀ
5 [*x* (*x x*) ^{m}*ul*?-*l*]*u-ba-a-a qaq-*⌞*qe-re*⌟
6 ⌜*pu-ṣi-e*⌝ *ša* ⌜É?⌝ ḪA.LA ⌜*x*⌝[(*x x*)]
7 ḪA.LA *ša* GIŠ.ŠAR *ša ur-*⌜*qi*⌝
8 *ú-piš-ma* ^{m}*man-nu-ki-i*-KUR-*aš-šur*
9 LÚ.GAL É TA* *pa-an* ^{m}*na-te-*⌜*ia*⌝
10 *ina* ŠÀ 52? MA.NA URUDU.MEŠ
11 *il-qi kás-pu ga-mur ta-d*[*in*]
12 A.ŠÀ *šu-a-tú za-rip laq-qi*
13 *tu-a-ru de-nu* KA.KA *la-š*[*u*]
14 *man-nu ša ina ur-kiš ina ma-*[*t*]*e-e*
B.E. 15 *lu-u* ^{m}*na-te-ia l*[*u*]*-u* ŠE[Š].MEŠ-*šú*
Rev. 16 *lu-u* DUMU.MEŠ-*šú lu-u mám-ma-nu-šú*
17 *ša* TA* ^{m}*man-nu-ki-i*-K[U]R-*aš-šur ù* ŠE[Š-*š*]*ú*
18 *de-nu* KA.KA *u*[*b-t*]*a-'u-ú-n*[*i*]
19 2 MA.NA KÙ.BABBAR 1 M[A.N]A GUŠKIN *sag-r*[*u*]
20 *ina bur-ki* ^{d}MAŠ *a-šib* ^{uru}*kal-ḫi* ⌜*i-šá*?-*kan*?⌝
21 GÚ.UN AN.NA.MEŠ *a-na* LÚ.EN.N[AM (URU-*šú*) SUM-*an*(?)]
22 [*kas-*]*pu a-na* 10.MEŠ *a-na* EN.MEŠ?-*šú*? [GUR(?)]
23 [*ina d*]*e-ni-šú* KA.KA-*ma la* T[I? (   )]
24 [I]GI ^{m}[*š*]*a*?-DINGIR-*gab-bu* ^{lú}*mu-kil-*[P]A.MEŠ
25 [I]GI ^{m}[(*x x*) *x*] *x x* LÚ.3.U$_5$ [(   )]
26 [IGI ^{m}]*la-qi-pu* LÚ.3.U$_5$
27 [IG]I $^{m.d}$AMAR.UTU.SUM.PAP.MEŠ
28 [(   )] LÚ.GAL *kal-la-bi*
29 [IGI ^{m}(*x*)]*x-bu-u-a* LÚ.A.BA
30 [(   )]2?-*i ṣa-bit ka-ni-ki*
31 [^{iti}*x* UD].13?.KA[M *li*]*m-mu*
T.E. 32 [^{m}*Ninurta*]-*še-zib-an-*⌜*ni*⌝

N.B.—The transliteration incorporates collations made after the copy.

Translation

1: [Instead of his] seal he impressed his nail. [Nail of N]atēya, owner of the land. (Nail marks.)

3: [An estate of x] homers 3 *sūtu* of land, in the hills, [(and) x homers 7?] *sūtu* in the valley, in all 4 homers of land, [adjoining(?) Ul]lubāyu(?), the clear ground for a house(?), a share of the . . . ., a share of the vegetable-garden—Mannu-kī-māt-aššur, the major-domo, contracted and took from Natēya in exchange for 53? minas of copper. 11: The price has been paid *in toto*, that land is legally acquired. There is no (further) withdrawal, lawsuit (or) litigation. Anyone who at any time in the future, whether Natēya, or his brothers, or his sons, or any (relative) of his, who [*sic*] initiates a lawsuit (or) litigation against Mannu-kī-māt-aššur or [his] brother, shall place 2 minas of silver (and) 1 mina of refined gold in the lap of Ninurta who dwells in Kalhu, [he shall give] a talent of tin to the governor [of his city] (and) shall [return] the price ten-fold to its owner. He shall plead in his lawsuit (but) not succeed.

24: Before Ša-ili-gabbu, rein-holder, before [. . .]. ., third rider, [before] Laqīpu, third rider, before Marduk-nādin-ahhē, chief *kallāpu*, [before . .]būa, the second? scribe, writer of the document.

31: [Month of . . . .], 13th? day, *limmu* of [Ninurta]-šēzibanni (754 B.C.).

Notes

1–3: The missing left-hand corner is very likely No. 49, which then supplies the missing beginnings of these lines.

8: It is obvious that here, as with the name of the governor of Guzāna known particularly from the Tell Halaf texts, the KUR must be read as part of the name; otherwise there would be no means of distinguishing " who is like Assyria " from " who is like the god Assur " (cf. E. Weidner, *AfO Beiheft* 6, p. 9, note 28).

24–8: All these witnesses are military personnel, and very likely come from the same administrative circle as the major-domo.

29: The traces permit neither *ṣ*]*a* or *n*]*a-bu-u-a*.

32: This is the only possible eponym.

Commentary

This is the first of our documents to distinguish between land in the " hills " (*mulû*) and land in the " valley " (*ušallu*). " Valley " is of course only a very rough approximation; coming as the word does from the south, it appears to mean flat, watered, and presumably water-laid ground, and in the region of Nimrud, and indeed all along the Upper Zab and Tigris rivers, it must have been the word used to describe the fields along the river and on its level, as opposed to the much less fertile ground through which the river valleys have cut.

No. 24 Plate 17 ND 473 + unn. frg.
IM 56861
$6{\cdot}5 \times 8{\cdot}8 \times 3{\cdot}2$ 27.xi.746

Governor's Palace, Room K.

Obv. 1 *ku-um* N[A_4.KIŠIB-*šú ṣ*]*u-pur-šú iš-kun*

2 *ṣu-pur* ^{m}[*tab-š*]*i*-SI.SÁ A ^{m}*qu-ú-a*
3 E[N] A.ŠÀ

(finger-nail impressions)

4 É 5-[BÁN] A.ŠÀ *ina ú-šal-li*
5 *ina* ^{uru}É.IM.DIR *ú-piš-ma*
6 ^{m}⸢*gi*⸣*-ri-tú* TA* IGI ^{m}*tab-ši*-SI.SÁ
7 *ina lìb-bi* 17 MA.NA URUDU.MEŠ *il-qi*
8 *kas-pu ga-mur ta-din* A.ŠÀ *šú-a-tú*
9 *za-rip la-qi tu-a-ru de-nu*
10 KA.KA *la-áš-šú man-nu ša ina ur-kiš*
11 *ina ma-te-ma lu-u* ^{m}*tab-ši*-SI.SÁ
12 *lu-u* DUMU.MEŠ-*šú lu-u* ŠEŠ.MEŠ-*šú*
13 *ša de-nu* KA.KA TA* ^{m}*gi-ri-te*
14 TA* DUMU.MEŠ-*šú* TA* ŠEŠ.MEŠ-*šú*
15 *ub-ta-u-ni*
16 1 MA.NA KÙ.BABBAR 1 MA.NA GUŠKIN
B.E. 17 *ina bur-ki* ^{d}MAŠ *a-šib* ^{uru}*kal-ḫi* GAR-*a*[*n*]
Rev. 18 1 GÚ-UN [AN.NA]
19 *kas-pu a-na* 10.[MEŠ-*te*?]
20 *ina de-ni-šú i-*⸢KA.KA⸣ [ ]

21 IGI ^{m}*šùl-mu*-PA[P.MEŠ?]
22 *ša* LÚ.EN.NAM [ ]
23 IGI $^{m.d}$*šùl*-[*m*]*a*-[*n*]*u*-[ ]
24 IGI ^{m}*rém-a-ni*-[*x*] ⸢LÚ⸣[ ]-⸤*a-a*⸥?
25 IGI ^{m}EN.DINGIR-*a-a ša* ^{uru}[(*x*) *x*]⸤*ú x x*⸥
26 IGI $^{m.d}$MAŠ.SU *ša* ^{uru}[(*x*)]*x-na*?
27 IGI ^{m}*gab-bu-a-mur* LÚ.ÌR
28 *ša* $^{m.d}$30.DI-*a-ni*
29 IGI ^{m}*rím-ut*-DINGIR-*ma* LÚ *ṣa-bit* [I]M
30 ^{iti}ZÍZ UD.27.KAM
31 [*l*]*im*-[*m*]*e* $^{m.d}$U.GUR.[P]AP-*ir*
32 [^{lú}]*šá-kìn* [^{ur}]^{u}*na-ṣi-bi-na*
L.E. 33 (two crossed wedges, of uncertain purpose)

N.B.—The top left-hand corner is supplied by a fragment stored with ND 480 (Inst. Arch. London).

Translation

1: Instead of [his seal] he impressed his nail. Nail of [Tabš]i-kittu, son of Qūa, owner of the land. (Nail marks.)

4: An estate of 5 [*sūtu*] of land in the valley(-land) in Bēt-šaššeri Girītu contracted and took from Tabši-kittu in exchange for 17 minas of copper. 8: The price has been paid *in toto*, that land is legally acquired. There is no (further) withdrawal, lawsuit, (or) litigation. Anyone who at any time in the future, whether Tabši-kittu, or his sons, or his brothers, initiates a lawsuit (or) litigation against Girītu, against his sons (or) against his brothers, shall place 1 mina of silver (and) 1 mina of gold in the lap of Ninurta who dwells in Kalhu. [He shall give(?)] 1 talent of [tin to the governor of his city, (and) he shall return] the price ten-[fold to its owner]. He shall plead in his lawsuit [(but) not succeed].

21: Before Šulmu-ah[hē(. . .), the . . . .] of the governor [. . . .], before Šulmānu-[. . . . . .], before Rēmāni-[. . .], the [. . . .], before Bēl-ilāya of the town of [. . . .], before Ninurta-(e)rība of the town of [. . .]na?, before Gabbu-āmur, slave of Sîn-šallimāni, before Rīmūt-ili-ma, the ⟨scribe⟩, writer of the tablet.

30: Month of Šabāṭu (XI), 27th day, *limmu* of Nergal-nāṣir, governor of Naṣibīna (746 B.C.).

Notes

2: *Tab-ši*–SI.SÁ poses problems: my use of *kittu* is intended to provide a feminine subject for *tabši*, but the name is perhaps better taken as an apocopated form of the mA *Ittabši*–SI.SÁ (*Iraq* 32 (1970), Pl. XXVI, BM 123367, rev. 8'), in which case *Tabši-mīšāru* would be preferable here.

4: For the restored price, compare No. 25; for *ušallu* see the commentary on No. 23.

5: The reading of É.IM.DIR as Bēt-šašširi, which is suggested by the comparison of this text with No. 25, is confirmed by the equation IM.DIR = *šar-še-ru* (A. Deimel, *ŠL* 399.100 e), and by the reflection that a plant (*šaršeru*) is more likely to be found in a place name than a cloud (*erpitu*). For *rš* becoming *šš* cf. W. von Soden, *GAG Erg.* § 35d. S. Parpola, *AOAT* 6, 81 (Bīt-erpitia) should be amended accordingly.

Bēt-šašširi is also found in I *R* 29, 46, in the list of cities which rebelled against Shalmaneser III, and in *RGD* No. 5 rev. 6, a text which seems quite likely to have come originally from Kalhu. As to the location of the city, it clearly lay on one of the two big rivers—Tigris or Upper Zab—, since in *RGD* No. 5 also there is mention of *ušallu*.

The sign DIR is lacking one vertical, but this is common in nA texts (cf. *Iraq* 32 (1970), Pl. XXVIII, No. 20, 4, where the sign is clearly DIR, so that the transliteration (p. 154) should be corrected).

6: Girītu is also the purchaser in No. 21.

28: d30-*de-e*!-*ni* is also possible, but seems less likely.

Commentary

See on No. 25.

No. 25 Plate 18 ND 472

8·5 × 6·0 cm. Austr. Inst. Arch. 28.i.744(?)

Governor's Palace, Room K.

Obv. 1 *ku-um* NA$_4$.KIŠIB-*šú ṣu-pár-šú iš-kun*
2 *ṣu-pur* m.dUTU.IGI.LÁ-*a-ni* EN A.ŠÀ
(finger-nail impressions)
3 É 5-BÁN A.ŠÀ *ina* URU.ŠE *ša* É-*šá-ši-ri*
4 *ina ú-šal-li ú-piš-ma*
5 m*gi-ri-tú ina* ŠÀ 17 MA.NA URUDU.MEŠ
6 TA* IGI m.dUTU-*a-mur-a-ni il-qi*
7 *kas-pu gam-mur ta-din* A.ŠÀ *x*
8 *šu-a-tú za-rip laq-qí tu-a-ru*
9 *de-e-nu* KA.KA *la-áš-šu*
10 *man-nu ša ina ur-kiš ina ma-te*!-*ma*

11 *lu-u* $^{\mathrm{m.d}}$UTU-*a-mur-a-ni lu-u* DUMU.MEŠ-*šú*
12 *lu-u* DUMU.DUMU.MEŠ-*šú lu-u* LÚ.ŠEŠ.MEŠ-*šú*
13 *lu-u* LÚ.DUMU.ŠEŠ.MEŠ-*šú lu-u* ^{ma}*mám-ma-nu-šú*
14 TA* ^{m}*gi-ri-tú* TA* DUMU.MEŠ-*šú*
15 TA* DUMU.DUMU.MEŠ-*šú de-e-*[*n*]*u*
16 KA.KA *ub-ta-u-ni* 1 [M]A.NA KÙ.BABBAR
B.E. 17 1 MA.NA GUŠKIN *a-na* ^{d}[*x* SUM]-*an*
Rev. 18 *kas-pu* [ ]
19 *ú*-GU[R(-*ra*) *ina de*]-⌜*ni*⌝-*šú* KA.[KA]-*ma*
20 *la i-laq*-[*qi* ( )]
21 IGI ^{m}*pu-x* [(*x*)] *x* LÚ.A.BA
22 IGI ^{m}*si-lim*-^{d}IM LÚ.SIPA MUŠEN.MEŠ
23 IGI $^{\mathrm{m.d}}$UTU.PAP.MEŠ.[*x* (. . . . .)]
24 IGI ^{m}DI.PAP.MEŠ[ ]
25 IGI ^{m}*mu-še-zib*-DINGIR[ ]
26 IGI $^{\mathrm{m.d}}$PA-*tak-bi-iS* LÚ.A.BA
27 *ṣa-bit* IM
28 ^{iti}BARAG UD.28.KÁM
29 *lim-me* ^{m}EN.KAL-*an*
30 ^{lú}*šá-kìn* ^{uru}*kal-ḫi*

Translation

1: Instead of his seal he impressed his nail. Nail of Šamaš-amurāni, owner of the land. (Nail marks.)

3: An estate of 5 *sūtu* of land in the village of Bēt-šašširi in the valley Girītu contracted and took from Šamaš-amurāni in exchange for 17 minas of copper. 7: The price has been paid *in toto*, that land . . . is legally acquired. There is no (further) withdrawal, lawsuit (or) litigation. Anyone who at any time in the future, whether Šamaš-amurāni, or his sons, or his grandsons, or his brothers or his brothers' sons, or any (relative) of his, initiates a lawsuit (or) litigation against Girītu, against his sons (or) against his grandsons, shall [pay] 1 mina of silver (and) 1 mina of gold to [DN]. He shall return the price [ten-fold to its owner], he shall plead [in his law]suit (but) not succeed.

21: Before Pu[. . .], scribe, before Silim-adad, bird-keeper, before Šamaš-ahhē-[. . .], before Šulmu-ahhē [. . . .], before Mušēzib-ilu[?(. . . .)], before Nabû-takbiṣ?, the scribe, writer of the tablet.

28: Month of Nīsānu (I), 28th day, *limmu* of Bēl-dān, governor of Kalhu (744/734 B.C.).

Notes

3: For Bēt-šašširi see on No. 24, 5.

7: The final sign in the line was collated by Professor D. J. Wiseman; I can only suggest MURUB_4! = *qablu*, which may refer in nA to a type of land or orchard (instances of syllabic spelling in *AHw* 888a, but logographic writings are not mentioned, e.g. *ADD* 751, 3, which do not support the suggestion (ibid.) that the word is *gablu* = *ǧabal* = hill). However, here we should not expect such a definition of the property to come at so late a stage in the document.

10: Text has *tu* (coll., D.J.W.).

14: Copy has *tú*, read perhaps rather *-te* (cf. No. 24, 13).

19: Traces are present on the tablet as indicated in the transliteration (coll. D.J.W.).

26: This name collated (D.J.W.); derivation from *kabāṣu* does not seem likely. Could this be for *kbt/d* with spirantization of the dental (cf. W. von Soden, *GAG Erg.* § 29f)?

29–30: 744 is the more probable date, not only because no mention of the second *pūru* is made, but also because it is closer in date to No. 24.

Commentary

This document and the preceding one both record purchases of land by Girītu in the valley-lands of Bēt-šašširi, for the sum of 17 minas of copper; hence I have restored the same area of land in No. 24 as we have here. It is particularly useful to compare the description of the land's situation in each case. In this text the land is " in the village of Bēt-š., in the valley "; now Bēt-šašširi is not a mere village (URU.ŠE), and we must have to do here with a village (or temporary habitations) belonging to the larger town. Therefore in No. 24, 5 *ina* must be understood as " in the territory of ", since the land will have been in the valley-land belonging to Bēt-šašširi, and not in the town itself or its immediate vicinity; it is highly probable that Girītu would acquire contiguous properties, and that the descriptions in these two texts could be exchanged. Hence I think we may reconstruct a picture in which the main town of Bēt-šašširi lay in the hills (*mulû*), some way above the level of the river, but owned lands and even a small settlement down on the alluvial river banks, where the richest agricultural land lay.

No. 26 Plate 18 ND 475

4·3 × 6·0 cm. Austr. Inst. Arch. 17.ix.743

Governor's Palace, Room K.

Obv. 1 *ku-um* NA$_4$.KIŠIB-*šú ṣu-pur-šú*
2 *iš-kun*
3 *ṣu-pur* ^{m}*mar-duk-a-te*
(finger-nail impressions)
4 É 2-BÁN A.ŠÀ *ina* KÁ URU
5 *ú-piš-ma* ^{m}*kur-ba-nu*
6 *ina lìb-bi* 12 MA.NA URUDU.MEŠ
7 TA* IGI ^{m}*mar-duk-a-te*
8 [*i*]*l-q*[*i*] *kas-*[*p*]*u ga-mur*
9 [*ta*]*-din* A.ŠÀ *šú-a-tú*
B.E. 10 *za-rip la-a-qi*
11 *tu-a-ru de-e-nu*
Rev. 12 KA.KA *la-áš-šu*
13 *man-nu šá ina ur-kiš*
14 *ina ma-te-ma lu-u* ⸤^{m}*mar*⸥*-duk-a-te*
15 *lu-u* PAP.MEŠ-*šú lu-u* ⸢DUMU⸣.MEŠ-*šú*
16 *lu-u* LÚ.EN.NAM URU-*šú*
17 ⸤*šá*⸥ *de-nu* KA.KA TA* ^{m}*kur-ba-ni*
18 [*ù*?] DUMU.MEŠ-*šú ub-ta-u-ni*
19 *kas-pu a-na* 10.TA.ÀM *ana* EN-*šú*

20 GUR-*ra ina de-ni-šú* KA.KA NU TI

21 IGI ^{m}*šùl-mu*-PAP.MEŠ
22 IGI ^{m}*ba-ri-ḫu*
T.E. 23 IGI ^{m}EN.BÀD
24 IGI ^{m}*x*[(*x*) *x*] *x*
25 IGI ^{m}DI.[KUD?-]*i?*
26 *ina* ^{iti}GAN UD.⌜17⌝.KÁM
L.E. 27 *lim-mu* ^{m}KU-*t*[*i*-]A.É.ŠÁR.RA
28 LUGAL KUR *aš-šur*^{ki}
29 IGI ^{m}*ke-ni-i* LÚ.A.B[A]
30 *ṣa-bit ka-ni-ki*

Translation

1: Instead of his seal he impressed his nail. Nail of Mardukāte. (Nail marks.) 4: An estate of 2 *sūtu* of land (with)in the gate of the city Kurbānu contracted and took from Mardukāte in exchange for 12 minas of copper. 8: The price has been paid *in toto*, that land is legally acquired. There is no (further) withdrawal, lawsuit, (or) litigation. Anyone who at any time in the future, whether Mardukāte, or his brothers, or his sons, or the governor of his city, initiates a lawsuit (or) litigation against Kurbānu (or) against his sons, shall return the price ten-fold to its owner. He shall plead in his lawsuit (but) not succeed.

21: Before Šulmu-ahhē, before Barihu, before Bēl-dūrī, before [. . . .], before Dayānī?.

26: In the month of Kislīmu (IX), 17th day, *limmu* of Tukultī-apil-ešarra, king of Assyria.

29: Before Kēnī, scribe, writer of the document.

Notes

4: *ina bāb āli* is presumably a way of saying " within the city walls " or " inside (a particular) gate "; the city in question must be Kalhu.

5: Kurbānu is also the purchaser in No. 27, of the same date.

18: Or [TA*].

25: The PN is restored after No. 3, 7, but is of course uncertain. The sign DI is confirmed by collation.

29: Kēnī is also the scribe of No. 5, of 754 B.C.

No. 27 Plate 19 ND 206
IM, for study
5·1 × 6·9 × 2·5 [—].ix?.743

Governor's Palace, Room K.

Obv. 1 *ṣ*[*u-pu*]*r* ^{m}⌜EN⌝.[BÀD]
2 ⌜EN⌝ A.ŠÀ [(*x x*)]

(finger-nail impressions)

3 ⌜É⌝ 1 ANŠE A.ŠÀ.GA
4 *ina* KUR-*e ú-piš-ma*

Obv. 5 ^{m}*kur-ba-nu ina lìb-bi*
6 16? MA.NA URUDU.MEŠ
7 TA* IGI ^{m}EN.BÀD *il-qi*
8 *kas-pu ga-mur ta-*⌜*din*⌝
9 A.ŠÀ *šú-a-tú* [*z*]*a-rip*
10 *la-qi tu-a-ru de-nu*
11 [K]A.KA *la-a-šú man-nu*
B.E. 12 *šá ina ur-kiš ina ma-te-ma*
13 *lu-u* ^{m}EN.BÀD
14 *lu-u* PAP.MEŠ-*šú lu-u* UN.MEŠ-*šú*
15 *lu-u* LÚ.GAR-*an-šú*
Rev. 16 *lu-u* LÚ.EN.NAM URU-*šú*
17 *šа de-e-nu* KA.KA
18 TA* ^{m}*kur-ba-ni u* DUMU.MEŠ-*šú*
19 *ù* [DU]MU.DUMU.MEŠ-*šú*
20 *ub-*[*ta-u*]*-ni* 1 MA.NA KÙ.BABBAR
21 1 MA.NA [GUŠKIN *ina bu*]*r-ki* ^{d}MAŠ
22 *a-šib* [^{uru}*kal-ḫi* GAR-*a*]*n*
23 (undeciphered)
24–7 (broken ; witnesses)
T.E. 28 ^{iti}G[AN UD.*x*.KAM]
29 *lim-*⌜*mu*⌝ ^{m}KU-*t*[*i*?-A.É.ŠÁR.RA]
30 MAN KU[R *aš-šur*]

Translation

1 : Nail of Bēl-[dūrī], owner of the land [(being sold)]. (Nail marks.)

3 : An estate of 1 homer of land, in the mountain, Kurbānu contracted and took from Bēl-dūrī in exchange for 16 minas of copper. 8 : The price has been paid *in toto*, that land is legally acquired. There is no (further) withdrawal, lawsuit, (or) litigation. Anyone who at any time in the future, whether Bēl-dūrī, or his brothers, or his family, or his officer(?), or the governor of his city, initiates a lawsuit (or) litigation against Kurbānu, or his sons or his grandsons, [shall place] 1 mina of silver (and) 1 mina [of gold in the] lap of Ninurta who dwells [in Kalhu] . . . . .

24 : (Witnesses' names.)

28 : Month of Kislīmu (IX) [xth day] *limmu* of Tukultī-[apil-ešarra], king of [Assyria (743 B.C.)].

Notes

4 : The precise connotations of *šadû* are uncertain ; it may be no more than a synonym of *mulû*, " raised ground, hills ", but it is perhaps more likely to refer to something more definite, although where such a locality should be sought in the Kalhu region is less clear.

6 : 18 MA.NA is also possible.

14 : In view of the absence of sons, Bēl-dūrī is probably a eunuch (K. Deller).

15 : LÚ.GAR-*an-šú* seems anomalous : we should expect *šakin-šu*, or more likely, *šaknu-šu*. K. Deller refers me to the similar ^{lú}*šá-kan-šú-nu* (*ABL* 610, 5) and *šá-ka-šú* (*ARU* 142, 7 ; 143, 10).

23 : The traces do not seem to correspond with any of the expected formulae.

29 : The restoration is guaranteed by the date of No. 26, also a sale text of Kurbānu.

No. 28 Plate 17 ND 275(e)
Inst. Arch. London
[—].x.743?

5·8 × (3·9) × 2·6

Governor's Palace, Room K.

Obv. 1 *ku-m[u* NA$_4$.KIŠIB-*š]ú ṣu-pár-šú* GAR
2 *ṣu-⌜pur* ^{m}⌝[*x x x* (*x x*)] EN É
(finger-nail impressions)
3 É *ep-šú a-di* GIŠ.ÙR.MEŠ-*šú*
4 [( ) *a*]-*di* GIŠ.[IG.MEŠ]-*šú*
5 [ ]*na*? [(*x*) *x*]*ú*?-*piš*
6 [L]Ú.GAL URU.MEŠ
7 [ ] *x x* [ ]
(remainder of obv. and upper part of rev. broken)
Rev. 1′ ^{iti}AB U[D.*x*.KAM]
2′ *lim-mu* ^{m}K[U-*ti*-]A?.É.⟨ŠÁR⟩.[R]A?
3′ LUGAL KUR [*aš-šur*(^{ki})]

Translation

1: Instead of his [seal] he impressed his nail. Nail of [PN], owner of the house. (Nail marks.)

3: A built house together with its beams (and) together with its [doors, PN], the village-inspector, contracted [(and) took in exchange for . . . . . . (long gap).

Rev. 1′: Month of Kanūnu (X), [xth] day, *limmu* of Tukul[tī-apil]-ešarra, king of [Assyria] (743 B.C.).

Notes

5: A possible restoration is [*ina libbi x* MA.NA AN].NA.[ME]Š; it would be possible, according to the traces, to read instead of *uppiš ú-tap-piš*, but since the name of a purchaser usually follows the preterite *u(p)piš*, but not the perfect *utappiš*, the restoration suggested is to be preferred.

Rev. 2′: No other royal name of the right period fits the traces, and therefore the emendation suggested —supplying ŠÁR—is unavoidable.

Commentary

So far as we can tell this is a perfectly ordinary house sale. In view of the title village-inspector (l. 6), the purchaser may have been Bēl-issīya.

No. 29 Plate 20 ND 276
IM 56838
[—.—].727

4·3 × 7·6 × 2·4

Governor's Palace, Room M.

Obv. 1 *ṣu-pur* ^{m}⌜*x x x*⌝[(*x*)]
(finger-nail impressions)

Obv. 2 EN *qaq-[q]e-r[e]* SUM-*u-n[i]*
3 30 GÍD.DA 14 DAGAL
4 *tu-piš-ma* ^{mí}*ia-u*?*-ta-tu*?
5 [*ina* Š]À ⌞10? MA⌟.NA ⟨URUDU?⟩.MEŠ *t[a]-al-qi*
6 ⌜*kas-pu ga*⌝*-mu[r t]a-din*
7 *qaq-qe-re* ⌜*šu*⌝*-a-tú-[nu]*
8 *za-rip-pu la-*⌞*qí*⌟*-ú*
9 *tu-a-*⌞*ru*⌟ *de-nu*
10 [K]A.K[A *l*]*a-áš-šú*
11 *man-nu ša* ⌜*i-na*⌝ *ur-k[iš]*
Rev. 12 *ina ma-[te-ma] i-za-qu-pa-ni*
13 *kas-pu* ⌜*a-na* 10⌝.MEŠ
14 *a-na* EN.MEŠ-*šú* GUR-*ra*
15 *ina de-ni-šú* KA.KA-*ma*
16 *la i-laq-qi*

---

17 IGI ^{m}DINGIR.SU
18 IGI ^{m}GUŠKIN-*i*
19 IGI $^{m.d}$*asal-lú-ḫi*-MU.PAP
20 IGI ^{m}DU-*i*
21 IGI ^{m}*aš-šur*-AŠ.PAP
22 IGI ^{m}*la-qi-pu*
23 IGI ^{m}*du-du-ú-a*
24 IGI $^{m.d}$[MA]Š?.TI.LA-*s[u-i]q-*⌞*bi*⌟
T.E. 25 *ṣa-bit* I[M ^{iti}*x*] UD.[*x*]
26 [*li*]*m-mu* ^{m}EN.KASKAL.EN.P[AP]
L.E. 27 ^{lú}*šá-kìn* ^{uru}*gu-za-na*

Translation

1: Nail of PN, (nail marks), owner of the ground being sold.

3: (Ground) 30 (cubits) long, 14 (cubits) wide, I(a)utātu? contracted and took, in exchange for 10? minas of ⟨copper⟩. 6: The price has been paid *in toto*, that ground is legally acquired; there is no (further) withdrawal, lawsuit, (or) litigation. Anyone who at any time in the future arises shall return the price ten-fold to its owners. He shall plead in his lawsuit, but not succeed.

17: Before Ilu-(e)rība, before Hurāṣī, before Asalluhi-šūmu-uṣur, before Kēnī, before Aššur-nādin-ahi, before Laqīpu, before Dudūa, before Ninurta?-balās-su-iqbi, writer of the tablet.

25: [Month of ...., xth] day, *limmu* of Bēl-harrān-bēlu-uṣur, governor of Guzāna (727 B.C.).

Notes

2: *qaqqerē*, as this transliteration implies, is plural, as is usual in nA legal texts; this is particularly clear in ll. 7–8. The plural of this noun is already in use in the middle Assyrian legal documents.

SUM-*u-n[i]* would be a very unusual spelling (cf. the list of spellings collected by K. Deller in *OrNS* 31 (1962), 229), and a possible alternative is to read SUM *q[a*!*-qe-re]* at the end of the line.

5: URUDU is more common than ZABAR at this date in the texts.

No. 30 Plate 90 ND 204
Austr. Inst. Arch.
7 × 10 cm. [—]

Governor's Palace, Room K.

Obv. 1 *ku-um* NA$_4$.KIŠIB-*šú-nu ṣu-pár-šú-nu i*[*š-ku-nu*]
2 ^{m}*ḫu-ub-uš-ka-a-a* ^{m}AD$^{!}$-*u*[*l*-ZU]
3 DUMU.MEŠ $^{m.d}$UTU-*še*-⌜*x*⌝ [( )]
(finger-nail impressions)
4 É 40 ANŠE A.ŠÀ *ina ma-za-ru-te*
5 É *ad-ru* GIŠ.ŠAR *ina* ^{uru}*sa-li-ma-a-ni*
6 *ina* ŠÀ 2 MA.NA KÙ.BABBAR *ina* ŠÀ 1 MA.NA *ša* MAN
7 ^{m}SUḪUŠ.15 *ú-piš-ma*
8 TA* IGI ^{m}*ḫu-bu-uš-ka-a-a*
9 TA* IGI ^{m}AD-*ul*-ZU *il-qi*
10 *kás-pu ga-mur ta-din*
11 A.ŠÀ *za-rip laq-qi*
12 *tu-a-ru de-e-nu* KA.KA *la-áš-šú*
13 *ina ur-kiš ina mat-e-ma*
14 *lu-u* ^{m}*ḫu-bu-uš-ka-a-a*
15 *lu-u* ^{m}AD-*ul*-ZU *lu-u* DUMU.MEŠ-*šú-nu*
16 *ša de-e-nu* KA.KA
17 TA* ^{m}*ub-ru*-15 *ú* DUMU.MEŠ-*šú*
18 *ub-ta-'u-ú-ni*

B.E. (uninscribed)

Rev. (broken, except for traces at the ends of the lines: l. 20$^{?}$: *a*]*n*$^{?}$; 21$^{?}$:]MAŠ$^{?}$; 23$^{?}$: *p*]*a*$^{?}$; 26$^{?}$:]*x-pi-di*; coll. D.J.W.).

Translation

1: Instead of their seals they [impressed] their nails. Hubuškāyu (and) Abu-ūl-[īdi], sons of Šamaš-šē[. . .]. (Nail marks.)

4: An estate of 40 homers of land in cultivation, a house, a threshing-floor, (and) an orchard, in the town of Salimāni, Ubru-ištar contracted and took from Hubuškāyu (and) from Abu-ūl-īdi in exchange for 2 minas of silver (weighed) by the royal mina. 10: The price has been paid *in toto*, the land is legally acquired. There is no (further) withdrawal, lawsuit, (or) litigation. At any time in the future (anyone), whether Hubuškāyu or Abu-ūl-īdi, or their sons, who initiates a lawsuit (or) litigation against Ubru-ištar or his sons [. . . . . (rest too broken for translation).

Notes

2: Copy (and collation) *ṣi*(!), but the emendation must be right.

4: For *maz*(*za*)*rūtu* see *Iraq* 32 (1970), 135.

7: In this line the purchaser's name is written SUḪUŠ.15, but in l. 17 he is *ub-ru*-15; both spellings were specifically collated and confirmed for me by Professor D. J. Wiseman. This shows that the correct reading of the sign SUḪUŠ in nA personal names can, and probably usually should, be not *išid* or *išdi*, but *ubru*. This solves some other problems: it explains the almost complete disappearance of the first element *ub-ru*, found in the texts from Tell Billa (*JCS* 7 (1953), 144a), from later nA texts—since it was written logographically—, and it provides an explanation for the variant writing of the name of the eponym for 763 B.C., which is normally written *bur-*^{d}*sa-gal-e*, but once SUḪUŠ?-*sa-[gal]-e* (see *RLA* II, 422–3). Although *ubru(m)* (**wabrum*) is already known in middle Assyrian as an onomastic element, it is not clear to me where the connection with SUḪUŠ arises. (See also on No. 248, 2′.)

16: There is a superfluous DIŠ between *ša* and *de* in this line (coll.).

17: as *ú* would be a very unusual way of writing *ū*, I am tempted to emend to TA*! (not collated).

Commentary

Ubru-ištar buys from two brothers a considerable area of land, which includes a house, a threshing-floor, and some trees. It is not clear if the two brothers own separate parts of this estate, or whether they are as yet undivided, joint holders of the land, which had presumably been the property of their father.

No. 31 Plate 21 ND 233

IM 56823

8·8 × 12·6 × (2·8) [—]

Governor's Palace, Room K.

Obv. 1 ⸢*ku-um* NA$_4$.KIŠIB-*šú ṣu-pur-šú*⸣ [*iš-kun*]

(finger-nail impressions)

2 [*ṣ*]*u-pur* ^{m}*ma-bi?-mu-*⌞*ú*⌟ DUMU $^{m.d}$⸢*x x*⸣ [ ]

3 DUMU ^{m}⸢*x*⸣*-a-a* LÚ *ša šar-ri*

4 É 40 ANŠE ŠE.NUMUN.MEŠ A.ŠÀ.[G]A?

5 *ina ma-[za-r]u-[t]e* ⸢*a*⸣*-na* ⸢*x x x x x*⸣

6 [*x*] *na* ⸢*x x x*⸣ URU ⸢*x x x x*⸣

7 [*ina*] ŠÀ 2 MA.[NA (*x*) *x*] *x* KÙ.BABBAR *a?-na* MA.NA *ša* LU[GAL]

8 [^{m}]$^{.d}$UTU-*ku-mu-a* LÚ.A.BA LÚ.NIMGIR [É.GAL(?)]

9 [T]A* IGI ^{m}*ma-bi?-mu-ú il-qí*

10 *kás-pu ga-mur ta-din* A.ŠÀ *za-rip* T[I]-⸢*qí*⸣

11 [*t*]*u-a-ru de-e-nu da-ba-bu la-áš-šú*

12 *man-nu ša a-na ur-kiš* EGIR UD-*me*

13 [*a-na ma-t*]*i-ma a-na* UD.UL.LÍ.A

14 [*lu*]*-ú* ^{m}*ma-*⌞*bi*⌟*-mu-ú* DUMU.MEŠ-⸢*šú*⸣

15 [*lu*]*-ú* DUMU.DUMU.MEŠ-*šú lu-ú* ŠEŠ.MEŠ-*šú*

16 [*lu-ú*]⸢DUMU⸣.ŠEŠ.MEŠ-*šú lu mám-ma qur-ub-šú*

17 [*lu-ú* E]N *il-ki-šú lu-ú* LÚ.GAR-*nu*

18 [*lu-ú š*]*a?-pi-ru lu-ú* ^{lú}*ḫa-za-an-nu*

19 [ ]*x ša i-za-qu-pa-a-ni*

20 [*de-e-nu da-b*]*a-bu* TA* $^{m.d}$UTU-*ku-mu-a*

21 [*ub*]*-ta-'u-ú-ni*

B.E. and rev. (broken)

Translation

1: Instead of his seal [he impressed] his nail. (Nail marks.) Nail of Mabimū?, son of . . . . ., son of . . . āyu, a " man of the king ".

4: An estate of 40 homers of sown land in cultivation .... Šamaš-kūmūa, the scribe (of?) the [palace(?)] herald, contracted and took from Mabimū? in exchange for 2 minas [(and x shekels?)] of silver (weighed) by the royal mina. 10: The price has been paid *in toto*, the land is legally acquired. There is no (further) withdrawal, lawsuit, (or) litigation. Anyone who in the future in after days [at] any time in distant days, [whether] Mabimū? or his sons, [or] his grandsons, or his brothers, [or] his brothers' sons, or any relative of his, [or] (someone) responsible for his *ilku*-duties, or an officer, [or] a representative(?), or a mayor, [.......]—who comes forward (and) initiates [a lawsuit (or) liti]gation against Šamaš-kūmūa [(or) against his sons .....

Notes

2: Here, and also in ll. 9 and 14, it might be possible to read the name m*ma-am*!*-mu-ú*; all the passages are too worn for certainty.

3: The man's title seems certain, although the syllabic writing of *šarru* is surprising. A title *ša šarri* has occasionally been looked for in nA texts (K. Deller refers me to *ABL* 1257, rev. 9–11, where ÌR.MEŠ *ša* MAN seems to have the Aramaic equivalent LÚ *di-mil-ki*; this is not a profession, though), but in fact the majority of instances are a profession *šá* U.U (or NÍG.U.U), which is definitely not to be confused with *ša šarri*, although its correct reading is unknown. From the contexts in which it is found it is clearly a profession connected with a craft such as stone or metal working; see *MSL* XII, 234, ii B 13 (do not emend !), where he appears with the copper-smith and workers in stone; *ADD* 868, 2′ (coll.), after a goldsmith and before stone-workers (*burgullu* and *kapšarru*); *ADD* 827, 5: MÍ.SIMUG.MEŠ mí*šá* U.U.MEŠ. Other instances are *Iraq* 19 (1957), 127–35: ND 5447, 11; 5452, 11; 5469, 20 (all the same man), and perhaps ND 2068 (*Iraq* 16 (1954), 32), *ADD* 50 rev. 6, and *ABL* 155, 4, 7. Unfortunately neither the logogram nor the contexts give a clue to the craftsman's exact trade; my guess is " furnace-man " or " fuel-man ".

5–6: These undeciphered lines presumably gave the land's location and precise description.

12–13: The unusual phrases in these lines are probably consciously literary; cf. *ina ár-kat* UD-*me* (*ARU* 96, 14) which is certainly a Babylonianism for Assyrian *ur-kat*.

18: *šāpiru* also occurs in *ARU* 96a, 6, and in No. 60 below.

Commentary

Note simply that a Šamaš-kūmūa is also purchaser in Nos. 17 and 57.

No. 32 Plate 22

ND 249+252(j)(+)275(g)
IM, for study
Inst. Arch. London (275(g))
[—]

(7·5) × (7·1) × 2·9
(2·7) × (3·0) × (1·6) (275(g))

Governor's Palace, Room K.

Obv. 1′ [ ].KÁM
2′ [-]*a?-a-e*
3′ ⌜É⌝ 29 ANŠ[E] A.ŠÀ.GA
4′ [*ina?* u]ru*ša-la-ḫi-ṭa?-a-a*
5′ [*tiḫ*]*i** GIŠ.ŠAR *ṭiḫi** ÍD
6′ [*ú-p*]*iš-ma* m.dUTU.DU-*ú-bal-li*[*ṭ*]
7′ [lú*š*]*a qur-bu-ti ša* m.dIM.ERÍN.GAB MAN [K]UR *aš-šur*
8′ [*ina lì*]*b-bi* 90 ⌞MA⌟.NA URUDU.MEŠ *il-qi*

Obv. 9′ [*kas-pu*] *ga-*⌞*mur*⌟ [*ta-din*] A.ŠÀ *za-*[*r*]*ip*
10′ [*laq-qi* (*tu-a-ru*) *de-e-n*]*u* KA.KA *la-a-šú*
11′ [ ]*ša* LÚ.ERÍN.MEŠ *an-nu-ti*
12′ [-]*šú-n*[*u l*]*u-u* DUMU.MEŠ-*šú-nu*
13′ [*l*]*u-u* EN *il-ki-šú-nu*
14′ [LÚ.GA]R?-*an*[-*šú-nu*(?)] *da-b*[*a*?-*bu*(?)]
15′ [ ]*x-ke-nu*-TI
16′ [*ub-ta-'u*]-*u-ni*
17′ [UD.K]A.BAR.MEŠ
18′ [-*a*]*n*?
19′ [ ]-*ma*
B.E. (broken; uncertain how many lines missing, if any)
Rev. 1 [ ]-*šá*
2 [^{m}*qu*]*r-di-*^{d}INANNA-*là-mur*
3 [.U]N.MEŠ
4 [ ].⌞MAN⌟.PAP
5–16? (last signs only; presumably ends of witnesses' names, etc.)
(remainder broken)

Translation

1′: [nail of . . . .]āyu, [nail of . . . .]-ēreš?.

3′: An estate of 29 homers of land [in] the village of Šalahiṭāya, [next] to an orchard, next to the river, Šamaš-kēnu-uballiṭ, officer of Adad-nērārī, king of Assyria, [con]tracted and took [in ex]change for 90 minas of copper. 9′: [The price has been paid] *in toto*, the land is legally [acquired]; there is no [(further) (withdrawal), lawsuit,] (or) litigation. [Anyone, whether one] of these men, [or] their [brothers] or their sons, [or their . . . . .] or those responsible for their *ilku*-duties, [or . . . . ., or their?] officer(?) [(who) initiat]es liti[gation(?) against Šamaš]-kēnu-uballiṭ [(or) against his sons(?)], shall [place/pay . . . .] of bronze [. . . . . . .].

Rev. 2: [before Qu]rdi-ištar-lāmur, [before . . . . .]-nišē, [before . . . .-]šarru-uṣur, [. . . . .

Notes

1′–2′: Since these lines precede the description of the estate being sold, it is clear that the traces surviving must be the ends of the names of the sellers, of whom we know from l. 11′ that there were more than one. There is no means of telling how much of the tablet is missing above l. 1′.

4′: This place name is derived from the PN Lā-hiṭāya attested in *JCS* 7 (1953), 169, No. 70, 8 (Tell Billa), and probably from Kalhu in ND 3432 (Photo, *Iraq* 17 (1955), Pl. XXVII; cf. K. Deller, *OrNS* 35 (1966), 193).

7′: For the title, see on No. 9, 15; the first sign preserved cannot be LÚ (coll.).

14′: The restoration is not entirely satisfactory, since we expect *dēnu dabābu* . . . .; however, the same objection affects an alternative restoration: . . . *ša i-za-qu-p*]*a-an-*[*ni*] *da-b*[*a-bu*]. For the writing LÚ.GAR-*an-šú-nu* (if correct), cf. No. 27, 15.

15′: The fragment with ll. 15′–19′ and Rev. 1–6 is in London and cannot therefore be joined physically to the rest of the tablet. That it does belong is indicated by the remains of Šamaš-kēnu-uballiṭ's name in l. 15′, and by the shape of the fragment. The shape of the fragment also seems to indicate that its first line follows on directly from l. 14′ on the main part of the tablet, as assumed here, but it is not impossible that the gap is wider.

Rev. 2: *là* (NU) is not a current value in nA texts of this type, and must be considered as eccentric here. K. Deller quotes me one further such writing: ^{m}IGI.15-*là*-IGI.LÁ (VAT 8643, 7, 15).

Commentary

Šamaš-kēnu-uballiṭ buys from 2 or more persons an area of 29 homers of land for 90 minas of copper. An unusual feature of the phraseology is that the sellers were named and referred to only at the head of the document, in the introductory section. There is not the usual resumptive phrase (such as *issu pān* LÚ.MEŠ *annūti*) in the main body of the text (l. 11′ being already part of the penalty clauses).

No. 33 Plate 23 ND 260
IM 56830
6·9 × 9·5 × 2·2 [—]

Governor's Palace, Room K.

Obv. 1 GIM NA$_4$.KIŠIB-*šú ṣu-pár-šú iš-ku-nu*
(finger-nail impressions)
2 *ṣu-pur* ^{m}*ia-ma-qi* EN A.ŠÀ
3 É 8 ANŠE A.ŠÀ *ina ma-za-ru-te*
4 GIŠ.BÁN *ša* 10 *qa* ^{uru}*ku-up-ru-na*
5 *ina lìb-bi* 8 MA.NA URUDU.MEŠ
6 ^{m}EN.KI-*a* LÚ.SAG *ša* ^{m}EN-*tar-ṣi*-DINGIR-[*ma*]
7 ^{lú}*šá-kìn* ^{uru}*kal-ḫi*
8 TA* IGI ^{m}*ia-ma-qi ú-tap-piš*
9 *i-si-qi kas-pu gam-mur ta-din*
10 A.ŠÀ *šú-a-tú za-rip laq-qi*
11 *tú-a-ru da-ba-bu la-áš-šú*
12 *man-nu ša ina ur-kiš lu* ^{m}*ia-ma-qi*
13 *lu* ŠEŠ.MEŠ-*šú lu* DUMU.MEŠ-*šú*
14 *lu* LÚ.MEŠ-*e* EN *il-ki-šú*
B.E. 15 TA* ^{m}EN.KI-*a* LÚ.SAG
Rev. 16 *de-nu* K[A.KA
17 ⌜2?⌝ MA.NA [
18 *a*-[*n*]*a* [
19 *kás-pu* [
20 *l*[*a*?
(remainder broken; T.E. and L.E. uninscribed).

Translation

1: Instead of his seal he impressed his nail. (Nail marks.) Nail of Iamāqi, owner of the land.

3: An estate of 8 homers of land in cultivation, (measured by) the *sūtu* of 10 *qa* (of) Kupruna, Bēl-issīya, eunuch of Bēl-tarṣi-ilu[ma], governor of Kalhu, has contracted and taken from Iamāqi in exchange for 8 minas of copper. 9: The price has been paid *in toto*, that land is legally acquired; there is no (further) withdrawal (or) litigation. Anyone who in the future, whether Iamāqi, or his brothers, or his sons, or the men responsible for his *ilku*-duties, [initiates] a lawsuit (or) liti[gation] against Bēl-issīya, the eunuch, [shall pay] 2? minas of [silver(?) . . . .] to [DN . . . ., he shall return] the price [ten-fold to its owner(s) . . . .

Notes

2: The PN should perhaps be normalized as Iamāqu, but this is made uncertain by l. 12, where it should be nominative.

4: The omission of *ina* at the beginning of the line is probably an error, since it occurs in the companion text No. 34, 4.

Kub/pruna (also No. 34, 4) is hardly identical with the town mentioned by Sennacherib in Bīt-dakkuri. As nothing is known of the town's location or character, there is no way of determining why it is mentioned here. At first sight it seems as if the scribe is referring to a special " Kupruna *sūtu*-measure ", like the " Assyrian *qa* " or the " Carchemish mina ", but since such a measure is never elsewhere attested, it may be rather that Kupruna is the village or town within whose territory the estate is situated.

12: The omission of *ina matē-ma* may be accidental.

15: The unusual repetition of the man's title is probably intended to explain why no relatives of his are mentioned, cf. No. 17, 12, with note.

Commentary

As far as l. 12, and apart from the necessary changes, this tablet is almost a sign by sign duplicate of No. 34. The two transactions must, I think, have been recorded by the same scribe, and they are very likely to have been close in date as well. Probably the lands were in the same area, if not contiguous, and they may well have been in the territory of a town or village Kupruna (see note on l. 4).

No. 34 Plate 23 ND 266
IM 56833
5·9 × 8·4 × (2·3) [—]

Governor's Palace, Room K.

Obv. 1 GIM NA_4.KIŠIB-*šú ṣu-pár-šú iš-ku-un*

(finger-nail impressions)

2 *ṣu-pur* ^{m}*ba-te-ia* EN A.ŠÀ
3 É 2 ANŠE A.ŠÀ *ina ma-za-ru-ti*
4 *ina* GIŠ.BÁN *ša* 10 *qa* ^{uru}*ku-up-ru-na*
5 *ina lìb-bi* 2 MA.NA URUDU.MEŠ
6 ^{m}EN.KI-*a* LÚ.SAG *ša* ^{m}EN-*tar-ṣ*[*i*-DINGIR-*ma*]
7 ^{lú}*šá-kìn* ^{uru}*kal-ḫi*
8 *ú-tap-piš* TA* IGI ^{m}*ba-te-ia*
9 *i-si-qi kás-pu gam-mur ta-din*
10 [A].ŠÀ *šú-a-tú za-rip laq-qi*
11 [*tu*]*-a-ru da-ba-bu la-áš-šú*
12 [*man-nu*] *ša ina ur-kiš ina ma-te-ma*

13 [*lu* ^{m}*ba*]-⌞*te-ia*⌟ *lu* ŠEŠ.MEŠ-*šú*
14 [ ]⌞LÚ?⌟[ ]
(Rev. broken, except for indecipherable traces).

Translation

1: Instead of his seal he impressed his nail. (Nail marks.) Nail of Batēya, owner of the land.

3: An estate of 2 homers of land in cultivation, (measured) by the *sūtu* of 10 *qa* (of) Kupruna, Bēl-issīya, eunuch of Bēl-tarṣi-[iluma], governor of Kalhu, has contracted and taken from Batēya in exchange for 2 minas of copper. 9: The price has been paid *in toto*, that land is legally acquired; there is no (further) withdrawal (or) litigation. [Anyone] who in the future at any time, [whether Ba]tēya, or his brothers, [or his sons, or] the men? [responsible for his *ilku*-duties ....

Notes and Commentary

See on No. 33.

No. 35 Plate 24 ND 264
Inst. Arch. London
[—]

7·5 × 10·4 × 3·0

Governor's Palace, Room K.

Obv. 1 *ku-um* NA_4.KIŠIB-⌜*šu*⌝-*nu* *ṣu-pár-šú-nu* [GAR?-*n*]*u*
(finger-nail impressions)
2 ⌜*ṣu*⌝-*pur* $^{m.d}$*gu-la-ba-la-ṭí* ⌜LÚ⌝.NAR
3 ⌜*ṣu*⌝-*pur* ^{m}É.IM.DIR-*a-a* L[Ú.N]AR
4 [*ṣu*]-*pur* ^{m}LUGAL.TI-*iq-bi* LÚ.NAR
5 [*ṣu-pu*]*r* $^{m.d}$MAŠ.PAP.MEŠ-*šal-lim?* LÚ.NAR
6 [*ṣu-pur*] ^{m}*kur-ba-ìl-a-a* LÚ.UŠ+[KU]
7 [É (*x*+)]15 ANŠE A.ŠÀ *ina ku-da-a-ri* [*ša* LÚ.NAR]
8 [*ina*] ^{uru}*kur-ba-ìl ina* GÚ.UN URUDU.M[EŠ]
9 ^{m}EN.KI-*ia* LÚ.GAL URU.MEŠ-*ni*
10 TA* *p*[*a-a*]*n* LÚ.MEŠ *šu-nu-ú-ti*
11 *ú*-⌜*piš*⌝-*ma* TI-*qí* *kás-pu*
12 *ga-mur* SUM-*ni* A.ŠÀ *za-ri-pi*
13 *la*-[*q*]*í tu-a-ru de-nu* KA.KA
14 *la-áš-šu ma-nu ša ina* ⌜*ur*⌝-*kiš*
15 *lu-u* TA* ŠÀ LÚ.MEŠ *šu-nu-ú-ti*
16 *lu-u* DUMU.MEŠ-*šú* TA* ^{m}EN.KI-*ia*
17 *de-nu* KA.KA *ub-ta-ú-ni*
18 1 MA.NA KÙ.BABBAR 1 MA.NA GUŠKIN
Rev. 19 *a-na* ^{d}IM [*a-ši*]*b* ^{uru}*k*[*u*]*r-ba*-⌜*ìl*⌝
20 ⌞SUM⌟-*an ina* [*de*]-*ni*-⌜*šu*⌝ KA.KA-*ma* NU TI-*qí*
21 [IG]I ^{m}EN.NUN.DINGIR.MEŠ LÚ.SANGA

22 IGI ^{m}⌜*si-par*⌝-*ra-a-nu* LÚ.GAL KUŠ.MEŠ
23 IGI ^{m}*aš-šur*-EN.[*x*] ^{lú}*láḫ-ḫi-nu*
24 I[GI ^{m}]EN.⌜KI-*ia*⌝ ŠEŠ-*šú ša* LÚ.SANGA
25 [IG]I ^{m}[(*x*) *x x*]-*a-a* ⌜ŠEŠ.AD⌝-*šú ša* LÚ.SANGA
26 [ ]-⌜15⌝ ⌞DUMU $^{m.d}$UTU?⌟.*x*.PAP
27 [ ]*x x-lu-u*-TI-*at*
28 [ ].MEŠ IGI $^{m.d}$IM.PAP.AŠ
29 [PAP *x* L]Ú IG[I].ME[Š] ^{uru}*kur*-[*b*]*a-ìl-a-a*
30 [IGI] ^{m}[(*x x*) *x*] *ak x x* [(*x x*) *x t*]*e*
(remainder of rev. traces only)

Translation

1: Instead of their seal they have [impressed] their nails. (Nail marks.) 2: Nail of Gula-balāṭī, the singer, nail of Bēt-šašširāyu, the singer, nail of Šarru-balāṭu-iqbi, the singer, [nail] of Ninurta-aḫḫē-šallim, the singer, [nail of] Kurbailāyu, the incantation-priest.

7: [An estate of (x+)] 15 homers of land in the ....-ground of the singer(s), [in] Kurbail, Bēl-issīya, the village-inspector, contracted and took from those men (in exchange for) one talent of copper. 11: The price has been paid *in toto*, the land is legally acquired; there is no (further) withdrawal, lawsuit, (or) litigation. Anyone who in the future, whether (one) from among those men, or his sons, initiates a lawsuit (or) litigation against Bēl-issīya, shall pay 1 mina of silver (and) 1 mina of gold to Adad [who dwells] in Kurbail. He shall plead in his lawsuit, but not succeed.

21: Before Bēl-rubā'-ilāni, the priest, before Siparrānu, the leather official, before Aššur-bēl-[...], the *laḫḫinu*, before Bēl-issīya, the brother of the priest, before [....]āyu, the paternal uncle of the priest, [before ....., before ....]-lū-balṭat?, [before .....], before Adad-ahu-iddina, [in all x] witnesses of Kurbail. Before .....

Notes

3: For the PN see note on No. 24, 5.
6–7: The signs restored at the end of these lines in the transliteration were present when Professor D. J. Wiseman made notes on the tablet in 1950. Since then a small fragment has become detached from the right edge. Note the association of the *kalû* priest with singers.
7: *ku(d)dāru*: see *AHw* s.v., also *RGD* No. 54.i.4′; a type of land.
8: It is probable that no number is written before GÚ.UN because the Akkadian would have read *ina bilat*; but it may be thought preferable to emend to ⟨*ina libbi*⟩ 1 GÚ.UN.
16: cf. No. 33, 15 and note.
21: Same witness as in No. 15, 34; on the present tablet the traces would also allow the reading NUN.ME.DINGIR.MEŠ (= *apkal-ilāni*), but the clear writing in No. 15 must take preference.
22: Same witness as in No. 15, 37.
23: *laḫḫinu* is also a temple employee, see *CAD* A Pt. 1, 296.
24: Same witness as in No. 15, 36.
28: Same witness as in No. 15, 39.
29: cf. No. 15, 42.

Commentary

Here, as in No. 15, Bēl-issīya buys land in the area of Kurbail from a consortium of sellers. In this case the previous owners are 4 singers and a lamentation-priest, and their association with the (Adad) temple at Kurbail is presumably one reason why the priest himself (*šangû*) is found as a witness. It is interesting that although the two texts are very similar in the transactions recorded, and in their witnesses, there are major differences in their formulation: where No. 15 has presumably *utappišu* . . . . . [*ittannu*], with the sellers as subject, here Bēl-issīya is the subject of *u*(*p*)*piš ilqi*, while the long penalties in No. 15 are absent here.

No. 36 Plate 25 ND 481
IM 56863
(8·0) × (9·0) × 2·0 [—]

Governor's Palace, Room K.

Obv. (not copied; traces are preserved of ll. 1 (indecipherable), 3: [ ].^{d}BE, and 4: [ ]*lu-ú*).

Rev. 1′ [ ] *x* [ ]
2′ [*a-šib*] ^{uru}*kur-*⌜*ba-ìl i*⌝*-šá-k*[*an*]
3′ [*bi-la*]*t* AN.NA *a-na* LÚ.EN.NAM URU-*šú* [SUM-*a*]*n*
4′ [*kas*]-*pu a-na* 10.MEŠ *a-na* EN-*šú* G[UR]-⌜*ár*⌝
5′ [*ina d*]*e-ni-šu-nu i-da-bu-ub la* TI-*ú*?
6′ [IG]I? ^{d}IM *ša* ^{uru}*kur-ba-ìl*
7′ [IGI $^{m.d}$E]N.A.⌞AŠ⌟ LÚ.SANGA *ša* ^{d}IM ⌜*ša* ^{uru}⌝[*kur-ba-*]⌞*ìl*?⌟
8′ [IGI ^{m}*ra*]-*ú-zu* IGI ^{m}U-*ku-mu-*⌜*ia*⌝
9′ [IGI ^{m}*ṭ*]*a-ab-li-pu-šú ša* É ^{lú}*tur-ta-ni*
10′ [IGI ^{m}*x*-P]AP?-*ia* IGI $^{m.d}$IM.SIPA-*ni* ^{uru}*kur-ba-ì*[*l*]
11′ [IGI ^{m}]$^{.d}$IM.A.AŠ *ša* É $^{m.d}$UTU.DU-*du-gul*
12′ [IGI ^{m}U(?)-*še-z*]*ib-an-ni* ^{lú}*šá* UGU É *ša* É ^{lú}*tar-ta-ni*
13′ [IGI ^{m}(*x*) *x*]-*ia* IGI ^{m}*a-gi-ra-a-a* ^{uru}*kur-ba-ìl*
14′ [PAP *x* ^{ur}]^{u}*kur-ba-ìl-a-a*
15′ [IGI ^{m}(*x*) *x*]*x-la-a-a ša* É ^{m}NUMUN?-*ki-x*[(*x x*)]
16′ [IGI ^{m} *x x*]-⌞*šal*⌟-*lim* KIMIN?-*ma*? [( )]
T.E. 17′ [ ]LÚ [*x x*]⌜*ša*⌝ [(*x x*)]
18′ [ ]*ṣa-bit* [ ]
19′ [ ].KÁM *l*[*i*]*m-me* ^{m}[ ]

N.B. The line-numbering on the copy is out by one.

Translation

Rev. 1′: [. . . . . . .] he shall place [in the lap of DN who dwells] in Kurbail. He [shall give one tal]ent of tin to the governor of his city. He shall return [the] price ten-fold to its owner. He shall plead [in] his lawsuit (but) not succeed.

6′: [Before(?)] Adad of Kurbail. [Before] Bēl-aplu-iddina, the priest of Adad of [Kurba]il, [before Ra]'ūzu, before Adad-kumūya, [before Ṭ]āb-lipūšu of the house of the *turtānu*, [before . . a]hūya?, before Adad-rā'īni (of) Kurbail, [before] Adad-aplu-iddina of the house of Šamaš-kēnu-dugul, [before Adad(?)-šēz]ibanni, the overseer of the house of the *turtānu*, [before . . . .]ia, before Agirāyu (of) Kurbail, [in all 9 men] of Kurbail. [Before . . . .]lāyu of the house of Zēr?-ki[. . . ., before . . . .]-šallim, ditto(?), [. . . ., before . . . ., the scribe], writer [of the tablet].

19′: [Month of . . . ., xth] day, *limmu* of [PN].

Notes

Rev. 6′: This appears to be the only possible restoration of the text; although of course common in old Babylonian texts, the witnessing of a contract by a god is rare in nA; cf. ND 2080 (*Iraq* 16 (1954), 54), which seems to be witnessed by the king's statue and also by Šamaš (ll. 11–12).

7′: Bēl-aplu-iddina is named as a witness in No. 15, 35, where he is the son of the priest of Adad. This tablet must therefore be later than 791 B.C.

8′: Ra'ūzu's name restored after No. 15, 41.

9′: This name is comparable to Hadi-lipūšu, for which see *AHw* 975a (*puāšu(m)*); the name Ṭāb-lipūšu shows that we should take the first part of Hadi-lipūšu as a predicative permansive, and these two instances suggest that perhaps *puāšu* (at least in nA) should mean not " sich ärgern ", but rather the opposite " to come to agreement ".

10′: As shown in the copy, there is an erased wedge after *ni*.

11′: Šamaš-kēnu-dugul, clearly an important man, since he has a " house ", must surely be the eponym for 749 B.C., see *APN* 211a.

12′: Adad- restored because of shortage of space.

15: NUMUN? may perhaps be rather *bi!*.

Commentary

Although the traces on the obverse are not sufficient to give any absolute proof that this is a land sale, the fact that parties from Kurbail are concerned, and the identity of some of the witnesses with those in the other Kurbail texts which are land sales, justify the text's inclusion here.

No. 37 Plate 25 ND 479(b)

IM, for study

[—]

(2·5) × (2·2) × (0·9)

Governor's Palace, Room K.

Obv. 1 [*k*]*u-um* N[A$_4$.KIŠIB-*šu*]

(finger-nail impressions)

---

2 *ṣu-pur* ^{m}*a-x*[ ]

3 É 50 ANŠE A.Š[À]

4 *ina* ŠÀ GIŠ.BÁN [ ]

5 [É(?)] *ad-ru* [ ]

6 [(*x*) *x*]⌞*x*⌟ GÚ.UN [ ]

7 [*u*(*p*)*piš-ma* (?) ^{m}]·⌞^{d}30⌟.K[AR-*ir*(?)]

(remainder of text broken)

Translation

1: Instead of [his seal he impressed his nail]. (Nail marks.) Nail of A[. . . .].

3: An estate of 50 homers of land [. . . . . . .] (measured) in the *sūtu* measure [of . . . *qa*, (including?) a house(?)], threshing-floor, [. . . . . in exchange for x] talent(s) of [. . . . .] Sîn-ē[ṭir(?) contracted and took . . .

Notes

7: The restoration of *uppiš* and of the PN is of course tentative. Sîn-ēṭir's name does however fit the traces, and he is quite a likely purchaser, since he is also found in Nos. 20 and 64, acquiring considerable areas of land.

No. 38 Plate 26 ND 272
IM, for study
[—]

4·8 × 6·3 × 2·5

Governor's Palace, Room K.

Obv. 1 ⌜*ṣu*⌝-[*pur*]
2 ⌞EN⌟ [ ]
(finger-nail impressions)
3 [*x*] *x*[ ]*x*
4 [*x*] GIŠ.Š[AR]
5 [( )]*a-na* É *ṣ*[*u-*]
6 [*ú*]-*tap*-⌞*piš*⌟[ ]
7 [ ]
B.E. 8 [*x x*]⌜*x*⌝[ ]
9 [*k*]*ás-pu gam*-[*m*]*ur* [*ta-din*]
Rev. 10 ⌜*qaq*⌝-*qe-re za-a*[*r-pu*]
11 *laq-qi-ú tú-a-r*[*u* (*dēnu*)]
12 *da-ba-bu la-a*-[*šu*]
13 *man-nu* [*ša*] *i-par-r*[*i-ku-u-ni*]
14 1 MA.[NA K]Ù.BABBAR *a-na* [ᵈ]⌜15⌝
15 (indecipherable)
(remainder broken; indecipherable traces of two lines on L.E.)

Translation

1: Nail [of PN], owner [of the ground(?)]. (Nail marks.)

3: [. . . . .], an orchard, [. . . . . . .] to the house . . .[. . . . PN] has contracted [and given/taken to/from PN_2 . . . .]. 9: The price has [been paid] *in toto*, the ground is legally acquired. There is no (further) withdrawal, [(lawsuit or)] litigation. Anyone [who] contra[venes (the agreement) shall pay] one mina of silver to Ishtar [. . . . .

Notes

7: Collation determines that there is only room for this one line between l. 6 and the first line on the B.E.

10: *qaqqerē*: see on No. 29, 2.

15: This line does not seem to contain the expected signs; there is very probably a ruling directly beneath it, so that the names of witnesses should begin in l. 16.

Commentary

The mention of *qaqqerē* (l. 10) implies that this is probably the sale of a building-plot within the town; on the other hand the property did include an orchard (l. 4). For a similar sale, of a plot of ground together with half an orchard, see *ARU* 348.

No. 39 Plate 26 ND 479(a)
IM, for study

6·5 × (7·7) × 2·8 [—]

Governor's Palace, Room K.

Obv. (beginning broken)

1′ [ ]*x* É *ep-šu*
2′ [GI]Š.⌞IG⌟.MEŠ-*šú*
3′ [ ] MA.NA URUDU.ME
4′ [ ] *ú-tap-piš*
5′ [*kaspu g*]*a-mur*
(remainder of obv., *c.* four lines, broken)

B.E. 1′ ⌜*x x*⌝ [ ]
2′ 1 MA.NA [ ]
Rev. 3′ *ina bur-ki š*[*a*]
4′ *i-šá-kan k*[*ás*?*-pu*]
5′ *a-na* ⌞EN⌟-[*šú ú-ta*]*-ra*
6′ [*i*]*na de-ni-šú i-*[*da*]*-bu-ub*
7′ *la i-laq-qi*
8′ IGI ^{m}[*a*]*š-šur-šal-l*[*im* (*x x*) *š*]*a*? ^{uru}*zu*?*-r*[*i*?]
9′ IGI ^{m}SUḪUŠ.⌜^{d}15⌝ IGI $^{m.d}$⌜EN?-*šal-lim*⌝
10′ [IGI] $^{m.d}$30-*ú*-TI.LA
11′ ⌜IGI⌝ ^{m}*ur-za-a-a*
12′ IGI $^{m.d}$UTU-*še-zib*
(blank space; then remainder broken)

Translation

1′: [. . . . . .] a built house, [. . . . . together with] its doors, [in exchange for . . .] minas of copper, [PN] has contracted [and taken]. 5′: [The price has been paid] *in toto*, [. . . . . . . (long gap) . . . Anyone who contravenes (the agreement)(?)] shall place 1 mina [of silver(?)] in the lap of [DN]. He [shall return the price ten-fold] to its owner. He shall plead in his lawsuit, (but) not succeed.

Rev. 8′: Before Aššur-šallim[(. . .)] of the village Zu?. . ., before Ubru-ištar, before Bēl?-šallim, [before] Sîn-uballiṭ, before Urzāyu, before Šamaš-šēzib.

[Date lost.]

Notes

Rev. 8′: -*šallim*[*anni*] possible; in the place name *ba* is possible instead of *zu* (coll.).

Commentary

That this text is a house sale is obvious from ll. 1′–2′. There is a slight problem as to the correct verb to be restored in l. 5′: *issiqi* or *ittidin* both seem possible at first sight. However, I think we may decide in favour of *issiqi* "taken" by considering the very little space available for PNs: since the seller will have been named in the superscript, and since there is room in l. 4′ for only one PN, that name must be the name of the buyer. It does occur occasionally elsewhere, that the name of the seller is not repeated in the body of the text.

No. 40 Plate 27 ND 275(f)

Inst. Arch. London

(6·0) × (8·1) × (2·6) [—]

Governor's Palace, Room K.

Obv. (beginning broken)

1′ [ ] *x* ⌜*x x*⌝[

2′ [ ]*x ú-p*[*iš-ma*]

3′ [mGI]Š.MI-*aš-šur* L[Ú?]

4′ [(*x*)]*x bi x*[(*x*)]*x* TA? *x*[ ]

5′ [*il*]-*qi ka*[*s*]-*pu gam*-[*mur*]

6′ [*ta-di*]*n* É *šu-a*-[*tu*]

7′ [*za-rip la-q*]*i tu*-[*a-ru*]

8′ [*de-e-n*]*u* K[A.KA]

9′ [ ]⌞*x x x x*⌟

(remainder broken)

Translation

2′: [. . .]Ṣil?-aššur, the [. . . . .], contracted [and] took [(from PN) in exchange for] . . . . 5′: The price [has been] paid *in toto*, that house [is legally acqu]ired; [there is no (further)] with[drawal, law]suit (or) liti[gation . . . .

Notes

5′: If [*ina lì*]*bʲ-bi* is restored at the beginning of the line, it is hard to extract a designation of the price from the signs that follow; similarly at the end of the line we might conjecture TA* I[GI PN], but the space is inadequate for this, while TA* I[GI-*šu*] is not particularly common. Reluctantly therefore I leave the line unresolved.

Commentary

It is clear from l. 6′ that this is a house sale.

No. 41 Plate 27 ND 275(d)
Inst. Arch. London
(5·0) × (5·6) × (2·7) [—]

Governor's Palace, Room K.

Obv. (beginning broken)
(finger-nail impressions)
1′ [ṣ]*u-pur* ^{m}⌜*na*?⌝-*x*[ ]
2′ [(*x*)] EN PAP.MEŠ ⌞DUMU⌟.MEŠ[ ]
3′ [*q*]*aq-qe-*⌜*re*⌝ *pu-*⌜*ṣe-e*⌝[ ]
4′ [GÍD].⌞DA⌟ 33? *ina* 1 K[ÙŠ DAGAL]
5′ [ ]⌞*x x x x*⌟[ ]
(remainder broken)

Translation

1′: Nail of Na?[. . . . .] owner? of(?) [his(?)] brothers (and) sons [. . . . .]. Clear ground, [x cubits] long, 33? cubits [wide . . . . .

Notes

2′: This is a most extraordinary line; what we expect is a phrase like "owner of the clear ground being sold", but this simply cannot be wrung from the tablet. Nor can the signs conceal another PN (which is not in any case required). As the line stands, it suggests that the seller was about to dispose of his brothers and sons, but that this is not so is shown by the ensuing lines. Possibly it refers in some way to the interests of the man's relatives in the property, but without parallels nothing more can be said. K. Deller suggests taking EN as *adi*, which is certainly a good idea, but does not resolve all difficulties.

No. 42 Plate 27 ND 232
Inst. Arch. London
(7·3) × 10·8 × 3·1 [—]

Governor's Palace, Room K.

Obv. (almost entirely broken; it is possible to distinguish a finger-nail impression at 3·5 cm. from the T.E., and below that (at 4·5 cm. from the T.E.), the sign É below a ruling).

Rev. 1 *l*[*u*?-*u*] *x x*[
2 ⌜TA*⌝ $^{m.d}$[30(?).K]AR-*ir* [(*x x x*)]
3 *da*?-*b*[*a*?-*bu*? (*x x*) *u*]*b*?-⌞*ta*?⌟ [-*u-ni*]
4 1? MA.N[A] ⌞KÙ⌟.⌜GI *a*⌝-*n*[*a*]
5 *x x x* [*x x*] *x x*[ ]
6 *kás-p*[*u*?]
7 [(*x*)] *x x*[ ]
8 IGI ^{m}[

9 IGI ^{m}*ki*$^{?}$-[
10 IGI ^{m}*šùl*$^{?}$*-mu*$^{?}$-[
11 IGI ^{m}*ša*$^{?}$*-x*[
12 IGI ^{m}*i-nu-x*[
13 IGI $^{m.d}$PA.[
14 IGI ^{m}KAB.⌞AD$^{?}$⌟.[
15 IGI ^{m}*mu-šal-*⟨*lim*⟩-^{d}AMAR.UTU DUMU ^{m}*x*[
16 [IG]I ^{m}TUR$^{?}$.[(*x*)].A.PAP *x*[
17 [ ]⌞*x x*⌟ KÁM$^{?}$ [
(remainder (T.E.) broken)

Translation

Rev. 1: .....] or [.......] initi[ates$^{?}$ a lawsuit] (or) litigation$^{?}$ against [Sîn$^{?}$]-ēṭir [shall pay] 1$^{?}$ mina of gold to [DN .... He shall return] the price [ten-fold to its owner ....].

8: Before [.....], before Ki[...], before Šulmu$^{?}$- [....], before Ša[...], before Inu[...], before Nabû-[...], before Kimir$^{?}$-.. [...], before Mušallim-marduk, son of [...., before] ...-aplu-uṣur .....

Notes

Obv.: The sign É (" estate ") in this position indicates that we probably have a sale of land, although it could also be a house sale. In any case it is a sale of property.

Rev. 2: The restoration of the name as that of Sîn-ēṭir is of course uncertain.

14: KAB as a logogram is very sparsely attested in nA PNs; apart from the names KAB.PAP.IGI (No. 17, 42), Dayānu-KAB-a[hhē$^{?}$] (83, 2′) and perhaps KAB.PAP.MEŠ [( )] (86, 2′; 91, 9), I can only quote from *APN* 200a Sîn-mu-KAB=mukammir(?). In all cases except perhaps this last we could suspect a miswriting of KAB for KÀD = *kiṣru*, although strictly KÀD should be *kaṣāru*.

No. 43 Plate 28 ND 228
Inst. Arch. London
[—].xii+i$^{?}$.[—]

5·2 × 7·8 × 2·4

Governor's Palace, Room M.

Obv. 1 ⌜*ṣu*⌝*-pur* ^{m}*ḫal-mu-si*
2 EN A.ŠÀ
(finger-nail impressions)
3 É 2 ANŠE 4$^{?}$-BÁN ⌜A.ŠÀ⌝
4 *ina* URU *šá* $^{m.d}$[*d*]*a*-⌜*gan*-EN⌝.PAP
5 *ú-piš-ma* ^{m}*aš-šur*-BÀD.PAP
6 *ina* ŠÀ 50 MA.NA URUDU.MEŠ
7 TA* *pa-an* ^{m}*ḫal-mu-si*
8 *il-qi kas-pu ga-mur*
9 *ta-din* A.ŠÀ *za-*[*rip*]
10 *laq-qi tú-a-ru* KA.KA
11 *la-áš-šu man-nu*

Rev. 12 *ša i*-GIL-*u-ni*
13 *kas-pu a-na* 10.MEŠ-*te*
14 *a-na* EN.MEŠ-*šú* GUR
15 *ina de-ni-šú* KA.KA
16 NU TI

17 IGI $^{m.d}$[MA]Š$^{?}$.APIN-*eš*
18 IGI ^{m}⌜*x*⌝[*x*]-*i* PAP-*šú*
19 [I]G[I] ^{m}BA[L-]⌞*a-a*⌟LÚ.NAGAR
20 [I]G[I] ^{m}[*x x x*]
21 [ ]*x lu*$^{?}$
22 [( )] ^{iti}Š[E] ⌞DIRIG$^{?}$⌟
23 [*x x*] $^{m.d}$[MA]Š$^{?}$.⌜*x*⌝
24 [ ]*x x*
L.E. 25 IGI ^{m}*ba*-⌜*ni*⌝-*i ṣa-b*[*it* IM]

Translation

1: Nail of Halmusu, owner of the land. (Nail marks.)

3: An estate of 2 homers 4$^{?}$ *sūtu* of land in the village of Dagan-bēlu-uṣur, Aššur-dūru-uṣur contracted and took from Halmusu in exchange for 50 minas of copper. 8: The price has been paid *in toto*, the land is legally acquired; there is no (further) withdrawal (or) litigation. Anyone who contravenes (the agreement) shall return the price ten-fold to its owners. He shall plead in his lawsuit, but not succeed.

17: Before Ninurta$^{?}$-ēreš, before [. . . .]ī, his brother, before Pilaqqāyu$^{?}$, a carpenter, before [. . . . .] . . . . .

22: Month of intercalary$^{?}$ Addāru (XII+I), [*limmu* of] PN [. . . . .].

25: Before Banī, writer [of the tablet].

Notes

1: I have used the nominative form of the name, Halmusu (cf. *APN* 84a), although it is not actually attested in this text.

19: Although one would expect GIŠ.BAL for *pilaqqu*, there is no space after BAL for another sign which would allow us to read e.g. Balṭāyu. I have therefore assumed that the GIŠ has been (consciously) omitted by the scribe.

23: The name, which must be that of the eponym, could also begin ^{d}PA, and so it does not seem worthwhile to speculate on the available dates. A decision may eventually be possible when more is known of the system of intercalary months in Assyria (assuming the restoration here of DIRIG is correct).

No. 44 Plate 28; Photo Plate 93a ND 258(a)
Inst. Arch. London
5·5 × 8·3 × (1·7) [—]

Governor's Palace, Room M.

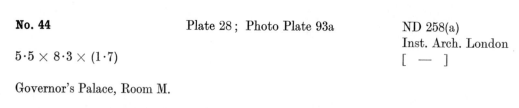

Obv. 1 [NA$_4$.K]IŠIB $^{m.d}$UTU.⌜SUM⌝-*na* ^{lú}*ḫa-za-nu ša* ^{ur}[^{u}]
(cylinder seal impression)

2 *ṣu-pur* ^{m}DUMU.15 E[N *q*]*aq-qe-re*
(finger-nail impressions)
3 [*qa*]*q-qe-re pu-ṣe-e* [1]5? *ina* 1 KÙŠ
4 [G]ÍD.DA 11 KÙŠ DAGAL
5 *ú-piš-ma* ^{m}EN.KUR.DINGIR L[Ú].KAŠ.LUL
6 [*š*]*a* MÍ.É.GAL *ina lìb-bi*? ⌜6 MA⌝.NA URUDU.MEŠ
7 [*qa*]*q-qe-re* TA* IGI ^{m}DUMU.15 [*i*]*l-qi*
8 [*k*]*as-pu ga-mur ta-din-*[*n*]*i*
9 [*qa*]*q-qe-re šu-a-tu za-rip laq-*⌜*qi*⌝*-ú*
10 [*t*]*u-a-ru de-*⌞*i*?⌟*-nu* KA.KA-*bu la-a-šú*
11 *man-nu ša ina ur-kiš ina ma-ti-ma*
12 [*i*]*-za-qu-pa-a-ni lu-u* ^{m}DUMU.15!
13 [*lu*]*-u* DUMU.MEŠ-*šú lu-u* DUMU.DUMU.MEŠ-*šú*
14 [*lu-u*] ŠEŠ.MEŠ-*šú lu-u* ⌞DUMU.ŠEŠ⌟.MEŠ-*šú*
B.E. 15 [*lu-u*]*-ni*?*-šú*
(remainder of B.E. and all rev. broken)

Translation

1: Seal of Šamaš-iddina, mayor of the village of [. . . . .]. (Cylinder seal impression.)
2: Nail of Mār-ištar, owner of the ground. (Nail marks.)
3: Clear ground, [1]5? cubits long, 11 cubits wide, Adi-māti-ilu, the queen's butler, contracted and took the ground from Mār-ištar in exchange for 6? minas of copper. 8: The price has been paid *in toto*, that ground is legally acquired; there is no (further) withdrawal, lawsuit, (or) litigation. Anyone who at any time in the future arises, whether Mār-ištar, or his sons, or his brothers' sons, [or his . . . . ., or] his [. . . . . . .

Notes

10: Both *de-i-nu* and KA.KA-*bu* are unusual writings; we should perhaps write rather *di-i-nu* (if the *i* is correct) though this would be un-Assyrian.
15: Not shown on copy.

Commentary

The only noteworthy feature of this text is that the tablet is sealed by the local mayor (*ḫazannu*), and that his name is placed before that of the seller. The owner was allowed to indicate his assent to the transaction by impressing his nail in the usual way, but only after the mayor's seal had been applied, and the space for his nails is squeezed between two lines. The reason for this is unclear: is the mayor concerned in his official capacity, or only as a private person? It is conceivable that in nA times local authorities took some part in sales of land which fell within their jurisdiction, but as far as I know no other evidence for it exists; on the other hand, there is no very obvious reason why a third party might be involved in a private capacity. Without further parallels a firm decision is difficult, but I prefer to think that the mayor is here acting officially, giving the consent of the village to the sale. Note that the mayor of the relevant town or village is found as a witness in Nos. 15 and 17.

No. 45 Plate 28 ND 803
Inst. Arch. London
5·2 × 9·5 × (2·1) [—]

Governor's Palace, Room M.

Obv. 1 *ṣu-pur* ^{m}*qur-di*-DIN[GIR.ME]Š-*ni*
2 ⌞*ṣu-pur*⌟ [^{m}*l*]*a*?-*q*[*i-p*]*u*?
3 [(PAP)] 2 LÚ.M[EŠ]
finger-nail impressions
4 É 1-BÁN *tab-ri-ú*[?]
5 *ú-piš-ma* [^{m}*qi-bi*]*t-aš-š*[*ur*]
6 TA* IGI L[Ú].MEŠ-*e*? [*annūte*]
7 [*t*]*ab-ri-ú ina* Š[À(-*bi*)]
8 [*x*] MA.NA UD.K[A.BAR.MEŠ *il-qi*]
9 [*ká*]*s-pu ga-mur* [*ta-din*]
10 [*tab-r*]*i-ú za-rip la-*[*qi*]
11 [*ma*]*n-nu šá ina ur-*[*kiš*] *ina ma-te-*⌜*ma*⌝
12 [*l*]*u-u* ^{m}*q*[*ur-d*]*i*-DINGIR.MEŠ
13 [*l*]*u-u* ^{m}*la-*[*q*]*i-pu*
14 [*l*]*u-u* ŠEŠ.MEŠ-*šú-*[*nu* ( )]
15 [*l*]*u-u* DU[MU.MEŠ(?)]-*šú-nu*
16 [*l*]*u-u* EN? *il-ki-šú-nu*
17 [*l*]*u-u mám-ma-nu-šú-nu*
18 *ša* TA* ^{m}[*q*]*i-bit-aš-šur*
19 [(*x*) *x* DUMU].MEŠ-*šú*
B.E. 20 [*d*]*e-nu* KA.KA [*ub-t*]*a-'u-u-ni*
21 1? MA.NA SÍG *q*[*er*]-*du* [ ]
(remainder broken; traces only of two lines on L.E.)

Translation

1: Nail of Qurdi-ilāni, nail [of L]aqīpu, [(in all)] 2 men, [owners of the . . . .]. (Nail marks.)

4: An estate of 1 *sūtu* . . . . [. . . . Qibī]t-ašš[ur] contracted and [took] the . . . . from [these] men in exchange [for x] mina(s) of bronze. 9: [The] price has [been paid] *in toto*, [the . . .]. . is legally acquired. Anyone who at any time in the future, whether Qurdi-ilāni, or Laqīpu, or their brothers, or their [sons(?)], or (those) responsible for their *ilku*-duties, or any (relative) of theirs, who initiates a lawsuit (or) litigation against Qibīt-aššur [or against] his [sons(?), shall eat] 1? mina of carded wool, [. . . . . . .

Notes

4: *tabriu* is a word which crops up occasionally in nA texts, and it must describe a special kind of property, like the well (PÚ) and threshing-floor (*adru*) with which it is also found. See *ARU* 46, 6 (5 homers of land, a quarter in(?) a threshing-floor, a quarter in 3 *tab-ri-a-te*); 117, 7; 120, 6, 20;

422, 6(?); 442, 3; 448, 18; *ADD* 741, 30(?); *ADD* 1195 (*AJSL* 42 (1925–6), 242), 5 (as here: É 1-BÁN *tab-ri-ú*?[ ); *ADD* 1196 (ibid., p. 244), 3, 32; no meaning can yet be ascertained for the word, although we may observe in passing that it is particularly frequent where long and detailed descriptions of a property's boundaries are given. Outside nA, see E. Cassin, *RA* 56 (1962), 72–5); E. Ebeling, *BVW*, p. 46; A. Deimel, *ŠL* 152.89 and 318.147; *AHw* s.v. *ablūtu*(*m*), *CAD* s.v. *ablum*. In these middle Assyrian and Nuzi references and the lexical texts, it seems to refer to a kind of hay, or a type of land.

7: For the curious repetition of the object sold at this juncture, cf. the repeated *qaqqerē* in No. 43, 7.

Commentary

Sale of a small area of land with some special characteristic by two men who are presumably joint owners in some way; cf. the very similar transaction *ADD* 1195, where however the price is probably much higher.

No. 46 Plate 27 ND 804(a)
IM, for study
(4·0) × (5·5) × 2·7 [—]

Governor's Palace, Room M.

Obv. 1 [ ]*ṣu-pár-šú-nu*
(finger-nail impressions)
2 [*š*]*a*? ^{m}DI.KUD.^{d}UT[U]
3 [ ]*ú*?-TI.LA
4 [-*b*]*i* É 70 ANŠE
5 [*k*]*ar-me*
6 [ ]*ú-tap-pi-š*[*ú*]
7 [ ]*x a x* [(*x*)]
(remainder of obv. broken; trace of one sign only on rev.)

Translation

1: [Instead of their seals (they impressed)] their nails. (Nail marks.) [Nail of . . . .] Dayān-šamaš, [nail of PN, nail of . . .]-uballiṭ [. . . . . . .]

4: An estate of 70 homers [. . . . . . .] corn heaps(?), [. . . . . these men] have contracted [and given(?) to . . . .

Notes

1–3: These lines show that there were three or four sellers, whose names are given in ll. 2–3; possibly the names extended into l. 4. These men must be the subject of *utappišu* in l. 6, and hence we should restore [*ittannu*] at the beginning of l. 7, as suggested by the translation.

4: It is tempting to restore *lìb-b*]*i* here, but the rest of the text is so uncertain that this cannot be justified; the sign could equally well be the end of a PN.

Commentary

Just enough of this fragment survives to tell us that the text concerned the sale(?) of a considerable area of land by three or more persons to another whose name is lost.

No. 47 Plate 29 ND 448
IM 56855
[—]

(5·7) × 9·0 × (3·0)

Governor's Palace, Room S.

Obv. 1 [ ]
2 [*ṣu-pur* $^{m.d}$UTU-*ša*]*l-lim* [ ]
3 [EN(?).MEŠ] [ ]
(space for finger-nail impressions)
4 [É *x*] ANŠE A.ŠÀ.GA *ina ma-za-ru-te*[
5 [ ]*x ša*? U AD *ina* ^{uru}*kap-ri* E[N
6 [*ina lìb-b*]*i* 1 *me* 60 MA.NA UD.KA.BAR.[MEŠ?]
7 [*ú-pi*]*š-ú-ma a-na* $^{m.d}$30.K[AR?
8 [LÚ.S]AG? LÚ.A.BA *i-ta-n*[*u*?]
9 [*kas-p*]*u ga-mur* ⌞*ta-din*⌟
10 [A.ŠÀ.G]A *šu-a-tú za-r*[*ip la*(*q*)-*qi*]
11 [*tu-*]*a-ru de-e-n*[*u da-ba-bu la-áš-šu*]
12 [*ina u*]*r-kiš ina ma-*[*te-ma*
13 [*lu-u* ^{m}]$^{\cdot d}$UTU-*š*[*al-lim*
14 [*lu-u*] DU[MU.MEŠ-*šú-nu*
15 [ ]-*ni*⌜*x x*⌝[
B.E. (uninscribed)
(rev. broken)

Translation

1: [Nail of PN, nail of Šamaš-ša]llim, [owners of the land]. (Unused space for nail marks.)

4: [An estate of x] homers of land in cultivation [. . . . .]. . . . . in the village of Bēl-[. . .], they (Šamaš-šallim and another) [con]tracted and have given to Sîn-ēṭ[ir(?), . . . eun]uch(?) (and) scribe, [in exchange] for 160 minas of bronze. 9: [The price] has been paid *in toto*, that [land] is legally [acquired; there is no (further) with]drawal, lawsuit, [(or) litigation]. In the future at any [time (anyone), whether] Šamaš-š[allim, or PN, or their] sons . . . . .

Notes

1: There is space for only one line at the top; this line must have contained the name of another seller besides Šamaš-šallim.

5: Could this line be read [*ina* GIŠ.BÁ]N *ša* 10-*at* ?

7: There is perhaps space to read [*ú-tap-pi*]*š-ú*, which would agree in tense with *ittannu*, and thus be preferable. The restoration of Sîn-ēṭir's name is again purely conjectural.

8: If the titles are correctly restored, then they must surely be parallel " eunuch and scribe ", and not " eunuch of the scribe ". K. Deller compares *TCL* 9, 58 rev. 45–6, where two men are respectively " eunuch (and) queen's scribe " and " eunuch (and) palace cook ".

No. 48 Plate 30 ND 482
IM 56864
[—]

(6·8) × (9·2) × (2·5)

Governor's Palace, Room K.

Obv. (beginning broken)
(finger-nail impressions)
1′ [ ] ⌜*x x x*⌝ *ni ša kap-ru x*[ ]
2′ [É]*x* ANŠE A.ŠÀ *ina ma-za-ru-te* [( )]
3′ [ ]*x-di-e* A.ŠÀ *ša* TA* [*p*]*a-a*[*n*]
4′ [*e-ti*(?)-*q*]*u-ú-ni ṭiḫi* ša* ^{m}*n*[*u*$^{?}$-]
5′ [*ú-pi*]*š-ma ina* ŠÀ 20 MA.NA 3-*su* [( )]
6′ [*a-na*] ^{m}AD.BU$^{?}$.SI$^{?}$ DUMU ^{m}PAP-*x*[ ]
7′ [*i*(*d*)-*di*]*n kás-pu ga-*[*mur ta-din* A.ŠÀ]
8′ [*za*]*-rip laq-qí a-píl z*[*a-ku*]
9′ [(*dēnu*)] *da-ba-a-bu la-á*[*š-šú*]
10′ [*man*]*-nu ša ina ur-kiš x*[ ]
11′ [(*x x*) *x x*].MEŠ-*šú lu-u* [ ]
12′ [*lu-u* E]N *il-k*[*i*
(remainder broken)

Translation

1′ : .....]... of the village [....].

2′ : [An estate of x] homers of land in cultivation [....]. ., the field which [pass]es in front of [.....], next to (the field) of P[N], [he contra]cted and gave [to] PN, the son of Ahu-x[...] in exchange for 20⅓ minas of [.....]. 7′ : The price [has been paid *in*] *toto*, [the field is] legally acquired, he is paid off and cleared. There is no (further) [withdrawal, (lawsuit,) (or)] litigation. [Any]one who in the future [....., whether PN, or] his [....]s, or [....., or (those) responsible for his] *ilku*-duties [..........

Notes

1′ : This line is presumably the end of the superscription which usually identifies the maker of the nail impression; the undeciphered signs may therefore be the remains of the seller's name, and this the second line of the original text.

3′ : The broken word at the beginning of the line must mean something like " near ", " adjoining "; frequent in such a sense are the signs GAB.DI, whose reading is not known. If these signs were in some way syllabic, this might be a form of the same word.

6′ : The PN in this line is uncertain; equally possible is AD.KUR.RA, but neither reading is very satisfactory.

The restoration of [*ana*] at the beginning of this line, which makes it necessary to read *iddin* in l. 7′, and makes AD.BU$^{?}$.SI$^{?}$ the purchaser, is necessary because if he were the seller (and the restorations were correspondingly changed), the name of the purchaser would not be given anywhere in the text; moreover if the seller were named at this stage in the document, it would normally be directly after *uppiš-ma*.

8′ : The archaic formula *apil zaku* crops up occasionally in nA texts (see *CAD* A Pt. 2, 158a), although not " passim " as stated there.

No. 49 Plate 16 ND 252 unn.
IM, for study
(2·5) × (3·1) × 2·0 [—].vii.[—]

[Governor's Palace, Room K/M.]

This small fragment, which must come from a property sale because of the É at the beginning of Obv. 3, does not merit full treatment. It may be the top left-hand corner of No. 23.

No. 50 Plate 29 ND 252 unn.
IM, for study
Fragment: (5·1) × (4·9) × (1·8) [—]
Inscr. surface: (3·1) × (3·7)

[Governor's Palace, Room K/M.]

(This fragment is shown to be part of a land sale by the only two decipherable lines: 2′:]A.ŠÀ.GA[, and 5′:]*ina* ŠÀ[(-*bi*)] 20 *x*[.)

No. 51 Plate 29 ND 263
Inst. Arch. London
7·9 × 11·7 × 3·0(?) —.i.797

Governor's Palace, Room K.

Obv. (entirely lost)
Rev. 1 *kás-pu a-na* 10.MEŠ-*te a-na* EN-*šú i-d*[*an*]
2 *ina de-ni-šú* KA.KA *la i-la-aq-qi*
3 IGI ^{m}DI.KUD.^{d}MAŠ LÚ.GAL É
4 IGI ^{m}*ku-ku-la-a-nu* ^{lú}*ša qur-bu-te*
5 IGI ^{m}Ì.GÁL.DINGIR.MEŠ LÚ.GAL *kal-la-pi*
6 IGI ^{m}GÌR^{ii}.LUGAL LÚ.MU
7 IGI $^{m.d}$PA.MU.DÙ LÚ.A.ZU
8 IGI ^{m}LUGAL-*mu-nam-ir* LÚ.SAG
9 IGI ^{m}EN.PAP.MEŠ LÚ.GAL KA.ŠÈR
10 IGI ^{m}ERÍN.MEŠ.SIG$_{5}$ ^{lú}*mu-šar-ki-su*
11 IGI ^{m}*mi-nu*-DÙ-*uš*-DINGIR ^{lú}*rak-su*
12 IGI $^{m.d}$IM-*na-áš-ḫi-ra* LÚ.A.BA
13 IGI $^{m.d}$IM.DÙ.PAP.MEŠ *ṣa-bit ṭup-pi*

14 ^{iti}BARAG *lim-mu* ^{m}EN.LÁ.DINGIR-*ma*
15 ^{lú}*šá-kìn* ^{uru}*kal-ḫi*

Translation

Rev. 1 : He shall give (back) the price ten-fold to its owner. He shall plead in his lawsuit (but) not succeed.

3 : Before Dayān-ninurta, the major-domo, before Kukulānu, the officer, before Ibaššiilāni, the chief *kallāpu*, before Šēp-šarri, the cook, before Nabû-šūmu-ibni, the doctor, before Šarru-munammir, the eunuch, before Bēl-ahhē, the chief tailor?, before Ṣābuda(m)qu, the *mušarkisu*, before Mīnu-ēpuš-ilī, the *raksu*, before Adad-našhira, the scribe, before Adad-bān-ahhē, the writer of the tablet.

14 : Month of Nīsānu (I), *limmu* of Bēl-tarṣi-iluma, governor of Kalhu (797 B.C.).

Notes

3 : For the reading of DI.KUD see on No. 3, 7.

10–11 : I leave the difficult words *mušarkisu* and *raksu* untranslated, since any translation would be misleading.

14 : Note the absence of a day date, and compare my note on No. 2, 22.

No. 52 Plate 31 ND 234
M 56824
23.i.788

7·2 × (10·9) × (2·6)

Governor's Palace, Room K.

Obv. (entirely lost, except for the ends of four lines on the right edge, and the end of the last line).

1′ [GAR]-*an*
Rev. 2′ 3 ANŠE.KUR.RA BABBAR-⌜*e*⌝ *ina* GÌR *aš-šur i-rak-kas*
3′ *kás-pu a-na* 10.MEŠ-*te a-na* EN-*šú*
4′ *ú-ta-ra a-na de-ni-šú*
5′ *i-da-bu-u*[*b*]
6′ *la i-la-qi*
7′ IGI ^{m}*la-qi-pu*
8′ IGI ^{m}DINGIR-*ḫa-na-na*
9′ IGI ^{m}*sa-la-ma-nu*
10′ IGI ^{m}*ga-ra-ši-ú*
11′ IGI ^{m}PAP.BA-*iš*?
12′ IGI ^{m}EN.NÍG.BA?-*ni*
13′ IGI ^{m}⌞*ub*⌟-*ru*-^{d}U.GUR
14′ IGI ^{m}[*x*]-*za-lu*
15′ [^{it}]^{i}BARAG UD.23.KÁM
16′ [*lim-m*]*e* ^{m}U-*mu-šá-mer*
(remainder blank to break)

Translation

1′ : [. . . in the lap of DN he shall] place. He shall offer 3 white horses at the feet of Assur. He shall return the price ten-fold to its owner. He shall plead in his lawsuit (but) not succeed.

7′: Before Laqīpu, before Ilu-hanāna, before Salamānu, before Garašiu, before Ahu-(i)qīš?, before Bēl-(i)qīšāni?, before Ubru-nergal, before [. .]zalu.

15′: Month of Nīsānu (I), 23rd day, [*limmu*] of Adad-mušammer (788 B.C.).

Notes

2′: K. Deller points out to me that this BABBAR-*e*, replacing the more usual BABBAR.MEŠ, would argue for a reading *puṣ(i)ē* (as in *qaqqerē puṣ(i)ē*, which is once written KI.MEŠ BABBAR.MEŠ, in VAT 8270, 2).

4′: Note *a-na* for the usual *ina*.

11′: Unusual writing; possibly PAP-*ba-da*.

12′: -*šuk*!-*na*!-*ni* also possible (collated), but less likely.

No. 53 Plate 30 ND 235
Inst. Arch. London
20.iii.778

(8·6) × (14·0?) × (2·8)

Governor's Palace, Room K.

Obv. (entirely lost)

Rev. 1′ [*x* M]A.NA KÙ.BABBAR L[UḪ]-*u* 1 MA.N[A GUŠKIN]
2′ [*sa*]*g-ru ina bur-ki* ^{d}MAŠ [*a-šib*]
3′ [^{u}]^{ru}[*kal-ḫ*]*i i-*⌞*šá*⌟*-kan* 2 ANŠE.[KUR.RA.MEŠ BABBAR.MEŠ]
4′ *ina* G[ÌR]^{II} *a*[*š-šu*]*r* ⌞*i-rak-kas*⌟ 2 ANŠE.[KUR.RA.MEŠ . . . . . .]
5′ *ina* GÌ[R^{II}] ^{d}[MAŠ].MAŠ *ú-še-rab k*[*ás-pu*]
6′ [*a-na* 10.MEŠ]-*t*[*e*] *a-na* EN.MEŠ-*šú ú-*[*ta-ra*]
7′ [*ina de-ni-š*]*u* KA.KA-*ma la i-l*[*aq*?-*qi*]

8′ [IG]I ^{m}*ra-*[']*u-zu* LÚ.DAM.G[ÀR]
9′ [I]GI ^{m}*mu-še-z*[*ib*]-DINGIR LÚ.SUM?.[GAR(?)]
10′ IGI ^{m}EN?.PAP.MEŠ KI[MIN]
11′ IGI ^{m}PAP.DU-*ka*? DUMU ^{mí}*m*[*u*?-]
12′ [IG]I ^{m}ERÍN.MEŠ.S[I]G$_{5}$ ^{lú}*da-a-a-l*[*u*?]
13′ [I]GI $^{m.d}$PA.MU.AŠ *ṣa-bit ṭup-p*[*i*]
14′ [I]GI ^{m}*di-di-i* LÚ.GÍR.LÁ [( )]

15′ [^{iti}]⌜SIG$_{4}$⌝ UD.20.KÁM *lim-mu* ^{m}EN.S[I]
16′ [LÚ.NIMGIR]⌞É⌟.[GA]L

Translation

1′: He shall place [1?] mina(s) of purified silver (and) 1 mina of refined [gold] in the lap of Ninurta [who dwells in Kalh]u; he shall dedicate 2 [white] horses at the feet of Assur, (and) introduce 2 [. . . . .] horses at the feet of [Ner]gal. He [shall return the price ten-fold] to its owners. He shall plead in his [lawsuit] but not succ[eed].

8′: [Before] Ra'ūzu, the merchant, before Mušēzib-ilu, the victualler(?), before Bēl?-ahhē, ditto, before Ahu-illaka(?), son of . .[. . .], before Ṣābu-da(m)qu, the runner, before Nabû-šūmu-iddina, writer of the tablet, before Didī, the butcher?.

15′: [Month of] Simānu, 20th day, *limmu* of Bēl-lēšir, the palace [herald] (778 B.C.).

Notes

3′–4′: These lines may be restored after No. 17, 21–2.

10′: Also possible would be KAB (cf. No. 42, 14).PAP.MEŠ (collated).

11′: For the name cf. No. 109; he is the son of a woman.

14′: GÍR.LÁ is a most unusual profession in nA texts, and as far as I have noticed, it is only found in *ARU* 455 and in Ass. Fd. Nr. 11789.i.24: ᵐPAP-*sa-pa* LÚ.GÍR.LÁL (K. Deller). The logogram is clearly glossed *ṭa-bi-ḫu* (*STT* 383 vii.6, see *MSL* XII, 234 iii.8), and the meaning " butcher " is therefore admissible. However, as K. Deller points out to me, it occurs twice in the other such list K 4935 (*MSL* XII, 238 ff.), once clearly as a butcher (v.29), but once (i.11) among eunuchs, bodyguards, etc., and there it is probably a functionary, perhaps to be read *nāš(i) patri*.

15′: S[I] stands for the expected SI.SÁ, and may be no more than an error.

No. 54 Plate 31 ND 210(a)
IM, for study
8·4 × 10·3 × 3·3 20.vii.771

Governor's Palace, Room K.

Obv. 1 [-*š*]*ú-nu*? *iš*?-*k*[*un*?]
(remainder of obv. broken)

Rev. 1 [A.Š]À? *za-rip la-q*[*i*]
2 [*t*]*u-a-ru da-ba-bu* ⌜*la*⌝-[*šú*]
3 [*man-m*]*a* TA *man-ma la i-da-bu-u*[*b*]

4 ⁱᵗⁱDUL UD.20.KÁM

5 *lim-me* ᵐ*aš-šur*-KAL-*an*
6 M[AN K]UR *aš-šur*ᵏⁱ

Translation

1: [Instead of their(?) seal they(?)] impressed their(?) [nails] . . . . .

Rev. 1: [The . . . .] is legally acquired; [there] is no (further) withdrawal (or) litigation. [No]-one shall litigate with anyone.

4: Month of Tašrītu (VII), 20th day, *limmu* of Aššur-dān, [king] of Assyria (771 B.C.).

Notes

1: Perhaps rather]-*šú*! *iš-k*[*un*], which would explain the seemingly singular verb, and give us but one seller.

Rev. 1: The traces at the beginning of this line are not clear enough to justify placing this text among the property sales.

No. 55 Plate 32 ND 239

IM 56825

(6·2) × (9·6) × (2·6) [—]

Governor's Palace, Room K.

Obv. (entirely broken)

Rev. 1 [ ]*x*.MEŠ[Š]
2 [ ]TA [ ]*x*
3 [*lu-ú*] ^{m}*li-x*[ ] *ta x x*[ ]
4 [*lu*]-*ú* $^{m.d(?)}$[ ]*bi*?
5 [*lu-ú* ER]ÍN?.MEŠ EN *i*[*l-ki-šú*]-*nu*?
6 [-*m*]*u*?-*šú-nu* ERÍN?[ ]*a*?
7 [ ]*x*.MEŠ-*šú-nu* TA ^{m}*ma*?[-*x x x*]
8 [*dēnu d*]*a-ba-bu* ⌜*ub*⌝-*ta-*'[*u*?]-*ú-n*[*i*?]
9 [*x* MA.NA KÙ].GI 3 MA.NA KÙ.BABBAR.MEŠ
10 [*ina bur*]-*ki* ^{d}MAŠ GAR-*an*
11 [*x* ANŠE.KUR.R]A.MEŠ BABBAR?.MEŠ *a-na aš-šur* SUM-*an*
12 [*x x* A]N.NA.MEŠ *a-na* LÚ.EN.NA[M URU]-*šú*
13 [SUM-*an kas-pu a-n*]*a* 10.MEŠ-*te a-n*[*a* E]N-*šú* GUR-*ra*

14 [ ]⌞*x x ša* ^{uru}⌟[*x*]-*ku*?-*a-ni*
15 [ ]*x-šú*? ^{uru}KIMIN
16 [ ] ^{uru}KIMIN
17 [*š*]*a* [^{ur}]^{u}EN-[*x x*]
(remainder broken)

Translation

3: .... [whether] Li[....., or] ...., [or the] people responsible for their? [*ilku*-duties, or] their [.....] people(?), [or] their [..... (who)] initiates [a lawsuit (or)] litigation against Ma[....], shall place [3? minas of go]ld (and) 3 minas of silver [in the lap of Ninurta. He shall give [x] white [horses] to Assur, (and) [he shall give(?) 1 talent of] tin to the governor of his [city]. He shall return [the price] ten-fold to its owner.

14: [Before .....], of the village [..]kuāni(?), [before .....].., ditto, [before .....], ditto, [before ....., of] the village Bēl-[.....].

Notes

12: A verb for this line is missing, unless we restore it (as suggested) at the beginning of l. 13; but there hardly seems room for it there.

Commentary

This is a purchase from more than one seller (their names are found in ll. 3–4, and the plural suffixes in ll. 6–7 confirm it). The fact that witnesses come from a named village suggest that this may have been a purchase of land in that area.

No. 56 Plate 32 ND 248
IM, for study
(7·5) × (8·0) × (2·6) [—]

Governor's Palace, Room K.

Obv. (entirely broken)

Rev. 1′ [ ] *x x x* [
2′ [ ]SUM$^{?}$-*an*[
3′ [10.ME]Š-*šú a-na* EN-*šu* GU[R]
4′ [K]A.KA-*ma* NU [TI]
5′–12′ (indecipherable traces of names of witnesses)

Translation

2′: [. . . . . . .] he shall give. He shall return [the price ten]-fold to its owner. He shall plead [in his lawsuit] but not [succeed].
5′: (Names of witnesses.)

No. 57 Plate 33 ND 480
Inst. Arch. London
7·0 × 8·8 × (2·9) [—]

Governor's Palace, Room K.

Obv. (entirely broken)
B.E. (uninscribed)
Rev. 1 *lu-u* ^{m}*bi-si-né-e* [( )]
2 *lu-u* DUMU.MEŠ-*šú lu-u* ŠEŠ.ME[Š-*šú* (*lu-u*)]
3 EN *il-ki-šú* TA* $^{m.d}$UTU-*ku-m*[*u-a*]
4 *u* ŠEŠ.MEŠ-*šú de-e-nu* KA.KA
5 [*u*]*b-ta-*⌜*ú*⌝*-n*[*i*]
6 1 MA.NA KÙ.[BA]BBAR 1 MA.NA GUŠKIN
7 *a-na* ^{d}MAŠ SUM-*an*
8 1 GÚ.UN AN.NA *a-na* LÚ.EN.N[AM]
9 SUM-*an kas-pu a-na* 10-*a-ti*
10 *a-na* EN-*šú* GUR *ina de-ni-šú*
11 KA.KA-*ma la* TI
12 IGI ^{m}*zi-zi-i* LÚ.SIMUG.KÙ.G[I]
13 IGI ^{m}NUMUN.ZI.GIŠ IGI ^{m}ZA-AD$^{?}$-IŠ$^{?}$
T.E. 14 [Ì]R$^{!}$ *ša* $^{m.d}$IGI.DU.PAP.A[Š$^{?}$]
15 [I]GI ^{m}*aš-šur-*E$^{?}$*-a-a*
16 [I]GI ^{m}⌞*x*⌟[*x*]-*a*[*š-š*]*ur* IGI ^{m}⌞*x a*⌟ *x*[

L.E. 17 [IG]I ^{m}*šùl-[mu*-E]N IGI ^{m}ḪÉ.SI_4.1[5]
18 [ ]*x* IGI ^{m}DÙ-*a*?[-*a*(?)]
19 [*l*]*im-mu* ${}^{m.d}$[

Translation

1: ..... whether Bisinē, or his sons, or [his] brothers, (or?) those responsible for his *ilku*-duties, (who) initiates a lawsuit (or) litigation against Šamaš-kūmū[a] or his brothers, shall give to Ninurta 1 mina of silver (and) 1 mina of gold; he shall give 1 talent of tin to the governor. He shall return the price ten-fold to its owner. He shall plead in his lawsuit but not succeed.

12: Before Zizī, the goldsmith, before Zēr-kitti-lēšir, before Za..., slave of Palil-ahu-idd[ina?], before Aššur-...āya, before ...-aššur, before ...... 17: Before Šulmu-bēl, before ...-ištar, [before .....], before Būnā[ya?].

19: [.........], *limmu* of [PN].

Notes

3: *lu-u* would be usual before this phrase; it may simply have been omitted by the scribe.

13: For the signs *ad*? and *iš*? see copy (collated; *sic*).

15: E? collated.

17: ḪÉ.SI_4-*ištar*: this name is found also in No. 101, rev. 6′, where it is clearly written ^{m}ḪÉ.DAR.^{d}INANNA; since neither writing offers any very convincing reading, it is difficult to determine which sign, SI_4 or DAR, was intended. A syllabic reading seems very unlikely, and the only possible logographic solution seems to be Libni-ištar (see *CAD* B 90b for the verb).

18: For the name Būnāya see on No. 17, 47.

No. 58 Plate 33 ND 252(f)+unn. frg.

IM, for study

(4·2) × (4·5) × (1·2) [—]

Governor's Palace, Room K/M.

Obv. (entirely broken)
Rev. 1′ [ ]⌜*x*⌝[
2′ [*tu-*]*a-ru de*[*-e-nu*
3′ [ ]*ša ina u*[*r-kiš*
4′ [ ]*ù* DUMU.MEŠ-*šú ù*[
5′ [*u*]*b-ta-'u-ni b*[*i*?*-lat*(?)
6′ [ ]*ina bur-ki* ^{d}MAŠ *a-š*[*ib*
7′ [ ]*de-ni-šú-nu* KA.[KA
(remainder broken)

Translation

2′: [There is no (further) with]drawal, law[suit, (or) litigation. Anyone] who in the future [.......] initiates [a lawsuit (or) litigation against PN] or his sons or [his brothers(?), shall place] a tal[ent(?) of tin(?) ...] in the lap of Ninurta who dwells [in Kalhu. They? shall plead in] their lawsuit [but not succeed].

No. 59 Plate 33 ND 275(b)
Inst. Arch. London
(6·0) × (7·8) × 2·4 [—]

Governor's Palace, Room K.

Obv. 1′–2′ (undeciphered)
3′ [ ]*x x ina lìb-bi* [( )]
4′ [MA.N]A URUDU.MEŠ *il*-[*qi*]
5′ [*za-ri*]*p* ⌞*la*⌟-*qi kás*-[*pu*]
6′–9′ (undeciphered)
10′ [ ]*x lu-u* D[UMU$^{?}$.MEŠ-*šú*]
11′ [*l*]*u-u* ŠEŠ.MEŠ-[*šú*]
12′–16′ (undeciphered)
Rev. (traces of four(?) lines towards base, undeciphered)

Translation

3′: ..... PN contracted and] took in exchange for [..... mi]nas of copper. [The ..... is legally] acquired, the price [has been paid *in toto* .... 8′: Anyone, whether PN .....] or [his s]ons(?) [.....] or [his] brothers [..........

No. 60 Plate 33 ND unn.
IM, for study
(3·4) × (2·8) × (0·6) [—]

N.B.—Dimensions are those of Fragment a, excluding the unjoined piece to its right. The script and general appearance of the other two fragments are so similar to those of Fragment a that they have been included under the same number as part of the same tablet.

[Governor's Palace, Room K/M.]

Obv. (entirely broken)

Rev. (Fragment a+c)
1′ [ ]*x*[
2′ [ ]⌜*laq*⌝-*qi-ú*[$^{?}$
3′ [KA.K]A *la-áš*$^{!}$-*šú* [
4′ [-*š*]*ú*$^{?}$ *lu-u* LÚ.[EN.NA]M$^{?}$ [
5′ [*š*]*a-pi-r*[*u*$^{?}$
6′ [ ]⌞*x x*⌟[

(Fragment b)
1′ [ ] *ša* ⌜*x*⌝[
2′ [*lu*]-*u* GAR-*nu x*[
3′ [*l*]*u-u* LÚ.MEŠ [
4′ [T]A $^{m.d}$30.[
5′ [*de-e*]-⌞*nu*$^{?}$⌟ [

Translation

Frag. a+c: [Those ..... are legally] acquired. There is no [(further) withdrawal, lawsuit, (or) liti]gation. [Anyone ..... whether PN, or] his [.....] or the governor? [of his city .....] or a representative(?), [.......

Frag. b: ....] or an officer [.......] or the men [responsible for his *ilku*-duties(?) ..... (who) initiates a law]suit? [(or) litigation] against Sîn-[..........

Notes

a+c.2′: If correctly restored, the plural form here shows that we must have a sale of ground (*qaqqerē*), or, less likely, of slaves.

5′: *šāpiru* is also probably in No. 31, 18.

b.: This fragment may well overlap with the other, to the left or right; there is practically no curvature of the surface to assist a decision.

Commentary

Purchase of some property by a certain Sîn-[....], who may be our familiar Sîn-ēṭir.

No. 61 Plate 33 ND unn.
IM, for study
[—]

(3·7) × (4·3) × (1·3)

[Governor's Palace, Room K/M.]

Obv. (entirely broken)

Rev. 1′ [ ]⌜*x x*⌝[
2′ [*ub*]-*ta*-'[*u*]-*ú*-[*ni* ( )]
3′ [*x* M]A.NA [K]Ù.BABBAR 1 M[A.NA GUŠKIN]
4′ [ ]ᵈMAŠ *ša* ᵘʳ[ᵘ
5′ [*x* ANŠ]E.KUR.⌞RA?⌟ BABBAR.M[E]Š [
6′ [ ] [
7′ [ ]⌞*x x*⌟[

Translation

1′: ..... Anyone who] initiates [a lawsuit (or) litigation .... shall place(?) x] mina(s) of silver (and) 1 m[ina of gold in the lap of(?)] Ninurta of [Kalhu ...... He shall dedicate x] white hor[ses to Assur ....

No. 62 Plate 34 ND 801
IM 56872
[—].iii.[—]

8·9 × 11·4 × (2·8)

Governor's Palace, Room S.

Obv. (entirely broken)

Rev. 1 [DUM]U.M[EŠ?]-⌜*šú*?⌝[

2 [*de-e-n*]*u da-ba-bu ub-t*[*a-'u-ni*]
3 [*x* MA].NA ⌞KÙ.BABBAR⌟ 1 MA.NA K[Ù.G]I
4 *a-na* ^{d}MAŠ *i-d*[*an*?]
5 15? GÚ.⌞UN⌟ AN.NA *a-na* LÚ.EN.N[AM]
6 URU-*šú i*-⌜*da*⌝-*an*
7 ⌜*kas*⌝-*pu a-na* 10.MEŠ *a-na* EN-*šú* G[UR]
8 *ina de-ni-šú i-da-bu-ub-ma*
9 *la i-laq-qi*
10 IGI ^{m}*ur*?-*du*-^{d}15 L[Ú].⌞EN?⌟ [ ]
11 IG[I] ^{m}PAP.SUM-*tu*? [( )]
12 IGI $^{m.d}$IM-*šal-li*[*m*
13 IGI $^{m.d}$PA.PAP.MEŠ.[
14 [IGI] ^{m}U.EN ^{lú}*mu*?-*x*[
15 [IGI] ^{m}EN-*la-m*[*ur*?
16 *ina* ^{iti}SIG$_4$ U[D.
17 [ ] *x x* [

Translation

Rev. 1: ..... who] initi[ates a lawsuit] (or) litigation [against PN or] his sons(?), [.....] shall [give 1 mi]na of silver (and) 1 mina of gold to Ninurta; he shall give 15? talents of tin to the governor of his city. He shall return the price ten-fold to its owner. He shall plead in his lawsuit but not succeed.

10: Before Urdu?-ištar, the ..[...], before Ahu-tidintu(?) [.....], before Adad-šalli[m ....], before Nabû-ahhē-[....., before] Adad-bēl, the ..[..., before] Bēl-lām[ur .....].

16: In the month of Simānu (III), [xth day, ...

No. 63 Plate 34 ND 240(a)
Inst. Arch. London
4·6 × (6·0) × 2·2 14.xii.[—]

Governor's Palace, Room K.

Obv. (very badly broken; not copied as useless)

Rev. 1′ [ ]⌜*x x*⌝[ ]
2′ ⌜2?⌝ MA.NA KÙ.G[I? ( ) *ina bur-ki*] ^{d}[IM?]
3′ EN ^{uru}*kàl-zi* [*išakka-a*]*n*?
4′ [IG]I ^{m}15?!-DINGIR-*a-a* IG[I ^{m}]*iq*?-[ ]
5′ [I]GI ^{m}*ub-ri*-15 I[GI ^{m}P]AP.ZU
6′ [I]GI ^{m}*iš-me*-DINGIR ⌜LÚ.NIMGIR?⌝ É.⌞GAL⌟
7′ [IG]I ^{m}*iš-ši*?-⌞*la*?⌟-*a-a*
8′ ⌜IGI⌝ $^{m.d}$30?-*mu*-DI LÚ.A.BA
9′ *ṣa-bit ṭup-pi*

Rev. 10′ [^{it}]^{i}⌈ŠE⌉ UD.14.[KÁM] *lim-mu*
11′ [*lim-m*]*u* $^{m.d(?)}$[ ]
12′ [( )] ⌈^{uru}*x*⌉[ ]

Translation

2′: He [shall place] 2? minas of gold? [in the lap of] Adad?, the lord of Kalzu.

4′: Before Ištar?-ilāya, before Iq[?. . . .], before Ubri-ištar, before Ahu-(i)le'i, before Išme-ilu, the palace herald(?), before Iššilāya(?), before Sîn?-mušallim, the scribe, writer of the tablet.

10′: Month of Addāru (XII), 14th [day], *limmu* of [PN, governor of . . . . .].

Notes

3′: For the restoration of Adad's name here, see *ARU* 460, 17.

6′: It seems a little unlikely that the palace herald should be listed here, after four other witnesses, but it is the restoration that best fits the traces; or LÚ.⌈UGU⌉ É.GAL ?

8′: The DN looks almost like ^{d}40, but one would hesitate to read it as Ea.

10′–11′: It seems certain that the scribe has repeated the signs *lim-mu* at the beginning of l. 11′.

Commentary

The small size of both tablet and script may point to a date late in the eighth century.

No. 64 Plate 34; Photo Plate 91b ND 231
IM 56822
[—]

9·4 × (10·9) × (2·5)

Governor's Palace, Room K.

Obv. 1 NA$_4$.KIŠ[IB]
2 ⌈EN⌉ [ ]
(cylinder seal impression)
3 ŠEŠ-*šú* *š*[*a*] ^{m}EN.LÁ.DINGIR-*ma* ^{lú}*šá-kì*[*n* ^{uru}*kal-ḫi*]
4 É 40 ANŠE A.ŠÀ.GA *tal-pi-tú* [( )]
5 *paṭ nar-ut-tu ina* ŠÀ *ki?-ri? ša ur-qi* [( )]
6 *ina* ^{uru}*bu-ru-qi* [(*x*)] *ša* KUR *ḫa-láḫ*-[*ḫi*]
7 $^{m.d}$30.KAR-*ir ú-piš-ma*
8 *ina* ŠÀ É ⌈30⌉ ANŠE A.ŠÀ É *ši*-⌊*qi*⌋
9 [*ù* (*x x*) É] *da-la-a-ni*
10 [*a-na* ^{m}*mu-ša*]*l-lim*-^{d}INANNA *id-din*
11 [*ṭiḫ*]*i**? ⌊*pu- ri?*⌋ *ša* ^{m}DÙG.IM.*x*[ ]
12 [ ] *x x x* [ ]
13 [ ]⌊*x x*⌋[ ]
(remainder of tablet broken)

Seal inscription

1 [*šá*(?) $^{m(.d)}$30.K]AR ŠEŠ! $^{m.d}$[EN-]
2 [LÁ(-*ṣi*)-DINGIR-*m*]*a?* *šá-kìn kal*-[*ḫi*]

Translation

1 : Seal [of Sîn-ēṭir], owner [of the land (. . . . .)], (Seal impression), brother of Bēl-tarṣi-iluma, governor [of Kalhu].

4 : An estate of 40 homers of . . . . . land, alongside the river-land(?), within(?) a vegetable-garden?, in the village of Būruqi(. .) of the land of Halahhu, Sîn-ēṭir contracted and gave [to Muša]llim?-ištar in exchange for an estate of 30 homers of land (watered by) canal [(and x homers)] (watered by) buckets [. . . . . next] to? the lot of Ṭāb-šār-[. . . .] . . . .

Seal inscription : (see note on ll. 1–3).

Notes

1–3 : The obvious restoration of these lines is that suggested in the translation : the so-called " seller ", who impresses the seal, must be Sîn-ēṭir, for reasons given below in the Commentary, and this is confirmed by the seal inscription, if rightly restored. Unfortunately the restoration is not entirely free from doubt, but it may be supported by the following considerations : l. 1 of the seal inscription seems to contain the sign KIŠIB (" seal "), but this would normally stand first, and the preceding sign is not NA_4. The reading K]AR, which agrees perfectly with the copy, makes it very probable that the KIŠIB is in fact miscopied for ŠEŠ—a not unlikely mistake—and we may then reconstruct the inscription as shown. The only remaining awkwardness is the division of Bēl-tarṣi-iluma's name over two lines, but this is no more unusual than the omission of the URU determinative before Kalhu. The translation of the seal inscription runs : [Seal of Sîn-ē]ṭir, brother of [Bēl-tarṣi-ilum]a, the governor of Kal[hu].

It seems that l. 3 was added as an afterthought, since it is abnormally written within the space ruled off for the seal impression.

4 : *talpittu* : this word, of unknown meaning, is quite often used in nA house sales, to describe the property being sold (see *ARU* 100, 2, 7 ; 128, 8 ; 178, 4 ; 339, 3 ; 341, 6 ; 352, 6 ; 354, 1 ; 444, 3 ; *ADB* No. 15, 1′ ; ND 2305 (*Iraq* 16 (1954), 36–7), 4, 11 coll.) ; *ARU* 105, 26 (*ta*]*l-pi-ta-a-te*, pl., coll.). Although it is applied merely to land in our text, in all these other passages it describes a house, whether sold by itself or as part of a larger estate. Elsewhere, though, the word is applied to consumptibles such as bread (ND 2789 (*Iraq* 23 (1961), 53), 2, 10 ; *ADD* 1023, 10 ; both times contrasted with NINDA.MEŠ *sadru*, " ordinary bread "), corn (ND 5457 (*Iraq* 19 (1957), 131), and wine (*KAV* 79 rev. 2), also for bread cf. H. Zimmern, *BBR* 66, 8 ; 67, 7 (K. Deller). *Talpit(t)u* is also found in the middle Assyrian texts of the sheep archive of Ninurta-tukulti-aššur (E. Weidner, *AfO* 10 (1935–6), 9 ff.), e.g. *KAJ* 206, 7–9 : PAP 4 UDU.MEŠ *tal-pi-tu ša* PN. Combining this last usage with the known (though admittedly old Assyrian !) meaning of *lpt* D, " to book (to someone) ", I would hesitantly suggest that *talpit(t)u* is used to indicate that the item referred to is recorded (elsewhere) : thus in the *KAJ* passage, the sheep would be " on PN's account ", " booked to his name ", while in the case of property, it may mean that the details of the house (etc.) are recorded, or even " registered ", whether in documents held by the authorities or privately.

5 : This line too is difficult. I assume that *nāruttu* is an (unattested) abstract formation from *nāru*, and that it may, like *ma'uttu* (*Iraq* 32 (1970), 135[6]) from *ma'û*, refer to a kind of land. However, this writing is unexpected, and the ending *-tu* in a word which should be genitive gives rise to further doubts.

6 : Halahhu is known to lie north-east of Nineveh, not far from the later Dūr-šarrukēn ; this Buruqi(/u) can therefore hardly be identical with that in a Tell Halaf text (*AfO Beiheft* 6, 82, s.v. Burudarri).

8–9 : *bēt šīqi* and *bēt dālāni* are technical terms describing the sort of irrigation the land receives. *Bēt šīqi* is already known from nA documents (*ARU* 187, 4 ; 211, 9 ; 444, 5), and refers to an area of land irrigated by water-flow from a river or canal, whereas *bēt dālāni* is only known otherwise from neo-Babylonian texts, and refers to land irrigated by the use of buckets, drawing water from wells or cisterns (see B. Landsberger, *MSL* I, 185).

In l. 9 we could restore either [(*ù*) *x* ANŠE É], or just [*ù* É].

11 : If my restoration of this line is correct—and it is hard to see what other function a third PN could have at this stage in the document—the description of the second plot of land exchanged is left until after the *iddin*, perhaps in order not to separate that verb too far from *uppiš*.

Commentary

In addition to the several curious points of detail in this text, it is remarkable as one of the very few nA exchange texts (cf. *Iraq* 32 (1970), 34, adding perhaps (according to K. Deller) Ass. Fd. Nr. 10005, see *OrNS* 33 (1964), 93). In exchange for 40 homers of land a long way from Kalhu to the north of Nineveh, Sîn-ēṭir gives Mušallim-ištar 30(+) homers of irrigated land, perhaps in the Kalhu area. Since the document is so phrased that Sîn-ēṭir appears in the role of " seller " and Mušallim-ištar as the " buyer ", the seal impression, which testifies that the " seller " has consented to the transaction, must be that of Sîn-ēṭir, who therefore appears to be Bēl-tarṣi-iluma's brother (for the significance of the text's formulation, see *Iraq* 32 (1970), 34). This tablet then should belong to the archive of Mušallim-ištar, but unfortunately we have no other information about him, and we cannot therefore say whether he is likely to have deposited his copy of the transaction in the governor's palace at Kalhu. Sîn-ēṭir, on the other hand, was a brother of the governor, and two tablets from the same provenance mention him as the purchaser of property (Nos. 20, 42, cf. 65), so that his archive clearly was housed in the governor's palace. In these circumstances it does seem possible that despite the formal arguments to the contrary, this tablet formed a part of his archive, and did not belong to Mušallim-ištar.

No. 65 Plate 35 ND 252(p)

IM, for study

(7·2) × (5·6) × (1·1) [—]

Governor's Palace, Room K/M.

Obv. 1′ [(*x*)]⌜LÚ.EN⌝[
2′ [*i*]*na* ŠÀ ^{uru}[
3′ É 70 ANŠE ⌜A⌝.[ŠÀ
4′ *a-na* $^{\mathrm{m.d}}$[3]0.KAR-*ir* ^{l}[^{ú}
5′ ⌜A⌝.ŠÀ.GA *ina* ŠÀ A.ŠÀ.[GA
6′ [(*x*)] *pu-tu*[*ḫ-ḫu*?] *ta-din* [
7′ [*tu-a*]-*r*[*u*] ⌞*da-ba*⌟-[*bu l*]*a*?-*á*[*š-šu*
(remainder broken)

Translation

2′: . . . in the village of [. . . . .] an estate of 70 homers of land [. . . . . . .] to Sîn-ēṭir the [. . . . . PN has given(?)]. Land [is taken(?)] in exchange for land, [(the land?)] has been given in exchange? [. . . . . There is] no (further) [with]drawal (or) litigation, [. . . . .

Notes

6′: The usual phrase at this stage of a land sale is of course *kaspu gammur tadin,* " the price has been paid *in toto* ", but there is obviously no place for such a phrase in an exchange document. In TR 4001 (see commentary below), the phrase is simply omitted; here it seems that an attempt has been made to supply a suitable equivalent. The signs *pu* and *tuḫ*, although damaged, have been collated and seem clear; there are in fact traces (as shown in the copy) of two verticals after *tuḫ*, which could constitute the remains of *ḫu*, and it is difficult to envisage any logogram of one sign only which might have stood between *tuḫ* and *tadin*. Despite the unexplained space at the beginning of the line, then, the suggested restoration seems probable, and the translation " exchanged (and) given " renders a fair equivalent of the usual sale text formula. For *putuḫḫu* see *AHw* 885a; this usage (where it must be a stative parallel to *tadin*) would seem to confirm the derivation from *puḫḫu* (876a).

Commentary

This text must be compared with No. 64, which is also a land exchange, but here the text is so phrased that Sîn-ēṭir is not, as there, the " seller ", but the " purchaser " (*ana* in l. 4′). We may therefore attribute this fragment to his archive with more confidence. The phraseology of the text, as far as it survives, is of some interest; apart from the phrase discussed above in the note to l. 6′, we meet *eqlu ina libbi eqli* just as in TR 4001 (*Iraq* 32 (1970), 31), 9.

No. 66 Plate 35; Photo Plate 95d ND 476

Inst. Arch. London

6·4 × 8·9 × 2·6 [—]

Governor's Palace, Room K.

Obv. 1 [N]A$_4$.KIŠIB ^{m}EN.LÁ-*ṣ*[*i*]-DIN[GIR-*ma*]
2 [*š*]*á-kìn* ^{uru}*kal-ḫi*
(inscribed cylinder seal impression)
3 [*q*]*aq-qe-*[*r*]*e pu-ṣe-e*
4 [*i*]*na* ^{uru}*k*[*ar*?-]Í[D?.ID]IGNA-*a-a*
5 [*in*]*a šid-d*[*i* ^{í}]^{d}*ḫi-ri-ti*
6 [^{m}E]N.LÁ-*ṣi*-DINGIR-*ma*
Rev. 7 [*šá-kìn*(?) ^{uru}*k*]*al*?-*ḫi*
8 [*a-na*] $^{m.d}$EN.⌜KAR⌝-*ir*
(remainder broken)

Seal inscription (see on No. 171)

1 [KIŠI]B ^{m}EN.LÁ.DINGIR-*m*[*a*]
2 [*š*]*á* SAG *šá* ^{m}U.ERÍN.GA[B]
3 [( )] MAN ŠÁR *šá-kìn* ^{uru}*kal-ḫi*
4 [ ] KUR *te-me-ni*
5 [KUR *ia-*]*lu-*[*n*]*a*
6 *a*[*t*]*-kal-ka*
7 *a*? [ ]*pa*

Translation

1: Seal of Bēl-tarṣi-iluma, governor of Kalhu. (Seal impression.)

3: Clear ground in the village of Kār?-(i)diglāyī, on the bank of the canal, Bēl-tarṣi-iluma, [governor of K]alhu, [has given(?) to(?)] Bēl-ēṭir? . . . . .

Notes

4: The first sign could be a flattened KAR, and this makes a plausible place-name: " quay of the Tigris-men ".

Commentary

This text has a number of features which make it unlikely to be an ordinary land sale. It may be a simple grant of land from Bēl-tarṣi-iluma to a subordinate.

If the text were a sale, the dimensions of the property would normally be given (although we might expect them also in a grant), and the seller would usually be designated as " owner of the land " after the superscript had identified his seal. Moreover, it is perhaps a little unlikely that Bēl-tarṣi-iluma should be selling the land and not buying it himself. It is true that the structure of the lines as preserved would accommodate a sale formula: PN$_1$ [*ana*] PN$_2$ [*utappiš ittidin*], as in No. 5, but even so the price should precede these verbs, and it appears to be entirely absent here.

Since the identity of the text as a grant must, however, remain very uncertain, there is little profit in discussing the possible implications of the existence of legal grants of land from a provincial governor to his subordinates.

No. 67 Plate 35 ND 250
Inst. Arch. London
[—]

3·9 × (5·6) × 2·2

Governor's Palace, Room K.

Obv. 1′ [*ṣ*]*u-p*[*ur*] ^{m}*ma-na*$^{?}$-[
(finger-nail impressions)
2′ EN LÚ [( )]
3′ TA* *lìb-bi zi-i-te*
4′ *ša* ŠEŠ-*šú-nu*
5′ [L]Ú *a-na* LÚ.GAL É
6′ [*i*]-*ta-nu*
7′ [(*x*) *x* ŠE]Š-*šú-nu*
B.E. 8′ [(*x x*) *x*]-*ak-te*
9′ [IGI ^{m}(*x*) *x x*]-*a-a ša* UGU É
Rev. 10′ [ ]É
(remainder, except for the end of one sign, broken)

Translation

1′: Nail of Mana[?. . .], (nail marks), owner(s) of the man. 3′: Out of the share of their brother, they have given a man to the major-domo. 7′: [. . . .] their brother, [. . . .]. . . .
9′: [Before . . . .]āyu, the house overseer, [before . . . . . the . . . . of the] house, [. . . . .

Notes

1′: It is uncertain how many lines are missing at the head of the tablet; from the text it appears that there must have been more than one owner, who must have been named before the nail marks.

3′: *zittu*, literally "a share", here clearly means "an inherited share". We cannot decide here whether the "share" in question is that inherited from the father by the (dead ?) brother along with the other sons, or the "share" = inheritance left by him at his own death.

Commentary

This curious little text seems to describe a joint action undertaken by two or more brothers after the death of another brother. Perhaps because he died without an heir, his brothers are able to dispose of some, at least, of his property, and here for some reason they are handing over a man (i.e. slave, presumably) to the "major-domo". The action may be in fulfilment of a debt left by the dead man, but of this there is no certainty.

No. 68 Plate 36 ND 262
Inst. Arch. London
21.iii.779

6·3 × 9·1 × 3·1

Governor's Palace, Room K.

Obv. 1? [ ] *la*? *iz* ⌜*x*⌝
2 [^{m}]*šùl-m*[*u*?]-⌞EN?⌟
3 [ ]*x* KA.MEŠ
4 [ ]SUM?-*an*
5 [ ]BAR
6 [ ] UTU[L?]
(remainder of obv. except last line broken)
1′ *la* [ ]
Rev. 2′ *ma-a* [U]TUL?.[MEŠ?] *ni-dan*
3′ *ma-a šum-ma* [*b*]*u-ru*
4′ [*in*]*a* KUR *aš-šur*^{ki} *i-tal-ka*
5′ TA* KUR *lu la i-*[*ḫ*]*a-ṣi-nu-na-š*[*i*]
6′ IGI ^{m}PAP-*šam-ši* ^{lú}*mu-šar-*⌜*ki*⌝-[*su*]
7′ IGI ^{m}*bur-zi-na-nu* LÚ.A.ZU
8′ IGI $^{m.d}$UTU-*ku-mu-a* LÚ.A.BA
9′ IGI ^{m}GIŠ.⌜MI⌝.^{d}ŠEŠ.GAL
10′ LÚ.GAL É.GAL *ša* É.GAL BE-*ti*
11′ IGI ^{m}GIŠ.⌞MI.15⌟ LÚ.GAL É.GA[L]
12′ *ša* É.GAL GIBIL
T.E. 13′ ^{iti}S[I]G_4 UD.21.KÁM
14′ [*limmu* $^{m.d}$]⌞AMAR.UTU⌟-*rém-ni*

Translation

(Obv. broken; mention of Šulmu-bēl, and perhaps of "shepherd-boy(s)".)

Rev. 2′: .....] saying: "We shall give the shepherd-boys, and if a famine comes in Assyria, let them not look after us from the palace?."

6′: Before Ahu-šamšī, the *mušarkisu*, before Burzinānu, the doctor, before Šamaš-kūmūa, the scribe, before Ṣil-nergal, the palace-overseer of the old palace, before Ṣil-ištar, the palace-overseer of the new palace.

13′: Month of Simānu (III), 21st day, [*limmu* of] Marduk-rēmāni (779 B.C.).

Notes

3′: The restoration of *būru* was only made after considering many alternatives; doubt exists as to the correct identity of both signs, and there is room for a small sign between the *bu* and the *ru*. However, the scribe does use extremely long horizontals, as in the line above, and hence the head of the wedge after *bu* can be the beginning of the *ru*. *Būru* is a strictly nA word (see the dictionaries), and although otherwise in semi-literary contexts, it clearly belongs to the vernacular and thus is not out of place here.

5′: *ḫaṣānu*, " to look after, protect ", is used in the nuance " to maintain, support " both of horses and of people (e.g. a slave-girl, ND 2307 (*Iraq* 16 (1954), 37–8, l. 45)).

Commentary

Not enough survives of this unique text to allow of any certain reconstruction, but none the less an attempt to account for the lines we do have must be made. That we have a legal document is obvious from the presence of witnesses, but there are no other resemblances to any known nA text. The main text, in so far as it remains, clearly records in the form of direct speech one side of an agreement; the identity of the speakers is lost, but since they seem to be in charge of " shepherd-boys " (UTUL.MEŠ), they are probably " shepherds ", or rather " herding-contractors ", who undertook to have flocks pastured and employed shepherd-boys to look after the animals. The other party to the agreement is presumably " the palace " (mentioned in l. 5′, and with at least two representatives among the witnesses), which term is used often to mean " the administration ", and it must be the palace which requires the shepherd-boys. The basic contract therefore seems to be for the provision of shepherd-boys by the " herding-contractors " for the palace flocks, but the clause about the consequences of a famine could only be explained if we knew what the other conditions were.

No. 69 Plate 35 ND 252(d)

8·2 × (5·2) × (1·8) IM, for study

[—]

Governor's Palace, Room K/M.

Obv. 1 [*ku-m*]*u*? ⌜NA₄.KIŠIB-*šú-nu ṣu*⌝-*pár-šú-nu*

(finger-nail impressions)

2 [*ṣu-p*]*ur* ᵐ*ku-na-a-a ṣu-pur* ᵐMU.GIŠ ᵐ*gab-b*[*u-a-m*]*ur*

3 [*ṣu*]-⌞*pur*?⌟[ᵐ(*x*)]-*ma-ak-ru ṣu-pur* ᵐ*šùl-mu*-PA[P.MEŠ]-*šú*

4 [ ]-*di ṣu-pur* ᵐKAM.ᵈ15

5 [*ṣu-p*]*ur* ᵐ*a-ḫi*?-*mi*?-*e*

6 [*ṣu-pur*] ᵐDINGIR-*a-a-ta*[*k*?-*lak*]

7 [ ]⌞*x x*⌟[

Translation

1: [Instead] of their seal (they impressed) their nail(s). (Nail marks.) 2: Nail of Kunāyu, nail of Šūmu-lēšir, nail of Gabbu-āmur, [nail of . .]makru, nail of Šulmu-ahhē-šu, [nail of . . . .]di, nail of Eršī?-ištar, [nail of . . . . ., nail of] Ahimie?, [nail of . . . . ., nail of Ilāya-ta[klak?] . . . . .

Notes

7: We might restore here EN.MEŠ] *ḫa-b[u-(ul-)li]*, " the debtors ", or a similar phrase, as in No. 92, 14.

Commentary

This long list of those impressing their nails could come from the beginning of a sale by several persons (e.g. No. 15), or from a debt-clearance text such as No. 92. If it belonged to the latter category, then the restoration suggested for l. 7 would become possible, and the list of names will have ended in the preceding line.

No. 70 Plate 35 ND 252(m)
IM, for study
(6·4) × (2·9) × (2·0) [—]

Governor's Palace, Room K/M.

Obv. (upper part broken)
1′ *[ṣu]-⌜pur⌝* mSUḪUŠ.d[IGI.D]U? *ṣu-p[ur*
2′ *ṣu-pur* m*rém-ni-[x (x)] ṣu-pu[r*
3′ *[ṣ]u-p[ur]* m*iq?-x[*
4′ *[ṣ]u-[pu]r* m*ḫa?-si?-n[i?*
B.E. 5′ (undeciphered)

Translation

1′: [Nail of] Ubru-[pal]il?, nail of [. . . . .], nail of Rēmāni-[. . . . .], nail of [. . . . .], nail of . .[. . . ., nail of . . . . .], nail of Hasin[i? . . . .

Commentary

This is a fragment from the bottom edge of a tablet, so that presumably the list of names constituting the superscription must have occupied the entire obverse of the tablet. As with No. 69, the nature of the transaction cannot be definitely established, but it seems very likely to have come from a debt-clearance.

No. 71 Plate 37 ND 252(a)
IM, for study
(5·1) × (3·6) × 2·2 [—].v.[—]

Governor's Palace, Room K/M.

Obv. (upper part broken)
1′ *x[*

Obv. 2′ *kás-p*[*u*?
3′ *i-ta-*[
4′ *ki-i x*[
B.E. 5′ IGI ^{m}PAP-*k*[*i*-
6′ IGI ^{m}*ti-ri-k*[*a*-
Rev. 7′ IGI $^{m.d}$PA-*rém-a*[*n-ni*]
8′ GAL *ú-ra-a-*[*te*?]
9′ IGI $^{m.d}$MAŠ-*rém-*[*an-ni*?]
10′ GAL ⌞*x x*⌟ [
(remainder of rev. broken)
L.E. 1″ ^{iti}NE U[D.
2″ *lim-mu* $^{m.d(?(}$[

Translation

2′:] price? [. . . . . . .] they have given? [. . . . . . .] as [. . . . . . .].

5′: Before Ahu-k[ēnu?], before Tirik[a . . .], before Nabû-rēma[nni], the chief of the teams?, before Ninurta-rēm[anni], the chief . . . . .

L.E.: Month of Abu (V), [xth] day, *limmu* of [. . . . .].

Commentary

The remains of the last three lines before the witnesses show that this was not a normal loan or sale; more than that we cannot say.

No. 72 Plate 37 ND 252(e)
IM, for study
[—]

(4·0) × (3·7) × 3·0

Governor's Palace, Room K/M.

Obv. 1 [*ṣ*]*u-pur* ^{m}[
2 [*ṣ*]*u-pur* ^{m}*di*[
3 [*ṣ*]*u-pur* ^{m}*a*[
(finger-nail impressions)
(remainder of obv. broken)
Rev. 1′ [ ] *x x*[
2′ [I]GI ^{m}*e*?-*ši*-[
T.E. 3′ [IGI] ^{m}*ši*?[
4′ [^{i}]^{ti} *x*[

Commentary

This is probably from a sale document, with three sellers named in the superscription; Rev. and T.E. have the remnants of the names of witnesses and of the date.

No. 73 Plate 37 ND 252(l)
IM, for study
(4·8) × (4·7) × (2·0) [—]

Governor's Palace, Room K/M.

Obv. (entirely broken)
Rev. 1 [ ]-⌜*ni*?⌝ *ú-ṭu-ru*
2 [ ] *la i-da-bu-ub*
3 [*tuāru de-e-*]*nu da-ba-bu la-áš-šu*
4 [L]Ú?.SANGA *ša* d[*x*]
5 [ ] GÚ.GAL [( )]
6 [ ]*x* LÚ.DAM.[GÀR]
(remainder broken)

Translation

1: . . . . they are [mutually] acquitted, [no one] shall plead [against anyone,] there is no [(further) withdrawal, law]suit, (or) litigation.

4: [Before PN], the priest of D[N, before PN], the "canal-inspector", [before PN], the merchant, [. . . . .

Notes

5: A *gugallu* (spelt apparently GU.GAL) is found in *ADD* 472 rev. 17.

Commentary

The *uṭṭuru issi aḫa'iš* clause is common in *Prozessurkunden*, but it does also occur in debt-clearance notes, of which this may have been an example.

No. 74 Plate 38 ND 236
IM, for study
7·2 × (10·5) × (1·7) [—.—].800(?)

Governor's Palace, Room K.

(Obv. and beginning of rev. broken)
Rev. 1′ [ ]*x* [ ] *x*[ ]
2′ [*x* MA.N]A? KÙ.BABBAR [ ]
3′ [I]GI m.dMAŠ-*šal-l*[*im-*]
4′ [GA]L É.GAL IGI[ ]
5′ IGI m*zi-za-a-*[*a*? ( )]
6′ IGI m*šùl-m*[*u-*]
7′ IGI mU.ḪAL.[(*x*)] IG[I]
8′ IGI mPAP.M[U?]
9′ IGI m*x*[ ]

Rev. 10′ IGI ^{m}[ ]
11′–12′ (entirely broken)
13′ [^{iti}*x* UD.*x*.KA]M
14′ [*limmu* ^{m}GÌ]R[^{ii}]$^{?}$.^{d}15
(sketch-map(?), see copy)

Translation

2′: . . . he shall pay(?) x minas of] silver [ ].

3′: Before Ninurta-šalli[m(anni)], palace overseer, before [. . . . .], before Zīzā[yu . . . . .], before Šulmu-[. . .], before Adad-išme[(anni)], before [. . . . .], before Ahu-. .[. . .], [before 4+ further witnesses].

13′: [Month of . . . . ., xt]h [day, *limmu* of Šē]p?-ištar (800 B.C.).

Notes

14′: A *limmu's* name is probable here, and the only two eponyms in roughly the right time bracket are Šēp-ištar (800), and Ṣil-ištar (787); the traces seem to favour the former, but the dating must be considered uncertain.

Commentary

Although there is no criterion in the actual text which would allow us to assign this fragment to a particular category, Professor D. J. Wiseman was doubtless right to suggest that this was a land sale, on the basis of the sketch at the base of the reverse (see *Iraq* 12 (1950), 191).

No. 75 Plate 38 ND 252(r)
IM, for study
[—]

(4·3) × (6·5) × 3·5

Governor's Palace, Room K/M.

Obv. (beginning broken)
1′–3′ (undeciphered traces)
4′ *x* [*x* (*x*)] *sa a*[*r*?
5′ TA [^{m}]15.KI-*i*[*a*?
6′ ^{m}*x*[
7′ IGI $^{m.d(?)}$[
B.E. 8′ LÚ.NINDA *ša* LÚ.[
Rev. 9′ IGI ^{m}*ga-lu-l*[*u*
10′ *ša* É LÚ.[
11′ IGI ^{m}*šá*-[
12′ IGI [
13′ IG[I
(remainder broken)

Commentary

Part of the end of a legal text, and the beginning of its list of witnesses; it mentions a penalty (*sartu*(?), l. 4′), and perhaps a man called Ištar-issīya (l. 5′).

No. 76 Plate 37 ND 275(h)
Inst. Arch. London

(3·3) × (1·8) × 2·3 [—]

Governor's Palace, Room K.

Obv. (beginning broken)
1′ [ ] *x*[
2′ DUMU $^{m.d}$[
3′ PAP 5 ERÍN.[MEŠ
B.E. 4′ EN ŠU^{ii}.[MEŠ?
Rev. 5′ *ša* 1 *me*(?)[
6′ *x*[
(remainder broken)

N.B.—cf. No. 124, which may be from the same tablet.

Translation

2′: ...] son of P[N ( )], in all 5 people [( )], guarantors [( )] of 100(?) [.........

No. 77 Plate 37 ND 275(i)
Inst. Arch. London

(2·1) × (1·6) × (1·3) [—]

(Top right-hand corner of a sale(?)-text: *ṣupur-šú*]-*nu iš-ku-nu*)

No. 78 Plate 38 ND 237
Inst. Arch. London

6·5 × (8·3) × (2·1) 24.xii.792/766

Governor's Palace, Room K.

Obv. (entirely lost)

Rev. 1′ [*tu-a*]-*ru d*[*e-e-nu*?]
2′ IGI ^{m}*mar-duk-ia-a* LÚ.*x*[ ]
3′ IGI ^{m}*ḫa-bíl*-DU LÚ.*x*[ ]
4′ IG[I ^{m}*aš*]-*šur-na-din*-PAP.MEŠ [( )]

Rev. 5′ IGI ^{m}*sa-la-ma-nu* DUMU ^{m}*li-pu-*[*šú*]
6′ IGI $^{m.d}$30.I LÚ.ASGAB
7′ IGI ^{m}SUḪUŠ.^{d}PA LÚ.A.BA
8′ [I]GI ^{m}*na-ni-i* ^{lú}*mu-tir-ṭè-me*
9′ [I]GI ^{m}*ib-ni-ia* LÚ.A.BA
10′ [I]GI ^{m}*ul-lu-ba-a-a* LÚ.A.BA
11′ [*ṣa*]*-bit ṭup-pi*
12′ [^{iti}Š]E UD.24.KÁM
13′ [*lim-me* ^{m}]*mu-šal-lim-*^{d}MAŠ

Translation

1′: [There is no (further) withdraw]al?, lawsuit? [(or) litigation(?) . . . . .].

2′: Before Mardukiā, the [. . . . .], before Hābil-kēni, the [. . . . .], before [Aš]šur-nādin-ahhē, before Salamānu, son of Lipū[šu], before Sîn-na'id the leather-worker, before Ubru-nabû, the scribe, before Nanī, the information-officer, before Ibnīya, the scribe, before Ullubāyu, the scribe, writer of the tablet.

12′: [Month of Ad]dāru (XII), 24th day, [*limmu* of] Mušallim-ninurta (792 or 766 B.C.).

No. 79 Plate 37 ND 230(b)
Inst. Arch. London
(5·7) × 7·2 × (2·4) 13.viii/ix.783

Governor's Palace, Room K.

Obv. (entirely broken except for traces of 4(+) lines on right edge, not deemed worth transliteration)
Rev. (beginning broken)
1′ [ ] LÚ.DAM.G[ÀR]
2′ [IGI ^{m}*ḫa*]*r-ma-ku*
3′ [IGI] ^{m}DINGIR-*ma*-ZU
4′ [IG]I ^{m}*ku-ku-la-nu*
5′ [^{it}]^{i}APIN GAN UD.13.KÁM
6′ [*li*]*m-mu* $^{m.d}$MAŠ.PAP-*ir*

Translation

1′: [Before PN], the merchant, [before Har]māku?, [before] Iluma-le'i, [bef]ore Kukulānu.

5′: [Month of] Arahsamnu (VIII) (/Kislīmu (IX)), 13th day, *limmu* of Ninurta-nāṣir (783 B.C.).

Notes

5′: It is impossible to tell whether the scribe wrote GAN after the month name for KÁM, instead of after the day date, or corrected the month to Kislīmu and forgot to erase the APIN.

No. 80 Plate 38 ND 269
IM 56835
6·0 × 7·8 × (2·9) 29.vi.803/775

Governor's Palace, Room K.

Obv. (entirely lost)
B.E. (blank except for ruling)
Rev. 1 IGI ^{m}ÌR.^{d}INANNA
2 IGI ^{m}*pu-[ṣ]i-i*
3 IGI ^{m}DÙG.GA-*a-ḫu-nu*
4 IGI [^{m}]*ki-qi-la-a-nu*
5 IGI $^{m.d}$30.PAP.AŠ
6 IGI ^{m}*k[a]-bi-lu*
7 IGI ^{m}PAP-*nu-ri*
8 ^{iti}KIN UD.29.KÁM
9 *lim-mu* $^{m.d}$IGI.DU.KAM

Translation

1: Before Urdu-ištar, before Puṣī, before Ṭāb-ahunu, before Kiqilānu, before Sîn-ahu-iddina, before Kabilu, before Ahu-nūrī.

8: Month of Ulūlu (VI), 29th day, *limmu* of Palil-ēreš (803 or 775 B.C.).

No. 81 Plate 39 ND 270
IM 56836
6·4 × 8·0 × (2·5) 19.vii.754

Governor's Palace, Room K.

Obv. (entirely lost)
Rev. 1 [IGI ^{m}(*x*) *x*-]*x-ri-i*
2 [IGI ^{m}]$^{.d}$PA-*ú-ṣal-la*
3 [GA]L LÚ.MU
4 [IGI ^{m}]*mu*-LÁ-*aš-šur*
5 [Ì]R *ša* LÚ.AGRIG
6 IGI $^{m.d}$[AMA]R.[U]TU.A.PAP
7 GAL [^{l}]^{ú}[*kal*]-*la-bi*
8 IGI $^{m.d}$PA-*tàk-lak*
9 IGI ^{m}*ḫi$^{?}$-ni-bi-ra-a*
10 ^{iti}DUL UD.19.KÁM *lim-mu*
11 $^{m.d}$MAŠ-*še-zib-an-ni*
12 ^{lú}*šá-kìn* ^{uru}RI-*mu-si*
T.E. 13 IGI $^{m.d}$PA-*šal-lim*-PAP.MEŠ LÚ.A.[BA]
14 [I]G[I] ^{m}*i-qa$^{?}$-la$^{?}$*[ ]

Translation

1: [before . . .]rī, [before] Nabû-uṣalla, [chief] cook, [before Mutaqqin-aššur], before Marduk-aplu-uṣur, the chief *kallābu*, before Nabû-taklak, before Hinibirā.

10: Month of Tašrītu (VII), *limmu* of Ninurta-šēzibanni, the governor of Rimūsi?.

13: Before Nabû-šallim-ahhē, the scribe, before Iqala? [. . . . .].

Notes

4: After the name, an erased ì[R], which confirms the restoration at the beginning of l. 5.

12: The doubt about the well-known place name Rimusu is whether it should not rather be read *tal-mu-su*, as proposed by A. Goetze, I believe, although I cannot trace the reference.

No. 82 Plate 39 ND 238

Inst. Arch. London

8·0 × (9·8) × (2·8) [—]

Governor's Palace, Room K.

Obv. (entirely lost)

Rev.
1 [IGI ^{m}]⌜*x*⌝-*si*⌜-*x*⌝[ ]
2 [IGI ^{m}]*ú-ra-ár-ṭa-a-a* ⌞^{lú}*x*⌟[( )]
3 [IG]I ^{m}*ḫa-di-li-pu-šú* DUMU ^{m}*ra-u-*⌜*zi*⌝ [( )]
4 [I]GI ^{m}*na-si-'i* ^{lú}*ḫa-za-nu*
5 IGI ^{m}ḪÉ.NUN.NA-*a-a* DUMU ^{m}*ru-ub-x*[(*x*)]
6 IGI ^{m}*man-nu-ki-*U IGI ^{m}*ub-ru-te*
7 IGI $^{m.d}$MAŠ.I GAL *da-a-a-li*
8 IGI ^{m}*ḫa-an-za-ru* ,,
9 IGI ^{m}*ma-an-ni-i* ^{lú}*qa-ti-en-nu*
10 IGI ^{m}*ḫi-iš-*DA-*nu* IGI ^{m}ḪI-*da-a* ,,
11 [IG]I ^{m}EN-*lu-*TI ^{lú}*ḫa-za-nu ša* ^{uru}*m*[*i*?-]
12 [I]GI ^{m}UD.7.KÁM-*a-a* IGI ^{m}*pa-na* ⌜LÚ ,,⌝
13 [*š*]*a* ^{uru}*m*[*u-*(*x*)-*x-*]*x* IGI ^{m} *x x* (*x*) *qi*?
14 [I]GI ^{m}PAP-*la-*⌜*mur* DUMU⌝ ^{m}*ṭu-ú-a*
15 [*š*]*a* ^{uru}*im-be-*^{m}*ra-ḫi-i*
16 [IGI ^{m}(*x*) *x-*]*muk*?*-tin* LÚ.3-*šu* U_5
17 [IGI ^{m}*man-n*]*u*?*-ki-a-ḫi-i* ,,
18 [^{l}]^{ú}*mu-kil-*KU[Š.PA(.MEŠ)]
(remainder broken)

Translation

1: [before] . . ṣi . .[. . . ., before] Urarṭāyu, the [. . . . .], before Hadi-lipūšu, son of Ra'ūzu, before Nasi'i, the mayor, before Nuhšāyu, son of Rub . . ., before Mannu-kī-adad, before Ubrūte, before Ninurta-na'id, the chief runner, before Hanzāru, ditto, before Mannī, the *qatinnu*, before Hišdānu, before Hidā?, ditto, before Bēl-luballiṭ, the mayor of M[i$^{?}$. . . .], before Sabāyu, before Pana(?), the ditto (i.e. mayor) of M[u . . . .], before . . . .qi, before Ahu-lāmur, son of Ṭūa, of the village of Imbe-rahī, [before . . .]-muktīn$^{?}$, the " third rider ", [before Mann]u-kī-ahī, ditto, [before . . . . .], the rein-holder, [. . . . .

Notes

15: This reading of the place name seems best after collation, although it is tempting to read *im-ba-ra-ḫi-i* instead.

16: The PN is most uncertain, since this form of *muk* is rather Babylonian, and the participle *muktīn* is not easy to explain. However, even an emendation to *sa*!*-din* would not assist.

The writing LÚ.3-*šu* U$_{5}$ is curious, since usually a syllabic complement of -*šu*, if it is used, is added to the second part of the logogram. Whether this new writing affects the now common identification of the logogram with *tašlišu* I leave undecided.

Commentary

The presence of mayors of different villages among the witnesses suggests that this comes from a land sale.

No. 83 Plate 39 ND 210(b)
IM, for study
(5·7) × (5·6) × (0·8) 5.vii.[—]

Governor's Palace, Room K.

Obv. (entirely lost)

Rev. (beginning broken)

1′ [IGI ^{m}*aš*]-*šur*-⌊]
2′ [IGI ^{m}]DI.KUD.KAB.P[AP.MEŠ$^{?}$]
3′ [IGI] $^{m.d}$MAŠ.[K]I-*a*
4′ [IG]I $^{m.d}$UTU.AŠ
5′ [I]GI ^{m}*kar-šá-a-nu*
6′ LÚ.A.BA
7′ [^{it}]^{i}⌜DUL⌝ UD.5.KÁM
8′ [ ]⌊*x x*⌋ *ni*$^{?}$

Translation

1′: [before Aš]šur-[. . . ., before] Dayān-kāmir$^{?}$-a[hhē$^{?}$], [before] Ninurta-issīya, [bef]ore Šamaš-iddina, before Karšānu, the scribe.

7′: Month of Tašrītu, 5th day, [*limmu* of P]N.

Notes

2′: For the PN cf. on No. 42 rev. 14.

5′: For this name cf. ND 2328 (*Iraq* 16 (1954), 43).

No. 84 Plate 39 ND 252(g)
IM, for study
[—]

(2·7) × (3·7) × 1·9

Governor's Palace, Room K/M.

Obv. (entirely lost)

Rev. (upper part broken)
1′ [ì]R? *ša* L[Ú.E]N.NAM
2′ [ ]ŠID? U
3′ [LÚ].NI.DUḪ
4′ [LÚ].SIMUG AN.BAR
5′ [ ] KIMIN
6′ [*š*]*a* ⌞LÚ.EN⌟.NAM
(remainder broken)

Translation

1′: . . .] slave of the governor, [. . . . .]. . ., [. . . . .], the doorkeeper, [. . . . .], the smith, [. . . . .], ditto, [. . . . . slave(?)] of the governor [. . . . .

Notes

2′: Hardly LÚ].SANGA U(= Adad) !

No. 85 Plate 32 ND 252(b)
IM, for study
[—]

(3·7) × (3·7) × (1·5)

Governor's Palace, Room K/M.

Obv. (entirely lost)

Rev. (upper part broken)
1′ [IGI m]·dMAŠ.⌜*x*⌝ [
2′ [IGI m(*x*)]*x-ka-qa*?[
3′ [IGI m]PAP.SIG₅.BI? L[Ú
4′ [IGI] m·dŠID.DÙ DUMU m*gi*[-
5′ IGI m*su-ú-li-i* LÚ[
6′ IGI mAD-*si-i*' LÚ[
7′ [IGI] m·dPA.PAP.MEŠ.S[U?
8′ [ ] *x*[
(remainder broken)

Translation

1′: [Before] Ninurta-. .[. . ., before . . .]. . kaqa$^{?}$[. . . . ., before] Ahu-damqu$^{?}$-. . ., the [. . . . ., before] Marduk-ibni, son of Gi[. . . . .], before Sūlī, the [. . . . .], before Abu-si’, the [. . . . ., before] Nabû-ahhē-(e)[rība$^{?}$, ...

Notes

7′–8′: If we compare No. 104, where the scribe is Nabû-ahhē-erība, we see that we may have the same man here, and that l. 8′ could perhaps be restored [*ṣa*]-*b*[*it ṭuppi*].

No. 86 Plate 39 ND unn.
IM, for study
[—]

(4·7) × (4·5) × (0·6)

Governor’s Palace, Room K/M.

Obv. (entirely lost)

Rev. (beginning broken)
1′ [IGI ^{m}*li*$^{?}$-*m*]*u-ru-x*[
2′ [IGI] ^{m}⌜EN$^{?}$⌝.PAP.ME[Š(-*šú*)
3′ [IGI] ^{m}SUḪUŠ.DINGIR.MEŠ-*ni*[
4′ [IGI] ^{m}GÌR^{II}.[(*x*)] GAL [
5′ [IGI ^{m}]$^{.d}$MAŠ.I [
(remainder broken)

Translation

1′: [before Līm]uru . .[. . ., before] Bēl$^{?}$-ahhē[(šu), before] Ubru-ilāni, [before] Šēp-[. . .], chief$^{?}$ [. . . . ., before] Ninurta-na’id [. . . . .

Notes

2′: ⌜KAB⌝ also possible; cf. on No. 42 rev. 14.

No. 87 Plate 39 ND unn.
IM, for study
[—]

(2·5) × (2·5) × (1·1)

Governor’s Palace, Room K/M.

Rev. 1′ [ ] *da* [
2′ [IG]I $^{m.d}$UTU-*m*[*u*$^{?}$-
3′ [IGI] ^{m}⌞*x x*⌟[
(remainder broken)

No. 88 Plate 32 ND unn.
IM, for study
5·7 × (4·9) × 2·7 [—]

[Governor's Palace, Room K/M]

(Beginnings of 8 lines from rev. giving names of witnesses; in l. 5′: ^{m}*Še*[. . . . .], in l. 8′: *Nabû-mu*[?. . . . .].)

No. 89 Plate 39 ND 406(a)
Inst. Arch. London
(2·7) × (3·0) × (1·6) [—]

Governor's Palace, Room S.

(Parts of 5 lines, including PNs; in l. 4′: *Ubru*-[. . . . .].)

No. 90 Plate 40 ND 216
Inst. Arch. London
8·0 × 9·5 × 3·5 26?.ii.803/775

Governor's Palace, Room K.

Obv. 1 *ḫa-bu-le ša* ^{m}*sa-ma-a*?-⸢*x* (*x*)⸣
2 ⸢*ša*⸣ ^{m}*ḫa-na-na*
3 *ša* ^{m}EN.⸤LÁ-*ṣi*⸥-DINGIR-*ma*
4 ^{lú}[*šá-k*]*ìn* ^{uru}*k*[*al-ḫ*]*i ú-šal-lim-ú-n*[*i*]

---

5 20 MA.NA *ša* $^{m.d}$30.PAP.AŠ LÚ.UŠ.⸢ANŠE⸣
6 15 MA.NA *ša* ^{m}*ku-ma*?-*a-a*
7 10 MA.NA *ša* ^{m}PAP-*ṭu-ri ša*? ⸢*x x x x*⸣
8 2 MA.NA *ša* ^{m}PAP-*le-i*
9 LÚ.ÌR *ša* ^{m}*li-pu-šú*
10 2 M[A].NA *ša* ^{m}*ba-ḫi-a-nu ša* ^{uru}*di-a-t*[*e*?]
11 1 MA.NA *ša* ^{m}*si-li* KUR *ar-ma*-⸢*a-a*⸣
12 $1\frac{1}{2}$ ⸢MA⸣.NA *ša* ^{m}*na-ni-i* LÚ.*x*[( )]
13 *ša pa-an* ^{m}EN.IGI[( )]
14 1? [M]A.NA *ša* ^{m}*bar-'a*-DINGIR[( )]
B.E. 15 [*x*] MA.NA *ša* ^{m}*bar*-⸢*x* (*x*)⸣ *a*[( )]
16 ^{lú}*ḫa*?-[*z*]*a*?-*nu* [( )]
Rev. 17 [ ]
18 PAP [ ]
19 *šá*/4 [*x* (*x*)]⸢*li*⸣?[ ]
20 ^{m}EN.LÁ-[*ṣi*-DIN]GIR-*m*[*a*?]

	21	IGI ^{m}*qu*-[(*x*) *x*]-*a* PAP?[
	22	DUMU ^{m}*x*[
	23	IGI $^{m.d}$⌜UTU⌝.[
	24	LÚ.MU-*šú* [ ]*x x*
	25	IGI $^{m.d}$UTU-*x*[
	26	[
	27	IGI ^{m}*ma*?-*a*[*n*?-
	28	[
	29	IGI ^{m}[
	30	[ ]*nu*? [
T.E.	31	[*l*]*u*? *ud a x*[
	32	[ ]*x* ÌR.ME *ša* ^{mí}*m*[*u*?-
		(finger-nail impressions)
L.E.	33	^{iti}[G]UD UD 26?.KÁM
	34	*lim-me* $^{m.d}$IG[I.D]U?.KAM[-(*eš*)]

Translation

1: The debts of Samā[. . .] (and) of Hanāna, which Bēl-tarṣi-iluma, governor of Kalhu, paid off in full.

5: 20 minas of Sîn-ahu-iddina, the donkey-driver; 15 minas of Kumāyu?; 10 minas of Ahu-ṭuri, of . . . . .; 2 minas of Ahu-le'i, the slave of Lipūšu; 2 minas of Bahiānu of the village of Diāt[e?]; 1 mina of Sili, the Aramaean; 1½ minas of Nanī, the [. . . .] who is under Bēl-lāmur(?); 1? mina of Bar'a?-ilu; [x] mina(s) of Bar?. . . . . ., the mayor [. . . . .

18: In all, [. . . . .] Bēl-tarṣi-iluma [(governor of Kalhu) paid off in full].

21: Before Qu[. .]a, brother? [. . . .], son of [PN], before Šamaš-[. . .], the cook of [PN(?)], before Šamaš-[. . . . .], before Man?[. . . . . 33: . .]slaves of F[PN].

34: Month of Ayāru (II), 26?th day, *limmu* of P[alil]-ēreš (803/775 B.C.).

Notes

10: *t*[*ú*] also possible at the end of the line, but -*t*[*e*] equally allowable (collated).

11: What exactly " an Aramaean " would mean at this date needs clarification.

18: This line will have given the total amount of the debts incurred by the two men, as in Nos. 93, 17 and 91, 27. The total of the individual debts preserved is 52½ minas, and not more than two further debts are recorded, so the total will have been slightly under a talent; it is not known if the medium of payment was bronze or copper.

19: Perhaps to be emended to *ḫ*[*a*'-*bu*(*l*)]-*le*[, after No. 91, 27.

21: Perhaps just ^{m}*qu*-[*ú*]-*a*, cf. No. 24, 2.

Commentary

This text records the payment by Bēl-tarṣi-iluma of debts incurred (apparently jointly) by the two men, Samā . . ., and Hanāna. There were nine or ten creditors, and the sums lent ranged from 20 minas to just 1 (or less). No particular reason is given why the governor should have paid their debts, but by analogy with No. 91, it is possible that they were members of his " household " or administration. Since the text is witnessed, it may be classed as a legal document; notice that as on No. 91, authentication is given in the form of finger-nail impressions, though here on the Top Edge.

No. 91 Plate 41 ND 261
IM 56831
8·0 × 11·2 × 3·9 27.xii.797

Governor's Palace, Room K.

Obv. 1 *ḫa-bùl-le ša* ^{m}ÌR.^{d}INANNA
2 LÚ.UŠ.BAR *bir-me ša* ^{m}EN.LÁ.DINGIR-*m*[*a*]
3 ^{lú}*šá-kìn* ^{uru}*kal-ḫi ú-šal-li-mu-ni*

---

4 *ku-um* ⌜NA$_4$.KIŠIB⌝-*šú-nu ṣu-pár-šú-nu*
(two rows of finger-nail impressions)
5 *ṣu-pur* ^{m}*ḫa-li-mu-si* ^{m}AD-*ul*-ZU
6 ^{m}*še*-⌜*lu*⌝-*bu* ^{m}IGI-*aš-šur*-IGI ^{m}*ḫa-ni-i*
7 ^{m}*la-qi-pu* ^{m}*dà-ri*-AD A ^{m}*šùl-mu*-EN.IGI
8 ^{m}EN-*e-mu-qi* A ^{m}*la-'i-ti*-DINGIR
9 ^{m}EN$^{?}$.PAP.MEŠ $^{m.d}$30.I ^{m}DINGIR-*bu-a*
10 ^{m}⌞*x*⌟-*bu-ku* ^{m}*du-la-a* ^{m}⌜*ḫi*⌝-*ni-du-ti*
11 ^{m}⌞*ba*⌟-*ni-ú* ^{m}*bu-sa-si-i* ^{m}GIŠ.MI.MAN
12 ^{m}U-[*x*]-*me*$^{?}$ ^{m}KAR.^{d}INANNA ^{m}*ḫa-an-bu-nu*
13 ^{m}DINGIR-*dà-ra-nu* PAP 23 LÚ.MEŠ-*e*
14 EN [*ḫ*]*a-bu-ul-le ša ṣu-pár-šú-nu*
15 [*i*]*š-ka-nu-ni*
Rev. 16 2$^{?}$ [MA.NA
17 1 M[A.N]A ^{m}[
18 1 ⌜MA.NA⌝ ^{m}*l*[*a*$^{?}$-
19 1 [M]A.NA ^{m}[ ]*a*$^{?}$[
20 1 [MA].NA [^{m}]*x*[
21 1½ M[A.N]A ^{m}[
22 1 MA.NA [MA.N]A$^{?}$ ^{m}*du*$^{?}$[-*la-a*(?)]
23 2 MA.NA ^{m}⌞*ḫi-ni-du*⌟-[*ti*
24 [*x*] MA.NA [
25 [*x* M]A.NA ^{m}[
26 [*x* M]A.NA ^{m}⌜*x x x x*⌝ 2$^{?}$[ ]-*ra*$^{?}$-*nu*$^{!?}$
27 PA[P] 53½ MA.NA ⌞UD⌟.KA.⌞BAR⌟.M[EŠ ( )]*ḫa-bùl-le*
28 ^{m}EN.LÁ-*ṣi*-DINGIR-*ma* ^{lú}*šá-kìn* ^{uru}*kal-ḫi*
29 *ú-šal-li-mu*-⌜*ni*⌝ [(*x*)]*x* ^{m}*x* [*x*] *x* LÚ.A$^{?}$.B[A$^{?}$]
30 IGI ^{m}EN.KAL-*an* ^{lú}*šá* UGU É *ša* É$^{?}$ ^{lú}*tur-ta-ni*
31 IGI ^{m}NUMUN.ZI.GI[Š] DUMU ^{m}A$^{?}$-*ia-a*
32 IGI ^{m}EN.KI-*a* LÚ.UŠ.BAR *ša* ^{uru}TAB.TAB.DINGIR
T.E. 33 IGI ^{m}*lid-bu-bu ša* ^{uru}*ku-me*
34 IGI $^{m.d}$UTU.PAP.AŠ LÚ.UŠ.BAR
35 IGI ^{m}SUḪUŠ.DINGIR.MEŠ-*ni* LÚ.UŠ.BAR *ša* É ^{lú}*tur-ta-ni*
36 IGI ^{m}EN-*i-si-a* KIMIN
L.E. 37 IGI ^{m}ZI.AN LÚ.NAGAR ^{giš}*mu-gir-re*
38 ^{iti}ŠE UD.27.KÁM
39 *lim-m*[*e*] ^{m}[E]N.LÁ.DINGIR-*ma*

Translation

1: The debts of Urdu-ištar, the weaver of coloured cloths, which Bēl-tarṣi-iluma, the governor of Kalhu, paid off in full.

4: Instead of their seal(s they impressed) their nail(s). (Nail marks.) Nail of Halimūsu, Abu-ūl-īdi, Šēlubu, Pān?-aššur, Hanī, Laqīpu, Dari-abu, the son of Šulmu-bēl-lāmur, Bēl-emuqī, the son of La'īti-ilu, Bēl?-ahhē, Sîn-na'id, Ilubūa(?), . . buku, Dulā, Hinidūti, Bāniu, Busāsī, Ṣil-šarri, Adad?-[. . .]me?, Eṭri?-ištar, Hanbunu, Ilu-darānu—13: in all 23 men, creditors, who impressed their nail(s).

16–26: (List of sums owed with creditors' names, now lost.)

27: In all, 53½ minas of bronze, debts which(?) Bēl-tarṣi-iluma, the governor of Kalhu, paid back in full.

29: [Before PN(?)], the scribe, before Bēl-dān, the household supervisor of the *turtānu's* household, before Zēr-kitti-lēšir, son of Aplāia(?), before Bēl-issīya, weaver of Arbailu, before Lidbubu of the town of Kumu, before Šamaš-ahu-uṣur, the weaver, before Ubru-ilāni, the weaver of the *turtānu's* household, before Bēl-issīya, ditto, before Kitti?-ili, the chariot-maker.

38: Month of Addāru (XII), 27th day, *limmu* of Bēl-tarṣi-iluma (797 B.C.).

Notes

7–8: In both these lines, one PN is separated from another by the sign A, "son" or "heir"; at first sight this would imply that the second man was father of the first, but as twenty-three creditors are mentioned in l. 13, the two men mentioned in second place must themselves be creditors. Consequently these two are not given their own names, but are identified by the names of their fathers; a possible reason for this is that the two fathers were the original creditors, and that they are here represented after their death by their sons.

8: La'ītu—see *AHw* 529a s.v. *la'ium*.

9: Also possible, mKAB!.PAP.MEŠ (cf. note on No. 42 rev. 14).

31: Also possible, m*za-ia-a*, cf. m*za-a-a* in ND 1120 (No. 246), Obv. 10 (G. van Driel, *The Cult of Aššur*, p. 200).

37: The reading of this PN is problematical; my suggestion follows the pattern of Kitti-ilāni (*APN* 116b). The name Kēni-ili which Tallqvist gives (*APN* 115b) does not in fact exist, since the passage concerned (*ADD* 676 rev. 6) reads m*ke-ni-i id*-[. . . .].

Commentary

Like No. 90, this tablet records debts paid off by Bēl-tarṣi-iluma on behalf of a third party, this time one man only, Urdu-ištar, who is a weaver. He has twenty-three creditors, and his total debts amount to 53½ minas of bronze; since those individual debts for which figures are preserved are small, it may be that, as in No. 90, there were two or three main creditors, with many lesser ones.

Like No. 90 the transaction is not only witnessed, but is also given validity by the impression of the finger-nails of the creditors (or their sons). The document therefore seems to fulfil two functions: it is on the one hand a receipt signed by the creditors, acknowledging that they have received what was due to them, while on the other hand it transfers the credit to Bēl-tarṣi-iluma, for whom this tablet becomes the proof of the debt henceforth owed to him.

No. 92 Plate 43; Photo Plate 92d ND 493

IM 56866

6·7 × 5·3 × 2·8 9.iv.795

Governor's Palace, Room M.

Obv.	1	*sa-ar-*⌞*tu*⌟ *ša* ^{m}*uš-šá-bi*
	2	LÚ.ÌR *ša* ^{m}MAN.IGI-*a-ni*
	3	1 GÚ.UN UD.KA.BAR.MEŠ
	4	*sa-ar-tu-šu* ^{m}MAN.IGI-*a-ni* EN-*šu*
	5	*a-na* ^{m}EN-*i-si-ia*
	6	*ú-sa-li-im*
	7	IGI ^{m}*man-nu-a-ki-i-aš-šur*
	8	LÚ.⌞MU?⌟ *ša* É ^{lú}*tur-ta-ni*
Rev.	9	IGI ^{m}*pu-šá-a-a*
	10	IGI ^{m}PA[P?]-*qàl-lu*
	11	[IG]I ^{m}*ba-la-ṭu*
	12	[LÚ.X *ša*]⌞LÚ.GAL⌟ É.GAL
	13–16	(traces only)
T.E.	17	⌜*ša qa-ṣi*⌝[*-bit-ti*]-⌜*šu?*⌝[( )]
	18	*iṣ-ba-tu-*⌜*ú*⌝*-ni*
	19	^{iti}ŠU UD.9.KÁM *lim-mu* $^{m.d}$[AMA]R.UTU.KUR-*ni*

Translation

1: The fine of Uššābu, slave of Šarru-amurāni?: Šarru-amurāni? his master has paid in full 1 talent of bronze, his fine, to Bēl-issīya.

7: Before Mannu-akī-aššur, the cook? of the *turtānu's* household, before Pušāyu, before Ahu?-qallu, [before] Balāṭu, [the . . .] of the palace-overseer . . . .

17: . . . . whom(?) they caught red-handed(?).

19: Month of Du'uzu (IV), 9th day, *limmu* of Marduk-šadūni (795 B.C.).

Notes

1: For the PN see *CAD* A Pt. 2, 460b, *aššābu*.

10: Despite the copy, made after collation, the first sign is to be read PAP = *aḫu* by comparison with the name *a-ḫu-qàl-lu* in *JCS* 7 (1953), 170, No. 72, 10 (coll. E. Leichty).

17–18: For this phrase, cf. in this volume No. 119, 20–3.

Commentary

This document records the payment of a fine by Šamaš-amurāni on behalf of his slave Uššābu. There is no sign in the main part of the text of how the man had incurred this penalty, but if the restoration of l. 17 is correct, then the reason, given after the witnesses' names, is that he was caught red-handed at some crime, very likely theft. However, if this was a criminal rather than a civil offence, it is not clear in what capacity Bēl-issīya was the recipient of the fine.

No. 93 Plate 42 ND 211
Inst. Arch. London
8·2 × 11·2 × 3·7 26.iii?.793

Governor's Palace, Room K.

Obv. 1 *ku-um* NA$_4$.KIŠIB-*šu-nu* [*ṣu-pár-šú*]-*nu*
(finger-nail impressions)
2 *ṣu-pur* ^{m}*k*[*i*]-*qi-la-nu* $^{m.u}$[^{ru}ŠÀ].URU-*a-a*
3 ^{mí}*ku-me-tum* $^{m.d}$*še-er*-⌞*ma*?-*a*?⌟-*'a-di*
4 $^{m.d}$AMAR.UTU-*rém-ni* $^{m.d}$*še-er-ḫa-na*-⌜*na*⌝
5 ^{m}*ka-bar* ^{m}*im-me-ra-a-nu* ^{mí}*la-ṣ*[*a-ḫ*]*i-tú*
6 LÚ.ÌR *ša* ^{mí}[*m*]*u-ra-a-a-i-te*
7 ^{m}⌜*ib*⌝-*ba-'a-a-mu* LÚ.ŠÀM *ša* ⌜ŠU? ^{m} *x*⌝-*ra-a*
8 PAP 11 LÚ.ERÍN.MEŠ EN *ḫa-bu*-⌜*le*⌝
9 *ša* ^{m}*sa-bi-ri* ⌞LÚ⌟.DAM.GÀR
10 22 MA.NA UD.KA.BAR.MEŠ ^{m}[*k*]*i-qi*-⌞*la*⌟-*nu*
11 10 MA.NA $^{m.uru}$ŠÀ.URU-*a-a* 12?⌜MA.NA⌝ [^{mí}*ku*]-*me-tum*
12 20 MA.NA $^{m.d}$*še-er-ma-'a-di* 2 ⌜MA.NA⌝ $^{m.d}$AMAR.UTU-*ré*[*m-n*]*i*
13 4 MA.⌜NA⌝ $^{m.d}$*še-er-ḫa*-⌜*na-na*⌝ 2 MA.NA ⌞^{m}⌟*ka-bar*
14 1 MA.NA ^{m}*im-me-ra-nu* 2 [M]A.NA ^{mí}*la-ṣa-ḫi-tú*
15 3 MA.NA LÚ.ÌR ⌜*ša*⌝ ^{mí}⌞*mu*⌟-[*ra-a*]-*a-i-ti*
16 2 MA.NA ^{m}*ib-ba-'a-a*[-*mu x x x x*] *x*
17 PAP 2 GÚ.UN 20 MA.NA [UD.KA.B]AR.MEŠ
18 [*ša*] ^{m}*sa-bi-ri* [*x x* (*x x*)]*x-ú-ni*
B.E. 19 [$^{m.d}$EN].LÁ-*ṣi*-DINGIR-*ma* ^{l}[^{ú}*šá-k*]*ìn* ^{uru}*k*[*al-ḫi*]
Rev. (upper part broken)
1′–5′ (witnesses; names broken)
6′ ^{iti}⌜SIG$_4$?⌝ UD.26.⌜KÁM⌝ [*lim-m*]*u* ^{m}*man-nu-ki*-KUR-*aš-šur*
7′ ^{lú}*šá-kìn* ^{uru}[*g*]*u-za*-[*n*]*a*

Translation

1: Instead of their seal(s they impressed) their [nail(s)]. (Nail marks.) Nail of Kiqilānu, Libbi-ālāyu, Kumītum, Šēr-mā'ādi, Marduk-rēmāni, Šēr-hanāna, Kabar, Immērānu, Laṣahītu, the slave of Murāyītu, Ibba'āmu, the "purchased man" under(?) . . . rā, in all 11 men, creditors of Sabiri, the merchant.

10: 22 minas of bronze—Kiqilānu; 10 minas—Libbi-ālāyu; 12 minas—[Ku]mītum; 20 minas—Šēr-mā'ādi; 2 minas—Marduk-rēmāni; 4 minas—Šēr-hanāna; 2 minas—Kabar; 1 mina—Immērānu; 2 minas—Laṣahītu; 3 minas—the slave of Mu[rayītu]; 2 minas—Ibba'ām[u . . . . . .].

17: In all, 2 talents 20 minas of [bronze, which] Sabiri [owes(?), Bēl-]tarṣi-iluma, [governor] of Kalhu [has paid off in full . . . .

Rev. 1′–5′: (witnesses).

6′: Month of Simānu? (III), 26th day, [*limmu*] of Mannu-kī-māt-aššur, governor of Guzāna (793 B.C.).

Notes

5: For Laṣaḫītu see K. Deller, *OrNS* 33 (1964), 91 (s.v. *ṣāḫittu*).

6: " The slave of Murayītu ", although not given a name of his own, is a creditor in his own right.

18: Restore perhaps [*ḫa-ab-l*]*u-ú-ni* or similar.

17: By simple addition of the individual debts, it appears that the sum of 2 talents and 20 minas is equivalent to 80 and not 140 minas. Consequently the talent in use here has only 30 and not 60 minas. A " short talent " of 30 minas has already been shown to exist in *ADD* 953 and 954, where it was used for wool (see *Iraq* 32 (1970), 159[11]), and we learn that it might also be used for silver from an inscribed sealing (*Iraq* 27 (1965), 16, No. 21, coll.), which records 1 GÚ *ina* QÀL-*si ša* MAN—" 1 talent in the small (talent) of the king ". (*Qallu* is used in Tell Halaf No. 67, 4 (*AfO Beiheft* 6, 42–3): *ina libbi* 1 MA.NA *qa-al-li*; a " short " mina is not otherwise attested to my knowledge.) The opposite of *qallu* is not surprisingly *dannu* " big "—thus we find in *ABL* 1194 rev. 3: 1 GÚ.UN KÙ.BABBAR *ina* KAL-*te* " 1 talent of silver in the big (talent) ", with similar instances, ibid., l. 16; *ADD* 676 rev. 4, 7, 9; 1105, 11–12; ND 5457 (*Iraq* 19 (1957), Pl. XXVII), 2 (for the *sūtu*).

Rev. 6′: The month might also be Ulūlu (VI).

Commentary

This text belongs with Nos. 90 and 91, in being a record of the payment of another person's debts by Bēl-tarṣi-iluma. Except for the absence of superscription such as that above the ruling in No. 91, this text is similar in structure to No. 91, and the missing parts should probably be restored accordingly.

No. 94 Plate 44 ND 254

5·4 × 4·1 × 2·3 Inst. Arch. London 12.viii.788

Governor's Palace, Room K.

Obv. 1 6?4 MA.NA UD.KA.BAR.MEŠ
2 mEN.KI-*ia*
3 *a-na* mDÙ *lu?* [(*x*)] *si?* SUM-*en*
4 *ḫa-bu-le x šu-nu*
5 *ú-sa-li-im*
B.E. 6 IGI m*ṣa-pu-nu*
Rev. 7 IGI mDU-*šal-lim* LÚ.NI.DUḪ
8 IGI m.dAMAR.UTU.TI.LA
9 *ša pit-ḫal-li*
10 itiAPIN! UD.12.KÁM
11 *lim-mu* mU-*mu-šam-mer*

Translation

1: 6?4 minas of bronze Bēl-issīya gave to PN, and(?) he has paid in full their(?) debts.

6: Before Ṣapūnu, before Kēnu-šallim, the door-keeper, before Marduk-uballiṭ, the cavalryman.

10: Month of Arahsamna (VIII), 12th day, *limmu* of Adad-mušammer (788 B.C.).

Notes

3: Instead of *lu* perhaps *qi*; the use of *en* as a complement instead of *in* is perhaps for reasons of space.

4: The undeciphered sign cannot be *e* or TA, nor is it obvious why the suffix is plural, since there can hardly be two PNs concealed in l. 3.

10: The APIN has an extra horizontal.

No. 95 Plate 44 ND 219

BM 131990

6·0 × 8·9 × 2·5 27.x.740

Governor's Palace, Room K.

Obv.	1	^{m}*še-lu-*[*b*]*u* DUMU-*šú*
	2	*šal-lu-*[*un*?]*-tú-šú* 80 MA.NA URUDU.MEŠ
	3	^{m}*aš-šur*-B[ÀD].PAP *ina* É LÚ.A.BA É.GAL
	4	*ú*?-[*sal*?]*-li-me* ⌜*x x* (*x*) *x x*⌝
	5	I[G]I $^{m.d}$MAŠ.MAŠ.I LÚ *qur-bu-te*
	6	^{uru}*par*-ḪA-*a-a*
	7	IGI $^{m.d}$PA.PAP-*ir* $^{lú(!)}$*šá* UGU URU
	8	IGI ^{m}ÌR-^{d}*al-la-a-a*
	9	^{lú}*ḫa-za-nu*
	10	IGI $^{m.d}$PA-*ú-a*
	11	^{lú}*mu-tir-ṭè-me*
	12	IGI ^{m}KAM-*eš*-DINGIR LÚ.GAL É.GAL!
Rev.	13	IGI ^{m}*ti*?-*ni*-DÙ?-*i*?
	14	^{uru}*ba-da-na-a-a*
	15	IGI $^{m.d}$PA-*rém-a-ni*
	16	EN ÚŠ.MEŠ *ša-du-ni*
	17	IGI $^{m.d}$PA-*ú*-TI.LA
	18	LÚ.A.BA *ṣa-bit ṭup-pi*
	19	^{i}[^{ti}A]B UD.27.KÁM
	20	*lim-me* [^{m}]$^{.d}$PA.KAR-*ir-a-ni*
	21	[L]Ú.GAL KAŠ.LUL
L.E.	22	IGI $^{m.d}$PA.S[U] LÚ.GAL ⌜URU⌝.MEŠ-*ni*
	23	[*ša*] LÚ.A.BA É.GAL

Translation

1: (For) Šēlubu, his son, Aššur-dūru-uṣur has [paid in] full his payment (of) 80 minas of copper, in the house of the palace scribe . . . .

5: Before Nergal-na'id, the officer, of Parnunna, before Nabû-nāṣir, the house overseer, before Urdu-allāya, the mayor, before Nabūa, the information-officer, before Ēreš-ilu, the palace-overseer, before Tini . . ., the Badanaean, before Nabû-rēmāni, owner of the blood(-money) being exacted, before Nabû-uballiṭ, the scribe, writer of the tablet.

19: Month of Kanūnu (X), 27th day, *limmu* of Nabû-ēṭirāni, the chief butler.

22 : Before Nabû-(e)rība, the village-inspector [of] the palace scribe.

Notes

16 : EN ÚŠ.MEŠ *šadduni* is of course parallel in construction to the well-known phrase *bēl eqli tadāni*, " owner of the field being sold ", or to *bēl kaspi našê* (No. 102, rev. 7′) ; the phrase should therefore be taken as a whole and does not contain the term *bēl damē*, which (except in Hittite texts) means " the shedder of blood " (see *CAD* D 80a). *Damē* then here means " blood-money " as elsewhere in nA (again, *CAD* D 79b). The use of the Š stem of *nadānu* is presumably because the money is not paid (at least directly) to Nabû-rēmāni, but " in the house of the palace scribe ". Was this because it was necessary for the authority which imposed the penalty to check the payment ? Certainly we must expect that the eventual recipient of the money was the relative of the dead person, since this seems to be the case in other nA texts, and the use of *šaddunu* seems to imply that the authority is " causing " the man " to pay " the money (for a third party). See Introduction, p. 18.

No. 96 Plate 45 ND 255

IM 56828

4·3 × 3·1 × 1·5 11.ii.737

Governor's Palace, Room K.

Obv. 1 2 *me* $17\frac{1}{2}$ MA.NA URUDU.MEŠ
2 $^{m.d}$MAŠ.KÀD-*an-ni*
3 *šal-lu-un-tu sa-ar-t*[*e*$^{?}$]
4 *ina* UGU ^{m}*sa-'i-*[*x*]
5 *ina* UGU ^{m}*ḫar-ma-ki-*⌜15⌝
6 *a-na* ^{m}*šul-mì-i*
7 *a-na* $^{m.d}$IM.EN
Rev. 8 *ú-sa-al-lam*

---

9 IGI $^{m.d}$AK.MU.AŠ LÚ.DAM.GÀR
10 IGI $^{m.d}$IM-*šal-lim* KIMIN
11 IGI ^{m}EN-*lu*-TI.LA ^{lú}*ša* UGU ⌞É⌟
12 *ša* É ^{lú}*ša* IGI É.GAL
13 ^{iti}GUD UD.11.KÁM
14 [*l*]*im-mu* ^{m}EN.IGI.LÁ-*ni*

Translation

1 : $217\frac{1}{2}$ minas of copper Ninurta-kuṣranni has paid to Šulmī and to Adad-bēl on behalf of Sa'i[. .] and on behalf of Harmāki-ištar, as full payment of the fine.

8 : Before Nabû-šūmu-iddina, the merchant, before Adad-šallim, ditto, before Bēl-luballiṭ, the household-overseer of the household of the palace-supervisor.

13 : Month of Ayāru (II), 11th day, *limmu* of Bēl-amuranni (737 B.C.).

Notes

8 : *usallam* appears to be a solecism for expected *usallim* ; or is it *usa'allam* for Dtt **uštatallam* (cf. *ta'alka* < *tatalka* in No. 199, 4)?

14: Clearly in the context of this archive the date 737 is to be preferred to either of the two possible seventh-century dates for an eponym of this name.

Commentary

A man called Ninurta-kuṣranni here pays a fine for two people, to two other persons; since none of the participants is given a title or profession, or is known from elsewhere, we cannot reconstruct the background to the text.

No. 97 Plate 43 ND 227
IM 56821

8·8 × (8·9) × 3·3 16?.[—.—]

Governor's Palace, Room K.

Obv. (entirely broken)

Rev. 1 1 MA.NA m[(*x x*) *x x*].PAP?.MEŠ? *x*[( )]
2 1 ˪MA.NA m˩ *x* (*x*) *x-bu* LÚ.UŠ.BAR
3 1? [MA.N]A m[*x*]-*m*[*u-ša*]*l-lim* ⌜LÚ?⌝.[" (?)]
4 3? [M]A.NA m[(*x*)]*x* *x* -SU? L[Ú.(*x*) *x*]*x*
5 1 [M]A.NA m⌜PAP⌝-*ši-na* lú*ša-nu-ú*
6 1 [MA].NA m*b*[*u?-n*]*i?-i* LÚ.NINDA
7 1? [M]A.NA m[ ]
8 3 M[A.N]A m[*š*]*a?*
9 iti[*x* UD].16?.KÁM *li*[*m-m*]*e* m[ ]⌜LÚ.SUKKAL?⌝

10 IG[I?]
(remainder broken)

Translation

1: 1 mina [. . . . .]-ahhē? . . ., 1 mina [. . . .]bu, the weaver, 1? mina [. . .]-mušallim, the [ditto?], 3? minas . . . ., 1 mina Ahu-šīna, the deputy, 1 mina Bunī?, the baker, 1 mina . . . . ., 3 minas . . . . . .

9: Month of [. . . .], 16?th day, *limmu* of [PN], the vizier?.

10: (witnesses' names (?)).

Notes

5: This title is usually written *šaniu*, but the signs seem clear.

10: It is of course uncertain whether this sign is indeed IG[I, but it seems most likely.

Commentary

This tablet has been included here because it seems likely that it belongs with Nos. 90, 91, and 93, and is a list of creditors. However, it may equally well have been an administrative text, and the only reason for placing it here rather than with the administrative texts, is the guess that a list of witnesses began in l. 10. In either case, the position of the date is unusual.

No. 98 Plate 46 ND 218
IM 56816
5·0 × 3·8 × 2·3 13.i.738

Governor's Palace, Room K.

Obv. 1 21 MA.NA URUDU.MEŠ
2 ^{m}*bar-ruq* LÚ.ÌR
3 *ša* ^{m}*di-lil*-15
4 ^{uru}*ša* ^{m}*lib-luṭ-a-a*
5 ⌞*ku*⌟*-um ig-re-šu*
6 [*i*]*t-ti-ši ú-ṭu-ru*
B.E. 7 *mám-ma* TA* *mám-ma la* K[A].KA

Rev. 8 IGI ^{m}*da-di-i*
9 LÚ.GAL *kal-la-pi ša* LÚ.EN.NAM
10 IGI ^{m}*ú-ra-ar-ṭa-a-a*
11 ^{lú}*za-ma-ru ša* LÚ.EN.NAM
12 IGI ^{m}SUḪUŠ.^{d}U.G[UR]$^{?}$
13 *ša* ^{uru}*pu-rat-ta-a-a* LÚ.GAL KAŠ.LUL
T.E. 14 ^{iti}BARAG UD.13.KÁM
15 IGI ^{m}AK.U LÚ.A.BA
L.E. 16 [*li*]*m-mu* ^{m}U.EN.D[U]
17 [*ina*$^{?}$] 2 *pu-ri*

Translation

Barruqu, the slave of Dilil-ištar of the village Ša-libluṭ, has taken 21 minas of copper instead of his wages. 6: They are quit, no-one shall plead against anyone.

8: Before Dadī, the chief *kallāpu* of the governor, before Urarṭāyu, the singer of the governor, before Ubru-n[ergal$^{?}$] of the village of Ša-puratti (of) the chief butler.

14: Month of Nīsānu (I), 13th day, 16: *limmu* of Adad-bēlu-ukīn, [in] his second term (lit. lot) (738 B.C.).

15: Before PN, the scribe.

Notes

15: No obvious reading for the name AK.U presents itself; perhaps, since it is a scribe writing his own name, we might consider reading *ak-bùr* (for *akburu*), which would yield a known name. However, the value *bùr* is not admitted in W. von Soden, *AS*² 47, 242.

17: Collation indicates that we should probably not restore a [*šú*] at the end of the line.

Commentary

This is a receipt to show that Barruqu has received "21 minas of copper instead of his wages". The text does not state from whom he received this, but since he is called the slave of Dilil-ištar, it must presumably have been from him. There are two surprising features here: one is that a slave should be said to receive wages (*igrē*) from his master, since this word is usually associated with the hiring of a free man on a voluntary basis;

the other curious feature is that he is said to receive copper " instead of his wages ". This seems to imply that his wages were normally paid in kind and that here he receives them in currency.

No. 99 Plate 45 ; Photo Plate 94a ND 241(a)
BM 131991

Tablet : 4·1 × 2·6 × 1·4 —
Envelope : 4·9 × 3·6 × 2·4

Governor's Palace, Room M.

N.B.—A copy is given of the envelope, since this has two extra lines ; I did not think it necessary to copy the tablet as well.

		Envelope			Tablet
T.E.	1	^{m}*aš-šur*-BÀD.PAP	Obv.	1	^{m}*aš-šur*-BÀD.PAP LÚ.SAG
	2	*ša* LÚ.SAG *ša* ^{m}EN.K[AL-*an*]		2	*ša* ^{m}EN.KAL-*an* LÚ.EN.NAM
Obv.	3	LÚ.EN.NAM *ša* ^{uru}[*kal-ḫi*]		3	*ša* ^{uru}*kal-ḫi*
	4	ŠE.PAD.MEŠ LUGAL-*e-šú*		4	ŠE.PAD.MEŠ LUGAL-*e-šú*
	5	*ma-ḫi-ir*		5	*ma-ḫi-ir*
	6	*mám-ma i-si-šú*	B.E.	6	*mám-ma i-si-šú*
	7	[*l*]*a i-da-*[*b*]*u-bu*		7	*la i-da-bu-bu*
	8	*qar-mat*	Rev.		(uninscribed)
B.E.	9	*qar-mat*			
Rev.		(cylinder-seal impression)			

Translation

1 : Aššur-dūru-uṣur, eunuch of Bēl-dān, the governor of Kalhu, has received his " king's corn ". 6 : No-one shall plead against him. (Envelope only) : It is covered.

Notes

4 : " King's corn " is also mentioned in two texts from Balawat, BT 116 and 117 (*Iraq* 25 (1963), 94–5) ; the term will be discussed in my study on nA taxation, and for the moment I will merely quote my conclusion, that it seems reasonable to surmise here that this issue is the result of an order made by the king, that the eunuch should receive corn from official sources, for some reason we cannot hope to define.

8–9 : *qarmat*, repeated twice, appears only on the envelope. Given the meaning of *qarāmu*, " überziehen mit " (*AHw* 902a), this remark must mean that " this is the envelope ". A similar comment is found on BT 124, for example (*Iraq* 25 (1963), 96), where the envelope has *kiṣirtu* (" envelope ").

Commentary

The nature of this transaction has already been described in the note to l. 4 ; it may be useful to point out that it is scarcely an ordinary legal document, since it has no witnesses, superscript, or date, and no mention is made of the person from whom Aššur-dūru-uṣur received the corn. There is however a fine seal impression on the envelope, and it is possible that this was the seal of Bēl-dān himself, the governor. Otherwise, we could perhaps expect that it was the seal of Aššur-dūru-uṣur, but because of the unusual nature of the document, which is clearly closely connected with the administration, we cannot be sure.

No. 100 Plate 47 ND 491
Inst. Arch. London

6·0 × 5·1 × 2·2 11.v.835

Governor's Palace, Room M.

Obv. 1 1 G[Ú.U]N UD.KA.B[AR.MEŠ ( )]
2 ^{m}EN.G[I]Š? *ša x*[ ]
3 *ina* ŠÀ ⌜3?⌝ MA?[ ]
4 IGI $^{m.d}$[(*x*) *x*].DINGIR.[ ]
5 IGI ^{m}*šú*? *'a*? *pi*? *si*? *x*[ ]
6 IGI $^{m.d}$UTU.[ ]⌞*x x*⌟
7 DUMU ^{m}*x*[
8 IGI ^{m}*aš-šur*-DÙ[
B.E. 9 LÚ SUM KÙ.BABBAR.MEŠ?
Rev. 10 SUM-*in kás-pi* ^{m}*bar-ra*-⌜*ra*?-*nu*?⌝
11 *ṣa-bit ka-ni-ki* ^{m}*ḫa-an-da*-⌜*šu*?⌝
12 ITI.NE UD.11.KÁM *li-mu* ^{m}GÌR.MAN

Translation

1: 1 talent of bronze Bēl-lēšir of [.......] in exchange for? [.......].

4: Before [...]-il[āya?], before ....., before Šamaš-[.....], son of [.....], before Aššur-bāni[? ...], giver of the silver. 10: Giver of the money: Barrarānu?; writer of the document: Handašu?.

12: Month of Ābu (V), 11th day, *limmu* of Šēp-šarri (835 B.C.).

Notes

9: Although the sign SUM is not identical with that in l. 10, it can hardly be anything else.

10: Presumably the scribe is consciously making the usual distinction between KÙ.BABBAR = silver and *kaspu* written syllabically = price. Leaving aside the question of whether there should be a reading for KÙ.BABBAR different from *kaspu*, it is clear that *kás-pi* of l. 10 can only refer to the bronze mentioned in l. 1. This would mean that we have an exchange of bronze against silver, and indeed we may plausibly restore 3[+] minas of silver as the commodity in l. 3 for which the bronze is given.

12: There seems to be no doubt as to the reading, nor therefore as to the date of the tablet.

Commentary

This text is really only classed with the loans because it cannot be considered a normal sale text. It appears to record the exchange of copper against silver, a transaction which would not under normal circumstances require any documentation at all, since neither substance requires documentary proof in order to establish ownership. It seems likely, therefore, that this is more in the way of an administrative record, but since it is also witnessed, I have classed it here under legal texts.

It will be noted that this is the earliest of our texts by some way, and this may in some degree account for its curious nature.

It is possible that the blank space on the reverse was intended for a seal impression, but if a seal was impressed, nothing is now discernible.

No. 101 Plate 46 ND 268

Inst. Arch. London

6·6 × (8·2) × 3·0 [—.—].798?

Governor's Palace, Room K.

Obv. 1 *ṣ[u]-pur* ^{m}*mu*-⌜*šal-lim*-^{d}AMAR.UTU⌝
2 *ṣ[u]-pur* ^{m}PAP.AŠ *ṣu-pur* ^{m}*ma-nu-ki*-PAP
(finger-nail impressions)
3 1 GÚ.UN UD.KA.BAR.MEŠ
4 $^{m.d}$EN.PAP ⌜GAL⌝.URU.MEŠ
5 *ina* I[GI?] ^{m}EN *x* [
6 *ku*-⌞*mu*?⌟ *x x x* [
7 *a-na*?! ^{m}PAP?-*x*[ ]^{uru}*kal-ḫa-a-a*
8 [*ina*] SAG ITI!?[
9 ⌜*x x*⌝[
10 5? MA.N[A
11 ⌞*x x*⌟[
(remainder of obv. and upper part of rev. broken)
Rev. 1′ [ ] ZU?
2′ [ ]*x* ^{uru}*ul-mu*?
3′ [ ]*x x x x*
4′ [I]GI ^{m}[*ḫ*]*a-bu-su*
5′ [I]GI ^{m}EN.URU
6′ IGI ^{m}ḪÉ.DAR.^{d}INANNA
7′ IGI ^{m}*e-ṣi-da-a-a*
8′ *ša* ^{uru}*gab-ri-na*
T.E. 9′ [L]Ú.ÌR *ša* ^{m}GÌR^{II}.1[5?]
10′ IGI ^{m}*qa-la-li-ú*?[( )]
11′ *ša* ^{uru}*šá-áš-li-e*?
L.E. 12′ ^{iti}[ ]
13′ *lim-me* ^{m}*m*[*u*?-*tak*?-*ki*]*l*?-^{d}AMAR.UTU

Translation

1: Nail of Mušallim-marduk, nail of Ahu-iddina, nail of Mannu-kī-ahi. (Nail marks.)

3: 1 talent of bronze Bēl-ahi(?), the village inspector . . . . (remainder of obv. too broken for translation).

Rev. 1′–3′: (too broken). 4′: before Habusu, before Bēl-āli, before . . . .-ištar, before Ēṣidāyu of Gabrīna, slave of Šēp-i[štar?], before Qalaliu of Šašlie?.

12′: Month of [. . . ., xth day], *limmu* of M[utakki]l?-marduk (798 B.C.).

Notes

Rev. 6′: For this name cf. note on No. 57, 17.

7′: Professor Deller quotes me two PNs ^{m}*e-ṣi-dà-a-a* (VAT 10696, 6) and ^{m}ŠE.KIN.KUD-*a-a* (VAT 9867, 3), which he suggests are identical with one another. He also suggests that they are identical with $^{m.iti}$KIN-*a-a*, but this cannot yet be proved.

9′: The name could also of course be ^{m}GÌR^{II}.M[AN]; if Šēp-ištar is the correct restoration, he might be the governor of Naṣibīna, eponym for 800 B.C.

Commentary

It is clear that this text is not a sale, and the opening line of the text proper (l. 3), which mentions a quantity of bronze, is reminiscent of loan texts. We should therefore expect that this was a loan from Bēl-ahi(?) to the three men whose nails are impressed above; but since the remainder of the obverse cannot be made out, this is very uncertain. We are probably justified, though, in classing this as a "loan-type" text, and it is interesting to note that instead of the usual practice of later nA texts of this kind, which is to impress the seal on an envelope, this tablet resembles rather a sale text, since the nail impressions are placed at the head of the single tablet, and no envelope is used; cf. on Nos. 106–7, and Introduction, pp. 18–9.

No. 102 Plate 45 ND 477

Inst. Arch. London

5·1 × 6·3 × 2·4 9.x.795

Governor's Palace, Room K.

Obv. (a few indecipherable traces only)

Rev. 1 *ša* $^{m.d}$AMAR.UTU.EN.PAP
2 *ša* É ^{lú}*tur-ta-ni*
3 IGI ^{m}*le-še-ru*
4 LÚ.KAŠ.LUL *ša* ^{m}*dan*$^{?}$*-ni-e*
5 IGI ^{m}DUMU.^{d}INANNA LÚ.NINDA
6 IGI ^{m}*ḫa-ma-qa-ti* LÚ.NINDA
7 EN *kas-pi na-še-e*
8 ^{iti}AB UD.9.KÁM
9 *lim-mu* ^{m}[$^{.d}$AM]AR.UTU.KUR-*ni*

Translation

[before PN, the .....] Rev. 1: of Marduk-bēlu-uṣur, of the household of the *turtānu*, before Lēšeru, the butler of Dannē?, before Mār-ištar, the baker, before Hamaqāti, the baker, owner of the money being borrowed(?).

8: Month of Kanūnu (X), 9th day, *limmu* of Marduk-šadūni (795 B.C.).

Notes

3: Although the name Lēšeru is not otherwise known, it is quite plausible and there is no justification for emending to ^{m}*li-mu*$^{!}$*-ru*. K. Deller quotes me a PN ^{m}*le-še-ri* from VAT 9758 obv. 5′.

7: For the construction of this line cf. note on No. 96, 16; the association of *kaspu* with *našû* seems to be sufficient grounds for classing the text as a loan, despite the absence of the main part of the text. However, the exact translation of this line must remain in doubt, especially since the principals in a transaction do not normally act as witnesses.

No. 103 Plate 47 ND 217
IM 56815
6·5 × 5·0 × 2·4 18.i.788

Governor's Palace, Room K.

Obv.	1	3 LÚ.ŠÁM.MEŠ
	2	10 MA.NA UD.KA.BAR.MEŠ
	3	*ša* ^{m}EN.KI-*ia*
	4	*ina* UGU ^{m}*ki-rib-ti*
	5	*ina* UGU ^{m}PAP.SUM-*na*
	6	IGI ^{m}*ab-di-i*
	7	A ^{mí}*bi-ia-a*
B.E.	8	IGI $^{m.d}$AMAR.UTU-*šal-lim*-PAP.ME[Š]
	9	LÚ.SANGA *ša* ^{d}MAŠ.MAŠ
Rev.	10	IGI ^{m}*i-ma-a-ru*
	11	A $^{m.d}$PA-*iq-bi*
	12	IGI ^{m}DUMU.^{d}INANNA
	13	LÚ.SANGA *ša* ^{d}GAŠAN.KUR-*ḫa*
	14	IGI $^{m.d}$[AM]AR.UTU-*na-din*-PAP.MEŠ
	15	A ^{m}*ba!-ar*-DINGIR
T.E.	16	^{iti}BARAG UD.18.KÁM
	17	*lim-mu* ^{m}U-*mu-šá-mer*

Translation

1: Three "bought men" (and) 10 minas of bronze, belonging to Bēl-issīya, owed by Kiribtu, owed by Ahu-iddina.

6: Before Abdī, son of Biyā, before Marduk-šallim-ahhē, priest of Nergal, before Imāru, son of Nabû-iqbi, before Mār-ištar, priest of Bēlat-nipha, before Marduk-nādin-ahhē, son of Bar-ili.

16: Month of Nīsānu (I), 18th day, *limmu* of Adad-mušammer (788 B.C.).

Notes

15: *ba!* is written over an erasure, perhaps of an original *bar*.

Commentary

This is a simple note of debt, noteworthy because of the curious items owed—three men and 10 minas of bronze—and because of the two priests among the witnesses, high ranking men.

No. 104 Plate 47 ND 205
BM 131989
—.iv.748/738

6·5 × 3·8 × 2·0

Governor's Palace, Room K.

Obv. 1 $18\frac{1}{2}$ MA.NA URUDU.MEŠ
2 *kas-pi ša* UDU.NITÁ.MEŠ
3 *ša* ^{m}*aš-š*[*u*]*r*-BÀD.PAP
4 *ina* IGI ^{m}*ḫu-ra-pi*
5 *ina* ^{iti}DUL SUM-*an*
B.E. 6 *šum-ma la* SUM-*in*
7 *i-ra-bi-u*
Rev. 8 IGI ^{m}*sa-al-ti*-DINGIR
9 IGI ^{m}*gír-tú*
10 IGI $^{m.d}$PA.PAP.MEŠ.SU
11 *ṣa-bit* IM ^{iti}ŠU
12 *lim-m*[*e*] ^{m}U.EN.DU

Translation

1: $18\frac{1}{2}$ minas of copper, the price of sheep, belonging to Aššur-dūru-uṣur, owed by Hurāpu. He shall give (it) in the month of Tašrītu (VII); if he does not give (it), it will accumulate (interest).

8: Before Salti-ili, before Girītu, before Nabû-ahhē-erība, writer of the tablet.

11: Month of Du'uzu (IV), *limmu* of Adad-bēlu-ukīn (748 B.C.).

Notes

12: Although Adad-bēlu-ukīn was also eponym for 738 B.C., I assume that if our text came from that year it would be mentioned that it was his second eponymate, as it is elsewhere (e.g. No. 99).

No. 105 Plate 90 ND 498
Aust. Inst. Arch.
24.i.742

6·7 × 4·8 cm.

Governor's Palace, Room M.

T.E. 1 10 ŠE.PAD.MEŠ *ina* UD? *x x* [(*x x*)]
Obv. 2 ^{m}*na-i* LÚ.DUMU GEMÉ É.GAL [( )]
3 TA* ^{m}*sa-mi-i' ina pu-u-ḫi i-ti-š*[*i*]
4 50 LÚ [*ina*(?)] UD KIN.KUD *i-d*[*an*?]
5 ŠE.PAD.MEŠ *a-na* É ^{lú}⌜*ša*?⌝ IGI É S[UM?]
6 BE-*ma* 50 LÚ.ŠE.KIN.KUD *la* SUM-*na*
7 ŠE.PAD.MEŠ *a!-na mit-ḫar t*[*a*]-GAL-*bi*
8 ^{iti}BARAG UD.24.KÁM *lim-mu*
9 $^{m.d}$PA.KAL-(*x*-)*a-ni* ^{lú}*tu*[*r-t*]*a*-[*nu*]

N.B.—This tablet was collated for me by Professor D. J. Wiseman, and the copy given has been corrected by me from those collations.

Translation

1: 10 (homers) of corn, ..., Nai, the " son of the palace servant-girl ", has taken from Sami' as a loan. 4: [He shall give(?)] 50 men at harvest-time(?), (and) [he shall give(?)] the corn to the household of the palace-supervisor(?). 6: If he does not give 50 harvesters, the corn will accumulate (interest) equally (i.e. at 100 per cent).

8: Month of Nīsānu (I), 24th day, *limmu* of Nabû-da'ināni, the *turtānu* (742 B.C.).

Notes

1: Instead of *ina* UD, perhaps *ina* ŠÀ . . . . .

2: This curious designation, " son of the servant-girl of the palace ", is also found in *ABL* 91, 16 and 99 rev. 13, and in *ADD* 675 rev. 23 (coll. W. G. Lambert, *CAD* A Pt. 2, 29a), where the man bearing the title appears to be of some importance.

3: TA* is needed, and although not shown in the copy, it is indicated in Professor D. J. Wiseman's transliteration of the text which he made available to me.

4: UD KIN.KUD for *ūm eṣādi?* Fifty is an unusually high number of harvesters, but as it occurs also in l. 6, it is not open to doubt. Possibly we should emend to 50 LÚ.ŠE!.KIN.KUD.

5: An alternative reading would be LÚ.⌜DUMU⌝ MÍ! É.GAL!!, but this requires doing more violence to the text, and MÍ É.GAL cannot without strong grounds be equated with GEMÉ É.GAL.

7: *a*! is written over an erasure.

9: The unwanted *nu* between KAL and *-a-ni* was not specially checked.

Commentary

This appears to be a loan of 10 homers of corn from Sami' to Nai, with a clause for the provision of harvesters instead of interest. The text has some unusual features, but its poor condition makes it difficult to assess the certainty of the suggested restorations.

No. 106 Plate 48 ND 215
IM 56814
4·5 × 3·5 × 2·3 13.i.738

Governor's Palace, Room M.

Obv. 1 1 MA.NA KÙ.BABBAR *ina*! *ša* MAN
2 ᵐ*ra-pa-la* TA* IGI
3 ᵐIGI.ᵈ15-*la-mur*
4 *ina pu-ḫi i-ti-ši*
5 *a-4-tú* G[AL]-*bi*

6 [I]GI ᵐ·ᵈPA.NUMUN?.DÙ
Rev. 7 IGI ᵐ*l*[*a*]-*qi-pu*
8 IGI ᵐ*bar*!-*zi-i*
9 IGI ᵐKUR-*a-a*
(finger-nail impressions)
10 ⁱᵗⁱBARAG UD.13.KÁM *lim-mu*
11 ᵐ·ᵈIM.EN.DU
T.E. 12 *ina* 2 *pu-ri-šú*

(There are meaningless scratches on the B.E., probably impressed after the clay had dried.)

Translation

1: One mina of silver (measured) by (the mina) of the king, Rapala has taken as a loan from Pān-ištar-lāmur. It will accumulate (interest) at a quarter.

6: Before Nabû-zēru$^{?}$-ibni, before Laqīpu, before Barzī, before Madāyu(?). (Nail marks.)

10: Month of Nīsānu (I), 13th day, *limmu* of Adad-bēlu-ukīn, in his second term (lit. lot) (738 B.C.).

Notes

1: *ina*$^{!}$ is written over an erasure.

6: MU$^{!}$ (= *šūmu*) is obviously possible here, but collation favoured NUMUN = *zēru*.

8: For the name Barzī, cf. BT 106, 22 (*Iraq* 25 (1963), 91).

9: Or rather Šadāyu ?

Commentary

A perfectly straightforward loan, but note that the nail marks are made directly on to the tablet, and there is no envelope (cf. commentary on No. 101). For the position of the nail marks, not (as in No. 101) at the head of the tablet, but before the date on the reverse, compare the position of the seal impression on No. 107, which also has no envelope.

No. 107 Plate 47; Photo Plate 92c ND 489

IM 56865

5·4 × 3·6 × 2·1 1.xii.737

Governor's Palace, Room M.

Obv. 1 1 MA.NA KÙ.BABBAR *ina* 1 MA.NA *ša* LUGAL
2 $^{\text{m.d}}$MAŠ.EN.PAP TA* *pa-an*
3 ^{m}EN.KUR-*u-a ina*$^{!}$ *pu-u-ḫi*
4 *i-ti-ši a-na* 4-*tu-šú*
5 *i-rab-bi*
6 ^{iti}ŠE UD.1.KÁM
Rev. 7 *lim-mu* ^{m}EN.IGI.LÁ-*a-ni*
(cylinder-seal impression)
8 ^{lú}*šá-kìn* KUR *ra-*[*ṣ*]*a-pa*

Translation

1: One mina of silver (measured) by the mina of the king, Ninurta-bēlu-uṣur has taken as a loan from Bēl-šadūa. It will accumulate (interest) at a quarter of it (the capital).

6: Month of Addāru (XII), 1st day, *limmu* of Bēl-am(u)rāni, (seal impression), governor of Raṣappa.

Notes

3: *ina*$^{!}$ written over an erasure.

Commentary

For the position of the seal impression, see the commentary to No. 106.

No. 108 Plate 48 ND 433
IM 56485
5·4 × 3·5 × 1·9 11.viii.728

Governor's Palace, Room S.

Obv.	1	30 MA.NA BÍL.EN.⸢ZU⸣
	2	⸢7⸣ MA.NA 8-*tú* AN.NA
	3	*ina* ŠÀ *a-sa-li* URUDU
	4	⸤*ša*⸥ 50 MA.NA URUDU
B.E.	5	[^{m}].^{d}⸢PA$^{?}$⸣.DINGIR-*a-a*
	6	[*a*]-*na* $^{m.d}$ŠID-*rém-ni*
Rev.	7	⸢LÚ⸣.EN.NAM *šá* ^{uru}*kal-ḫa*
	8	SUM-*an šúm-mu* UD.15.KAM
	9	[*š*]*a* ^{iti}APIN *la-a* SUM-*ni*
	10	⸤2⸥.TA SUM-*an*
	11	[IG]I ^{m}*aš-šur*-KUR-*ka*-GUR IGI $^{m.d}$UTU.KI-*ia*
T.E.	12	[IG]I ^{m}*na-din-e-a* IGI ^{m}*x*[(*x*)]-*a-a*
	13	IGI ^{m}*aš-šur-še-zib-a-ni* I[GI$^{?}$ ^{m}*x x* (*x*)]-*a-a*
L.E.	14	[^{it}]^{i}APIN UD.11.K[AM]
	15	[*lim-me*] ^{m}BÀD-*aš-šur*

Translation

1: 30 minas of .....-metal, (and) 7⅛ minas of tin, in exchange for a copper bowl of 50 minas of copper, Nabû$^{?}$-ilāya shall give to Marduk-rēmāni, the governor of Kalhu.
8: If (by) the 15th of the month of Arahsamnu (VIII) he has not given (it), he shall give double.

11: Before Aššur-mātka-tirri, before Šamaš-issīya, before Nādinea, before ... āya, before Aššur-šēzibāni, b[efore ...]āya.

14: [Month] of Arahsamnu (VIII), 11th day, [*limmu*] of Dūr-aššur (728 B.C.).

Notes

1: BÍL/BIL.EN.ZU is also attested with other metals in ND 2774 (*Iraq* 23 (1961), 50, Pl. XXVI), l. 1 (200 talents) and rev. 7′ (180 talents). I know of no clue to the identity of the substance.

3: It would of course be possible to translate *ina libbi* as " inside ", and make the copper bowl part of the loan to Nabû$^{?}$-ilāya; but comparison with No. 109 suggests the translation given above.

5: ^{d}⸢MAŠ⸣ is perhaps also possible.

10: 2.TA is perhaps to be read *eṣṣip*, for which see K. Deller, *WZKM* 57 (1961), 35–7.

Commentary

Although this text uses the basic phraseology and structure of a loan, it is clear that it is not strictly speaking one. Apart from the absence of the phrase *ina pūḫi*, which is almost invariably used for true loans, ll. 3–4 show that some kind of exchange is involved, of which only one side has been completed. Further, the payment by Nabû$^{?}$-ilāya is required within only four days. If we did not have ll. 3–4, or if they are rather to be understood as suggested in the note to l. 3, we could suppose that this is in fact a work contract for the governor, or perhaps even a novation of a work contract; but we should need to know Nabû$^{?}$-ilāya's profession to be more confident of this.

No. 109 Plate 48 ND 275(c)
Inst. Arch. London
4·8 × 4·0 × 1·6 [—]

Governor's Palace, Room K.

Obv.	1	2$^{!}$ GÚ.U[N] UD.K[A.BAR(.MEŠ)]
	2	*ina* ŠÀ 7 ZI.MEŠ
	3	^{m}PAP.DU-*ka* L[Ú].*x*[
	4	*ša* ^{uru}*im-gúr*-^{d}BE
	5	⌞*x*⌟ *i-ti-ši*
	6	IGI $^{m.d}$UTU.DINGIR-*a-a*
	7	IGI $^{m.d}$MAŠ.ZU
B.E.	8	IGI ^{m}DUMU-*ba-nu-te*$^{?}$
	9	[ ] *x* SU$^{?}$
Rev.		(almost entirely broken; possibly finger-nail impressions on T.E.)
L.E.	1′	*ki-m*[*a*] ⌜NA$_4$.KIŠIB⌝-*šú*
	2′	*ṣu-pár-šu*
	3′	*ša* ^{m}PAP.DU-*ka*

Translation

1: Two talents of bronze in exchange for 7 persons Ahu-illaka$^{?}$, the . . . . ., of Imgur-enlil, has taken.

6: Before Šamaš-ilāya, before Ninurta-(i)le'i, before Mār-banūte, ...

L.E. 1′: Instead of his seal, the nail of Ahu-illaka$^{?}$.

Notes

1: 2$^{!}$ is written over an erased " correcter " horizontal 2 sign.

4: Imgur-enlil is of course modern Balawat.

5: The trace at the beginning of the line is probably an erased IGI.

L.E. 1′–3′: It is possible that these lines are added as an afterthought, and should have been at the beginning of the text; but equally they may have been left intentionally to this late stage of the document, cf. the commentary to No. 106.

Commentary

Again with this text the structure and phrasing are that of a loan, but the transaction cannot strictly be classed as one. The *ina pūḫi* phrase is absent, and there is no doubt that the sum " borrowed " is owed in exchange for the seven persons mentioned. It almost seems therefore as if this text is an incidental document to a sale text: the new owner of the seven persons is not named, but may perhaps be assumed to be a member of the administration. Ahu-illaka impresses his nail not only on the sale text which would attest his consent to the transfer of ownership, but also apparently to this small tablet which gives confirmation to the purchasers that they have indeed paid the sale price to the previous owner. Why a text of this kind should have been required we cannot tell; possibly it would be made out when the two halves of the transaction—transfer of the purchased object and transfer of the purchase price—took place at different times.

No. 110 Plate 48 ND 214
Inst. Arch. London
—

5·4 × 7·8 × 2·4

Governor's Palace, Room M.

Obv. 1 ŠE.PAD.MEŠ *ša pu-ḫi*
2 *ša* m.dUTU.AD.PAP

3 10 ANŠE m*ḫi-ni-im-me*
4 IGI mDINGIR-*a*-[*x* L]Ú?.ÌR *ša* m.dMAŠ-*tàk-lak*
5 IGI m*bu-s*[*i*?]-*lu* lú*kal-la-pu*
6 IGI m*ḫa-da*?-*a-a ša* É lú*tar-ta-ni*
7 IGI m⌞*ba*?⌟-*ia-a*
8 IGI m[(*x*) *x*]-*a-a* lú*ḫa-za-nu*
9 PAP [*x*] *ša* URU-*šú*

10 10 ANŠE m*ka-ku-ú-su*
11 [IG]I m.dUTU.NIGIN

Rev. 12 PAP 20 ANŠE ⌜ŠE⌝.PAD.MEŠ
13 SAG.DU
14 *a-na* 1 ANŠE 5-BÁN-*a-a*

Translation

1: The corn borrowed by/from Šamaš-abu-uṣur:

3: 10 homers—Hinimme, before Ilā[ya?], slave of Ninurta-taklak, before Busilu?, the *kallāpu*, before Hadāya?, of the *turtānu's* household, before Bayā, before [. . .]āya, the mayor. In all [x (men)] of his village.

10: 10 homers—Kakūsu, before Šamaš-(u)pahhir.

12: In all, 20 homers of corn, capital; (it will accumulate interest) at 5 *sūtu* each per homer.

Notes

1: Probably what is meant is the corn lent by Šamaš-abu-uṣur, rather than the corn borrowed by him.

4–8: These names are probably those of the witnesses mentioned on the original loan text from which the details are taken.

Commentary

This is probably not strictly a legal text at all, but is a simple note recording two debts, no doubt copied from two separate loan texts. Note the absence of any nail marks or seal impressions, and of the date, besides the usual legal phraseology.

No. 111 Plate 90 ND 432
[E]
—

4 × 2·7 cm.

Governor's Palace, Room S.

Obv. 1 ᵐPAP-*la-maš-ši*
2 LÚ.UŠ *kib-si*
3 UD.3.KÁM *ina* U[GU?] NAM
B.E. 4 LÚ.EN.NAM
Rev. 5 *ša* ᵘʳᵘRI-*mu-si*?!
6 *šá-pi-ir*

N.B.—This tablet was assigned to the Expedition, but I have as yet been unable to trace it; Professor D. J. Wiseman's copy is therefore given here.

Translation

Ahu-lamašši, the tracker, was sent on the 3rd day (of the month?) to the province of the governor of Rimūsu?.

Notes

3: *ina* U[GU] NAM: NAM (= *pāḫutu*) is probably not to be taken as "province", in a geographical sense, but rather more vaguely as "responsibility, authority".
5: RI-*mu-su*! also possible; for the name of the town see note on No. 82, 12.

Commentary

This kind of text is perhaps best classed as a memorandum; for the phrasing, which uses the permansive, cf. No. 112.

No. 112 Plate 49 ND 442
IM 56852
[—].i?.[—]

(4·8) × 3·4 × 1·9

Governor's Palace, Room S.

Obv. 1 ᵐ*da-a'-zi-n*[*a* ( )]
2 KUR *ú-ra-ár-ṭa-a*[*-a*]
3 *pa-an* ᵐ·ᵈPA.ŠU.G[UR]
4 LÚ.GAL 50 *ša* ˡᵘ́*t*[*ur-ta-ni*(?)]
B.E. 5 *pa-qi-di* [( )]
Rev. 6 ⁱᵗⁱBA[RAG? UD.*x*.KÁM]
7 *lim-mu* ᵐEN.*x*[

Translation

1 : Da'zin[a], the Urarṭaean, has been appointed to be under Nabû-gimillī-t[irri], the captain of fifty of the *t*[*urtānu*?].

6 : Month of Nī[sānu(?), xth day], *limmu* of Bēl-[. . . .].

No. 113 Plate 49 ND 451
IM, for study
—

4·6 × (4·0) × 1·6

Governor's Palace, Room S.

Obv. (beginning broken)
1′ [DUMU]U?.MÍ-*šú*
2′ [^{m}]*rab-ba*-DINGIR D[UMU] 5 *ru*
3′ [^{m}DIN]GIR-*a-a-ta-ka*-[*r*]*a*? DUMU 4
4′ [^{m}]*ga-me-ú* DUMU 4
5′ [^{m}]*ri-ib-si-ru* DUMU *ša* GAB
6′ [^{m}]⌜*e*⌝-*bi-su* DUMU.MÍ 4 *ru*
7′ [^{m}]*sa-ia-a* GEMÉ-*šú* ⌜*x*⌝
B.E. 8′ [( )] PAP 8

Rev. 9′ [ ]⌞*x* MÍ É? *ta*? *ša*?⌟
10′ [ ]⌜*x*⌝.[ME]Š?-*šú*
11′ [ ] 5 *ru*
12′ [*ba*]-*tú-su*
13′ [DUMU.M]Í 4 *ru*
14′ [ ]
15′ [-]⌞*ta*?⌟-*la-a* MÍ-*šú*
(remainder broken)

N.B.—The original ND 451 has since been joined to an unnumbered fragment which constitutes the right edge; it is possible that obverse and reverse should be exchanged, but not likely.

Translation

1′ : [PN] his daughter?; Rabba-il, s[on], 5 half-cubits; [I]lāya-takara?, son, 4 (half-cubits); Gameu, son, 4 (half-cubits); Ribsiru, son, unweaned; Ebisu, daughter, 4 half-cubits; Sayā, his slave-girl, . . . In all, 8.

9′ : . . . ., his . . . . .; [PN, ...], 5 half-cubits; [PN, girl], adolescent; [PN, daugh]ter?, 4 half-cubits; [. . .]talā, his wife; [. . . . .

Notes

2′ : *ru* is a known abbreviation for *rūṭu*, for which see on No. 212, 2′.

5′ : *ša* GAB, literally "of the breast", here replaces the more frequent DUMU GA or DUMU *ša* GA, "milk child", and refers to a baby which has not yet been weaned.

Commentary

Although the purpose of this list is lost, it is clearly similar in its phraseology to the " Harran census ", published by C. H. W. Johns in *ADB*. It lists first boys according to their size, then girls—an observation which serves to justify the restorations in ll. 2′ and 14′. Before each child there is a personal name, which presumably belongs to the father. This makes the total of eight in l. 8′ rather puzzling: if both parent and child are counted, then the total should be at least twelve, and it therefore seems clear that only one of each pair is counted. If it is the parents, there is no obvious reason why the children should be mentioned at all, and it is surprising that the list is arranged according to the sex and age of the children. It seems, therefore, more likely that the total of eight refers to the children, and that the list is devoted to them, and that the fathers' names were given only in order to identify the children.

No. 114 Plate 49 ND 471 + 431(a)

IM 56860 (ND 471)

4·8 × (7·2) × 2·5 (ND 471) Inst. Arch. London (ND 431(a))

(3·6) × (3·7) × 2·1 (ND 431(a)) —

Governor's Palace, Room S.

N.B.—The join has not been physically confirmed, but the juxtaposition of the two fragments, especially the interlocking of l. 11, confirms it sufficiently.

Obv. 1 ^{m}EN.DIN-*iṭ* ⸢LÚ.SANGA?⸣ 4 DUMU.MEŠ-*šú*
2 *ša* ŠU^{ii} LÚ.AGRIG
3 ^{m}SUḪUŠ.KASKAL ^{m}*ḫ*[*a*]-*li-mu*
4 PAP 2 LÚ.SIMUG KÙ.[GI? *š*]*a* ^{m}*da-da-a*
5 ^{m}*ḫat-ti-i-a-nu* LÚ.ŠIM×NINDA
6 ^{m}*man-nu-ki-i-*^{d}IM DUMU-*šú*
7 [P]AP 3 ^{uru}*bi?-ḫa-*[(*x*-)]*a-a*
8 ^{m}*mu*-LÁ.DINGIR LÚ.SIP[A? (*x x*) Ì]R?
9 *ša* $^{m.d}$PA-*šar-ḫi*-DI[NGIR.MEŠ?]
10 [^{m}]*x* (*x*)-PAP.MEŠ LÚ.[ ]
11 ^{m}DINGIR-*da-la-a* L[Ú.]
12 *ša* $^{m.d}$MAŠ.DINGIR-[*a-a?* ( )]
13 [^{m}E]N.BÀD ^{m}SUḪUŠ.^{d}[ ]
Rev. 14 ^{m}DINGIR?.AD.P[A]P? *x*[ ]
15 ^{m}⸢*x x* 15⸣ *ti?* [
16 PAP 5 *ša* LÚ.EN.N[AM
17 $^{m.d}$IM.⸤DÙ?⸥-*uš?*[
18 (traces only)
(remainder of rev. uninscribed)

Translation

1: Bēl-(l)uballiṭ, the priest(?), his 4 sons, in the charge of the steward; 3: Ubru-harrān,

Halimu, in all 2 [gold?-]smiths, of Dadā; 5: Hattiānu, the brewer, Mannu-kī-adad, (and) his son, in all 3 men of Bihu(?); 8: Mutaqqin-ilu, the shepherd? [(. . . .) the] servant? of Nabû-šarhi-il[āni]; . . . .-ahhē, the [. . . .]; Ilu-dalā, the [. . . .] of Ninurta-il[āya? . . . .], Bēl-dūrī, Ubru-[. . . .], Ilu-abu-uṣur(?) [. . . .], . . .-ištar? . . .[. . . .], in all 5 of the governor; 17: Adad-ēpuš, [. . . . .].

Notes

1: The restoration of the man's title as "priest" is doubtful, especially since we should not expect him then to be "under" the steward.

4: The space rather favours KÙ.[BABBAR], but since silver-smiths do not seem to have existed as such, they are almost certainly gold-smiths.

No. 115 Plate 49 ND 456
Inst. Arch. London
—

3·4 × (3·9) × 2·1

Governor's Palace, Room S.

Obv. (beginning broken)
1′ PAP 3[
2′ m ÌR?.DINGIR? *x*[
3′ m*tu*?-*li*?-[
4′ PAP 2 LÚ? *ša*? [
5′ m.d⌜*x* *x* *x*⌝
6′ m*šùl-mu*-E[N]
7′ PAP 2 LÚ *x*
Rev. (space)
8′ 6 LÚ?.MEŠ
9′ [ ] *x* (*x*) MEŠ

No. 116 Plate 50 ND 463
IM 56859
—

4·8 × 3·0 × 1·8

Governor's Palace, Room S.

Obv. 1 mPAP-*l*[*e*]-⌜*i*⌝
2 *ša* uru*za-li-qi-e*?
3 m*ku-ú-a-ri*
4 *ša* uru*su-ni-gi-e*?

Translation

Ahu-le'i of Zaliqē?, Kuwāri of Sunigē?.

No. 117 Plate 50 ND 470
IM, for study
—

(2·4) × 2·5 × 1·4

Governor's Palace, Room S.

Obv. 1 ᵐ*ḫal-di*-E[N
2 ᵐ*man-nu-ki*-ᵈ[
3 ᵐ*ḫa-an-ṭu*-[
4 ᵐDINGIR-*ia*-[
5 PAP 4? ⌞*x*⌟ MEŠ?[
B.E. (broken ; perhaps uninscribed)
Rev. 6 ᵐ·ᵈ*nin?*-[
7 LÚ.Ì[R
(remainder broken)

Translation

Haldi-bē[l], Mannu-kī-[. . .], Hanṭu[. . .], Ilu-ia[. . .], in all 4 . . . . . 6 : Nin[. . . . .], slave [. . . . . . .

No. 118 Plate 50 ND 423
Inst. Arch. London
—

2·8 × 4·5 × 2·0

Governor's Palace, Room S.

Obv. 1 [ᵐ]*lu*-[T]I?.DINGIR.MEŠ-⌜*ni*⌝
2 ⌜LÚ⌝.[B]UR.G[U]L
3 ᵐDINGIR-*ma*-Z[U? ( )]
4 ᵐEN.AD.PAP [( )]
5 ᵐ·ᵈMAŠ-*tàk-lak*
6 A ᵐ*a*-DA-*bu-i*
7 LÚ.SIMUG GUŠKIN
8 A ᵐ*i-tu-a-a*
9 ᵐ·ᵈIM-*ša*[*l*]-*l*[*im*]
10 ᵐGIŠ?.MU.[ ]

Rev. (long space)
11 PAP 8

Translation

1 : Luballiṭu?-ilāni, the stone-[worker], Ilu-ma-l[e'i(?)], Bēl-abu-uṣur, Ninurta-taklak, the son of Ad/ṭabui, the gold-smith, the son of Itu'āyu, Adad-šallim, . . . mu[. . .].
11 : In all, 8.

Notes

10: Also possible: ^{m}UD.MU[ ].

Commentary

A list of eight persons, two of whom are given professions, and two of whom are identified only by their fathers' names.

No. 119 Plate 51 ND 259
IM 56829

7·5 × 9·9 × 3·2 —

Governor's Palace, Room K.

Obv. 1 ^{m}*sa-[a]b-ḫar-ru*
2 ^{m}*id-na-a-ni*
3 ^{m}DINGIR-⸢*x*⸣-QI
4 ^{m}*nap-'a-d[u]-lu*
5 ^{m}*mu-da-da*
6 ^{m}*me-'i-i-*⸢*su*⸣
7 ^{m}*ḫa-ra-a-nu*
8 PAP 7 ^{lú}*ru-qa-ḫa-a-a*
9 *ša* ŠU ^{m}*ia-da-a'*-DINGIR
10 ^{lú}*na-si-ku*
11 *ša* ^{lú}*na-qi-ra-a-a*
12 $^{m.uru}$KASKAL-*a-a*
13 ^{m}*ḫa-ra-a-nu*
Rev. 14 ^{m}*ub-ru-*^{d}[U]TU$^{?}$
15 A ^{m}*da-di-ia-a*
16 $^{m.d}$UTU.PAP.PAP A ^{m}*bu-si-i*
17 PAP 4 *ša* ^{uru}*si-i'-al*$^{?}$*-ta*$^{?}$*-ru*$^{?}$
18 PAP-*ma* 11 ^{lú}*sa-ru-ti*^{meš}
19 70 UDU.MEŠ *ig-da-az*$^{?}$*-lu*
(two lines erased)
20 UDU.M[EŠ] *q[a-a]t ṣi-bit-ti-šú*
21 ŠU ^{m}*ia-da-a'*-DINGIR
22 DUMU ^{m}*ú-ka-tur*$^{?}$*-me*
23 *ṣab-tu*

Translation

1: Sabharru, Idnāni, Ilu-. . . ., Nap'adulu, Mudāda, Me'īsu, Harānu—in all 7 Ruqahaeans, in the charge of Iada'-ilu, the sheikh of the Naqiraeans. 12: Harrānāyu, Harānu, Ubru-šamaš?, son of Dadiyā, Šamaš-ahu-uṣur, son of Busī—in all 4 men of Si'altāru?.

18: All in all, 11 criminals—they carried off 70 sheep. 20: The sheep were taken in the hands of Iada'-ilu son of Uka . . me, red-handed.

Notes

3: cf. perhaps *Ilu-mu-ki-in* (*APN* 98b).

10: For *nasiku* see J. A. Brinkman, *An.Or.* 43, 274–5.

18: For the use of *sarru* in nA administrative texts, see K. Deller, *OrNS* 30 (1961), 255–7.

19: The verb here posited, **gazālu*, is not attested in Akkadian; however, the general meaning is clear, and my translation can seek support in the west Semitic root *gzl*, well attested in Biblical Hebrew and occurring in Aramaic.

20: For *qāt-ṣibitti* see most recently *Iraq* 32 (1970), 133, note to l. 4, with references. Here also the Akkadian idiom, though clear, is difficult to render both accurately and grammatically in English.

21: Trace at end of line probably erased (coll.).

Commentary

The text lists eleven Aramaeans who had undertaken a raid and carried off seventy sheep. One group of Ruqahaeans, a tribe which is usually associated with the area on the Tigris near Assur (see E. O. Forrer, *Provinzeinteilung*, p. 12), is said to be " in the charge of " Iada'-ilu who is surprisingly then described as a " sheikh of the Naqiraeans ", a tribe which is otherwise unknown; possibly it was a sub-division of the larger group called Ruqahaeans. This Iada'-ilu is probably the same man as that in l. 21, who was actually caught with the stolen sheep, but curiously he is not counted in the total of " 11 criminals ". It is interesting that of the four men coming from a village, two have Assyrian names (but fathers with probably Aramaic ones), whereas all (except perhaps the second) of the Ruqahaeans have uncompromisingly Aramaic names.

No. 120 Plate 51 ND 213
Inst. Arch. London
—

6·7 × 9·9 × 3·2

Governor's Palace, Room K.

Obv. 1 [^{m}]⸤*x*⸥-*lid*$^{?}$-*pi*-SI.SÁ
2 ^{m}*mu-šal-lim*-DINGIR
3 ^{m}*ab-di-i*
4 ^{m}*ka-bi-lu*
5 ^{m}*ḫa-ma-a-ni*
6 ^{m}DINGIR-*ia-a-ab*
7 ^{m}*aš-šur*-AŠ
8 ^{m}*a-du-ru*
9 ^{m}*si-i'-ra-mu*
10 ^{m}EN.IGI.LÁ-*ni*
11 ^{m}*pa-ri-su*
12 ^{m}*qa-ri*-DINGIR
13 ^{m}*iq-bi*-DINGIR
14 ^{m}*tar-di-t*[*i*]-⸢15⸣
Rev. 15 ^{m}*ia-ta-'*[*a*] ŠEŠ-*šú*
16 [^{m}]*sa-la-ma-nu*
17 ^{m}*e-da-a*

18 ^{m}*ṣa-pu-nu*
19 ^{m}*i*[*q*?-*b*]*i*?-DINGIR
20 A $^{m.d}$[*x*.PA]P?.SUM-*na*
21 ^{m}*id*?[- *x* (*x x*)]-*a-nu*
22 ^{m}*si*-[*lim*?-^{d}M]AŠ?.MAŠ
23 ^{m}*ga*-[*x* (*x*)]*x*-DIR?
24 [^{m}]*a*
25 [-*b*]*u*
26 [ ]*x-nu*
27 [ ]*da*? ŠEŠ-*šú*
28 [ ]*x-a-nu*
29 [ ]*x*
T.E. 30 [ ]ERÍN.M[E]Š
31 [(*x*) *x*]⌜*x x x x*⌝-*bi-na-a-a*

Translation

1: . . .-lēšir?, Mušallim-ilu, Abdī, Kābilu, Hamāni, Ilu-ia'ab, Aššur-iddina, Aduru, Si'-ramu, Bēl-amurāni?, Parisu, Qari-ilu, Iqbi-ilu, Tardīti-ištar, Iata'a, his brother, Salamānu, Edā, Ṣapūnu, I[qb]i-ilu(?), son of [. . .-ah]u?-iddina, I[d?. . .]ānu, Si[lim-ne]rgal?, Ga[. . .]. . . . ., his brother, ...

30: [In all . . . .]people, [. .]. . . binaeans.

Notes

1: Copy accurate (coll.); perhaps [^{m}]*šá*!-*liṭ-pi-kitti*, or similar.

19–20: Presumably the man's father is specified to distinguish him from the other Iqbi-ilu mentioned in l. 13; this confirms the restoration here.

31: Consultation of the Reverse Index in S. Parpola, *AOAT* 6, shows that Nūr-abīnu is the only suitable toponym; this could be accommodated here by restoring]⌜*x* KUR ZALAG-*a*⌝-*bi-na-a-a*, but it is not likely, since some of the PNs are characteristically Assyrian, and could not come from the south.

No. 121 Plate 90 ND 208
Aust. Inst. Arch.

4·2 × 6·8 cm. —

Governor's Palace, Room M.

N.B.—The tablet was collated for me by Professor D. J. Wiseman, and any deviations from the copy are the result of this collation.

Obv. 1 ^{m}*a-bu-ú-a* [( )]
2 *ku-um* 2 GUD.MEŠ
3 ^{m}*si-na-a* ^{lú}*ḫa-za-nu*
4 ^{m}*ú-ru*?!-*ku-na*
5 ^{uru}*ia-lu-na-a*-[*a*]
6 ^{m}*a-qa-ta* : LÚ.DUMU-[*š*]*ú* PAP 2
7 ^{u}[^{ru}]*a-ri-ra-a-a*
8 ^{mí}*a-bu-ta*

Obv. 9 ^{mí}⌜*x*⌝-*ṣi-a-na-a-a*
10 ^{mí}*ṣi-ri-a-na*
11 LÚ.DUMU.MÍ-*sa*
12 PAP 4 ^{uru}*ia-lu-na-a-a*
B.E. 13 ^{mí}*a-ni-ni-a*
14 URU.ŠE ^{m}*ba-bu-u*

Rev. (space of five lines)
15 PAP 9 LÚ.ZI.MEŠ
16 *ša* URU.MEŠ

Translation

1: Abūa, instead of 2 oxen, Sinā, the mayor, Urukuna?, the Ialūnaean, Aqata, his son, in all 2 Ariraeans. 8: Abuta, . . . ṣianāyu, Ṣiriāna, her daughter, in all 4 Ialunaeans. Aniniya, (of) the village of Babū.

15: In all 9 persons of the villages.

Notes

15: LÚ.ZI is to be taken simply as " soul " (**napištu?*), cf. E. Ebeling, *SVAT*, p. 4, and has no connection with *nasāḫu* " deport "; it is used where a total includes different sexes.

16: It is perhaps a little unfair to describe Ialūna as a mere village, but the other places named probably are such.

Commentary

This motley collection of people has no obvious unifying characteristic. Perhaps this was a note of persons asking for audience with the governor, or with some equally coincidental factor in common.

No. 122 Plate 50 ND 241(b)
Inst. Arch. London

(5·2) × 3·7 × 2·0 —

Governor's Palace, Room M(?).

N.B.—The number of 241(b) seems to have been assigned to this tablet after the compilation of the dig catalogue, and its provenance is therefore not necessarily the same as that of No. 100 (ND 241(a)).

Obv. 1 [^{m}PAP?]-*u-a*-SU
2 [^{m}*x*]-*lu*-[*d*]*i-e*
3 [^{m}]*aš-šur*-KAR-*ir*
4 ^{m}*ša-la-ma-ši-e*
5 ^{m}*na-ga-ḫa*
6 [^{m}]*a-gu-su*
B.E. 7 [ ]*x-a*
(remainder of B.E. and all of rev. broken; trace of one sign only on T.E.)

Translation

[Ah]ūa-erība, [. .]ludie, Aššur-ēṭir, Ša-lamašie, Nagaha, Agūsu, ...

No. 123 Plate 52 ND 488
Inst. Arch. London

5·6 × 7·5 × 2·6 —

Governor's Palace, Room M.

Obv. 1 mGAL?[ ] m*ḫa?-lut?*
2 mEN?-⌜*ni?*⌝ *x*[ ]*bi?*
3 D[UM]U? mŠÀ?.[ ]
4 m*mu-šal-lim*-[(*x*) *x*]
5 m*ku-ma-a-a* m*ur*-⌞*x*⌟-*a*
6 mUD? ⌜*x* (*x*) *za?*⌝ m⌜*x* (*x*) *x*⌝
7 m*na-ni-i di? te?* DINGIR
8 m.dAMAR.UTU.EN.PAP
9 mDINGIR-*ir?-te?*-APIN-*eš*
10 m⌜*x x*⌝ *sal* m*man-nu-a-ki*-MAN
11 m*ina*-IM.EN.DU KUR?
12 m.dMAŠ.MAŠ.MU.AŠ
13 *la maḫ-ru-ti*
(rev. uninscribed)

Translation

1–3: (broken). 4: Mušallim-[. . .], Kūmāyu, Ur . . ā, ..., Nanī, ..., Marduk-bēlu-uṣur, Ilu-irte?-ēreš, ..., Mannu-akī-šarri, Ina-šār-bēli-allak . . ., Nergal-šūmu-iddina—not received.

Notes

11: No obvious way of incorporating the sign at the end of the line, KUR or MAN, into the PN presents itself.

13: *maḫrūti* probably from *maḫru*, not *maḫrû*; I am tempted to suggest that *maḫru* here means " present ", so that *lā maḫrūti* means " absent, missing ". *Maḫru* also occurs in 79–7–8, 200, a piece of a historical or possibly administrative text with a list of various professions, where l. 1 reads: 3 DUMU.MEŠ *maḫ-ru-u-te* . . . ., but the context is not sufficient to determine the meaning.

No. 124 Plate 50 ND 275(j)
Inst. Arch. London

(1·5) × (2·0) × 2·0 —

[Governor's Palace, Room K.]

(Top left-hand corner with the beginning of 3 PNs; rev. of fragment uninscribed. Possibly part of ND 275(h) = No. 76.)

No. 125 Plate 52 ND 445
Inst. Arch. London
16. [—].—

5·4 × 3·5 × 1·8

Governor's Palace, Room S.

Obv. 1 1 ANŠE.KUR.RA GÙN.MEŠ
2 2 ,, SA$_5$.MEŠ
3 8 ,, *ir-gi-nu*
4 1 ,, SA$_5$ *me-ṣi-ra-nu*
5 1 ,, *ir-gi-nu me-ṣ[i-ra-nu(?)]*
6 PAP 13 ANŠE.KUR.RA.ME[Š]
B.E. 7 *ša* $^{m.d}$Š[ID].P[AP$^?$].AŠ
Rev. 8 [LÚ.GAL] ⌞URU$^?$⌟.MEŠ
9 [( )] ^{it}[^{i}*x* U]D.16.KÁM

Translation

1: 1 roan horse, 2 bay horses, 8 grey$^?$ horses, 1 banded$^?$ bay horse, 1 banded$^?$ grey$^?$ horse. 6: In all, 13 horses, of Mar[duk]-ahu$^?$-iddina, [the] village-[inspector$^?$].

9: Month of [. . . .], 16th day.

Notes

1: For the reading of GÙN in this context, K. Deller refers me to ANŠE.KUR.RA *bar-ru-mu* in a nA list of various animals (Ass. Fd. Nr. 10804 obv. 14); for the logogram GÙN.A = *barmu* see *CAD* B 112b. The meaning is " spotted " or " multi-coloured ".

Roan is defined (*Chambers's Twentieth Century Dictionary*, 1959) as " bay or dark, with spots of grey or white: of a mixed colour, with a decided shade of red ".

The use of MEŠ here is presumably an error, as there is only one animal of this colour.

2: SA$_5$ = *sāmu?* Bay is defined (ibid.) as " reddish brown inclining to chestnut ".

3: The colour of *irginu* is still unknown, see commentary below.

4: *meṣerānu* is presumably an adjective from *miṣ(i)ru*, a " band " or " stripe ".

8: The restoration is suggested by comparison with No. 127, 4, etc.

Commentary

The colours of horses in nA terminology have not been fully studied, and here is not the place to start. However, that terminology is fairly consistent, in that bay (SA$_5$), black (GI$_6$), and *irginu* are much the commonest terms used. Comparison with the coloured wall-paintings from Til-barsip (e.g. A. Parrot, *Nineveh and Babylon* (London, 1961), pp. 268 ff.) shows that there the horses are most commonly black, red, or blue in colour. It is therefore easy—perhaps too easy—to identify the blue horses with those called *irginu*, and assume that the blue is used to render grey, which is quite plausible.

No. 126 Plate 52 ND 446
IM 56854
15.[—].—

(5·1) × 3·0 × 2·1

Governor's Palace, Room S.

Obv. 1 [*x* AN]ŠE.KUR GI$_6$.MEŠ

2 [*x*]ANŠE.KUR SA$_5$.MEŠ
3 [*x*]ANŠE.KUR ḪAR.MEŠ
4 [PAP]9? ANŠE.KUR *ša* LÚ.⌞DAM.GÀR⌟
B.E. 5 [*ša*? ^{m}]EN.IGI.LÁ-[*ni*]
Rev. 6 [( )] UD.15.K[ÁM]

Translation

1: [x] black horses, [x] bay horses, [x] .... horses, [in all] 9? horses of the merchant(?) [of] Bēl-am(u)r[āni?].

6: [(Month of ....)] 15th day.

Notes

3: ḪAR.MEŠ is probably a typical nA abbreviation for the word elsewhere written out *ḫar-ša-a-a* (*ABL* 466, 9; *ADD* 1103, 2; and *ADD* 988, 12: *ḫar-ša!* (copy: RA)-*a-a*). There is a toponym Ḫaršu associated with Namri, of which this could be the gentilic (see S. Parpola, *AOAT* 6, 154).

5: The restoration of a PN seems necessary; it is probably mere coincidence that *ADD* 1103, 5, mentions a PN]-am(u)rāni.

Commentary

For the colours see No. 125; this text may come from the day previous to that text, each being a daily report.

No. 127 Plate 52 ND 430
Inst. Arch. London
—

(4·5) × 3·2 × 2·1

Governor's Palace, Room S.

Obv. 1 [*x* ANŠE.KUR.(RA.)]MEŠ ANŠE.NUN.NA TU.MEŠ

2 [ ]*x* 4? 1
3 [ ]^{m}*man-nu-ki*-DINGIR
4 [( ) LÚ.GA]L URU.MEŠ-*ni*
5 [ ] *ra-da-ni*
6 [LÚ.E]N?.NAM *ša* ^{uru}*ar-zu-ḫi-na*
Rev. 7 [AN]ŠE.KUR.MEŠ
8 [ ]-*si-im-ti*
9 [ ]*x* URU.MEŠ
10 [š]*a*? ^{m}*aš-šur*-U.PAP
11 [ ]*x* 10? *ša* $^{m.d}$MAŠ.DINGIR-*a-a*

Translation

1: [Horses] and mules which have come in.

2: ....[.....] Mannu-kī-ili, the village-inspector, [.....]radāni, [..... the] governor of Arzuhīna, [. . . . .] horses, [. . . . .]-simti, [. . . . .] villages [. . . . . o]f$^{?}$ Aššur-bēlu-uṣur, [. . . . .]. . 10$^{?}$ of Ninurta-ilāya.

Notes

2: Possibly four (horses) one (mule), although it is unclear what would then have occupied the beginning of the line; alternatively, we might consider four (mules), with the DIŠ wedge indicating a repetition of the logogram from the line above.

5: With the mention of Arzuhīna in the line below, it is possible that this is the river Radānu.

6: This governor of Arzuhīna must be the same as Ninurta-ilāya mentioned in l. 11, who was eponym for 802 B.C.

10: Aššur-bēlu-uṣur is probably the governor of Kalhu who functioned as eponym for 772 B.C., although a man of the same name was governor of Kirruri and eponym for 797 B.C.

No. 128 Plate 53 ND 427

BM 131997

3·9 × 2·4 × 1·5 —

Governor's Palace, Room S.

Obv. 1 11 ANŠE.KUR.RA.MEŠ
2 *ša* LÚ.EN.NAM
3 [*š*]*a* ^{uru}*ḫal-ṣu*
4 [*š*]*a z*[*i*$^{?}$]
5 [ ]*me x*[ ]
B.E. (broken; perhaps uninscribed)
Rev. 6 [ ]*x d*[*a x*]
7 [ ] *x x ki rim*$^{?}$
8 [( ) *š*]*a* LÚ.EN.NAM
9 [( ) *š*]*a* ^{uru}*ta-ma*$^{?}$*-nu-n*[*i*$^{?}$]
10 [( ) ^{m}]*šùl-mu*-PAP.MEŠ
11 [( )] LÚ.GAL URU.MEŠ-*ni-šú-nu*
T.E. (crossed lines; significance unknown)

Translation

1: 11 horses of the governor of Halṣu, ... 8: of the governor [of] Tamanūni?, [(. .)]Šulmu-ahhē, their village-inspector.

Notes

3: Halṣu is probably the province on the north-eastern borders of Assyria, see E. O. Forrer, *Provinzeinteilung*, 113.

9: Tamanūni, if that is the correct form of the name, is unknown. However, since in the next two lines one man is said to be " their village-inspector ", Tamanūni may be close to Halṣu, which would allow one official to act for both provinces.

No. 129 Plate 52 ND 447
Inst. Arch. London
—

4·6 × 3·2 × 1·5

Governor's Palace, Room S.

Obv. 1 [()]32 ANŠE.KUR.RA.MEŠ
2 ^{m}*aš-šur*-NUMUN?.PAP
3 ⌞*ša*?⌟ *ma-ḫa-za-a-ni*
(rev. damaged, but probably uninscribed)

Translation

32? horses—Aššur-zēru?-uṣur, the village-inspector(??).

Notes

3 : The fact that *māḫāzu* does occasionally occur spelt syllabically in nA texts (see e.g. L. Waterman, *RCAE* IV, 80b) makes one wonder whether the GAL URU.MEŠ(*-ni*) should not be read *rab* or *ša māḫāzāni*. This would be convenient in that we already have the village-inspector in Nos. 125(?), 127, and 128. Otherwise we must fall back on the infinitive of *ḫaṣānu*, which is unlikely.

No. 130 Plate 53 ND 452
Inst. Arch. London
—

3·2 × 5·7 × 2·2

Governor's Palace, Room S.

Obv. 1 [ ] *x*[ ]
2 ⌜*ša* LÚ? *x* (*x*) GUD.MEŠ⌝

---

3 ⌞13⌟ ANŠE.KUR.RA
4 ⌜3 ANŠE.GÌR⌝.NUN.NA
5 4 ANŠE.NITÁ.MEŠ
6 2 GUD.MEŠ PAP 22 :
7 *ša* ^{m}*ia-*⌞*na*?⌟*-di*

---

8 10 ANŠE.KUR.MEŠ *ša* ^{m}*mar-*^{d}15
9 9 : *ša* ^{m}*si-na-a'*-DINGIR

---

10 [2] ANŠE.KUR.MEŠ 4 ANŠE.NITÁ.MEŠ
11 [PAP]6 : ^{m}*bal-ṭi-nu-ri*

Rev. (space)
12 PAP 34 ANŠE.KUR.MEŠ
13 3 ANŠE.GÌR.NUN.NA

Rev. 14 8 ANŠE.NITÁ.MEŠ
15 2 GUD.MEŠ

Translation

. . . . and oxen.
3 : 13 horses, 3 mules, 4 donkeys, 2 oxen, in all 22 : of Ianādi.
8 : 10 horses of Mār-ištar, 9 (horses) : of Sina'-ilu.
10 : [2] horses, 4 donkeys, [in all] 6 : of Balṭi-nūrī.
12 : In all 34 horses, 3 mules, 8 donkeys, 2 oxen.

Notes

2′ : This cannot be emended to ⌜*ša* ANŠE.KUR . . .⌝ or similar (coll.), but ⌜LÚ.GAL GUD.MEŠ⌝ is possible.

No. 131 Plate 53 ND 278
Inst. Arch. London
—

2·9 × 1·8 × 1·3

Governor's Palace, Room B.

Obv.	1	1	KAL
	2	1	3
	3	2	2
	4	17	U_8
	5	PAP 10	NI[M]
B.E.	6	1!	MÁ[Š]
	7	1	3
	8	2	2
Rev.	9	15	Ù[Z]
	10	PAP 8	MÁŠ.TUR
	11	PAP	ÁB? (erased ?)
	12		^{m}*ri-'a-a-nu*

Translation

1 : 1 full-grown (sheep), 1 3-(year-old sheep), 2 2-(year-old sheep), 17 ewes, a total of 10 lambs.
6 : 1? he-goat, 1 3-(year-old goat), 2 2-(year-old goats), 15 she-goats, a total of 8 kids.
11 : In all (. . .) ; Ri'ānu.

Commentary

This laconic text is a brother to No. 233, which uses the same terminology and is similar in script and general appearance.

No. 132 Plate 54; Photo Plate 96c–d, f ND 494
IM 56867
—

6·7 × 5·5 × 2·2 (greatest thickness at centre)

Governor's Palace, Room M.

1 [( )] UDU.U$_8$.MEŠ [
2 [( )]*ša* IGI ^{m}*ba-ni-i* LÚ.SI[PA
3 [( )] *ša* ^{uru}*sa-me-*[

Translation

[(. . .)] flocks [(. . . .)] which are under Banī, the shepherd [(. . .)] of the village of Same[. . .].

Commentary

For both the text, and the docket *per se*, see the discussion in the Introduction (pp. 20–1); for the seal inscription see on No. 172.

No. 133 Plate 54 ND unn.
IM, for study
[—]

(4·9) × (4·7) × (2·4)

Governor's Palace, room uncertain.

1 [( ) UD]U.NITÁ.MEŠ *á*[*š*?-
2 [( ) *š*]*a ina* IGI [
3 [( )]*ša ina* IGI [
(seal impression)
(remainder broken)

Commentary

Like No. 132, a docket recording the sheep (here male sheep) under the charge of shepherds (here two of them); for further discussion of this sort of docket, see Introduction (pp. 20–1).

No. 134 Plate 54 ND 497
Inst. Arch. London
1.viii.733

6·3 × 4·8 × 2·4

Governor's Palace, Room M.

Obv. 1 60 AMA.MEŠ MUŠEN.MEŠ GAL.MEŠ
2 10 NITÁ.MEŠ

Obv. 3 PAP 70 ᵐ*ba-su-su*
4 ⁱᵗⁱAPIN UD.1.KÁM
5 *lim-mu* ᵐ*aš-šur*-KAL-*an-ni*
(rev. broken, but presumably uninscribed)

Translation

1: 60 mother ducks, 10 drakes, in all, 70, Basusu.
4: Month of Arahsamnu (VIII), 1st day, *limmu* of Aššur-da'inanni (733 B.C.).

Notes

1: For MUŠEN.GAL = duck, see B. Landsberger, *Die Welt des Orients* 3 (1966), p. 260, and *CAD* I/J 214b.

No. 135 Plate 54 ND 273
IM 56837
—

(4·4) × 2·9 × 1·6

Governor's Palace, Room K.

Obv. 1 [ ] *ina lìb-bi* 4 *pa-da-ka-ti*
2 [*m*]*e*? *ina lìb-bi* 10 *kar-me*
3 [ ]2 *lim ina* URU.ᵈIM
4 [*x l*]*im* 1 *me ina* ᵘʳᵘ*kap-ri*
5 [( )]⌞*ša*⌟ GAL URU
(rev. damaged but probably uninscribed)

Translation

1: [. . . . homers] in 4 (grain-)bins(?), [x +]100 (homers) in 10 (grain-)heaps, [x +]2,000 (homers) in Āl-adad, [x +]1,100 (homers) in the village of the town commandant?.

Notes

1: *padakku*: (*AHw* 807b): some kind of building or container in which grain could be stored, and which could be closed, because in *ABL* 1070 (the only other occurrence), the writer's complaint is that the *padakkus* have been opened and grain removed from them.

2: *karmu*, a grain heap, is of frequent occurrence in nA; it does have the plural *karmāni*, as in the title *rab karmāni*, but it is probably not necessary here to read KAR.ME(š) = *karmāni*.

Commentary

This is a note of grain stored in various ways and places; cf. No. 136 and e.g. ND 2791 (*Iraq* 23 (1961), 54).

No. 136 Plate 55 ND 416
Inst. Arch. London
—

4·3 × 3·0 × 1·8

Governor's Palace, Room S.

Obv. 1 ⌜9⌝ ŠE *pa-ru-ga-ni*
2 *za-ri-ú*
3 34 ŠE *pa-ru-ga-ni re-ḫu*
4 6 ŠE *pa-ru-ga-ni*
5 *ša* ŠE.PAD.MEŠ BABBAR.MEŠ *re-ḫu*
B.E. 6 5 GÌR^{II} GUD *ša*⌞ŠE.PAD.MEŠ⌟
7 BABBAR.MEŠ *re-ḫu* [( )]
Rev. 8 9 *pi-*⌞*ni*⌟*-gi* GÌR^{II}(?) G[UD]
(space)
9 PAP *an-ni-u*
10 *ina* ŠÀ *ú-šal-li*

Translation

1: 9 piles(?) sown (out), 34 piles(?) remaining. 6 piles(?) of white corn remaining.
6: 5 " ox-feet(?) " of white corn remaining, 9 . . . . . [" ox(?)]-feet(?) ".
9: All this in the valley.

Notes

1: *parūgu*: see *AHw* 837b " ein Saatgetreidebehälter ? ", obviously on the basis of this passage. However, the lexical parallels and equivalences of the word (e.g. *raḫīṣu*, *tara(m)mu*) suggest that it means rather " a pile (of corn) ", and this is not impossible, since the corn could be stored in this way, and taken straight from the pile to be sown.

8: *pinigu* is an uncertain restoration; the word is connected by R. Borger (*Asarhaddon* 94, 26) with *pannigu*, and he is followed by *AHw* 818b. This is not, however, necessarily correct, and W. von Soden is probably nearer the truth when he separates off the Esarhaddon reference and translates " eine Art Mehl "; add also an occurrence in the ritual text published in G. Van Driel, *The Cult of Aššur* (see W. G. Lambert, *OrNS* 40 (1971), 91, on Col. IX 1).

Note that if the restoration is correct, some kind of measure has to be supplied.

No. 137 Plate 54 ND 429
Inst. Arch. London
—

3·7 × 7·1 × 2·8

Governor's Palace, Room S.

Obv. 1 [1?] *me* 2 ANŠE 1-BÁN! 7
2 $^{m.d}$PA.⌞BÀD.PAP⌟
3 1 *me* 24 ANŠE $^{m.d}$[ ]
4 1? *m*[*e*]10 ANŠE ^{m}*dan-nu*[ ]
5 ⌞1? *me* 14⌟ [ANŠ]E ^{m}*ša-aš-*⌜*šur-du*⌝*-bu*
(space)

Obv. 6 [P]AP (*x*+)4? *me* 50 ANŠE 1-BÁN 7 *qa*
7 [(*x*)]SUM-*tú*
(rev. largely damaged, but probably uninscribed)

Translation

1: [1]02 homers 1 *sūtu* 7 (*qa*)—Nabû-dūru-uṣur; 3: 124 homers [PN]; 1?10 homers Dannu[?(. . .)]; 1?14 homers, Ša-aššur-dubbu.
6: In all, (x+) 450 homers, 1 *sūtu*, 7 *qa* (. . .) issue(d).

Notes

6: For SUM-*tú* cf. ND 2451 (*Iraq* 23 (1961), 28–30), 23, rev. 3′.

Commentary

A list of dry quantities, probably grain. Land is excluded because of the mention of *qa*, which is not used for surface measurement. It may list contributions from high officials, even governors, since Ša-aššur-dubbu was governor of Tušhān and eponym for 707 B.C., while a Nabû-dūru-uṣur was governor of Parnunna, and eponym for 697 B.C.

No. 138 Plate 54 ND 434
IM 56846
—

(3·2) × 2·3 × 1·4

Governor's Palace, Room S.

Obv. 1 60 ŠE.GIŠ.IÀ.MEŠ [
2 m*ab-da*-U.U [
3 66 ANŠE ŠE.GIŠ.[IÀ.MEŠ
4 4 ANŠE 1-BÁN IÀ.[MEŠ?
B.E. 5 LÚ.UŠ ANŠE.NITÁ.[MEŠ
Rev. (space)
6 PAP 1 *me* 26 ANŠE Š[E.GIŠ.IÀ.MEŠ]
7 4 ANŠE 1-BÁN IÀ.M[EŠ?

Translation

1: 60 (homers) of sesame, Abda-adad-milki [( )], 66 homers of ses[ame (and)] 4 homers 1 *sūtu* of oil [( )], the donkey driver.
6: In all, 126 homers of [sesame (and)] 4 homers 1 *sūtu* of oil.

No. 139 Plate 55 ND 419
IM 56841
—

6·4 × 3·3 × 2·2

Governor's Palace, Room S.

Obv. 1 7 GÚ.UN *a-na* mKASKAL-*a-a*
2 7 m.uru[KÁ].DINGIR-*a-a*

	3	7?	^{m}DÙ.PAP.MEŠ
	4	7	^{m}*e-ṣi-da-a-a*

	5	PAP 1 *lim* 2 *me ziq-pu*
	6	*ina* ŠU^{II} $^{m.d}$UTU.KAL-*in-an-ni*
	7	[*i*]*na* ^{uru}*kal-ḫa* UD.5.KÁM *ša* ^{iti}ŠE
Rev.	8	3 *me* 50! *ziq-pu* GIŠ.NU.ÚR.MA
	9	4 *me* *ziq-pu* GIŠ.PÈŠ
	10	4 *me* 50 *ziq-pu* GIŠ.ŠENNUR
	11	PAP 1 *lim* 2 *me ziq-pu*

Translation

1: 7 talents to Hūlāyu?, 7 (talents to) Bābilāyu, 7 (talents to) Bān?-ahhē, 7 (talents to) Ēṣidāyu.

5: A total of 1,200 saplings in the charge of Šamaš-da'inanni, in Kalhu, 5th day of the month of Addāru (XII).

8: 350 pomegranate saplings, 400 fig saplings, 450 medlar saplings. In all, 1,200 saplings.

Notes

1: The *a-na* is written small, and is presumably a later addition; the *na* lacks its final vertical.
8: Although there are seven wedges in the 50 sign, the addition shows that 50 was intended.

Commentary

This tablet seems to record two entirely separate matters. In the second part there is a note of some fruit-tree saplings, but above the ruling four persons are named who receive(?) 7 talents each. Since it is not stated what the substance so measured is, it is impossible to tell whether this might have been connected with the second part.

No. 140 Plate 54 ND 428
BM 131998

3·7 × 2·3 × 1·5 —

Governor's Palace, Room S.

Obv.	1	[1]/2 MA.NA	^{giš}*eri-nu*
	2	⌜1/2⌝ MA.NA	GIŠ.ŠUR.MAN
	3	,,	^{giš}*dáp-ra-nu*
	4	,,	GIŠ.ŠEŠ
B.E.	5	,,	GIŠ.MAN.DU
Rev.	6	,,	GIŠ.LI
	7	,,	GI.DÙG.GA

Translation

1 : $\frac{1}{2}$ mina of cedar, $\frac{1}{2}$ mina of cypress, ditto of juniper, ditto of myrrh, ditto of elder, ditto of juniper, ditto of " sweet reed ".

Notes

1, 6 : For these two trees, *daprānu* and *burāšu*, see *CAD* D 190a and *CAD* B 328b ; in the earlier volume *daprānu* is identified as *Juniperus drupacea*, and *burāšu* as *Juniperus oxycedrus*, but *CAD* B is more cautious.

I have translated the remaining trees after the identifications of R. C. Thompson, *A dictionary of Assyrian botany*.

Commentary

A list of amounts of essences derived from the trees named.

No. 141 Plate 55 ND 453
IM 56856
—

2·7 × 4·9 × 1·9

Governor's Palace, Room S.

Obv. 1 [*i*]*l-k*[*u*]
2 [*x* D]UG.ŠAB [*š*]*a*$^{?}$ GEŠ[TIN].MEŠ
3 ⌜2?⌝ ANŠE 1-[BÁN?] NINDA.MEŠ
4 2$^{?}$ ANŠE KAŠ.MEŠ
5 [5]-BÁN ŠE *ki-su-tú ša* UD-*me*
6 2$^{?}$ MA.NA URUDU *ša* IÀ.MEŠ
7 *ša* ^{giš}*bu-ṣi-ni*
8 PAP *an-ni-u ša ana* KASK[AL]-*šú*

9 90 MA.NA URUDU.MEŠ
10 [*š*]*a*$^{?}$ 30 LÚ *ku-tal* ERÍN.MAN
11 [*x* A]NŠE ŠE.PAD.MEŠ
12 ⌜5⌝ ANŠE ŠE *ki-*⌞*x x*⌟[( )]
13 *ina* MU.AN.NA[(*x x x*)]
B.E. 14 *i-ma-ḫ*[*ar* ( )]

Rev. 15–19 (traces only)
(remainder uninscribed)

Translation

1 : *Ilku* [of . . . . .] : [x] bowl(s) of wine, 2$^{?}$ homers 1 *sūtu* of bread, 2$^{?}$ homers of beer, 5 *sūtu* of fodder—per day. 6 : 2 minas of copper for oil for the lamp(s). All this for his expedition.

9 : 90 minas of copper for 30 reserves of the " king's men ", [x ho]mers of corn, 5 homers of . . . .-corn, he shall receive in the year [(. . . . .)]. . . . .

Notes

1: The restoration of *ilku*, which fits the traces, is based on a comparison with ND 3467 (for which see commentary below).

7: ^{giš}*bu-ṣi-ni*: although this should strictly mean a plant of some kind (*CAD*: mullein) or the wick made from it, I think there can be no doubt here that this is an abbreviation for *bēt buṣinni*, a lamp. The *bēt* is also omitted in *ADD* 964 rev. 15.

8: That this is approximately the correct rendering of the line is shown by a comparison with ND 3467, 23–4: PAP *an-nu-u ša ina* KASKAL-*šú*. Strictly it may be that *ša ana ḫūli-šu* should be read as a single unit, meaning roughly "expedition-materials", since otherwise the use of both *ša* and *ana* seems otiose.

10: For *ša kutalli* "a reserve" (not "substitute"), and for *ṣāb šarri* (soldier), I refer to my study of nA taxation and conscription.

Commentary

That portion of the tablet which is preserved lists two groups of contributions: in ll. 1–8 there are items "for his expedition", mostly quoted per day, but in the case of the oil, a once-for-all amount. In ll. 9–14, the man is said to receive 90 minas of copper and two amounts of corn per annum.

The background to this is too complex to be elucidated in full here, and it will be dealt with in my study of nA taxation and conscription. It will be shown there that this is probably a list of *ilku* contributions to be paid to a *rab kiṣri* or similar officer, for the maintenance of his regular corps and his reserves during the course of a year. Similar texts are ND 3467 (*Iraq* 15 (1953), Pl. XIII) and *ADD* 1095.

No. 142 Plate 56 ND 271
IM, for study

7·2 × (4·9) × (2·6) —

Governor's Palace, Room K.

Obv. (entirely lost)

B.E. 1′ $\frac{5}{6}$ MA.NA *a* ⌜*x*⌝[(*x x*)]
Rev. 2′ PAP 8 MA.NA 3-*su x*[
3′ *ša* 14 *ú-di-e*
4′ 1[(+*x*) M]A.NA 5-*su* AN.NA-*šú-nu*
5′ [(*x*) *x* MA].NA *ša* AN.NA *a-na* 4-*šú*
6′ [(*x*) *x* (*x*+)]1 MA.NA 3-*su* URUDU
7′ [ ]UD$^{?}$-*šú-nu*
(remainder of rev. broken)

Translation

1′: $\frac{5}{6}$ mina .... In all 8$\frac{1}{3}$ minas [.....], of 14 vessels, their tin being 1$^{?}\frac{1}{5}$ minas; [x min]as$^{?}$ of tin 4 times, [.....]1(+x) $\frac{1}{3}$ minas of copper, [.....] their .... [.........

Notes

1′: A possible restoration is A.BARAG (lead).

7′: Also .N]A could be restored after the break; if UD is right, however, then a word ending in *-tú* is probably required, e.g. *šaqultu* (unless KÙ].BABBAR).

Commentary

The breaks in the text make it impossible to restore the sense of the original, which is particularly aggravating, since the juxtaposition of copper and tin suggests that the scribe was noting the relative quantities of these metals in the fourteen vessels he mentions.

No. 143 Plate 56 ND 258(b)
Inst. Arch. London
(5·7) × 3·3 × (4·5) —

Governor's Palace, Room M.

1 KAK.ME

Translation

Nails (or: arrows).

Notes

The docket shows string impressions, and probably came from the neck of a large jar in which the nails or arrows were stored.

No. 144 Plate 57 ND 223
IM 56818
3·7 × 2·6 × 1·5 30.[—].711

Governor's Palace, Room K.

Obv. 1 3-*su* GUŠKIN
2 $\frac{5}{6}$ MA.NA *ša* 1 GÍN LÁ
3 m⌞*ba*⌟-*ṣi-id-qi-i*
4 *a-na* ⌞*ki*⌟-*ir-ki*
Rev. 5 iti[*x*] UD.30.KÁM
6 *lim-m*[*u* m]·dMAŠ.DU.IGI

Translation

1: $\frac{1}{3}$ (mina) of gold, $\frac{5}{6}$ minas minus 1 shekel—Baṣidqī, for rolls.

5: Month of [. . . .], 30th day, *limmu* of Ninurta-ālik-pāni (711 B.C.).

Notes

1–2: It is hard to see why these two amounts are not totalled (presumably to 1 mina $\frac{1}{6}$ minus 1 shekel). They may be from separate sources as in No. 148.

4: *kirku* is also found in No. 145; elsewhere it is used to describe rolls of papyrus or cloth (see *AHw* 468a), and possibly gold-leaf, which is almost unmanageable, was rolled to make it easier to control.

Commentary

This small " cigar-shaped " tablet, together with at least the next five, comes from the transactions of a certain Baṣidqī, who may well have been a goldsmith, but was certainly in charge of the operations of the goldsmiths. The texts probably all record the transfer of gold from one division of the administration to another.

No. 145 Plate 57 ND 221
Inst. Arch. London
17?.iii.710

3·9 × 2·2 × 1·8

Governor's Palace, Room K.

Obv.	1	2 GÍN GUŠKIN
	2	TA* ŠÀ *gi-za-a-ti*
	3	*a-na ki-ir-ki*
B.E.	4	*ša tam-lit*
Rev.	5	*ša ur-ki ša-ku?-ri*
	6	[it]iSIG$_4$ [UD].17?.[KA]M
	7	⌜*lim*⌝-*mu* m.dUTU.U.PAP

Translation

1: 2 shekels of gold, out of the clippings, for rolls for the inlay of the back of the .....
6: Month of Sīmānu (III), 17th [day], *limmu* of Šamaš-bēlu-uṣur (710 B.C.).

Notes

2: *gizzāti*: also in No. 148, 2, and, also clearly meaning gold " clippings " or scraps, in *ABL* 1458 rev. 5 and *ADD* 676 rev. 11 (both singular, *gizzutu*).
3: For *kirku* cf. note on No. 144, 4.
5: For the description of the purpose for which the gold is destined, cf. No. 149. The last sign is unclear, perhaps *ri* or *ti*; if *ša-ku-ri* is correct, this is nA for *šukurru*, and must refer to a spear emblem.

No. 146 No copy ND 222
[E]
—.xii+i.710

2·6 × 1·5 cm.

Governor's Palace, Room K.

Obv.	1	2 GÍN *a-na tam-lit*
	2	m*ba-ṣi-id-qi-i*
	3	itiDIRIG.ŠE

B.E. 4 *lim-mu*
Rev. 5 m.dUTU.U.PAP

N.B.—This tablet was assigned to the Expedition, but I have as yet been unable to trace it; fortunately, however, Professor D. J. Wiseman's rough copy shows all that is needed, and has been used to provide the transliteration given above.

Translation

1: 2 shekels for inlay—Baṣidqī.
3: Month of intercalary Addāru (XII+I), *limmu* of Šamaš-bēlu-uṣur (710 B.C.).

No. 147 Plate 57 ND 252(n)
IM, for study
3·0 × 2·0 × 1·3 11.i?.710

Governor's Palace, Room K.

Obv. (broken, except for final wedge of last line)
Rev. 1′ ⌜itiBARAG?⌝ UD.11.KAM
2′ *lim-mu* m.dUTU.U.PAP

Commentary

Both from its characteristic cigar shape, and from its date, this clearly belongs with the other gold dockets.

No. 148 Plate 57 ND 252(i)
IM, for study
3·9 × (2·2) × (1·4) [—]

Governor's Palace, Room K.

Obv. 1 [6? GÍ]N? ⌜KÙ⌝.[GI]
2 ⌜TA*⌝ ŠÀ *gi-za-[a-ti]*
3 4 GÍN.MEŠ TA* IGI m*aš-šur*-⌜DÙ?⌝
4 PAP 6-*su* KÙ.GI
Rev. (entirely broken)

Translation

1: [6 shekels] of gold, from out of the clippings, 4 shekels from Aššur-bā[ni(?)]. In all $\frac{1}{6}$ (mina) of gold.

Notes

1: The restoration of 6 shekels is based on the assumption that the one-sixth mina of l. 4 is equivalent to 10 shekels. If the mina in use were of 30 shekels only, we should have to restore here 1 shekel instead, but as yet I know of only the Tell Halaf passage (quoted above, note to No. 94, 17) which would lead us to posit the existence of a short mina.

2: For *gizzāti* see on No. 145, 2.

3: If the restoration of the name as Aššur-bāni is right, then he is probably the governor of Kalhu of that name, eponym for 713 B.C.

No. 149 Plate 57 ND 220
IM 56817
—

3·7 × 2·3 × 1·5

Governor's Palace, Room K.

Obv. 1 4-*tú* GUŠKIN TA* É ⌜(*x*) *x*⌝-*si*?
2 *a-na tam-lit ša pu-u-te*
3 *ša qi-im-me*
4 *ša né-me-di*
Rev. 5 10? ½ GÍN TA* ŠÀ *gi-za-ti*
6 *a-na tam-lit*
7 PAP ½ MA.NA 1? ½ GÍN LÁ
8 m*bi-ṣi-id-qi-i*

Translation

1: ¼ (mina) of gold from the house of ....., for the inlay of the front of the ..... of the throne?; 10? ½ shekels from out of the clippings for inlay.

7: In all, ½ mina minus 1½ shekels—Biṣidqī.

Notes

2: *pūtu*, "front": cf. *urku* "back" in No. 145, 5.

3: *qimmu* is an unknown word; any attempt to determine its meaning on the basis of this single occurrence would be futile, though one may suspect a relationship with *qimmatu*.

4: *nēmedu* (Ass. *nēmudu*) can be a throne or altar-base.

6: There are erasures at the end of this line.

7: This total does not agree with that expected, since a quarter mina should be 15, added to 10½, making 25½ shekels. The only way of juggling the figures to fit seems to be to read in l. 7 4'½ GÍN LÁ, which is just possible (collated).

No. 150 Plate 57 ND 274
Inst. Arch. London
—

3·6 × 2·0 × 1·5

Governor's Palace, Room K.

Obv. 1 1 *me kam-ma-t*[*e*]
2 30 *ia-ri*?-⌜*x*⌝
3 5 *sa-'u-ra-te*

B.E. 4 *dal-lul-te*
Rev. 5 ANŠE.KUR.[R]A

Notes

1: The word whose plural form is *kammāte* is given under *AHw* 433a, *kammu(m)* I, and translated " Schmuckplättchen ". However, in ND 11,305 (unpub., courtesy P. Hulin), the first line reads KUŠ *a-ri-tú ša kam-me-te*, which suggests that the nA singular form may rather be *kammutu*.

2: The shape of the sign after *ia* favours *ri*, but I cannot detect the extra vertical required. One naturally thinks of the word *(a)iaru* (*CAD* A Pt. 1, 229), but I cannot restore the final sign satisfactorily.

3: This word is found elsewhere in a list of booty taken by Assur-nāṣir-apli (*sa-'u-ru* (var. *-ri*) GUŠKIN *ša tam-li-te*, *AKA* 365), and in texts from Nineveh dealing with gold (*ADD* IV 317b), but as far as I know its exact meaning has not been established.

4: *dallulūtu*: here I think we must have the abstract noun " trappings ".

Commentary

The note lists three types of decoration for horses, presumably of gold, as it seems more than likely that it belongs with No. 151 in particular, and Nos. 144–9 as well.

No. 151 Plate 57 ND 225
IM 56820
—

3·5 × 1·7 × 1·2

Governor's Palace, Room K.

Obv. 1 37 *ka-ma-te!*
2 GUŠKIN
B.E. 3 *ša* SAG.DU ANŠE.⌞KUR⌟
(rev. uninscribed)

Translation

37 discs(?) of gold, for the head of a horse.

Notes

1: For *kammu* or *kammutu* see note on No. 150, 1.

No. 152 Plate 58 ND 245
Inst. Arch. London
—

4·8 × 8·1 × 2·3

Governor's Palace, Room K.

Obv. 1 6 [T]ÚG.GÚ.LÁ.M[EŠ]
2 5 túg*ma-ak-lil!*
3 *qàl-pu-te*
4 ⌞6 *qul?-pa?-ni?* KAD?⌟
(space)

5 1 ⸤^{túg}⸥*dáp-pa-as-tú* LÁ-*e*
6 1 ^{túg}*ma-ak-lul* LÁ-*e*
7 2 *qiri-me* LÁ-*e*
8 [1] *qiri-mu* GIBIL LÁ-*e*
B.E. 9 2? *k*[*i*?-]⸢*x*⸣*-pa-a-te* LÁ-*e*
10 ⸢2?⸣ *qiri-me* LÁ-*e* KAD
Rev. 11 ^{túg}*ma-*[*ak-lul*(?)] L[Á]-*e*
12 [*qà*]*l*?-*pu*
(remainder of rev. (uninscribed) shows textile impressions)

Translation

1: 6 wraps(?), 5 worn? shawls(?), 6 linen? . . . s.

5: 1 rug, missing; 1 shawl(?), missing; 2 . . . . s, missing; 1 new . . . ., missing; 2 . . . . . s, missing; 2? linen . . . s, missing; (1) sh[awl(?)], missing, [wor]n?.

Notes

1: TÚG.GÚ.LÁ is not listed in the usual sources, but is found in *PVA* 236 = *ḫu-la-nu*; it is referred to by A. Deimel, *ŠL* 106, 34, but I cannot find his other references to it. The logogram, which is not listed, except for the *PVA* passage, under *ḫullānu* by the dictionaries, is also found in *ADD* 957, 6 (2 GÚ.LÁ *ṣu-pu*); the word itself is quite well attested.

2: *maklelē* is the plural of *maklulu* already in mA (see *AHw* 590a); the form of the LIL is slightly, but not very, abnormal.

3: *qalpu*, literally " peeled " is well known as applied to textiles (*AHw* 895a), although not as yet in nA. My translation " worn " is an attempt to allow for the apparent contrast with *eššu* " new " in No. 155, col. v, 16–17. This contrast between GIBIL and *qalpu* is also found in VAT 8659 (K. Deller).

5: The meaning of LÁ-*e* " missing " in this and following lines is not doubtful, but the reading remains to be established. It seems that it is not an adjective, since it always appears either in the genitive or as a plural; hence I would suggest the word *muṭā'ū* (*AHw* 691b) as a candidate, so that the LÁ-*e* in each case would stand in apposition to the object missing. I believe that *muṭā'ū* is spelt logographically already in middle Assyrian times: LÁ.MEŠ in *KAJ* 112, 1. In nA S. Parpola refers me to the writings *mu-ṭe-e* in *LAS* 35, 11 and 58, 19, r. 4.

No. 153 Plate 58 ND 277
IM 56839
—

2·2 × 4·0 × 1·7

Governor's Palace, Room C.

Obv. (one line erased)
1 ⸢40?⸣[+*x*] *x* SA$_5$ KUR
2 32 *ša* IŠ *su-*⸢*ni*⸣
3 5 ,, NU *su-ni*
4 3 IB.MEŠ GÙN
5 45 AN.TA.[( )]
6 12 IB SA$_5$
B.E. 7 11 [K]I *ḫal*
8 [ ]

Rev. 9 2[ ]GÙN?
10 3[š]a *duk*?-*di*
11 3[ ]*x*
12 1 [ ]
13 2 *am*?[(*x*)]*x*
14 *ina* IGI m·dPA.⌜A?⌝.PAP

Translation

1 : 40[+x] red . . . . s ; 32 . . . . . s, with breast-piece ; 5 . . . . . s, without breast-piece ; 3 multi-coloured sashes(?) ; 45 " upper " garments ; 12 red sashes(?) ; 11 " lower " garments, rolled ; . . . . ; 2 multi-coloured . . . . . s ; . . . .

14 : — at the disposal of Nabû-aplu?-uṣur.

Notes

2 : cf. *ADD* 758, 8 : 2 *šá* IŠ 2 KI *ḫal*meš(!) GI6 ; this shows that the *ša* is syllabic, but there is no way of telling whether IŠ is too.

4 : (TÚG).IB(= DARÁ) is known from *PVA* 264 to be a writing for *nēbettu* (*AHw* 774a) ; the logographic writing is also found in *AfO* 17 (1954–6), p. 8, l. 18 (60 TÚG.IB.MEŠ *ša bi-ir-mu*), among a list of gifts (*nāmurāti*) sent to the king of Elam. This suggests that the GÙN here might well be read *ša birme*, a phrase which is used with other textiles in nA (see *PVA* 222, 266). TÚG.IB is presumably not to be confused with TÚG.ÍB.LÁ (= *nēbeḫu*), but confusion is introduced by the occurrence of a TÚG.IB.LÁ in *ADD* 953.ii.16 (coll.).

5 : (TÚG).AN.TA.(MEŠ) are quite well known (see *CAD* E 114a (s.v. *elû* B), and add *ADD* 683, 4) ; the reading is probably not *elû* but *elītu* (pl. *el(i)āti*), because of 9 TÚG *e-la-a-ti* in the same list of gifts to the king of Elam (*AfO* 17 (1954–6), p. 8, l. 16).

7 : KI *ḫal* : this is an abbreviation for TÚG.KI.TA.MEŠ (= *šapliāte?*, cf. TÚG.AN.TA.MEŠ) *ḫallupāte*, a frequently occurring item. For the singular, see TÚG.KI.TA *ḫal-lu-up-tú* (*ADD* 1095, 12) and 1 TÚG.KI *ḫal-up-tú* (*ADD* 956, 7) ; for the plural, see 2 TÚG.KI.TA.MEŠ *ḫal-lu-pat* (*ADD* 1040, 4) and various stages of abbreviation—*ADD* 974, 5 ; 977.iii.12 ; 956, rev. 3–4 (3 TÚG.KI *ḫal-pat bir-*[*še*]) ; 781, 4 (*ḫal-lu-pa*meš) ; 973.iii.3, 5 (singular or plural ?) ; ND 2687 (*Iraq* 23 (1961), Pl. XXIII), 9 (TÚG.KI.TA *ḫal- x - x*). Clearly *ḫalluptu* is a fem. adjective agreeing with TÚG.KI.TA ; other epithets attested are black (2 KI *ḫal*meš GI6, *ADD* 758, 8 (coll.), cf. 3) and white (*Iraq* 32 (1970), 154, No. 20, 1) ; cf. also 4 TÚG.KI.TA.MEŠ, VAT 8657 (quoted by K. Deller, *WZKM* 57 (1961), 37).

10 : *dukdu*, a type of fruit, seems out of place here ; cf. for the word G. van Driel, *The Cult of Aššur* 119 ad 21′.

No. 154 Plate 56 ND 461 + unn.
Inst. Arch. London
—

5·1 × (4·0) × 2·5

Governor's Palace, Room S.

N.B.—ND 461 has been joined to an unnumbered fragment in the Iraq Museum (IM, for study) ; the join has been confirmed with a cast of the Iraq Museum fragment, and the dimensions given above apply to the resulting piece.

Obv. 1 12 MA.NA [( )] KÙ.BABBAR
2 60 ANŠE [(*x x*)]*x an gi*

3 50 ANŠE [ ].MEŠ
4 PAP 1 *me* 10 ANŠE 1-BÁ[N?]-*a-a* [( )]
5 *ina* ŠÀ *kás-pi* *x*[*x* (*x* *x*)]

---

6 [ ]⌞4?⌟ AN[ŠE
(remainder of obv. and upper part of rev. broken)
Rev. 1′ [ ]52? ⌜TÚG?⌝.[
2′ [*x*] TÚG *gu-l*[*i*]-⌜*na-a-te*⌝
3′ [*x*] TÚG *dáp-pa-*[*s*]*a-a-te*
4′ [*x*] TÚG *bur?-*[*x* *x*] ḪÉ.MED
5′ ⌞*x*⌟ [TÚ]G *qa-*[( )]*-ra-ni*
T.E. 6′ [P]AP *an-ni-ú*
7′ *a-nu-ut* É
8′ *ša* uru*kal-ḫi*

Translation

1: 12 minas [( )] of silver, 60 homers of . . . . ., 50 homers of [. . . . .]—in all 110 homers, 1 *sūtu* each(?), in exchange for money [. . . . . . .].

Rev. 1′: [ ]52 [. . . .]-cloths, [x] cloaks(?), [x] rugs, [x] . . . .-cloths, of red wool, x . . . .-cloths—all this (is) the domestic equipment, of Kalhu.

Notes

2: The sign before *an-gi* is either *a*]*r* or *ri*; neither seems very helpful, and the obvious restoration *kurangu* is excluded.

Rev. 4′: For ḪÉ.MED (= *tabribu*) see note on No. 1, 6′.

5′: The only textile which might fit seems to be *qarrāru* (*AHw* 905b), but there does not appear to be space for the extra sign; however, the space available may be deceptive, since no actual join has been made.

Commentary

This is obviously an inventory of some kind, but the long break prevents a more accurate classification. On the obverse there are details of silver and land, and on the reverse the items listed are textiles, qualified as the equipment of a house in Kalhu, which clearly does not apply also to the items on the obverse.

No. 155 Plates 59–60; Photo Plate 91a

ND 459 + 450
BM 132012 (ND 459)
IM, for study (ND 450)
—

14·2 × (9·3) × 3·2 (ND 459)
(3·4) × (3·8) × 2·3 (ND 450)

Governor's Palace, Room S.

N.B.—The join has been checked and the copies united by means of a cast of ND 450 made for me by the Iraq Museum.

Obverse
Col. I 1 [ ]
2 [ ]⌜*x*⌝ [*x*] *u*[*r*]
3 [(*x* *x*) *x* m].d⌜PA?⌝.ZALÁG-*ka-la-*[*m*]*ur*

Obverse

Col. I

4 [( )] LÚ.ÌR.É.GAL
5 [(*x x*) *x* ${}^{\text{m.d}}$P]A?.ŠU^{ii}.DIB-*bat*
6 [ ]*x kap-ru*
7 [ ]*x x na?-ba*
8 [ ]*x x x x x*
9 [ ]*x* PAP-*u?-[n]i?*
10 [${}^{\text{m.d}}$*x*]-*rém-a-*⸢*ni*⸣ LÚ.NIMG[IR]
11 [ ]-*mal?-ka* LÚ.TÚG.ŠÈ[R]
12 [.B]ÀD?.EN-*ia* LÚ.ASGAB
13 [ ]^{m}*me?-ni-i*
14 [ ]*x* ⸢DUMU UD?.MEŠ⸣ 6 MÍ.MEŠ
15 [(*x*)*x*] LÚ.ZI.MEŠ

---

16 [5-B]ÁN(?) *ša* GIŠ.ŠE *ḫar-ṣu-te*
17 [ ]2? *ša* ,, 1 *ša* KASKAL?
18 [ ]⸤*ša*⸥ ${}^{\text{giš}}$*ṭar-pi-'i* [(*x*)]
19 [ ] ⸤*x*⸥ *šá* [(*x*)]
(remainder of column (? 3–4 lines) broken)

Col. II

1 [ ]*x x*
2 ⸢2?⸣[ ]
3 1 *x*[ ]*x*
4 6 GIŠ [(*x*) *x*]*x ša ma* ⸢*a?*⸣ [(*x*)]
5 1 GIŠ ⸢*x*⸣ -*nu* ⸤*x x x*⸥
6 *rit-ti* UR.MAḪ
7 2 GIŠ.É.ÚR
8 4? GIŠ.É.IÀ.MEŠ
9 4 GIŠ.GU KAL
10 2? ${}^{\text{giš}}$*na-as-re*
11 4 ${}^{\text{giš}}$*a-ri-a-te*
12 *ša ku-tal* ⸢É⸣ KI.KAL
13 12 ${}^{\text{giš}}$*kap-pe da[n]-nu-te*
14 *š[a] a-ka-li*
15 14 ,, QÀL.MEŠ
16 34 ${}^{\text{giš}}$*saḫ-ḫa-ra-a-te*
17 3 ${}^{\text{giš}}$*[k]ap-pe ša maš-q[i]-te*
18 ⸢5?⸣ GIŠ *šá kar ir dan-nu-te*
19 4 ,, QÀL.MEŠ
20 [ ]⸤*x x*⸥-*ni* KAL.MEŠ
(remainder of column (? 2–3 lines) broken)

Col. III

1 [ ]
2 2 *x*[ ]
3 6 ⸢*x x*⸣ [ ]
4 10 ,, *ṣ[u?-(x-)]-*⸢*pu*⸣-*te*

5 2 a-ga-⌜na⌝-te URUDU
6 ša maš-qi-te
7 2 da-a-le URUDU
8 3 na-ḫa-bi-⌞e⌟ URUDU
9 1 mu-sa-l[i-i]ḫ?-[t]ú? URUDU
10 3 áš-ḫe-l[e (x)] URUDU
11 1 qa-ab-ḫu [(x)] URUDU
12 1 mu-šá-ḫi-nu [U]RUDU
13 1 ZA.ḪUM [U]RU[DU]
14 3 šá A.MEŠ ŠU^{II}[URU]DU
15 2 qa-⌜bu⌝-a-te URUDU
16 1 ,, ša É ra-ma-[k]i
17 1 É bu-ṣi-ni URUDU
18 1 du-u-du URUDU
19 5 NAGAR.MEŠ [U]RUDU
20 ⌞1? mu⌟-li-⌜x⌝ URU[DU]
21 [ ]x
(remainder of column (? 2 lines) broken)

Col. IV
1 [ ]qa?-tú A[N.BAR]
2 [ ].MEŠ AN.B[AR]
3 4 k[a]l-la-pe AN.B[AR]
4 10! ḫa-[d]a?-ni A[N.BAR(?)]
5 3 ma-ṣ[a?-n]i? A[N.BAR(?)]
6 ša LÚ.S[IMUG(??)]
7 3 KAK AN.BA[R ( )]
8 3 ši-a?-r[e? (x) AN.BAR]
9 3 up sa ša x[ ]
10 1 ka-⌞si?⌟-mu[ ]
11 1?[ ]x-nu [AN.BA]R?
12 3[(x)]x zi [AN.B]AR
13 1[0?(+x) q]a?-šá-ni? ⌜AN.BAR⌝
14 3 ⌜mu⌝-tir-re AN.BAR
15 5 qa-az-pe AN.BAR
16 1 me 3 GAB.GUR AN.BAR
17 6-šú a-ru-ut-ḫe AN.BAR
18 5? ⌞in⌟-gal-a-te AN.BAR
19 2-te ṣib-ta-⌜te⌝ ⌞AN.BAR.KAL.ME⌟
20 3-šú ,, QÀL.M[E]Š
21 [ ]x [
(remainder of column (? 1 line) broken)

Reverse
Col. V
(upper part broken)
1′ [ ]-te?
2′ [ ]x x te

Reverse

Col. V	3′	[-]*ru-te*
	4′	[*ša(?)*] *la* ZAG
	5′	[ ] *ša* ⌞UGU⌟ [ ]*x*
	6′–9′	(traces only)
	10′	⌜1?⌝ TÚG.⌜AN⌝.TA[
	11′	*ša* ZAG.MEŠ [( )]
	12′	5? TÚG.KAD.MEŠ [( )]
	13′	4 TÚG *šá-di-ni* KAD.[MEŠ]
	14′	4 TÚG [SA]GŠU.MEŠ *qàl(!)-pu(!)-te*
	15′	[ ]*x ki-ra-te*
	16′	[ ] GIBIL.MEŠ
	17′	⌜10⌝ ,, *qàl-pa-te*
Col. VI		(traces only; insufficient survives even to determine the type of object listed)
Col. VII		(3–5 lines broken)
	1′	⌜2⌝ GIŠ[?
	2′	2 [G]IŠ[?
	3′	3 GIŠ *x*[
	4′	24? *x*[
	5′	*š[a*
	6′	2 Z[A]G?.MEŠ [
	7′	*x x* [
	8′	1[(*x*) *x*] *ša* GIŠ MAN? *x*[( )]
	9′	[ ]3 *ki-ṣir*^{meš}
	10′	[ ]*rat*? ^{meš}
	11′	⌜2?⌝ GIŠ É *k[i-*
	12′	*ša* [*x*] ERÍN [
	13′	[(*x*)] ŠU? *n[a*?
	14′–16′	(broken)
	17′	[ ].MEŠ
Col. VIII	1′	[GIŠ.ŠAR(?)] Ú.SAR
	2′	[$^{ur]u}$*kal-ḫi*
		———
	3′	[ ]*x-u*
	4′	[ ]UD BE A KU?
		———
	5′	⌜4 MÍ.MEŠ⌝ ⌞1 DUMU⌟ 1 DUMU.MÍ
	6′	PAP 6 ZI ⌜*ša*⌝ ⌞$^{m.d}$ENŠADA(?)-*rém*?-*ni*?⌟
	7′	GIŠ.ŠAR *ša* ^{giš}*til-lit*
	8′	*ina* URU(?) É? *x x x*
		(space)
	9′	(undeciphered)

Translation

(Since so much of the text consists of untranslateable items, those lines which can be translated are included in the notes below.)

Notes

i.2 : Probably the end of a PN.

3–4 : Nabû (or less likely : Ninurta-)nūr-ka-lāmur, palace slave.

5 : Nabû-qātā-ṣabat.

6 : It is unclear whether]*kapru* belongs to Nabû-qātā-ṣabat's title, or is part of another PN.

9 : PN :]ahūni(?).

10 : PN :]-rēmāni, the herald.

11 : PN :]-malka?, the tailor(?) ; instead of *mal* also epigraphically possible is *uš*.

12 : PN :]-dūr-bēliya, the leather-worker.

14–15 : These lines probably give the total of the dependants of the men mentioned above by name : [x] weaned boys, 6 women, [in all, x] persons. DUMU.UD (= *pir*) is a common abbreviation for *pirsu* " weaned child ", e.g. ND 2744 (*Iraq* 23 (1961), Pl. XXIV), 5 ; ND 2497 (ibid., Pl. XVIII), 7 ; and *ADB* often.

16 : I can only interpret this as GIŠ.ŠE = ŠE.GIŠ.IÀ and *ḫarṣūte* = *ḫalṣūte*.

17 : KASKAL possibly rather BI (= KAŠ, beer).

ii.6 : " (with) lion's feet "—clearly the object listed in ii.5 is a piece of furniture with legs.

7 : For GIŠ.É.ÚR I can only compare TÚG.É.ÚR.MEŠ (? = *meḫṣūtu*), *PVA* 285, and this does not assist the translation.

8 : Presumably an oil container of some kind.

9 : " 4 large chairs ", if GIŠ.GU is an abbreviation for GIŠ.GU.ZA.

11–12 : " 4 shields, (which are) behind the fortified(?) house " ; *dannutu* (**dannatu*) is used in neo-Assyrian times for a fortress, but as far as I know, the compound *bēt danniti* is not known.

13–15 : " 12 large eating bowls, 14 small ditto ".

16 : For the vessel *sa/iḫḫāru* see recently K. Deller, *WZKM* 57 (1961), 34.

17 : " 3 drinking bowls ".

18 : Even emending the *ir* in this line to *ni*(!) would not yield a known item.

iii.4 : *ṣuppu* : see K. Deller, *OrNS* 33 (1964), 95 ; probably " polished " or " smoothed ".

5–6 : " 2 copper drinking basins ".

7 : " 2 copper buckets ".

8 : " 3 copper pails ".

9 : " 1 copper sprinkling vessel ".

10 : " 3 copper boxes(?) " ; the word *ašḫulu* (**ašḫalu*) has a long history, but is also found in *PVA* 447 (of bronze). The possibility of reading *ma-ḫe-le* (from *maḫḫalu* (*AHw* 582b) was considered but rejected.

11 : *qab/pḫu* : this reference is quoted *AHw* 886b. The word is almost certainly found also in *PVA* 452 (*x-ap-ḫu*), where the initial sign can very well be a [*q*]*a*.

12 : " 1 copper brazier ".

13 : ZA.ḪUM : cf. *PVA* 451 : [Z]A.ḪUM „ (= UD.KA.BAR) = *šá-a-ḫu* ; see also for nA B. Parker, *Iraq* 23 (1961), 34 (also Alalakh references), and for the earlier periods A. Deimel, *ŠL* 586.122, and H. Limet, *Métal*, p. 233, No. 153. The reading ZA.ḪUM is indicated by the entry *dug.za.ḫu.um* (*MSL* VII, 200.41), and it is possible that the word is an Akkadian loan into Sumerian, and the same word that became *šá-a-ḫu* in nA.

14 : " 3 water-vessels (with) copper handles ".

15–16 : " 2 copper beakers, 1 ditto for the bathroom ".

17–18 : " 1 copper lamp, 1 copper kettle ".

19 : " 5 copper ' carpenters ' " ; there does not appear to be any suitable meaning or reading of NAGAR.

20 : A possible, though not probable, restoration is 1 *mu-li-lum* URUDU ; cf. for *mullilu*(*m*) " cleaner " *AHw* 670b (mainly cultic).

iv.3: *kalappu* is not usually spelt with a double *l*, but the meaning "pick(-axe)" is suitable.

4: 10! is written over an erased 9; for the object cf. perhaps *ḫadānu* ("ein Gerät", *AHw* 307a).

5–6: The object, if correctly restored, is unknown; the reading of S[IMUG] "smith" is of course a mere guess.

7: "3 iron nails/arrows".

8–13: Various unknown utensils.

14: "3 iron fire-rakes(?)" (so *AHw* 688a "eine Schürstange").

15: *qas/zpu*: *AHw* 906a quotes only this instance.

16: The identity of GAB.GUR is unknown to me; it is less likely but possible that we should read MU.GUR.

17: A third instance of the word *aruthu*; the writing 6-*šú* is probably intended to convey a multiplicative (W. von Soden, *GAG* § 71a), and indicates that *aruthē* is used in the plural, which explains why the final sign is still *-ḫi* when only one is mentioned (cf. *CAD* A Pt. 2, 324a). We should therefore render "6 sets/pairs of *aruthē*" (cf. note on iv.19–20).

18: "5 iron tablets" (? = ingots).

19–20: "2 sets of large iron chains(?), 3 sets of small ditto"; *ṣibtāti* is probably the nA for the known nB *ṣibtētu* (*CAD* Ṣ 158a). This may support the interpretation of *ṣib/ptu* (written MÁŠ) as a "chain" and not a "setting" (see *Iraq* 32 (1970), 157 ad l. 7).

v.10′–11′: "1 (or 4) 'upper garments', with arms [red(?)]"; for TÚG.AN.TA see note on No. 153, 5. ZAG = *aḫu* "arm or sleeve of a garment", and is most often followed by DIR ("red", so SA_5) which is often misunderstood as KAL (e.g. by me, *Iraq* 32 (1970), 154); see references *CAD* A Pt. 1, 209a. Occasionally, however, it is qualified by GI_6 ("black"), e.g. *ADD* 682, 3; 684, 1–2.

12′–13′: "5 linen cloths, 5 linen . . . . . s"; *šaddinu* is of course well known, but its exact meaning is not yet established.

14′: "14 worn(?) hats"; for *qalpu* cf. note on No. 152, 3.

15′–16′: "[x] new [. . . .]s, 10 worn(?) ditto"; this seems to give the contrasting pair "new" and "worn" (*qalpu*), cf. note on No. 152, 3.

vii: (wooden items; none clearly identifiable).

viii.1′–2′: ". . . . a vegetable-[garden(?) in (?)] Kalhu".

3′–4′: Traces perhaps in l. 4′ of a PN.

5′–6′: "4 women, 1 son, 1 daughter, in all 6 persons of Nusku(?)-rēmāni(?)".

7′–8′: "a vineyard in the village? of . . . . .".

9′: It would be possible to read the beginning of a date in this line: ⌞UD.16?.KAM⌟, but I can still not interpret the ensuing traces.

Commentary

This long inventory is regrettably much less useful than it would have been complete, since it has lost any introduction it may have had, while the final lines are also unclear. The items listed are quite logically arranged, each major category seeming to occupy about one column: people (i) and edibles(?), also (i); wooden tools and vessels (ii); "copper" vessels, etc. (iii); iron objects (iv); textiles (v); Col. vi is lost; more wooden items of uncertain character (vii); and then perhaps again persons, and land (viii).

No. 156 Plate 58 ND 422
IM 56844
—

4·2 × 2·6 × 1·9

Governor's Palace, Room S.

Obv. 1 É 15? ANŠE 3-BÁN ŠE!.NUMUN

2 *qa-qu-ru ra-qu*
3 *qa-ab-si* URU
(rev. uninscribed)

Translation

An estate of 15? homers 3 *sūtu* of arable land, empty ground within the town.

Notes

2: *qaqquru raqu* presumably means " bare, unbuilt on, ground ".

No. 157 Plate 58 ND 458
IM, for study
—

(3·3) × (1·7) × 1·6

Governor's Palace, Room S.

Obv. (beginning broken)
1′ [ ]ANŠE ^{uru}*sip?-r*[*u*
2′ [ ] SAG [
3′ [ ]10 ^{uru}*ar-rak?*[-
4′ [ ]ANŠE ^{uru}*ki-d*[*i?*
Rev. 5′ [ ]ANŠE ^{uru}*ša-sa-*[
6′ [ ]PAP 40 ^{m}DUMU?.*x*[
7′ [*x*+]4? ANŠE ^{uru}*ḫar-*BE-*x*[
(remainder broken)

Notes

3′: Possibly Arrakdi (in the Sulaimaniyah area).
7′: For place names beginning Harbe- or Harbat-, see S. Parpola, *AOAT* 6, 149–50, and *RGD* No. 27, 8, and 19–20.

Commentary

A note, probably not much bigger when complete than the surviving fragment, listing areas of land and persons associated with them in some way.

No. 158 Plate 56 ND 256
Inst. Arch. London
[—].i.[—]

4·9 × 3·1 × 2·4

Governor's Palace, Room K.

Obv. 1 13 *x*[
2 *x*[
(remainder of obv. broken)

Rev. 1 6 *be*? *ma*? *lul*?
2 *ša* 60? KUŠ.MEŠ
3 *a-na* [(*x*) *x* B]AR?.RA
4 IGI m*la*?-⌜*x* (*x*)⌝-*a*
T.E. 5 itiBARAG[
6 m.d[

Commentary

Note apparently concerned with leather skins (rev. 2), and possibly even witnessed (rev. 4).

No. 159 Plate 61 ND unn.
IM, for study
—

(2·1) × (2·8) × 1·6

Governor's Palace, room uncertain.

Obv. (beginning broken)
1′ ⌜*x*⌝[
2′ ŠE *k*[*i*-
3′ *ša* m[

4′ *lu*?[
B.E. 5′ [
6′ *ḫi-x*[
Rev. 7′ m15[?.

8′ 2 *qa* [
9′ ⌜*x*⌝[
10′ 50 [
11′ ⌞PAP?⌟ [
(remainder broken)

Commentary

Presumably an administrative note concerning issues or receipts of corn and perhaps other commodities.

No. 160 Plate 56 ND 449
IM, for study
—

(4·6) × (5·0) × (2·5)

Governor's Palace, Room S.

Obv.(?) (entirely lost)
Rev.(?) 1′ [ ]*x* [ ]

2′ [(*x*) *x*. ME]Š? *ša* ANŠE.NITÁ
(space)
3′ PAP 24 UD LÁ ⌞*x x*⌟ [(*x*)]
4′ 25 MA.NA *x*[*x* (*x x*)]
(remainder blank to break)

Commentary

Nature of text quite uncertain.

No. 161 Plate 61 ND 457
IM, for study
(3·6) × (4·9) × 2·5 —

Governor's Palace, Room S.

(Surface cracked and worn; mention of "purchased men" (LÚ.ŠÁM.MEŠ) in A.3 and B.5′, but nature of text uncertain.)

No. 162 Plate 56 ND 412
Inst. Arch. London
(3·6) × (3·7) × 2·1 —

Governor's Palace, Room S.

(Note with the beginnings of four PNs preserved; reverse uninscribed.)

No. 163 Plate 61 ND 224
IM 56819
3·6 × 2·0 × 1·4 —

Governor's Palace, Room K.

(Obverse destroyed except for end of one line; B.E.: ⌜*at*⌝-*ta-nu*; reverse blank. The size, and ND number of this piece suggest that it may belong with Nos. 144–51.)

No. 164 Plate 61 ND 226
IM, for study
3·4 × (2·0) × 1·5 —

Governor's Palace, Room K.

(Obverse remains of three lines (l. 3′: *ta-ad-ni*); reverse uninscribed. Like No. 163 this may belong with Nos. 144–51.)

No. 165 Plate 25 ND unn.
IM, for study
(3·0) × (5·4) × (2·2) —

(Fragment from right of ? administrative text; provenance uncertain.)

No. 166 Plate 61 ND 431(c)
Inst. Arch. London
(1·9) × (2·7) × (1·1) —

Governor's Palace, Room S.

(Fragment from centre of an administrative or epistolary text ?)

No. 167 Plate 61 ND unn.
IM, for study
(1·7) × (1·2) × (0·6) —

(Fragment from centre of an administrative or epistolary text; cf. in l. 2′: *e*]-*gír*-*t*[*i*.)

No. 168 Plate 61 ND 406(b)
Inst. Arch. London
(2·0) × (1·9) × (1·3) —

Governor's Palace, Room S.

(Fragment from B.E.; found with ND 403–5 (Nos. 208–9, 212); type uncertain.)

No. 169 Plate 61 ND 406(c)
Inst. Arch. London
(1·9) × (1·2) × (1·8) —

Governor's Palace, Room S.

(As No. 168.)

No. 170 Plate 62; Photo Plate 95c ND 252(k)
IM, for study
(4·2) × (3·8) [—.—].808?

Governor's Palace, Room K/M.

One large and one small fragment of a sealing, with inscribed cylinder and stamp seal impressions, and cuneiform text. For the seal impressions see Appendix.

Inscribed text

UD.*x*+]4.KÁM [*l*]*im-me* $^{m(!).d}$MAŠ.M[AŠ.DI]NGIR-*a*[$^{?}$-*a*]

Seal inscription

1 [( ) K]IŠIB [^{m}]EN.LÁ.DINGIR-*m*[*a*]
2 [( )] *šá* S[AG] *šá* ^{m}U.[ER]ÍN.GA[B]
3 [MAN ŠÁR *šá-kìn*] ^{uru}*kal-*[*ḫi*]
4–5 (broken)
6 [-*k*]*a*
7 [ ]*pa*$^{?}$

Notes

For the name of the *limmu* no other reading seems possible; Nergal-ilāya was eponym for 817 and again in 808, which is clearly to be preferred here.

The seal inscription is to be restored after No. 66 and No. 171 q.v.

No. 171 Plate 62; Photo Plate 95a–b ND 240(b)
Inst. Arch. London
(4·7) × (5·9) × (2·2) 13?.[—.—]

Governor's Palace, Room K.

One large and one small (1·7 × 1·8 cm.) fragment of a sealing, impression on back, of object sealed, broken away. As with No. 170, the clay bears the impression of both an inscribed cylinder seal (three or more times), and a stamp seal. Presumably it was also inscribed similarly, as the remains of a day date survive: UD.]13$^{?}$.KÁM [.

Seal inscription

The seal is the same as that impressed on No. 170 and No. 66 (see p. 248 for the design). Three different parts of the inscription survive here (ll. 3–5, 6–7, and l. 1), while No. 170 has ll. 1–3 and 6–7, and No. 66 has parts of all seven lines. Making use of the combined evidence of all these, the reconstructed inscription runs:

1	KIŠIB ^{m}EN.LÁ.DINGIR-*ma*	Seal of Bēl-tarṣi-iluma,
2	*šá* SAG *šá* ^{m}U.ERÍN.GAB	eunuch of Adad-nirārī,
3	MAN ŠÁR *šá-kìn* ^{uru}*kal-ḫi*	king of the world, governor of Kalhu,
4	[S]AG$^{?}$ KUR *te-me-ni*	[. . .]. . of *māt* Temeni,
5	[KUR *i*]*a-lu-na*	(and) Ialūna;
6	*at-kal-ka*	I have trusted on you,
7	*a*[*-a-ba*(?)]-*áš* ^{d}PA	may I not be put to shame, o Nabû.

In l. 4 the traces at the beginning of the line as preserved resemble the end of a DI or a SAG (i.e. a PA preceded by a vertical); traces are also visible on No. 171 of l. 7 which may confirm the suggested restoration. Similar phrases are found elsewhere, but not, as far as I can see, this exact one.

It may cause surprise that this inscription only associates Bēl-tarṣi-iluma with Kalhu, *māt* Temeni, and Ialūna, whereas his Nabû temple statue inscriptions mention also Hamedi and Sirgāna (I *R* 35.2). However, if the date of 808 B.C. for No. 170 is correct, the seal was already in use very early in Adad-nirārī's reign, and Bēl-tarṣi-iluma's provincial domain may have been much smaller than it later became.

No. 172 | Plate 62; Photo Plate 96e | ND 275(a)
Inst. Arch. London
(5·0) × (5·0) × 2·8 | [—]

Governor's Palace, Room K.

Fragment of a sealing with cylinder seal impression; the upper side is gently rounded and the underside flat, probably with wood impressions where preserved. There is nothing to show whether the label bore an inscribed text like No. 173, which is similar and has the same seal.

Seal inscription

1: [*šá*] ^{m}M[A]N.BÀ[D]; 2: [^{lú}]*šá-kìn*; 3: [^{uru}]*kal-ḫi*. This identifies the seal as that of Šarru-dūrī, on whom see above, p. 11. The restoration of the inscription is confirmed by the impression of the same seal on No. 132, which has the text: 1: [*š*]*á* ^{m}[ ]; 2: [^{l}]^{ú}*š*[*á-kìn*]; 3: [^{u}]^{ru}*kal*-[*ḫi*]. For the seal design, see Appendix on No. 173.

No. 173 | Plate 62; Photo Plate 96a–b | ND 275(k)
Inst. Arch. London
(7·0) × (4·0) × (2·2) | [—]

[Governor's Palace, Room K.]

Fragment of a clay label with the impression of the same cylinder seal as is found on No. 172. No part of the inscription of the seal here survives, but at the edge of the fragment there are the traces of two inscribed signs which show that the label bore a cuneiform inscription. On the underside of the fragment there is the impression of a flat surface rising at the centre to a knob or neck (see Photo Plate 96b). Another fragment is stored with this one (dimensions (3·3) × (2·9) × (2·3)), since it carries the same impression on the underside; no impression or inscription survives on its upper surface.

No. 174 | Plate 63 | ND 479(c)
IM, for study
c. (4·0) × (2·1) | [—.—].733?

Governor's Palace, Room K.

Fragment from the end of a legal(?) text, with the remains of the date only: [*limmu* m*aš-š*]*ur*?-KAL-*an-ni x*[ ] (Aššur-da'inanni, eponym for 733 B.C.).

No. 175 Plate 63 ND 252(q)
IM, for study
26.i.726?

(6·0) × (3·9) × (2·3)

Governor's Palace, Room K/M.

As with No. 174, fragment with remains of date only:

1′ [it]i⌜BARAG⌝ UD.26.KÁM [( )]
2′ ⌞*lim*⌟-*mu* m.d[ŠÚ].EN.PAP LÚ.[

No. 176 Plate 63 ND 252(o)
IM, for study
[—]

(3·7) × (3·2) × (0·9)

Governor's Palace, Room K/M.

Fragment with parts of two lines; the script, which is large and clear, and the flatness of the surface, mark it out as probably a fragment from an early eighth century legal text, similar e.g. to No. 65 (in appearance).

No. 177 Plate 63 ND unn.
IM, for study
[—]

(2·8) × (2·6) × (0·8)

Small fragment, possibly from a legal document concerning a house; it comes from the top of the tablet's reverse, but the signs preserved cannot be easily fitted into the normal legal formulae.

No. 178 Plate 63 ND unn.
(IM 56831)
[—]

Fragment from the same box as No. 92 (IM 56831, with which it is now), but not part of the same tablet; probably legal (*i-da*]-*bu-u*[*b*).

No. 179 Plate 63 ND 275(l)
Inst. Arch. London
[—]

(2·0) × (1·8) × (1·0)

[Governor's Palace, Room K.]

Perhaps a fragment from a legal text.

No. 180 Plate 64 ND unn.
IM, for study
—

4·0 × (4·0) × 1·5 (main fragment)

[Governor's Palace, Room S.]

Obv. 1 *a-na* LUGAL EN-*iá*
2 ⌞ÌR⌟-*ka* ^{m}*ḫu-na-a-nu*
3 [*aš-š*]*ur* ^{d}UTU *a-na* [LUGAL] EN-*iá lik-ru-bu*
4 [*š*]*a*$^{?}$ É [(*x*) *x*] *e*$^{?}$-*ri-ši*
5 [*tè*$^{?}$-]*e*$^{?}$-*mu a*-⌜*ra*⌝-*ši-ma*
6 [ ]*x* [ ]⌞*x* (*x*) *x*⌟ S[I]G$_5$ *a-dan-niš*
7 [ ]*i-ta-aḫ-za*
8–10 (traces at end of lines only)
(remainder of obv. broken)

Rev. 1′ [ ] *ta*$^{?}$
2′ [ ]*al-k*[*an*$^{?}$]-*ni*
3′ [ ]*x-ni* : *šá* LUGAL ⌜EN?⌝
4′ [*i*]*š*$^{?}$-*pur-a-ni*
5′ *a-na-ku* ŠU^{ii}-*a-a*
6′ *i-se-šú-nu a-ta-la-ka*
7′ É *i*-[*b*]*a-šu-u-ni*
8′ *i-su*-[*u*]*k* SUM-*u-ni*
9′ ŠE.AL *šá* LUGAL EN *i-di-nu-ni*
T.E. 10′ É : *i-ba-šu-ni la* SUM
11′ É *la-šu-u-ni a-ti-di-ni*

Unplaced fragment a′ *iš*]-⌜*pur-a*⌝-[*ni*
b′]*kal*$^{?}$: *a-t*[*i*$^{?}$-
c′] *a-t*[*i*$^{?}$-

Translation

1: To the king, my lord, your servant Hunānu; may Assur (and) Šamaš bless [the king] my lord.

4: [. . . . .] . . . . is cultivated?; I shall take a dec[ision?] . . . . is very good. [. . . . . . .] he has taken [. . . . . . .

Rev. 3′: ..... the ....] of which the king my lord wrote to me—I went along with them in person, (and) wherever there was (any) they would assign and give (it) to me, (and as for) the ....-corn which the king my lord had given me—wherever there was (some already) I did not give (any out), (but) wherever there was none, I gave (some out).

Notes

2: For the PN cf. Billa No. 72, 24 (*JCS* 7 (1953), 170) ^{m}*ḫu-na-a-ni*.

Rev. 5′: *qātāya* is used in this way in NL 31 (*Iraq* 18 (1956), 47), 9–10: *a-na-ku* ŠU^{ii}-*a-a ina* UGU ÍD *at-tu-rid*, doubtless correctly rendered by Saggs " I personally . . ." ; so also in a similar context *qa-ta-a-a*, *ABL* 138 rev. 8, 638, 3 (ŠU.MEŠ-*a-a*).

8′: For *issuku iddunūni* (ventive, not subjunctive); present, since preterite is excluded in a main clause (S. Parpola).

9′: The logogram ŠE.AL is not found in the lists, but does occur in TH No. 58 (*AfO Beiheft* 6, 38–9), where quite large quantities are recorded. That text and the occurrence here suggest that the logogram does not so much describe a rare and exotic type of grain, as define the use to which it was put, just as ŠE.PAD.MEŠ is used to indicate that the corn is for eating. ŠE.AL may therefore be a typical nA abbreviation for the word *aldû*, attested so far only in old Babylonian and meaning corn set aside for seed and other purposes. Also possible (coll.): ŠE *tab*+*ku* (S. Parpola).

a′–c′: Although this fragment does not actually join, it is certainly from the same tablet, probably from the upper part of the reverse.

Commentary

This is the only letter addressed *to* the king, and as it is written very well on fine clay, it should possibly be kept separate from the rest of the archive. Hunānu, the writer, although otherwise unknown, is clearly an official, and since he writes to the king on at least two different subjects, we are justified in assuming that he was quite highly placed in the administration.

No. 181 Plate 64 ND 426
Inst. Arch. London
—

2·9 × 4·5 × 2·0

Governor's Palace, Room S.

Obv. 1 ⌜*a*⌝-*bat* LUGAL
2 *a-na* ^{lú}[*um*?]-⌞*ma*-⌟*ni*
3 *ša* ^{uru}*kal-ḫi*
4 *x x x x*
5 [*x*]*x ka*
6 [(*x*) *x*] *ka*
7 [*t*]*a-dan*
8 ⌞8?⌟ *qa* ŠE *ki-su-*⌜*tu*⌝
9 ⌞*a-na*?⌟ 1-*a*[?-*a*?]
B.E. 10–11 (broken)
Rev. 12–13 (broken)
14 ^{m}UD?[
15 ⌜*ša*? *x* (*x*)⌝ *be ši*

Rev. 16 *ša* S[A]L?
17 *ta-d[a]-na*
18 *bi-ti-[i]q-tú*
19 [*ša(?)*] Ú.ME?
20 [*la(?)*] *ta-da-na*

Translation

1: The king's command to the scribe? of Kalhu: ....
5: Your [.....] your? [.....] give! [Give(?)] 8? *qa* of fodder [to each] one? [.....
15: Give ... for ..... (and?) for a woman?; [(but) do not(?)] give the loss on plants(?)!

Notes

2: If *ummānu* is correctly restored, it must be used here for "scribe", and we should compare the well-known "city-scribe" (LÚ.A.BA URU). Whether this allows us to identify the logogram A.BA with *ummānu* cannot be discussed here, though it seems distinctly possible.

4–6: Possibly restore (with S. Parpola): 4: *š[ùl-mu] ia-ši!*. 5: [*lìb-b]a-ka*. 6: [*lu ṭa-ab]-ka*, but collation does not favour *ia-ši* in l. 4.

18: *bitiqtu* is probably also to be recognized for nA in ND 2386+ (*Iraq* 23 (1961), Pl. XI), iii.24′; commoner in nA (though perhaps in fact the same word) is *batiqtu* "losses" (e.g. in battle).

19: Examples of Ú.ME(Š) = "assorted plants", which is a typical nA term, will be given in my study on nA taxation; it is hardly necessary to stress that the restoration and consequently the translation are exceedingly hypothetical.

No. 182 Plate 65 ND 435
IM 56847
—

3·6 × 2·3 × 1·6

Governor's Palace, Room S.

Obv. 1 *a-b[at]* LUGAL
2 *a-n[a]* mŠU.DINGIR-*gab-bu*
3 *ša* [u]ru*kal-ḫa*
4 ⌜3 *lim*⌝ ŠE.PAD.MEŠ
5 *ina qa-ab-si*
B.E. 6 [K]UR? *ša? pi-te-ka*
7 *i-ma-du-du*
Rev. 8 [(*x*)]*x ma ḫa ru x x*
9 [*ina*] UGU EN-*i-ka*
10 [*liš-ṭ]u?-ru*
(space for one further line but probably uninscribed)

Translation

1: The king's command to Qāt-ili-gabbu of Kalhu:
4: They will measure out 3,000 (homers) of corn inside the palace?, under your authority(?). ..... [Let them] write (it) on your master's account.

Notes

8: Possibly, with S. Parpola, a form of *maḫāru*—" pay out (and) receive ", like *nadānu* + *maḫāru*.

9: " your lord " is probably the governor of Kalhu, as whose deputy Qāt-ili-gabbu was acting in his absence.

No. 183 Plate 65; Photo Plate 92e ND 440
IM 56850

3·4 × 6·1 × 2·0 —

Governor's Palace, Room S.

Obv. 1 *a-bat* LUGAL
2 *a-na* ^{m}EN.KAL-*an*
3 Ú.ZÀ.ḪI.LI.SAR
4 SIG$_{5}$.MEŠ
5 *ša* ^{uru}*za-ban*
6 *ina* ^{uru}*ši-iš-li*
7 *ina* ^{uru}*ḫar-ḫum-ba*
8 *lu ma-a'-da*
9 *le-ru-šu*
10 *ki*? [*x*] *x -an-ni*
11 [*x x x*]-*mar*
Rev. 12 [(*x*) *x ma*]-*a'*(?)-*da*?
13 [ ]*x*
(remainder uninscribed)

Translation

1: The king's command to Bēl-dān:

3: Let them cultivate good Zabban cress? in Šišlu and in Harhumba, much of it ..... (remainder too broken for translation).

Notes

3: S. Parpola tells me that this writing of *saḫlû* (with both Ú as determinative and SAR as post-determinative) is regular.

6: For the town Šišlu see *Iraq* 32 (1970), 139; the reading of the name Har(i)humba in this line was established in *AOAT* 6, 151.

No. 184 Plate 65 ND 444
IM 56853

3·7 × 5·9 × 2·3 —

Governor's Palace, Room S.

Obv. 1 ⌜*a-bat* LUGAL⌝
2 *a-na* ^{m}EN.KAL-*an*

Obv. 3 *šùl-mu ia-a-ši*
4 *lìb-ba-ka*
5 *lu ṭa-ab-ka*
6 *šu-uḫ* UN.MEŠ
7 [*š*]*a taš-pur-an-ni*
8 [*g*]*ab-bu a-n*[*a*?-*ka*?]
(one to two lines broken)
Rev. 1′ [ ]⌜*ša*?⌝[( )]
2′ [TA(?)] ⌜uru *ši*/*pi-ku-ki*?⌝ [( )]
3′ [*ú*]-*ṣ*[*u*]-*ni-n*[*i*?]
4′ [*gab*]-*bu šu-ṭur*
5′ ⌜*ša*⌝ [*pa*]-*né-e-ka*(!)
6′ *lu šá* KI-*ia*
7′ [*ki*?-]*ma*? *at-tal-ka*(!)
8′ [*lu*(?) *ina p*]*a-né-e-a*
(remainder broken; perhaps uninscribed)

Translation

1: The king's command to Bēl-dān; I am well, may your heart be glad.

6: About the people of whom you wrote to me, all (of them) ..... here? [.......... Those(?)] Rev. 1′: who? came [out of] the town of .....—write (them) all down, 5′: (both) those under you and those with me. 7′: [When?] I come [let them(?)] be under me [..........

Notes

Rev. 8′: An alternative restoration is [*ša ina p*]*anēya*, " [those] under me ".

Commentary

Clearly the background to this letter is the matter of the distribution of captives from a military campaign who had " come out " of a besieged settlement (cf. the use of **wṣ*' in No. 195, and perhaps also No. 187 A Rev. 3′). It is particularly sad therefore that the name of the place is lost.

No. 185 Plate 66 ND 437
BM 132000

3·6 × 7·0 × 2·2 —

Governor's Palace, Room S.

Obv. 1 ⌜*a-bat* LUGAL⌝
2 *a-na* ᵐMAN.BÀD
3 *šul-mu ia-a-ši*
4 ŠÀ-*ka* ⌜*lu*⌝ DÙG.GA-*ka*
5 *am-mar* ERÍN.MEŠ.MAN-*ni*
6 *gab-bu ša ina* IGI-*ka*

7 1 ANŠE-*a-a* ŠE.PAD.MEŠ
8 *di-na-áš-šú-nu*
9 3-BÁN-*a-a a-na* ZÍD.KASKAL.MEŠ-*šú-nu*
10 ⌞*liš-ši-ú*⌟
B.E. (broken; but probably uninscribed)
Rev. 11 ⌜7-BÁN-*a-a*⌝
12 *ina* IGI UN.MEŠ-*šú-nu*
13 *lu-ra-am-me-u*

Translation

1: The king's command to Šarru-dūrī; I am well, may your heart be glad:

5: Give to all the "king's-troops" who are under you 1 homer of corn each. 9: Let them take 3 *sūtu* each as their campaign-flour, (and) leave 7 *sūtu* each at the disposal of their families.

Notes

5: ERÍN.MEŠ.MAN-*ni* indicates the plural *ṣāb-šarrāni*, analogous in formation to e.g. *rād(i)-kibsiāni* "trackers". For this technical term—"king's-troops", and for "campaign-flour", cf. note on No. 141, 10 (referring to my study of nA taxation and conscription).

9: For ZÍD.KASKAL.MEŠ cf. K. Deller, *OrNS* 33 (1964), 94 s.v.*ṣidītu*; the correct reading of the sign KASKAL was suggested to me by S. Parpola.

No. 186 Plate 66 ND 454
IM, for study
—

3·3 × 7·0 cm.

Governor's Palace, Room S.

Obv. 1 [*a-bat* LUGAL]⌜*a-na*⌝ ^{m}[MAN].⌜BÀD$^{?}$⌝
2 [*šùl-m*]*u ia-a-ši*
3 [*lìb-ba-k*]*a* [*lu*] DÙG.GA-*ka*
4 [ ] ^{lú}⌜*e*⌝-[*m*]*u-qe-ka*
5 [*ša taš*]-*pu-ra-an-ni* [( )]
6 [*ma-*]*a*$^{?}$ [*m*]*i-i-nu*
7 [*i*(*l*)-*l*]*u-ku-u-ni*
8 [*ki-i*] *an-ni-i*$^{?}$ *a-na* ^{m}⌜*x x*⌝
9 *a-*[*n*]*a* ^{m}EN.MU.KÁM$^{?}$ *a-sa-p*[*ar*]
10 *nu-u*[*k*] *e-*[*m*]*u-qe ša* É.EN.MEŠ-*š*[*ú-n*]*u*
11 [*x x*]*x ša* ^{uru}*kal-ḫ*[*a*]
12 [ ]*x x ina* ^{uru}*ḫal-z*[*i*$^{?}$]
13 [*p*]*u-uḫ-ru nu-u*[*k*]
14 [*x*] *x x* 1-*en lu* [*la i-ma-ṭ*]*i*
15 [*nu-u*]*k*$^{?}$ *a-du bi-i*[*t*$^{?}$ ( )]
B.E. (uninscribed)
Rev. 16 [ ]*a*$^{?}$-*sap-rak*$^{!}$-*k*[*u-nu-ni*(?)]

Rev. 17 U[D$^?$-*mu*(?) ( )] *an-ni-u*
18 *ina* ^{uru}[*šá-b*]*i-ri-šú i-da-tu-u-*[*a*$^?$]
19 *i-sa*$^!$*-pa*$^?$*-ru-u-*[*ni*]⌜*ma-a*$^!$⌝ LÚ.EN.N[AM]
20 *i-sa-ap-ra ma-a e-mu-q*[*e*]
21 [*lil*$^?$*-l*]*i-ku-u-ni a-ša*[*p-pa-ra*(?)]
22 [ ]*x-ni ša* ⌜*bi*$^?$⌝ *sal* [ ]
23 [-*n*]*a*$^?$*-ni ina* UG[U]
24 [-*t*]*i*$^?$ *ma-a i-da-a-*[*t*]*e*
25 [*i-sa-ap*]*-ra ma-a a-na me-i-ni*
26 [*e-m*]*u-qe il-la-ku-u-ni*
27 [*e-m*]*u-qe e*[*-ta*]*r-ba-ni*
28 [*m*]*a*$^?$*-ṣi-ni*

Translation

1: [The king's command] to [Šarru]-dūrī$^?$; I am [well], may your [heart] be glad:
4: [About] your troops [of which] you wrote to me [saying:] "What (troops) [are] coming?" It is [like] this, I wrote to [PN] (and) to Bēl-šūmu-ēreš$^?$, saying: "The troops belonging to their superior departments ..... of Kalhu ..... in Halzi$^?$ .... are assembled", and saying: "Let one [...] not be missing .... 17: Today$^?$ from Šabirēšu they wrote after me, saying: The governor has written, saying: "[Let] the troops come", (and) I sent [.......]..... 24: saying: "[He sent] afterwards to me saying: 'Why are the troops coming? The troops have arrived(?), and are sufficient for me(?).'"

Notes

10: *-kunu* ("your") also possible (S. Parpola); *bēt bēlē* "master's house" is a phrase used (with suitable change of the suffix), to refer to the administrative department under which a person works. For some references, see *CAD* B 195a and K. Deller, *OrNS* 35 (1966), 312, although in neither place is a serious attempt made to define the phrase's meaning.
13: *puḫru* is stative: see *AHw* 810b s.v. *paḫāru*(*m*) II G 1 d).
25: It is unclear if *mā* introduces a new speech or continues the old.
27–8: If the restorations are correct, *emuqē* here appears to have become singular!

No. 187 Plate 67 ND unn.
IM, for study
—

A: (2·7) × (2·7) × 1·7
B: (2·1) × (1·9) × 1·7

[Governor's Palace, Room S.]

A: Obv. 1 *a-bat* [
2 *a-na* ^{m}MAN.[BÀD(?)]
3 ^{m}*lu*-D[I$^?$
4 *ša* ^{uru}[
(remainder of obv. of A broken)
B: Obv. 1′ [PA]P ⌜40⌝ [

2′ [L]Ú.GA[L?
3′ *ša* uru[
4′ *ša* LÚ.EN.[
Rev. 5′ [3]8 ANŠE? [
6′ [( )] *ša la* [
7′ ⌜4⌝ ANŠE.NU[N
8′ [PAP(?)] 72?[
(remainder of B broken)
A: Rev. 1′ [*š*]*a*? [
2′ [*š*]*a*? ur[u(?)
3′ *še-ṣi-a a-*[
4′ *ina* UGU KÁ[
5′ *lil-li-k*[*u*

Commentary

Although these two fragments do not join, they are so alike both in physical appearance and in their content to justify placing them under one number. Insufficient remains to give a translation, but we can say that this was an order of the king to Šarru-[dūrī] (l. 2), on the subject of mules (B. 7′; and horses?), and their towns or villages. Instructions regarding their movements are given in A Rev.

No. 188 Plate 67 ND 436
BM 131999

3·4 × 6·0 × 2·5 —

Governor's Palace, Room S.

Obv. 1 ⌜IM LÚ⌝.GAR KUR
2 *a-na* mLUGAL.BÀD
3 *lu šùl-mu a-na* ŠEŠ-*ia*
4 IZI? LÚ.ÌR.MEŠ-*ka*
5 *ina m*[*u*]*-da-bir*
6 *ik-tar-ru*
7 *a-di* UGU KUR *s*[*u-ḫ*]*i*
8 *a-di* UGU KU[R] *ḫa-d*[*a*]*l-li*
9 *mu-da-bur gab-bu*
10 *ta-ta-kal*
11 *šá-*⌞*a'-la ú-ṣi-ṣi*⌟
B.E. 12 ⌜*x x x x x*⌝
13 *ša* IZI?
Rev. 14 *x* [*x x*] *x ni*?
15 *la-a i-šá-mu-u-ni*
16 *a-sa-*[*pa*]*r-ka*

Translation

1 : Tablet of the governor of (Assur) province to Šarru-dūrī ; health to my brother :

4 : Your subjects have set the desert on fire, and as far as the land of Sūhu and as far as the land of Hadallu, it has eaten up the whole desert. 11 : Make enquiries ..... 13 : Who [ ] the fire? . . . they will not obey, I am writing to you.

Notes

4, 13 : IZI seems the best reading of the sign in these two lines, as suggested to me by S. Parpola ; I had originally read *bi-is*, but reading IZI provides an object for *karāru*, and a subject for *tatakal*. The only slight awkwardness is the word order which is unusual for nA.

Commentary

A letter from the governor of Assur province to his counterpart in Kalhu province, complaining that the subjects of the province of Kalhu have set fire to the desert and thus destroyed the desert (i.e. presumably the grazing) in his own area. This shows that the land between Assur and the Euphrates was under him, as we might have deduced from the correspondence of another(?) governor of Assur, Ṭāb-ṣil-ešarra, which concerns affairs in Hindānu (*ABL* 93 ; 547 ; 1433).

No. 189 Plate 67 ND 417
IM 56840

2·9 × 4·7 × 1·7 —

Governor's Palace, Room S.

Obv. 1 IM LÚ.GAR KUR
2 *a-na* ᵐMAN.BÀD(!)
3 *lu šùl-mu*
4 *a-na* ŠEŠ-*iá*
5 *ina* UGU GIŠ.MES!.MÁ.KAN.NA
6 *ša* ŠEŠ-*u-iá*
7 *iš-pur-a-ni*
8 *ki-ma* ⌜*x* (*x*)⌝
B.E. 9 [ ] *x*[ ]
Rev. 10 *i*[*na* U]GU-*iá*
11 *e-te-li*
12 *ma-a'-da*
13 *a-na-ku a-na*
14 ŠEŠ-*ia*
15 *u-še-ba-la*

Translation

1 : Tablet of the governor of (Assur) province to Šarru-dūrī ; health to my brother :

5 : About the sissoo-wood of which my brother wrote to me—when it has come up to me, I shall send a large quantity to my brother.

Notes

2: Since the recipient of the letter is shown by the author's use of " my brother " to be his equal in rank, and since the letter was found at Nimrud, we need not doubt that the emendation of the PN is correct.

9: The B.E. may in fact be uninscribed, and the apparent wedges mere scratches; another line is not needed for the translation.

13: Is the use of *anāku* here intended to make it clear that the verb is 1st and not 3rd person ?

No. 190 Plate 68 ND 418
BM 131995

2·5 × 4·4 × 1·6 —

Governor's Palace, Room S.

Obv. 1 IM LÚ.EN.NAM
2 *a-na* ^{m}*ṣil*-LUGAL
3 UD.15 *ša* ITI.ŠE
4 *at-ta* EN LÚ.ERÍN.MEŠ-*ka*
5 *ina* ^{uru}*ši-šil*
6 *lu-u at-ta*
7 1-*en lu-u la-a*
B.E. 8 *i-ma-ṭi*
(rev. uninscribed, but has the impression of a stamp seal, diameter *c.* 2·0 cm., very faint)

Translation

1: Tablet of the governor to Ṣil-šarri:

3: On the 15th day of the month of Addāru (XII), you, together with your troops, are to be in Šišil. Let not one be lacking.

Notes

4: EN for *adi*, unusual in this sort of text.

5: For Šišil, see note on No. 183, 6.

No. 191 Plate 68 ND 421
IM 56843

3·0 × 5·0 × 2·0 —

Governor's Palace, Room S.

Obv. 1 ⸢*a*⸣-*na* LÚ.E[N.N]AM
2 [I]M ^{lú}*šá* IGI É.GAL
3 ^{giš}*mu-gir-ri*
4 [*š*]*a* ^{giš}*šá-da-di*
5 *am-mi-u*

Obv. 6 *ár-ḫiš*
7 KÙ.BABBAR
8 *li-il-bi-u*
B.E. (two faint seal impressions or thumb marks)

Translation

1: To the governor—tablet of the palace supervisor:
3: Let them quickly cover that drawing-chariot with silver.

Notes

1–2: Note that when an equal writes, his name or title is put first, but that when writing to a higher authority, it is obviously etiquette to place his name or title first by reversing the order of the first two lines (cf. No. 192).

3–5: It is perhaps probable that the correcter translation for these lines is "the chariots (and) that drawing-chariot"; for it is hard to see how the two items, *mugirru* and *ša šadādi* could be combined into one. For the *ša šadādi*, a light chariot drawn by men, cf. A. Salonen, *Landfahrzeuge*, 64 ff. Perhaps, with S. Parpola, *mugirru* here means a wheel.

No. 192 Plate 68 ND 438
IM 56848
—

3·5 × (3·2) × 2·0

Governor's Palace, Room S.

Obv. 1 *a-na* LÚ.EN.NAM
2 IM LÚ.GA[L *m*]*u-gi*
3 *lu-u šùl-mu a-na* EN-*iá*
4 *ina* UGU LÚ [*š*]*a* EN
5 *iš-pu-ra-ni*
6 [(*x*) *x x*] *x tú*? [*a*/*i*]-*ta-har*
(remainder (more than half) of obv. and upper part of rev. broken)
Rev. 1′ ⌜*ša* ŠU ^{m}*na*?⌝-[(*x x*) *x x*]
2′ ^{m}*ki-me-e ina pa*-⌜*ni-i*⌝[*a*?]
3′ ^{m}*a-a-am-mu* ,, EN
4′ *li-iṣ-bat*
5′ *lu-u-še-bi-la*

Translation

1: To the governor—tablet of the *rab mūgi*; health to my lord:
4: About the man of whom (my) lord wrote to me, [. . . . . he/I] presented him/myself before [. . . . .
Rev. 1′: . . . .] in the charge of [PN], ... may (my) lord seize and send to me Kimē, under [me?], and Ayammu, ditto.

Notes

1–2: From the order of these lines (see note on No. 191, 1–2), and of course from the use of *bēlī* " my lord ", it is clear that the *rab mūgi*, a military official of some kind, is a subordinate of the governor.

Commentary

There is a bare possibility that this fragment should be joined with No. 209, but it does not seem likely.

No. 193 Plate 69 ND 420
IM 56842

3·8 × 6·3 × 2·0 —

Governor's Palace, Room S.

Obv. 1 *a-na* LÚ.EN.NAM EN-*ia*
2 ÌR-*ka* $^{m.d}$MAŠ.DINGIR-*a-a*
3 UD.20.KÁM *ša* ITI.BARAG
4 ^{lú}*ú-ra-se it-tal-ku-ni*
5 *a-na pa-an* KÁ.GAL
6 *ša* KUR *hal-zi* ⌜*i*⌝-*sak-nu*
7 1 *me* LÚ.ERÍN.MEŠ ŠU ^{m}EN.TI
8 *ina* ^{uru}NINA *i-tú-bíl*
9 *ú-sa-áš-ki*!-*in*
10 *ma-a* ^{m}DINGIR-*a-a*-EN
11 *iq-ṭí-bi-a*
12 [*m*]*u*?-*uk*? *nu* SIG$_4$
13 [*i*]*na* KAR? URU *ni-šá-ha-aṭ*
Rev. 14 $^{[l]ú}$*ú*!-*ra*!-*se*! *li-ši*-⌜*u*?⌝
15 ŠE-*ú ṭé*-⌜*mu*⌝ *i-tú-qut*
16 [*i*]*t-tal-ku* ŠE-*ú*
17 *ú-še-lu-ú*
18 ^{lú}*ú-ra-se ša* ^{m}*ki-ṣir-aš-šur*
19 *it-tal-ku-ú-ni*
20 *a-na* ŠÀ ⌜*dib-bi*⌝ [*a*]*m-mu-ti*
21 *ša* MURUB$_4$ URU *lu-šá-áš-ki-in*
22 UD.26.KÁM LÚ.DUMU *šip-ri*
23 UGU EN-*ia i*-⌜*tú*⌝-*ṣi-a*

Translation

1: To the governor, my lord, your servant Ninurta-ilāya:

3: On the 20th day of Nīsānu (I), the building-overseers arrived (and) they set (to work) on the front of the gate of the land of Halzu.

7: Bēl-(l)uballiṭ has brought his 100 men from Nineveh, (and) has set (them to work), saying: " Ilāya-bēl gave me (these) instructions ", (to which I replied) saying: " We shall mould the bricks on the city quay, (and) the building-overseers will take (them from there)."

15: The corn—a message arrived (and) they have gone (and) are removing the corn. The building-overseers of Kiṣir-aššur have come, (and) I shall set (them to work) on those affairs inside the city.

22: On the 26th day the messenger left (the city) to (go to) my lord.

Notes

2: A Ninurta-ilāya was author also of NL 15; 34; and 37 (*Iraq* 17 (1955), 133, and 18 (1956), 49, 52); a man of this name was also governor of Naṣibīna and eponym for 736, and again eponym for 722. Here the writer is clearly not a governor, and unfortunately the other Nimrud letters (all from the North-west Palace) do not show clearly whether their author held the rank of a governor or not.

4: *urāsu* (plural regularly *urāsē*), see K. Deller, *OrNS* 35 (1966), 194, on ND 2705. Some connection with the building trade is certain, but possibly " (mud-brick) masons " would be closer than " building-overseers ". I suspect that *urāsu* = **warrāsu*, and is connected with *ursūtu* " a deposit ".

12: The restoration of [*m*]*u-uk* is made uncertain by the *nu* which follows it, and which seems unwanted. I can only suggest that *nu* is a written or spoken abbreviation for *nēnu* " we ", and that it is used here to point the contrast with the subject of the following verb.

13: Possibly MURUB$_4$ URU (K. Deller—S. Parpola); *šaḫāṭu* = " glaze " according to A. Salonen, *BiOr* 28 (1971), 24.

14: Reading uncertain, even after collation; also possible is LÚ.MÁ.LAḪ$_6$ (= DU.DU) ŠE *li-ši-u*.

14–16: ŠE(-*ú*) probably refers to the straw needed for the bricks, the writer talking loosely of " corn " not " straw ".

Commentary

This is a report from a subordinate to the governor (presumably of Kalhu), on the subject of building operations. The work is on a town of considerable size—it has a gateway, a quay, and a " centre "—and presumably is therefore at Kalhu itself. This means that the governor must be absent from his capital, and this letter must have been brought back with him after his absence.

No. 194 Plate 69 ND 424
BM 131996
—

2·8 × 5·1 × 2·6

Governor's Palace, Room S.

Obv. 1 [*a*]-⌜*na*⌝ LÚ.EN.NAM EN-*ia*
2 ÌR-*ka* $^{\text{m.d}}$U.GUR.KAR-*ir*
3 *lu-u* ⌜*šùl*⌝-⌞*mu*⌟ *a-na* LÚ.EN.NAM EN-*ia*
4 ⌜*šùl-mu*⌝ *a-na a-*[*ṣ*]*a-pe*
5 *a-na* LÚ.ÌR.MEŠ-*ni*
6 *ša* LÚ.EN.NAM EN-*ia*
7 TA* *lìb-bi šal-le-te*
8 *ša tu-ṣa-an-ni*
9 [*ub*]-⌞*ta*⌟-'*i* 30 LÚ.Z[I].MEŠ
10 [*ina lìb-b*]*i a-ta-mar*

11 ⌜*ina pa*⌝-*an* ^{lú}*tur-ta-ni*
12 *a-ti-it-zi*
13 *i-ta-an-na*
Rev. 14 TA* ŠÀ *šal-le-te*
15 *ša* ŠÀ ⌜^{uru}⌝*ra-pi-qi*
16 *ša tu-ṣa-an-ni*
17 10 LÚ.ZI.MEŠ *ina lìb-bi-šú-nu*
18 *a-ta-mar lib-bu*
19 *š*[*a* ^{l}]^{ú}*tur-ta-ni la* D[ÙG].GA
20 *ina pa-ni-šú la a-zi-zi*
21 *ki-i ina* É.GAL
22 *i-lak-an-ni*
23 *be-lí li-qi-ba-áš-šú*

Translation

1: To the governor, my lord, your servant Nergal-ēṭir; health to the governor my lord; the animals and the servants of the governor my lord are well:

7: Out of the captives who came out I have searched and chosen 30 persons [from] them. I applied to the *turtānu*, (and) he has given (them) to me. 14: Out of the captives who were inside Rapīqu, who came out, I have chosen 10 persons from them, (but) the *turtānu* was not in a good mood, (and) I did not apply to him. When he comes into the palace, may my lord speak to him.

Notes

2: Nergal-ēṭir is too common a name for us to identify the author; note that a man of this name is to be found in NL 35 (*Iraq* 18 (1956), Pl. XI), 8.

7, 14: *šallutu* " booty " clearly refers here specifically to the human part of the spoils (cf. -*šunu*, l. 17); for the verb **wṣ'* see No. 184 rev. 3′ and perhaps No. 187 A rev. 3′.

11–12: Here and in l. 20 the Assyrian is literally " I stood before ".

15: Rapīqu is the well-known Babylonian border town on the Euphrates; no direct military activity against it seems to be attested under Tiglath-pileser III or Sargon, although it is named among Aramaean tribes by Tiglath-pileser (cf. J. A. Brinkman, *An.Or.* 43, 270–1).

Commentary

The officer entrusted with the military contingent of the governor of Kalhu here reports back to him on his success in securing for the governor a share of the booty resulting from the campaign led by the *turtānu*.

No. 195 Plate 68 ND 462
IM 56858

2·7 × 4·1 × 1·7 —

Governor's Palace, Room S.

Obv. 1 ⌜*a-na*⌝ L[Ú.EN.NAM E]N-*ia*
2 ÌR-*ka* $^{\text{m.d}}$I[M?].KAR-*ir*

Obv. 3 *lu-u šùl-mu a-na* LÚ.EN.NAM EN-*ia*
4 *i-na* KUR *da-ú-na-ni*
5 *šak-na-a-ni*
6 ŠE.IN.NU.MEŠ
7 ŠE *ki-su-tú*
8 *ma-a'-da*
9 *nu-šá-dan*
Rev. 10 [*š*]*ùl-mu a-na a-ṣap-pe*
11 *ša* EN-*ia*

Translation

1: To [the governor], my lord, your servant Adad?-ēṭir; health to the governor my lord:

4: We are situated in the land? of Da'unāni, (and) we are collecting much straw and fodder. The animals of my lord are well.

Notes

2: Šamaš(dU[TU])-ēṭir is also possible.

4: Da'unāni, whether land or mountain, is unknown; it does not seem to improve the sense if we take *da'unāni* as a D stative from **dnn*.

9: One may hesitate between *nu-šá-dan* and *nu-ša-kal*; although the Š stem of **ndn* does not seem to occur in nA with its common earlier meaning " to collect (taxes) ", I have preferred this reading because it does not seem likely that the only purpose of the writer's visit to Da'unāni, wherever it may be, was to feed the animals, nor that he would be feeding them both on straw and on " fodder ".

Commentary

If my interpretation of l. 9 is correct, this is a report to the provincial governor from one of his officials who has been sent out to undertake the collection of agricultural taxes. This suggests that the unknown place, Da'unāni, is within the province of Kalhu, and is probably therefore a mountain rather than a land.

No. 196 Plate 70; Photo Plate 93d ND 413

BM 131992

—

3·5 × 6·3 × 2·1

Governor's Palace, Room S.

Obv. 1 *a-na* LÚ.EN.NAM
2 EN-*ia*
3 ÌR-*ka* m*aš-šur-tak-lak*
4 *ši-pir-tu ša* LÚ.EN.NAM
5 *ša* uru*ar-zu-ḫi-na*
6 *ina* UGU m*na-ni-i*
7 ⌜*ta*⌝-*tal-ka*
8 *ma-a* ŠE *nu-sa-ḫe*meš

9 [*š*]*a* LÚ.EN.NAM
10 [*š*]*a* ^{uru}*kal-ḫi ú-su-ḫu*
B.E. 11 [*m*]*a-a šum-*⌜*ma*⌝
12 [ŠE *nu-*]⌞*sa*⌟*-ḫe*^{meš}
Rev. 13 [ ]*x*
14 [*x* (*x x*)].MEŠ
15 [*ina*? *l*]*ìb-bi* URU.MEŠ.ŠE-*ia*
16 [LÚ.E]NGAR.MEŠ
17 [*a*]*-se-me*
18 [^{m}.]^{d}UTU.EN.PAP LÚ.EN.NAM
19 ⌜*x* (*x*) *x*⌝ *i-ṣa-bat*
20 ŠE *nu-*⌜*sa*⌝*-ḫe*^{meš}*-ni*
21 *la na-as-ḫu*
22 *a-ta-a ina* MU.AN.NA
23 *an-ni-tú* ŠE *nu-sa-ḫe-ni*
T.E. 24 *i-na-su-ḫu*
L.E. 25 [L]Ú.ERÍN.MEŠ-*šú*
26 [*an*?]*-na-k*[*a*] *ša* ⌜UD⌝*-me ša* UD*-me*
27 [( )]URU?.ME *i-la-bi*

Translation

1: To the governor, my lord, your servant Aššur-taklak:

4: A message of the governor of Arzuhīna has come for Nanī, saying: "Levy the corn-taxes of the governor of Kalhu", (and) saying: "If the [corn-]taxes .... 15: [In] my villages [I] have heard the farmers (say): "Šamaš-bēlu-uṣur, the governor, is taking ....." 20: Our corn-taxes are not levied—why are they levying our corn-taxes this year? [.......] his troops, here? day by day(?) .... are going round the villages(?).

Notes

8: The corn tax *nusāḫē* is discussed in my study of nA taxation.

10: *ú-su-ḫu* for *usuḫ*.

18–24: There is a little doubt as to who is speaking in these lines: if ll. 18–19 are the words of the farmers, as I have suggested, a *mā* would be expected. If the *mā* is not needed, however, then it would be possible to interpret the following lines also as part of the farmers' speech. On the other hand, we could take *aseme* as referring back to something lost in the preceding break, and dissociate ll. 18 ff. from the farmers altogether. However, my preferred rendering is certainly that given in the translation.

17: Possibly [*ú*]*-se-šib* "he has appointed"; if so, [GAL.EN]GAR.MEŠ should be considered for l. 16.

18: Šamaš-bēlu-uṣur is known as eponym for 710 B.C. and governor of Arzuhīna (A. Ungnad, *RLA* II, 455).

19: ⌜*x*⌝.MEŠ *i-ṣa-bat* possible (coll.); BE-*qu* not possible.

20: i.e. "corn-taxes are not (usually) levied from us".

26: For *ša ūmi ša ūmi*, not known to me from elsewhere, cf. *ša* MU.AN.NA *ša* MU.A[N.NA (K 4279 7′, unpub., courtesy S. Parpola).

Commentary

At first sight this letter described a dispute as to which provincial authority was entitled to exact taxes in certain villages—the governor of Kalhu or the governor of Arzuhīna. However, it is hard to conceive any way in which these two provinces could have bordered on one another, and a closer examination of the wording of the letter shows that the governor of Arzuhīna is instructing his subordinate to collect the taxes not of the province of Kalhu, but of the governor of that province. Since we have other instances where one provincial governor owns considerable estates in a different province (cf. *RGD*, pp. 58–9), the solution seems to be that the governor of Kalhu has private property in the province of Arzuhīna, and that the governor of that province has suddenly decided to levy taxes on that property whereas it had previously been exempt. The author of the letter is probably therefore the governor's private " estate agent ", perhaps the *abarakku*.

No. 197 Plate 70 ND 490
BM 132002

2·7 × (5·2) × 2·0

Governor's Palace, Room S.

Obv. 1 *a-na* LÚ.EN.NAM EN-*iá*
2 ÌR-*ka* ^{m}DUMU.^{d}15
3 LÚ.IÀ.SUR.MEŠ
4 *an-nu-te a-na me-i-ni*
5 ^{lú}*šá* UGU URU
6 *ú-⌜ba?⌝-a-šú-nu*
7 *ina* UGU GUD
8 *an-nu-te-ma*
9 GIŠ.ÙR.MEŠ
10 ⌞*li*⌟*-zi-bi-lu*
11 [(*x*) *x x*] *dul-*[*l*]*u?-šú-nu*
B.E. (broken; up to 4 lines missing)
Rev. 1′ [*x*]⌜*x ni?*⌝[*x* (*x x*)]
2′ *ina muḫ-ḫi-šú-nu*
3′ *ma-a-da a-da-ni-iš*
4′ *ina* UGU ^{lú}*šá* UGU URU
5′ *li-iš-pur-u-ni*
6′ *i-se-šú-nu*
7′ ⌜*lu*⌝ *la al-ka*

Translation

1: To the governor, my lord, your servant Mār-ištar:

3: These oil-pressers—what does the town overseer want them for? Let them transport these beams also on oxen(?) . . . their work [. . . . .

Rev. 2′: . . . .] about them very much. Let them write to the town overseer (but) let me not come with them.

Notes

7: The MEŠ is omitted; in 8 it is not clear to what *annūte-ma* refers.

Rev. 3′: It is possible that *ma'da adanniš* qualifies *lišpurūni*, and that the break does not come at the end of this line.

7′: For *lu lā allaka*. Also possible is *lu la* KA!.KA.

No. 198 Plate 71 ND 414
BM 131993
—

3·3 × 5·6 × 1·8

Governor's Palace, Room S.

Obv. 1 [*a-na* LÚ.E]N.NAM EN-*iá*
2 [ÌR-*ka*] ᵐSUḪUŠ.ᵈPA(?)
3 [*lu*] *šùl-mu a-na be-lí-i*[*á*]
4 [*i*]*na* UGU ᵍⁱˢ*ziq-pe*
5 [*š*]*a be-lí iš-pur-an-ni*
6 ᵍⁱˢ*ziq-pu dan-*⌜*nu-ti*ˀ⌝
7 *ša mar* MU.AN.NA-*šú*[(-*nu*)]
8 *i-na-šú*!*-u*ˀ*-ni*!
9 *ina* UGU : KA-*e*
10 *ša be-lí-ia*
11 *ú-se-bi-la*
12 [*x*+]20 ⌞GIŠ⌟.ŠENNUR
B.E. 13 ⌜*x x x x* (*x*)⌝
Rev. 14 GIŠˀ[ ].MEŠ
15 *ma*ˀ[ ] *ši*ˀ [( )]
(up to 3 lines broken; remainder of rev. blank)

Translation

1: [To the] governor, my lord, [your servant] Ubru-nabû(?); health to my lord:
4: About the saplings of which my lord wrote to me. I have sent big saplings which ..... a year (in age), according to my lord's instructions. 12: [x+]20 medlars ....

Notes

2: The divine name in the PN is written over an erasure, and perhaps also itself partly erased.
6: *ziq-pu* would appear to be plural!
8–10: These lines are written over erasures, and in l. 8 in particular it is difficult to tell what is erased and what not; the verb might be *inaššūni* but a present tense followed at once by a perfect creates suspicion.
12: For medlar (and other) saplings in an administrative text, cf. No. 139.

No. 199 Plate 71 ND 455
Inst. Arch. London
—

3·6 × 7·8 × 1·8

Governor's Palace, Room K.

Obv. 1 *a-na* LÚ.EN.NAM ⌜EN-*iá*⌝
2 ÌR-*ka* ᵐU.PAP.AŠ
3 *lu šùl-mu a-na* EN-*iá*

Obv. 4 *ú-qu* LUGAL
5 *ina* UGU-*a ta-a-a[l]-ka*
6 UGU ⌞*ki*⌟-⌜*i-ti-ki-te*⌝
7 [*š*]*a*? É?! [lú]*tar-ta-a-ni*
8 1 LÚ.MU 1 [L]Ú.NINDA.SUM
9 1 LÚ.NINDA *ma-a*
10 *re-su-nu i-ši*
11 *ma-a bi-su-n*[*u*]
Rev. 12 *ma-a pa*?*-an* [m][*x x* (*x*)]
13 *ša-a-zi-i-*[*zi*]
14 *ú-ma-a la-*[*x x* (*x x*)]
15 *a-na ka-na-*[*šú-nu*]
16 ⌜*a*⌝*-sa-par* ⌜*x x x* (*x*)⌝
17 *ma-*⌞*a*⌟ *lìb-bi-šu-nu*
18 UGU ANŠ[E]⌜*ú*?⌝*-ra*[meš]*-te*
19 *ša* KUR URI[ki(!)] [( )]
20 ⌜*x*⌝ *še-bi-la-*⌜*ni*?⌝
21 *la i-ma-gúr-ru*
22 *la i-ma-ḫu-ru*
23 *ma-*[*a*] *a-na* [uru]NINA
24 [*x*]*-da* SUM ⌞*x* (*x*) *x*⌟
T.E. 25 ⌜*i*⌝*-qa-*⌜*bi*⌝ [ ]
26 [*liš*?*-d*]*u-du*

Translation

1: To the governor, my lord, your servant Adad-ahu-iddina; health to my lord:

4: A royal document has come to me about employees of the house of the *turtānu*—1 cook, 1 victualler, 1 baker—saying: "Take them under your command, (and) assign their families to [PN]." 14: Now I am writing to you, ..., saying: "Send? (some?) of them on the horse teams(?) of Akkad"—but they will not consent and do not present themselves, saying: '....... to Nineveh .... he will say ... let them haul.

Notes

4: *ú-qu*: the sign is definitely *ú* and not *un*. This form is comparable to *daqu* for *damqu* in the PN Ṣābu-damqu. *Unqu* means a ring, then the seal on a ring, and then a document stamped with that seal; here it refers (as elsewhere) to a royal letter (rather than a sealed decree), and the letter itself may not even have been sealed at all, to judge from other surviving royal letters. The word *unqu* is feminine—cf. *un-qa-a-te* in ND 2307 (*Iraq* 16 (1954), 37), 12, and for the singular, *ABL* 486 rev. 14–15; 533, 8–11. *Ta-a-al-ka* = *ta'alka* for *tatalka* ?

6: It appears from this line that *kitkitû* includes domestic or culinary professions.

10: For *rēšu našû* see *AHw* 763a s.v. *našû*(*m*) II, G I 3) d) γ).

16–17: The *mā* of l. 17 shows that the undeciphered phrase at the end of l. 16 must have introduced an instruction from the king or another person, and not an utterance of the writer's.

19: URI could also of course refer to Urarṭu.

25–6: Restorations proposed by K. Deller.

Commentary

The writer, who has received instructions from the king, is unable to get co-operation from the men of whom he has been ordered to take charge, and he therefore writes for assistance to the governor, who is presumably his immediate superior, rather than admit failure to the king.

No. 200 Plate 70 ND unn.
IM, for study
—

3·4 × (2·2) × 1·9

[Governor's Palace, Room S.]

Obv. 1 ⌜*a*⌝-*na* LÚ.EN.NAM [E]N-*iá*
2 [ÌR]-*k*[*a*]
(remainder broken)

The beginning of a letter to the governor.

No. 201 Plate 72 ND 415
BM 131994
—

4·0 × 6·3 × 2·0

Governor's Palace, Room S.

Obv. 1 *a-na* m.dEN-*da-a-ni*
2 *qí-bi-ma um-ma*
3 m.d*mi-šar-rum*-ŠEŠ-*ir* ⌜*x* (*x*) *x*⌝
4 *a-na ka-a-šá lu-ú šul-mu*
5 *um-ma-a a-na* AD-*iá-a-ma*
6 *i-na šar-re-e*
7 uru*ka-làḫ* É-*ni šú-ú*
8 *am-me-ni en-na*
9 AD-*ú-a*
10 *ú-maš-šèr-an-na-ši*
11 *a*?-*na* UGU *mi-ni-i*
12 *ḫi x* AD-*ú-a*
13 [*i*]*m*?-*maš-x x*[*x* (*x x*)]-*ra*?
(1–2 lines broken)
Rev. 1′ *šá x*[*x* (*x*)] *x šá*
2′ PAP ⌜*x x* (*x*)⌝ *a*
3′ *ù*?[*x*]*x x x*
4′ PAP ⌜*en*⌝-*na-a* AD-*ú-a*
5′ *lu-še-bi-la*

Translation

1: To Bēl-dān say, thus Mišārum-nāṣir . . . . .; health to you; saying to my father:

6: Our family is from the kings of Kalhu—(so) why has my father now deserted me? To what purpose . . . . . my father . . . .

Rev. 4′: Let my father send all (this) to me now.

Notes

3: Here and in No. 202, 3, there are two or three signs after Mišārum-nāṣir which I cannot decipher; they must be either his title or description (" your son " or similar), or the end of the PN (Mišārum-nāṣir-. . . . .).

6–7: The precise implications of the phrase " kings of Kalhu " are not clear to me; it is obviously quite possible that Bēl-dān was connected to the Assyrian royal house.

12: The word at the beginning of the line may be identical with that in No. 202, 8, but the second sign here does not closely resemble the apparent *rat* there.

Commentary

See on No. 202.

No. 202 Plate 72 ND 441

IM 56851

—

3·6 × 6·1 × 1·9

Governor's Palace, Room S.

Obv. 1 *a-na* ᵐ·ᵈEN-*da*-⌜*a*⌝-[*ni*]
2 *qí-bi-ma um-ma*
3 ᵐ·ᵈ*mi-šar-rum*-ŠEŠ-*ir* ⌜*x* (*x*) *x*⌝
4 *a-na ka-a-šá lu-u šùl-mu*
5 *um-ma-a a-na* AD-*iá-a*-⌞*ma*⌟
6 *áš-šú ṣi-bu-t*[*i*]
7 *šá* ⌜AD⌝-*ú-a iš-pu*-[*r*]*a*?
8 *hi rat*? [(*x*) *x*] *x*
9 AD-*ú-a la áš-bu*
10 *a-na* AD-*ia*
11 *la ú-še-bi-la*
12 *en-na ki-i*
13 [A]D-*ú-a*
Rev. 14 *iḫ-ḫi-sa* AD-*ú-a*
15 *liš-pu-ram-ma*
16 *a-na* AD-*ia lu-še-bi-la*

Translation

1: To Bēl-dān say, thus Mišārum-nāṣir . . . . .; health to you; saying to my father:

6: About the requirement of which my father wrote to me—. . . .[. . .] my father was not residing, I did not send (it) to my father. 12: Now, when my father has got back, let him write to me, and I will send (it) to my father.

Notes

3: For the name cf. note on No. 201, 3.
8: Cf. No. 201, 12.

Commentary

These two letters (Nos. 201–2) were sent to Bēl-dān (clearly, in view of their provenance, the governor of that name), by Mišārum-nāṣir(-. . . . .), who addresses him as his father. Each is concerned with sending things, once to and once from the writer, and both are written in Babylonian script and dialect. Clearly, therefore, the son must have been resident in Babylonia, but whether this should allow us to guess that he was being given a scribal education there is uncertain. Note in passing that the divine name Mišārum is uncommon (if not actually unattested) in both nA and contemporary Babylonian names.

No. 203 Plate 73 ND 439
IM 56489
—

3·9 × (4·5) × 2·4

Governor's Palace, Room S.

Obv. (beginning broken)
1′ [(*x*) *x*]*x-a-a* ⌜LÚ.ERÍN$^{?}$⌝.[(*x*)]
2′ [*re-eš*(?)] ^{giš}BE-*le-šu-nu*
3′ [*liš*$^{?}$-*š*]*i*$^{?}$-*ú* ZÍD.DA.KASKAL.MEŠ-*šú-nu*
4′ ⌜*lu*⌝ *tar-ṣa* LÚ.SAG.MEŠ-*ka*
5′ *ina muḫ-ḫi-šú-nu pi-qi-di*
6′ ^{m}LUGAL.BÀD LÚ.E[N.N]AM
7′ [*š*]*a* ^{uru}*kal-ḫi ina qa-*⌜*an*⌝-*ni*
8′ [*a*]*s-s*[*a*]-*pa*[*r*]-*šú*
9′ [*is-se*]-⌜*šú*⌝ *il-lu-ku*
Rev. 10′ [(*x*) *x* *x*] UD-*mu*
11′ [*ša* L]Ú.A.KIN-*šú ta-am-ma-ru-*⌜*ni*⌝
12′ [*l*]*u-nam-mi-šú is-se-šú*
13′ *lil-li-ku a-na*
14′ LÚ.SAG.MEŠ-*ka ša is-se-šú-nu*
15′ [*i*]*l-la-ku-ni ṭè-e-mu*
16′ [*ta-*]*šak-kan* ⌞*ma-a*⌟ *ka-a-a-ma-ni*
17′ [*a-na*(?) ^{m}]⌞LUGAL⌟.BÀD
18′ [*ta-šam-m*]*a*$^{?}$-*a*
19′ [*ta*]-*šak-ka-n*[*a*]
(remainder broken)

Translation

1′: . . . . troops?, [let them take charge of(?)] their equipment, and see that their " campaign-flour " is good. Appoint your eunuchs over them. 6′: Šarru-dūrī, the governor of Kalhu, (is?) in the area(?); I have written to him and they will go with him [. . . ;] the day [that] you see his messenger, they should get moving and go with him. 13′: You should give instructions to your eunuchs who are going with them, that they should constantly [obey(?)] Šarru-dūrī [. . . . .

Notes

2′: According to *CAD* B 199a, the word should be *tillū* (connected with *alālu* Gt).

3′: For "campaign-flour" see on No. 185, 9; note that the word is here construed as feminine plural.

16′–17′: The writer is probably asking his correspondent to ensure that his subordinates will obey Šarru-dūrī's command; ll. 17′–18′ are restored on this assumption.

Commentary

The general tone of the letter suggests that it was written by the king. The recipient is being told to send troops to Šarru-dūrī, but the way in which the title of "governor of Kalhu" is specified in full seems to show that the recipient of the letter is not a member of Šarru-dūrī's own administration. Since the man also has charge of several eunuchs, he was probably a man of some importance, perhaps another provincial governor, but there is no reason why this letter should have been found at Kalhu unless the recipient forwarded it together with the troops to Šarru-dūrī.

No. 204 Plate 74 ND unn.
IM, for study
—

4·6 × (7·8) × 3·0

[Governor's Palace, Room S.]

Obv. (beginning broken)
1′ [*x p*]*a*? *m*[*u*?] *na* UD[ ]
2′ ⸢*ma*⸣-*a* ⸢*ki*⸣-*i x*[
3′ *ma-ḫi-ru ša ma*-⸢*ti*?⸣-[*ia*(?)
4′ ⸢*ma-a*⸣ *ša* GUD *ki-i* [
5′ *m*[*a*-]*a ša* UDU *ki-i*[
6′ *m*[*a*-]*a ša* KUR.MEŠ *ku-din* ⸢*x*⸣
7′ [*m*]*a-a* LÚ-*ti* ,, ,,
8′ [*m*]*a-a* GIŠ.ME BUL+BUL *in-ta-ḫar*?
9′ [*m*]*a-a* GIŠ.ME BUL+BUL *ú-ma*-⸢*x x*⸣
10′ [ ] *di*? *ina* IGI *ma*? [*x*]*x*
11′ [ ]*šá* IGI É.GAL
12′ [ ]*bil*? *in-bu*? [(*x*)]
B.E. 13′ [ ]-*nu* [( )]
Rev. 14′ [ ]
15′ [*š*]*a*? [*x*] *hu*
16′ [ ] 2-*šú*
17′ [ ]*x te-ta*-⸢*šar*⸣

(remainder of rev. blank to break)

Notes

3′: *maḫīru ša māt*[*iya*]: for a report on prices (or rates of exchange) for different commodities, cf. NL 52 (*Iraq* 21 (1959), 162); prices were fixed, according to that letter, for different towns or provinces, and other references make it clear that each province might have a different rate of exchange.

4′–9′: These lines presumably gave the situation with regard to differing commodities, viz. oxen (l. 4′), sheep (l. 5′), horses and mules (l. 6′), slaves (*amēlūti* or corresponding nA form, cf. *ARU* 658, l. 7′), and woods (ll. 8′–9′); however the ends of the lines which gave the rates are unfortunately lost.

8′–9′: I can only suppose that BUL+BUL here, as in literary texts, means "such and such", and that the general sense is: "some woods (did this), other woods (did something else)".

17′: "has gone well" (suggestion of K. Deller).

Commentary

Regrettably the text is too broken for translation, but it does reveal the existence of recognized rates for various commodities.

No. 205 Plate 73 ND unn.
IM, for study
—

3·1 × (5·2) × 1·7

[Governor's Palace, Room S.]

Obv. 1 ⸢*a-na*⸣ [
2 ÌR-[*ka*
3 *lu-u šùl-*[*mu*
4 *ia-u-ti* LÚ ⸢*x*⸣ [
5 [(*x*) *x*] ^{m}ERÍN.⸢MEŠ?⸣.15 ⸢*ša*?⸣ [
6 [(*x*) *š*]*a*? ⸢*x x x x*⸣ [( )]
7 [(*x*) *x*] ⸢*ša*?⸣ NAM? [(*x*) M]EŠ?-*šú*
8 [(*x x*) *x*] *šá*? *li-di-na*
9 [ ]*na*? [*i*]*a-u-ti*
10 ⸢*ši*? (*x*) *di*? *be*?⸣ *ni a si na ḫa bi ša*?
11 [*l*]*i*?-*ma-x* LÚ.NIMGIR? *a-li-a*/*e*
12 [(*x*) *x* B]ÀD? *ni lu* ÌR.ME-*ma*?[( )]
13 [ ]*x* ERÍN.MEŠ.15 *lu x*[
B.E. 14 [ ] *la a*? -*za* [(-*x*)]
15 [ ]⸢*x x x*⸣
16 [ ]*a x x* UD?-*me*
Rev. 17 [-*š*]*ú-nu dul-lu* [( )]
18 ⸢*šu*?-*a*?-*tú*⸣ *ur-ta-me-*[*u*?]
19 *me-me-ni* SIG$_4$.ME[Š(-*šú*)]
20 *la ú-qa-ra-ba* [*x* (*x*)]
21 *a-na* 6-*šú ri-ṣip*?-*x*[
22 [*ina*?] UGU *mu-kar-r*[*i*?-*si*(?)
23 [(*x*) *x*] *na*? *ur* ⸢*x*⸣ NA$_4$[
24 [*š*]*a* ^{uru}TAB.TAB-*ḫa-a*[-*a*(?)]
25 *ina pa-ni-ia aq-qur*? [ ]

Rev. 26 *a-na-ku* KASKAL? *a*-[
27 ⌜*x x x*⌝ *di*? [
28 *dul-lu x*[
29 *z*[*a*
(remainder of rev. broken)
L.E. 1′ [ ]*mu*? *ṣa li*? *x*[

Translation

1: To [. . . . ., your] servant [PN]; health to [. . . . .]:
4: My [. . . . .]-men [. . . . . . .] Ṣābu-ištar? . . . . 8: May he give me . . . . my . . . .
17: . . . . . they have abandoned that work, (and) no one is bringing up [his?] bricks; 6 times the masonry(?) [. . . . . (remainder too broken for translation).

Note

5: The restoration of the PN is made likely by l. 13, where it probably recurs.

Commentary

This was clearly a report on building activities, perhaps once similar to No. 193, but since both the addressee and the writer are lost, it is practically useless.

No. 206 Plate 74 ND 443
IM, for study
3·6 × 6·1 × (2·4) —

Governor's Palace, Room S.

Obv. (beginning broken)
1′ ⌜*ina muḫ-ḫi* ŠE?⌝ L[Ú]
2′ *ša* ^{uru}*ur*?-*bi*[*l*?]
3′ *a-sa-pár-ka* : ⌜*la*?⌝ *ta-pa*?-*q*[*í-di*?]
4′ *a-na* ⌜*x* (*x*)⌝ ŠE?-*ú*
5′ ⌜A⌝.ŠÀ.⌜GA⌝ *an-ni-*⌜*u*⌝
6′ ⌜*a*⌝-*ki ina* IGI-*ma ina* ⌜ŠÀ⌝ [(*x*)]⌜*x x*⌝
7′ *tu-ru*?-*u-ni* : ^m⌜*x x*⌝
8′ ⌜*ša*?⌝ [*x*] *ru x x*
(remainder almost entirely broken)

Translation

1′: about the corn(?) of the [. . . .-men] of the city of Urbi[l . . .]—I wrote to you (but) you did not make an appointment . . . . corn?; 5′: this land is returned into . . . . . as it was in the past . . . .

Note

6′: *ina* IGI-*ma* probably *ina pānīte-ma*.

No. 207 Plate 75 ND 425
Inst. Arch. London
—

(3·9) × (4·6) × 2·2

Governor's Palace, Room S.

Obv. (beginning broken)
1′ *iḫ-[tal-qu*$^{?}$ ( )]
2′ *a-na-k[u] ša* ^{u}[^{ru} *x x* (*x*)]
3′ *ar-ti-di-pi*
4′ *ú-sa-ḫi-ra* ^{m}*x*[*x* (*x x*)]
5′ *ša* URU.ŠE *ṣ[i*$^{?}$*]-id-[q]i*$^{?}$*-[i*$^{?}$*]*
6′ *ir-ti-di-p[i*$^{?}$ *i]ḫ*$^{?}$*-[tal-qu(?)]*
7′ *la-áš-šú la* ⌜*i*⌝*-[ma-gúr(?)]*
8′ *la ú-šu-bu* [( )]
B.E. 9′ [Š]E.NUMUN-*šú-nu la i-*⌜*ma-gúr*⌝
10′ *la i-ru-šu*
Rev. 11′ ŠE *kur-an-gu ša i-za-r[u*$^{?}$*-u-ni]*
12′ *ur-ta-me-ú e-ta-x*[(*x*) *x*]
13′ ⌜*ša*⌝ LÚ.MU.MEŠ ⌞*ša*⌟ [ ]
14′ *be-lí e-mar te-lit ad-r[i]*
15′ *a-mar ú-še-rab-u-n[i]*
16′ *š[ú]m-ma be-lí i-sa-ap*$^{?}$*-r[a(?)]*
17′ *ina* UGU ^{giš}*za-qi-pe* [( )]
18′ [T]A* *lìb-bi*$^{!}$*-šú-nu i-*⌞*x*⌟*-[x* ( )]
(remainder of rev. broken)
L.E. 1″ *ina* UG[U E]N-*ia i-ta-*⌜*ra*⌝*-[ṣa*$^{?}$
2″ *be-l[í] lu-še-bi-la-šú* UD[
3″ *ina* ŠU^{ii}*-šú lu-ḫa[l*$^{?}$*-*

Translation

1′: ....] they [fled? (.....)]; I chased (those) of the village? [of .....] (and) brought (them) back; [PN] chased (those) of the village of Ṣidqī, (but) [they escaped]. None of them [agree] to stay, (and) they will not agree to cultivate their sown corn; they have abandoned the rice they were sow[ing?], and have [....]. 13′: My lord will see the yield of the threshing-floor of the cooks (and) of [.....], how much they bring in. If my lord writes? about the stakes [.......

L.E.: It was unpleasing to my lord [.....] let my lord send it [.......] let him destroy? (it) from his hands.

Notes

11′: *-r[u* (suggested by S. Parpola) is admissible (collated).
12′: The final sign is accurately copied, and no obvious restoration suggests itself.
L.E. 1″: Assuming that the verb is from *marāṣu*, in its sense of " be displeasing to, annoy ".

Commentary

The surviving part of the letter seems to cover two topics: in ll. 1′–12′ it is a question of some villagers who abandoned their homes and crops to flee authority, and possibly ll. 13′–15′ belong with this incident as well. From l. 16′ onwards the writer is concerned with stakes (or less likely, saplings). The L.E. is too broken to assess.

No. 208 Plate 74 ND 405
Inst. Arch. London
—

(3·3) × (3·9) × (2·0)

Governor's Palace, Room S.

1′]*qar* ⌜*x x*⌝
2′ -]*ši-ib-an-ni*
3′ AN]ŠE.KUR.RA.ME
4′ -*q*]*i lu la i-la-qi*

Translation

2′: ... has] appointed me(?), [.......] horses, [.......] let him not take.

Note

2′: Presumably a form of *šēšubu* "to appoint (to a post)".

Commentary

This is the bottom right-hand corner of a tablet, but there is no way even of telling whether the face that survives is obverse or reverse.

No. 209 Plate 75 ND 403
Inst. Arch. London
—

3·2 × (2·9) × 1·9

Governor's Palace, Room U.

Obv. (beginning broken)
1′ *a-k*[*i*?]⌜*x x x*⌝[*x* (*x x*)]
2′ *is-se-niš ki-i a*[*t*?-*ta*(?)]
3′ *taq-ban-ni ma-a* ⌞ERÍN⌟.[MEŠ]
4′ *ú-šal-lam a-da-n*[*a*]
5′ *ina* É.GAL *aq-ṭí-b*[*i*]
6′ *ú-ma-a* ERÍN.MEŠ *la-á*[*š-šú*]
7′ *be-lí ki-i šá e-pa-šú-ni*
B.E. 8′ *le-pu-uš*
9′ [lú]*ha-za-nu-ma*

10′ *la a-mur*
Rev. 11′ LÚ.GAL URU.MEŠ-*ni-ma*
12′ *la a-mur* ᵐGÌR[ii].15
13′ *šu-u i-se-ia am-me-ni*
14′ *a-na* EN-*ia i-sa-li*?-*u*[(-*ni*)]
15′ *at-ta ina* É.GAL
16′ *taq-ṭí-bi ma-a* ERÍN.ME[Š]
17′ ⸢*ú-šal-lam*⸣ [*i-da-na*]
(remainder broken)

Translation

2′: ..... just as [you?] told me that you would give the full complement of troops, so I told the palace. 6′: Now there are no troops, and my lord may do as he will. I have not seen even a/the mayor or a/the village-inspector. Šēp-ištar (remonstrates?) with me: "Why did they lie? to my lord, and why did you tell the palace that [he would give?] the full complement of troops? [..........

Notes

2′: *issēniš kī* obviously means "equally as, just as" here.

7′–8′: The exact connotation of "my lord will do as he will do" is probably "he will be justified in taking any action against me as he pleases"—in other words "you" (the recipient) "have exposed me to his wrath".

13′: The interpretation of *šū issēya* as "he (remonstrates) with me" is of course open to doubt. It is prompted by the fact that the *atta* of l. 15′ is performing the same actions as (and is therefore the same person as) the man who is speaking in the 1st person in l. 5′. This person is the author of the letter, and if he refers to himself in the 2nd person in l. 15′, we must suppose he is quoting another person's speech.

14′: The subject of *isaliū*(*ni*) must be a 3rd person plural, referring to people in general, if the reconstruction just made is correct. *Salā'u* "to tell lies" is fairly common in nA letters.

Commentary

The letter seems to be from one official to another, and blames the recipient for not living up to his word and having failed to provide the troops which he had promised to the writer, and which the writer in turn had promised to the palace. The immediate source of wrath would seem to be the person referred to as "my lord", who is probably the provincial governor; a man called Šēp-ištar who intervenes is probably an intermediary between the guilty officials and the governor.

No. 210 Plate 75 ND 431(b)
Inst. Arch. London
—

(2·3) × (3·0) × (1·7)

Governor's Palace, Room S.

A small fragment, presumably from a letter because of the EN-*ia* in l. 3′.

No. 211 | Plate 75 | ND unn.
IM, for study
—

(1·8) × (3·8) × (1·4)

[Governor's Palace, Room S.]

A small fragment from the left edge of a tablet, probably a letter.

No. 212 | Plate 76 | ND 404
Inst. Arch. London
—

(3·7) × (5·5) × (1·7)

Governor's Palace, Room S.

Obv.? (beginning broken)
1′ [*x*]2?-[*u*?]-*te*?[
2′ [*x r*]*u-ṭu* [
3′ [*a-n*]*a* É ^{giš}*šur-mi-n*[*i*
4′ 2 2-*u-te* 2 *ina* 1 KÙŠ *pu-u*[*š*?-*ku*?
5′ *a-na* KÁ *zi-*⌜*qi ša* É⌝[
6′ P[A]P 10 *ša* É *ḫi-l*[*a*?-*ni*
7′ 2 ⌜KAL⌝.MEŠ *a-na* KÁ *x*[
8′ ⌞*ša*⌟ É GIŠ.KAL 3 *ina* 1 K[ÙŠ
9′ [1 *r*]*u-ṭu pu-uš-ku* 2[?
10′ ⌞2?⌟ 2-*u-te a-na* É [
(rev.? broken)

Translation

2′: . . .] a half-cubit [. . . . .] for the house of cypress wood [. . . . .]; 2, small, of 2 cubits and 1/6th [. . . . .] for the window? of the house [of . . . .-wood(?)]; in all 10, of the *bīt-ḫil*[*āni* . . . . .].

7′: 2, large, for the [. . . . .] gate of the house of willow?, of 3 cubits [( )], a half-cubit and 1/6th cubit [. . . . .]; 2?, small, for the house [of . . . . .-wood(?) . . . .

Notes

2′: The use of *rūṭu* here, in the same system as the cubit (*ammutu*) and its fraction *pušku*, implies that it was a definite fraction of the cubit. The cubit (*ammutu*) is generally taken as about 0·50 m., and if the *rūṭu* is half that, it would be 0·25 m. This length is satisfactory, since the maximum number of *rūṭu* used when measuring children is 5, i.e. 1·25 m., which gives a sensible result. Hence I would suggest that *rūṭu* is to be taken as half an *ammutu*.

4′: *šaniūte* here is clearly contrasted with KAL.MEŠ in l. 7′, and must therefore mean " of secondary size, smaller "; since the exact length of each piece is defined, it is possible that *šaniu* and *dannu* refer to its breadth or thickness.

5′: *bāb zīqi*, according to *CAD* Z 133b, occurs only once elsewhere, in Sargon's inscription describing his rebuilding of the juniper (*daprānu*) palace in Aššur-naṣir-apli's North-west Palace (H. Winckler, *Die Keilschrifttexte Sargons*, I, p. 170; A. H. Layard, *ICC*, Pl. 33, 17).

9′: *pušku* (also in l. 4′) has previously been identified only in neo-Babylonian texts; it is identified by W. von Soden as an Aramaic loan word meaning "one-sixth of a cubit" (*OrNS* 37 (1968), 263, No. 116).

Commentary

This appears to be a list of beams, with their sizes and lengths, which were required for the building of doors and windows in a palace. It is probably hopeless to attempt to identify the palace concerned, although the occurrence of *bīt ḫilāni* and the phrase *bāb zīqi* make us think inevitably of Sargon, and the text's discovery at Nimrud suggest that this *might* be for a reconstruction of the North-west Palace of Assur-nāṣir-apli, which had different "houses" of different woods.

The tablet would naturally have been classed as "administrative" but for the text's physical appearance: it is very well written, on a finely made and possibly baked tablet with a flat surface and the general look of a library text.

No. 213 Plate 77 ND 822
[E]

5·2 × 3·0 cm. —

Governor's Palace, Room S.

A rough copy of this text by Professor D. J. Wiseman is given, since I cannot at the moment trace the tablet itself. The lines copied do not give much clue to the text's identity; according to Professor Wiseman's notes, the tablet had 12 + [x] + 13 + 1 (left edge) lines.

No. 214 Plate 76 ND 411
Inst. Arch. London

(6·2) × (6·0) × 2·9 —

Governor's Palace, Room S.

Obv. 1 [^{d}UT]U ⌜EN⌝ *di-nim* ^{d}IM EN *b*[*i-ri*]
2 ^{d}UTU *mi-gir* ^{d}*a-nim mi-na*(!) *kit*$^{?}$[ ]
3 DUMU.UŠ ^{d}EN.LÍL LUGAL *kiš-šat* UN.MEŠ *mi-na x*[ ]
4 LUGAL *šá-ma-mi* LUGAL *sip-par*^{ki} LUGAL *a-x*[
5 *mun-nar-bu mu-zak-ru* LUGAL *gi-mir* [
6 *e*[*r*]*-ba-am-ma ina né-re-bi šá* KUR-*i ši-te*[*m-me*$^{?}$
7 [(*x*) *x x*]*-a-nu iš-ku-nu tu-q*[*u-un-tu*
8 [(*x*) *x x*]*-at-ka iš-ku-nu pi-*[
9 [(*x*) *x x*] UN.MEŠ *sa-paḫ ma-a-ti iš-k*[*u-nu*
10 [(*x*) *x š*]*u-a-te i-ḫi-il-lu ki-ma z*[*a-*
11 [^{d}*iš-*]*tar šar-ra-tú ú-šar-ri-i*[*r*$^{?}$
12 [GIŠ.M]I$^{?}$ EDIN *it-ta-ra-aṣ a-*[*na*$^{?}$

(remainder of obv. and upper part of rev. broken)

Rev. 1′ [(*x*) *x*]*x ir-tak*?*-ka*?*-*⌜*bu*⌝ [
2′ [*x*]-⌜*x-ru*?⌝*-ma* UR.SAG.MEŠ *ina bi-*[*r*]*i-šú-n*[*u*?]
3′ *mu-ú* [( )]
4′ *ul ú-ad-di ina* SUḪ ŠEŠ *x*[
5′ *ù šá ú-ir-tu i-pu-šú ul i-*[

6′ 40 MU.MEŠ NUN? *e*[

Notes

5: *muzzakru* (i.e. N Participle of *zakāru*) appears to be unique.

Rev. 6′: The subscript informs us that the tablet had forty lines, so that over half is lost; the remainder of this line is unclear, but it obviously does not quote the text's opening words.

Commentary

A literary text consisting of an address to the gods Šamaš and Adad, invoked in divination texts and *tamītu* texts. However, it does not fall into either of those categories, and after the introduction describes wars and disaster. Professor W. G. Lambert informs me that he knows of no parallel texts.

No. 215 Plate 77 ND 460
IM 56857
—

(8·2) × (15·1) × 3·0 (main piece)
(4·2) × (4·1) × (1·7) (lower left-hand corner)

Governor's Palace, Room S.

Obv. (only the ends of a few lines survive, together with some very worn signs on the obverse proper rather than the right edge. Enough remains to show that the obverse contained similar material to the reverse)

Rev. 1′ [ ]*x* [ ]
2′ [ ]*a-na b*[*a-ma-te*]
3′ [ ]DUB-*a*[*k* ( )]
4′ [ ]*a-na ba-m*[*a-te*]
5′ [ ]*sa 'a t*[*i*? ( )]
6′ [ ] *za d*[*u* ( )]

7′ [ ]KI.LÁ *ša* Š[I]M.ŠEŠ
8′ [ ]*x ú r*[*a*? ( ) *m*]*an*?

9′ [ ](*x*) *x ina p*[*a-an*?] LUGAL
10′ [*ta-ḫa-r*]*a-aṣ* 2 *qa* IÀ.[MEŠ] ŠIM.GÍR
11′ [B]ABBAR.MEŠ *in*[*a*] ⌜UGU?⌝ ^giš^*tal-tal-li-šu* [*ta*?]-*šá-*⌜*kan*⌝
12′ [ ]*x ina bat-te-šu ta-ḫa-ra-aṣ i*[*na*?] A.MEŠ
13′ [ ]*a-na* 10 UD.ME-*šu* A.MEŠ *ša* ^giš^*tal-t*[*al*]-*li*

14′ [ ]x-e DUB-ak 2 qa IÀ.MEŠ ŠIM.GÍR TA* ^{giš}tal-tal-li-šú
15′ [ ]x IZI tu-um-mad a-di É i-ba-šal-ú-ni
16′ [ina muḫ-ḫ]i$^{?}$ NÍG.NA ^{šim}qu-nu-bu tu-lab-bak ina muḫ-ḫi ta-za-ri[q]
17′ [ina mu-k]a$^{?}$-ri-si 5/6$^{?}$ MA.NA ŠIM.ŠEŠ ta-ma-raq
18′ [ ]x ta-ga-mar a-na 2-šú ta-bat-taq
19′ [t]a-kar-ra-ár-šú 10 GÍN.MEŠ ina ša KUR gar-ga-miš
20′ [ ]x-qu ta-ma-raq a-na 2-šú-ma ta-bat-taq
21′ [x]⌜DUG⌝ [ ]ta-kar-ra-ár i-bi-ia-da
22′ [a-n]a 2-e[ ].ME-šú ta-ṣa-ḫa-at tu-ul-⌜la⌝

(remainder of rev. blank)

Commentary

This is a fragment from a long text giving recipes for the preparation of perfumes from spices and aromatic woods. Similar texts may be found in e.g. E. Ebeling, *Parfümrezepte und kultische Texte aus Assur*, from the middle Assyrian period.

No. 216 Plate 77 ND 279
IM, for study
—

(4·0) × (3·8) × 2·4

Governor's Palace, Room H.

Right-hand edge fragment, probably from a lexical text.

No. 217 Plate 74 ND 201
IM, for study
—

(10·5) × (9·2) × 6·7

Outside Governor's Palace (see below).

Obv. (beginning broken)
1′ ku-dúr-ru e-me-[su-nu-ti
2′ ú-šúm-gal-lu ek-[du
3′ mu-la-it ek-[ṣu-te
4′ MAN kàl mal-ke^{meš}[
5′ ⌞ka$^{?}$⌟ [
(remainder of obv. and upper part of rev. broken)
Rev. 1′ DÙ.A.BI GE[ŠTIN.MEŠ
2′ DUL la-be-ru [
3′ lu ú-šá-pí[l
4′ BÀD-šú ana eš-šú-[te
5′ [x x]ri[$^{?}$

Commentary

This seems to be a fragment from a duplicate of the "inscription from the wall of Calah" (*AKA* 177 ff.); our Obv. 1′–5′ correspond to Obv. 31–6 (*AKA* 181–2), our Rev. 1′–5′ to Rev. 14–18 (*AKA* 185–6).

The piece was "found in ash rubbish outside southern external wall of bathroom" (of Governor's Palace) "about 2·00 m. above the level of the floor, possibly from the ruins of Shalmaneser's" (= Governor's ?) "palace, but may have been thrown out from elsewhere" (quotation from excavation catalogue).

No. 218 Plate 78 ND 202
Inst. Arch. London

(3·0) × 3·6 × 2·0 —

A 49.

Docket with five lines on obverse, two on reverse; ends of lines only preserved, not adequate to warrant transliteration or to permit classification, but presumably administrative.

No. 219 Plate 78; Photo Plate 94c ND 409
Inst. Arch. London

4·7 × (6·2) × 2·1 [x+]4.x.post-can.

A 50, Room 7.

Obv. 1 [NA$_4$.KIŠIB ^{m}(*x*)]-*x-ad-du*
2 [EN DUMU.M]Í-*šú ta-*⌜*da*⌝*-a-ni*
(stamp-seal impressions)
3 $^{\text{mí.d}}$*ba-ni-tum-*[*šar-ra*]*t*? DUMU.MÍ-*su*
4 4 *ru-ú-ṭu ú*?[*-piš-*]*ma*
5 ^{m}*man-nu-ki-*^{d}MAŠ [*ina lìb-b*]*i*
6 5 GÍN.MEŠ KÙ.BABBAR *x*[*x*]⌞*x x*⌟
7 *ina kal-la-ú-t*[*i il-qi*(?)]
8 *kás-pu ga-mur t*[*a-din*]
9 ⌜MÍ⌝ *šu*!*-a-te* ⌞*za*⌟*-a*[*r-pat*]
10 [*la*(*q*)]*-qi-at tu-a*[*-ru* (*dēnu*)]
11 [KA.K]A *la-áš-šú man-n*[*u x x x*]
12 [*ina ma-te-*]*ma*? *i-za-qu-*[*pa-ni*]
13 [KÙ].⌞BABBAR?⌟ [
(remainder of obv. and beginning of rev. (*c.* 5 lines in all), broken)
Rev. 1′ ⌜IGI⌝ $^{\text{m.d}}$PA.*x*[
2′ IGI $^{\text{m.d}}$UTU.[
3′ ⌞IGI ^{m}⌟ *ke*?*-e*?[-
4′ IGI [^{m}GÌ]R^{II}.^{d}15 [( )]

5′ IGI [^{m}]*ṣal*$^{?}$*-mu* [( )]
6′ IGI [^{m}]*s*[*u*$^{?}$-(*x*)-]*x-qu* [( )]
7′ IGI [^{m}]*man-*[*nu-ki-i-*^{d}]15-*ia*
8′ IGI $^{m.uru(?)}$*pa-*⌜*x*⌝*-a-a*
9′ IGI [^{m}]$^{.d}$⌞PA$^{?}$⌟.KAL-*in-a-ni*
10′ IG[I ^{m}]*ga-lul* [LÚ].⌜A.BA⌝
11′ ITI.AB UD.[(*x*+)]4.KÁM
12′ [*lim*]-*me* ^{m}*aš-šur*-ŠU.GUR

Translation

1 : [Seal of . . .]addu, [owner of] his daughter (who is) being sold. (Seal impressions.)

3 : Mannu-kī-ninurta has [contracted] and [taken] Banītum-[šarra]t?, his (. . . addu's) daughter, 4 half-cubits (in height), as a bride, in exchange for 5 shekels of silver [. . . . . . .].
8 : The price has been [paid] *in toto*, that [woman] is legally acquired. There is no (further) withdrawal, [(lawsuit) or liti]gation; anyone who [at any time in the future] comes forward (to litigate) [. . . . .

Rev. 1′ : Before Nabû-[. . . . .], before Šamaš-[. . . . .], before Kē[. . .], before [Šē]p-ištar [. . . . .], before Ṣalmu?, before Su[. . . .]qu, before Ma[nnu-kī-]ištaria, before . . . . āyu, before Nabû?-da'ināni, before Galulu, the scribe.

11′ : Month of Kanūnu (X), [x+]4th day, *limmu* of Aššur-gimillī-tirri (early post-canonical).

Notes

4 : For *rūṭu* see on No. 212, 2′.

7 : *kallaūti* : this can only be the abstract noun from *kallatu*, a bride or daugher-in-law. If this form is not a mere freak, it would seem to show that the root of the word is *kl'*, and despite the Assyrian forms like *kallutu*, *kalliti*, which because of their vowel harmony argue for a short second syllable, it suggests that the word is originally *kallā'tum*, which, with a firm alef, would give an abstract *kallā'ūtum*. However, we should not exclude the possibility of Aramaic influence as well.

The phrase *ina kallā'ūti* probably indicates that Mannu-kī-ninurta bought the girl not for himself but for his son, so that an equally valid English rendering would be " as a daughter-in-law ". Instead of *ina* it is possible we should read *anà*, but not certain.

Commentary

Sale of a daughter for eventual marriage, probably to the purchaser's son. Sales of daughters are not infrequent in nA times (cf. Nos. 4, 5, 11, and perhaps 13, and e.g. *ARU* No. 37), but not, as far as I know, with this specification of the sale's purpose. On the tablet's provenance, see Introduction, p. 7.

No. 220 Plate 79 ND 408
IM, for study
(7·4) × (5·2) × (2·3) 1?.[—].?

A 50, Room 7.

Obv. (entirely lost)

Rev. (perhaps 1 line broken at top)

Rev. 1′ [ ]*me* UD!.MEŠ ⌜*sa*?⌝-*a*[*r-tú* ( )]
2′ [*a-n*]*a* *x* *x* MU.AN.N[A?!
3′–4′ (undeciphered)
5′ [KA.K]A *la* T[I? ( )]

6′ [IGI] m*šùl-mu*-[*x* *x* (*x*)] *x*[ ]
7′ [IGI] m *x* *x* *x* [
8′ [IGI] m*gi-da*?-*a*[?-*a*?
9′ [IGI] m*ab-da-a*[?-*a*?
10′ [IGI] mPAPii-*šu*?-*x*[
11′ [IGI] m*rém-a*?-*x*[
12′ [IGI] mNUMUN?-*u-a* L[Ú?
13′ [IGI] m*za-a-a* [( )]
14′ [ITI.]*x* UD.⌞1?⌟.KÁ[M]
15′ [ ] DINGIR E[( )]
(remainder broken but probably uninscribed)

Translation

.... (is guaranteed against) sickness and seizure. 1′: for] 100 days (and against) criminal [charges for] all? years? [..........;] he shall plead [in his lawsuit (but)] not suc[ceed].

6′: Before Šulmu-[...., before] ....., [before] Gidāya?, [..., before] Abda[...., before] Ahu-šu?-[...., before] Rēmā[...., before] Zērūa?, the? [...., before] Zāya [.....].

14′: [Month of ....], 1st? day, [.....] Ilu-iqbi(?).

Note

15′: Ilu-iqbi, or ...]-šamê is presumably the name of the eponym or part of it, but I cannot find a *limmu* who would fit these traces.

Commentary

This fragment must be the remains of a slave sale, if the very broken lines at the beginning are correctly restored. In view of the date of No. 219, with which it was found, it is probably seventh century in date.

No. 221 Plate 78 ND 407

IM, for study

(3·3) × 3·7 × 1·8 20.i.[—]

A 50, Room 7.

Obv. 1–3 (broken)
4 [*x* *x* *x*] *pu* *u* *x*[
(stamp-seal impressions)
5 m*man-nu-ki*-⌜*i*⌝-d[
B.E. 6 ⌞*kás-pu*⌟ [*gam*]-*mur* [*ta-din*]

	7	*tú-a-ru* [K]A.[KA *laššu*]
Rev.	8	*mám-ma* TA* *mám-*[*ma*
	9	*man-nu ša* GI[L-*u-ni*
	10	EN *u* ᵈMAŠ *a-*[*di*ˀ*-e*(?)
	11	⌜*lu-u*⌝*-ba-'u-šú*[
	12	ITI.BARAG UD.20.K[ÁM
	13	IGI ᵐKUR.DINGIR-*a-x*[
	14	I[GI] ᵐ*la* ⌜*x*⌝ *man*ˀ[
T.E.	15	IGI ᵐ*qur-di-a*[*š-š*]*ur*ˀ[
	16	[ ]
L.E.	17	IGI ᵐ⌞*x x x*⌟
	18	IGI *x* [ ]

Translation

5: . . .] Mannu-kī-[. . . has taken]. 6: The price [has been paid] *in toto*, [there is no (further)] withdrawal, lawsuit, [(or) litigation]. No one [shall plead] with anyone. Whoever contra[venes (the agreement)], may Bēl and Ninurta (and) the [oaths? of the king (and king's son)] seek (requital) [from his hands].

12: Month of Nīsānu (I), 20th day, [*limmu* of . . . . .].

13: (6 witnesses, including Qurdī-aššur, l. 15).

Notes

10–11: For this sort of clause, see K. Deller, *WZKM* 57 (1961), 29 ff.

13: To be read Šadu-ilāya ? (assuming KUR.DINGIR-*a-i*[*a*]).

Commentary

Although outwardly the tablet has the appearance of a loan text, ll. 6–9 cannot belong to a loan transaction, and ll. 8–9 in particular point to a receipt of some kind; in this case Mannu-kī-[. . .] must have been the payer, and the name of the recipient is lost. Although the *limmu* name is broken, script and general size and appearance of the text suggest seventh century, which agrees with No. 219 from the same provenance, post-canonical in date.

No. 222 Plate 80 ND 465
IM, for study
—

7·1–7·6 × (3·7) × 3·0

B 50, Room vii.

A	1′	[ ]*x* 1 GUD ⌜MÍ?⌝ *x*[
	2′	⌜1⌝ GUD 25 *gi-zi* ᵐSUḪUŠ.ᵈ[ ]
	3′	1 ANŠE 20 *gi-zi* ᵐ·ᵈPA.PAP-*š*[*al*ˀ*-lim*(?)]

A 4′ 1 GUD *ku-um x*[*x*]*x* m.d*šùl-ma-nu*-PAP

5′ 1 MÍ.ḪÚB m.dAMAR.UTU-[(*x*)-*x*-]*lu* LÚ.MU

6′ [ ]*x* ⌞UD.KA.BAR.M⌟[EŠ]
(remainder of this face broken)

B 1′ ⌜É? 40?⌝[(+*x*)
2′ ⌜É 20?⌝ URU 2 LÚ.EN[GAR(.MEŠ)] ⌜É 60?⌝ uruDUL-⌜*x* (*x*) *x*⌝
3′ 1 GIŠ.ŠAR *ina* KUR-*e* 1 *ina* uru*né-med*-dINANNA
4′ *mim-ma an-ni-ú* m⌞EN?⌟.ERÍN-*šu?*

5′ 2? GÚ.UN URUDU[ ]⌞*x x*⌟ .MEŠ
(remainder of this face broken)

L.E. 1 [ ]*an-ni-u* m*da-x*[
2 [*i*]*na lìb-bi* LÚ.Ì[R?

Translation

A 1′: .....] 1 ox, ..[.....]; 1 ox, 25 goats, Ubru-[.....]; 1 donkey, 20 goats, Nabû-ahu-š[allim?]; 1 ox instead of ....., Šulmānu-nāṣir; 1 mare, Marduk-[...]lu, the cook; [.......] bronze [..........

B 1′: an estate of 40 [(+x) (homers) ....]; an estate of 20? (homers in) the town(?), 2 farmers; an estate of 60? (homers) in Til-....; 1 orchard in the hills, 1 (orchard) in Nēmed-ištar—all this, Bēl?-ṣābi-šu.

5′: 2? talents of copper [..........

L.E. 1: .. all] this, Da[..........

Notes

A 2′: For *gizzu*, here clearly a kind of goat, and not "shearing", see, besides the dictionaries, B. Landsberger, *MSL* VIII/1, pp. 31, 59. *Gizzu* or *kizzu*, "a shearling (goat)" is apparently not attested in nA before (unless in *Iraq* 25 (1963), 99, BT 131,6).

B 2′: The only known place name which might fit the traces is Til-līni (DUL-⌜*li!-ni*⌝), see S. Parpola, *AOAT* 6, 357.

Commentary

This text, listing animals, land, and amounts of metals, can hardly be a normal census of any kind. In A 4′ an ox is said to be "instead of" something else (unfortunately lost), but this hints that perhaps we have a list of contributions paid. Admittedly it is a little surprising to find land among the other items, but this does not disprove the idea. We may note the similarity to *ADD* 942, which also has rulings to separate the contributions of the different people (who are in that case provincial governors).

No. 223 Plate 80 ND 467
IM, for study
—

7·6 × 6·7 × 3·1

B 50, Room vii.

Obv. 1 [ ]*x* SÍG.M[E]Š

2 [( ) L]Ú?.[S]AG *ša* [N]IN?.É
3 ⌞2⌟[( )] GÚ.UN m*x*[(*x*)]-*ri-i*
4 [( ) L]Ú.ASGAB
5 [*x* GÚ.U]N L[Ú].SAG
6 [*ša* (LÚ).GA]L?.É.GAL
Rev. 7 [(*x*+)]20 MA.NA m*gab-bu*-IGI

Translation

1: [x talents . . .] wool—the eunuch of the " mistress of the house "; 2 talents (of wool) —[. . .]rī, the leather-worker; [x tal]ents (of wool)—the eunuch of the palace-[overseer(?)]; [(x+)]20 minas (of wool)—Gabbu-āmur.

Note

6: Perhaps rather *ša* M]Í É.GAL—" of the queen "; if so, the identity of the " mistress of the house " becomes problematical.

Commentary

This administrative list of issues of wool looks very much as though it comes from an official archive, since the recipients may all be members of the palace staff.

No. 224 Plate 80 ND 469
IM, for study
—

5·8 × 4·7 cm.

B 50, Room vii.

Obv. 1 2 TÚG.AN.TA.MEŠ
2 5 túg*ma-aq-lul*
3 [*i*]*na* ŠÀ *ša la* ZAG
4 [(*x x*) *x*]⌞TAR?⌟ LÁ
5 2[(*x x*) *x x*].MEŠ
6 ⌜*x x x*⌝ SÍG
7 *x na?* LÚ? [*ḫ*]*ar?* *r*[*a* ( )]
B.E. 8 1-*te* [(*x*)] *ud ud* [ ]
Rev. (blank space)
9 [ ]⌞AB?⌟[ ]
10 [( )]IGI m*ú-ṣa-mir-ak-šu-du!*

Translation

1: 2 " upper " garments, 5 shawls(?), among (them? some?) without arms, ...
10: . . . . at the disposal of Uṣammir-akšudu.

Note

10: The final sign is uncertain; *ak-šu-ud!* might also be considered.

Commentary

An administrative note about textiles, perhaps, in view of their common provenance, from the same office as No. 223.

No. 225 Plate 79 ND 468
IM, for study
—

6·4 × (3·9) × 2·5

B 50, Room vii.

Obv. 1 [(*x*)]*x* [G]AL? *ši* BÀ[D?]
2 [*x* M]A.NA KÙ.GI 2 GÚ.UN [( )]
3 [*x* GÚ.U]N AN.NA.MEŠ
4 [(*x*) *x* *x* *l*]*i* 1 *me* 70 *kap-pe* UR[UDU?]
5 [UD.K]A.BAR
(remainder of obv. broken; rev. uninscribed as far as preserved)

An administrative note concerned with quantities of gold (l. 2), tin (l. 3), copper bowls (l. 4, 170 of them), and bronze (l. 5).

No. 226 Plate 81 ND 464(a)
Inst. Arch. London
—

(5·0) × (5·0) × 3·2

B 50, Room vii.

Fragment from near bottom right-hand corner of an unusually thick tablet; script coarse, three lines on Face A and five (one erased) on Face B.

No. 227 Plate 81 ND 464(b)
Inst. Arch. London
—

(3·4) × (4·2) × (1·8)

B 50, Room vii.

Fragment from left-hand side of large tablet, perhaps a list of objects; beginnings of three lines only survive.

No. 228 Plate 81 ND 464(c)
Inst. Arch. London
—

(3·6) × (2·6) × (2·2)

B 50, Room vii.

Fragment from bottom left-hand corner of a large, coarsely written tablet; what survives of other face uninscribed. Parts of two lines only.

No. 229 Photo Plate 98f–g ND 483
Inst. Arch. London
—

(4·6) × (3·5) × (0·7) (Frag. a)
(2·0) × (3·1) × (0·6) (Frag. b)

B 50, Room vii.

Two fragments of one or more clay strips bearing the impression of a cylinder seal (see p. 251); this was probably a test strip with no other function, cf. No. 264.

No. 230 Plate 79 ND 466
Inst. Arch. London
—

3·9 × (3·3) × 2·2

B 50, Room ix.

Obv. 1 [*a-na* LÚ].EN.NAM E[N-*ia*]
2 ⌜ÌR-*ka*⌝ $^{m.d}$PA.SIG$_5$⌜-*eq*$^?$⌝
3 *lu šùl-mu a-na* EN-*a*
4 LÚ.GAL SUM.GAR *i-da-bu-ub*
5 [*m*]*a-a ana-ku* ^{m}DI.EN-*l*[*a-mur*$^?$]
6 [*at-ta*$^?$]-*ḫar a-na* ^{uru}[ ]
(remainder of obv. and upper part of rev. broken)
Rev. 1′ ⌜*pi*$^?$⌝[ ]*x*
2′ *ša x*[ ]*ma*$^?$
3′ [*x x x*] *ina* UGU-*i*[*a*$^?$]
T.E. 4′ [(*x*) *x x*] *i-tal-k*[*u*]
L.E. 5′ [ ]*ú*[ ]
6′ [ ]*pa-na-tú*[ ]

Translation

1: [To the] governor, [my] lord, your servant, Nabû-deiq; health to my lord:

4: The chief victualler says: "I [appl]ied to Šulmu-bēl-l[āmur? ....], to the town [..... (remainder too broken for translation).

Commentary

Since this letter is addressed to the provincial governor, it is tempting to suppose that it belongs with the archive of the Governor's Palace, which includes several letters to the governors (Nos. 183–200). The tablet's provenance is given as B 50, which would dissociate it from the others, but I note that there was some slight doubt as to the provenance, since in the site register of tablets Professor D. J. Wiseman at one point assigned the tablet to the Governor's Palace, Room S. However, this is corrected both in the register and in the published catalogue (*Iraq* 13 (1951), 113), and this corrected provenance should certainly be accepted.

No. 231 Plate 63 ND 1114
Inst. Arch. London
—

(4·8) × (3·1) × 2·2

Burnt Palace, Long Room.

Obv.	1	DIŠ LÚ.MEŠ LUL DI[Š
	2	DIŠ LÚ.MEŠ UD.LUL? D[IŠ
	3–5	DIŠ LÚ.MEŠ [
		(remainder of obv. and upper part of rev. broken)
Rev.		(what survives is uninscribed; possibly a ruling at break)
T.E.		SU?[

It is uncertain if this text is administrative and not rather vaguely "literary"; the initial vertical wedges are hard to explain in an administrative context, and doubts are further enhanced because the script is Babylonian.

No. 232 Plate 82 ND 1116
IM 56879
—

2·0 × 1·7 × 1·1

Burnt Palace, Room viii.

Obv.	1	3	KAL
	2		3
	3	4	2
	4	19	U_8
	5	9	NIM
B.E.	6	3	MÁŠ
	7		3
Rev.	8	1	2
	9	4	ÙZ
	10	12	MÁŠ.TUR
	11	PAP	
	12	^{m}*ḫal-bu-u-ri*	

Translation

1: 3 full-grown (sheep), 0 3(-year-old sheep), 4 2(-year-old sheep), 19 ewes, 9 lambs.
6: 3 he-goats, 0 3(-year-old goats), 1 2(-year-old goat), 4 she-goats, 12 kids.
11: All—Halbūri.

Commentary

The classification of the animals, and the order in which they are listed, are identical with those of No. 131, which was found in Room B of the Governor's Palace, at the south-west end of the building and apart from the main Governor's Palace archive. Both dockets agree in dividing both sheep and goats into males, females, and young animals, and the males further into fully-grown, 3-year-old, and 2-year-old animals. Each then has a personal name, perhaps that of the shepherd-boy to whom they were assigned. It therefore seems likely that the two dockets belong together, and that No. 232 was found closer to their original home, while No. 131 had somehow strayed across. Cf. a similar note, ND 3418 (*Iraq* 15 (1953), Pl. XI).

No. 233 Plate 81 ND 1117
Inst. Arch. London

6·1 × 7·1 × 2·0 —

Burnt Palace, Room viii.

1 ^{m}*sam-si-im-me* [( )]
2 ŠU ^{m}DINGIR-*a-a-ra-me* [( )]
(royal stamp-seal impression)

Note

The reading of *ú* as *sam* follows the excellent suggestion of K. Deller.

The reverse bears the impression of a jar-neck, very similar to that on the reverse of No. 234; a sketch to show how the clay must have been applied, reconstructed from the impression of the reverse of this sealing, is given on Plate 82. The diameter of the cylindrical jar-neck must have been *c.* 6·0 cm.

For discussion of the text, and of this type of sealing, see on No. 239.

No. 234 Plate 81; Photo Plate 98a–b ND 1118
Inst. Arch. London

6·7 × (7·3) × 1·5 —

Burnt Palace, Room viii.

1 ^{m}⌜*x* (*x*)⌝-*a-a*
2 ŠU ^{m}*sa-a*-MAŠ
(royal stamp-seal impression)

On the reverse there is the impression of the neck of a jar-like object, which shows clear fibrous or wooden impressions; the diameter of the cylindrical jar-neck? must have been *c.* 5·0 cm.

For discussion of the text, and of the type of sealing, see on No. 239.

No. 235 Plate 81; Photo Plate 98c–d ND 1119
IM, for study
—

(4·9) × (5·3) × 2·3

Burnt Palace, Room viii.

1 ^m^TI-*x*[(*x x*)]
2 ŠU^ii^ ^m^[ ]
(royal stamp-seal impression)

The reverse bears impressions similar to those of Nos. 233–4; for discussion of the text and of the type of sealing, see on No. 239.

No. 236 Plate 81; Photo Plate 98e ND 1124
IM 56881
—

6·0 × 5·8 cm.

Burnt Palace, Room viii.

1 ^m^*k*[*u*-]
2 ŠU [ ]
(royal stamp-seal impression)

The sealing resembles Nos. 233–5; see on No. 239.

No. 237 Plate 82; Photo Plate 97a–b ND 1125(c)
Inst. Arch. London
—

(4·5) × (2·5) × 1·8

[Burnt Palace, Room viii.]

1 [( )] ^m^DINGIR-*da-na-ni* ŠU^ii^ *m*[ ]
(royal stamp-seal impression)

The sealing resembles Nos. 233–6; see on No. 239.

No. 238 Plate 82; Photo Plate 97d–e ND 1125(a)
Inst. Arch. London
—

(3·5) × (3·5) × 2·0

Burnt Palace, Room viii.

1 [( )] ^m.d.d^EN.LÍL.GA[R? ( )]
2 [ŠU^ii^ ^m^( )]*ka?-du-x*[ ]
(royal stamp-seal impression)

The reverse of the sealing is smooth and flat, giving it the shape of a half-olive; it bears the impression of string along its longer axis, as does No. 239, but there is no way of telling to what the clay was attached.

For the text, see on No. 239.

No. 239 Plate 81; Photo Plate 97g–h ND 1125(b)

(4·5) × (3·3) × 2·5 Inst. Arch. London

[Burnt Palace, Room viii.] —

1 [( )] 1 QAR ^{m}ZALÁG.$^{d \cdot d}$EN.[LÍL ( )]
2 [ŠU^{ii} ^{m}( )]*ku*?-*šal-mu-la*-[ ]
(royal stamp-seal impression)

The reverse is smooth and flat, with string impressions, like No. 238, and the sealing is half-olive shaped like that number.

Note

1: It is hard to see how 1 QAR can be incorporated into the following signs to make a single PN. Here, as in No. 238, the scribe has written the DINGIR before EN twice: once normally, and once in ligature with EN in the Babylonian fashion. The same scribe doubtless wrote both sealings.

Commentary

This is the last of a group of sealings from the Burnt Palace, all of which name a man who is said to be "in the hand of" (*qāt*; ŠU, ŠU^{II}) another person; except perhaps for No. 239, that is the entire inscription, and the sealings have only a royal stamp-seal impression in addition on their obverse.

In his publication of the text of the sealings (*Iraq* 14 (1952), 65–6), Professor D. J. Wiseman suggested that the clay had been attached to a papyrus scroll, and that the inscriptions gave the name of first the addressee, and second, the name of the messenger in whose hand (*qāt*) the letter was sent. However, an examination of the reverse of all these sealings shows that they were applied to an object which had the shape of a jar-neck swelling out below into a spherical body (see sketch, Plate 82); usually, if not always, the part of the sealing which was attached to the cylindrical neck shows impressions of a fibrous material, or possibly of wood, since the grain runs in one direction only. Each sealing also had string between it and the jar-neck?, and sometimes actually within the body of the sealing itself, and they were therefore certainly used to seal up the contents of the jars which had previously been covered with a cloth(?) and secured by string. Whether the fibrous impressions can have been caused by a textile of some kind, which is the simplest answer, or whether the jars themselves were in wood, can presumably be determined by scientific examination. In either case, we know that the diameter of the jars' necks was in the region of 5 to 6 cm. (see Nos. 233–4).

Nos. 238–9, which are both "half-olive" shaped, with a flat impression on their reverse, do not give us any clue as to the shape or size of the objects to which they were applied.

It thus appears that the impressions on the reverse of these sealings do not support the idea that they were attached to papyrus scrolls, and it is therefore preferable to try and explain the *qāt* in its usual nA sense of " in the charge of ", " under the command of ". This can be done if we assume that the men first mentioned in each case are the recipients of the jar (with its contents), while they are identified as being " under " the officer or official with whom they serve. Since the sealings bear the " royal " seal, which identifies items as " palace " or government property, the issues were presumably made and authorized by the palace itself, perhaps in the Burnt Palace, where the sealings were found. As to the jars' contents, we are in the dark, but oil is a likely candidate, since we know that it might be issued to soldiers going on campaign.

No. 240 Plate 83 ND 1111
BM 132008

3·9 × (6·1) × (1·7) —

Burnt Palace, Room vii.

Obv. 1 *a-na* LUGAL EN-*ia*
2 ÌR-*ka* ᵐDÙG.GA-*ṣil-é-šár-ra*
3 *lu šùl-mu a-na* LUGAL EN-*ia*
4 *aš-šur* ᵈNIN.LÍL *a-na* LUGAL EN-*ia*
5 *lik-ru-bu ša* LUGAL EN *iš-pur-ni*
6 *ma-a ina* UGU BURU_5 *du-a-ki*
7 *ma-a a-na* ᵘʳᵘA.MEŠ DÙG.GA.MEŠ
8 *a-na* ᵘʳᵘ*am-an-te*
9 *ma-a a-du* ᵘʳᵘ*ka-sa-pa šá-lik*
10 $\text{BURU}_5^{\text{mušen}}$ *an-na-⌞ka⌟*[( )*ina l*]*ìb-bi* KUR
11 *bir-⌞te⌟*[ ]*x* KUR GAL-*e*
12 *x*[ ]*ú*?*-ta-li*
13 [ ]*da*
(remainder of obv. broken)
Rev. (broken, except for the ends of several lines written round on to right edge, including one ending ᵘʳ]ᵘŠÀ.URU)

Translation

1: To the king, my lord, your servant Ṭāb-ṣil-ešarra; health to the king my lord, may Assur and Ninlil bless the king my lord:

5: As to what the king (my) lord wrote to me, saying: " With reference to killing the locusts, have them(?) go to Mê-ṭābūte (and) to Amantu (and) as far as Kasapa "—10: the locusts (are?) here in the centre of the land within [. . . . . . .] great mountain(?) [. . . . . . .] I have removed [. . . . .

Notes

2: Ṭāb-ṣil-ešarra, governor of the province of Assur, is (as noted already by Professor D. J. Wiseman) the author of other letters known from the Kouyunjik collection and published in *ABL*.

4: For the possibility that ᵈNIN.LÍL should be read *muli(s)su*, see *BSOAS* 34 (1971), 390a with note 1.

6: *du-a-ki* could also be interpreted as DU-*a-ki* = *alāki* (so Professor D. J. Wiseman, *Iraq* 14 (1952), 64), but the sense of the letter seems to favour *duāku*; this verb is also used in *ABL* 910, 6, of killing locusts (*am-mar ta-du-ka-ni*).

9: Kasappa is known otherwise (S. Parpola, *AOAT* 6, 202–3), and has been plausibly identified with Tell Keshef (Kashaf, Kushaf), on the Upper Zab almost due south of Nimrud, but I cannot trace the originator of the suggestion.

šālik presumably means "make (the men) go", rather than "make (the locusts) go", since the latter is impossible.

No. 241 Plate 83 ND 1113
IM 56878
—

3·8 × (4·7) × 2·1

Burnt Palace, Room viii.

Obv. 1 *a-na* LUGAL EN-*ia*
2 ÌR-*ka* ᵐ*aš-šur-ba-ni*
3 *lu šùl-mu a-na* LUGAL EN-*ia*
4 [*ina*] UGU É *tu-'i-in-te*
5 [*ša ki*]-*sa-al-li* É *ra-ma-ki*
6 [*ša* LUG]AL *be-lí iš-pur-an-ni*
7 [*ma-a k*]*a-ri-in-tu-ú ši-i*
8 [*lā*? *k*]*a-*[*r*]*i-in-tu ra-ṣip*
9 [*ka-r*]*i*?*-in-tu-ma*
10 [ ]*x*
11 [-*r*]*u*?*-u-ni*
12 [-*k*]*is*?
(remainder of obv. and upper part of rev. broken)
Rev. 1′ [*šulmu ana* (?)] ⌜*ma-a-ti*⌝
(remainder of rev. uninscribed)

Translation

1: To the king, my lord, your servant Aššur-bāni; health to the king my lord:

4: About the gate-house(?) of the [court]yard of the bath-house, of which [the] king my lord wrote to me, [(asking)]: "Is it behindhand?"—8: [it is certainly not?] behindhand, it is built. [If(?)] it is [behind]hand, ...

Rev. 1′: The land (i.e. province) [is well].

Notes

2: Assur-bāni was governor of Kalhu under Sargon, and eponym for 713 B.C.

4: *bēt tu'inte* is clearly connected with the root *t'm*, "twin", for which see for the time being F. Delitzsch, *Hwb.* 697b, and (referring to doors) *ADD* 756, 3, 5. In view of the root's constant association with double doors, it is possible that the *bēt tu'inte* was a structure accommodating double doors or gates, here leading into a courtyard through its surrounding wall.

7: It is hardly necessary to point out that the *plene* writing here indicates a question.

8: Is *raṣip* here an error for *raṣpat*?

No. 242 Plate 83 ND 1108
BM 132007
—

3·4 × (3·0) × 1·7

Burnt Palace, Room viii.

Obv. 1 [*a-n*]*a* LU[GAL] EN-*ia*
2 [ÌR-*k*]*a* ^{m}MAN.IG[I].LÁ-*an-ni*
3 [*lu šù*]*l-mu a-na* ⌜LUGAL⌝ EN-*ia*
4 ⌜*ša*⌝ LUGAL EN *iš-pur-an-n*[*i*]
5 *ma-a ma-'a-at* ^{m}MAN.IGI.LÁ-[*an-ni*(?)]
6 *il-la-ka i-qa-*[*bi*( )]
7 *ma-a* BÀD *ša* ^{uru}BÀ[D.]
8 ⌞*x x*⌟ [ ]
(remainder of obv. (more than half) and upper part of rev. broken)
Rev. 1′ $^{m.d}$ŠID-⌜*rém-ni*⌝ L[Ú?]
2′ *ana-ku ina* ŠÀ-*ma ana-ku š*[*a*]
3′ *ša* ^{m}BA-*šá*-^{d}ŠID? IGI?[ ]
4′ *ša is-se-šú a-*⌜*na*⌝*-ku*? *a*[*ḫ*?-]
5′ *a-du me-ni ša* LUGAL *i-šá*?*-ma*?-[*ni*?]
6′ *a-se-me ma-a* ^{m}MAN.IGI.LÁ-⌜*an*⌝*-ni*
7′ [*x*]*-tal-ka ma-a ina* ^{uru}⌜*x*⌝[ ]
T.E. 8′ [(*x*)]*x ma*[*n*?] *ma-a du*[*l-lu*]
9′ [( )]*i-ba-ši šak*?*-x*[ ]

Translation

1: [To] the king, my lord, [your servant] Šarru-am(u)ranni; [health] to the king my lord:

4: As to what the king (my) lord wrote to me, saying: "Who (do you think) you are? Šarru-am(u)ranni? is coming to me and say[ing to me?]: 'The wall of the town of Dūr-[. . . . .' . . . ."

Rev. 1′: Marduk-rēmāni, the [. . . . .], I am in it too(?), I [. . . . .] of (I)qīša-marduk, [. . . . .] who (is?) with him . . . . . I have heard whatever the king hears—that Šarru-am(u)ranni has come, that . . . . . in the town of [. . . . .], that there is work . . . . .

Notes

2: A man named Šarru-am(u)ranni is known as author of letters to Sargon—e.g. *ABL* 310–21, 757–63—and there is obviously a good chance that this is the same man.

5: The form *ma-'a-at* has to be compared with *ABL* 196, 23, *ma-'a-at-tú-nu*, which has been recognized by W. von Soden (*AHw* 603a) as nA for **mannu-attūnu*, "who are you?"; *ma-'a-at* here is thus for *mann-āta*, a 2nd sing. permansive, and this form allows us to see in the *ABL* passage not *ma'u attunu* (*AHw*) but rather *mannātunu*, 2nd pl. permansive.

Rev. 5′: The combination *adu mēni ša* . . . . . does not appear to be common; the implication of this and the ensuing lines seems to be that Šarru-am(u)ranni has heard all the rumours about himself that have reached the king, some of which he quotes in ll. 6′–9′. If he is quoting accusations made against him, it explains the otherwise curious fact, that he refers to himself by his own name, and not in the first person.

No. 243 Plate 84 ND 1107
IM 56877
—

(2·9) × (4·4) × 2·2

Burnt Palace, Room viii.

Obv. (beginning broken)
1′ ⌜*x x*⌝ [
2′ *šul-mu a-*⌜*na*⌝ [
3′ *šul-mu a-na* ^{u}[^{ru}]
4′ *ina* UGU *ṭè-e-me a*[*m*$^{?}$*-*]
5′ *ša* LUGAL *be-lí i*[*š-pur-an-ni*]
6′ *ma-a ṭè-mu ḫur-ṣ*[*a*$^{?}$
7′ KUR *g*[*i*]*-*⌞*mir*⌟*-*[*a-a*
8′ *m*[*a*$^{?}$*-a*
(remainder of obv. and upper part of rev. broken)

Rev. 1′ [ ]*x ú* L[Ú$^{?}$]
2′ [ ]*ša* ^{m}*a-r*[*a-*]
3′ [*m*]*aḫ-ru x*[
4′ ⌜*x*⌝ *ma ʾa - gu-ru ni*(-)*ir-t*[*u-bu*(?)]
5′ KUR *gi-mir-a-a ina muḫ-ḫi x*[ ]
6′ *ina* ŠÀ KUR *ú-ṣu-na-li* [ ]
7′ *i-sa-kan ṭè-e-mu* [ ]
8′ TA* KUR *ḫu-ub-buš*$_{x}$*-*[*ka*
9′ UGU ^{m}*ur-za-na a-*[
10′ *mu-uk ṭè-e*[*-mu*
11′ *ḫur-ṣa* [
(remainder of rev. (a few lines) broken)

L.E. 1′ *a-d*]*i*$^{?}$ *la-a a-šá-me*[*-*
2′ *l*]*i*$^{?}$*-iš-pa-ru-u-ni* [( )]

Translation

2′: . . .] it is well with [. . . . .], it is well with [the fortresses(?) . . . . .].

4′: As to that? report of which the king my lord [wrote to me], saying: “ Make the report exactly [. . . . . . .], the Cimmerians [. . . . .

Rev. 4′:]. . . . . we trembled(?); the Cimmerians [. . . . .] against [. . . . .], within the land? of Uṣunāli he camped?. A report [. . . . . . .] from the land of Hubuš[kia?] I [sent?] to Urzāna, saying: “ Make an exact report [. . . . .

L.E. 1′:]until I hear[? . . . . ., let] them send [. . . . .

Notes

3′: Perhaps to restore is ^{u}[^{ru}*ḫal.ṣu*^{meš}] or similar.

4′: Probably a form of *ammiu* “ that ” to be restored.

Rev. 4′: I cannot do anything with the beginning of the line—perhaps the first sign is [*šu*]*m* or [*mi*]*m*; for *ruābu* in letters, cf. *ABL* 128, 19.

8′: For KASKAL = *buš* see W. von Soden, *An.Or.* 42, p. 21; here the sign is followed by an apparent A, which must, however, be a dual sign, occasionally found in nA texts after KASKAL when used as a logogram.

Commentary

This fragment clearly belongs with the several letters of the Kouyunjik archive which refer to events on the Assyrian-Urarṭian frontier during the reign of Sargon.

No. 244 Plate 83 ND 1112
IM, for study
—

(1·4) × (2·4) × 2·2

Burnt Palace, Room xii.

Obv. (beginning broken)
1′ ⸢*x* (*x*)⸣ [
2′ *i-la-k*[*a*?
3′ *ina* ŠÀ KUR[
4′ KUR-*e* *i*-[
5′ SAG.DU GIB[IL
6′ *ina* KUR *mu-ṣa*?[-
7′ *e*[-
(remainder of obv. broken; rev. blank as far as preserved)

Perhaps part of a letter, but uncertain.

No. 245 Plate 90 ND 1109
[E]
—

6·3 × 2·2 cm.

Burnt Palace, Room viii.

1′ [( )]⸢*ša*? LUGAL? *iq*?⸣-[*bu-u-ni*(?)]
2′ [( ) *m*]*a-a a-ta-*[*a*]
3′ [( )] NA_4 AN.KAL×BAD *ti* [ ]
(remainder broken)

A fragment from the bottom edge of a letter, which seems to be addressed to the king, on the subject of stone winged genii (*šēdu*, l. 3′); similar letters are known from the Kouyunjik archive, and there is one on this subject from Nimrud (NL 16 (*Iraq* 17, Pl. XXXIII)).

No. 246 ND 1120
IM 56880
22.ix/x.714

(10·4) × (9·9) × 3·0

c. 10 m. east of Burnt Palace, Room viii.
(Square D 12.)

A copy of this tablet is to be found in *Iraq* 14 (1952), Pl. XXIII, and it seems pointless to repeat it here. The text has recently been edited by G. van Driel (*The Cult of Aššur*, pp. 198–205), and I therefore give below the results of a collation of the tablet whenever it proved possible to confirm an emendation or improve his edition:

Obv. 1: *ina t*]*ar-ṣi* . . . . .
4: *i-šá*!*-da-du-ni* (with copy)
7: last sign is *ṣu*
10: tablet has *-šal-l*]*im-šú-nu*, emendation not therefore necessary; tablet has LUGAL (not LÚ as copied)
11: *né-pa-šu-ni*! (verb !)
12: *up-ta-ṭi*!*-ru* (not *ši*)
13: .M]EŠ GEŠTIN.MEŠ . . . . .
14: *-lu* at end correct
16: BAḪAR$_2$ probably correct
19: the sign after TUR, given by van Driel as *ri*!, appears to be TUK
23: probably K]AL.MEŠ
25:]*e-si-*⌞*iḫ*⌟*-ti-šú-nu*; at end, L[ÀL.MEŠ]
27: perhaps]*ú-sa-ši-ri* . . . . .
Rev. 3′:]*-šú-ri* probable
6′:]*x* DIR (rather than KAL)
7′: G]UD.MAḪ
18′: m.dA.LÁL+SAR(= *aššur*)*-ki-na-ni*
19′: *-kab*!*-tu* correct

With regard to van Driel's remarks (ibid., p. 199) about the amount of space missing from the beginning of each line, by observing the curvature of the surface I estimate the original width of the tablet as *c*. 16·0 cm. (surviving max. width 10·2 cm.), and its original height as *c*. 12·0 cm. (surviving max. height 10·0 cm.); but it must be stressed that these proportions cannot be relied on too heavily when making restorations.

No. 247 Plate 84 ND 815
IM 56876
4·7 × 8·0 × 2·1 [—]

North-west Palace, Room DD.

Obv. (beginning broken)
1′ MÍ[?
2′ *a-n*[*a*
3′ *na-ṣ*[*u*?-
4′ *il-*⌜*qí*?⌝ [*šum-ma*]
5′ m*a-t*[*a*]*-ra-x*[*-x*]
6′ MÍ *ina muḫ-ḫi-*⌜*ša*⌝
B.E. 7′ *e-ta-ḫa-a-za*

Rev. 8′ *am-mar ša qa-nu-u-ni*
9′ *ta-na-áš-ši tal-lak*
10′ *tu-ú-ṣa*
11′ *šum-ma* ^{m}*a-ta-ra-*⌜*x - x*⌝
12′ KÙ.BABBAR *ina pu-u-ḫi i-na-áš-ši*
13′ MÍ *ina lìb-bi la tu-ra-ta*

14′ IGI ^{m}KA.^{d}1[5?.PA]P?
15′ IGI ^{m}*ia-t*[*a*?]-⌜*a*(-*x*)⌝
16′ IGI ^{m}*še-*⌜*ka*⌝*-a-nu*
17′ IGI ^{m}*si-li-mu*
18′ [ ]⌞*ša*? *x*⌟-*i* LÚ.A.BA
(remainder broken)

Translation

1′: ....]woman [......] to ...... he took. 4′: [If] Atara[. .] takes a woman in addition to her, she may take away whatever has been acquired, (and) may go and leave. 11′: If Atara . . borrows money as a loan, the woman shall not be concerned(?) in (the affair).

14′: Before Abat-i[štar?-lāṣ]ur?, before Iata'a?, before Šekānu, before Silimu, [before? . . .]i, the scribe [. . . . .

Note

13′: *tu-ra-ta*: the signs, and the general sense, are clear, but the word's derivation is less so. Unless it comes from an unrecognized root, it must be a 3 fem. permansive of *tuāru* G, with an " otiose " final *a*, but I cannot quote any instance of *tuāru* used in the sense proposed.

Commentary

Clearly the main part of this text consisted of a marriage contract, although all we have left are two clauses defining the wife's rights. Similarly in ND 2307 (*Iraq* 16 (1954), 37–8) a marriage contract (largely consisting of a list of the dowry) is concluded with certain conditions in the form of *šumma* clauses (ll. 41–50), although their content is very different from those we have here. However, in ND 2316 (*Iraq* 16 (1954), 40), ll. 7–13, we have a clause which excludes the wife from responsibility for the husband's eventual debts, such as here ll. 11′–13′, although the phrasing is very different. The clause here concerning the taking of a second wife (ll. 5′–10′) cannot be paralleled from the very scant material available on marriage in nA times.

No. 248 Plate 85; Photo Plate 93c ND 487
BM 132001
7·5 × (7·2) × 3·2 [—]

North-west Palace, Room OO.

Obv. (beginning broken)
1′ ^{m} PAP ⌜*x x*⌝ [(*x*)] ⌜^{m}DINGIR-*mu-šab-ši*⌝

2′ ^{m}*še-'i*-^{d}INANNA ^{mí}*ú-bur-tu*-PAP.MEŠ-*ša*
3′ ^{mí}*ḫa-di*-AD-*ša* ^{mí}*ri-šu-tú*
4′ PAP 6 ZI.MEŠ *ša* ^{m}EN.URU
5′ DUMU ^{m}*mu-še-zib*-DINGIR LÚ.A.BA
6′ É.DINGIR *ša* ^{uru}ŠÀ.URU
7′ *up-piš-ma ina lìb-bi* 2 MA.NA KÙ.BABBAR
8′ *ina* ŠÀ 1 MA.NA *ša* LÚ.DAM.GÀR
9′ *a-na* $^{m.d}$PA-*tuk-la-tu*-⌜*ú-ṣal-li*⌝
B.E. 10′ LÚ.DUB.SAR É.GAL ⌜*i*⌝-*d*[*in*]
11′ *kás-pu ga-mur* SUM-*n*[*i*]
12′ UN.MEŠ ⌞*za-ar*⌟-*pu la*-[*qi-u*]
Rev. 13′ *šúm-mu* U[N].⌜MEŠ *ša-tu-nu*?⌝
14′ *ina du-ra-ri ú-ṣu-ú*
15′ ^{m}EN.URU *kás-pu a-na* EN.MEŠ-*šú*
16′ *ú-ta-a-ra*

17′ IGI ^{m}*mu-še-zib-aš-šur* IGI ^{m}BÀD-*aš-šur*
18′ IGI ^{m}*iš-ma-ni*-^{d}INANNA IGI ^{m}AD.DÙG.GA
19′ PAP 4 DUMU.MEŠ $^{m.d}$MAŠ.UN.MEŠ-*ka*-PAP
20′ ŠEŠ.MEŠ-*šú* ^{m}ŠEŠ.DINGIR-*a-a*
21′ IGI ^{m}DINGIR.ZU LÚ.A.BA *ki-si-ti*
22′ [I]GI ^{m}*mu-še-zib*-⌞*aš-šur* LÚ.NI.DUḪ⌟ *šá* É.GAL
(remainder broken)

Translation

1′: Ahu-. . . ., Ilu-mušabši, Še'i-ištar, Uburtu-ahhē-ša, Hadi-abu-ša, Rīšūtu—4′: in all 6 persons belonging to Bēl-āli, son of Mušēzib-ilu, the temple scribe of the inner city (= Assur), he (Bēl-āli) contracted and gave to Nabû-tuklātu-uṣalli, the palace scribe, in exchange for 2 minas of silver (measured) with the mina of the merchant(s). 11′: The price has been paid *in toto*, the people are legally acq[uired]. 13′: If [those] people leave (their condition of slavery) in an " amnesty ", Bēl-āli will return the money to its owners.

17′: Before Mušēzib-aššur, before Dūr-aššur, before Išmāni-ištar, before Abu-ṭāb, in all 4 sons of Ninurta-nišē-ka-uṣur, the brothers (of?) Ahu-ilāya. 21′: Before Ilu-le'i, the family scribe, before Mušēzib-aššur, the palace door-keeper [. . . . .

Notes

2′: The name Uburtu-ahhē-ša is clearly the fem. counterpart of the male name written SUḪUŠ-ahhē-šu (K. Tallqvist, *APN* 103b), and this provides further support for reading SUḪUŠ as *ubru* (see on No. 30, 7).

8′: The " mina of a/the merchant " is known already (*ARU* 54; 159; 192).

13′–16′: This clause evidently provides for the contingency that the sale might be effectively cancelled because of an *(an)durāru*. Evidence for the operation of this sort of economic " amnesty " or seisachtheia is scarce in nA times (see J. Lewy, *Eretz Israel* 5 (1958), 21* ff., esp. 31* on this particular text), but it is clear that the king might initiate an " amnesty ", and that this would lead to the cancellation of enslavement for debt. Thus in *ABL* 387 rev. 17–21 (*CAD* A Pt. 2, 116 h), the Babylonians are said to have complained to the king (*ittalkūni ana maḫirte*) that " when the amnesty was imposed by the king, he caused (or: it caused) many people to leave their possession " (*issu pāni-šunu . . . . . uṣēṣia*). See also No. 10.

20′: For *aḫḫēšu* ⟨*ša*⟩ PN ?

Commentary

This text is basically a slave sale, transferring the possession of three men and three women from Bēl-āli (whose father is the temple scribe at Assur), to Nabû-tuklātu-uṣalli (who is described as "the/a palace scribe", and who probably was resident at Kalhu). The clause in ll. 16′–20′, discussed above, provides that if an amnesty was passed, the effects of the sale would be annulled. This clearly does not mean that the people would return to the possession of Bēl-āli, the previous owner, but rather that the "slaves" are released absolutely from the debts which must have been the cause of their enslavement in the first instance. Thus the six people would no longer be slaves, and Nabû-tuklātu-uṣalli is refunded the price he gave for them.

No. 249 Plate 85 ND 1110
Inst. Arch. London
4·8 × 3·6 × 1·6 [—].vii.718

North-west Palace, Room AH.

Obv. 1 [*x* MA].⌜NA URUDU⌝.[MEŠ?] SAG.DU
2 [*š*]*a* ᵐSUḪUŠ!⌜-*x* - *x* - *x*⌝
3 ᵐ*gab-bu-a-mur* L[Ú]
4 *i-ti-ši ina* ITI.*x*[ ]
5 [*šú*]*m-ma la i-din* [ ]*x*
6 [*i*]-*rab*-⌜*bi*⌝-*u*
Rev. 7 [IGI] ᵐ*sa-ni-i*
8 ⌜IGI⌝ ᵐ*pu-ṣa-nu*
9 IGI ᵐ·ᵈAMAR.UTU.A.[*x* (*x*)]
10 ITI.DUL UD.⌞10⌟[(+*x*).KAM]
11 [*l*]*im-me* ᵐNUMUN.DÙ
12 [ˡ]ᵘ*šá-kìn* ᵘʳᵘ*ra-ṣa-pa*

Translation

1: [x mi]nas of copper, capital, belonging to Ubru-. . . . ., Gabbu-āmur, the [. . . . .] has taken [as a loan(?). He shall (re)pay it] in the month of [. . . . .]; if he does not pay it [the copper] shall increase [(x-fold)].

7: [Before] Sanī, before Puṣānu, before Marduk-aplu-[. . .].

10: Month of Tašrītu (VII), [xth] day, *limmu* of Zēru-ibni, governor of Raṣappa (718 B.C.).

No. 250 Plate 85 ND 805
Inst. Arch. London
2·7 × 1·7 × 1·2 —.ii.717

North-west Palace, Room HH.

Obv. 1 5 ᵐⁱ*a-na-qa-te*

2 [š]*a* ANŠE.A.AB.BA
3 *ina* IGI ᵐ*man-nu-ki-i*-DINGIR
B.E. 4 ITI.GUD *lim-mu*
Rev. 5 ᵐDÙG.GA.IM-*aš-šur*

Translation

1: 5 she-camels, under Mannu-kī-ili. 4: Month of Ayāru (II), *limmu* of Ṭāb-šār-aššur (717 B.C.).

Note

2: There is some doubt as to the first sign of this line; Professor D. J. Wiseman read it 32, but repeated collation leads me to prefer *ša*; presumably the scribe is defining the type of camel involved, ANŠE.A.AB.BA (= *ibilu*?), as opposed to *gammālu*, where *anaqāte* does not specify which.

No. 251 Plate 85 ND 800
IM 56871
—

2·8 × 2·1 × 1·5

North-west Palace, Room HH.

Obv. 1 3 *me* 15 ANŠE
2 ŠE.PAD.MEŠ
3 3 *me* 15 ANŠE
4 ŠE.GIG.MEŠ
5 10 ANŠE IÀ.MEŠ
B.E. 6 10[ ]
Rev. 7 *šá*? *na*? *sal*? *tú* [( )]
8 NÍG.KA₉ ⌜*la*⌝ *ep*-⌜*šu*⌝

Note

8: cf. on No. 256, 2.

Translation

315 homers of barley, 315 homers of wheat, 10 homers of oil, 10 [. . . . .]. . . . ., accounts not done.

No. 252 Plate 85 ND 499
IM 56870
—

(3·0) × 2·3 × 1·5

North-west Palace, Room HH.

Obv. 1 7 *me* 70 T[ÚG?]
2 SÍG.MEŠ [ ]

3 GÚ.UN SÍG?[ ]
(rev. uninscribed)

A note concerning quantities of wool.

No. 253 Plate 85 ND 1101
Inst. Arch. London
—

2·8 × 1·6 × 1·1

Text: TÚG.AN.TA.MEŠ "Upper garments" (cf. on No. 153, 5).

No. 254 Plate 85 ND 810
IM 56874
—

2·7 × 1·5 × 1·8

North-west Palace, Room HH.

Obv. 1 1 *lim* 2 *me* 50? MA.NA
2 SÍG.MEŠ
3 1 *me* [( )]90 MA.NA
B.E. 4 SÍG.ÙZ.MEŠ
Rev. 5 (1 erased(?) wedge only)
(remainder uninscribed)

Translation

1,250 minas of wool, 190 minas of goats' hair.

No. 255 Plate 85 ND 486
Inst. Arch. London
—.i.715

2·5 × 1·5 × 1·5

North-west Palace, Room HH.

Obv. 1 56? GÚ.UN URUDU?
2 IGI m.dMAŠ-*ku*?-⌜*x*⌝
B.E. 3 ITI.BARAG
Rev. 4 *lim-mu*
5 m*tak-lak-ana*-EN

Translation

56 talents of copper, at the disposal of Ninurta-.... 3: Month of Nīsānu(I), *limmu* of Taklak-ana-bēl (715 B.C.).

No. 256 Plate 86; Photo Plate 97f ND 806
IM, for study
—

(5·0) × 3·2 × 1·4

North-west Palace, Room HH.

1 [*x*] *me* 40 UDU.NITÁ.ME(Š) MÁŠ.MEŠ
(stamp-seal impression)
2 [ ]*x* NÍG.KA$_9$.MEŠ *la ep-šú*

Translation

[x] hundred and 40 sheep (and) goats, [. . . .] the accounts not done.

Note

2: For the "accounts not done" cf. No. 251, 8; the reverse is noted in *ADD* 993.iii.27 (coll.): NÍG.KA$_9$ *ep-šú*!

The sealing is half-olive shaped, with a flat reverse which shows the marks of string and perhaps of some textile.

No. 257 Plate 86; Photo Plate 97k ND 807
IM 56873
16.i.716

6·5 × 4·8 × 1·6

North-west Palace, Room HH.

N.B.—This sealing was originally assigned the number ND 807 (so in the excavation catalogue and *Iraq* 13 (1951), 118); in *Iraq* 17 (1955), Pl. XXII, etc., the number ND 807 is ascribed to an uninscribed sealing (No. 263 below), while the present sealing is given as ND 808. It seems preferable, despite the risk of confusion, to retain the original numbering.

1 [ ]35 UDU.MEŠ *ṣib-ti*
2 [ ] LÚ.SIPA.MEŠ *ša* $^{m.d}$PA.BÀD.EN-*id*
(stamp-seal impression)
3 ITI.BARAG UD.16.KÁM
4 *lim-mu* ^{m}DÙG-*ṣil*-É.ŠÁR

Translation

1: [(x+)]35 sheep, *ṣibtu*, [under?] the shepherds of Nabû-dūr-bēlīya. 3: Month of Nīsānu (I), *limmu* of Ṭāb-ṣil-ešarra (716 B.C.).

Notes

1: For the difficult word *ṣibtu*, I refer to my treatment of it in my study of nA taxation; here it must mean either "stock, holding" or "tax (on increase)".

2: We should perhaps restore [*ša* (*ina*) IGI] or similar, following Nos. 132–3, of which at least the former comes from the Governor's Palace.

The sealing is roughly half-olive shaped, and shows on the reverse not the usual flat surface, but the impression of a jar neck, with a small part of the rounded jar body at the base of the sealing. It therefore seems (like Nos. 233 ff.) to have been applied to a small jar, sealing the string with which the jar was closed, but I am unable to suggest what purpose a jar could have served in this case.

No. 258 Plate 86 ND 809
Inst. Arch. London
(2·8) × (3·6) × 2·0 [—]

North-west Palace, Room HH.

1 [ ]*x li ma š*[*i*?]
2 [ ]ŠÀ?
(stamp-seal impression)

Inscription useless; the sealing is half-olive shaped, with the reverse roughly flattened, but with only the impression of string clear to see.

No. 259 Plate 86; Photo Plate 97c ND 1115
IM, for study
(6·4) × (3·1) × 2·2 —

North-west Palace, Room HH.

Fragment of a half-olive shaped sealing, with originally one or more lines of inscription, now useless. The reverse is smooth and flat, string holes are visible within the body of the clay; stamp-seal impression below the first line of the inscription.

No. 260 Plate 86; Photo Plate 97j ND 1106(a)
IM, for study
(5·5) × (4·3) × 1·8 [—].iv.[—]

North-west Palace, Room HH.

1 ITI.ŠU U[D.
(stamp-seal impression)
(uncertain whether further lines of inscription)

This sealing belongs with Nos. 261–2, which bear the same fine oval stamp-seal impression, and are presumably from the same provenance. Here the inscription may have given nothing more than the date.

All these three sealings (260–2) are roughly circular, and have string holes and the impression of a jar neck on the reverse (cf. No. 257, 233 ff.). They very likely all date from 719 B.C., like No. 261; there is no clue as to their purpose.

No. 261 Plate 86; Photo Plate 97i ND 1106(b)
IM, for study
4·9 × (4·2) × 2·8 —.iv.719

[North-west Palace, Room HH.]

1 [( )] ITI.ŠU *l*[*im*?-]*mu* ᵐMAN.GIN
(stamp-seal impression)
(uncertain whether further lines of inscription)

See on No. 260; the provenance is taken to be the same, although the catalogues do not mention more than one fragment under ND 1106.

No. 262 Plate 86 ND 1106(c)
IM, for study
(2·9) × (4·0) × 3·6 [—]

[North-west Palace, Room HH.]

1′ [ ]*x* [ ]
2′ [*ka*]*l*?-*ḫa ša* ⌜UGU? (*x*) *x*⌝ KÁ DINGIR.MEŠ
(stamp-seal impression)
(probably no further inscription)

See on No. 260–1; probably l. 1′ here was indeed the first line and contained the date. I cannot interpret the surviving signs here in a satisfactory way; it does not seem very likely that we have a reference to Babylon at the end of the line, more probable is a PN.

No. 263 ND 808
Inst. Arch. London
4·3 × 2·8 cm. —

North-west Palace, Room HH.

Small sealing, uninscribed, with the same seal impressed as ND 802, photo published in *Iraq* 17 (1955), Pl. XXII.1 (under the wrong number ND 807, see on No. 257).

No. 264 Photo Plate 95e ND 813
Inst. Arch. London
—

8·6 × 4·6 × 2·2

North-west Palace, Room FF.

Rough strip of clay with stamp-seal impressions, design indecipherable.

No. 265 Plate 86 ND 818
Inst. Arch. London
—

(2·2) × (2·4) × 1·2

North-west Palace, Room QQ.

Top left-hand corner of a letter in Babylonian script; parts of five lines on obverse and three lines on reverse.

No. 266 ND 1104
Mosul Museum 3
—

104·5 × 128 × 57 cm.

North-west Palace, Room EA.

This is the inscribed stele of Assur-nāṣir-apli published by Professor D. J. Wiseman in *Iraq* 14 (1952), 23–39. It is now on display in the Mosul Museum, and by kind permission of the Director of the Museum I was allowed to collate the stele. This was particularly useful for the damaged lower right-hand corner of the obverse, where some improvements could be made to the published copy which was prepared in difficult conditions. Apart from minor details, where doubtful signs were confirmed, the following corrections can be made: corrections to the transliteration and translation are included, although minor discrepancies between copy and transliteration (such as *-ti* for *-te* or a wrong accent) are not listed; see also R. Borger, *HKL* I, 638, and J. A. Brinkman, *An.Or.* 43, p. 391, note 2188.

3: *d*[*an-n*]*i*! and *dan-ni*! (with copy)
5: *a-di-ru*! (with copy)
10: insert MAN ("king") between MEŠ and *šá* (with copy)
12: *a-di* is not (!) repeated!
14: KUR *ú-ra-ar-ṭí* ŠU-*su*
17: read *ḫa*! (not *ḫar*)-*ru-tu* (with copy)
21: read È-*a* (i.e. *ušēṣ*(*i*)*a*)

23 : read *kal-ḫu*$^{!}$ (with copy)
24 : read DUL *la-be-ru* (with copy ; no *-šu*)
27 : insert *ú-si-im* after *ad-di* (with copy)
31 : at end read *e-ṣir* (not *sir*) (with copy)
33 : at end ^{uru}⌜*kap*⌝*-ra-bi* (so S. Parpola, *AOAT* 6, 195, confirmed)
34 : insert a *šá* between *gimri-ša* and KUR (with copy) ; read KUR *šup-ri-e* (and not KUR [*kir*]*-ru-ri-e*)
35 : read ^{m}*lu-bar-na* (with copy ; BAR is in fact written PA)
36 : ÍD*-tu* probably not *ḫirītu* but *nartu* ; AN.TA (not *elīta*^{ta})
37 : better *Patti-nuḫši* (S. Parpola, *AOAT* 6, 276)
39 : read in centre *áš-ḫu-ut* SAG.MEŠ, and translate " I drew wine and libated the ' first-fruits ' to Assur . . . ." (see *CAD* ṣ 60b)
41 : *a-tam-ma-r*[*u*$^{!}$
47 : ^{giš}ZIB$^{!}$ (not ḪI)*-b/pu-tu* ; at end, ^{giš}*ḫa-am-*[*bu*]*-qu-qu*
48–52 : I give a new transliteration and translation of this passage, with all due reserve, since it obviously contains some unusual topoi :

48 : ^{giš}*nu-*ḪAR*-tu* ^{giš}*ur zi nu u* GIŠ.ŠIM.GIG ÍD*-tu iš-*[*tu*] *e-le-na* ⌜*a-na*⌝ GIŠ.ŠAR.MEŠ
49 : *tu-ug-da-ša-ra i-ri-šu ma-la-ka-ni i-x*[(*x*)]*-lu na-at-*⌜*ba-ka*⌝*-ni* ⌞A.MEŠ⌟ *ki-ma*
50 : MUL AN*-e ina* GIŠ.ŠAR *ṣi-ḫ*[*a*]*-te i-ḫa-nu-*⌜*nu*⌝ [GIŠ].NU.ÚR.[MA(.MEŠ?)] *šá ki-*[*ma*] GIŠ.KIN.GEŠTIN
51 : *sa-an-bu-ku lab-šu* LÍL *ina* GIŠ.ŠAR *si-ḫa*?(/[*p*]*iš*)*-te* ⌜*tu*⌝*-lal-la* [*anāku*(?) ^{m}]⌜*aš-šur-*PAP.A *ina*⌝ GIŠ.ŠAR
52 : *ri-šá-te u'-ta-nab ki pi-ia-z*[*i*? . . . .

(End of list of trees). The canal comes rushing(?) from above to the orchards ; the paths [are full(?)] of scent ; the channels of water flow like the stars of heaven in the garden of pleasure ; the pomegranate-tree(s), which are clothed with clusters(?) like vines, make the wind rich in the garden of . . . . . [I], Assur-nāṣir-apli, gather fruit in the garden of delights like a mouse [. . . . . . .

Notes

49 : See the dictionaries for other instances of *gšr* Dt ; the verb after *mālakāni* is uncertain, the second sign is not *ḫ*[*al*] (so *CAD* Ḫ 54b), as the second horizontal wedge is higher than the first ; perhaps *k*[*a*] or similar.

50 : *ḫanānu* is given *CAD* Ḫ 76b as " to flow " ; the dictionaries restore here *i-ḫa-nu-b*[*a*, but *-nu* seems better after collation.

51 : *sanbuku* is found in *ADD* 1031 rev. 2, where the meaning " bunch " or " cluster " is not unlikely ; *tu-lal-la* is derived from the denominative verb *lullû* (*AHw* 562b); the fem. form is hard to explain in view of the masc. *labšu*.

52 : A denominative (')*unnubu* from *inbu* is known in lexical lists (see *AHw* 217a) ; here the meaning " to gather in fruit constantly " (*u'tannab* for *u'tanannab* ?) is imposed by the context.

55 : Read ^{d}*é-a-*MAN (with copy) ; for Ea-šarru see R. Frankena, *Tākultu*, 86
57 : Read *Bēlat-*KUR*-ḫi* (= *nipḫi* or *natḫi*)
58 : Read, with copy, É ^{d}*kad-mu-ri* (no Ištar)
59 : Read *šu-bat* (with copy) instead of *ma-mit*

70: There is no -*u* complement to ZA.GÌN

73–5: To be understood thus: "I established its festivals in Šabāṭu and Ulūlu, the name of its Šabāṭu festival (MU *i-si-ni-šú ša* ITI.ZÍZ) I called its name (MU-*šá ab-bi-ma!*) rejoicing (*tašriḫtu*), and I established lustration (*sir-qu*) and incense for them."

78: Read *na-ṭu!-te* (taken by *AHw* 768a to mean "suitable"; not clear to me, perhaps rather from *naṭû* II (ibid.) "geschlagen")

90: *ú-na-pi!-is*; *šub-ti* (not *miqti*), "a trap"

93–4: Read . . . [TA KUR]-*e*. 94: *u* GIŠ.TIR.[MEŠ *i-n*]*a?* š[U? (*x x*)]*x ú-ṣab-bi-ta* (cf. *AKA* 202, 25–7)

101: UN.MEŠ *a-na-sa*[*ḫ!*] *ú-rad-di*

107: At end, UDU.ZEḪ is indeed written DAM.GÀR, as in copy!

109: *si-sir!-ḫu* (with copy); presumably the same word as *sisalḫu* (*AfO* 18 (1957–8), 340 IIIa 11) used of sheep and oxen (in *ADD*)

112: 1 *lim me-su-ki*^{mušen}

118: 3 *me* IÀ+GIŠ!.MEŠ

119: 3 *me* Ú *ra-qu-tú*

134: At end, *ḫa-ba-qu-qi!* (copy -*ku*)

138: ^{giš}*ḫa-še!-e*

139: 10 ANŠE BÍL.LI.MEŠ sic! (not BÍL.SAR)

145: With copy, KUR *ṣur!-ra-a-a*

148: With copy, *za-ri-qi*^{meš}

153: With copy, *ḫa-de-e a-na*. . . . .

No. 267

ND 1122
Mosul Museum 1
—

247 × 336 × 36·5 cm.

North-west Palace, Room B.

Throne base slab uncovered by Layard and now moved to the museum at Mosul (see D. J. Wiseman, *Iraq* 14 (1952), 66); inscription partially published by Layard (in *ICC*, Pls. 43–5), but it seems worthwhile to give the whole text here. Lines 1–43 are entirely on the upper step, ll. 44–9 are partly on the lower step, with a central portion inscribed on the projecting part of the upper step, and ll. 50–62 occupy most of the remaining space on the lower step; Layard's line numbering in *ICC*, Pls. 43–5, begins with l. 21 of the text.

1 É.GAL ^{m}*aš-šur*-PAP.A SANGA *aš-šur ni-šit* ^{d}BE *u* ^{d}MAŠ *na-ra-am* ^{d}*a-nim ù* ^{d}*da-gan ka-šu-uš* DINGIR.MEŠ GAL.MEŠ MAN *dan-nu* MAN ŠÚ MAN KUR *aš-šur*

2 DUMU IGI+DUB.^{d}*nin-urta*(*wr*.UR!) MAN GAL-*e* MAN *dan-ni* MAN ŠÚ MAN KUR *aš-šur* DUMU U.ERÍN.GAB MAN ŠÚ MAN KUR *aš-šur-ma eṭ-lu qar-du šá ina* GIŠ.KU-*ti aš-šur* EN-*šú* DU.DU-*ku-ma*

3 *ina mal-ke*^{meš} *šá kib-rat* 4-*ta šá-nin-šú la-a* TUK-*ú* LÚ.SIPA *tab-ra-te la a-di-ru* GIŠ.LÁ *e-du-ú gap-šú*

4 *šá ma-ḫi-ra la-a* TUK-*ú* MAN *mu-šak-niš la kan-šu-te-šú šá nap-ḫar kiš-šat* UN.MEŠ

i-pe-lu NITÁ *dan-nu mu-kab-bi-is*

5 GÚ *a-a-bi-šú da-a-iš kul-lat* KÚR.MEŠ *mu-pa-ri-ru ki-iṣ-ri mul-tar-ḫi* MAN *šá ina* GIŠ.KU-*ti* DINGIR.MEŠ

6 GAL.MEŠ EN.MEŠ-*šú* DU.DU-*ku-ma* KUR.KUR.MEŠ DÙ-*ši-na* ŠU-*su* KUR-*ud ḫur-šá-ni* DÙ-*šu-nu i-pe-lu-ma*

7 *bi-lat-su-nu im-ḫu-ru ṣa-bit li-i-ṭí šá-kín li-i-te* UGU DÙ-*ši-na* KUR.KUR.MEŠ *e-nu-ma aš-šur* EN

8 *na-bu-ú* MU-*ia mu-šar-bu-ú* MAN-*ti-ia* GIŠ.KU-*šú la pa-da-a a-na i-da-at* EN-*ti-ia*

9 *lu-ú it-muḫ* ERÍN.ḪI.A.MEŠ KUR *lu-ul-lu-me-e* DAGAL.MEŠ *ina qí-rib tam-ḫa-ri ina* GIŠ.KU.MEŠ *lu ú-šam-qit*

10 *ina re-ṣu-te šá* ^{d}*šá-maš u* ^{d}IM DINGIR.MEŠ *tik-li-ia* ERÍN.ḪI.A.MEŠ KUR.KUR *na-i-ri* KUR *ḫab-ḫi* KUR *šu-ba-re-e*

11 *u* KUR *né-reb* GIM ^{d}IM *ra-ḫi-ṣi* UGU-*šú-nu áš-gu-um* MAN *šá* TA *e-bir-tan* ÍD.IDIGNA *a-di* KUR *lab-na-na*

12 *u* A.AB.BA GAL-*te* KUR *la-qe-e ana si-ḫír-ti-šá* KUR *su-ḫi a-di* ^{uru}*ra-pi-qi ana* GÌR^{ii}-*šú ú-šík-ni-šá*

13 TA SAG *e-ni* ÍD *su-ub-na-at a-di* KUR *ú-ra-ar-ṭí* ŠU-*su* KUR-*ud* TA KUR *né-reb šá* KUR *kír-ru-ri a-di* KUR *gíl-za-ni*

14 TA *e-bir-tan* ÍD *za-ba* KI.TA *a-di* ^{uru}DUL-*ba-a-ri šá el-la-an* KUR *za-ban* TA ^{uru}DUL-*šá-za-ab-da-ni*

15 *u* ^{uru}DUL-*šá-ab-ta-a-ni* ^{uru}*ḫi-ri-mu* ^{uru}*ḫa-ru-tu* KUR *bi-ra-a-te šá* KUR *kar-du-ni-áš ana mi-iṣ-ri* KUR-*ia ú-te-ri*

16 TA KUR *ni-ir-bi šá* KUR *ba-bi-te a-di* KUR *ḫal-mar a-na* UN.MEŠ KUR-*ia am-nu ina* KUR.KUR.MEŠ *šá a-pe-lu-ši-na-ni* LÚ.GAR-*nu-te-ia al-ta-kan*

17 *ur-du-ti ú-pu-uš* ^{m}*aš-šur*-PAP.A NUN-*ú na-a-du pa-líḫ* DINGIR.MEŠ GAL.MEŠ *ú-šúm-gal-lu ek-du ka-šid* URU.DIDLI *u ḫur-šá-ni*

18 *paṭ gim-ri-šú⟨-nu⟩ ina* MAN EN.MEŠ-*e mu-la-iṭ ek-ṣu-te a-pi-ir šá-lum-ma-te la-di-ru* GIŠ.LÁ *ur-šá-nu la pa-du-ú*

19 *mu-rib a-nun-te* MAN *ta-na-da-a-te* LÚ.SIPA *ṣa-lu-ul* UB.MEŠ MAN *šá ina qí-bit* KA-*šú uš-ḫar-ma-ṭu* KUR.MEŠ-*e*

20 *u* A.AB.BA.MEŠ *šá ina qi-it-ru-ub* EN-*ti-šú* MAN.MEŠ-*ni ek-du-te la pa-du-te* TA *ṣi-it* ^{d}*šam-ši a-di*

21 *e-reb* ^{d}*šam-ši pa-a* 1-*en ú-šá-áš-kín e-ta-tiq* KUR.MEŠ-*e dan-nu-te a-tam-mar du-rug šap-šá-qi šá* DÙ-*ši-na* UB.MEŠ

22 *ú-šá-az-ni-ni nab-li mul-mul-li* UGU *mal-ke*^{meš} *šá nap-ḫar* DÙ URU.DIDLI *si-qir* KA-*ia e-ta-nam-da-ru*

23 *ú-sa-pu-ú* EN-*ti ana-ku* ^{m}*aš-šur*-PAP.A *er-šu mu-du-ú ḫa-si-su pe-et uz-ni né-me-qi* ^{d}*é-a* MAN ZU.AB *iš-ma-ni a-na iá-ši*

24 DINGIR.MEŠ GAL.MEŠ *šá* AN-*e ù* KI-*tim ina ke-e-ni* ŠÀ-*šú-nu ú-du-ni-ma* MAN-*ti* EN-*ti kiš-šu-ti ina* KA-*šú-nu* KÙ *ú-ṣa-a* KUR.KUR.MEŠ

25 *u ḫur-šá-ni dan-nu-te ana pe-e-li šuk-nu-še ú šá-pa-ri a-gi-iš ú-ma-'i-ru-ni ina qí-bit aš-šur* EN GAL-*e* EN-*ia*

26 *u* ^{d}*nin-urta*(*wr.*UR$^{!}$) ÁG SANGA-*ti-ia a-na* KUR *lab-na-na lu-ú a-lik ana* A.AB.BA GAL-*te lu-ú e-li ina* A.AB.BA GAL-*te*

27 GIŠ.KU.MEŠ-*ia lu ul-lil* UDU.SIZKUR.MEŠ *a-na* DINGIR.MEŠ-*ni-ia lu aṣ-bat ina* UD-*me-šú-ma ma-da-tú šá* MAN.MEŠ-*ni šá ši-di tam-di*

28 *šá* KUR *ṣur-ra-a-ia* KUR *ṣi-du-na-a-ia* KUR *a-mur-ra-a-a* KUR *gu-bal-a-ia* KUR *ma-ḫal-la-ta-a-a* KUR *ka-i-ṣa-a-a*

29 KUR *ma-i-*ZA*-a-a u* ^{uru}*ar-ma-da šá* MURUB$_4$ *tam-di* KÙ.BABBAR.MEŠ GUŠKIN.MEŠ AN.NA.MEŠ UD.KA.BAR.MEŠ UTÚL.MEŠ UD.KA.BAR

30 TÚG *lu-búl-ti bir-me* TÚG.KAD.MEŠ ZÚ.MEŠ *na-ḫi-ri bi-nu-ut tam-di am-ḫur ina* UD*-me-šu-ma pa-ga-a-te* GAL.MEŠ

31 *pa-ga-a-te*^{meš} TUR.MEŠ *it-ti ma-da-ti-šú-nu am-ḫur-šu-nu a-na* KUR*-ia aš-šur lu ub-la-ši-na i-na* ^{uru}*kal-ḫi*

32 *mar-ši-si-na ana ma-a'-diš ú-šá-li-di* UN.MEŠ KUR*-ia* DÙ*-ši-na ú-šab-ri ina ti-ri-ṣi* ŠU*-ia*

33 *ú šu-uš-mur* ŠÀ*-ia* 15 UR.MAḪ.MEŠ KAL.MEŠ TA KUR.MEŠ*-e ù* GIŠ.TIR.MEŠ *ina* ŠU*-te* DIB*-bat* 50 *mu-ra-ni*

34 UR.MAḪ.MEŠ *lu áš-šá-a ina* ^{uru}*kal-ḫi ù* É.GAL.MEŠ KUR*-ia ina* É *e-sir lu ad-di-šú-nu mu-ra-ni-šu-nu*

35 *a-na ma-a'-diš ú-šá-li-di* UR *mi-in-di-na-áš* TI.LA.MEŠ «MEŠ» *ina* ŠU.MEŠ *ú-ṣab-bi-ta su-gul-lat* GUD.AM.MEŠ

36 AM.SI.MEŠ UR.MAḪ.MEŠ GÁ.NU$_x$(ŠIR).MUŠEN.MEŠ *pa-ge-e pa-ga-a-te* ANŠE.EDIN.NA.MEŠ MAŠ.DÀ.MEŠ DARA$_3$.BAR.MEŠ *a-sa-a-te*^{meš}

37 *ni-im-re*^{meš} *se-en-kur-ri*^{meš} *ú-ma-am* EDIN KUR*-e* DÙ*-šú-nu ina* URU*-ia* ^{uru}*kal-ḫi lu-ú ak-ṣur* UN.MEŠ

38 KUR*-ia* DÙ*-šú-nu ú-šab-ri* NUN*-ú* EGIR*-ú ina* MAN.MEŠ*-ni* DUMU.MEŠ*-ia ša aš-šur i-na-bu-šu lu-ú* UN.MEŠ

39 EGIR.MEŠ *lu-ú* ^{lú}*um-ma-an* MAN *lu-ú* LÚ.GAL*-ú lu-ú* ^{lú}*šá* SAG *la ta-ṭa-píl ina pa-an aš-šur* ZI *ši-i-ti*

40 ^{d}*nin-urta*(*wr.* UR!) *ù* ^{d}IGI.DU *ša* SANGA*-ti* ÁG*-mu* MÁŠ.ANŠE EDIN *ú-šat-li-mu-ni e-peš ba-'u-ri iq-bu-ni*

41 30 AM.SI.MEŠ *ina šub-ti a-duk* 2 *me* 57 GUD.AM.MEŠ KAL.MEŠ *ina* GIŠ.GIGIR.MEŠ*-ia pa-tu-te ina qi-it-ru-ub*

42 EN*-ti-ia ina* GIŠ.KU.MEŠ *ú-šam-qit* 3 *me* 70 UR.MAḪ.MEŠ KAL.MEŠ GIM MUŠEN.MEŠ *qu-up-pi ina* ^{giš}*pu-aš-ḫi a-duk*

43 *ina* ITI.GUD UD.8.KÁM TA ^{uru}*kal-ḫi at-tu-muš* ÍD.ḪAL.ḪAL *e-te-bir a-na* ^{uru}*gar-ga-miš ša* KUR *ḫat-te*

44 *aq-ṭí-rib* NÍG.GA É.GAL*-šú* ḪI.A.MEŠ *ša* KI.LÁ*-šú* NU *ṣab-ta-at am-ḫur-šú* MAN.MEŠ*-ni ša* KUR.KUR.MEŠ DÙ*-šú-nu*

45 *ana muḫ-ḫi-ia* DU*-ku-ni* GÌR^{ii}*-a iṣ-ṣab-tu li-ṭí-šú-nu aṣ-bat pa-na-tu-ia uk-ti-lu a-na* KUR *lab-na-na* DU*-ku*

46 TA ^{uru}*gar-ga-miš at-tu-muš ina bi-rit* KUR *mun-zi-ga-ni* KUR *ḫa-mur-ga a-ṣa-bat* KUR *a-ḫa-nu a-na* KAB*-ia ú-ta-šèr*

47 *a-na* ^{uru}*ḫa-za-zi ša* ^{m}*lu-bar-na* KUR *ḫat-ti-na-a-a aq-ṭí-rib* KÙ.BABBAR GUŠKIN TÚG *lu-búl-ti* TÚG.KAD.MEŠ *at-ta-ḫar e-te-tiq* ÍD *ap-re-e*

48 *e-te-bìr a-sa-kan be-dak* TA UGU ÍD *ap-re-e at-tu-muš a-na* ^{uru}*ku-nu-lu-a* URU MAN*-ti-šú ša* ^{m}*lu-bar-na* KUR *ḫat-ti-na-a-a aq-ṭí-rib*

49 TA IGI GIŠ.KU.MEŠ*-a ez-zu-te* MÈ*-ia šit-mu-ri ip-láḫ-ma a-na šu-zu-ub* ZI.MEŠ*-šú* GÌR^{ii}.MEŠ*-a iṣ-bat* 20 GÚ.UN KÙ.BABBAR.MEŠ 1 GÚ.UN GUŠKIN.MEŠ 1 *me* GÚ.UN AN.NA.MEŠ

50 1 *me* GÚ.UN AN.BAR.MEŠ 1 *lim* GUD.MEŠ 10 *lim* UDU.MEŠ 1 *lim* TÚG *lu-búl-ti bir-me* TÚG.KAD.MEŠ ^{giš}*né-mat-ti* GIŠ.KU.MEŠ *ša tam-li-te uḫ-ḫu-za-te*

51 GIŠ.NÁ.MEŠ GIŠ.KU.MEŠ GIŠ.NÁ.MEŠ ZÚ.MEŠ *ša tam-li-te* GAR.RA.MEŠ *ú-nu-tú* É.GAL-*šú* ḪI.A.MEŠ *ša* KI.LÁ-*šá* NU *ṣab-ta-at am-ḫur-šú*

52 ^{uru}*kal-ḫu maḫ-ra-a šá* $^{\mathrm{m.d}}$*šùl-ma-nu*-SAG MAN KUR *aš-šur* NUN *a-lik pa-ni-ia* DÙ-*uš* URU *šu-ú e-na-aḫ-ma iṣ-lal*

53 URU *šu-ú ana eš-šú-te ab-ni* UN.MEŠ *ki-šit-ti* ŠU-*ia šá* KUR.KUR.MEŠ *šá a-pe-lu-ši-na-ni šá* KUR *su-ḫi*

54 KUR *la-qe-e ana si-ḫír-ti-šá* ^{uru}*sir-qu šá né-bir-ti* ÍD *pu-rat-te* KUR *za-mu-a ana paṭ gim-ri-šá*

55 KUR É-*a-di-ni u* KUR *ḫat-te paṭ*(/*u šá?*) ^{m}*lu-bar-na* KUR *ḫat-ti-na-a-a al-qa-a ina lìb-bi ú-šá-aṣ-bit* DUL *la-be-ru*

56 *ú-na-kir*$_7$ *a-di* UGU A.MEŠ *lu ú-šá-píl* 1 *me* 20 *tik-pe ina muš-pa-li lu ú-ṭa-bi* É.GAL GIŠ.ERIN.NA

57 É.GAL GIŠ.ŠUR.MAN É.GAL ^{giš}*dáp-ra-ni* É.GAL GIŠ.TASKARIN.MEŠ É.GAL GIŠ.MES.KAN-*ni* É.GAL ^{giš}*bu-uṭ-ni u* ^{giš}*ṭar-pi-'i*

58 *a-na šu-bat* MAN-*ti-ia ana mul-ta-'i-it* EN-*ti-a šá da-ra-a-te ina lìb-bi ad-di ú-ma-am* KUR.MEŠ-*e*

59 *u* A.AB.BA.MEŠ *šá* NA$_4$ *pe-li* BABBAR-*e u* NA$_4$ *pa-ru-te* DÙ-*uš ina* KÁ.MEŠ-*šá ú-še-zi-iz ú-si-im-ši ú-šar-riḫ-ši*

60 *si-kat kar-ri* UD.KA.BAR *al-me-ši* GIŠ.IG.MEŠ ^{giš}*e-re-ni* GIŠ.ŠUR.MAN ^{giš}*dáp-ra-ni* GIŠ.MES.KAN-*ni ina* KÁ.MEŠ-*šá ú-re-ti*

61 KÙ.BABBAR.MEŠ GUŠKIN.MEŠ AN.NA.MEŠ UD.KA.BAR.MEŠ *ki-šit-ti* ŠU-*ia šá* KUR.KUR.MEŠ *šá a-pe-lu-ši-na-ni*

62 *a-na ma-a'-di-iš al-qa-a ina lìb-bi ú-kín*

No. 268 — Plate 87 — ND 812(a)

IM, for study

—

(6·7) × (7·8) × 2·6

North-west Palace, Room FF.

Obv. (entirely broken, except for the traces of single signs in three of four lines)

Rev. (upper part broken)

	1′	] ⌜*x x x x*⌝ [
	2′	*ma-*]*a*? ⌜*a-lik*⌝ *a*!-*na* DING[IR.MEŠ] *gab-bu pa*!?-*s*[*i*!-
	3′	] ⌞*iḫ*?⌟-*di*-[
A.62	4′	(traces)] DINGIR?.MEŠ ⌞AD.MEŠ⌟-*šú šu-nu e*[?-
A.63	5′	]^{d}*gu-la ina* [UGU(-*ḫi*)]-*šú ta*-⌜*šap*?⌝-[*pa-ra*
A.64–5	6′	]*ú-še-b*[*al*]-*áš-ši né-mi-i*[*l ana šá*]-*a-šú* [*l*]*a ú*-⌜*šar*?⌝-[*u-šú-ni*]
A.66	7′	*la-á*]*š-šú* [*š*]*a*? ⌜*la*⌝ E[N ( )] *ta-sa-b*[*u-u'*]
A.67	8′	*ba-k*]*i-su ši-i* [TA] URU *ta-*[*la-bi-a*]
A.68	9′	]*e-tar-ba* GIŠ.IG [*ina pāni*]-*šú e-*[*te-di-li*]
A.70	10′	*ṭu*]*p-pu a*[*n-ni-*]*ú*? *e-ma*[*r-ra-qu-u-ni*
A.71	11′	]*ù em-mar-u-ni a-*[*na ša la ú-du-ni*
A.72–3	12′	^{d}15 *ša* NINA^{k}]^{i} ^{d}15 *ša* ^{uru}TAB.TAB.DINGIR ⌞*x x*⌟ [

A.74	13′	KUR *aš-šur*^{ki}]	*ka-li-*[*šu-nu*
A.76	14′		*š*]*a lab-bi* [*liškunu*]

15′–16′/17′ (undeciphered traces; presumably colophon)

This text is the duplicate of the Assur version of the " Marduk Ordeal " composition, to which I referred in *ZA* 60 (1969), 127. The lines of our text are given above their corresponding line numbers in the Assur (A.) text as edited by W. von Soden (*ZA* 51 (1955), 132–41); for the later additions to the Ninevite recension of the composition see W. von Soden, *ZA* 52 (1957), 222–34 (esp. ll. 33–4, for l. 4′ here), and J. N. Postgate, *ZA* 60 (1969), 124–7.

Unfortunately the tablet is so badly preserved that only those lines with clear duplicates have been satisfactorily deciphered; particularly galling is the loss of the colophon.

No. 269 Plate 88 ND 812(b)
IM, for study

(7·2) × (8·7) × 2·6 —

North-west Palace, Room FF.

Part of a presumably " literary " text in Babylonian script, perhaps the end of obverse and upper part of reverse; it seems worth while to give a copy in the hope that someone will be able to identify the text, even if that hope is distant.

No. 270 Plate 89 ND 821(a)
BM 132004

(7·4) × (6·6) × 2·9
North-west Palace, Room FF. —

Central part of the right-hand side of an unidentified incantation and ritual text; on face A incantation (ll. 1′–6′) and ritual instructions (7′–12′), contents of the six lines partly surviving on face B unclear.

No. 271 Plate 87 ND 821(b)
BM 132005

(6·4) × (8·9) × (3·5) —

North-west Palace, Room FF.

A thick fragment in small script, in at least two columns, and probably from a lexical text.

No. 272 Plate 87 ND 821(c)
BM 132006

(4·1) × (4·3) × 2·0 —

North-west Palace, Room FF.

Fragment from centre of bottom (or top) edge of a tablet in script similar to that of No. 271; probably four columns, presumably lexical, but it cannot form part of the same tablet as No. 271 because it is much less thick. Face B (not copied) does show traces of cuneiform signs, but is extremely badly worn.

APPENDIX: SEAL IMPRESSIONS (Plates 91–8)

The major seal impressions from this group of tablets have already been published by B. Parker (*Iraq* 17 (1955), 110–14; Pls. XX–XXII). However, since it seemed worth while to illustrate some of those not dealt with there, I have taken this opportunity to give new photographs of most of the seal impressions from the first three seasons, as well as some illustrations of characteristic or noteworthy tablets. Not illustrated are Nos. 133, 233, 258, 262, and 263, either because adequately illustrated in *Iraq*, or because they are so similar to others; in addition, Nos. 1, 10, 100, 191, and 221 once had seal impressions which are now lost. Below I give what details may be helpful, but it is not intended to give a full publication, for which I have not hesitated to refer back to B. Parker's original article where relevant. Seal inscriptions have been dealt with in the main body of the edition; the list is in the order of the texts' numbers.

No. 13 (ND 257) Plate 92a

Stamp seal, circular (dia. ±1·3 cm.); impressed probably three times.

Design: Two, or more likely three, hollow lozenge-shaped motifs, placed horizontally one above the other (length of central lozenge 0·9 cm., breadth 0·3 cm.). The motif is hardly intended for lips, possibly they are stylized eyes; for a discussion of this lozenge motif, cf. B. Parker, *Iraq* 17 (1955), 106.

No. 18 (ND 209) Plate 94a

Cylinder seal (ht. very roughly 4·0 cm. (est. from photograph); circ. not estimated); impression fair but badly broken and encrusted.

Design (taken from photograph): Goddess seated on throne, facing right, behind her two standards of which the right-hand one is surmounted by a plain disc. Remainder of design could perhaps be discerned from the tablet; on the extreme right the base of the standards may be repeated on the extension of the impression, but this is uncertain.

The seal belonged to Aššur-aplu-uṣur, son of . . . . ni (l. 1).

Date: 778 B.C.

No. 44 (ND 258(a)) Plate 93a

Cylinder seal, impression extending beyond ruled space above and below; ht. of ruled space 2·65 cm.; min. ht. of seal 2·95 cm.; est. circ. of seal ±4·7 cm.

Design: A four-winged human figure, wearing a plain head-dress with narrow band round forehead, confronts a rearing, two-winged unicorn, whose right fore-hoof he grasps in his left hand (note the stylized mane represented by drill holes). With his right hand he holds the fore-paw of a winged lion, who rears up on the other side. Between the backs of the two animals there is a meaningless cuneiform sign, like an incorrect NU or PAP; Miss E. Porada informs me that this is a known kind of filling motif in nA glyptic.

To judge from the remainder of the archive, and more specifically from the size and ductus of the script, the text belongs roughly to the time of Tiglath-pileser III.

The seal was the property of Šamaš-iddina, mayor of a village whose name is lost; for discussion of why his seal was impressed, see commentary on the text.

No. 64 (ND 231) [*Iraq* 17, 110; Pl. XX.2] Plate 91b

Cylinder seal, impression extending beyond ruled space; min. ht. of seal 2·4 cm., circ. ±5·1 cm.

Design: See *Iraq* 17, 110; note that the figure to the right in the impression is unbearded and probably therefore a eunuch. The object between the two figures seems to be an offering stand or brazier rather than a cult symbol.

The seal inscription is unclear, but according to my reconstruction of the transaction, the seal should have belonged to Sîn-ēṭir, brother of Bēl-tarṣi-iluma.

No. 66 (ND 476) [*Iraq* 17, 110–11; Pl. XXI.1] Plate 95d

Cylinder seal, overall ht. 3·55 cm., ht. of impression without borders 2·7 cm. (i.e. metal caps 0·4–0·45 cm. each); est. circ. ±5·0 cm. (width of this impression 5·1 cm.). The main part of the seal is occupied by the inscription (*c*. 3·0 cm.), while the design has but *c*. 2·0 cm.

Design: See *Iraq* 17, 110–11; since other instances of this seal are found below, it seems worth while to quote the description given there at some length: "The impression shows a god mounted on a horned lion, which may have a scorpion tail as on the Maltai reliefs ..... The god holds an axe and a ring in his lowered hand and the other is raised in acknowledgment of devotions rendered by a worshipper, probably the owner of the seal, who stands before him. The god wears a sword, the point of which is marked by five small stars; there are stars on either side of his head, which probably mark the end of bow and quiver slung over his shoulders. The worshipper standing before him wears the usual Assyrian dress of which no details can be seen; he appears to be beardless. ... In the field above is an unusual emblem comprising a crescent on a staff which is encircled by a ring; is this an attempt to represent both the crescent and the full moon?"

The new impressions (Nos. 170–1) alter the picture very little; it seems to me that the animal is not a horned lion, but a unicorn or possibly bull, and that the "staff" bearing the crescent and ring is rather a short spear-like object with a leaf-shaped blade suspended point downwards. It is certain that the worshipper is beardless, and he must surely be, as B. Parker suggests, the owner of the seal, who we know to have been Bēl-tarṣi-iluma, and who is expressly described as a eunuch in the seal inscription. The worshipper appears as a eunuch also in Nos. 64, 132, and 172–3.

Date: Since the seal is found on No. 170, it must date to or before 808 B.C., assuming the *limmu* date is correctly restored there. In any case it belongs to the governorship of Bēl-tarṣi-iluma, viz. between 808 and 772 B.C.

No. 99 (ND 241(a)) Plate 94b

Cylinder seal, dimensions not preserved, rolled twice but faintly on the uninscribed reverse of the envelope which measures 4·9 × 3·6 cm.

Design: Bearded, winged, figure facing left, hand raised to acknowledge gesture from a second, unbearded figure, who is probably the seal's owner. Behind him, to the left, another bearded and winged figure, facing right, visible on lower impression. In field above "eunuch" a winged disc, above first bearded figure, crescent moon and probably stars. Line of cap or rim at top of impression.

Date: During the governorship of Bēl-dān, to whom the seal might belong, although it could also belong to Aššur-dūru-uṣur.

No. 107 (ND 489) Plate 92c

Cylinder seal (ht. 2·3 cm. +; circ. 4·8 cm. +); the impression is extremely faint and damaged in its lower part.

Design: A human figure, standing full-face, holds in one hand a horse's foreleg, and in the other probably the front leg of a winged figure visible on the right of the impression. Between the backs of the horse and the winged figure (which may be a female centaur), there is a symbol in the shape of a pillar(?), or tapering offering stand, with a star-like shape above it.

Date: 737 B.C.

The seal probably belonged to Ninurta-bēlu-uṣur; for the position of the impression—on the reverse of the tablet—cf. commentary to No. 106.

No. 132 (ND 494) [*Iraq* 17, 111; Pl. XXI.2; Fig. 1 (p. 111)] Plate 96c, df,

(1) Cylinder seal (ht. 2·5 cm. +; circ. ±6·0 cm.); top and bottom of impression missing because of curvature of clay.

Design: See *Iraq* 17, 111; as indicated there in Fig. 1, there *appears* to be the back of a third figure directly to the right of the god, of which no further detail can be made out. However, when the inscription of this impression is compared with that of the seal used on Nos. 172–3, it becomes apparent that this is the same seal, that of Šarru-dūrī, and that the indistinct object to the god's right is in fact the staff(?) held by the worshipper, with part of his hand perhaps accounting for one of the bulges. The design is described below, under No. 173.

(2) Stamp seal, circular or slightly elliptical; max. dia. 1·9 cm.; impression good but missing at sides.

Design: A mace or sceptre, across the diameter of the circle.

A similar seal is found on Nos. 170 and 171 q.v., but that stamp seal was smaller, and its design is carved in reverse, so that it is not the identical seal. This raises an interesting point: both here, and on Nos. 170 and 171, the sealing has the impression of an inscribed cylinder seal of the governor of Kalhu (Bēl-tarṣi-iluma or Šarru-dūrī), but in each case there is also on one side a single impression of a stamp seal, which, although portraying a sceptre, is different for the two different governors. Did they both have an official cylinder seal and stamp seal, and if so, were both needed to lend validity to certain transactions? And is there any special symbolism behind the use of a sceptre as the design for the stamp seals? cf. No. 133.

No. 133 (ND unn.) Not illustrated

Stamp seal, only about one-quarter survives, dia. *c.* 2·0 cm.

Design: In centre of field probably a single sceptre or similar symbol, details broken.

The dimensions of this seal, and what remains of the design, make it probable that it was the same as that impressed on No. 132, which like this sealing dealt with sheep. It is not possible to tell if No. 133 also had a cylinder seal impression, since the greater part of the sealing is now lost.

No. 170 (ND 252(k)) Plate 95c

(1) Cylinder seal, inscribed with the name and titles of Bēl-tarṣi-iluma, and evidently the same as that impressed on No. 66 q.v.; this particular impression adds little to Nos. 66 and 171.

(2) (On separate small fragment, not photographed; cf. sketch on Pl. 62): Stamp seal, circular, dia. ±1·2 cm. (also on No. 171).

Design: A mace or sceptre, across the diameter of the circle; the impression of the sceptre is sunk into the clay, hence on the seal itself the background must have been cut away to make the design, leaving the sceptre in relief. For the use of this stamp seal in conjunction with the cylinder seal, see my comments on No. 132.

Date: Possibly 808 B.C.

No. 171 (ND 240(b)) Plate 95a–b

(1) Cylinder seal, impressed at least three times in different parts. Inscription and design show that this is the same seal as that on Nos. 66 and 170 qq.v. The main impression on this sealing shows clearly that the god is standing not upon a lion, but on a unicorn; it also confirms that the worshipper is indeed beardless (i.e. a eunuch), and shows that animal's tail rather more clearly.

(2) Stamp seal, circular, slightly over half preserved; identical with the stamp seal on No. 170 q.v.

No. 172 (ND 275(a)) Plate 96e

Cylinder seal; inscription and design identify this seal with that found on Nos. 132 and 173 q.v.

No. 173 (ND 275(k)) Plate 96a–b

Cylinder seal, from its design identical with that on Nos. 132 and 172; for a description of part of the design see No. 132. The combination of evidence from all three impressions gives further information: min. ht. 3·4(+) cm., + border (metal cap) (2x) 0·5 cm. (i.e. total height *c.* 4·5 cm. or a little more); circ. *c.* 6·0 cm.

Design: The god (see *Iraq* 17, 111) is now seen to be standing on a winged animal, possibly a lion, with up-curving tail done in drill-holes, perhaps intended as that of a scorpion. Before him is the robed figure of a eunuch (seen best on No. 132, Pl. 96c, but also appearing on Nos. 172–3), who is probably holding a staff (see No. 173); the detail of the upper part of the staff is lost. The remainder of the field, between the backs of the god and the worshipper, is partly occupied by a three-line inscription and partly blank. The inscription identifies the seal as that of Šarru-dūrī, governor of Kalhu; it is possible that the blank space was once devoted to further titles which were later erased (cf. the Introduction, p. 11).

Date: Since there is no fixed date in the governorship of Šarru-dūrī, the seal cannot be dated closer than *c.* the third quarter of the eighth century (see the Introduction, p. 11).

No. 219 (ND 409) Plate 94c

Stamp seal, dia. ±1·0 cm.; impressed faintly three times.

Design: Geometrical pattern in the form of a wheel with eleven spokes and a reserved central hub. Probably the design is a stylized floral motif with the petals in negative (on the impression); cf. the stamp seal on BM 121043 (*Iraq* 32 (1970), Pl. XXXIb), where the petals do not appear in negative.

Date: Late seventh century (according to M. Falkner's scheme for the post-canonical eponyms, 641 B.C.).

No. 229 (ND 483) Plate 98f–g

Cylinder seal, impressed on two non-joining fragments of clay; ht. of larger piece 3·5 cm., dimensions of seal not reconstructible.

Design: A bearded figure, probably the king, shoots from chariot at enemy whose head is turned back over his shoulder. To right of larger fragment, the heads of the horse(s) and chariot driver; "Pleiades" in field above, and unidentified lozenge-shaped object between back of chariot and falling enemy. For similar scenes of battle, cf. E. Porada, *Corpus*, Nos. 659–63.

No. 233 (ND 1117) Not illustrated

Royal stamp seal; impression obliterated. See on No. 239.

No. 234 (ND 1118) Plate 98a–b

Royal stamp seal; see on No. 239.

No. 235 (ND 1119) Plate 98c–d

Royal stamp seal; left side of impression only. See on No. 239.

No. 236 (ND 1124) Plate 98e

Royal stamp seal; dia. 3·0 cm. See on No. 239.

No. 237 (ND 1125(c)) Plate 97a–b

Royal stamp seal; upper left-hand corner only, with clear guilloche border. See on No. 239.

No. 238 (ND 1125(a)) Plate 97d–e

Royal stamp seal; part of upper half only. See on No. 239.

No. 239 (ND 1125(b)) Plate 97g–h

Royal stamp seal; (?) part of lower half only.

Nos. 233–9: All of these sealings have the impression of the royal stamp seal (in varying degrees of certainty), on which see A. J. Sachs, *Iraq* 15 (1953), 167–70, and A. R. Millard, *Iraq* 27 (1965), 12–16. Because of the variation in the way in which the seal was impressed, and the varying states of preservation of the sealings themselves, it is impossible to be certain if the identical seal was used on each occasion. Even the apparent absence of a guilloche border (clearly visible on No. 237, for example) is not decisive, since close inspection of No. 234 shows that the seal used there also had a guilloche border, although it scarcely shows in the impression.

Date: This group of sealings comes from the same room in the Burnt Palace as some letters from the reign of Sargon, and they are therefore probably likewise from his reign. This agrees well with the date of K 3781a (*Iraq* 15 (1953), Pl. XIX.5), which is dated to 719 B.C. and is similar to our examples in general appearance and size ($1\frac{1}{4}$ in. = 3·2 cm.).

No. 256 (ND 806) [*Iraq* 17, 112–13; Pl. XXII.2; Fig. 3, p. 112] Plate 97f

Stamp seal, elliptical (2·2 × *c.* 1·9 cm.). See the better preserved impression of the same seal on No. 258.

No. 257 (ND 807!) [*Iraq* 17, 114; Pl. XXII.5—" ND 808 "] Plate 97k

Stamp seal, elliptical; 3·5 × 2·8(+) cm.; with raised rim.

See *Iraq* 17, 114; a very similar, if not identical, seal was impressed on Nos. 260–2. For the ND number, see the main text on No. 257.

No. 258 (ND 809) [*Iraq* 17, 112–13; Pl. XXII.4; Fig. 3, p. 112] Not illustrated

Stamp seal, as on No. 256. See *Iraq* 17, 112–13.

No. 259 (ND 1115) Plate 97c

Stamp seal; small part only survives, possibly showing the legs of the figure of the king from a royal stamp seal (cf. No. 239).

No. 260 (ND 1106(a)) Plate 97j

Stamp seal, elliptical; 3·8 × ±2·9 cm., with raised rim.

Design: The design on this unusually large stamp seal is extremely similar to that on No. 257, and I cannot determine with certainty whether they are the same seal or not. The greatest apparent difference between the two impressions seems to be in the king's head-dress, which looks tiered and conical on No. 257, whereas here it is the usual fez shape with the streamer behind; there also seem to be differences in the shape and position of the king's beard. In general the figures in the impression on No. 257 are more elongated than here, and this impression is marginally larger than that on No. 257.

It is hard to attribute all these differences to different impressions of the same seal, and I therefore incline to the view that on Nos. 260–2 (from which the above details are drawn) we have a different seal to that on No. 257, although the two seals must have been extremely similar.

Details on Nos. 260–2 which would not in any case have been discernible on No. 257 because of its poor preservation are the head of the attendant (best seen on No. 261), who is clearly unbearded and therefore a eunuch, and the presence of a scorpion in the field above the goddess (on the unillustrated part of No. 261).

No. 261 (ND 1106(b)) Plate 97i

Stamp seal, as No. 260.

The photo shows only the top left-hand corner of the sealing: the right half (as shown in the copy, Pl. 86) was only joined to this piece subsequently.

No. 262 (ND 1106(c)) Not illustrated

Stamp seal, as No. 260; right half only.

No. 263 (ND 808!) [*Iraq* 17, 111–12; Pl. XXII.1; Fig. 2, p. 111—" ND 807 "] Not illustrated

Stamp seal, impressed three times on uninscribed sealing; see *Iraq* 17, 111–12; for the ND number see the main text on No. 257.

No. 264 (ND 813) Plate 95e

Stamp seal, roughly elliptical (2·5 × 1·65 cm.); impressed twice on a rough strip of clay. No details of the design can be made out.

CATALOGUE OF TEXTS

(BY EXCAVATION NUMBER)

NOTES TO CATALOGUE

1st Column: ND number: ND 201–287 are from first season (1949).
ND 400–499, 800–831 are from second season (1950).
ND 1101–1131 are from third season (1951).

I have used square brackets thus: 464[a], to indicate that the letters identifying separate pieces catalogued under a single ND number have been assigned by me, for convenience of identification. Letters in round brackets, e.g. 230(a), were already assigned at the time of excavation (in the catalogue or field notes).

Unnumbered pieces: a considerable number of fragments from the first two seasons were not assigned individual ND numbers. These fragments were assigned to the Iraq Museum, and I have placed them last in the catalogue above. From their character, and because some of them have been joined to numbered pieces, it is obvious that they come from Rooms K, M, and S, with the rest of the archive. Those of a legal nature probably belong under the number ND 252, which included thirty-seven small fragments of which eighteen only have been identified. Some of the unnumbered pieces were from letters, and these must belong to the archive found in the second season in Room S, which contained the other letters; they may well belong under ND 802, a number assigned to miscellaneous fragments from Room S, of which only the sealing, which bears that number in the catalogue, has been identified.

2nd Column: *either* number of text in the present edition, *or*, where the item is not included here, primary place of publication.

3rd Column: present location of piece, and museum number where relevant.

Austr. Inst. Arch. = The Australian Institute of Archaeology, Melbourne.

BM = British Museum, Department of Western Asiatic Antiquities.

[E] = piece assigned to the Expedition when division was made, not located by me.

IM = Iraq Museum, Baghdad; "for study" applies to tablets not given a separate IM number, but stored with the other Nimrud tablets.

Inst. Arch. London = Institute of Archaeology, 31–34 Gordon Square, London, W.C.1.

4th Column: *either* details of joins:

+ = physical join made.

(+) = either physical join presumed, but not made, or no physical join, presumed to be from same tablet.

Or, where item is not included in this edition, a brief description.

5th Column: provenances, details taken from catalogues both published and unpublished; for further information on the find spots, see in the Introduction, p. 3 ff.

CATALOGUE OF TEXTS (BY EXCAVATION NUMBER)

ND	*No.*	*Museum*	*Notes*	*Provenance*	*ND*
201	217	IM, for study		Ash rubbish outside south external wall of bathroom of Governor's Palace, *c.* 2·00 m. above level of floor	201
202	218	Inst. Arch. London		Found at west end of Trench A 49 on topmost brick floor	202
203	15	IM 56810		Governor's Palace, Room K; against east wall underneath rubbish of a party-wall subsequent to Shalmaneser III	203
204	30	Austr. Inst. Arch.		Governor's Palace, Room K	204
205	104	BM 131989		Governor's Palace, Room K	205
206	27	IM, for study		Governor's Palace, Room K	206
207	19	IM 56811		Governor's Palace, Room K	207
208	121	Austr. Inst. Arch.		Governor's Palace, Room M	208
209	18	IM 56812		Governor's Palace, Room K	209
210[a]	54	IM, for study		Governor's Palace, Room K	210[a]
[b]	83	IM, for study		Governor's Palace, Room K	[b]
211	93	Inst. Arch. London		Governor's Palace, Room K	211
212	5	IM 56813		Governor's Palace, Room K	212
213	120	Inst. Arch. London		Governor's Palace, Room K	213
214	110	Inst. Arch. London		Governor's Palace, Room M	214
215	106	IM 56814		Governor's Palace, Room M	215
216	90	Inst. Arch. London		Governor's Palace, Room K	216
217	103	IM 56815		Governor's Palace, Room K	217
218	98	IM 56816		Governor's Palace, Room K	218
219	95	BM 131990		Governor's Palace, Room M	219
220	149	IM 56817		Governor's Palace, Room K	220
221	145	Inst. Arch. London		Governor's Palace, Room K	221
222	146	[E]		Governor's Palace, Room K	222
223	144	IM 56818		Governor's Palace, Room K	223
224	163	IM 56819		Governor's Palace, Room K	224
225	151	IM 56820		Governor's Palace, Room K	225
226	164	IM, for study		Governor's Palace, Room K	226
227	97	IM 56821		Governor's Palace, Room K	227
228	43	Inst. Arch. London		Governor's Palace, Room M	228
229	23	Inst. Arch. London	(+) No. 49(?)	Governor's Palace, Room K	229
230(a)	20	Inst. Arch. London		Governor's Palace, Room K	230(a)
(b)	79	Inst. Arch. London		Governor's Palace, Room K	(b)

ND	*No.*	*Museum*	*Notes*	*Provenance*	*ND*
231	64	IM 56822		Governor's Palace, Room K	231
232	42	Inst. Arch. London		Governor's Palace, Room K	232
233	31	IM 56823		Governor's Palace, Room K	233
234	52	IM 56824		Governor's Palace, Room K	234
235	53	Inst. Arch. London		Governor's Palace, Room K	235
236	74	IM, for study		Governor's Palace, Room K	236
237	78	Inst. Arch. London		Governor's Palace, Room K	237
238	82	Inst. Arch. London		Governor's Palace, Room K	238
239	55	IM 56825		Governor's Palace, Room K	239
240(a)	63	Inst. Arch. London		Governor's Palace, Room K	240(a)
(b)	171	Inst. Arch. London		Governor's Palace, Room K	(b)
241[a]	99	BM 131991		Governor's Palace, Room M	241[a]
[b]	122	Inst. Arch. London		Governor's Palace, Room M	[b]
242	7	IM, for study		Governor's Palace, Room K	242
243	10	IM 56826		Governor's Palace, Room K	243
244	12	Inst. Arch. London		Governor's Palace, Room K	244
245	152	Inst. Arch. London		Governor's Palace, Room K	245
246	11	IM 56827		Governor's Palace, Room K	246
247	16	Inst. Arch. London	(+) 275[m]	Governor's Palace, Room K	247
248	56	IM, for study		Governor's Palace, Room K	248
249	32	IM, for study	+ 252(j) (+) 275[g]	Governor's Palace, Room K	249
250	67	Inst. Arch. London		Governor's Palace, Room K	250
251	6	Inst. Arch. London		Governor's Palace, Room M	251
252				" Collection of fragments which may join with pieces from Rooms M and K "	252
(a)	71	IM, for study			(a)
(b)	85	IM, for study			(b)
(c)	—	—	(descr. in *Iraq* 12 ; exact fragment not identified		(c)
(d)	69	IM, for study			(d)
(e)	72	IM, for study			(e)
(f)	58	IM, for study	+ unn. frgt.		(f)
(g)	84	IM, for study			(g)
(h)	21	IM, for study			(h)
(i)	148	IM, for study			(i)
(j)	32	IM, for study	+ 249 (+) 275[g]		(j)
[k]	170	IM, for study			[k]

ND	*No.*	*Museum*	*Notes*	*Provenance*	*ND*
[l]	73	IM, for study			[l]
[m]	70	IM, for study			[m]
[n]	147	IM, for study			[n]
[o]	176	IM, for study			[o]
[p]	65	IM, for study			[p]
[q]	175	IM, for study			[q]
[r]	75	IM, for study			[r]
253	3	Inst. Arch. London		Governor's Palace, Room K	253
254	94	Inst. Arch. London		Governor's Palace, Room K	254
255	96	IM 56828		Governor's Palace, Room K	255
256	158	Inst. Arch. London		Governor's Palace, Room K	256
257	13	Inst. Arch. London		Governor's Palace, Room M	257
258[a]	44	Inst. Arch. London		Governor's Palace, Room M	258[a]
[b]	143	Inst. Arch. London		Governor's Palace, Room M	[b]
259	119	IM 56829		Governor's Palace, Room K	259
260	33	IM 56830		Governor's Palace, Room K	260
261	91	IM 56831		Governor's Palace, Room K	261
262	68	Inst. Arch. London		Governor's Palace, Room K	262
263	51	Inst. Arch. London		Governor's Palace, Room K	263
264	35	Inst. Arch. London		Governor's Palace, Room K	264
265	4	IM 56832		Governor's Palace, Room K	265
266	34	IM 56833		Governor's Palace, Room K	266
267	1	IM 56834		Governor's Palace, Room K	267
268	101	Inst. Arch. London		Governor's Palace, Room K	268
269	80	IM 56835		Governor's Palace, Room K	269
270	81	IM 56836		Governor's Palace, Room K	270
271	142	IM, for study		Governor's Palace, Room K	271
272	38	IM, for study		Governor's Palace, Room K	272
273	135	IM 56837		Governor's Palace, Room K	273
274	150	Inst. Arch. London		Governor's Palace, Room K	274
275				Collection of 12 fragments of tablets; may join some of the tablets ND 259–74. All these fragments found in south-west corner of Room K. [Some useless fragments not included here]	275
(a)	172	Inst. Arch. London			(a)
(b)	59	Inst. Arch. London			(b)
(c)	109	Inst. Arch. London			(c)

ND	*No.*	*Museum*	*Notes*	*Provenance*	*ND*
[d]	41	Inst. Arch. London			[d]
[e]	28	Inst. Arch. London			[e]
[f]	40	Inst. Arch. London			[f]
[g]	32	Inst. Arch. London	(+) 249 + 252(j)		[g]
[h]	76	Inst. Arch. London			[h]
[i]	77	Inst. Arch. London			[i]
[j]	124	Inst. Arch. London			[j]
[k]	173	Inst. Arch. London			[k]
[l]	179	Inst. Arch. London			[l]
[m]	16	Inst. Arch. London	(+) 247		[m]
276	29	IM 56838		Governor's Palace, Room M, near door into Room K	276
277	153	IM 56839		Governor's Palace, Room C, near door of Room E	277
278	131	Inst. Arch. London		Governor's Palace, Room B, next to red tripod-bowl (ND 15 = IM 55311)	278
279	216	IM, for study		Governor's Palace, Room H, opposite door to Room P, close to west wall	279
280	*Iraq* 12, 197	BM 131981	Amulet	Governor's Palace, Room K, adjacent to the tablets	280
281	*Iraq* 12, 197	IM 55349	Brick	Governor's Palace, Room K, pavement	281
282	*Iraq* 12, 197[6]	Inst. Arch. London	Brick	Governor's Palace, Room K, pavement	282
283A	*Iraq* 12, 197[6]	IM 55350	Brick	Governor's Palace, Room I, pavement	283A
B	*Iraq* 12, 197[6]	[E]	Brick	Governor's Palace, Room I, pavement	B
284	*Iraq* 12, 197	IM 55351	Brick	Rubbish at south end of Governor's Palace	284
285	*Iraq* 12, 197	IM 55352	Brick	Rubbish over top of Governor's Palace, out of position	285
286A	—	IM 55353	Brick	Incorporated into Parthian burnt-brick grave, G.2, over top of Governor's Palace	286A
B	—	[E]	Brick	Incorporated into Parthian burnt-brick grave, G.2, over top of Governor's Palace	B
287	—	IM 55354	Brick	Provenance not recorded	287
400	*Iraq* 13, 21–4	BM 131982	Historical	Governor's Palace, Room U, upper fill	400
401	14	Inst. Arch. London	+ 402	Governor's Palace, Room U, upper fill	401
402	14	Inst. Arch. London	+ 401	Governor's Palace, Room U, upper fill	402
403	209	Inst. Arch. London		Governor's Palace, Room U, upper fill	403
404	212	Inst. Arch. London		Governor's Palace, Room S, 0·20 m. above Level II, near west door in fill	404
405	208	Inst. Arch. London		Governor's Palace, Room S, 0·20 m. above Level II, near west door in fill	405
406[a]	89	Inst. Arch. London		Miscellaneous fragments found with ND 404–5	406[a]

ND	*No.*	*Museum*	*Notes*	*Provenance*	*ND*
[b]	168	Inst. Arch. London			[b]
[c]	169	Inst. Arch. London			[c]
407	221	IM, for study		A 50, Room 7, Level II (in fill by door into Room 3, associated with cache of small objects—pedestal vase, furniture bronze, etc.)	407
408	220	IM, for study			408
409	219	Inst. Arch. London			409
410	*Iraq* 13, 107	IM 55742	Stone vase	Trench d 13, outside north-west corner of Governor's Palace, in upper fill	410
411	214	Inst. Arch. London		Governor's Palace, Room S; under brick mastaba over mud-brick floor level in south-west corner, 1·00 m. to left of door in south wall	411
412	162	Inst. Arch. London		As 411	412
413	196	BM 131992		As 411	413
414	198	BM 131993		As 411	414
415	201	BM 131994		As 411	415
416	136	Inst. Arch. London		As 411	416
417	189	IM 56840		As 411	417
418	190	BM 131995		As 411	418
419	139	IM 56841		As 411	419
420	193	IM 56842		As 411	420
421	191	IM 56843		As 411	421
422	156	IM 56844		As 411	422
423	118	Inst. Arch. London		As 411	423
424	194	BM 131996		As 411	424
425	207	Inst. Arch. London		As 411	425
426	181	Inst. Arch. London		As 411	426
427	128	BM 131997		As 411	427
428	140	BM 131998		As 411	428
429	137	Inst. Arch. London		As 411	429
430	127	Inst. Arch. London		As 411	430
431[a]	114	Inst. Arch. London	(+) 471	As 411	431[a]
[b]	210	Inst. Arch. London		As 411	[b]
[c]	166	Inst. Arch. London		As 411	[c]
432	111	[E]		As 411	432
433	108	IM 56845		As 411	433
434	138	IM 56846		As 411	434
435	182	IM 56847		As 411	435
436	188	BM 131999		As 411	436

ND	*No.*	*Museum*	*Notes*	*Provenance*	*ND*
437	185	BM 131200		As 411	437
438	192	IM 56848		As 411	438
439	203	IM 56849		As 411	439
440	183	IM 56850		As 411	440
441	202	IM 56851		As 441	441
442	112	IM 56852		As 411	442
443	206	IM, for study		As 411	443
444	184	IM 56853		As 411	444
445	125	Inst. Arch. London		As 411	445
446	126	IM 56854		As 411	446
447	129	Inst. Arch. London		As 411	447
448	47	IM 56855		As 411	448
449	160	IM, for study		As 411	449
450	155	IM, for study	(+) 459	As 411	450
451	113	IM, for study	+ unn. frgt.	As 411	451
452	130	Inst. Arch. London		As 411	452
453	141	IM 56856		As 411	453
454	186	IM, for study		As 411	454
455	199	Inst. Arch. London		As 411	455
456	115	Inst. Arch. London		As 411	456
457	161	IM, for study		As 411	457
458	157	IM, for study		As 411	458
459	155	BM 132012	(+) 450	As 411	459
460	215	IM 56857		As 411	460
461	154	Inst. Arch. London	(+) unn. frgt.	Governor's Palace, Room S; (perhaps as 411)	461
462	195	IM 56858		Governor's Palace, Room S; in bricked-in doorway on west side	462
463	116	IM 56859		Governor's Palace, Room S; in bricked-in doorway on west side	463
464[a]	226	Inst. Arch. London		B 50, Room VII, below Level I	464[a]
[b]	227	Inst. Arch. London		B 50, Room VII, below Level I	[b]
[c]	228	Inst. Arch. London		B 50, Room VII, below Level I	[c]
465	222	IM, for study		B 50, Room VII, below Level I	465
466	230	Inst. Arch. London		B 50, Room IX, second floor [see on No. 230, p.]	466
467	223	IM, for study		B 50, Room VII, between Floors I and II	467
468	225	IM, for study		B 50, Room VII, between Floors I and II	468
469	224	IM, for study		B 50, Room VII, between Floors I and II	469

ND	*No.*	*Museum*	*Notes*	*Provenance*	*ND*
470	117	IM, for study		Governor's Palace, Room S; south-west corner, in wall	470
471	114	IM 56860	(+) 431(a)	Governor's Palace, Room S; south-west corner, in wall	471
472	25	Austr. Inst. Arch.		Governor's Palace, Room K, Level II	472
473	24	IM 56861	(+) unn. frgt.	Governor's Palace, Room K, Level II	473
474	9	IM 56862		Governor's Palace, Room K, Level II	474
475	26	Austr. Inst. Arch.		Governor's Palace, Room K, Level II	475
476	66	Inst. Arch. London		Governor's Palace, Room K, Level II	476
477	102	Inst. Arch. London		Governor's Palace, Room K, Level II	477
478	8	Inst. Arch. London		Governor's Palace, Room K, Level II	478
479[a]	39	IM, for study		Governor's Palace, Room K, Level II	479[a]
[b]	37	IM, for study		Governor's Palace, Room K, Level II	[b]
[c]	174	IM, for study		Governor's Palace, Room K, Level II	[c]
480	57	Inst. Arch. London		Governor's Palace, Room K, Level II	480
481	36	IM 56863		Governor's Palace, Room K, Level II	481
482	48	IM 56864		Governor's Palace, Room K, Level II	482
483	229	Inst. Arch. London	Seal impression	B 50, Room VII, between I and II	483
484	*Iraq* 13, 115; *N &R* I, pp. 117–18	IM 55753	Pazuzu plaque	North-west Palace, Rooms OO and QQ	484
485	*Iraq* 13, 115	IM 55698	Jar sherd	North-west Palace, Room HH; fill above Floor I	485
486	255	Inst. Arch. London		North-west Palace, Room HH; 5 cm. above Floor III, 2·80 m. deep near east wall, 2·10 m. from south-east corner (with ivory cow)	486
487	248	BM 132001		North-west Palace, Room OO, Level III	487
488	123	Inst. Arch. London		Governor's Palace, Room M, Level II	488
489	107	IM 56865		Governor's Palace, Koom M, Level II	489
490	197	BM 132002		Governor's Palace, Room M, Level II	490
491	100	Inst. Arch. London		Governor's Palace, Room M, Level II	491
492	2	BM 132003		Governor's Palace, Room M, Level II	492
493	92	IM 56866		Governor's Palace, Room M, Level II	493
494	132	IM 56867		Governor's Palace, Room M, Level II	494
495	22	IM 56868		Governor's Palace, Room M, Level II	495
496	17	IM 56869		Governor's Palace, Room M, Level II	496
497	134	Inst. Arch. London		Governor's Palace, Room M, Level II	497
498	105	Austr. Inst. Arch.		Governor's Palace, Room M, Level II	498
499	252	IM 56870		North-west Palace, Room HH, on floor	499
800	251	IM 56871		North-west Palace, Room HH, on floor	800

ND	*No.*	*Museum*	*Notes*	*Provenance*	*ND*
801	62	IM 56872		Governor's Palace, Room S	801
802	*Iraq* 17, 113–14	IM, for study	Sealing	Governor's Palace, Room S	802
803	45	Inst. Arch. London		Governor's Palace, Room M, Level II	803
804[a]	46	IM, for study		Governor's Palace, Room M, Level II	804[a]
[b]	—	IM, for study	**Uninscr. frgt.**	Governor's Palace, Room M, Level II	[b]
805	250	Inst. Arch. London		North-west Palace, Room HH, Floor III	805
806	256	IM, for study		North-west Palace, Room HH, Floor III	806
807	257	IM 56873		North-west Palace, Room HH, Floor III	807
808	263	Inst. Arch. London		North-west Palace, Room HH, Floor III	808
809	258	Inst. Arch. London		North-west Palace, Room HH, Floor III	809
810	254	IM 56874		North-west Palace, Room HH, Floor III	810
811	*Iraq* 13, 118	IM 55744	Historical	North-west Palace, Room FF, just below Floor III	811
812[a]	268	IM, for study		North-west Palace, Room FF, in box, Floor III	812[a]
[b]	269	IM, for study		North-west Palace, Room FF, in box, Floor III	[b]
813	264	Inst. Arch. London		North-west Palace, Room FF, Level IV	813
814	*Iraq* 13, 24–6	IM 56875	Historical	North-west Palace, Room OO, 0·23 m. above Level III, to right of door	814
815	247	IM 56876		North-west Palace, Room DD, Level III	815
816	*Iraq* 13, 118	[E]	Historical	North-west Palace, Room DD, covering grave below Level III	816
817	*Iraq* 13, 118	IM 55745	Historical	North-west Palace, Room DD, covering grave below Level III	817
818	265	Inst. Arch. London		North-west Palace, Room QQ, Level III	818
819	*Iraq* 13, 119	IM 55743	Historical	North-west Palace, Room GG, Level III	819
820	*Iraq* 13, 119	[E]	Historical	North-west Palace, pavement at end of Passage P	820
821(a)	270	BM 132004		North-west Palace, Room FF, Level III; north-west corner	821(a)
(b)	271	BM 132005		North-west Palace, Room FF, Level III	(b)
[c]	272	BM 132006		North-west Palace, Room FF, Level III	[c]
822	213	[E]		Governor's Palace, Room S, Level II	822
823	*Iraq* 13, 119	[E]	6 bricks	North-west Palace/Governor's Palace	823
824	*Iraq* 13, 119	IM 55759	2 bricks	North-west Palace/Governor's Palace	824
		IM, for study	1 brick		
		Mosul Museum	2 bricks		
825	*Iraq* 13, 119	IM 56167	Brick	North-west Palace/Governor's Palace	825
826	*Iraq* 13, 119	[E]	Brick	North-west Palace/Governor's Palace	826
827	*Iraq* 13, 119	[E]	Brick	North-west Palace	827

ND	*No.*	*Museum*	*Notes*	*Provenance*	*ND*
828	*Iraq* 13, 119	Mustansiriyah, Baghdad	Brick	North-west Palace	828
829	*Iraq* 13, 119	[E]	7 bricks	North-west Palace	829
830	*Iraq* 13, 119	IM 55760a–b	2 bricks	North-west Palace	830
		IM 55761	1 brick		
		Mosul Museum	3 bricks		
831	*Iraq* 13, 119	IM 55701	Plaque	(Originally?) Balawat (inscr. ^{uru}*im-gúr*-^{d}BE)	831
1101	253	Inst. Arch. London		North-west Palace, Entrance E, 1·00 m. above courtyard pavement, in filling against blocked doorway into EB	1101
1102	*Iraq* 14, 63	IM, for study	Ostrich egg	North-west Palace, Room B; behind slab 23 in east wall	1102
1103	*Iraq* 14, 63	BM 131980	Amulet	Trench in Square E 3, 0·30 m. below surface	1103
1104	266	Mosul Museum 3	Stele	North-west Palace, recess EA	1104
1105	*Iraq* 14, 63	IM, [for study?]	Diorite frgt.	Ground south of south-east wing of North-west Palace	1105
1106[a]	260	IM, for study		North-west Palace, Room HH, in upper fill, Level I	1106[a]
[b]	261	IM, for study		North-west Palace, Room HH, in upper fill, Level I	[b]
[c]	262	IM, for study		North-west Palace, Room HH, in upper fill, Level I	[c]
1107	243	IM 56877		Burnt Palace, Room viii, upper fill	1107
1108	242	BM 132007		Burnt Palace, Room viii, upper fill	1108
1109	245	[E]		Burnt Palace, Room viii	1109
1110	249	Inst. Arch. London		North-west Palace, Room AH	1110
1111	240	BM 132008		Burnt Palace, Room vii	1111
1112	244	IM, for study		Burnt Palace, Room xii	1112
1113	241	IM 56878		Burnt Palace, Room viii	1113
1114	231	Inst. Arch. London		Burnt Palace, Room viii (near door to xviii, north wall)	1114
1115	259	IM, for study		North-west Palace, Room HH (cupboard in east wall)	1115
1116	232	IM 56879		Burnt Palace, Room viii	1116
1117	233	Inst. Arch. London		Burnt Palace, Room viii (centre)	1117
1118	234	Inst. Arch. London		Burnt Palace, Room viii	1118
1119	235	IM, for study		Burnt Palace, Room viii	1119
1120	246	IM 56880		Outside south-west corner of Burnt Palace, *c.* 10 m. east of Room viii, Square D 12	1120
1121	*Iraq* 14, 66	[E]	Historical	North-west Palace, Room B; on floor by east wall below fallen fresco	1121
1122	267	Mosul Museum 1		North-west Palace, Room B (east end), west of Slab 23	1122
1123	*Iraq* 14, 66	BM, on loan	Historical	As for 1120	1123
1124	236	IM 56881		Burnt Palace, Room viii, floor	1124
1125[a]	238	Inst. Arch. London		Burnt Palace, Room viii, floor	1125[a]

ND	*No.*	*Museum*	*Notes*	*Provenance*	*ND*
[b]	239	Inst. Arch. London		Burnt Palace, Room viii, floor	[b]
[c]	237	Inst. Arch. London		Burnt Palace, Room viii, floor	[c]
1126	*Iraq* 14, 54–8	BM, on loan(?)	Historical	Not from Nimrud	1126
1127	*Iraq* 14, 67	IM 56283	Brick	North-west Palace, Room SS	1127
1128	*Iraq* 14, 67	BM 132265	Brick	North-west Palace, Room SS (Level III)	1128
1129	*Iraq* 14, 67	[E]	Brick	Trench east of Ishtar Temple and ziggurrat	1129
1130	*Iraq* 14, 67	IM 56282	Brick	Burnt Palace, Room xviii (north end, upper level)	1130
1131A	*Iraq* 14, 67	Gulbenkian Museum, Durham	Brick	North-west Palace	1131A
B	*Iraq* 14, 67	IM 56281	4' bricks	North-west Palace	B
Unnumbered pieces				[Probably all from Governor's Palace, Rooms K, M, or S; see p. 254]	
	24	Inst. Arch. London (with 480)	(+) 473		
	49	IM, for study	(+) 229(?)		
	50	IM, for study			
	58	IM, for study	+ 252(f)		
	60	IM, for study			
	61	IM, for study			
	86	IM, for study			
	87	IM, for study			
	88	IM, for study			
	113	IM, for study	+ 451		
	133	IM, for study			
	154	IM, for study	(+) 461		
	159	IM, for study			
	165	IM, for study			
	167	IM, for study			
	177	IM, for study			
	178	With IM 56831			
	180	IM, for study			
	187	IM, for study			
	200	IM, for study			
	204	IM, for study			
	205	IM, for study			
	211	IM, for study			

INDEX OF PERSONAL NAMES

Note

The index includes names from No. 246, but not Nos. 266–72.

Names of *limmus* are marked with an asterisk, and the day and month dates given in brackets.

Dots indicating breaks are classed last alphabetically.

Besides the reference, the entries give:

(1) Function in the text—i.e. witness; buyer, seller, sold; slave, owner; creditor, debtor; author, addressee (letters).

(2) Relatives.

(3) Profession or other description.

(4) Provenance (" from GN ").

br. = brother
d. = daughter
f. = father
gov. = governor (*šakin*)
m. = mother
ow. = owner
s. = son
scr. = scribe
s.i. = seal impression
sl. = slave
w. = witness

Abat-iš[tar?-lā]ṣur? 247, 14′ w.
Abdā[. . .] 220 r. 9′ w.
Abda-adad-milki 138, 2
Abdī 103, 6 w.; s. of ^{f}Biyā
120, 3
Abūa 121, 1
Abu-ilāya 11 r. 5′ w.; nephew of Ha(m)šāyu; ^{lú}*ḫa-za-nu*
248, 20′
Abu-lēšir 17, 40 (*bis*) w.; f. of Itu'āyu
22, 31 w.; ^{lú}*š[e-l]ap-pa-a-a*
Abu-si' 85, 6′ w.
^{f}Abuta 121, 8 from Ialūna
Abu-ṭāb 248, 18′ w.; s. of Ninurta-nišēka-uṣur
Abu-ūl-īdi 3, 5 sold; br. of Ubru-ahhē
30, 2, 9, 15 seller; s. of Šamaš-šē[. . .], br. of Hubuškāyu
91, 5, creditor
Adabui 118, 6 f. of a LÚ.SIMUG GUŠKIN
Adad-ahu-iddina 15, 39 w.; from Kurbail
35, 28 w.; from Kurbail
199, 2 author
Adad-ahu-uṣur 15, 4 seller
Adad-aplu-iddina 16, 2 seller
36, 11′ w.; *ša* É Šamaš-kēnu-dugul; from Kurbail
Adad-bān-ahhē 51 r. 13 w.; (scr.) writer of tablet
Adad-bānu 17, 46 w.; ^{uru}*kal-ḫa-a-a la-bi-ru*
Adad-bēl 62, 14 w.; ^{lú}*mu?-x*[ ]
96, 7 creditor
*Adad-bēlu-ukīn 98, 16 (13.i; 2nd *pūru*)
104, 12 (—.iv)
106, 11 (13.i)
Adad-ēpuš? 114, 17
Adad?-ēṭir 195, 2 author
Adad-ibni 11 r. 7′ w.; from HARšu
[Ad]ad-iqbi 6, 22 w.
Adad-išmāni? 74, 7′ w.
Adad-kūmūya 36, 8′ w.; from Kurbail
*Adad-mušammer 52, 16′ (23.i)
94, 11 (12.viii)
103, 17 (18.i)
Adad-našhira 51 r. 12 w.; scr.
Adad-nērārī 17, 7 [LUGAL K]UR *aš-šur*
32, 7′ MAN [K]UR *aššur*
66(/170/171) s.i. 2 MAN ŠÁR
Adad-rā'īni 36, 10′ w.; from Kurbail
Adad-ṣa'du-iddin 11 r. 3′ w.; LÚ.3.U_5
[Adad-šē]zibanni 36, 12′ w.; ^{lú}*šá* UGU É *ša* É ^{lú}*tar-ta-ni*; from Kurbail
Adad-šallim 96, 10 w.; LÚ.DAM.GÀR
118, 9
Adad-šall[im(-. . .)] 62, 12 w.
Adad-[. . .]me 91, 12 creditor
AD.BU?.SI? 48, 6′ buyer; s. of Ahu?-. .[. . .]
Adi-māti-ilu 44, 5 buyer; LÚ.KAŠ.LUL *ša* MÍ É.GAL
Aduru 120, 8
Agirāyu 36, 13′ w.; from Kurbail
Agūsu 122, 6
Ahimē? 69, 5 debtor(?)
Ahūa-(e)rība 4, 1 seller; sl. of LÚ.AGRIG GAL
122, 1(?)
Ahuānu 4, 18 w.; ^{lú}*ḫa-za-nu ša* URU.ŠE ^{lú}*tur-ta-ni*
Ahu-damqu?-. . . 85, 3′ w.
Ahu-iddina 101, 2 debtor
103, 5 debtor

Ahu-ilāya 248, 20′ br. of 4 witnesses(?)
Ahu-(i)le'i 63, 5′ w.
90, 8 creditor; sl. of Lipūšu
116, 1 from Zaliqē?
Ahu-illaka? 53, 11′ w.; s. of fMu[...]
109, 3, L.E. 3′ debtor; from Imgur-ellil
Ahu-(i)qīš? 52, 11′ w.
Ahu-ke[...] 71, 5′ w.
Ahu-lamašši 111, 1 LÚ.UŠ *kib-si*
Ahu-lāmur 9, 1, 4 seller; s. of Kisī(ya)
82, 14 w.; s. of Ṭūa; from Imberahī
Ahu-uballiṭ 11 r. 11′ w.; f. of Qanasī; lú*kar-ka-di-nu*
Ahu-M[U...] 74, 8′ w.
Ahu-nūrī 80, 7 w.
Ahu?-qallu 92, 10 w.
Ahu-rība (246 r. 17′)
Ahu-šamšī 68, 6′ w.; lú*mu-šar-ki-[su]*
Ahu-šīna 97, 5 creditor(?); lú*ša-nu-ú*
Ahu-šu?[...] 220 r. 10′ w.
Ahu-tidintu? 62, 11 w.
Ahu-ṭuri 90, 7 creditor
Ahu-[...] 48, 6′ f. of AD.BU?.SI?
101, 7(?)
248, 1′ sold
Akburu(?) 98, 15 (wr. AK.U) w.; scr.
Ampāru? 15, 43 w.; sl. of fṢarpanītum-šarrat
fAninia 121, 13 (from) URU.ŠE m*ba-bu-u*
Aplayā? 91, 31 f. of Zēr-kitti-lēšir (wr. A?-*ia-a*)
Aqata 121, 6 from Ariru
Aribu? 3, 26 w.; LÚ.ŠÀM
Asalluhi-šūmu-uṣur 29, 19 w.
Aššur-aplu-uṣur 15, 44 ow. of Šamaš-ahu-iddina
18, 1, 7 seller; s. of ... ni
Aššur-bāni 100, 8(?) w.; LÚ.SUM KÙ.BABBAR.MEŠ?
148, 3(?)
241, 2 author
*Aššur-bašti-ēkurri 14, 28 (18.xii)
Aššur-bēl-ilāni (246 r. 19′)
Aššur-bēlu-uṣur 127, 10
Aššur-bēl(u)-[...] 35, 23 w.; lú*láh-hi-nu*; from Kurbail
*Aššur-da'inanni 134, 5 (1.viii)
174(?)
*Aššur-dān 54 r. 5 (20.vii) M[AN K]UR *aš-šur*ki
Aššur-dūru-uṣur 43, 5 buyer
95, 3 f. of Šēlubu
99, 1 (*ša*) LÚ.SAG *ša* Bel-dān LÚ.EN.NAM *ša* uru*kal-hi*
104, 3 creditor
Aššur-E?-a-a 57 T.E. 15 w.
Aššur-ēṭir 122, 3
*Aššur-gimillī-tirri 219 r. 12′ (4+.x)
Aššur-iddina 120, 7
Aššur-idnāni (246 r. 20′)
Aššur-kinnāni (246 r. 18′)
Aššur-le'i 11 r. 8′ f. of Harmāku and Mumī
Aššur-mātka-tirri 108, 11 w.
Aššur-nādin-ahhē 78, 4′ w.
Aššur-nādin-ahi 29, 21 w.
Aššur-nāṣir 11 r. 10′ w.; LÚ.MU
Aššur-rēmāni 9, 17 w.; *mu-tir⟨ṭe⟩-mi*
*Aššur-šallimanni 6, 27 (28.—); [gov.] of uru*ár-x*[...]
Aššur-šallim[(...)] 39 r. 8′ w.; from Zur[i?]
Aššur-šēzibāni 108, 13 w.
Aššur-taklak 14, 4, 9 buyer; LÚ.GAL É
196, 3 author
Aššur-zēru?-uṣur 129, 2 [*š*]*a*? *ma-ha-za-a-ni*
Aššur-[...] 83, 1′ w.
Atara[...] 247, 5′, 11′
Ayammu 192 r. 3′
A[...] 37, 2 seller

Bābilāyu 19, 19 w.
139, 2
Babû 121, 12 (URU.ŠE B.)
Bahiānu 90, 10 creditor; from Diāt[e?]
Balāṭu 92, 11 w.; [... *ša*] LÚ.GAL É.GAL
Balṭi-nūrī 130, 11
Bān?-ahhē 139, 3
Bānī 43, 25 w.; (scr.) writer of tablet
132, 2 LÚ.SI[PA]; from Same[(...)]
fBānītum-[šarra]t 219, 3 sold; d. of [...]addu
Bāniu 91, 11 creditor
Bar'a-ilu 90, 14 creditor
Barihu 26, 22 w.
Bar-ili 103, 15 f. of Marduk-nādin-ahhē
Barrarānu? 100, 10 SUM-*in kas-pi*
Barruqu 98, 2 recipient; sl. of Dilil-ištar
Barzī 106, 8 w.
Bar[...] 90, 15 creditor; lú*ha?-za?-nu* [...]
Basusu 134, 3
Baṣidqī 144, 3 (*ba-*)
146, 2 (*ba-*)
149, 8 (*bi-*)
Batēya 34, 2, 8 seller
Bau-ahu-iddina (246 r. 16′)
Bayā? 110, 7 w.
Bēl-abu-uṣur 118, 4
Bēl-ahhē 51 r. 9 w.; LÚ.GAL KA.ŠÈR
53, 10′ w.; LÚ.SUM?.[GAR(?)]
86, 2′(?) w.
91, 9(?) creditor
Bēl-ahi (cf. Bēl-nāṣir) 2, 1, 4 s. of HARṭunāyu; ow. of [...]ta'a
101, 4 creditor(?); GAL URU.MEŠ
Bēl-āli 9, 16 w.; GAL lú*kal-la-pi*
101 r. 5′ w.
248, 4′, 15′ seller; s. of Mušēzib-ilu

*Bēl-am(u)ranni 96, 14 (11.ii)
107, 7 (1.xii) gov. of KUR [*r*]*a-ṣa-pa*
Bēl-am(u)ranni 120, 10
126, 5
Bēl-aplu-iddina 15, 35 w.; s. of Bēl-rubā'-ilāni; from Kurbail
36, 7′ w.; LÚ.SANGA *ša* ^{d}IM *ša* ^{uru}[*kur-*]*ba-il*
Bēl-būnāya 20, 2, 12 seller
*Bēl-dān 25, 29 (28.i) gov. of Kalhu
Bēl-dān 91, 30 w.; ^{lú}*šá* UGU É *ša* É ^{lú}*tur-ta-ni*
99, 2 LÚ.EN.NAM *ša* ^{uru}*kal-ḫi*
183, 2 addressee
184, 2 addressee
201, 1 addressee; f. of Mīšarrum-nāṣir(-. . .)
202, 1 addressee; f. of Mīšarrum-nāṣir(-. . .)
Bēl-dūrī 22, 26 w.; ^{lú}*mu-kil*-KUŠ.PA.MEŠ
26, 23 w.
27, 1, 7, 13 seller
114, 13
Bēl-emūqī 91, 8 creditor
Bēl-ēpuš 12, 5′ seller
Bēl-ēṭir$^{?}$ 66, 8 recipient
*Bēl-harrān-bēlu-uṣur 29, 26 gov. of Guzāna
Bēl-iddina 22, 27 w.; LÚ.GAL *x*[(*x*)] *ša* MAN
*Bēl-ilāya 4, 25 (13.i)
Bēl-ilāya 24, 25 w.; from . . . u . . .
*Bēl-(i)qīšāni 3, 31 (3.xi)
15, 51 (15.vii) gov. of Šibhiniš
16 r. 7′ gov. of Šibh[iniš]
Bēl-(i)qīšāni$^{?}$ 52, 12′ w.
Bēl-issīya 4, 4 ow. of buyer
7, 6 buyer; LÚ.GAL URU$^{?}$.MEŠ$^{?}$
8, 6 buyer
9, 3, 9 buyer
15, 11, 22 buyer; LÚ.GAL URU.MEŠ-*ni* [*ša* . . . P]N gov. of Kalhu
15, 36 w.; br. of Bēl-rubā'-ilāni; from Kurbail
22, 2 ow. of Kiqilānu; [L]Ú.GAL URU.MEŠ-*ni*
33, 6, 15 buyer; LÚ.SAG (*ša* Bēl-tarṣi-iluma gov. of Kalhu)
34, 6 buyer; LÚ.SAG *ša* Bēl-tarṣi-iluma gov. of Kalhu
35, 9, 16 buyer; LÚ.GAL URU.MEŠ-*ni*
35, 24 w.; br. of Bēl-rubā'-ilāni; from Kurbail
91, 32 w.; LÚ.UŠ.BAR of Arbail
91, 36 w.; LÚ.UŠ.BAR *ša* É ^{lú}*tur-ta-ni*
92, 5 creditor
94, 2 creditor
103, 3 creditor
Bēl-lāmur$^{?}$ 62, 15 w.
90, 13
*Bēl-lēšir 18, 28 (15.i) LÚ.NIMGIR *ša* Šulmānu-ašārēd [king] of Assyria
53, 15′ (20.iii) [LÚ.NIMGIR] É.[GAL]
Bēl-lēšir(?) 13, 12 w.
100, 2 debtor
Bēl-(lu)balliṭ/balāṭ 82, 11 w.; ^{lú}*ḫa-za-nu ša* ^{uru}*m*[*i*$^{?}$ . . .]
96, 11 w.; ^{lú}*ša* UGU É *ša* É ^{lú}*ša* IGI É.GAL
114, 1 LÚ.SANGA$^{?}$
193, 7
Bēl-nāṣir (cf. Bēl-ahi) 6, 4 f. of Marduk-aplu-uṣur
Bēl-nūrka-lāmur 5, 6 buyer
Bēl-rubā'-ilāni 15, 34, 36 w.; f. of Bēl-aplu-iddina, br. of Bēl-issīya; LÚ.SANGA *ša* Kurbail
35, 21 w.; br. of Bēl-issīya, nephew of [. . .]āyu; LÚ.SANGA
Bēl-ṣābišu$^{?}$ 222 B 4′
*Bēl-šadūa 22, 30 (26.ii) gov. of Parnunna
Bēl-šadūa 107, 3 creditor
Bēl-šallim 39 r. 9′ w.
Bēl-šūmu-ēreš$^{?}$ 186, 9
*Bēl-tarṣi-iluma 51 r. 14 (—.i) gov. of Kalhu
91, 39 (27.xii)
Bēl-tarṣi-iluma 33, 6 gov. of Kalhu
34, 6 gov. of Kalhu
64, 3 br. of [Sîn-ēṭir](?); gov. of Kalhu
64, s.i.(?)
66, 1, 6 donor(?); gov. of Kalhu
66(/170/171) s.i. 1 *šá* SAG *šá* Adad-nērārī
90, 3, 20 gov. of Kalhu
91, 2, 28 gov. of Kalhu
93, 19 gov. of Kalhu
(?)15, 12 gov. of Kalhu
(*)Bēl-[. . .] 101, 5
112, 7 (—.i$^{?}$)
Bēt-šašširāyu 35, 3 seller; L[Ú.N]AR
^{f}Biyā 103, 7 m. of Abdī
Bibī(?) 5, 14 w.
Birtāyu 17, 37 w.; LÚ.A.ZU *ša* LÚ.GAL.SAG
Bisilu 17, 41 w.; ^{lú}*ḫa-za-nu ša* ^{uru}*du-'u-ú-a*
Bisinē 57 r. 1 seller
Biṣidqī see Baṣidqī
Būnāya$^{?}$ 17, 47 w.; scr.
57 L.E. 18 w.
Būnī$^{?}$ 97, 6 creditor(?); LÚ.NINDA
Burki-. . . 18, 15 w.; s. of Ninurta-iqbi
Burzinānu 68, 7′ w.; LÚ.A.ZU
Busāsī 91, 11 creditor
Busī 119, 16 f. of Šamaš-ahu-uṣur
Busilu$^{?}$ 110, 5 w.; ^{lú}*kal-la-pu*

Dadā 114, 4
Dadī 98, 8 w.; LÚ.GAL *kal-la-pi ša* LÚ.EN.NAM
Dadiyā 119, 15 f. of Ubru-šamaš$^{?}$
Dagan-bēlu-uṣur 43, 4 (URU *šá*)
Dannē 102 r. 4
Dannu-[. . .] 137, 4
Dari-abu 91, 7 creditor

Dayānī 3, 7, 9 buyer
26, 25(?) w.
Dayānu-kāmir?-a[hhē?] 83, 2′ w.
Dayān-ninurta 51 r. 3 w.; LÚ.GAL É
Dayān-šamaš 46, 2 seller
Da'zīn[a] 112, 1 KUR *ú-ra-ár-ṭa-a-[a]*
D[a . . .] 13, 1 seller
222 L.E. 1
Didī 3, 29 w.; LÚ.ŠÀM
53, 14′ w.; LÚ.GÍR.LÁ
Dilil-ištar 98, 3 ow. of Barruqu; from "village of Libluṭu"
Dudūa 29, 23 w.
Dulā 91, 10, 22? creditor
*Dūr-aššur 108, 15 (11.viii)
Dūr-aššur 248, 17′ w.; s. of Ninurta-nišēka-uṣur

Ebisu 113, 6′
Edā 120, 17
Ellil-. .[. .] 238, 1
Ēreš-ilu 22, 25 w.
95, 12 w.; LÚ.GAL É.GAL
Eršī?-ištar 69, 4 debtor(?)
Esaggil-aplu-uṣur 6, 25 w.; scr. writer of tablet
Eši?[. . .] 72 r. 2′ w.
Ešra'āyu? (UD.20.KÁM-*a-a*) (246 r. 16′)
Ēṣidāyu 101 r. 7′ w.; sl. of Šēp-i[štar?]; from Gabrīna
139, 4
Etel-pī-marduk (246 r. 21′)
Eṭrī?-ištar 91, 12 creditor

Gabbu-āmur 24, 27 w.; sl. of Sîn-šallimāni
69, 2 debtor(?)
223, 7
249, 3 debtor
Gabbu-ana-ištar 4, 20 w.; LÚ.TIN.NA
Galulu 75, 9′ w.; [. . .] *ša* É LÚ.[. . .]
219 r. 10′ w.; scr.
Gameu 113, 4′
Garašiu 52, 10′ w.
Ga[. . .]DIR? 120, 33
Gidāya? 220 r. 8′ w.
Girītu 24, 6, 13 buyer
25, 5, 14 buyer
104, 9 w.
Gi[. . .] 85, 4′ f. of Marduk-ibni
Gula-balāṭī 35, 2 seller; LÚ.NAR
Gung[u . . .] 19, 21 w.

Hābil-kēni 78, 3′ w.; LÚ.*x*[. . .]
Habusu 101 r. 4′ w.
Hadāya? 110, 6 w.; *ša* É [lú]*tar-ta-ni*
Hadē-[. . .] 19, 23 w.
[f]Hadi-abuša 248, 3′ sold
Hadi-lipūšu 82, 3 w.; s. of Ra'ūzu
Halbūri 232, 12
Haldi-bēl(-. . .) 117, 1
Halimu 114, 3 LÚ.SIMUG KÙ.[GI]
Hal(i)musu 43, 1, 7 seller
91, 5 creditor
Halutu(?) 123, 1
Hamāni 120, 5
Hamaqāti 102 r. 6 w.; LÚ.NINDA; *bēl kaspi našê*
Ha(m)šāyu 11 r. 6′ w.; uncle of Abu-ilāya
Hanāna 90, 2 debtor
Hanbunu 91, 12 creditor
Handāšu? 100, 11 *ṣābit kanīki*
Hanī 91, 6 creditor
Hanini(?) 70, 4′ debtor(?)
Hanṭu[. . .] 117, 3
Hanzāru 82, 8 w.; GAL *da-a-a-li*
Harānu 119, 7 [lú]*ru-qa-ḫa-a-a*
119, 13 from Si'-altāru?
Harmāki-ištar 96, 5 debtor
Harmāku 11 r. 8′ w.; s. of Aššur-l[e'i?]
14, 24 w.
79, 2′(?) w.
Harrānāyu (cf. Hūlāyu) 119, 12 from Si'-altāru?
HARṭunāyu 2, 2 f. of Bēl-ahi
Hattiyānu 114, 5 from Biha?[. . .]
ḪÉ.DAR/SI$_4$-ištar 57 L.E. 17 w.
101 r. 6′ w.
Hi'āyu 15, 46 w.; LÚ.DUMU *ši-pír ša* GAL.LÚ.SAG.MEŠ
HIbāni 18, 26 f. of Nabû-šūmu-iddina
Hidā? 82, 10 w.; *qatennu*(?)
Himbu(?) 17, 35 w.; LÚ.SANGA *ša* [d]ŠEŠ.GAL
Hinibirā 81, 9 w.
Hinidūti 91, 10, 23 creditor
Hinimme 110, 3 debtor(?)
Hišd/ṭānu 82, 10 w.
Hubuškāyu 30, 2, 8, 14 seller; s. of Šamaš-šē[. . .], br. of Abu-ūl-īdi
Hulāyu? 3, 27 w.; from Bēl-lībur
139, 1 (KASKAL-*a-a*)
Hunānu 180, 2 author
Hurāpu 104, 4 debtor
Hurāṣī 29, 18 w.
Huṭusu 4, 14 w.; LÚ.KA.ŠÈR *ša ša* IGI É.GAL

Iada'-ilu 119, 9, 21 s. of Ukaturme?; [lú]*na-si-ku ša* [lú]*na-qi-ra-a-a*
Iamāqi 33, 2, 8, 12 seller
Ianādi 130, 7
Iata'(a) 120, 15 br. of Tardīti-ištar
247, 15′(?) w.
Ibašši-ilāni 51 r. 5 w.; LÚ.GAL *kal-la-pi*
Ibba'āmu 93, 7, 16 creditor; LÚ.ŠÁM *ša* ŠU? [. . .]*rā*

Ibnī 2, 18 w.; s. of Šamaš-ēṭir
Ibnīya 78, 9′ w.; scr.
Idnāni 119, 2 ^{lú}*ru-qa-ḫa-a-a*
Ilāya-bēl 193, 10
Ilāya-rame 233, 2
Ilāya-takara? 113, 3′
Ilāya-ta[klak?] 69, 6 debtor(?)
Ilu-abu-uṣur(?) 114, 14
Ilu-a[. . .] 110, 4 w.; sl. of Ninurta-taklak
Ilubua 91, 9 creditor
Ilu-dalā 114, 11 [. . .] of Ninurta-il[āya?]
Ilu-danāni 237, 1
Ilu-dārānu 2, 14 f. of Urdu-ilāni
91, 13 creditor
Ilu-eppaš 17, 2, 11 seller; LÚ.SAG *ša* L[Ú.GAL.SAG(?)]
Ilu-(e)rība 8, 2, 4 seller; ow. of [. . .]dulu; from Hamath
29, 17 w.
Ilu-hanāna 52, 8′ w.
Ilu-i(a')āb 120, 6
Ilu-ia[. . .] 117, 4
Ilu-(i)le'i 248, 21′ w.; LÚ.A.BA *ki-si-ti*
Ilu-iqbi(?) 220 r. 15′
Ilu-irte?-ēreš 123, 9
Iluma-le'i 79, 3′ w.
118, 3(?)
Iluma-[. . .] 16, 3 seller
Ilu-mušabši 248, 1′ sold
Ilu-[. . .] 119, 3 ^{lú}*ru-qa-ḫa-a-a*
199, 12
Imārī 9, 15 w.; *ša qurbūti*
Imāru 103, 10 w.; s. of Nabû-iqbi
Immerānu 93, 5, 14 creditor
Ina-šulmi-nāṣir(?) 11 r. 14′ w.; [scr., writer] of tablet
Ina-šār-bēli-allak 123, 11
Inu[. . .] 42 r. 12 w.
Iqala?[(. . .)] 81, 14 w.
Iqbi-ilu 17, 45 w.; ^{uru}*kal-ḫa-a-a la-bi-ru*
120, 13
120, 19(?) s. of [. . .-ah]u-iddina
(I)qīša-marduk? 242 r. 3′
Iq[. . .] 63, 4′ w.
70, 3′ debtor(?)
Irnīya 15, 45 w.
Išdi-. . . see Ubru-. . .
Išmāni-ištar 248, 18′ w.; s. of Ninurta-nišēka-uṣur
Išme-ilu 14, 21 w.
63, 6′ w.; LÚ.NIMGIR? É.GAL
Iššilāyu(?) 63, 7′ w.
*Ištar-dūrī (246, 2, r. 22′)
Ištar?-ilāya 63 r. 4′ w.
Ištar-issīya 75, 5′
Ištar-tarība 18, 14 f. of U[b . . .]
Ištar-[. . .] 15, 5(?) seller
159, 7′(?)
Itu'āyu 17, 40 w.; s. of Abu-lēšir
118, 8
^{f}Iutātu? 29, 4 buyer
Izbu-lēšir 15, 47 w.; *ša qurbūti*

KAB . . . . see Kimir . . . .
Kabar 93, 5, 13 creditor
Kabilu 80, 6 w.
120, 4
Kakūsu 110, 10 debtor(?)
Kāmir?-. .[. . .] 42 r. 14 w.
Karšānu 83, 5′ w.; scr.
Kēnī 5, 17 w.; scr.
26, 29 w.; scr., writer of tablet
29, 20 w.
Kēnu-šallim 94, 7 w.; LÚ.NI.DUḪ
Kimē 192 r. 2′
Kimir?-aḫi-lāmur 17, 42 w.; from Du'ūa
Kimir-. . . . 42 r. 14 w.
Kiqilānu 22, 1, 8, 15 seller; sl. of Bēl-issīya LÚ.GAL URU.MEŠ-*ni*
80, 4 w.
93, 2, 10 creditor
Kiribtu 2, 17 f. of Šūmu-lēšir
103, 4 debtor
Kisī(ya) 9, 1, 4 f. of Ahu-lāmur
Kiṣir-aššur 193, 18
Kiṣrāyu(?) 3, 26 w.
Kitti?-ili 91, 37 w.; LÚ.NAGAR ^{giš}*mu-gir-re*
Kuāri 116, 3 from Sunigē?
Kukulānu 51 r. 4 w.; *ša qurbūte*
79, 4′ w.
Kukunātu 19, 3 seller; s. of Ṣābūya
Kumāyu 90, 6 creditor
123, 5
^{f}Kumētum 93, 3, 11 creditor
Kunāya 69, 2 debtor(?)
Kurbailāyu 35, 6 seller; LÚ.GALA
Kurbānu 26, 5, 17 buyer
27, 5, 18 buyer

La'īti-ilu 91, 8 f. of creditor
Lamariyānu 10, 2′, 9′ sold; sl. of [. . .]
Laqīpu 2, 20 w.; ^{lú}*še-lap-pa-a-a*
23, 26 w.; LÚ.3.U$_5$
29, 22 w.
45, 2, 13 seller
52, 7′ w.
91, 7 creditor
106, 7 w.
^{f}Lāṣahittu 93, 5, 14 creditor
La . . . a 158 r. 4 w.(?)
Lēšeru 102 r. 3 w.; LÚ.KAŠ.LUL *ša* Dannē

Libbi-ālāyu 93, 2, 11
Libluṭ(u) 98, 4 (URU *ša*)
Lidbubu 91, 33 w.; from Kume
[Līm]uru 86, 1′ w.
Lipūšu 78, 5′ f. of Salamānu
90, 8 ow. of Ahu-le'i
Li[. . .] 55 r. 3 seller(?)
Luballiṭu?-ilāni 118, 1 LÚ.[B]UR.G[U]L
Lu . .[. .] 187 A 3

Mabimū(/Mammū) 31, 2, 9, 14 seller; grandson of [. . .]āya; LÚ *ša šar-ri*
Madāyu? 106, 9 w.
Mana[. . .] 67, 1′ donor
Mannī 82, 9 w.; lú*qa-ti-en-nu*
Mannu-akī-aššur 92, 7 w.; LÚ.MU? *ša* É lú*tur-ta-ni*
Mannu-akī-šarri 123, 10
Mannu-kī-adad 82, 6 w.
114, 6 from Biha?[. . .]
Mannu-kī-ahhē 17, 44 w.; uru*kal-ḫa-a-a la-bi-ru*
Mannu-kī-ahī 82, 17 w.; LÚ.3-*šu* U5
101, 2 debtor
Mannu-kī-ili 127, 3 [LÚ.GA]L? URU.MEŠ-*ni*
250, 3
Man[nu-kī-iš]tāria 219 r. 7′ w.
*Mannu-kī-māt-aššur 93 r. 6′ (26.iii?) gov. of Guzāna
Mannu-kī-māt-aššur 23, 8, 17 buyer; LÚ.GAL É
Mannu-kī-ninurta 219, 5 buyer
Mannu-kī-[. . .] 117, 2
221, 5
Mār-banūte 109, 8 w.
Marduk-ahu-iddina? 4, 12 (dNA4.ŠÚ-) w.; LÚ.KA.ŠÈR *ša ša* IGI É.GAL
125, 7 [LÚ.GAL]⌜URU?⌝.MEŠ
Marduk-aplu-uṣur 6, 4 buyer; s. of Bēl-nāṣir
81, 6 w.; GAL lú[*kal*]-*la-bi*
Marduk-aplu-[. . .] 249, 9 w.
Mardukāte 26, 3, 7, 14 seller
*[Marduk]-bēlu-uṣur 175, 2′(?) (26.i)
Marduk-bēlu-uṣur 102 r. 1 *ša* É lú*tur-ta-ni*
123, 8
Mardukiā 15, 49 ow. of Ubru-šamaš
78, 2′ w.
Marduk-ibni 85, 4′ w.; s. of Gi[. . .]
Marduk-kabtu-ahhēšu (246 r. 19′)
Marduk-nādin-ahhē 23, 27 w.; LÚ.GAL *kal-la-bi*
103, 14 w.; s. of Bar-ili
*Marduk-rēmāni 19, 27 (20.xii+i?)
20 L.E. 4′ (11.—)
68 r. 14′ (21.iii)
Marduk-rēmāni 93, 4, 12 creditor
108, 6 creditor; LÚ.EN.NAM *šá* uru*kal-ḫa*
242 r. 1′
*Mdaruk-šadūni 92, 19 (9.iv)
102 r. 9 (9.x)
Marduk-šallim-ahhē 103, 8 w.; LÚ.SANGA *ša* dMAŠ.MAŠ
Marduk-(u)balliṭ 94, 8 w.; *ša pit-ḫal-li*
Marduk-[. . .]lu 222 A 5′ LÚ.MU
Mār-ištar 15, 38 w.; lú*ḫa-za-nu ša* uru*kur-ba-ìl*
15, 40 w.; GAL MÍ.MAŠ.MEŠ *ša* É lú*tur-ta-ni*; from Kurbail
44, 2, 7, 12 seller
102 r. 5 w.; LÚ.NINDA
103, 12 w.; LÚ.SANGA *ša* dGAŠAN-*nat-ḫa*
130, 8
197, 2 author
Mār?-[. . .] 157, 6′
Māt-mandiāyu(?) 22, 22 w.
Me'īsu 119, 6 lú*ru-qa-ḫa-a-a*
Meni'i 14, 2, 10 seller
155 i.13(?)
Mīnu-ēpuš-ilī 51 r. 11 w.; lú*rak-su*
Mīšarrum-nāṣir(-. . .) 201, 3 author; s. of Bēl-dān
202, 3 author; s. of Bēl-dān
Mudāda 119, 5 lú*ru-qa-ḫa-a-a*
Mumī 11, 9′ w.; s. of Aššur-l[e'i?]
fMurāyītu 93, 6, 15 ow. of creditor(?)
Mušallim-ilu 120, 2
[Muša]llim-ištar 64, 10 "buyer" (exchange)
Mušallim-marduk 17, 50 w.; LÚ.3.U5 *ša* LÚ.GAL.SAG
42 r. 15 w.
101, 1 debtor
*Mušallim-ninurta 78, 13′ (24.xii)
Mušallim-ninurta 18, 19 w.; lú*mu-tir-ṭe-me ša* LÚ.EN.NAM *ša* Kalhi
Mušallim?-šamaš 7, 5, 8 seller; ow. of Šamaš-abu-[. . .]
Mušallim-[. . .] 123, 4
Mušēzib-aššur 248, 17′ w.; s. of Ninurta-nišēkauṣur
248, 22′ LÚ.NI.DUḪ *ša* É.GAL
Mušēzib-ilu 25, 25(?) w.
53, 9′ w.; LÚ.SUM?.[GAR(?)]
248, 5′ f. of Bēl-āli; scr. of É.DINGIR *ša* uruŠÀ.URU
Mušēzib-ninurta 2, 7 buyer; gov. of Kalhu
*Mutakkil-marduk(?) 101 r. 13′
Mutaqqin-aššur 81, 4 w.; sl. of LÚ.AGRIG
Mutaqqin-ilu 114, 8 sl. of Nabû-šarhi-[ilāni]; LÚ.SIP[A?]
fM[u . . .] 53, 11′ m. of Ahu-illaka?
90, 33

Nabūa 95, 10 w.; lú*mu-tir-ṭè-me*
Nabû-ahhē-(e)rība 85, 7′(?) w.
104, 10 w.; (scr.) writer of tablet
Nabû-ahhē-[. . .] 62, 13 w.
Nabû-ahu-š[allim?] 222 A 3′
Nabû-aplu?-uṣur 153, 14

Nabû-bēl-ili (246 r. 17′)
*Nabû-da'inanni 105, 9 (24.i) ^{lú}*tu[r-t]a-[nu]*
Nabû?-da'inanni 219 r. 9′ w.
Nabû-de'iq 230, 2 author
Nabû-dūr-bēlīya 257, 2
Nabû-dūru-uṣur 137, 2
Nabû-(e)rība 95, 22 w.; LÚ.GAL URU?.MEŠ-*ni* [*ša*] LÚ.A.BA É.GAL
*Nabû-ēṭ(i)rāni 95, 20 (27.x) LÚ.GAL KAŠ.LUL
Nabû-gimillī-tirri 112, 3 LÚ.GAL 50 *ša* LÚ[...]
Nabû?-ilāya 108, 5 debtor
Nabû-iqbi 103, 11 f. of Imāru
Nabû-kēnu-dugul? 17, 49 w.; writer of tablet
Nabû-MU[?...] 88, 8′ w.
Nabû-nādin-ahhē 17, 46 w.; (^{uru}*kal-ḫa-a-a la-bi-ru*)
Nabû-nāṣir 95, 7 w.; ^{lú}*ša* UGU URU
Nabû?-nūrka-lāmur 155.i.3 LÚ.ÌR É.GAL
Nabû?-qātē-ṣabat 155.i.5
Nabû-rēmāni 71, 7′ w.; GAL *ú-ra-a-[te?]*
95, 15 w.; EN ÚŠ.MEŠ *ša-du-ni*
Nabû-šallim 17, 39 w.; scr.
Nabû-šallim-ahhē 81, 13 w.; scr.
Nabû-šallim-šunu (246, 6, 10)
Nabû-šarhi-il[āni] 114, 9 ow. of Mutaqqin-ilu
Nabû-šūmu-ibni 51 r. 7 w.; LÚ.A.ZU
Nabû-šūmu-iddina 18, 26 w.; s. of HIbani; writer of tablet
53, 13′ w.; (scr.) writer of tablet
96, 9 w.; LÚ.DAM.GÀR
Nabû-takbis 25, 26 w.; scr., writer of tablet
Nabû-taklak 81, 8 w.
Nabû-tuklātu-uṣalli 248, 9′ buyer; palace scr.
Nabû-uballiṭ 95, 17 w.; scr., writer of tablet
Nabû-uṣalla 81, 2 w.; [GA]L LÚ.MU
Nabû-zēru?-ibni 106, 6 w.
*Nabû?-[...] 43, 23 (—.xii+i?)
Nabû-[...] 13, 13 w.
19, 25 w.; (scr.) writer of tablet
42 r. 13 w.
219 r. 1 w.
Nādinea 108, 12 w.
Nagaha 122, 5
Nagāyu 5, 1, 5 seller; f. of ^{f}[..]nāya
Nai 105, 2 debtor(?); LÚ.DUMU GEMÉ.É.GAL
Nanī 78, 8′ w.; ^{lú}*mu-tir-ṭè-me*
90, 12 creditor; LÚ. *x*[ ] *ša pān* Bēl-lāmur?
123, 7(?)
196, 6
Nap'adulu 119, 4 ^{lú}*ru-qa-ḫa-a-a*
Nasi'i 82, 4 w.; ^{lú}*ḫa-za-nu*
^{d}NA$_4$.ŠÚ-ahu-iddina 4, 12′ w.; LÚ.KA.ŠÈR *ša ša* IGI É.GAL
Natēya 23, 2, 9, 15 seller
Na[...] 41, 1′ seller
192 r. 1′
Nergal-.... see also Palil-....
*Nergal-ilāya 2, 23 (—.xii)
170 (4(+).—)
Nergal-na'id 95, 5 w.; LÚ *qur-bu-te*; from Parnunna
*Nergal-nāṣir 24, 31 (27.xi) [*šakin* ^{u}]^{ru}*na-ṣi-bi-na*
Nergal-nāṣir 194, 2 author
Nergal-šūmu-iddina 123, 12
Nergal-šūmu-uṣur 15, 50 w.; (scr.) writer of tablet
16 r. 6′ w.; [scr.]
Ninuāyu 6, 2, 3 seller; ow. of [...]qi; LÚ.TÚG.K[A.ŠÈ]R
Ninurta-ahhē-šallim? 35, 5 seller; LÚ.NAR
Ninurta?-ahu-uṣur 6, 23 w.
*Ninurta-ālik-pāni 144, 6 (30.—)
Ninurta?-balassu-iqbi 29, 24 w.; (scr.) writer of tablet
Ninurta-bēlu-uṣur 107, 2 debtor
Ninurta?-ēreš 43, 17 w.; br. of [...]ī
Ninurta-(e)rība 24, 26 w.; from .... na
Ninurta-ilāya 114, 12(?) [ow.?] of Ilu-dalā
127, 11
193, 2 author
Ninurta-(i)le'i 109, 7 w.
Ninurta-iqbi 18, 15 f. of Burki-...
Ninurta-issīya 83, 3′ w.
Ninurta-kuṣranni 96, 2
Ninurta-na'id 4, 22 w.; (scr.) writer of tablet
22, 28 w.; (scr.) writer of tablet
82, 7 w.; GAL *da-a-a-li*
86, 5′ w.
*Ninurta-nāṣir 17, 48 (6.ii)
79, 6′ (13.viii/ix)
Ninurta-nišēka-uṣur 248, 19′ f. of 4 witnesses
Ninurta-qātē-ṣabat? 14, 25 w.
Ninurta-rēm[āni] 71, 9′ w.; GAL ...
Ninurta-šall[im(-...)] 74, 3′ w.; [GA]L É.GAL
*Ninurta-šēzibanni 5, 19 (2.vii)
23, 32 (13?.—)
81, 11 (19.vii) gov. of Rimusi
Ninurta-taklak 110, 4 ow. of Il(u)a[...]
118, 5
*Ninurta?-[...] 43, 23 (—.xii+i?)
Ninurta-[...] 85, 1′ w.
255, 2
Nuhšāyu 82, 5 w.; s. of Rub[...]
Nuqsā 15, 48 w.; *ša* É ^{lú}*sar-ten-ni*
Nūrānu 3, 28 f. of Urdu-ištar
Nūr-el[lil] 239, 1
Nusku?-rēmāni(?) 155 viii.6′

Palil-ahu-idd[ina] 57 T.E. 14 ow. of ZA.AD?.IŠ?
*Palil-ēreš 21 T.E. 6′
80, 9 (29.vi)
90, 34(?) (26?.ii)

Pāna 82, 12 w.; *ḫazanu* [*š*]*a* ^{uru}*m*[*u* . . .]. .
Pān-aššur 91, 6 creditor
Pānāya 22, 24 w.
Pān-ištar-lāmur 106, 3 creditor
Parisu 120, 11
Pa[. . .]āyu 219 r. 8′ w.
Pilaqqāyu? 43, 19 w.; LÚ.NAGAR
Puṣānu 249, 8 w.
Puṣī 80, 2 w.
Pušāya 18, 22(?) w.; EN . . . . *ša* ^{uru}*kap-ru da-lal*
92, 9 w.
Pušhī 5, 16 w.
Pu[. . .] 25, 21 w.; scr.

Qalaliu 101 r. 10′ w.; from Šašlē
Qanasī 11 r. 12′ w.; s. of Ahu-luballiṭ
Qari-ilu 120, 12
Qaruru 3, 29 w.
Qāt-ili-gabbu 182, 2 addressee; from Kalhu
Qibīt-aššur 45, 5, 18 buyer
Qūa 24, 2 f. of Tabši-kittu
Qunīya 15, 2 seller
Qurdi-aššur? 221, 15 w.
Qurdi-ilāni 45, 1, 12 seller
Qurdi-ištar 11 r. 13′ w.
[Qu]rdi-ištar-lāmur 32 r. 2
Qu[. . .]a 90, 21 w.

Rabba-il? 113, 2′
Rapala 106, 2
Raši-ilu 2, 15 w.; ^{lú}*mu-kil*-KUŠ.PA.MEŠ
Ra'ūzu 15, 41 w.; s. of Sanini; from Kurbail
36, 8′ w.; from Kurbail
53, 8′ w.; LÚ.DAM.G[ÀR]
82, 3 f. of Hadi-lipūšu
Rēmāni-ilu 17, 42 w.; from Du'ūa
Rēmāni-[. . .] 24, 24 w.; LÚ [. . .]āyu?
70, 2′ debtor(?)
220 r. 11′(?) w.
Ri'ānu 131, 12
Rīb-marduk 19, 6, 8 buyer
Ribsiru 113, 5′
Rīmūt-ili-ma 24, 29 w.; (scr.) writer of tablet
^{f}Rīšūtu 248, 3′ sold
Rub[. . .] 82, 5 f. of Nuhšāyu

Sa('a)lti-ilu 104, 8 w.
Sabāyu 82, 12 w.
Sabiri 93, 18 debtor; LÚ.DAM.GÀR
Sa'i[. . .] 96, 4 debtor
Salamānu 18, 21 w.
18, 24 w.; LÚ.GAL KA.ŠÈR *ša* ^{lú}*rak-su-te*
52, 9′ w.
78, 5′ w.; s. of Lipūšu
120, 16

Sā-MAŠ 234, 2
Samā[. . .] 90, 1 debtor
Sami'i 105, 3 creditor
Samsi-imme 235, 1
Sāmūtu 17, 39 w.; LÚ.ḪAL LUGAL
Sanī 249, 7 w.
Sanini 15, 39, 41 w.; f. of Ra'ūzu; from Kurbail
Sapharru 119, 1 ^{lú}*ru-qa-ḫa-a-a*
Sayā 113, 7′
Silim-adad 25, 22 w.; LÚ.SIPA MUŠEN.MEŠ
Silim-aššur 3, 25 w.; ^{lú}[*x*]-*pur*?
Silim-nergal? 120, 22
Silimu 247, 17′ w.
Silu 90, 11 creditor; KUR *ar-ma-a-a*
Sinā 121, 3 ^{lú}*ḫa-za-nu*
Sîn-ahu-iddina 80, 5 w.
90, 5 creditor; LÚ.UŠ ANŠE
Sina'-ilu 130, 9
Sîn-aplu-iddina (246 r. 18′)
Sîn-ēṭir 17, 36 w.; LÚ.GAL É *ša* LÚ.GAL.SAG
20, 5, 15
37, 7(?) buyer(?)
42 r. 2(?) buyer
47, 7(?) buyer; [LÚ.SA]G? LÚ.A.BA
60 b.4′(?) buyer
64, 7 " seller " (exchange); br. of Bēl-tarṣi-iluma(?)
65, 4′ " buyer " (exchange)
Sîn-iqbi 19, 20
Sîn?-mušallim 63, 8′ w.; scr., writer of tablet
Sîn-na'id 13, 16(?) w.
78, 6′ w.; LÚ.ASGAB
91, 9 creditor
Sîn-šallimāni 24, 28 ow. of Gabbu-āmur
Sîn-uballiṭ 39 r. 10′ w.
Sîn-[. . .] 60 b.4′ buyer
Siparrānu 15, 37 w.; GAL KUŠ.MEŠ of Kurbail
35, 22 w.; LÚ.GAL KUŠ.MEŠ; from Kurbail
Si'-ramu 120, 9
Sisī(ya) 4, 17 w.; LÚ.NINDA
14, 26 w.; A.BA? URU?
Sūlī 85, 5′ w.
^{f}Suni[. . .] 19, 24 w.
S[u . . .]qu 219 r. 6′ w.

Ṣāb-ištar? 205, 5, 13
Ṣābu-da(m)qu 4, 16 w.; LÚ.TIN.NA
18, 16 f. of Šulmu-šarri
22, 6, 17 buyer
51 r. 10 w.; ^{lú}*mu-šar-ki-su*
53, 12′ w.; ^{lú}*da-a-a-l*[*u*?]
Ṣābūya 19, 4 f. of Kukunāte
Ṣalmu[(. . .)] 219 r. 5′ w.
Ṣapūnu 94, 6 w.
120, 18

ᶠṢarpanītum-šarrat 15, 43
Ṣaṣī 4, 24 w.
Ṣidqī 207, 5′ (URU.ŠE)
Ṣidqi-ilu 17, 42 w.; from Du'ūa
Ṣil-aššur 40, 3′ buyer
Ṣil-ištar 4, 21 w.
68, 11′ w.; LÚ.GAL É.GAL *ša* É.GAL GIBIL
Ṣil-nergal 68, 9′ w.; LÚ.GAL É.GAL *ša* É.GAL BE-*ti*
Ṣil-šarri 91, 11 creditor
190, 2 addressee
ᶠṢiriāna 121, 10 from Ialūna

Ša-aššur-dubbu 137, 5
Šadu-il[āya?] 221, 13 w.
Ša-ili-gabbu 23, 24 w.; [lú]*mu-kil*-PA.MEŠ
Ša-la-mašê 122, 4
Šallim-ilu 7 L.E. 3′ w.; LÚ.SAG
Šamaš-abu-uṣur 110, 2 creditor(?)
Šamaš-abu-[. . .] 7, 4 sold; sl. of Mušallim?-šamaš
Šamaš-ahhē-[. . .] 25, 23 w.
Šamaš-ahu-iddina 15, 44 w.; sl. of Aššur-aplu-uṣur
91, 34 w.; LÚ.UŠ.BAR
Šamaš-ahu-uṣur 119, 16 s. of Busī; from Si'-altāru?
Šamaš-am(u)rāni 25, 2, 6, 11 seller
*Šamaš-bēlu-uṣur 145, 7 (17?.iii)
146, 5 (—.xii+i)
147, 2′ (11.i?)
Šamaš-bēlu-uṣur 196, 18 LÚ.EN.NAM
Šamaš-da'inanni 139, 6
Šamaš-ēṭir 2, 19 f. of Ibnī
Šamaš-iddina 44, 1 [lú]*ḫa-za-nu ša* [ur][u. . .]
83, 4′ w.
Šamaš-ilāya 109, 6 w.
Šamaš-(i)le'i 15, 3 seller
Šamaš-issīya 108, 11 w.
Šamaš-kēnu-uballiṭ 32, 6′, 15′ buyer; *ša qurbūti* of Adad-nērārī
Šamaš-kūmūa 17, 7, 17 buyer; LÚ.SAG of Adad-nērārī
31, 8, 20 buyer; scr. of LÚ.NIMGIR [É.GAL(?)]
57 r. 3 buyer
68, 8′ w.; scr.
Šamaš-m[u . . .] 87, 2′ w.
Šamaš-nādin-šūmi? 22, 23 w.; s. of . . . . ālik-pāni
Šamaš-nūr[u?] 13, 14 w.
Šamaš-šallim 14, 22 w.; [lú]*mu-kil ap-pa-te*
47, 2, 13 seller
Šamaš-šēzib 22, 7, 17 buyer
39 r. 12′ w.
Šamaš-šē[. . .] 30, 3 f. of Hubuškāyu and Abu-ūl-īdi
35, 26
Šamaš-upahhir 110, 11 w.
Šamaš-[. . .] 90, 23, 25 w.
100, 6 w.
219 r. 2′ w.
Šamaš-[. . .]-uṣur(?) 35, 26 f. of [. . .]-ištar
Šarru-am(u)rāni 92, 2, 4 ow. of Uššābu
242, 2, 5, r. 6′ author
Šarru-balāṭu-iqbi 35, 4 seller; LÚ.NAR
Šarru-dūrī 132/172 s.i. 1 gov. of Kalhu
185, 2 addressee
186, 1(?) addressee
187 A.2(?) addressee
188, 2 addressee
189, 2 addressee
203, 6′, 17′ LÚ.E[N.N]AM [*š*]*a* Kalhi
*Šarru-kēn 261, 1 (—.iv)
Šarru-kēn (246, 1, r. 23′)
Šarru-munammir 51 r. 8 w.; LÚ.SAG
Ša[. . .] 42 r. 11(?) w.
75, 11′ w.
Še'i-ištar 248, 2′ sold
Šekānu 247, 16′ w.
Šēlubu 91, 6 creditor
95, 1 debtor; s. of Aššur-dūru-uṣur
Šēp-aššur-aṣbat 17, 45 w.; [uru]*kal-ḫa-a-a la-bi-ru*
*Šēp-ištar(?) 74, 14′
Šēp-ištar 209, 12′
219 r. 4′ w.
*Šēp-šarri 100, 12 (11.v)
Šēp-šarri 51 r. 6 w.; LÚ.MU
Šēp-[. . .] 86, 4′ w.; GAL [. . .]
101 r. 9′ ow. of Ēṣidāyu
Šēr-hanāna 93, 4, 13 creditor
Šēr-ma'ādi 93, 3, 12 creditor
Šē[. . .] 88, 5′ w.
Šulmānu-ašarēd 18, 29 [king] of Assyria
Šulmānu-nāṣir 222 A.4′
Šulmānu-[. . .] 24, 23 w.
Šulmī 96, 6 creditor
Šulmu-ahhē 4, 11 w.
26, 21
128, 10 LÚ.GAL URU.MEŠ-*ni-šú-nu*
Šulmu-ahhē-šu 69, 3 debtor(?)
Šulmu-ah[hē(-. . .)] 24, 21 w.; [. . .] *ša* LÚ.EN.NAM
25, 24 w.
Šulmu-bēl 68, 2(?)
115, 6′
Šulmu-bēl-lāmur 4, 15 w.; GAL *ši-ma-ni*
57 L.E. 17 w.
91, 7 f. of creditor
230, 5(?)
Šulmu-šarri 18, 16 w.; s. of Ṣābu-da(m)qu
Šulmu-[. . .] 42 r. 10(?) w.
74, 6′ w.
220 r. 6′ w.
Šūm-adad-milki(?) 10, 5′ buyer
Šūmu-lēšir 2, 17 w.; s. of Kiribtu
69, 2 debtor(?)
Šunu-qardu 17, 47 w.; LÚ.NU(=KAŠ).LUL MAN

Tabši-kittu/mēšāru 24, 2, 6, 11 seller; s. of Qūa
*Taklak-ana-bēl 255, 5 (—.i)
Tardīti-ištar 120, 14 br. of Iata'
Ta[. . .]qa? 3, 24 w.
Tini . . . 95, 13 w.; from Badana
Tirik[a . . .] 71, 6′ w.
TI[. . .] 235, 1
*Tukultī-apil-ešarra 26, 27 (17.ix) king of Assyria
27, 29 (—.ix?) king of [Assyria]
28 r. 2′ (—.x) king of [Assyria]
Tuli?[. . .] 115, 3′

Ṭāb-ahūnu 80, 3 w.
[Ṭ]āb-lipūšu 36, 9′ w.; *ša* É [lú]*tur-ta-ni*; from Kurbail
*Ṭāb-ṣil-ešarra 257, 4 (16.i)
Ṭāb-ṣil-ešarra 240, 2 author
*Ṭāb-šār-aššur 250, 5 (—.ii)
Ṭāb-šār[. . .] 64, 11
Ṭābūs[u(. . .)] 19, 22 w.
Ṭūa 82, 14

Ubri-ištar 63 r. 5′ w.
Ubru-adad? 16, 3 seller
Ubru-ahhē 3, 2, 10, 11 seller; sl. of *ša* LÚ.UGU É; br. of Abu-ūl-īdi
Ubru-harrān 114, 3 LÚ.SIMUG KÙ.[GI]
Ubru-ilāni 86, 3′ w.
91, 36 w.; LÚ.UŠ.BAR *ša* É [lú]*tur-ta-ni*
Ubru-ištar 13, 15(?) w.
30, 7, 17 buyer
39 r. 9′ w.
63 r. 5′ (*ub-ri-*; sandhi ?) w.
Ubru-nabû 17, 38 w.; scr. of LÚ.GAL.SAG
78, 7′ w.; scr.
198, 2(?) author
(246 r. 16′)
Ubru-nergal 52, 13′ w.
98, 12(?) w.; *ša* [uru]*pu-rat-ta-a-a* LÚ.GAL KAŠ.LUL
Ubru-[pal]il? 70, 1′ debtor(?)
Ubru-šamaš 15, 49 w.; sl. of Mardukiā
119, 14(?) s. of Dadiyā; from Si'-altāru?
Ubrūte 82, 6 w.
Ubru-[. . .] 16, 5 seller
18, 14(?) w.; s. of Ištar-tarība
89, 4′
114, 13
222 A.2′
249, 2 creditor
[f]Uburtu-ahhē-ša 248, 2′ sold
Ukaturme? 119, 22 f. of Iada'-ilu
Ullubāyu 78, 10′ w.; scr., writer of tablet
Ūm-. . . see Ha(m)šāyu, Sabāyu, Ešra'āyu
Urarṭāyu 82, 2 w.
98, 10 w.; [lú]*za-ma-ru ša* LÚ.EN.NAM
Urdu-allāya 95, 8 w.; [lú]*ḫa-za-nu*
Urdu-ilāni 2, 13 w.; s. of Ilu-dārānu
Urdu-ištar 3, 28 w.; s. of Nūrānu
18, 17 w.; [lú]*ḫa-za-nu* of Kalhu
62, 10(?) w.; LÚ.EN?[. . .]
80, 1 w.
91, 1 debtor; LÚ.UŠ.BAR *bir-me ša* Bēl-tarṣi-iluma
Urdu?-[. . .] 115, 2′
Urukuna(?) 121, 4 from Ialūna
Urzāna 243 r. 9′
Urzāya 39 r. 11′ w.
Ur[. . .]a 123, 5
Uṣammir-akšudu 224, 10 w.(?)
Uššābu 92, 1 debtor; sl. of Šarru-am(u)rāni

Zāya 220 r. 13′ w.
(246, 10)
ZA.AD?.IŠ? 57 r. 13 w.; sl. of Palil-ahu-id[dina?]
Zēr-kitti-lēšir 57 r. 13 w.
91, 31 w.; s. of Aplayā?
Zēr-ki[. . .] 36, 15′
Zērūa? 220 r. 12′ w.
*Zēru-ibni 249, 11 (10+.vii) gov. of Raṣappa
Zīzāyu 74, 5′ w.
Zizī 57 r. 12 w.; LÚ.SIMUG KÙ.[GI]

[. . .]-adad 16, 6 seller
[. . .]addu 219, 1 seller; f. of Banītum-[šarr]at
[. . .]-ahhē 97, 1 creditor(?)
114, 10
[. . .]ahīya? 36, 10′ w.; from Kurbail
[. . .-ah]u-iddina 120, 20 f. of Iqbi-ilu?
[. . .]-ahūni? 155 i.9
[. . .]a-ilu 14, 17 w.
[. . .]-ālik-pāni? 22, 23 f. of Šamaš?-nādin-šūmi
[. . .]ānu 120, 21, 28
[. . .]-aplu-uṣur 42 r. 16 w.
[. . .]-aššur 6, 19 w.
57 T.E. 16 w.
(246 r. 18′)
[. . .]'atu . . . 11 r. 1′ w.; [lú]*mu-kil* KUŠ.PA.ME
[. . .]āya/u 31, 3
32, 2′ seller
35, 25 w.; uncle of Bēl-rubā'-ilāni; from Kurbail
67, 9′ w.; *ša* UGU É
108, 12 w.; 13 w.
110, 8 w.; [lú]*ḫa-za-nu*
234, 1
[. . .]-bēl 21 r. 5′ w.
[. . .]bu 97, 2 creditor(?); LÚ.UŠ.BAR
[. . .]. . būa 23, 29 w.; LÚ.A.BA 2-*i*, writer of tablet
[. . .]buku 91, 10 creditor
[. . .]dulu 8, 3 sold; sl. of Ilu-(e)rība
[. . .-d]ūr-bēlīya 155 i.12 LÚ.ASGAB

[. . .]-ellil 36, 3
[. . .]-ērēš(?) 32, 1′ seller
[. . .]hisu 15, 45 w.
[. . .]ī 43, 18 w.; br. of Ninurta$^{?}$-ērēš
[. . .]ibni$^{?}$-ahu 11, 6 buyer
[. . .]-ilāni 21 r. 2′ w.
[. . .]-ištar 35, 26 w.; s. of Šamaš$^{?}$-. . .-uṣur; from Kurbail
[. . .]kadu[(. . .)] 238, 2
[. . .]kaqa$^{?}$[. . .] 85, 2′ w.
[. . .]lāya 36, 15′ w.; *ša* É Zēr-ki[. . .]
[. . .]-lēšir 120, 1(?)
[. . .]. . li 21 r. 1′ w.
[. . .]-lū-balṭat 35, 27 w.; from Kurbail
[. . .]ludē 122, 2
[(. . .)]makru 69, 3 debtor(?)
[. . .]malka$^{?}$ 155 i.11 LÚ.TÚG.ŠÈ[R]
[. . .]muktīn$^{?}$ 82, 16 w.; LÚ.3-*šu* U$_{5}$
[. . .]-mušallim 97, 3 creditor(?)
^{f}[. . .]nāya 5, 3 sold; d. of Nagāyu
[. . .]ni 18, 1 f. of Aššur-aplu-uṣur
[. . .]-nišē 32 r. 3 w.
^{f}[. . . p]ušu 11, 2 sold; d. of [. . .]-šūmu-ērēš$^{?}$
[. . .]qī 5, 15 w.
6, 3 sold; sl. of Ninuāyu
82, 13 w.
[. . .]rā 93, 7
[. . .]rāya(. . .) 16 r. 4′ w.
[. . .]rēmāni 155 i.10 LÚ.NIMGIR
[. . .]rī 81, 1 w.
223, 4 [L]Ú.ASGAB
[. . .]si[. . .] 82, 1 w.
[. . .]-simti 127, 8
[. . .]simu$^{?}$ 14, 18 w.
^{f}[. . .]ṣianāya 121, 9 from Ialūna
[. . .]-šākin-šūmi (246 r. 19′)
[. . .]-šallim 36, 16′ w.
[. . .]. .-šalmu-la[. . .] 239, 2
[. . .]-šarru-uṣur 32 r. 4 w.
[. . .]-šūmu-ērēš(?) 11, 1, 4 seller; f. of ^{f}[. . . p]ušu
[. . .]ta'a 2, 3 sold; sl. of Bēl-ahi
^{f}[. . .]talā$^{?}$ 113, 15′
[. . .]. . tua 16, 2 seller
[. . .]-uballiṭ 46, 3 seller
[. . .]-uṣur 14, 19 w.; [LÚ].SAG *ša* LÚ.EN.NAM
[. . .]zalu 52, 14′ w.

INDEX OF PLACE NAMES

Note: the index includes gentilics and some PNs which are gentilics in form. In the arrangement the signs KUR and URU are ignored, even where they are certainly to be read as part of the name (as in *māt Sūḫi*).

Adad (*Āl-*)
URU.^{d}IM 135, 3
Akkad (*Māt-*)
KUR.URI$^{ki(!)}$ 199, 19
^{uru}*am-an-te*
240, 8
Arba'il
^{uru}TAB.TAB.DINGIR 17, 32; 91, 32
^{uru}*a-ri-ra-a-a*
121, 7
^{kur}*ar-ma-a-a*
90, 11
^{uru}*ar-rak$^{?}$*-[. . .]
157, 3′
Arrapḫa
^{uru}*ar-x*-[. . .] 6, 28
^{uru}TAB.TAB-*ḫa-a*-[*a*] 205, 24
^{uru}*ar-zu-ḫi-na*
127, 6; 196, 5
Aššur
KUR *aš-šur*$^{(ki)}$ 17, 8; 18, 30; 26, 28; [27, 30]; [28 r. 3′]; 32, 7′; 54 r. 6; 68, 4′
^{uru}ŠÀ.URU 17, 28; 240 r.; 248, 6′
^{uru}ŠÀ.URU-*a-a* (PN) 93, 2, 11
^{uru}*ba-da-na-a-a*
95, 14
Bēl-lībur (*Āl-*)
URU EN-*li-bur* 3, 27
Bēl-[. . .]
[UR]U.EN.[. . .] 55 r. 17
Bēt-šašširi
URU.ŠE *ša* É-*šá-ši-ri* 25, 3
^{uru}É.IM.DIR 24, 5
^{m}É.IM.DIR-*a-a* (PN) 35, 3
^{uru}*bi$^{?}$-ḫa*-[(. .)]-*a-a*
114, 7
^{uru}*bu-ru-qi*
64, 6
^{kur}*da-ú-na-ni*
195, 4
^{uru}*di-a-t*[*e$^{?}$*]
90, 10

Dūr-[. . .]
^{uru}BÀD.[. . .] 242, 7
^{uru}*du-'u-ú-a*
17, 5, 41, 43
^{uru}*gab-ri-na*
101 r. 8′
Gargamiš
KUR *gar-ga-miš* 215 r. 19′
^{uru}*gar-ga-miš* 1, 16′
^{kur}*gi-mir-*[*a-a*
243, 7′, r. 5′
^{uru}*gu-za-na*
29, 27; 93 r. 7′
$^{ku[r]}$*ḫa-d*[*a*]*l-li*
188, 8
^{kur}*ḫa-láḫ-*[*ḫi*]
64, 6
^{uru}*ḫal-ṣu*
128, 3
Ḫalzi
^{uru}*ḫal-z*[*i*?] 186, 2
KÁ.GAL *ša* KUR *ḫal-zi* 193, 6
^{kur}*ḫa-ma-t*[*a*?*-a-a*]
8, 2
^{uru}*ḫar*-BE-[. . .]
157, 7′
^{uru}*ḫar-ḫum-ba*
183, 7
Ḫarrān
$^{m.uru}$KASKAL-*a-a* (PN) 119, 12
^{uru}ḪAR-*ša-a-a*
11 r. 7′
ḪAR.MEŠ 126, 3
$^{m.uru}$ḪI-*a-a* (PN)
15, 46
Ḫubuškia
KUR *ḫu-ub-buš*$_x$(KASKAL^{ii})-[. . .] 243 r. 8′
^{m}*ḫu-bu/ub-uš-ka-a-a* (PN) 30, 2, 4, 18
Ialūna
[KUR *i*]*a-lu-na* 65(/170/171) s.i. 5
^{uru}*ia-lu-na-a-a* 121, 5, 12
^{uru}*im-be-*^{m}*ra-ḫi-i* (?)
82, 15
Imgur-ellil
^{uru}*im-gúr-*^{d}BE 109, 4
^{m}*i-tu-*('*a*-)*a-a* (PN)
17, 40; 118, 8
Kalḫu
^{uru}*ka-làḫ* 201, 7
^{uru}*kal-ḫa* 108, 7; 139, 7; 182, 3; 186, 11; 196, 10; 203, 7′; 262, 2′(?)
^{uru}*kal-ḫa-a-a* 17, 44; 101, 7
^{uru}*kal-ḫi* 3, 4; 14, 14; 15, 12, 30; 17, 20, 27; 18, 18, 20; 23, 20; 24, 17; 25, 30; 33, 7; 34, 7; 51 r. 15; [53, 3′]; 64, [3], s.i. 2; 65, 2, 7; 65(/170/171) s.i. 3; 90, 4; 91, 3, 28; 93, 19; 99, 3; 154, 8′; 155 viii.2′; 172–3 s.i. 3; 181, 3
^{uru}*kàl-zi*
63 r. 3′
^{uru}*kap-ri* (. .) *ša* GAL URU(?)
135, 4–5
kap-ru
155 i.6
kap-ru [. . .]
48, 1′
Kapru-Babû
URU.ŠE ^{m}*ba-bu-u* 121, 14
Kapru-bēl-[. . .]
^{uru}*kap-ru*-E[N . . .] 47, 5
^{uru}*kap-ru-da-lal*
18, 23
Kapru-ṣidqī(?)
URU.ŠE *ṣ*[*i*]*-id-*[*q*]*i*?-[*i*?] 207, 5′
Kapru ša Bēt-šašširi
URU.ŠE *ša* É-*šá-ši-ri* 25, 3
Kapru-turtāni
URU.ŠE ^{lú}*tur-ta-ni* 4, 19
Kār-diglāyē
^{uru}*k*[*ar*?-]Í[D.ID]IGNA-*a-a* 65, 4
^{uru}*ka-sa-pa*
240, 9
^{uru}*ki-d*[*i*?-. . .]
157, 4′
Kumme
^{uru}*ku-me* 91, 33
^{m}*ku-ma-a-a* (PN) 90, 6; 123, 5
^{mí}*ku-me-tum* (FPN) 93, 3, 11
^{uru}*ku-up-ru-na*
33, 4; 34, 4
^{uru}*kur-ba-ìl*
15, 24, 29, 34, 37, 38; 17, 30; 35, 8, 19; 36, 2′, 6′, 7′, 10′, 13′
^{uru}*kur-ba-ìl-a-a* 15, 42; 35, 29; 36, 14′
^{m}*kur-ba-ìl-a-a* (PN) 35, 6
Libbi-āli see *Aššur*
Mē-ṭābūte
^{uru}A.MEŠ DÙG.GA.MEŠ 240, 7
^{uru}*m*[*i* . . .]
82, 11
^{kur}*mu-ṣa*?-[*ṣir*(?)]
244, 6
^{uru}*m*[*u* . . .]
82, 13
^{lú}*na-qi-ra-a-a*
119, 11
^{uru}*na-ṣi-bi-na*
24, 32
Nēmed-ištar
^{uru}*né-med-*^{d}INANNA 222 B.3′

Nīnua
^{uru}NINA 6, 12; 193, 8; 199, 23
$^{m.uru}$NINA-*a-a* (PN) 6, 2, 3
Parnuna
^{uru}*par-*ḪA*-na* 22, 30
^{uru}*par-*ḪA*-a-a* 95, 6
$^{m.uru}$*pa-x-a-a* (PN)
219 r. 8′
^{uru}*pu-rat-ta-a-a*
98, 13
[^{íd}]*ra-da-ni* (?)
127, 5
^{uru}*ra-pi-qi*
194, 15
$^{kur/uru}$*ra-ṣa-pa*
107, 8; 249, 12
^{uru}RI*-mu-si*
81, 12; 111, 5
^{lú}*ru-qa-ḫa-a-a*
119, 8
^{uru}*sa-li-ma-a-ni*
30, 5
^{uru}*sa-me-*[. . .]
132, 3
^{uru}*si-i'-al?-ta?-ru?*
119, 17
^{uru}*sip?-ru-*[. . .]
157, 1′
^{kur}*s*[*u*]*-ḫi*
188, 7
^{uru}*su-ni-gi-e?*
116, 4
^{uru}*šá-áš-li-e?*
101 r. 11′
Ša-Dagan-bēl-uṣur (*Āl-*)
URU *šá* $^{m.d}$[*d*]*a-gan-*EN.PAP 43, 4
^{uru}*ša-la-ḫi-ṭa?-a-a*
32, 4′
^{uru}*ša-*^{m}*lib-luṭ-a-a*
98, 4
^{uru}*ša-sa-*[. . .]
157, 5′
URU.ŠE . . . see *Kapru* . . .
^{uru}*šib-ḫi-ni-iš*
15, 51; 16 r. 7′
Šišlu
^{uru}*ši-šil* 190, 5
^{uru}*ši-iš-li* 183, 6
^{uru}*ta-ma?-nu-n*[*i?*]
128, 9
^{kur}*te-me-ni*
65(/170/171) s.i. 4
Til-[. . .]
^{uru}DUL*-x* (*x*) *x* 222 B.2′
^{uru}*ul-mu?*
101 r. 2′
^{kur}*ú-ra-ar-ṭa-a-*[*a*]
112, 2
[^{m}]*ú-ra-ár-ṭa-a-a* (PN) 82, 2
^{m}*ú-ra-ar-ṭa-a-a* (PN) 98, 10
^{uru}*ur?-bi*[*l?-*. . .]
206, 2′
^{kur}*ú-ṣu-na-li*
243 r. 6′
^{uru}*za-ban*
183, 5
^{uru}*za-li-gi-e?*
116, 2
^{uru}*zu?-r*[*i?*]
39 r. 8′
. . . .*-bi-na-a-a*
120, 31
^{uru}[. . .]*-ku?-a-ni*
55 r. 14(–16)
^{uru}[. .]. .*-na?*
24, 26
^{uru}[. . .]*-ú-*. . .
24, 25

INDEX OF PROFESSIONS

Note: This list gives all professions and similar designations, but not family terms. The examples are arranged thematically by the context in which the term appears. Where convenient, the commonest writing is used to form the heading for each word, and in the ensuing examples the initial letter of the word stands for that writing, and only that writing; other writings are explicitly indicated. Thus under EN *il-ki*, LÚ.SAG E.*-šú* stands for LÚ.SAG EN *il-ki-šú*. Logographic writings are placed after syllabic, and the sign LÚ, whether rendered in Akkadian or not, is ignored.

[*ba*]*-tú-su*
113, 12′
^{lú}*da-a-a-lu*
PN **d.** 53, 12′
PN GAL *da-a-a-li* 82, 7–8

e-mu-qe
186, 4 (^{lú}e.), 10, 20, 26–7
^{lú}*ḫa-za-nu*
PN ḫ. 11 r. 5′; 21 T.E. 4′; 82, 4; 90, 16(?); 95, 9; 110, 8; 121, 3
PN ḫ. of Du'ūa 17, 41
PN ḫ. of Kalḫu 18, 17
PN ḫ. of Kurbail 15, 38
PN ḫ. of M[i...] 82, 11
PN ḫ. of M[u...] 82, 12
PN ḫ. of URU.ŠE ^{lú}*tur-ta-ni* 4, 18
PN ḫ. of [...] 44, 1
in clauses: *lū* ḫ. 15, 20; 17, 13
lū ^{lú}*ḫa-za-an-nu* 31, 18
ḫ.-*ma lā āmur* 209, 9′
^{lú}*kal-la-b/pu*
PN k. 110, 5
PN GAL ^{lú}*kal-la-pi* 9, 16
PN LÚ.GAL *kal-la-pi* 51, 5
PN LÚ.GAL *kal-la-pi ša* LÚ.EN.NAM 98, 9
PN LÚ.GAL *kal-la-bi* 23, 28
PN GAL [^{l}]^{ú}[*kal*]-*la-bi* 81, 7
^{lú}*kar-ka-di-nu* (cf. LÚ.SUM.NINDA)
PN k. 11 r. 11′
(^{lú}*ku-tal* see *ša kutalli*)
^{lú}*láḫ-ḫi-nu*
PN l. 35, 23
^{lú}*mu-kil ap-pa-te*
PN m. 14, 23
PN ^{lú}*mu-kil*-KUŠ.PA.ME(Š) 2, 16; 11 r. 2′; 22, 26; 82, 18(?)
PN ^{lú}*mu-kil*-[P]A.MEŠ 23, 24
^{lú}*mu-šar-ki-su*
PN m. 51, 10; 68, 6′
^{lú}*mu-tir-ṭè-me*
PN m. 78, 8′; 95, 11
PN ^{lú}*mu-tir-ṭe-me ša* LÚ.EN.NAM of Kalhu 18, 19
PN ^{lú}*mu-tir-*⟨*ṭe*⟩*-mi* 9, 17
^{lú}*mu*[...]
PN m. 62, 14
^{lú}*na-si-ku*
PN n. *ša* ^{lú}*na-qi-ra-a-a* 119, 10
^{lú}*qa-ti-en-nu*
PN q. 82, 9
^{lú}*qe-pu*
in clauses: *lū* q. 17, 14
(^{lú}*qurbūtu* see *ša qurbūti*)
^{lú}*rak-su*
PN r. 51, 11
PN LÚ.GAL KA.ŠÈR *ša* ^{lú}*rak-su-te* 18, 23
^{lú}*sar-ten-ni* (Genit.)
PN *ša* É s. 15, 48
^{lú}*sa-ru-ti*^{meš}
PAP-*ma* 7 s. 119, 18
^{lú}*ša* IGI É
É š. 105, 5(?)
^{lú}*šá* IGI É.GAL
PN š. 191, 2 (author); 204, 11′
PN LÚ.KA.ŠÈR *ša ša* IGI É?.GAL 4, 13
PN ^{lú}*ša* UGU É *ša* ^{lú}*ša* IGI É.GAL 96, 12
ša kutalli
30 LÚ *ku-tal* ERÍN.MAN 141, 10
ša muḫḫi ... see *ša* UGU ...
ša pet-ḫal-li
PN š. 94, 9
ša qur-bu-ti
PN š. 9, 15
PN ^{lú}š. 15, 47
PN ^{lú}*ša qur-bu-te* 51, 4
PN [^{lú}]š. *ša* PN (king) 32, 7′
PN LÚ *qur-bu-te* ^{uru}*par*-ḪA-*a-a* 95, 5
^{lú}*ša šar-ri*
PN š. 31, 3
ša UGU É
PN š. 67, 9′
PN ^{lú}š. *ša* É ^{lú}*ša* IGI É.GAL 96, 11
PN ^{lú}*šá* UGU É *ša* É ^{lú}*tur-ta-ni* 91, 30
LÚ UGU É *ša* LÚ.EN.NAM of Kalhu 3, 3
^{lú}*šá* UGU URU
PN š. 95, 7
197, 5, r. 4′
šaknu A (^{lú}*šá-kìn* (+GN) = "governor")
PN š. ^{uru}*gu-za-na* 29, 27; 91 r. 7′
PN š. ^{uru}*kal-ḫi* 2, 8; 25, 30; 33, 7; 34, 7; 51, 15; 64(/170/171) s.i. 2; 65, 2, [7], s.i. 3; 90, 4; 91, 3, 28; 93, 19; 132(/172) s.i. 2
PN LÚ.GAL URU.MEŠ-*ni* [*ša* P]N š. ^{uru}*kal-ḫi* 15, 12
PN [š.] ^{uru}*na-ṣi-bi-na* 24, 32
PN š. ^{uru}*par*-ḪA-*na* 22, 30
PN š. $^{kur/uru}$*ra-ṣa-pa* 107, 8; 249, 12
PN š. ^{uru}RI-*mu-si* 81, 12
PN š. ^{uru}*šib-ḫi-ni-iš* 15, 51; 16 r. 7′
IM LÚ.GAR KUR (author) 188, 1; 189, 1
šaknu B (an official)
in clauses: *lū* ^{lú}*šak-nu* 15, 20; 17, 14
lū LÚ.GAR-*nu* 31, 17; 60 b.2′
lū LÚ.GAR-*an-šú* 27, 15; cf. 32, 14′(?)
^{lú}*ša-nu-ú*
PN š. 97, 5
šāpiru
in clauses: *š*]*a*?*-pi-ru* 31, 18
š]*a-pi-r*[*u*? 60 a+c.5′
^{lú}*še-lap-pa-a-a*
PN š. 2, 21; 22, 31
^{lú}*turtānu*
PN ^{lú}*tu*[*r-t*]*a-*[*nu*] 105, 9
ina pān ^{lú}*tur-ta-ni* 194, 11, 19
.... ^{lú}*tar-ta-a-ni* 199, 7
URU.ŠE ^{lú}*tur-ta-ni* 4, 19
PN LÚ.GAL 50 *ša* ^{lú}*t*[*ur-ta-ni*(?)] 112, 4
PN *ša* É ^{lú}*tur-ta-ni* 36, 9′; 102 r. 2; 110, 6 (*tar-*)
PN GAL MÍ.MAŠ.MEŠ *ša* É ^{lú}*tur-ta-ni* 15, 40

PN *ša* UGU É *ša* É [lú]*tur-ta-ni* 91, 30; 36, 12′ (*tar-*)
PN LÚ.UŠ.BAR *ša* É [lú]*tur-ta-ni* 91, 35(–6)
[lú][*um*]-*ma-ni*
181, 2
[lú]*ú-ra-se* (pl.)
193, 4, 14?, 18
[lú]*za-ma-ru*
PN Z. *ša* LÚ.EN.NAM 98, 11
[lú][*x*]-*pur*?
3, 25

LÚ.A.BA (= *ummānu*(?) cf. LÚ.DUB.SAR)
PN A. *ṣābit* IM 6, 25; 25, 26
PN A. *ṣābit kanīki* 26, 29
PN A. 2-*i*(?) *ṣābit kanīki* 23, 29
PN A. *ṣābit ṭuppi* [11 r. 14′]; 63 r. 8′; 78, 10′; 95, 18
PN A. (prob. writer of tablet) 5, 17; 68, 8′(?); 81, 13; 83, 6′; 93, 15; 219 r. 10′; 247, 18′(?)
PN A. 17, 39, 47; 25, 21; 47, 8; 51, 12; 78, 7′, 9′; 91, 29(?)
PN A.BA? URU? 14, 26
PN A. *ša* LÚ.GAL.SAG 17, 38
PN A. LÚ.NIMGIR [É.GAL(?)] 31, 8
ina É A. É.GAL 95, 3
PN LÚ.GAL URU.MEŠ-*ni* [*ša*] A. É.GAL 95, 23
PN LÚ.A.BA É.DINGIR *ša* [uru]ŠÀ.URU 248, 5′
PN A. *ki-si-ti* 248, 21′
scribes not so designated, but writers of tablet:
PN *ṣābit* IM 15, 50; 22, 28; 29, 24; 103, 10
PN LÚ.⟨A.BA⟩*ṣābit* IM 24, 29
PN *ṣābit ṭup-pi* 17, 49; 18, 26; 19, 26; 51, 13; 53, 13′
PN *ṣāb*[*it* . . .] 43, 25
ṣābit ka-ni-ki PN 100, 11
[L]Ú.A.KIN (= *mār šipri*; cf. LÚ.DUMU *šipri*)
ūmu [*ša*] A.-*šú tammarūni* 203, 11′
LÚ.A.ZU (= *asû*)
PN A. 51, 7; 68, 7′
PN A. *ša* LÚ.GAL.SAG 17, 37
LÚ.AGRIG
PN ÌR *ša* A. 81, 5
PN LÚ.ÌR *ša* A. GAL 4, 2
. . . *ša* ŠU[II] A. 114, 2
LÚ.ASGAB
PN A. 78, 6′; 155 i.12; 223, 4
LÚ.[B]UR.G[U]L
PN B. 118, 2
LÚ.DAM.GÀR
PN D. 53, 8′; 73 r. 6; 79, 1′; 93, 9; 96, 9–10
x ANŠE.KUR *ša* D. 126, 4
ina ŠÀ 1 MA.NA *ša* D. 248, 8′
LÚ.DUB.SAR (cf. LÚ.A.BA)
PN D. É.GAL 248, 10′
LÚ.DUMU GEMÉ É.GAL
PN D. 105, 2
LÚ.DUMU *šip-ri* (cf. LÚ.A.KIN)
193, 22
PN LÚ.DUMU *ši-pir ša* GAL.LÚ.SAG.MEŠ 15, 46
EN *il-ki*
in clauses: *lū* E.-*šú*(-*nu*) 31, 17; 32, 13′; 45, 16; 48, 12′(?); 57 r. 3
[*l*]*ū* LÚ.ERÍN.MEŠ EN[.MEŠ] *il-ki-šú-nu* 15, 19
[*lū* ER]ÍN?.MEŠ EN *i*[*l-ki-šú-*]*nu*? 55 r. 5
lū LÚ.MEŠ-*e* E.-*šú* 33, 14
lū LÚ.SAG E.-*šú* 17, 13
LÚ.EN.NAM (*bēl pāḫiti*; cf. *šaknu* A)
PN E. 196, 18
IM E. (author) 190, 1
letters *ana* E. 191–200; 230, 1; cf. also 194, 3, 6; 195, 3
PAP 5 *ša* E. 114, 16
LÚ . . . . *ša* E. 186, 19
PN [. . .] *ša* E.[24, 22
[PN . . .] *ša* E. 18, 3; 84, 1′, 6′
PN LÚ.GAL *kal-la-pi ša* E. 98, 9
PN [lú]*za-ma-ru ša* E. 98, 11
[P]N [LÚ.]SAG *ša* E. 14, 20
E. *ša* [uru]*ar-zu-ḫi-na* 127, 6; 196, 4
E. *ša* [uru]*ḫal-ṣu* 128, 3
E. *ša* [uru]*kal-ḫi* 196, 9
PN E. *ša* [uru]*kal-ḫa/i* 108, 7; 203, 6′
PN *ša* LÚ.SAG *ša* PN E. *ša* [uru]*kal-ḫi* 99, 3
PN *mutīr-ṭēmi ša* E. *ša* [uru]*kal-ḫi* 18, 20
LÚ UGU É *ša* E. *ša* [uru]*kal-ḫi* 3, 4
E. *ša* [uru]RI-*mu-si*? 111, 4
E. *ša* [uru]*ta-ma*?-*nu-n*[*i*?] 128, 8
in clauses: *ana* E. *iddan*(?) 57 r. 8
ana E. URU-*šu iddan* 6, 16; 14, 15; 23, 21; 36, 3′; 55 r. 12; 62, 5
lū E. 17, 15; 60 a+c.4′(?)
lū E. URU-*šú* 26, 16; 27, 16
EN ŠU[II][.MEŠ(?)]
76, 4′
EN . . . .
PN EN *x x me ša* GN 18, 23
PN L[Ú].EN? [. . .] 62, 10
LÚ.EN[. . .] 65, 1′
ša LÚ.EN[. . .] 187 B.4′
LÚ.ENGAR
[LÚ.E]NGAR.MEŠ [*a*]*seme* 196, 16
2 LÚ.EN[GAR(.MEŠ)] 222 B.2′
(LÚ.)ERÍN.MEŠ (= *ṣābu*; cf. PN Ṣābu-da(m)qu)
E. [GN]-*a-a* 120, 30
sold: 9, 2; 12, 6′
PAP 11 E. EN *ḫa-bu-li* 93, 8
PAP 5 ERÍN.[MEŠ? . . .] 76, 3′

in clauses: *lū* E. *annūte* 15, 17; 32, 11′
lū E. EN(.MEŠ) *il-ki-šú-nu* 15, 19; 55 r. 5–6
lū LÚ.MEŠ ERÍN (for EN ?).MEŠ[20, 14
"troops":
196, 25 (E.-*šú*); 203, 1′(?); 206, 3′, 6′, 16′
100 E. *ša* ŠU PN 193, 7
atta EN E.-*ka* 190, 4
"king's troops":
ERÍN.MEŠ.MAN-*ni* 185, 5
30 LÚ *ku-tal* ERÍN.MAN 141, 10
GAL see also [lú]*da-a-a-lu*; [lú]*kal-la-bu*; KA.ŠÈR; LÚ.KAŠ.LUL; LÚ/MÍ.MAŠ; LÚ.MU; LÚ.SUM.NINDA
LÚ.GAL É
PN G. 14, 4; 23, 9; 51, 3
PN G. *ša* LÚ.GAL.SAG 17, 36
LÚ *ana* G. [*it*]*tannu* 67, 5′
LÚ.GAL É.GAL
PN G. 74, 4′; 95, 12
PN G. *ša* É.GAL BE-*ti* 68, 10′
PN G. *ša* É.GAL GIBIL 68, 12′
PN [. . . *ša*?] G. 92, 12
GA]L? É.GAL 223, 6
GAL KUŠ.MEŠ
PN G. *ša* Kurbail 15, 37
PN LÚ.G. 35, 22
LÚ.GAL *mu-gi*
IM G. (author) 192, 2
GAL *ši-ma-ni*
PN G. 4, 15
GAL *ú-ra-a-*[*te*?]
PN G. 71, 8′
GAL URU.MEŠ
PN G. 101, 4; 125, 8(?)
PN LÚ.G. 7, 7(?); 28, 6
PN LÚ.G.-*ni* 35, 9; 127, 4(?)
PN LÚ.G.-*ni* [*ša* P]N gov. of Kalhu 15, 11
PN LÚ.G.-*ni* [*ša*] LÚ.A.BA É.GAL 95, 22
PN ÌR *ša* PN [L]Ú.G.-*ni* 22, 3
PN LÚ.G.-*ni-šú-nu* 128, 11
PN [*š*]*a*? *ma-ḫa-za-a-ni* 129, 3
[uru]*kap-ri ša* GAL URU(?) 135, 5
in clauses: *lū* LÚ.G. 17, 14
LÚ.G.-*ni-ma lā āmur* 209, 11′
LÚ.GAL 50
PN G. *ša* [lú]*t*[*ur-ta-ni*(?)] 112, 4
(LÚ.)GAL [. . .]
PN G. 71, 10′; 86, 4′(?); 187 B.2 (?)
PN LÚ.GAL *x* [(*x*)] *ša* MAN 22, 27
LÚ.GALA
PN G. 35, 6
LÚ.GAR see *šaknu* A and B and LÚ.NINDA
GEMÉ
PN — G.-*šú* 113, 7
PN LÚ.DUMU G. É.GAL 105, 2
LÚ.GÍR.LÁ
PN G. 53, 14′
GÚ.GAL
[PN] G. [( )] 73 r. 5
LÚ.ḪAL
PN Ḫ. LUGAL 17, 39
LÚ.IÀ.SUR
I.MEŠ *annūte* 197, 3
(LÚ.)IGI
PAP 8 IGI.MEŠ 3, 30
PAP 9 LÚ.IGI.MEŠ-*ti* [uru]*kur-ba-ìl-a-a* 15, 42
(LÚ.)ÌR
PN (LÚ.)ÌR (*ša* . . .) 4, 4; 10, 10′; 15, 43, 44, 49; 24, 27; 81, 5′; 84, 1′(?); 90, 9; 92, 2; 93, 6, 15; 98, 2; 101 r. 9′; 110, 4; 114, 8(?); 117, 7
PN (LÚ.)ÌR sold: 2, 4; 3, 3; 4, 2; 6, 3; 8, 3
ÌR-*ka* PN (introd. to letters): 180, 2; 193, 2; 194, 2; 195, 2; 196, 3; 197, 2; [198, 2]; 199, 2; [200, 2]; 205, 2; 230, 2; 240, 2; 241, 2; [242, 2]
PN LÚ.ÌR É.GAL 155 i.4
ÌR.ME *ša* [f]P[N] 90, 33
LÚ.ÌR.MEŠ-*ni ša* LÚ.EN.NAM . . . 194, 5
ÌR.ME-*ma*?[205, 12′
LÚ.ÌR.MEŠ-*ka* 188, 4
i]*na libbi* LÚ.Ì[R? . . . 222 L.E. 2
KA.ŠÈR (also LÚ.TÚG.(KA.)ŠÈR)
[P]N K. ÌR *ša* PN 6, 3
PN LÚ.K. *ša ša* IGI É.GAL 4, 13, 14
[P]N LÚ.TÚG.ŠÈ[R] 155 i.11
PN LÚ.TÚG.K[A.ŠÈ]R 6, 2
PN LÚ.GAL K. 51, 9
PN LÚ.GAL K. *ša* [lú]*rak-su-te* 18, 24
LÚ.KAŠ.LUL (= *šāq*(*i*)*u*)
PN K. *ša* PN 102 r. 4
PN K. *ša* MÍ.É.GAL 44, 5
PN LÚ.NU(= KAŠ?).LUL MAN 17, 47
PN LÚ.GAL KAŠ.LUL 95, 21
[P]N *ša* GN LÚ.GAL KAŠ.LUL 98, 13
LUGAL (cf. MAN)
letters from L.: 181–5; [186–7]
letters to L.: 180, 1, [2], r. 3′, 9′; 240, 1, 3, 4, 5; 241, 1, 3, 6; 242, 1, 3, 4, r. 5′
u(*n*)*qu* L. 199, 4
[*šumm*]*u* L.(!) *andurāru* [*iša*]*kkan*? 10, 8
PN L. KUR *aš-šur*([ki]) 17, [8]; 18, 29; 26, 28; 28 r. 3′
PN LÚ.ḪAL L. 17, 39
PN LÚ.SAG *ša* PN [L.] 17, [8]
ŠE.PAD.MEŠ-LUGAL-*e-šú* 99, 4
MA.NA *ša* L. 31, 7′; 107, 1
ritual: *ina p*[*ān*] L. 215 r. 9′
lit.: DN L. . . . 214, 3–5

MAN (cf. LUGAL)
PN M. KUR *aš-šur*(ki) 27, 30; 32, 7′; 54, 6
PN LÚ.NU(= KAŠ?).LUL M. 17, 47
PN LÚ.GAL *x* [(*x*)] *ša* M. 22, 27
PN [*š*]*a qurbūti ša* PN M. 32, 7′
(MA.NA) *ša* M. 30, 6; 106, 1
hist.: M. *kàl malkē* 217, 4′
(LÚ/MÍ.)MAŠ
PN GAL MÍ.MAŠ.MEŠ *ša* É lú*tur-ta-ni* 15, 40
in clauses: 7 LÚ.MAŠ.MEŠ 7 MÍ.MAŠ.MEŠ 15, 25; 17, 30
MÍ É.GAL
PN LÚ.KAŠ.LUL *ša* M. 44, 5
LÚ.MU
PN M. 11 r. 10′; 16 r. 4′(?); 51, 6; 222 A.5′
[PN] M. *ša* GAL.SAG 21 T.E. 3′
PN M.? *ša* É lú*tur-ta-ni* 92, 8
1 M. 199, 8
M.-*šú* 90, 24
ša M.MEŠ 207, 13′
PN [GA]L M. 81, 3
LÚ.NAGAR
PN N. 43, 19
PN N. giš*mu-gir-ri* 91, 37
cf. 155 iii.19
LÚ.NAR
PN N. 35, 2, 3, 4, 5
ina ku-da-a-ri [*ša* N.] 35, 7
LÚ.NI.DUḪ
PN N. 84, 3′; 94, 7
PN N. *ša* É.GAL 248, 22′
LÚ.NIMGIR
205, 11(?)
PN N. 155 i.10
PN N. *ša* PN (king) 18, 29
PN [N.] É.[GAL] 53, 16′
PN N.? É.GAL 63 r. 6′
PN LÚ.A.BA N. [. . .] 31, 8
NIN É (?)
223, 2
LÚ.NINDA (cf. *šaknu* A and B)
PN N. 4, 17; 97, 6; 102 r. 5, 6
[PN?] N. *ša* LÚ.[. . .] 75, 8′
1 N. 199, 9
LÚ.SAG (= *ša rēši*)
PN S. 7 L.E. 3′; 33, 15; 51, 8; 47, 8′(?) (+LÚ.A.BA)
PN S. *ša* PN (king) 17, 7
PN [*š*]*á* SAG *šá* PN (king) 65(/170/171) s.i. 2
PN S. *ša* PN (gov.) 33, 6; 34, 6; 99 tab. 2
PN *ša* S. *ša* PN (gov.) 99 env. 2
PN [LÚ.]SAG *ša* LÚ.EN.NAM 14, 20
PN S. *ša* L[Ú.GAL.SAG(?)] 17, 2
PN S. [*ša* (LÚ.)G]AL? É.GAL 223, 6
PN S. *ša* [N]IN?.É 223, 2
S.MEŠ-*ka* 203, 4′, 14′
in clauses: *lū* S. EN *il-ki-šú* 17, 13
LÚ.GAL.SAG
PN LÚ.GAL.É *ša* G. 17, 36
PN LÚ.A.ZU *ša* G. 17, 37
PN LÚ.A.BA *ša* G. 17, 38
PN LÚ.3 U_5 *ša* G. 17, 50
PN LÚ.SAG *ša* L[Ú.GAL.SAG(?)] 17, 2
PN LÚ.DUMU *ši-pir ša* GAL.LÚ.SAG.MEŠ 15, 46
LÚ.SANGA
PN S. 35, 21, 24, 25; 114, 1(?)
PN S. *ša* DN 17, 35; 36, 7′; 73, 4; 103, 9, 13
PN S. DN(?) 84, 2′
PN S. *ša* Kurbail 15, 34
LÚ.SIMUG
PN S. GUŠKIN 57 r. 12; 118, 7
PAP 2 S. KÙ.[GI] 114, 4
[PN] S. AN.BAR 84, 4′
cf. 155 iv.6(?)
LÚ.SIPA
PN S. 114, 8; 132, 2
PN S. MUŠEN.MEŠ 25, 22
]S.MEŠ *ša* PN 257, 2
(LÚ/MÍ).SUḪUR.LÁ
in clauses: 7 LÚ.SUḪUR.LÁ.MEŠ 7 MÍ.SUḪUR.LÁ.MEŠ 17, 31
LÚ.SUKKAL
[PN] S.? 97, 9
LÚ.SUM.NINDA (prob. = *karkadinu* q.v.)
PN S. 53, 9′(?)
1 S. 199, 8
LÚ.GAL SUM.NINDA 230, 4
LÚ.ŠÁM/ŠÀM
PN LÚ.ŠÀM 3, 26, 29
PN LÚ.ŠÁM (NINDÁ X A.AN) *ša* ŠU PN 93, 7
3 LÚ.ŠÁM (NINDÁ X AN).MEŠ 103, 1; cf. 161 A.3, B.5′
LÚ.ŠE.KIN.KUD
50 Š. 105, 6
LÚ.ŠIM X NINDA (= BAPPIR)
PN Š. 114, 5
LÚ.TIN.NA
PN T. 4, 16, 20
PN [L]Ú.TIN?[( )] 6, 21
LÚ.TÚG.KA.ŠÈR see KA.ŠÈR
UN.MEŠ
sold: 248, 12′, 13′
in clauses: *lū* U.-*šú* 27, 14
U.-*šú-nu* ("family") 185, 12
šuḫ U. ("people") 184, 6
LÚ.UŠ
PN U. *kib-si* 111, 2
PN U. ANŠE.(NITÁ.)(MEŠ) 17, 5; 90, 5; 138, 5
LÚ.UŠ.BAR
PN U. 91, 34; 97, 2

PN U. *ša* Arbail 91, 32
PN U. *ša* É [lú]*tur-ta-ni* 91, 35, 36
PN U. *bir-me ša* PN (gov.) 91, 2
UTUL
68, 6(?), r. 2′ (U.MEŠ)
ZI.MEŠ
109, 2
LÚ.Z. 121, 15; 155 i.15; 194, 9, 17
PAP 6 ZI *ša* PN 155 viii.6′
sold: 9, 2; 248, 4′
LÚ.3 U_5
PN **3.** 11 r. 4′; 23, 25, 26
PN LÚ.3-*šu* U_5 82, 16, 17
PN **3.** *ša* LÚ.GAL.SAG 17, 50

INDEX OF WORDS

N.B.—This list includes only those new words or meanings discussed in the notes or commentary. A complete index would, of course, be ideal, but did not prove practicable, and in any case would be more valuable if it could include past and future publications of texts from Nimrud.

(an)durāru 10 comm.; 248, 13′–16′
apālu 48, 8′
aruthē 155 iv.17
ašḫulu 155 iii.10
bāb zīqi 212, 5′
bašītu 15, 52
bēt bēlē(-šunu) 186, 10
bēt dālāni 64, 8–9
bēt danniti 155 ii.11–12
bēt qāti 22, 11
bēt šīqi 64, 8–9
bēt tu'inte 241, 4
bitiqtu 181, 18
būru 68, 3′
buṣinnu 141, 7
dallulūtu 150, 4
dannu 93, 17
dukdu 153, 10
durāru see *andurāru*
elītu 153, 5
gazālu 119, 19
gizzu 222 A.2′
gizzutu 145, 2
ḫallup(t)u 153, 7
ḫanānu 266, 50
ḫarṣu 155 i.16
ḫaṣānu 63, 5′
ḫullānu 152, 1
ḫulsu 1, 11′
irginu 125 comm.
kalappu 155 iv.3
kallā'ūtu 219, 7
kammutu 150, 1
kirku 144, 4
kiṣiptu 1, 5′
ku(d)dāru 35, 7
labīru 17, 44
maḫīru 204, 3′
maḫru 123, 13
maklulu 152, 2
mannu(ma'āta) 242, 5
mēṣirānu 1, 14′; 125, 4
mullilu 155 iii.20
(m)uššuru 17, 30
muṭā'ē 152, 5
muzzakru 214, 5
nāruttu 64, 5
nu 193, 12
padakku 135, 1
parūgu 136, 1
pinigu 136, 8
puāšu 36, 9′
pušku 212, 9′
putuḫḫu 65, 6′
qab/pḫu 155 iii.11
qallu 93, 17
qalpu 152, 3; 155 v.14′–16′
qaqquru 29, 2; 156, 2
qarāmu 99, 8–9
qātāya 180 r. 5′
qā(t)ṣibitti 92, 17–18; 119, 20
qimmu 149, 3
rāqu 156, 2
rūṭu 113, 2′; 212, 2′
sanbuku 266, 51
sa'urāte 150, 3
ṣibtāti 155 iv.19–20
ṣibtu 11, 8; 155 iv.19–20
ša GAB 113, 5′
ša ḫilli 1, 6′
ša IŠ 153, 2
ša māḫāzāni 129, 3
ša puškāyi 1, 5′
ša qurbūti 9, 15
ša šarri 31, 3
ša U.U 31, 3

šāḫu 155 iii.13
šāpiru 31, 18
šimānu 4, 15
tabriu 45, 4
talpittu 64, 4
tu-ra-ta 247, 13′
ubru 30, 7
uklu 15, 52
ummānu 181, 2
ummudu 17, 16
'unnubu 266, 52
u(n)qu 199, 4
uppušu 2, 6
urāsu 193, 4
zakû 48, 8
zarāpu 2, 6 ; 22, 11 (*za-pat*)
zittu 67, 3′

BIL.EN.ZU 108, 1
BUL+BUL 204, 8′–9′
DIR 14, 13 ; 24, 5 ; 155 v.10′–11′
DUMU UD 155 i.14–15
GAB.GUR 155 iv.16
GIŠ.É.ÚR 155 ii.7
GIŠ.GU 155 ii.9
GIŠ.ŠE 155 i.16
GÚ.GAL 73, 5
GÚ(.UN) 93, 17
GÙN 125, 1 ; 153, 4
ḪAR(.MEŠ) 126, 3
ḪÉ.MED 1, 6′
IM.DIR 24, 5
KAB 42 r. 14
LÁ(-*e*) 152, 5
NAGAR 155 iii.19
SA_5 see DIR
SIG 4, 16
SIP.PUR 3, 25
(LÚ/MÍ).SUḪUR.LÁ 15, 25
SUḪUŠ 30, 7
ŠE.PAD.MEŠ LUGAL(-*e-šu*) 99, 4
ŠE.AL 180 r. 9′
TÚG.AN.TA 153, 5
TÚG.GÚ.LÁ 152, 1
TÚG.IB 153, 4
TÚG.KI.TA 153, 7
TÚG.PA 1, 12′
TÚG.SI.LUḪ 1, 4′
Ú(.ME) 19, 5 ; 181, 19
ÚŠ.MEŠ 95, 16
UTUL 68 comm.
ZA.ḪUM 155 iii.13
ZAG 155 v.10′–11′
(LÚ.)ZI 121, 15
ZÍD.KASKAL.MEŠ 185, 9 ; 203, 3′

2.TA 108, 10

5

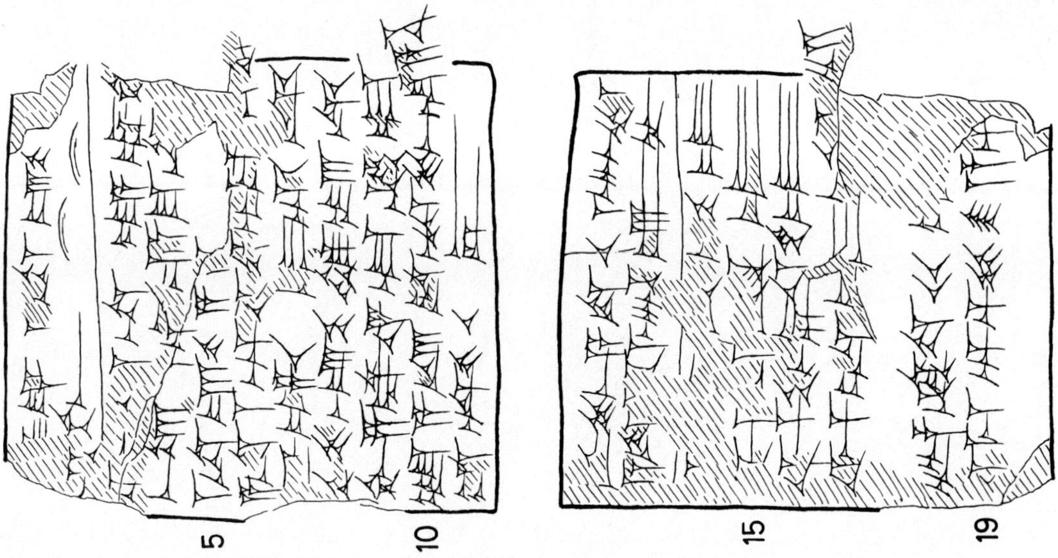

1

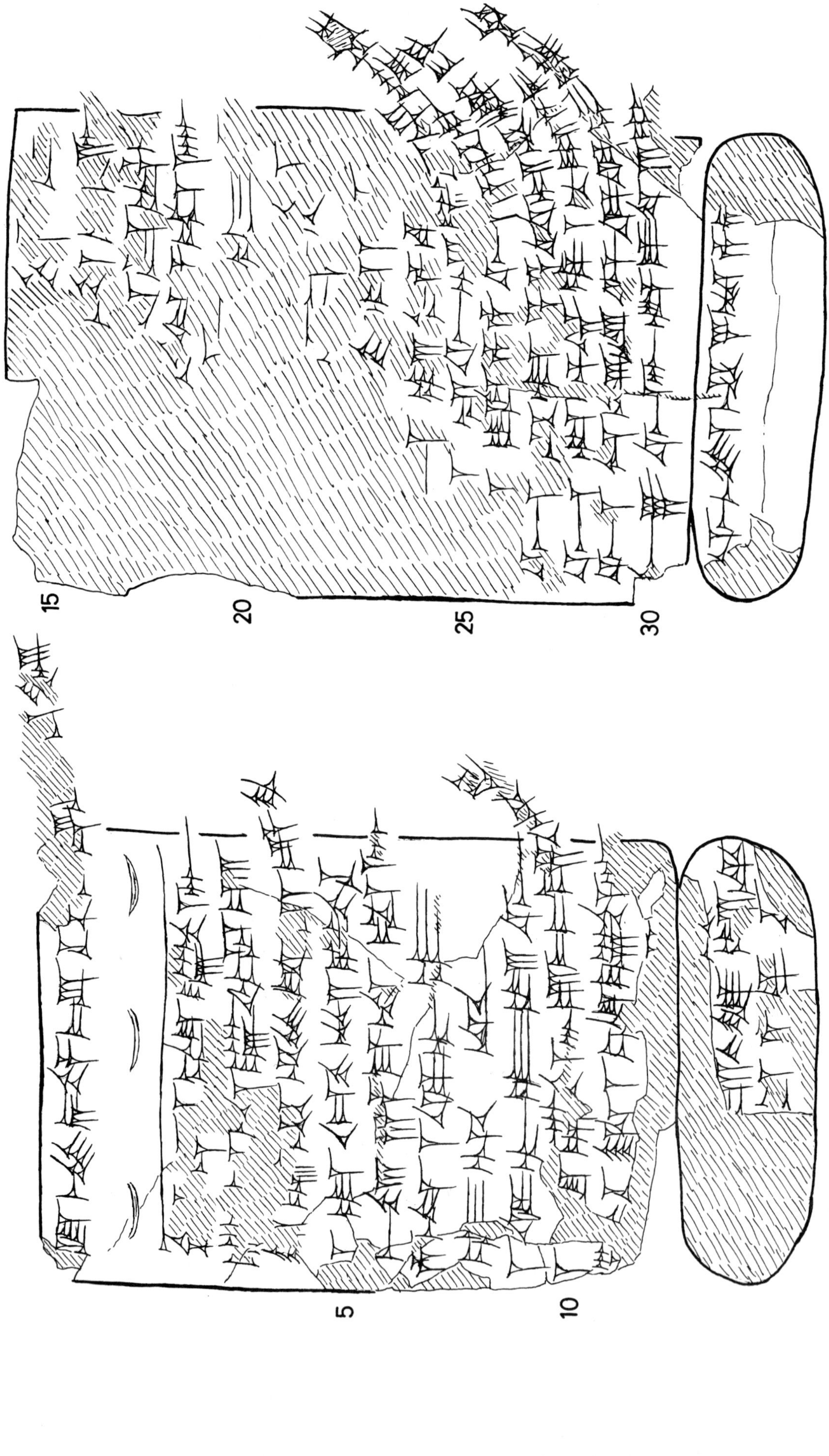
3

2

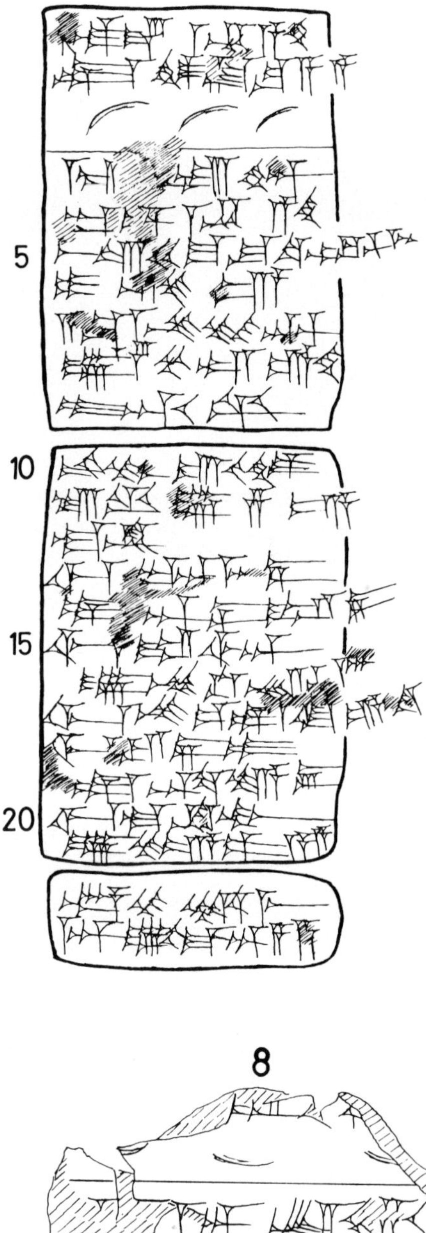

4

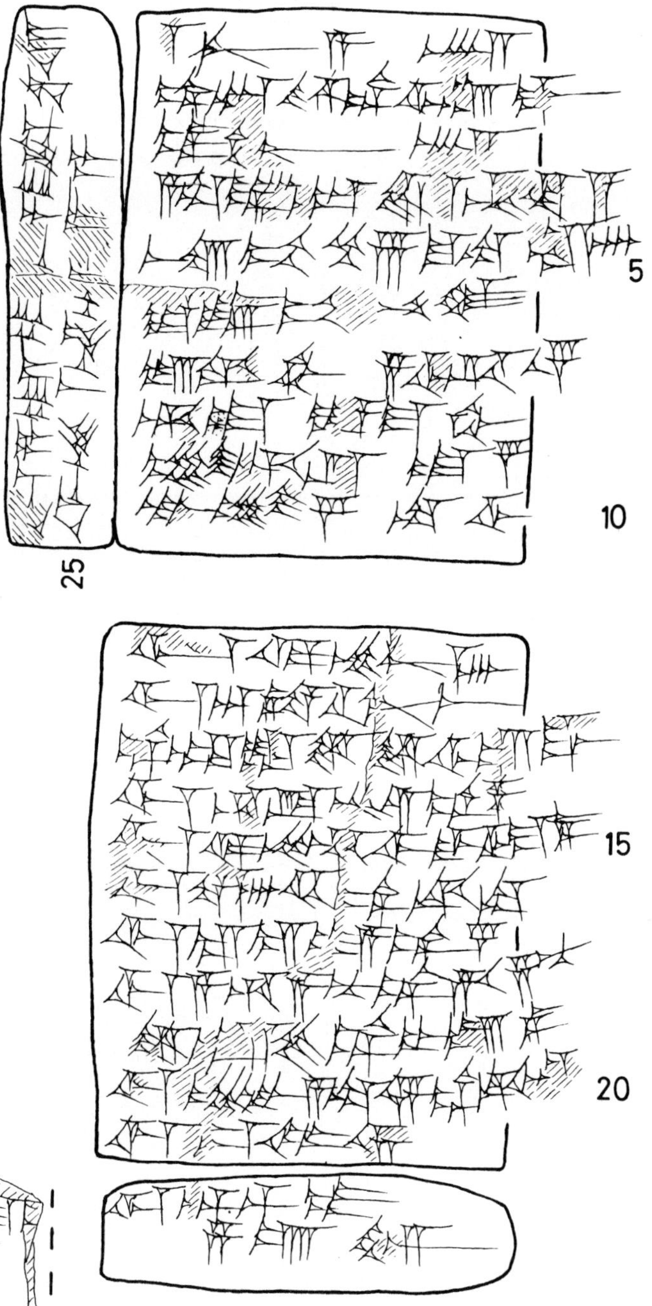

8

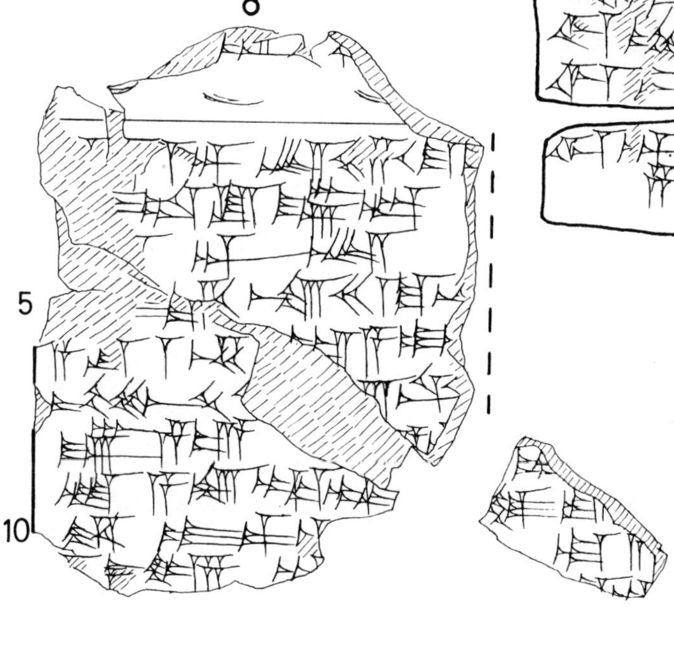

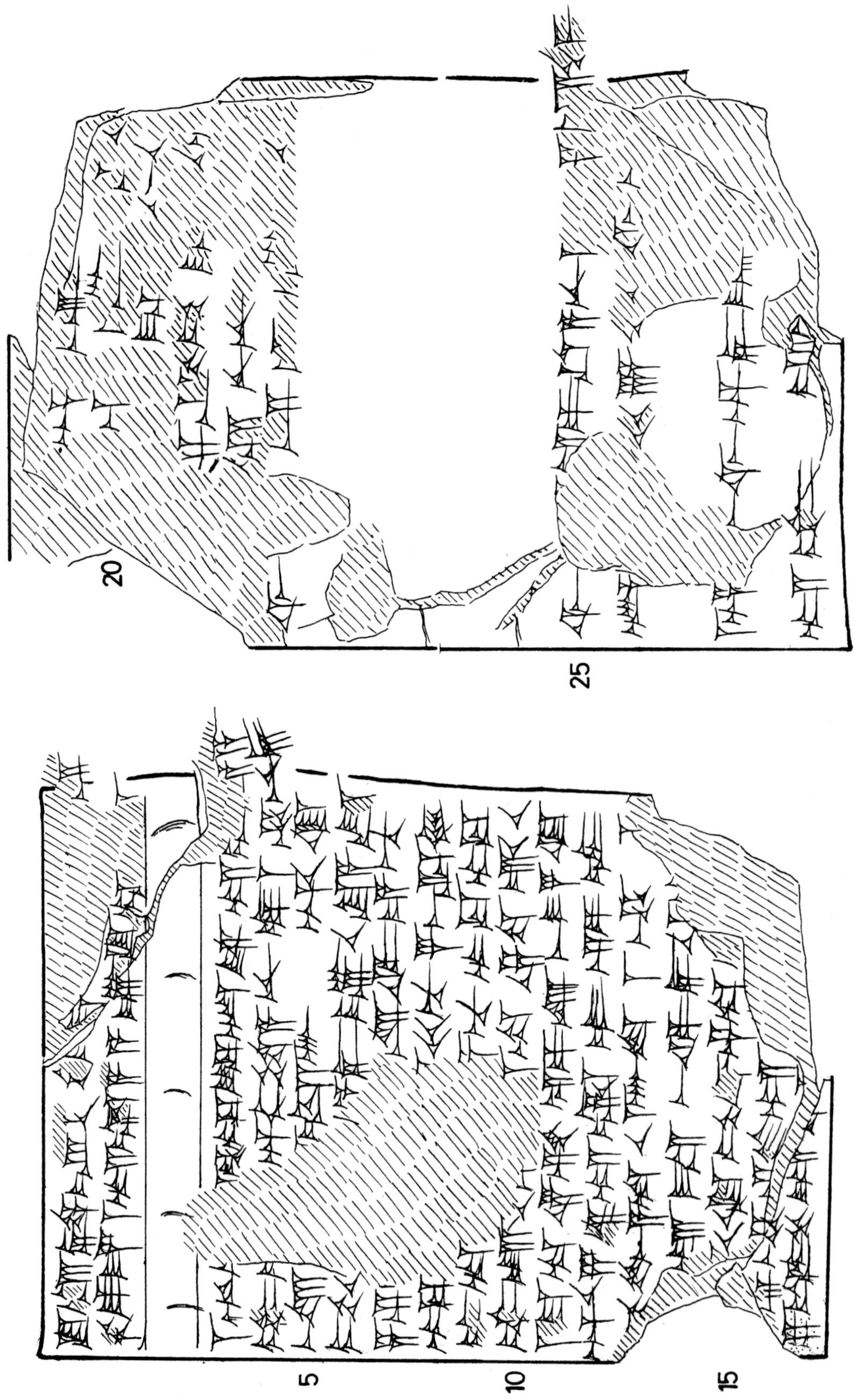

6

7

10

11

obv

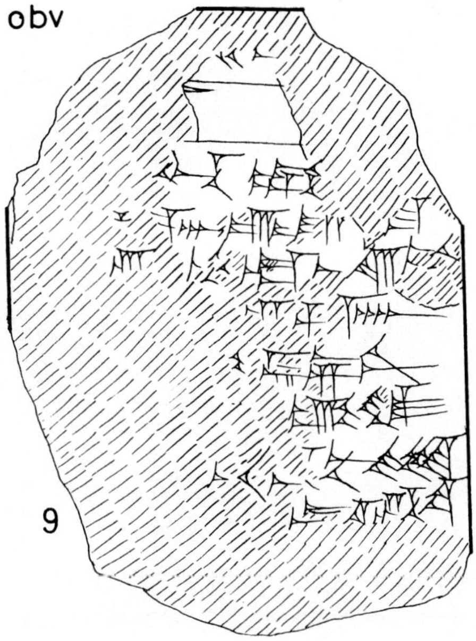

11 rev

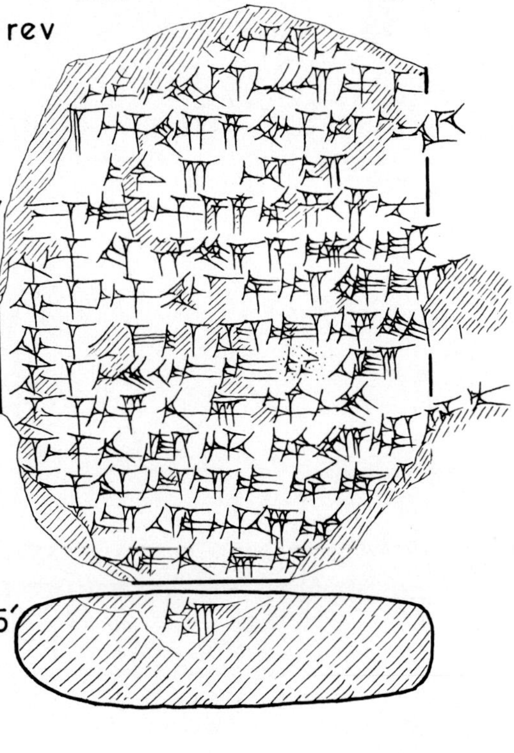

9

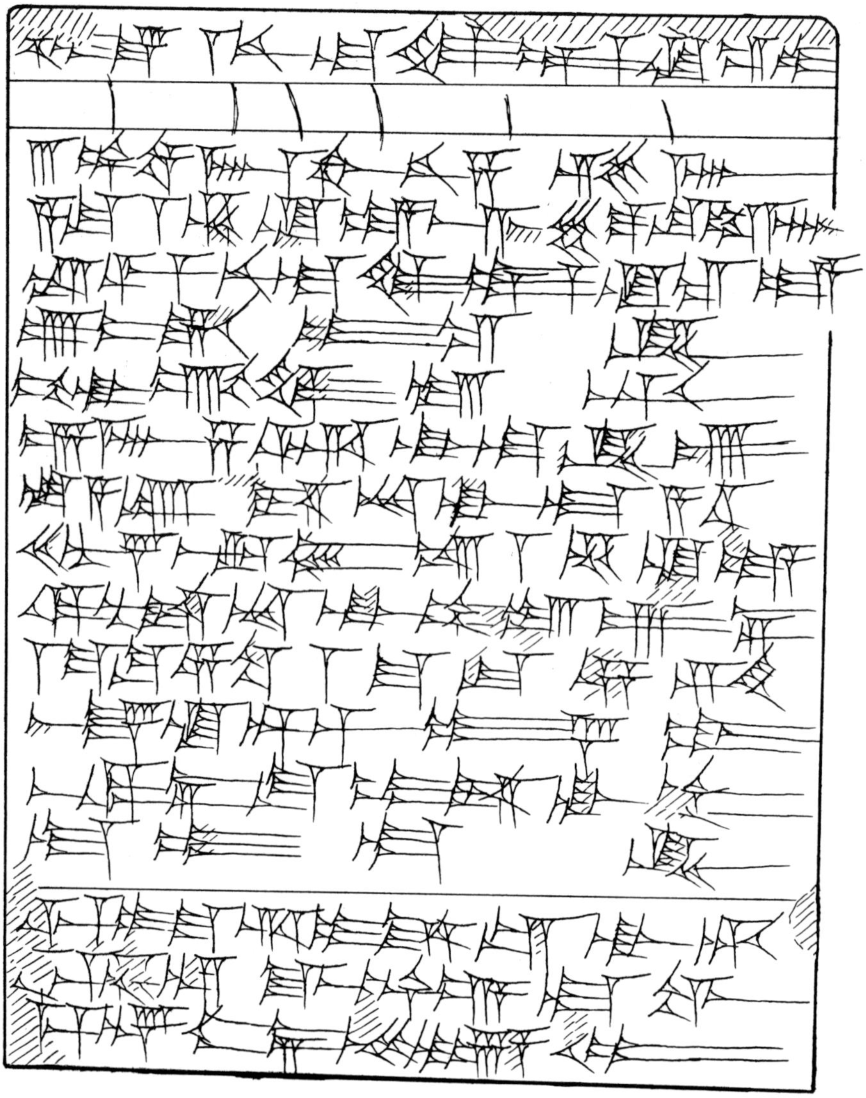

13

10

12

rev

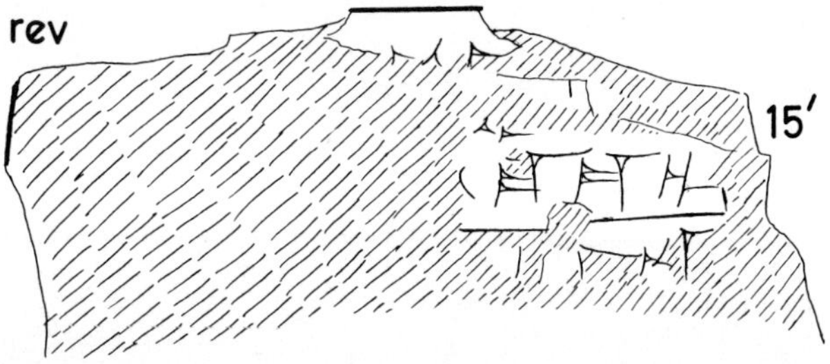

obv

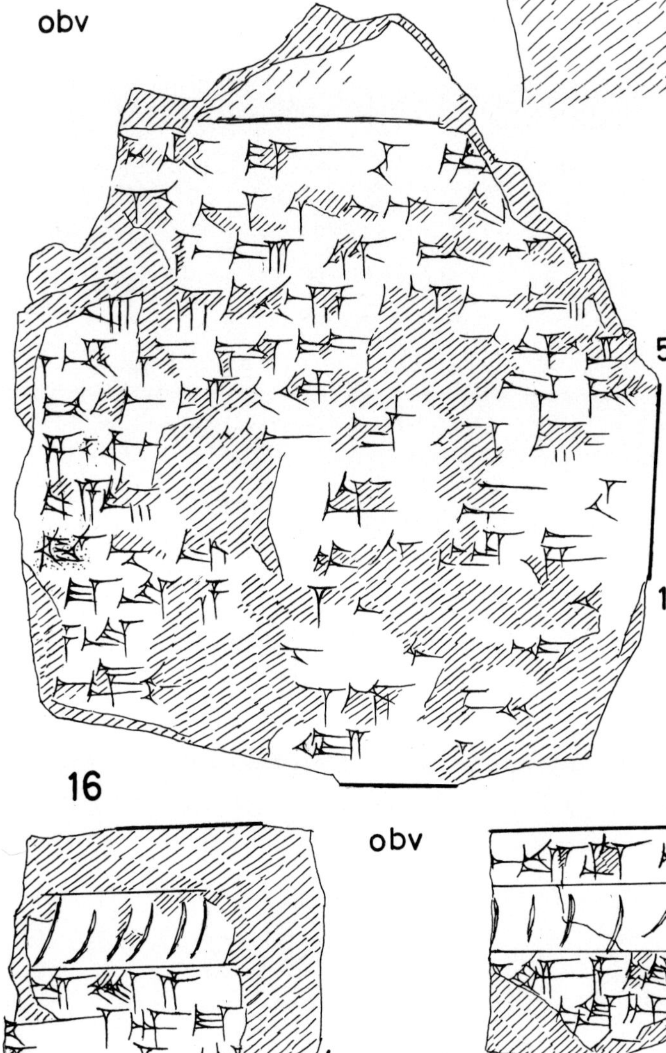

16

obv

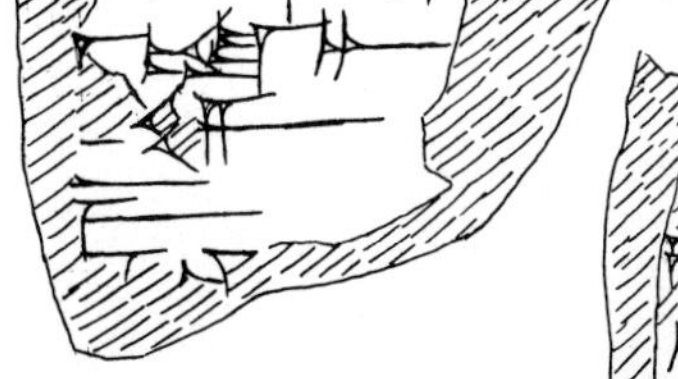

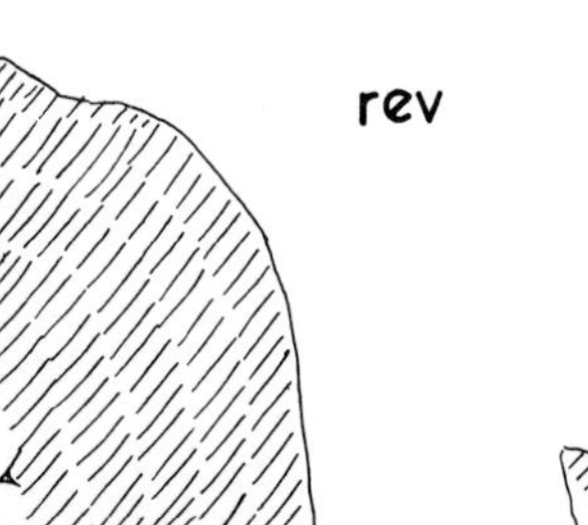

ND 275(m)

rev

ND 247

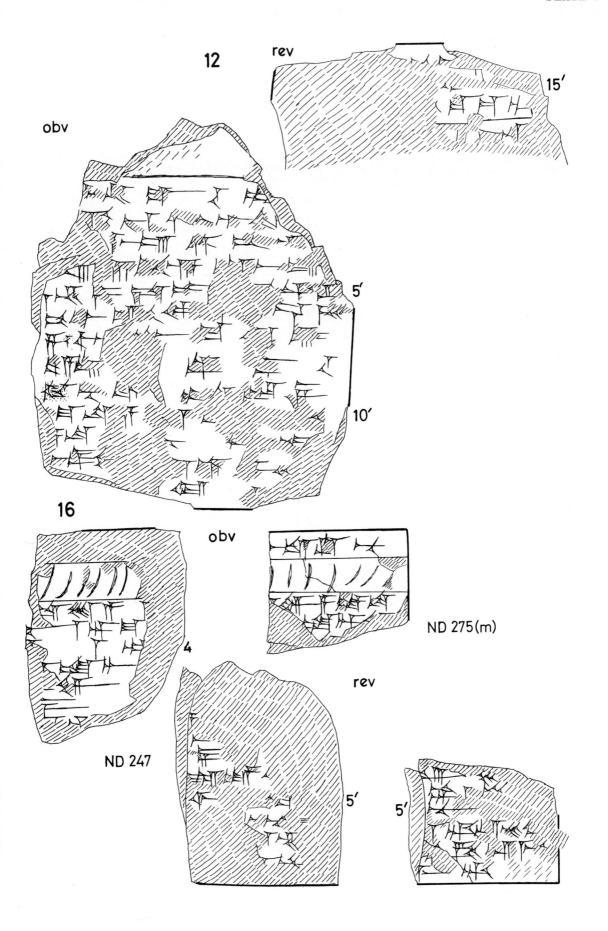

14

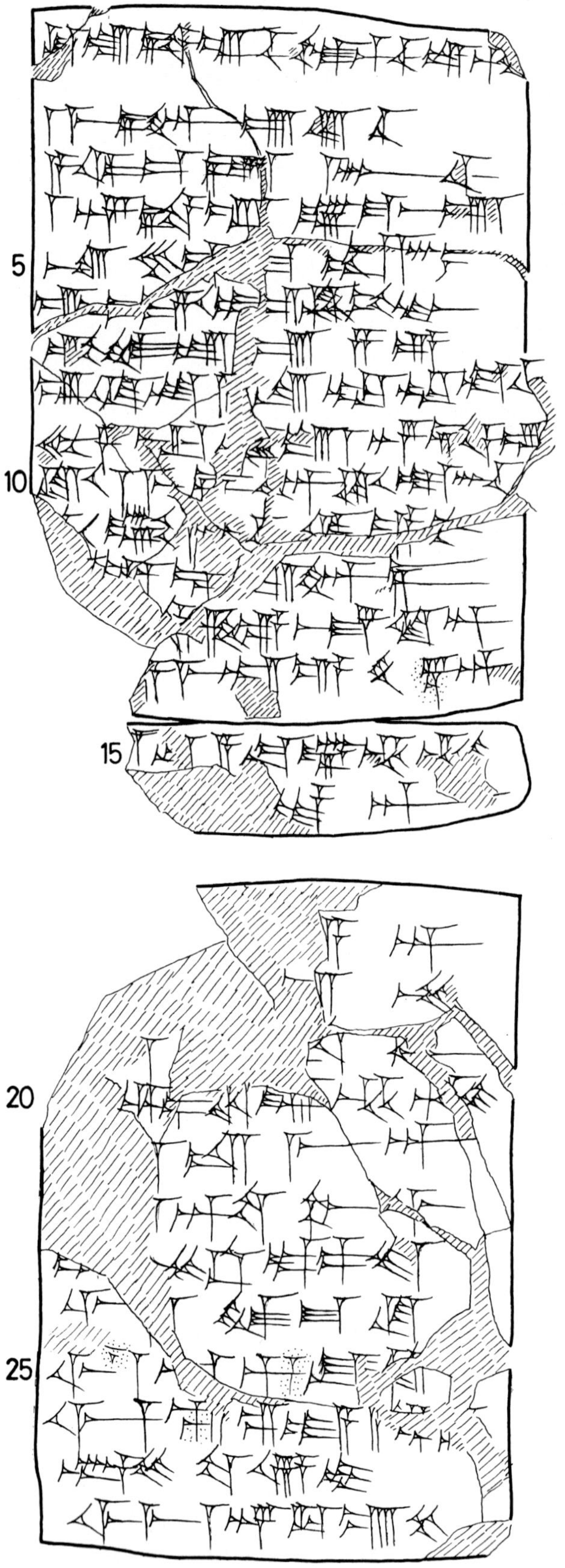

19

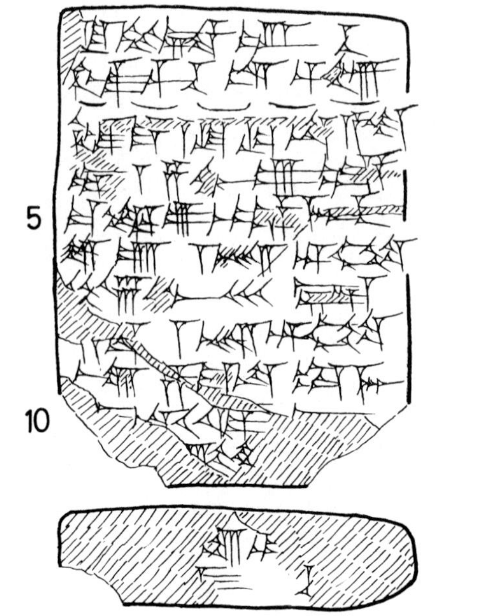

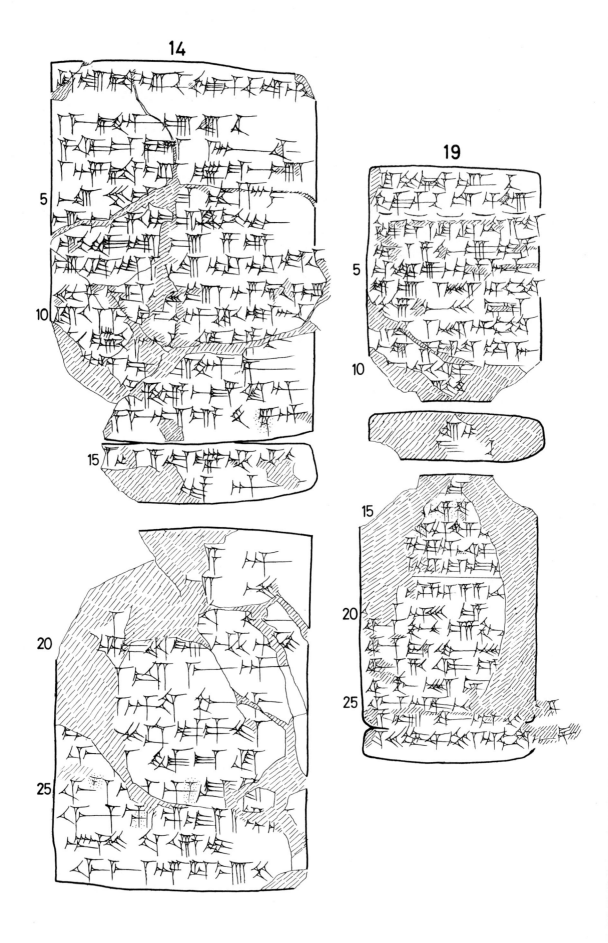

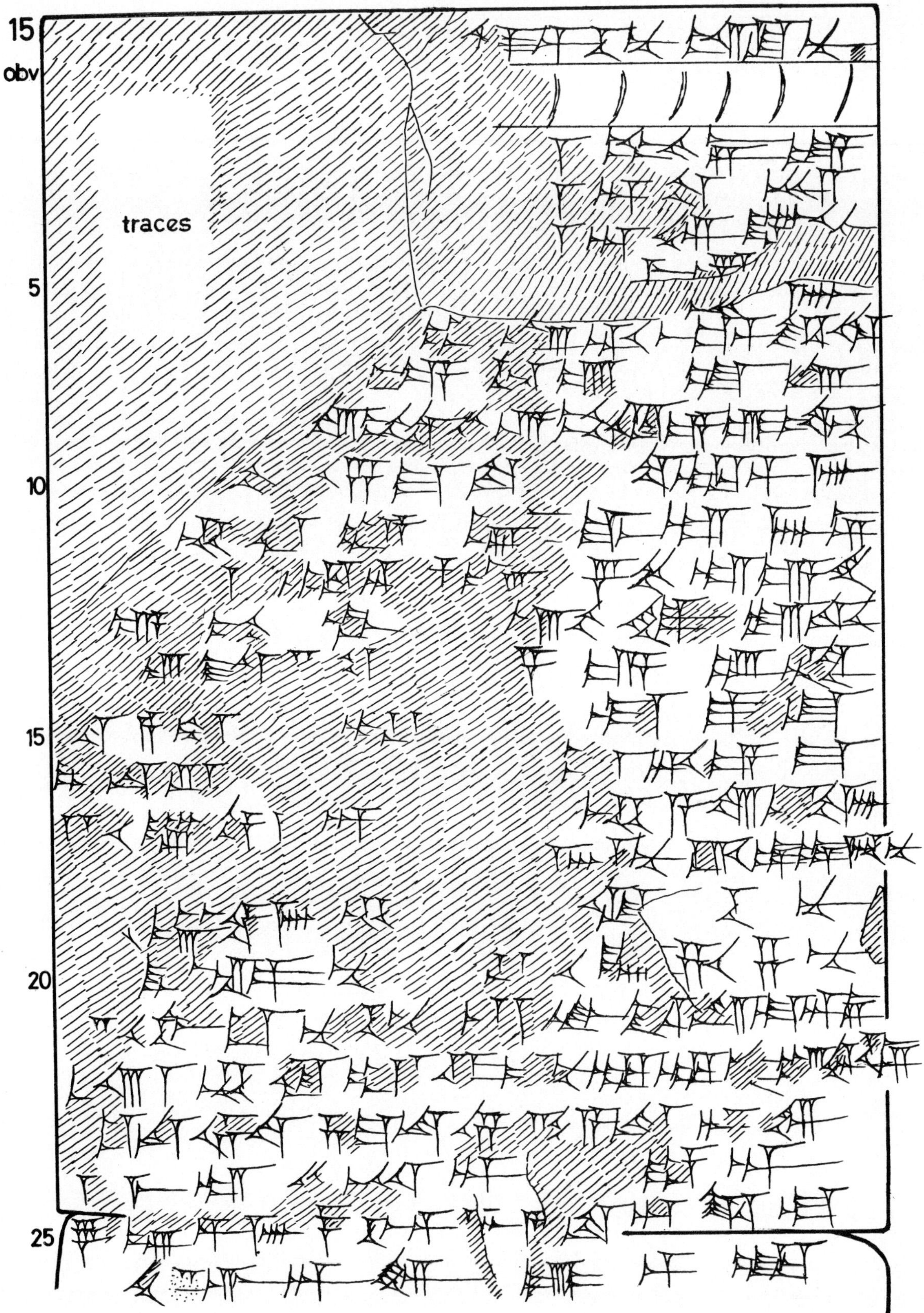
15
obv
traces

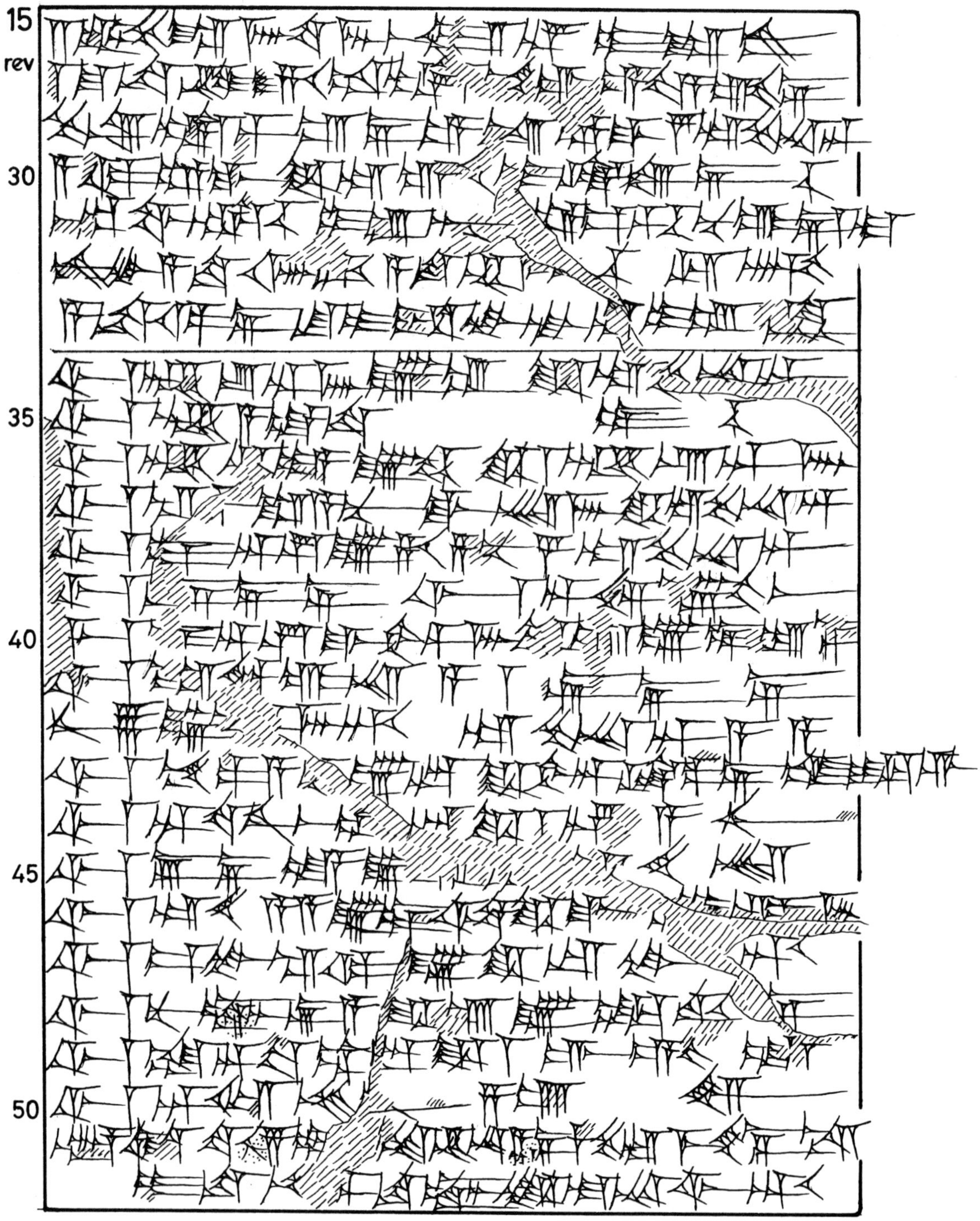
rev

17

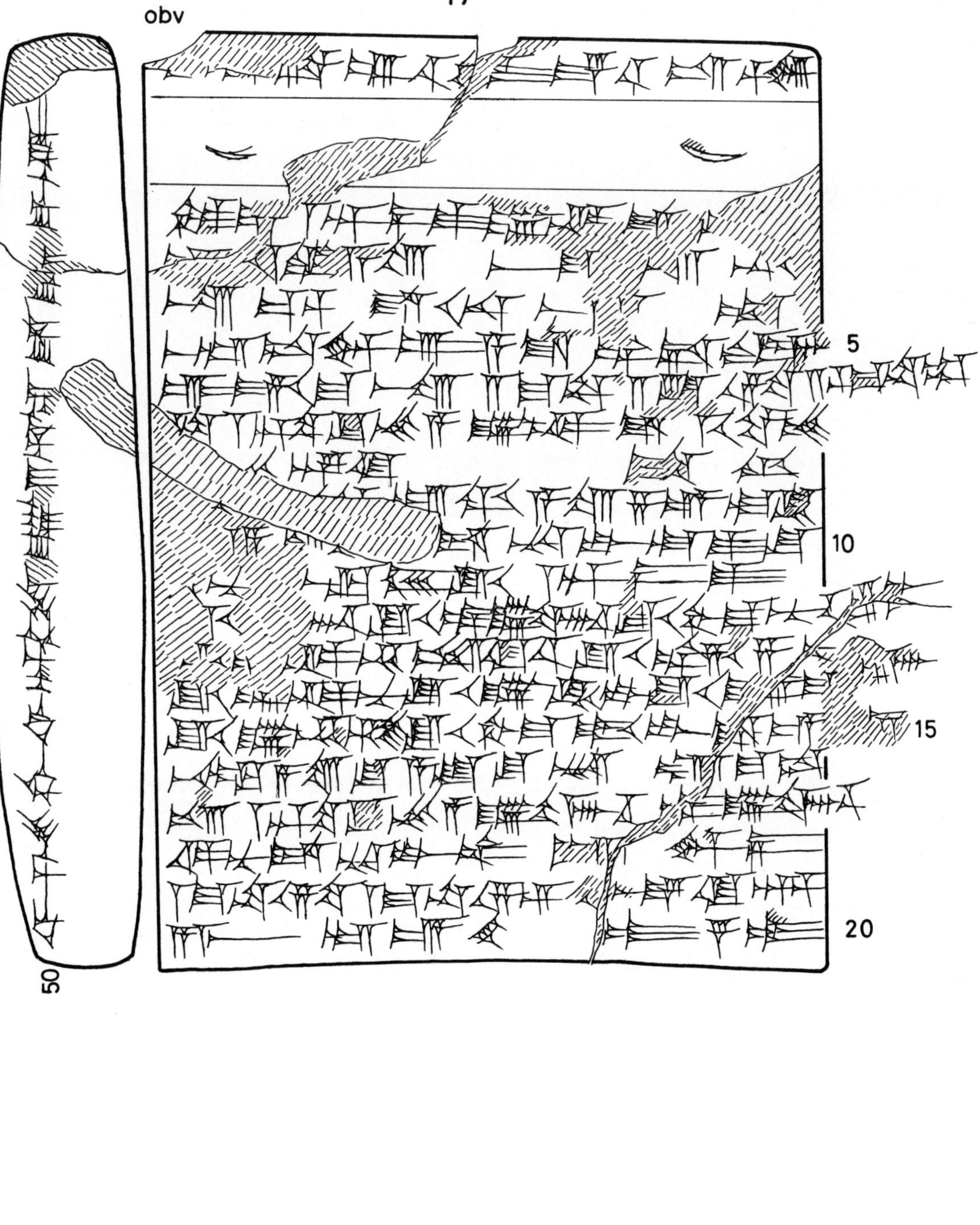

17

rev

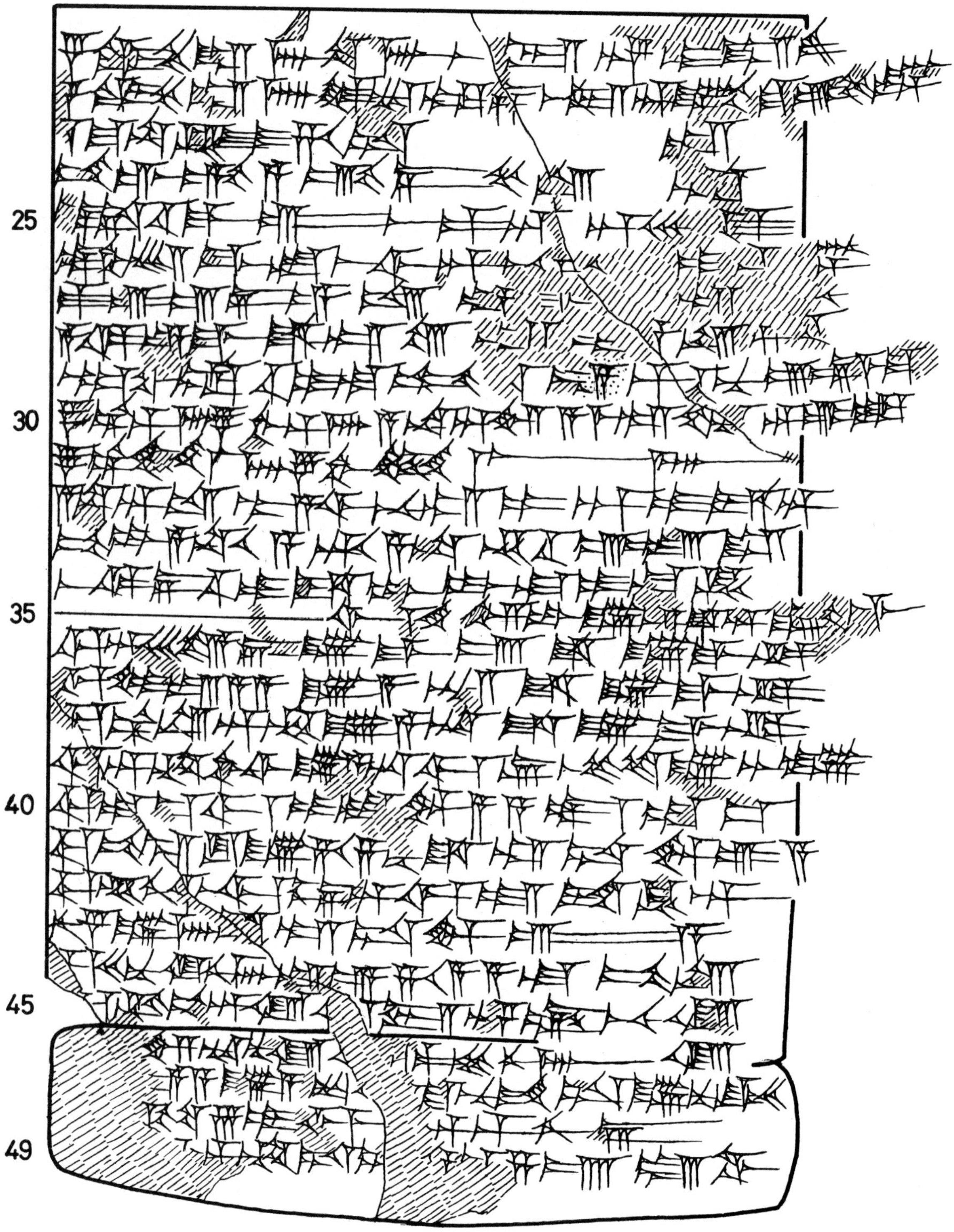

18

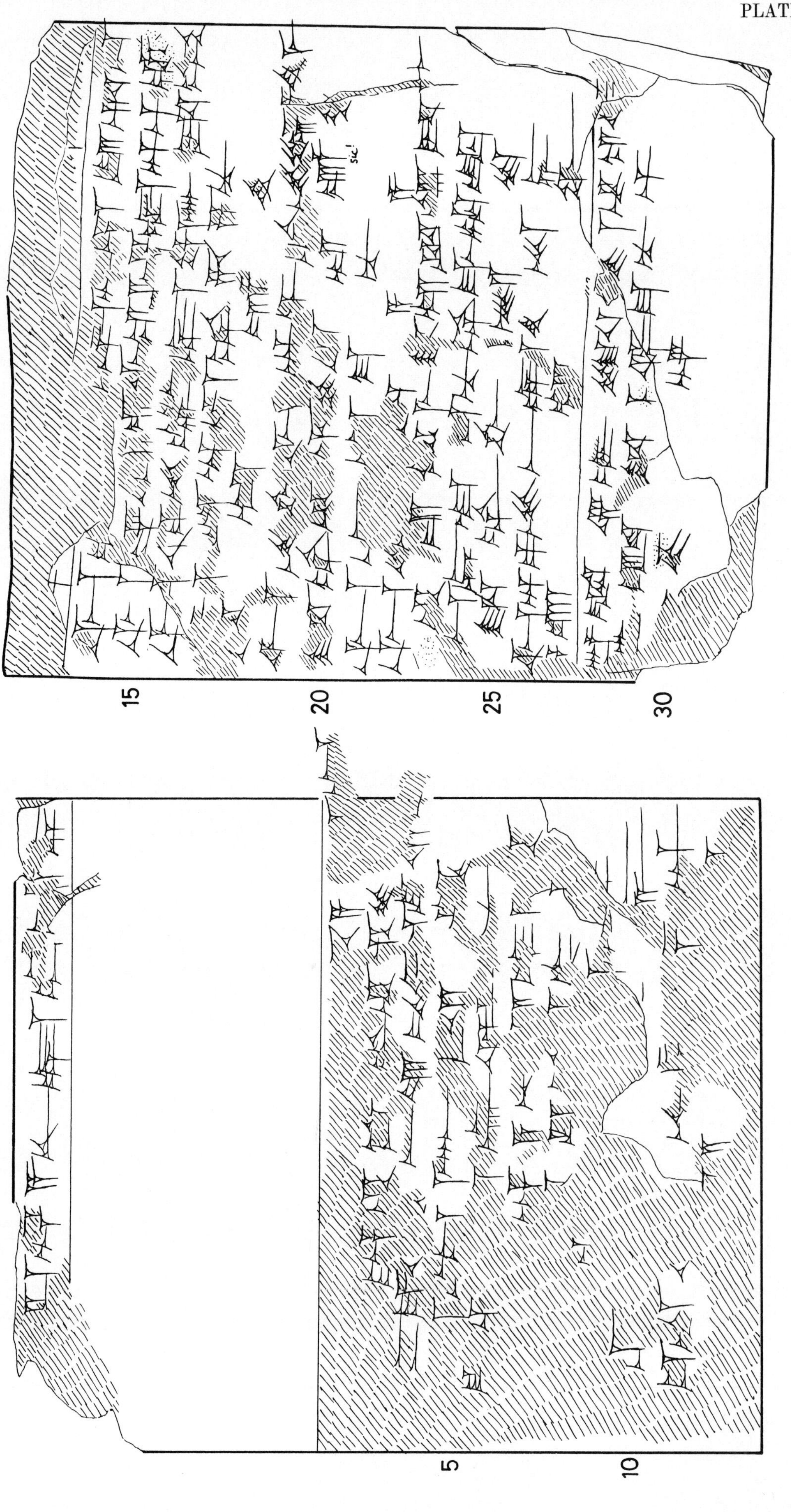

20

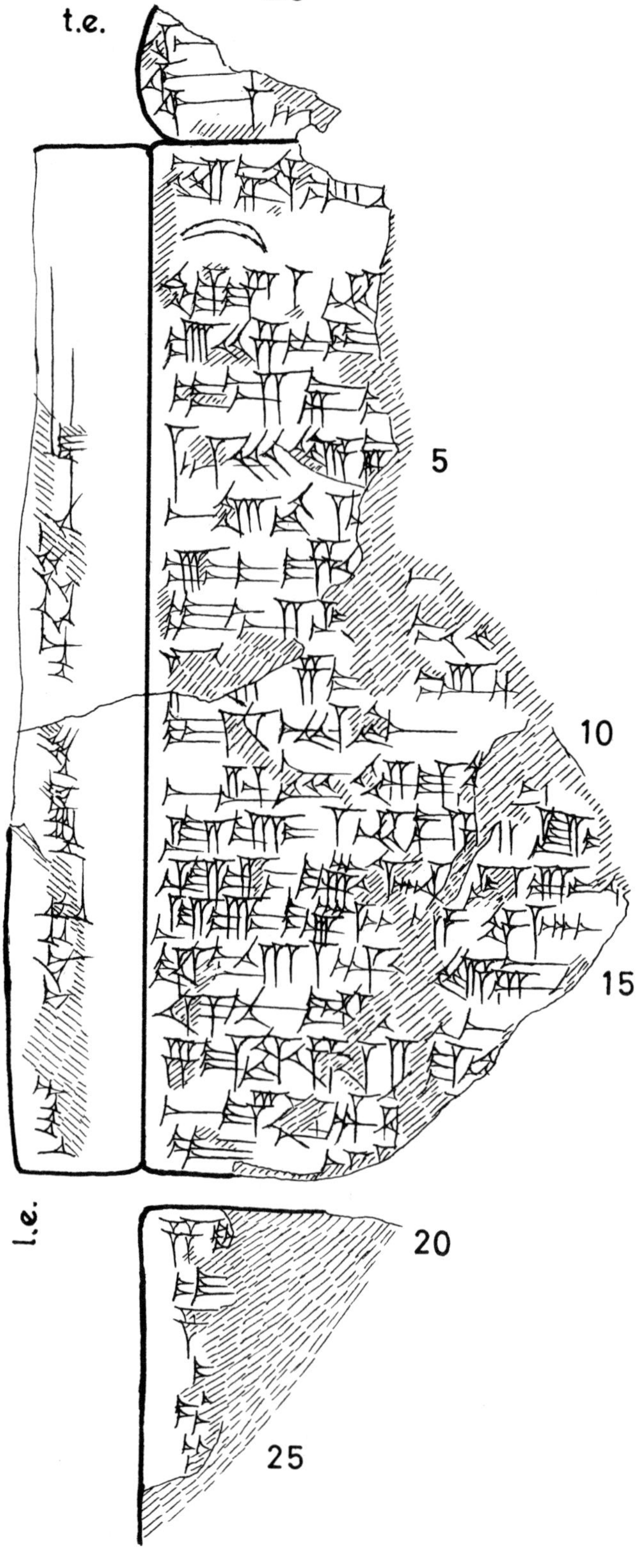

21

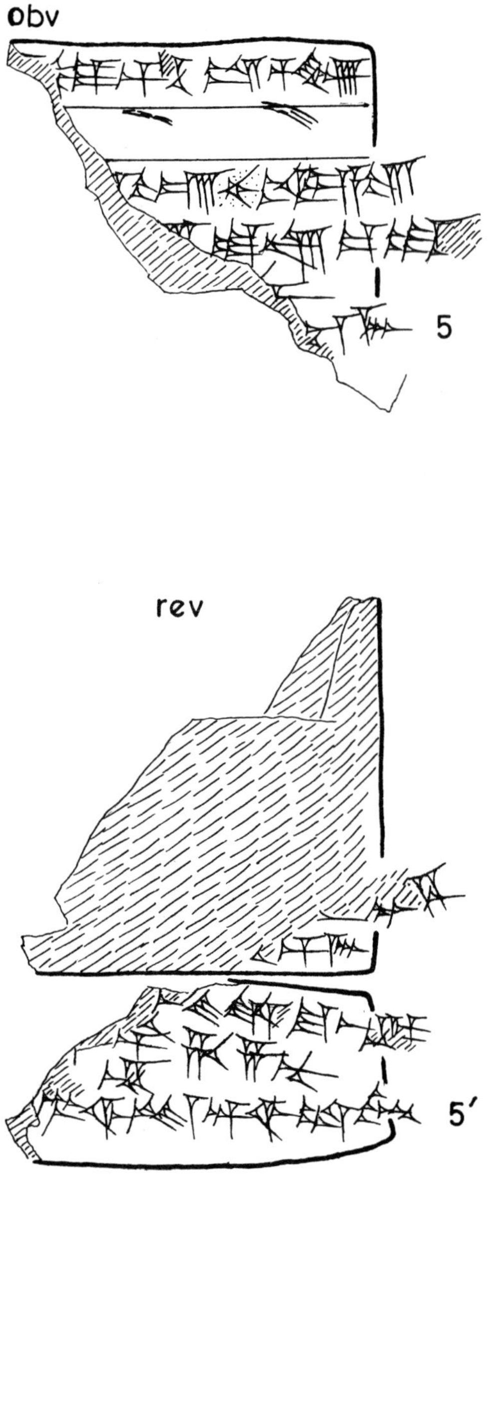

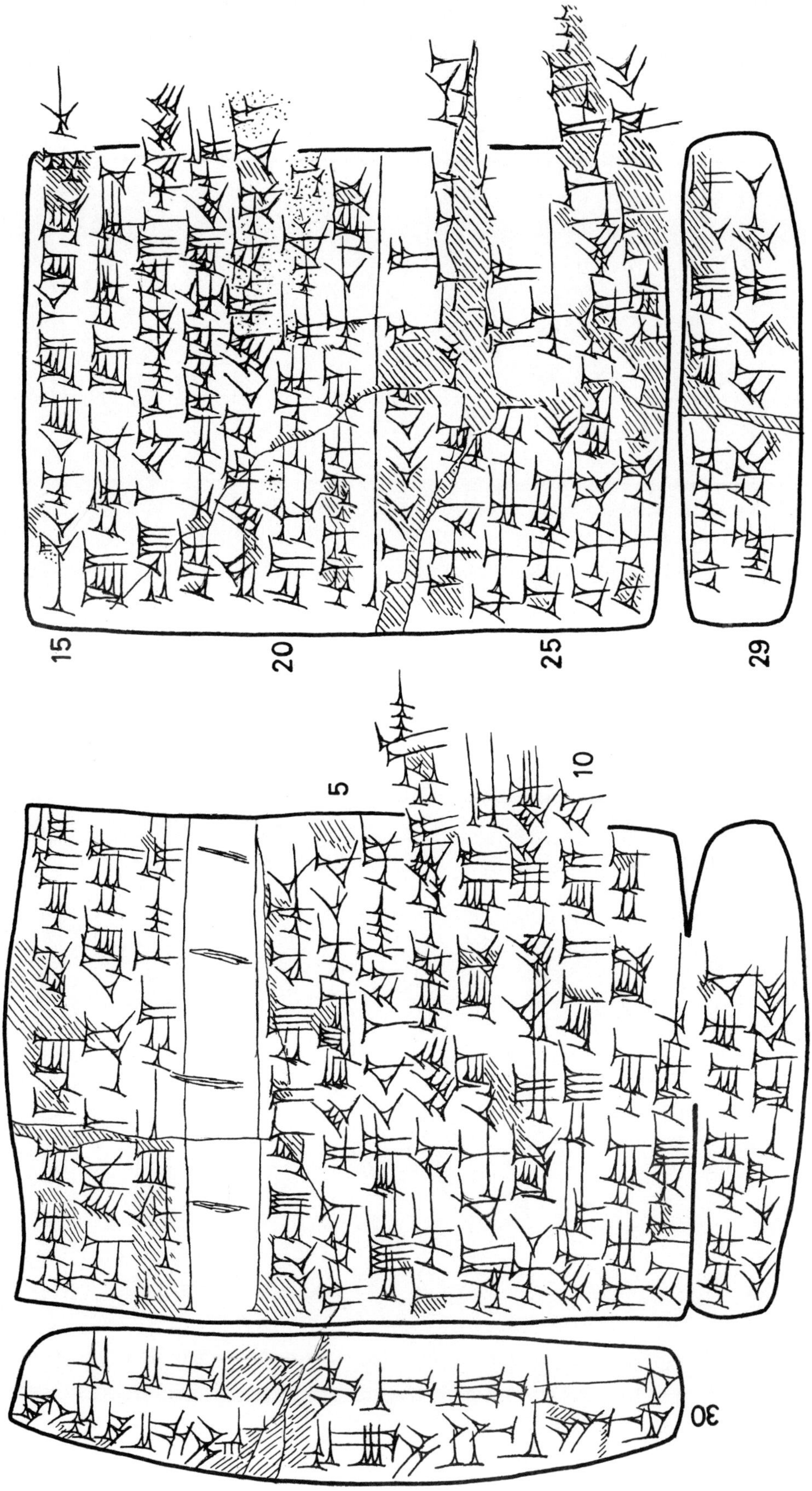

22

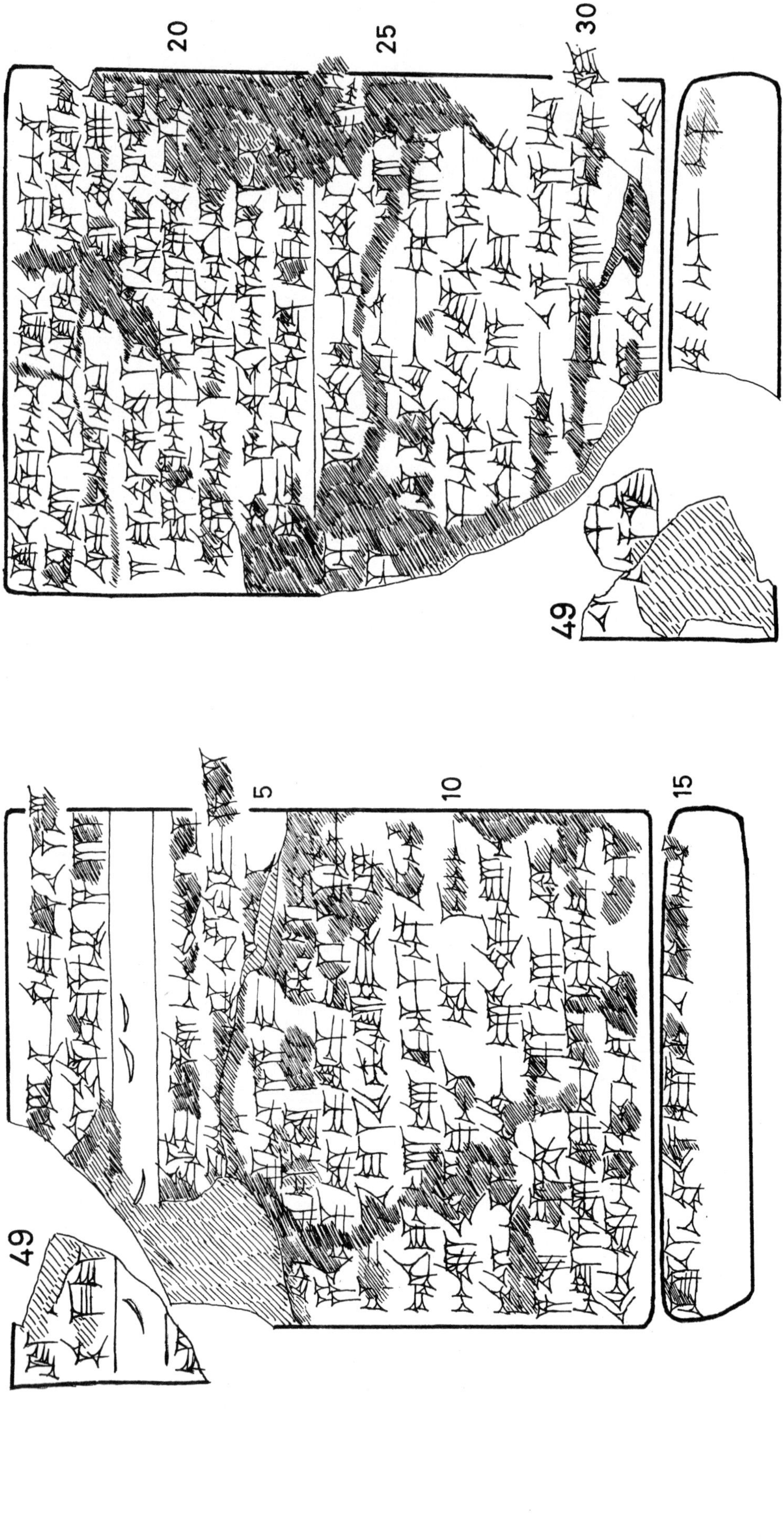

23

24

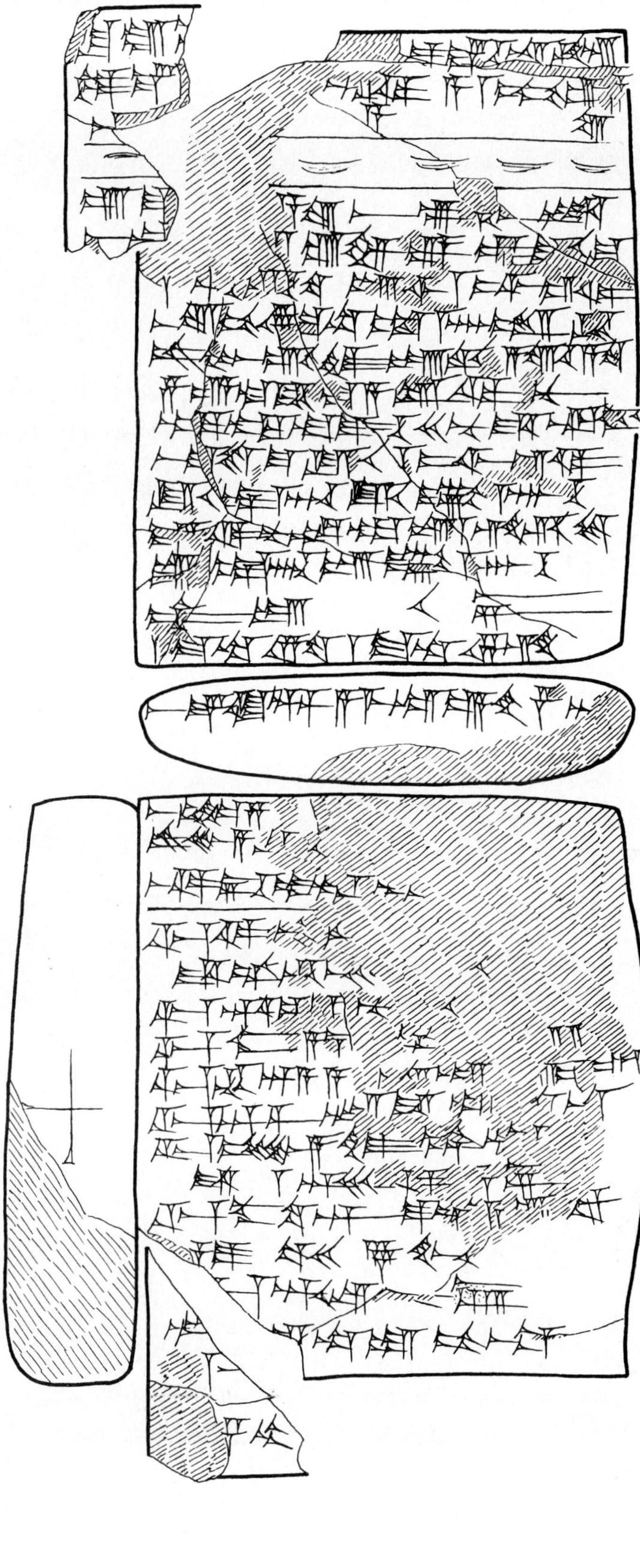

25

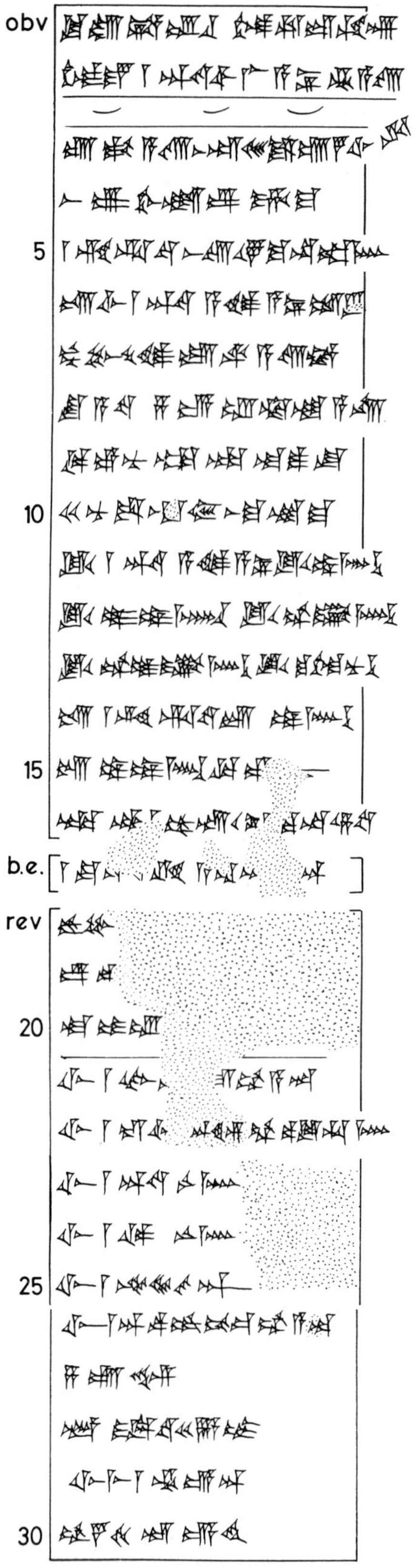

26

27

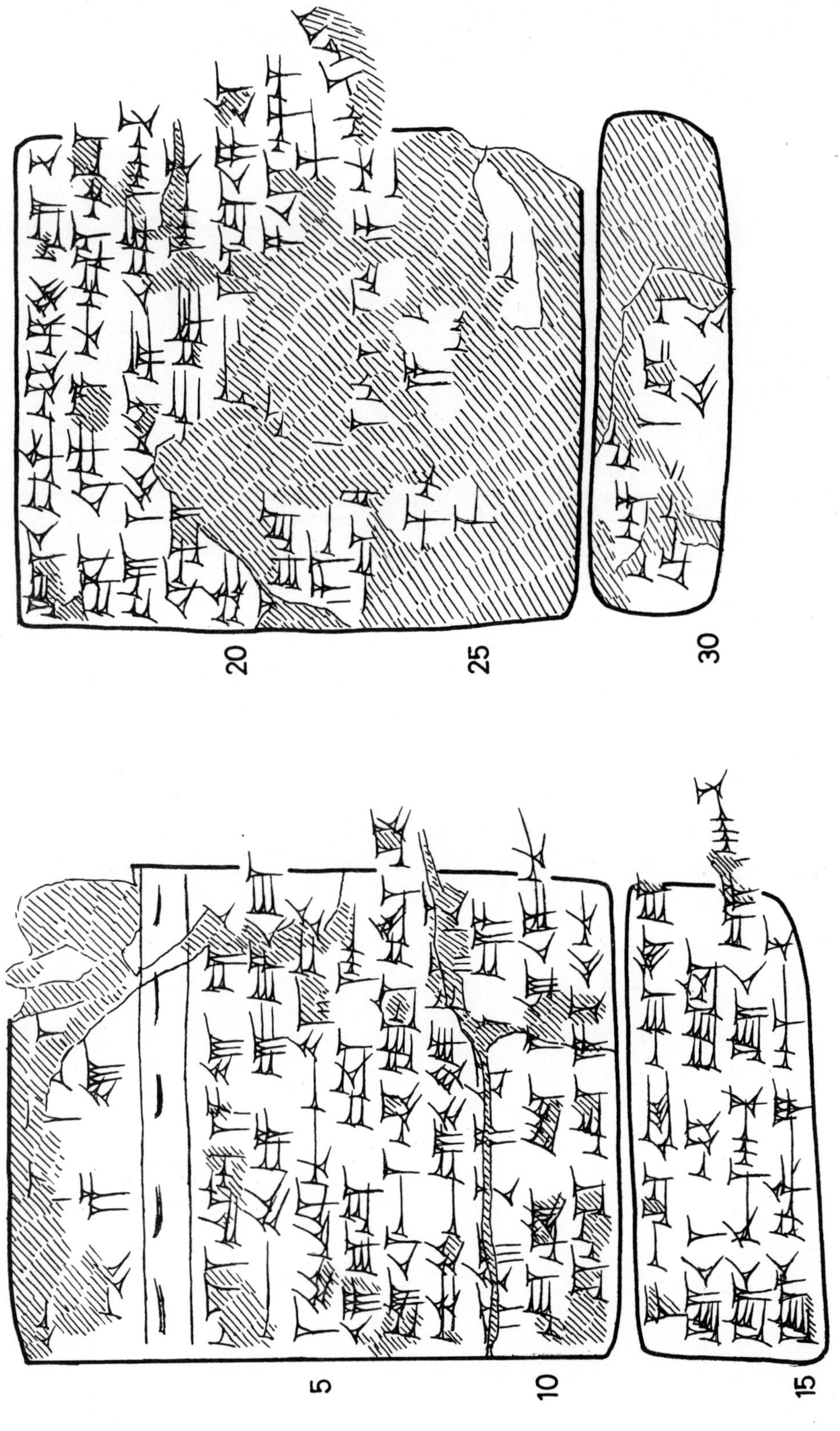

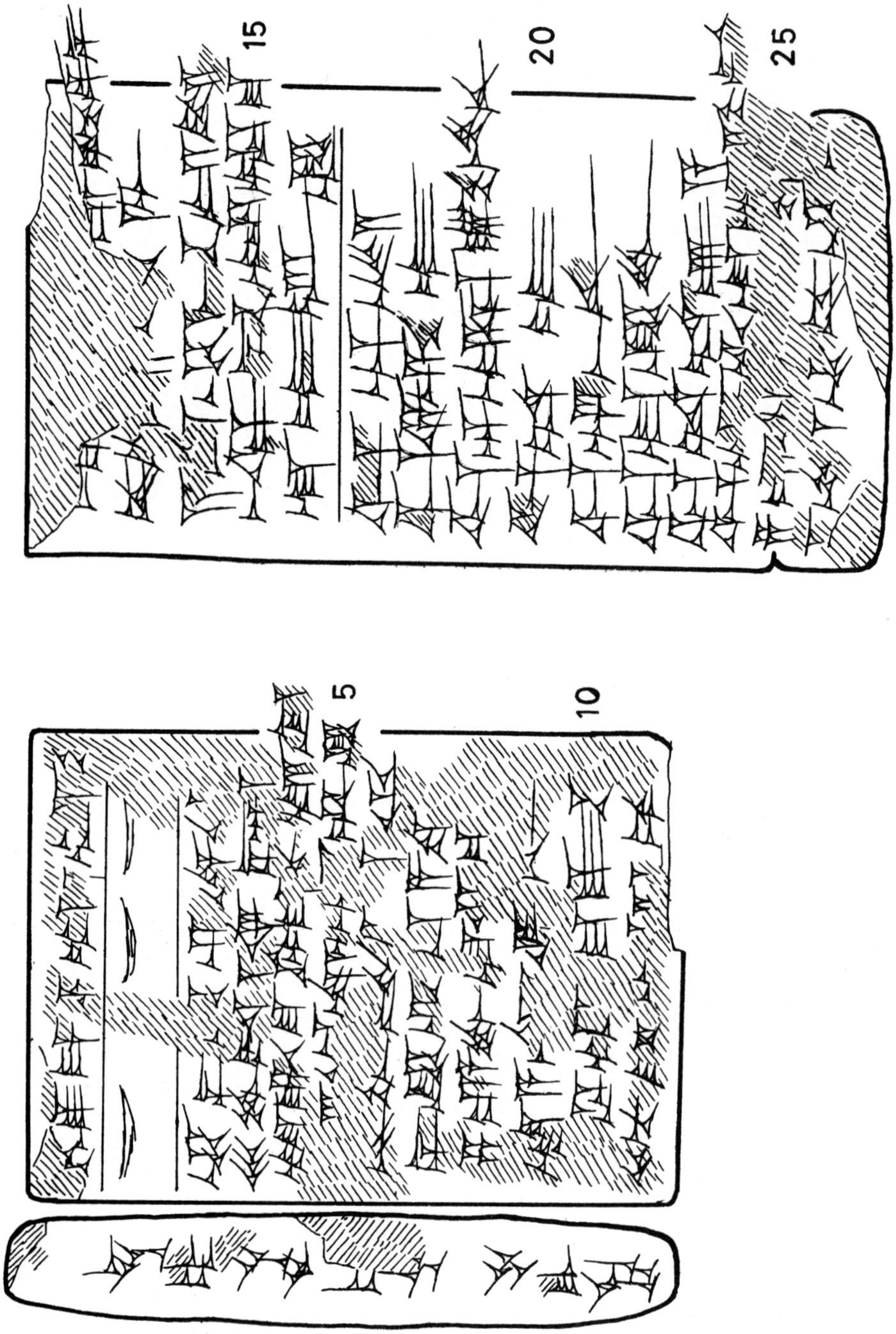

29

31

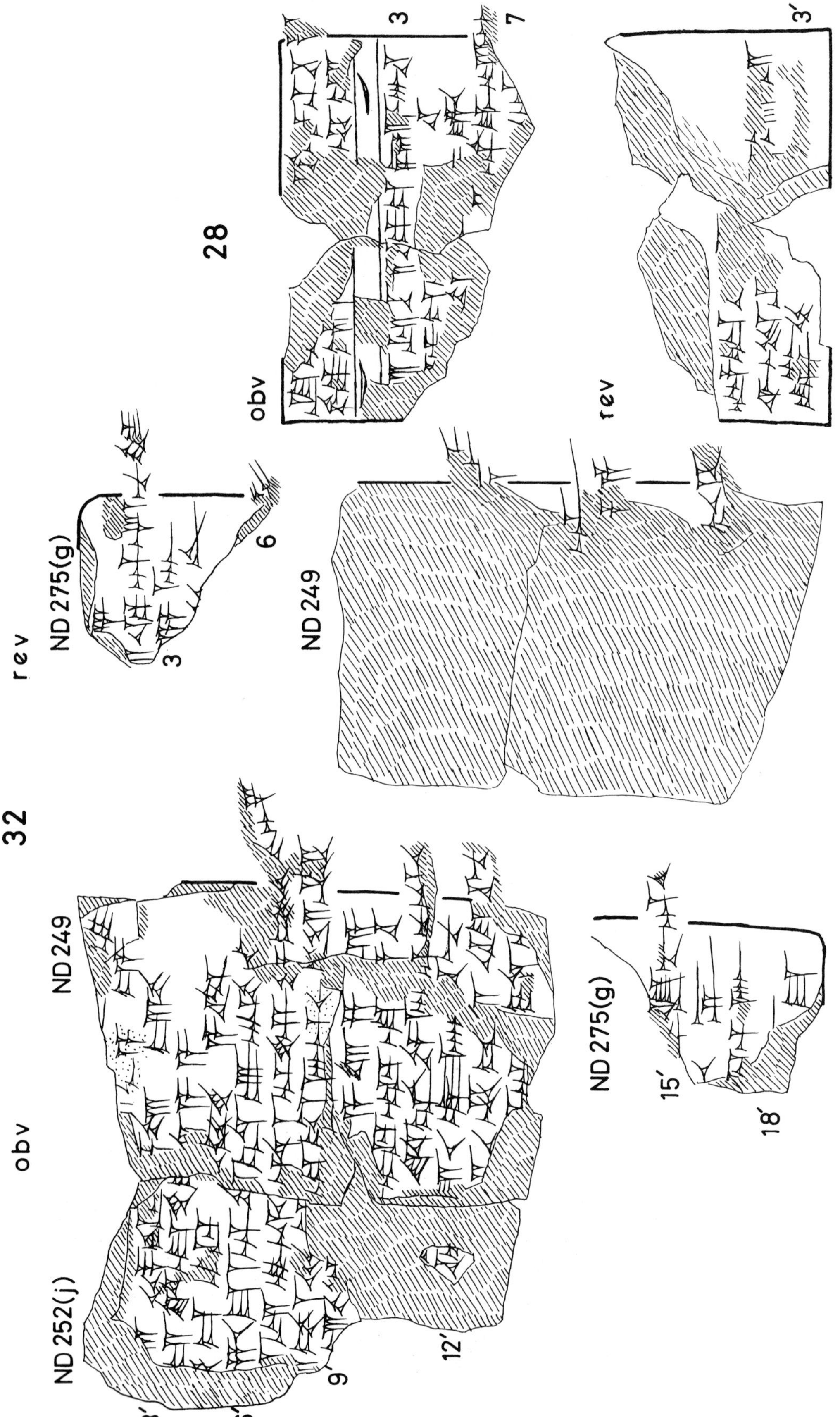
32
obv
ND 249
ND 252(j)
3′
6′
9′
12′
ND 275(g)
15′
18′
rev
ND 275(g)
3
6
ND 249
28
obv
3
7
rev
3′

34

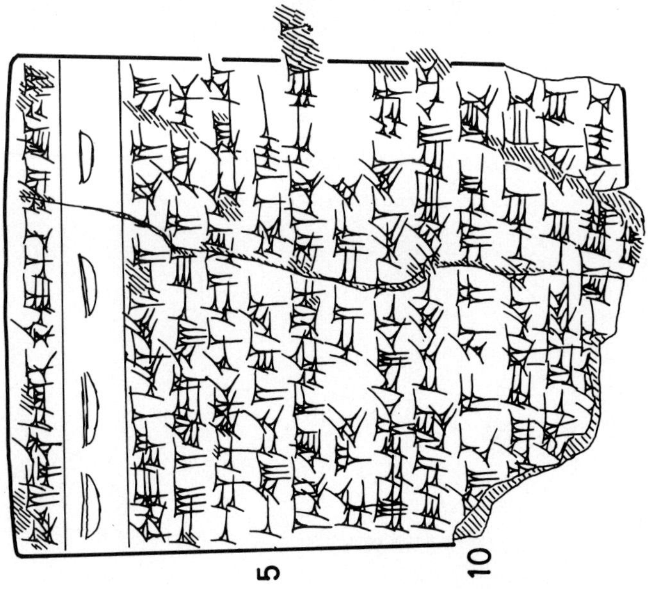

33

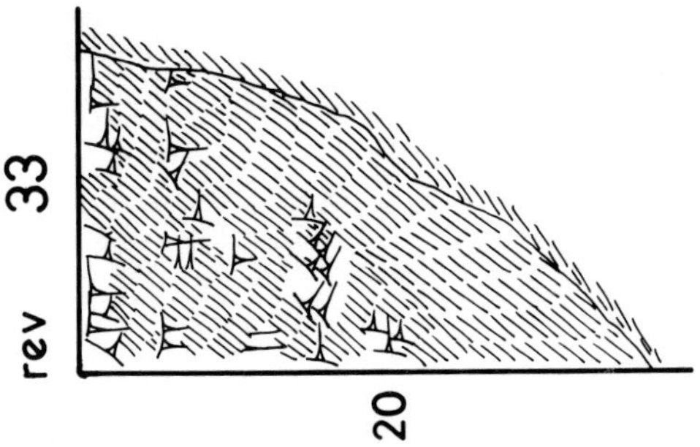

33

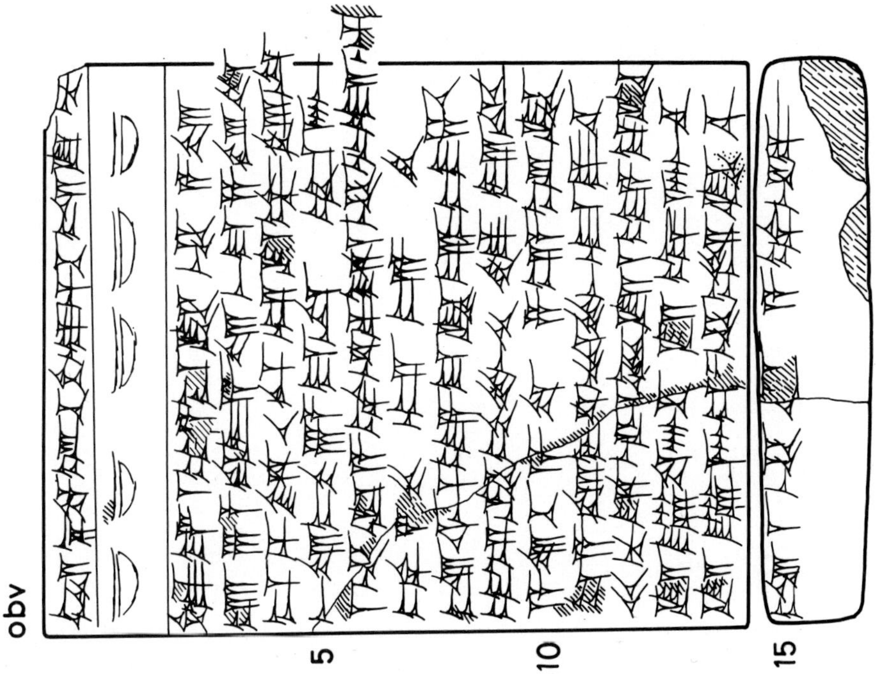

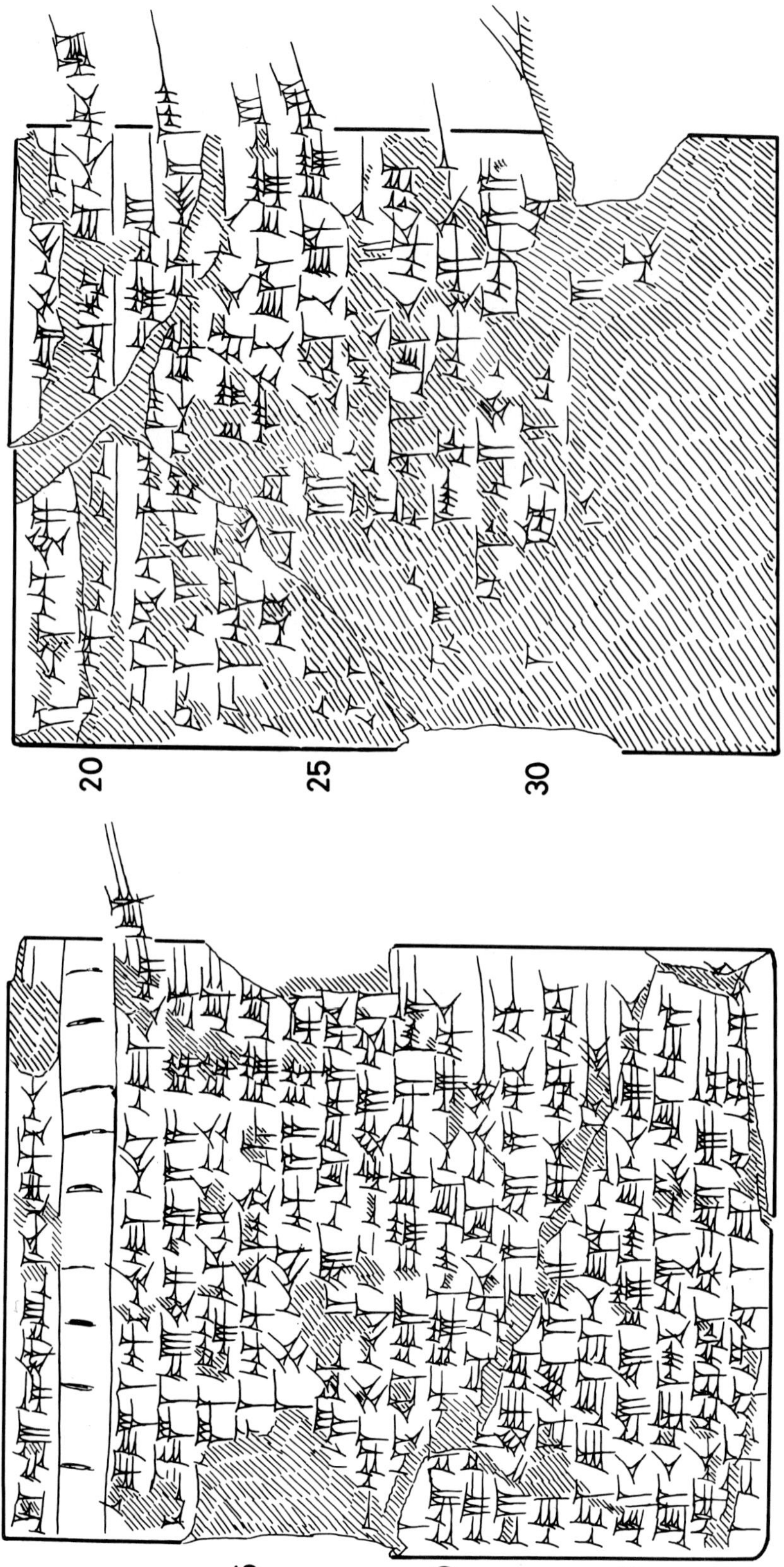

35

36

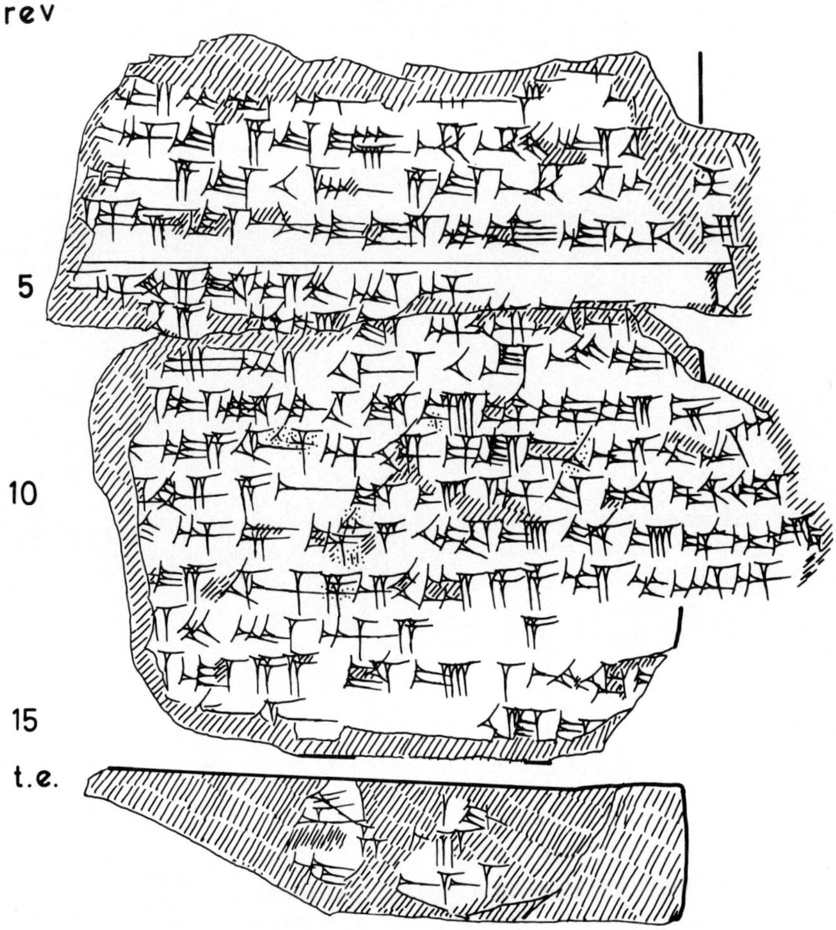

37

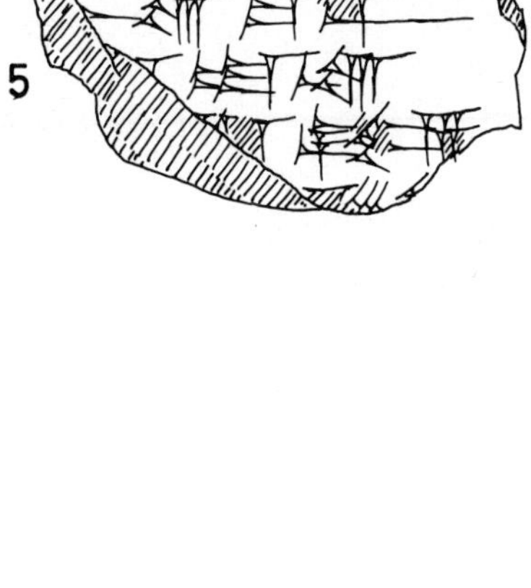

165

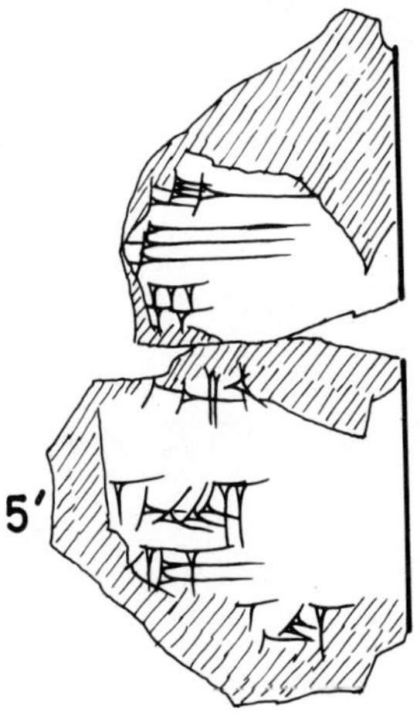

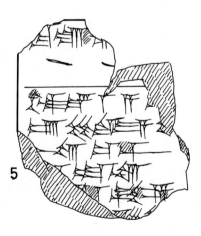

38

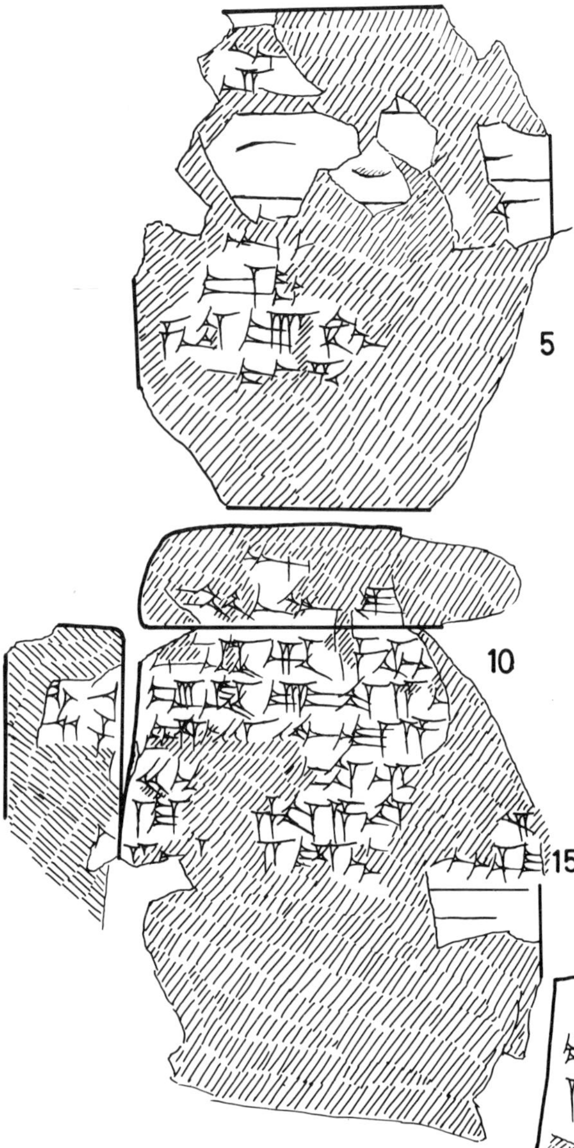

39

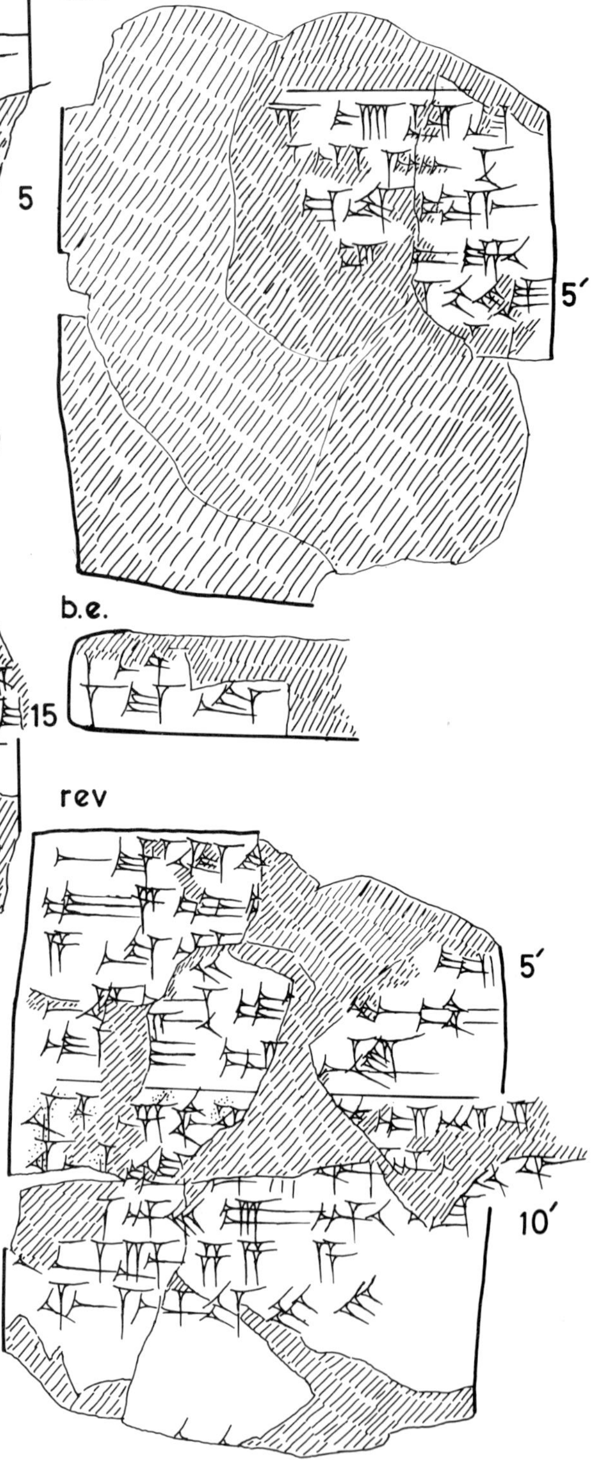

40

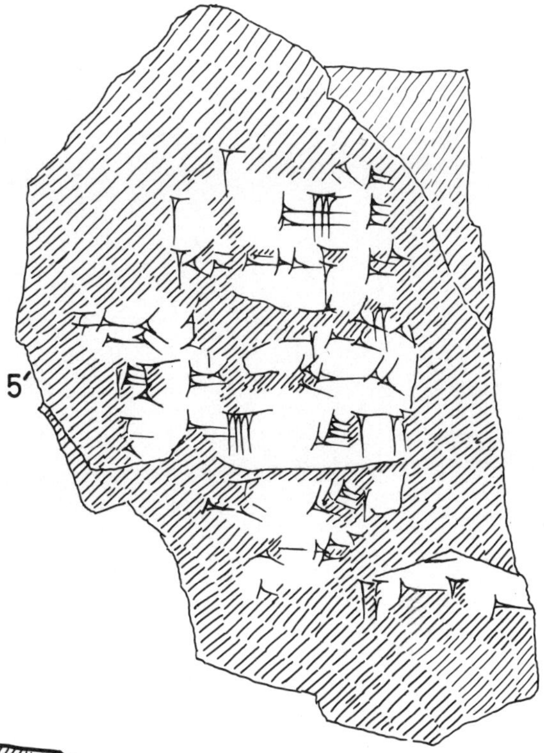

41

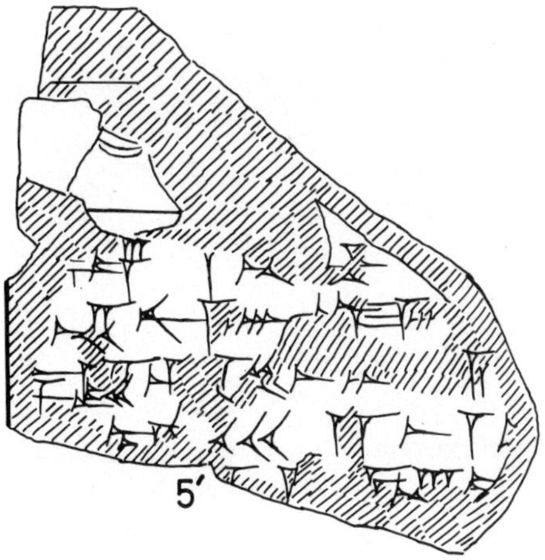

42

rev

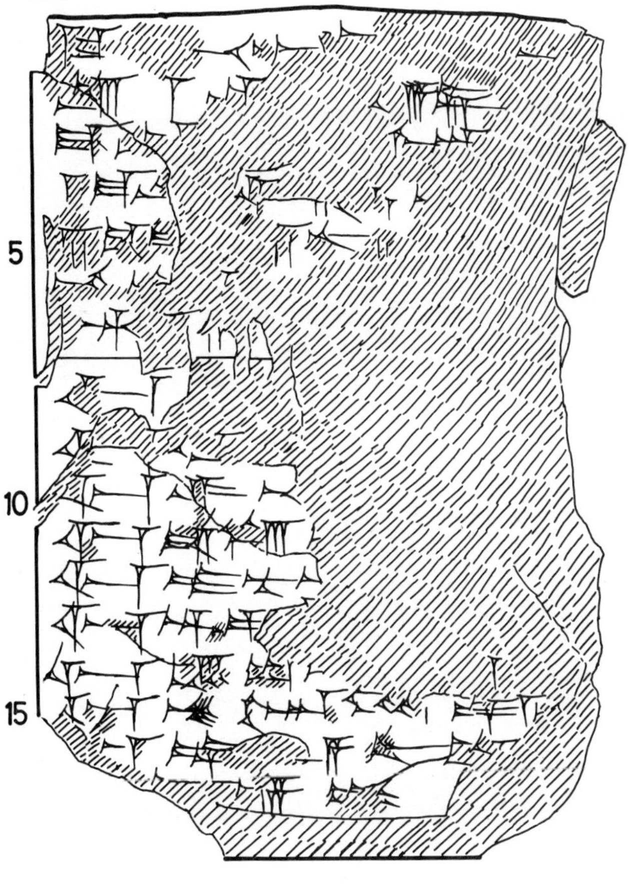

46

obv

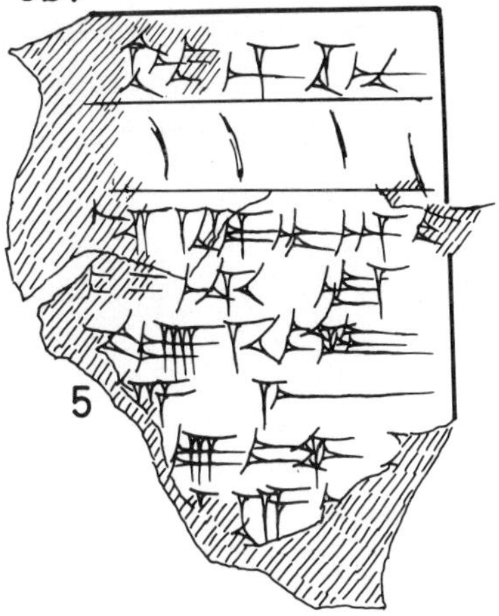

rev

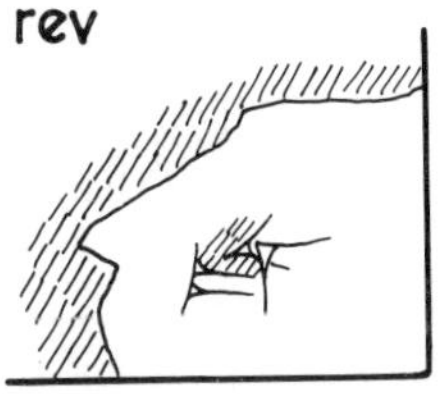

43

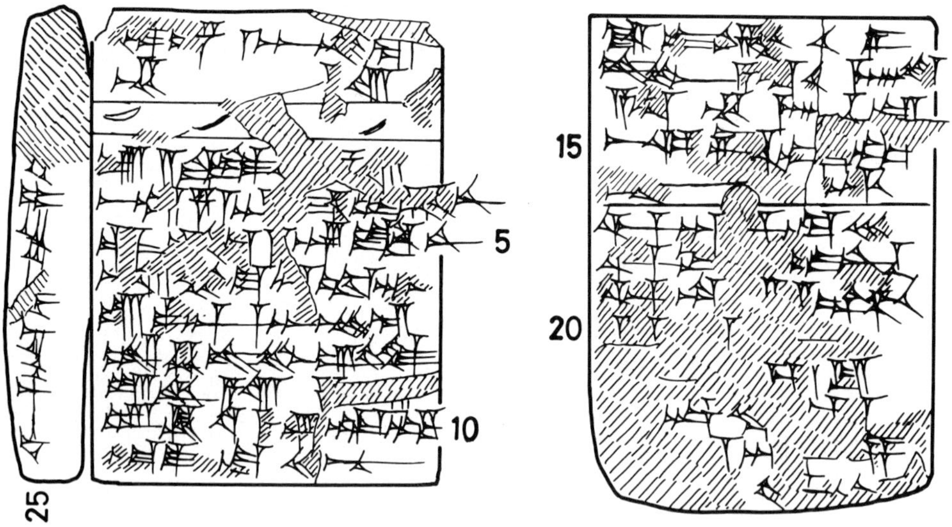

44

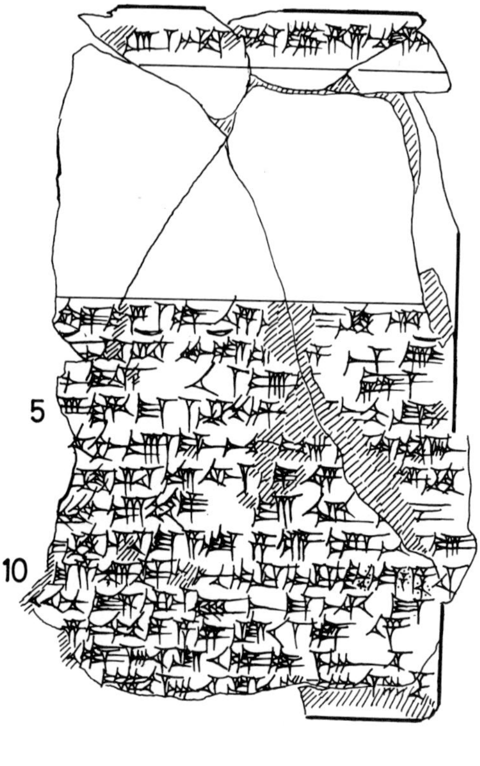

45

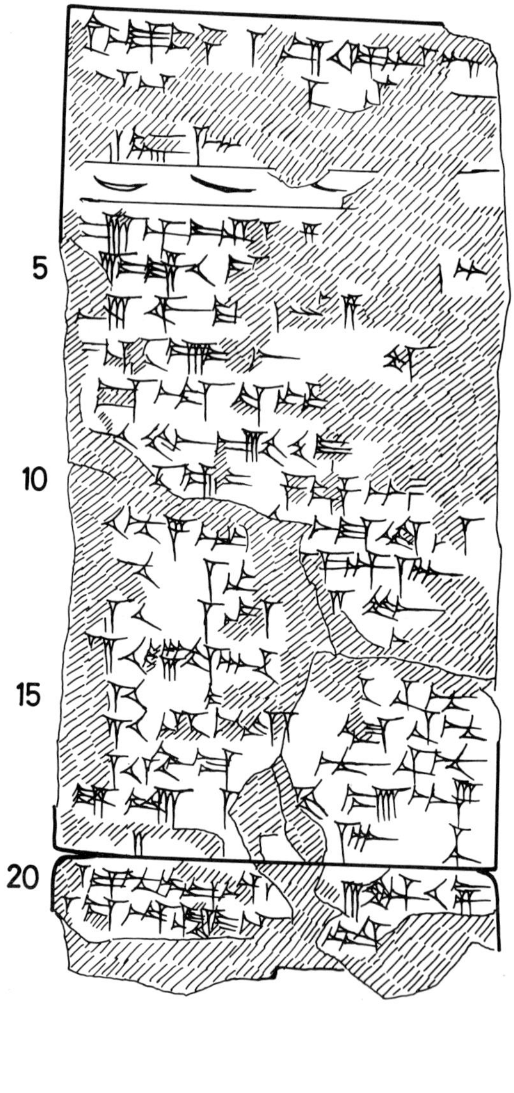

47

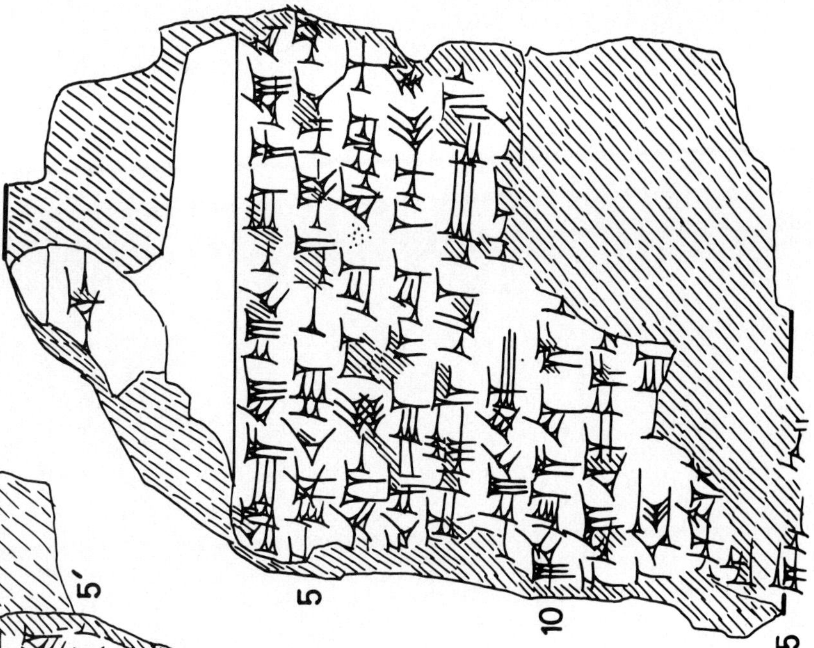

50

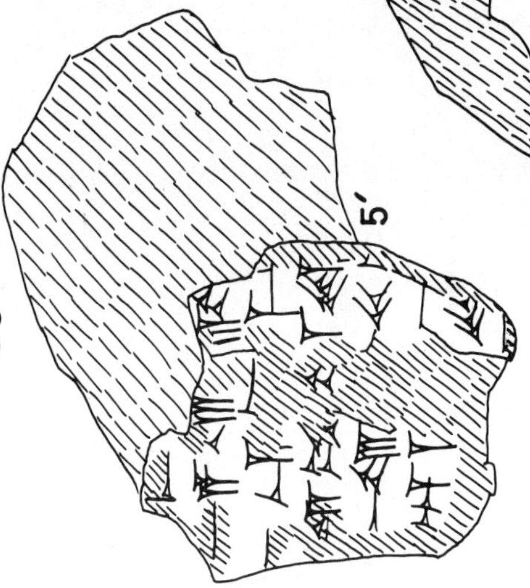

51

rev

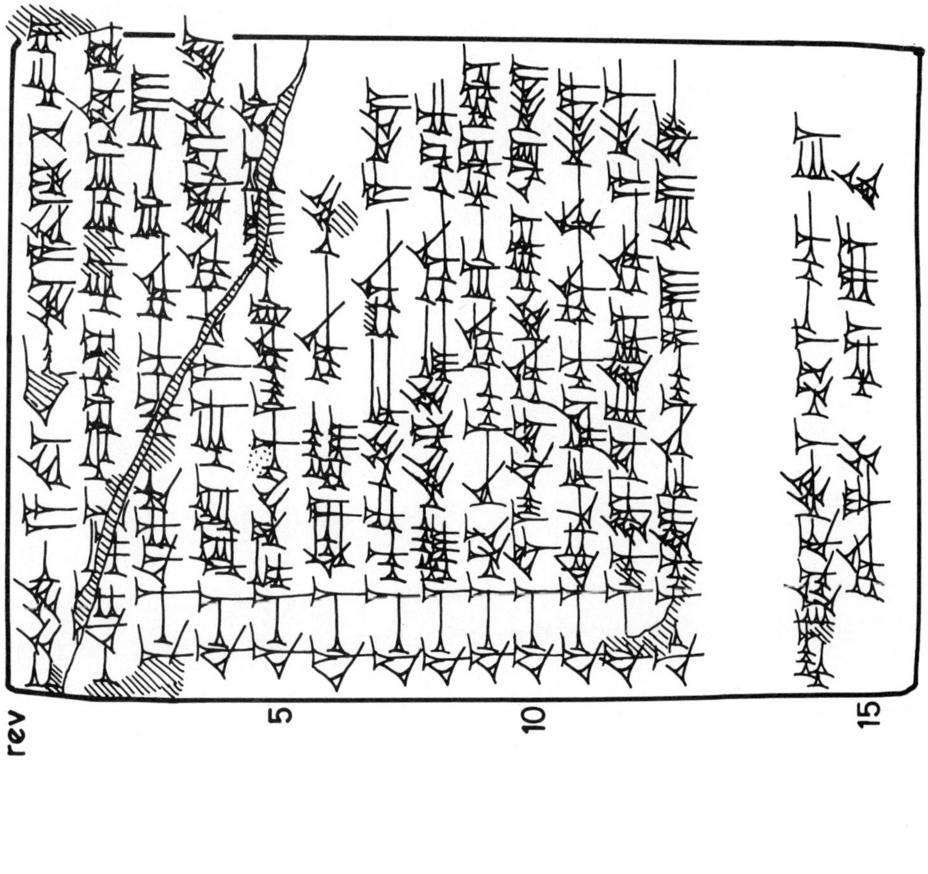

53

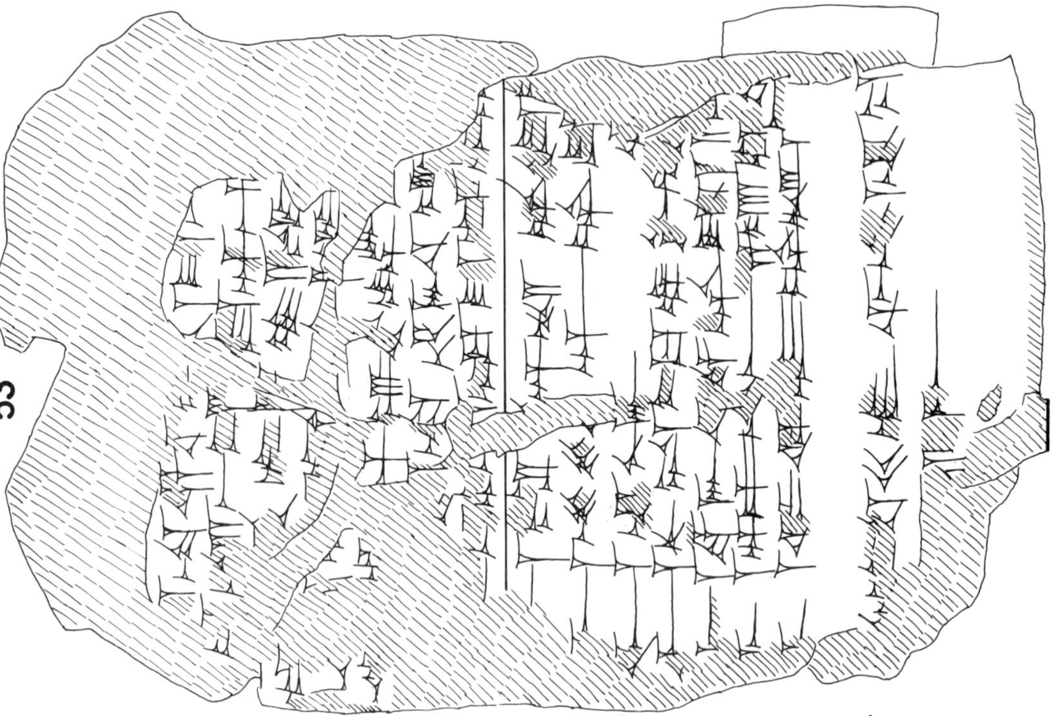

48

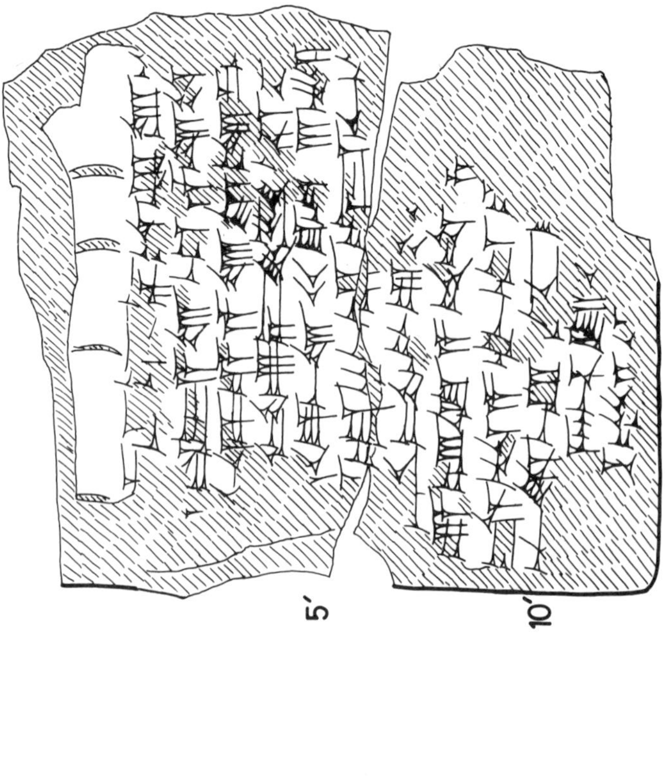

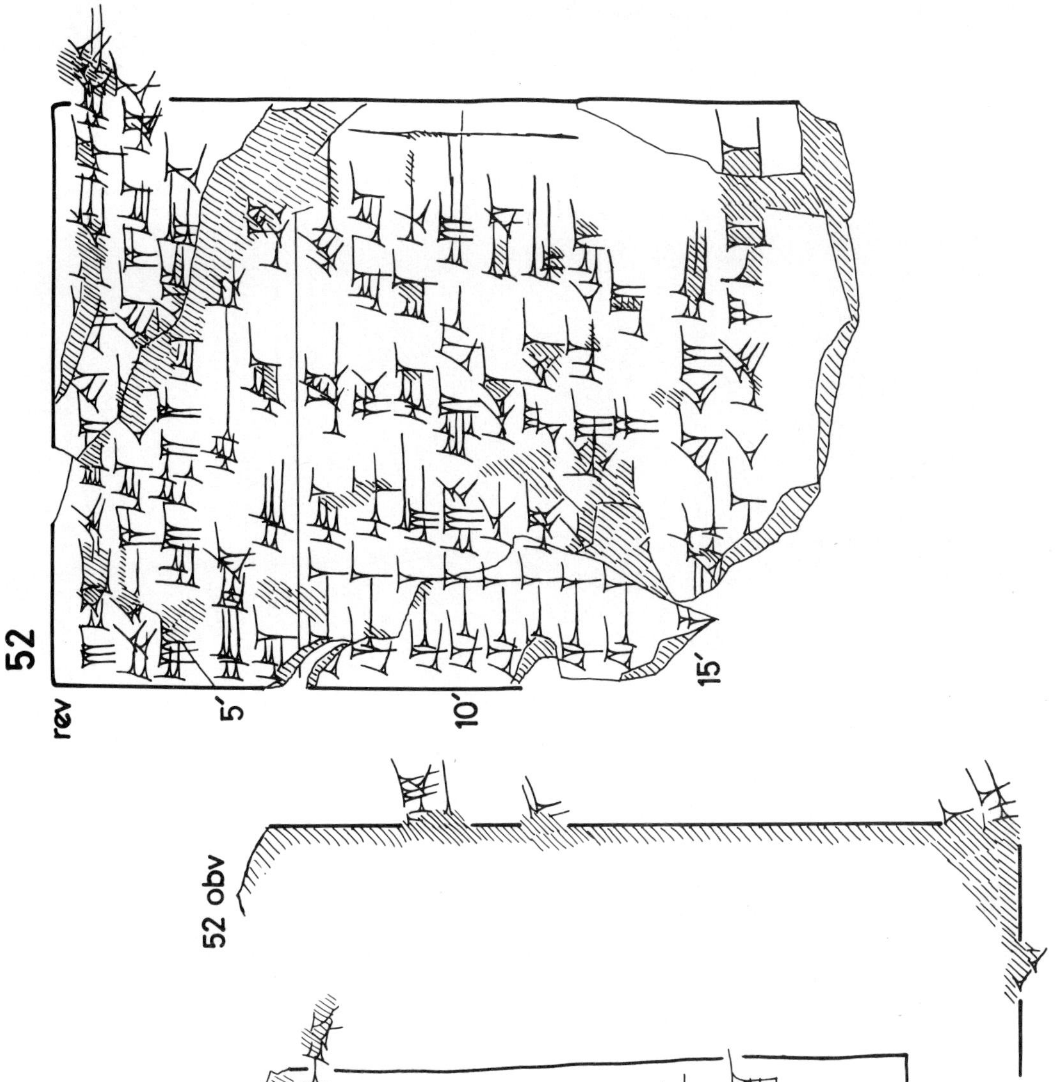
52
rev
5'
10'
15'
52 obv

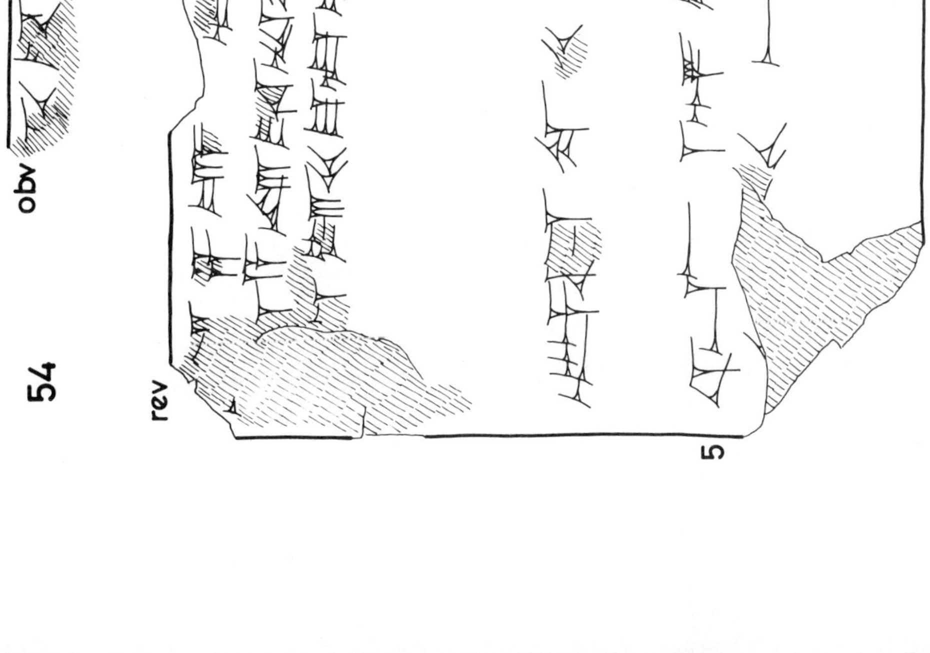
54
obv
rev
5

55

rev

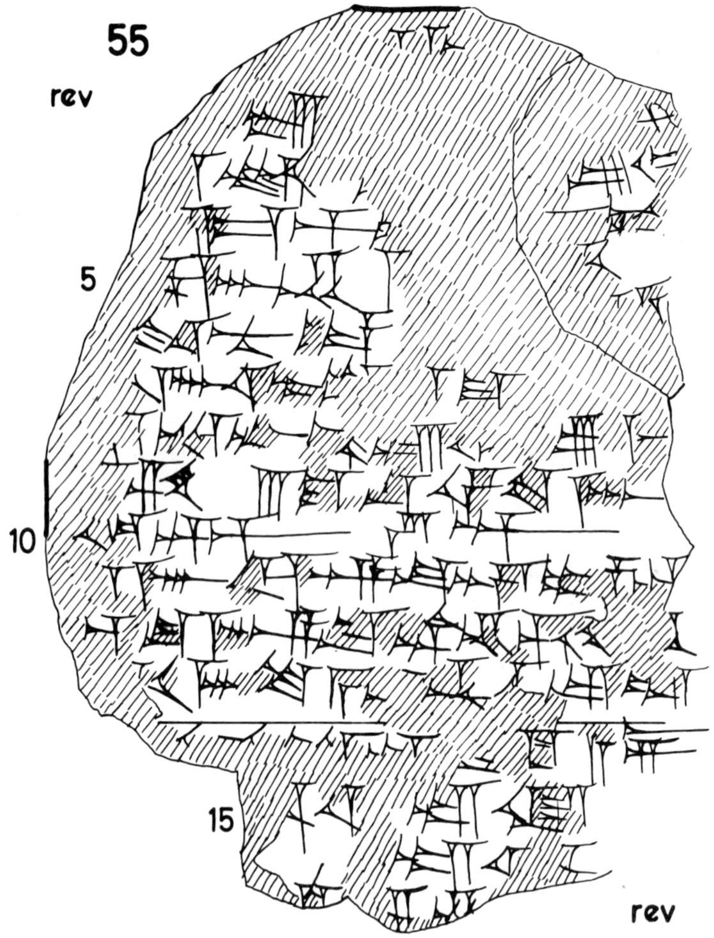

88

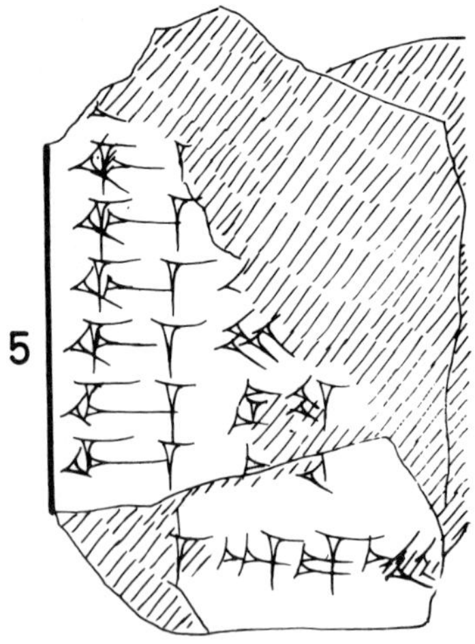

56

rev

85

rev

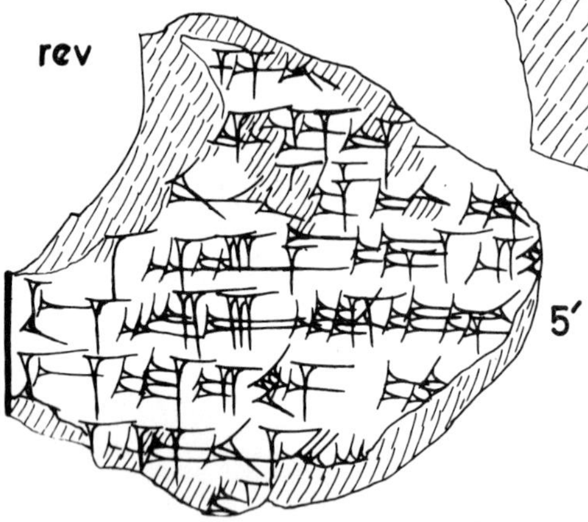

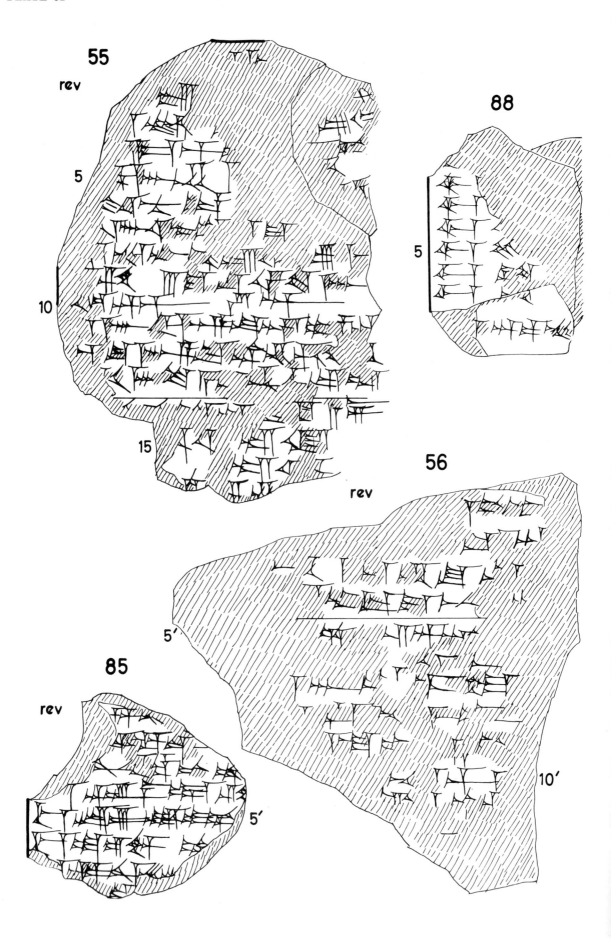

57

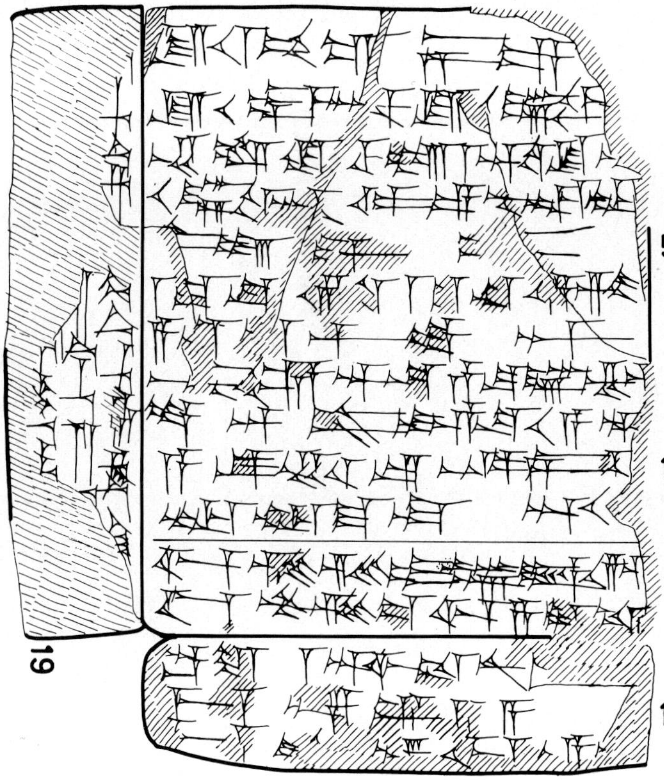

58

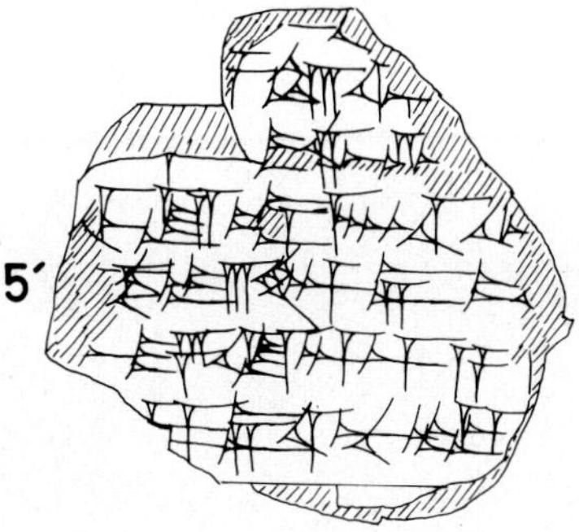

61

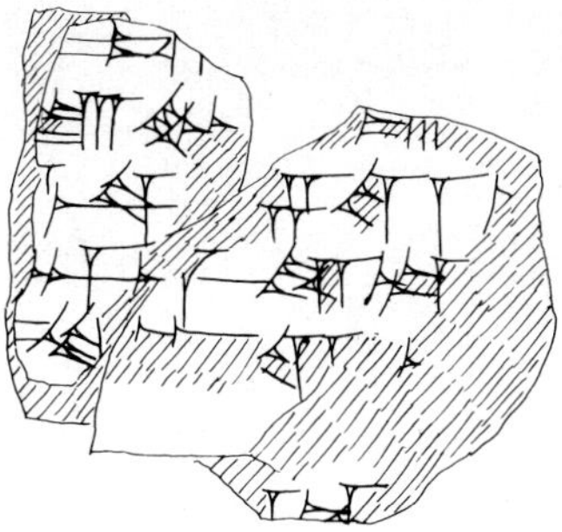

60

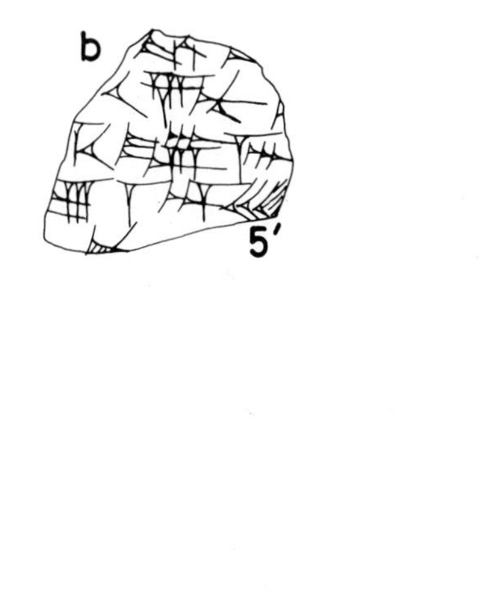

59

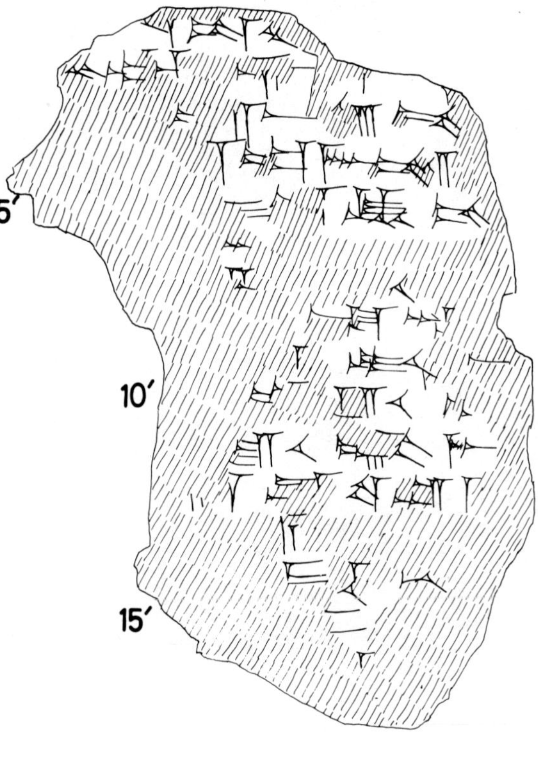

62

rev

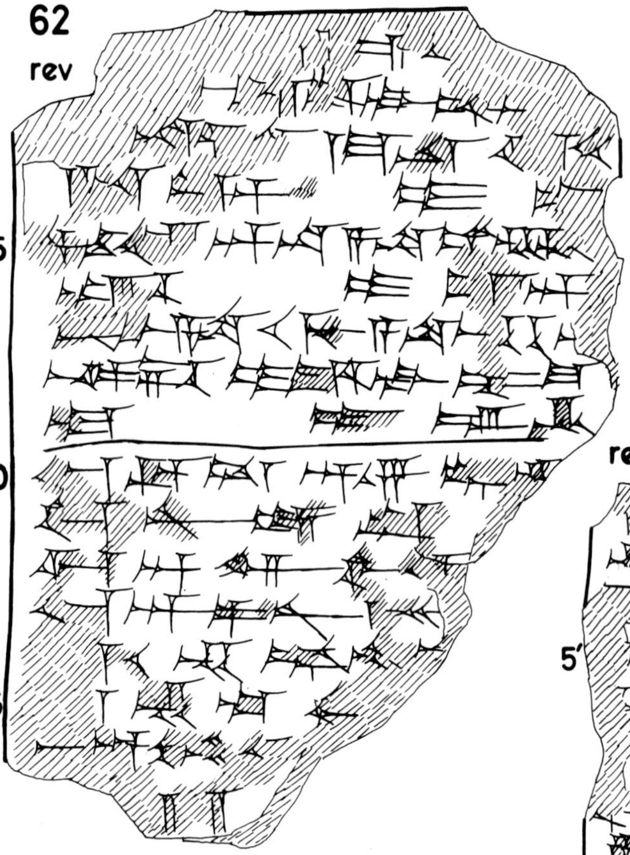

63

rev

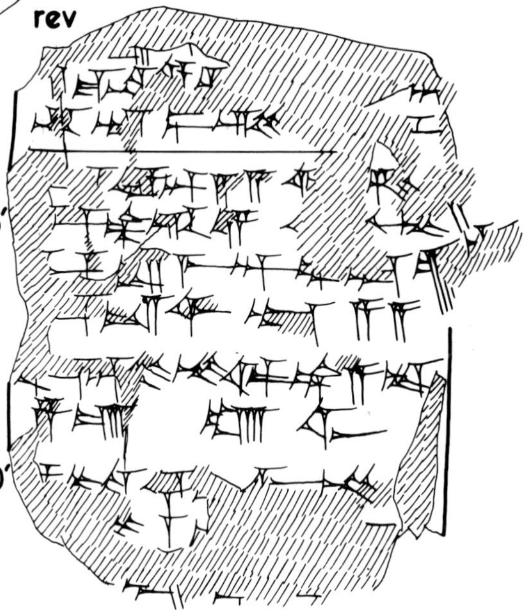

64

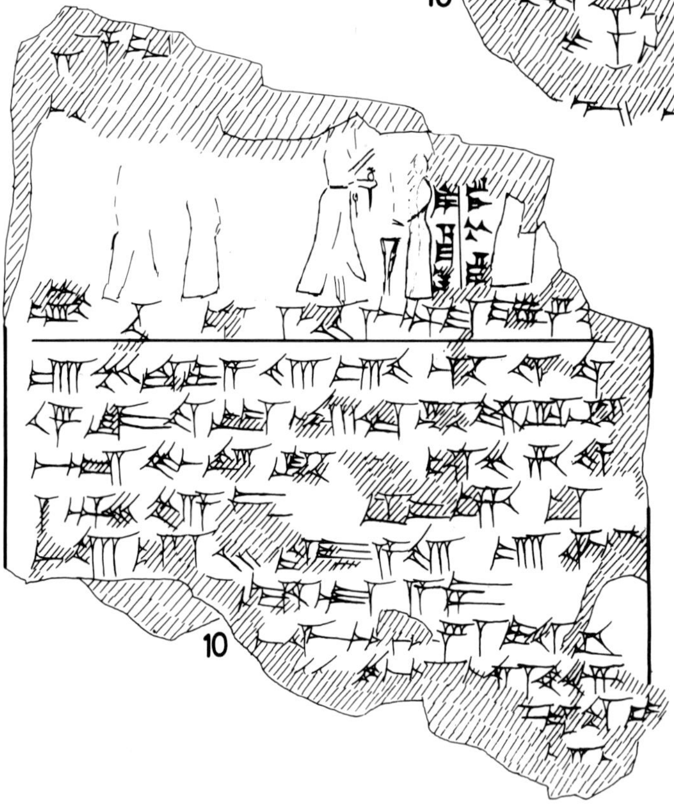

66

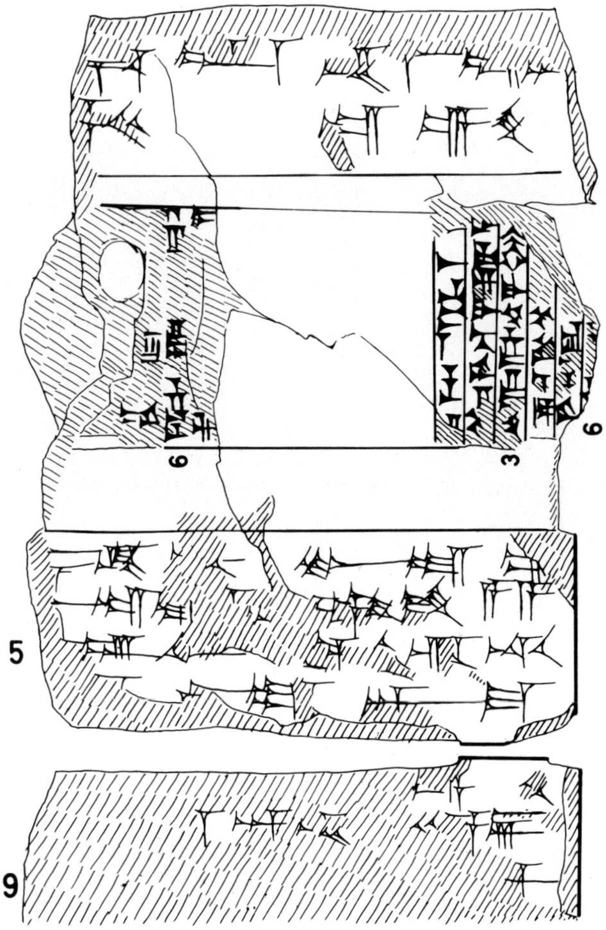

67

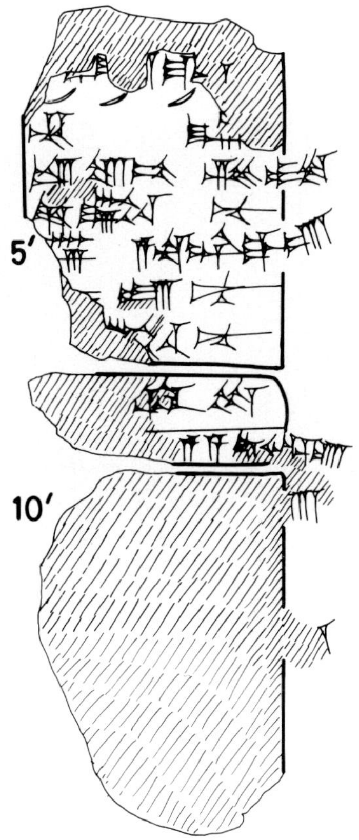

69

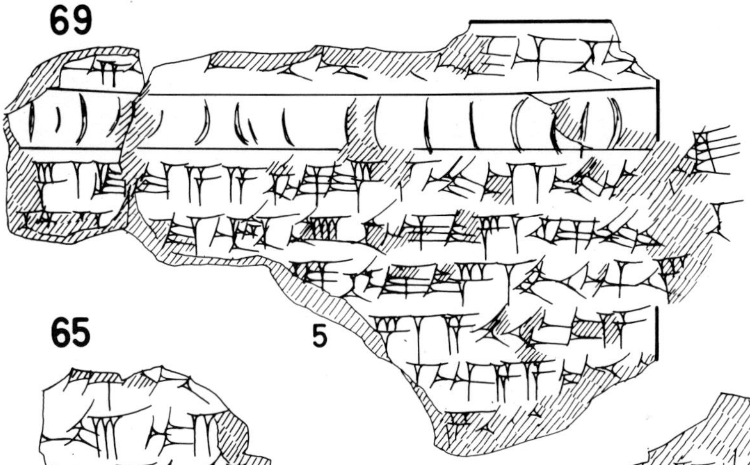

65

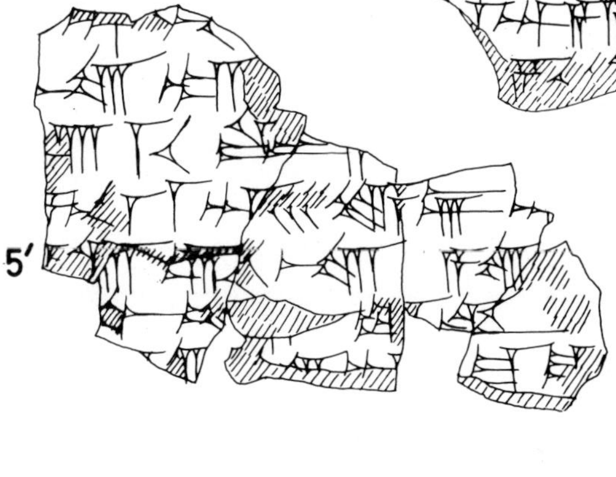

70

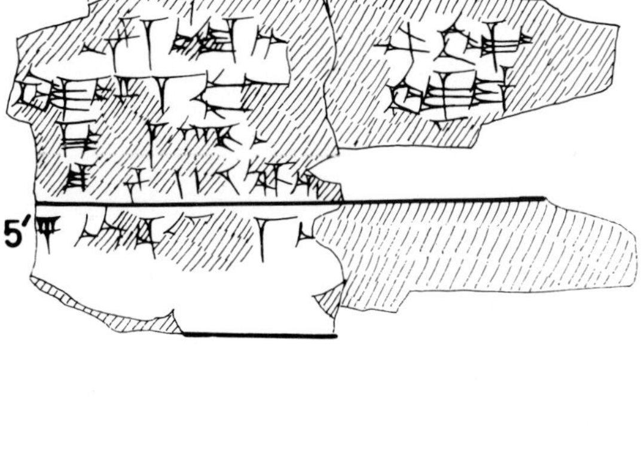

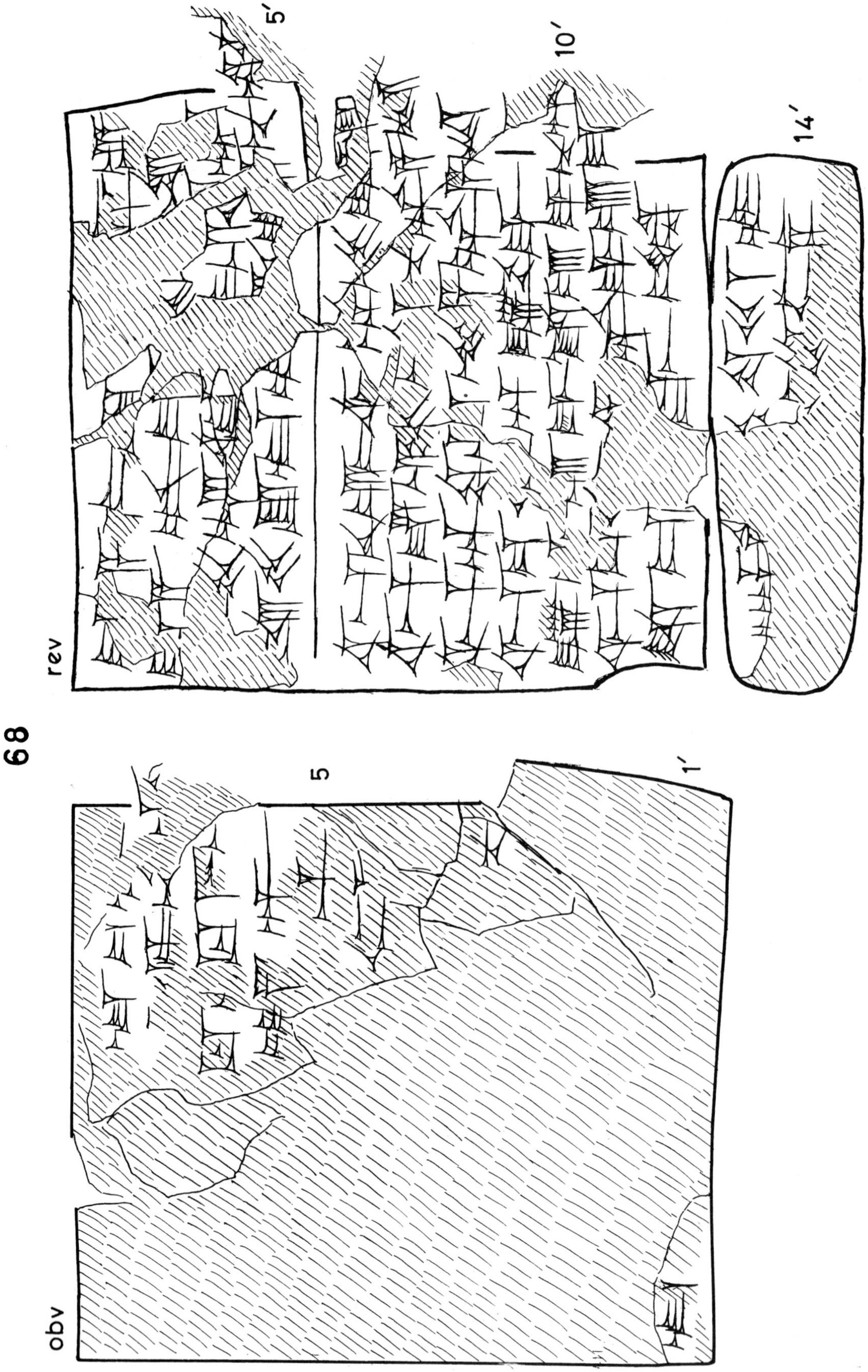
68
obv
5
1′
rev
5′
10′
14′

71

72

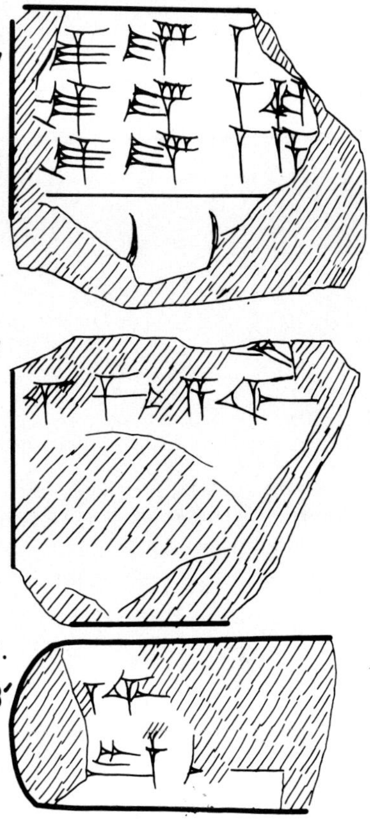

76

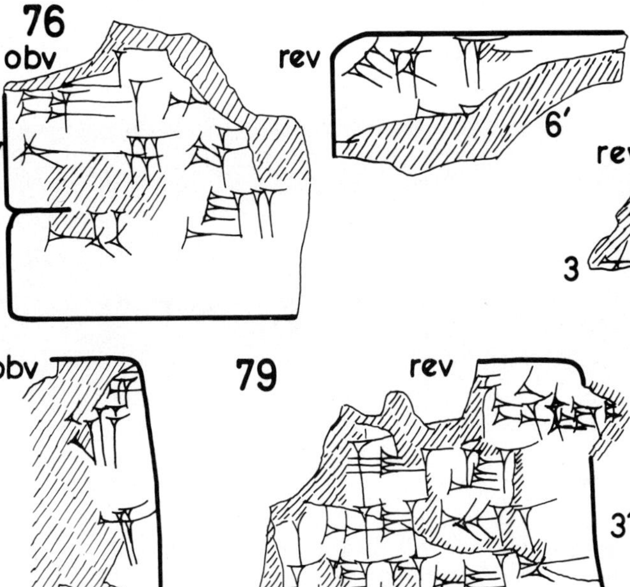

73

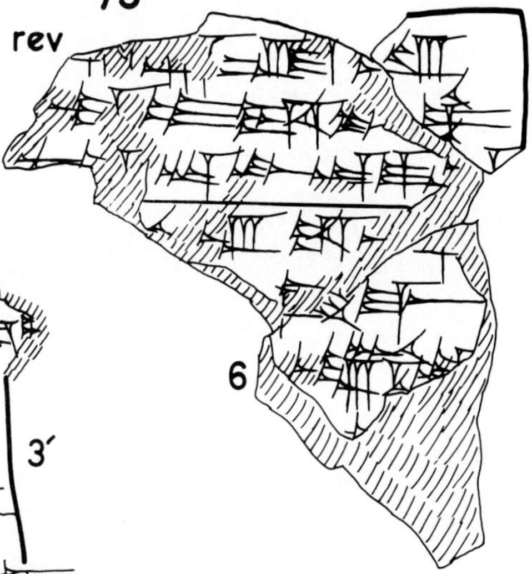

79

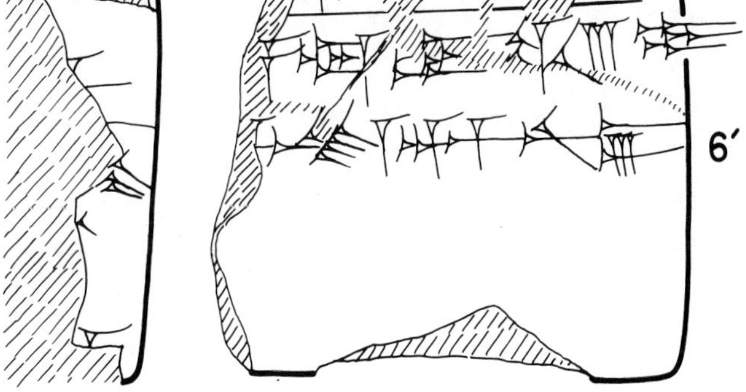

77

80

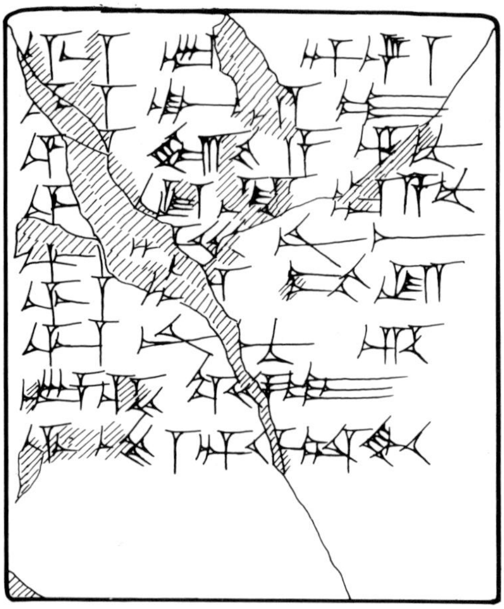

74

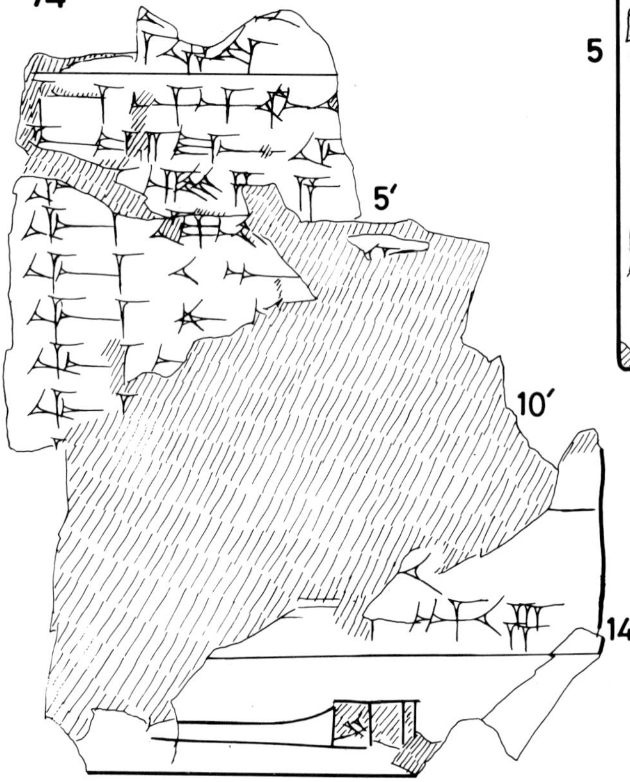

75

78

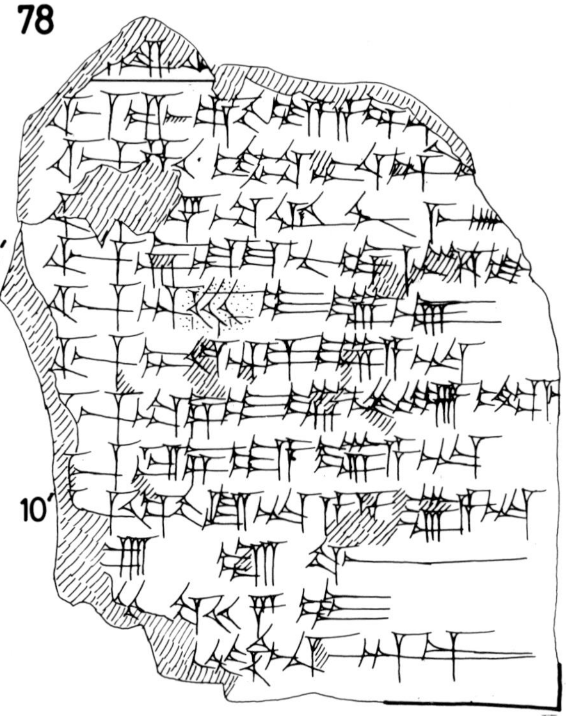

81

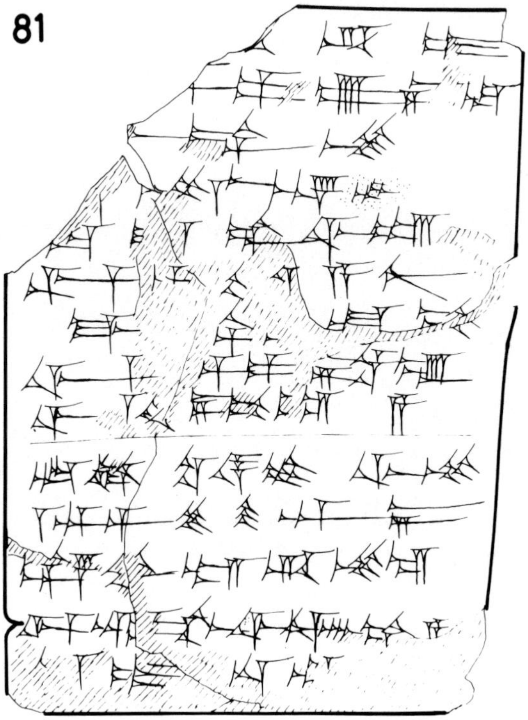

86

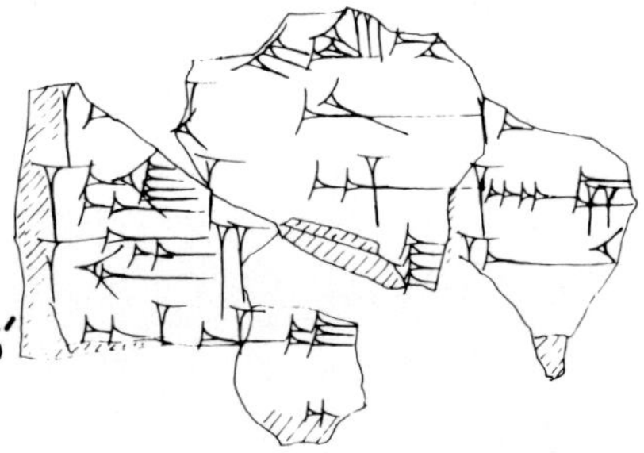

87

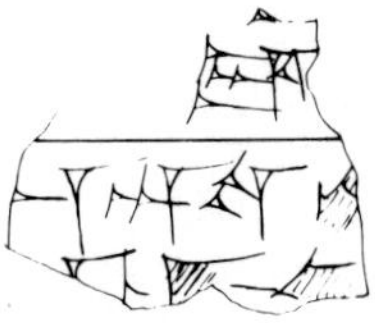

83

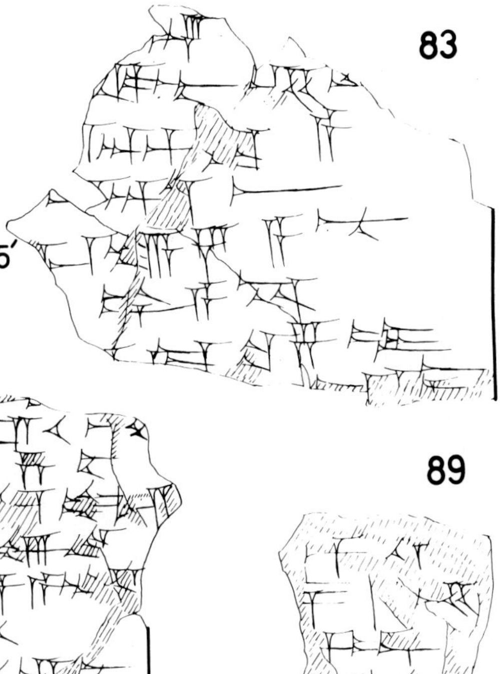

82

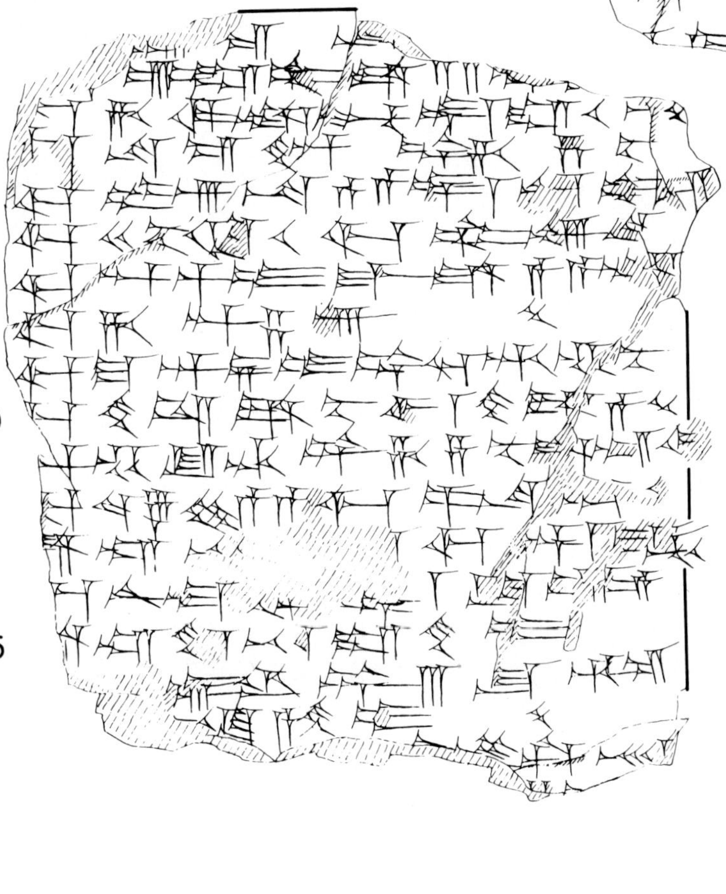

89

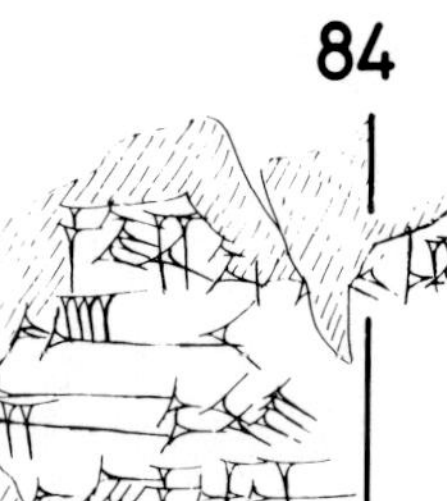

84

90

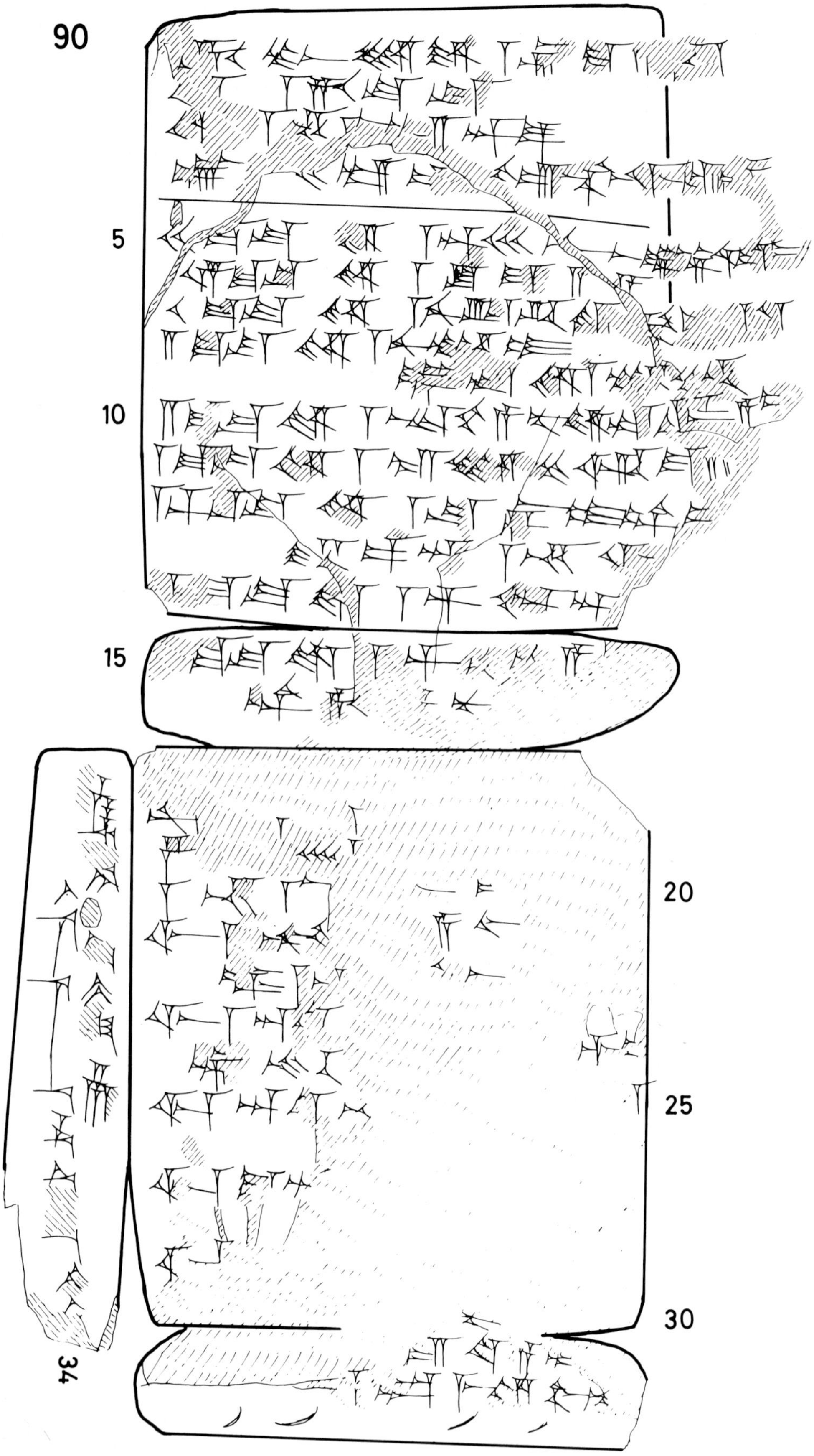

91

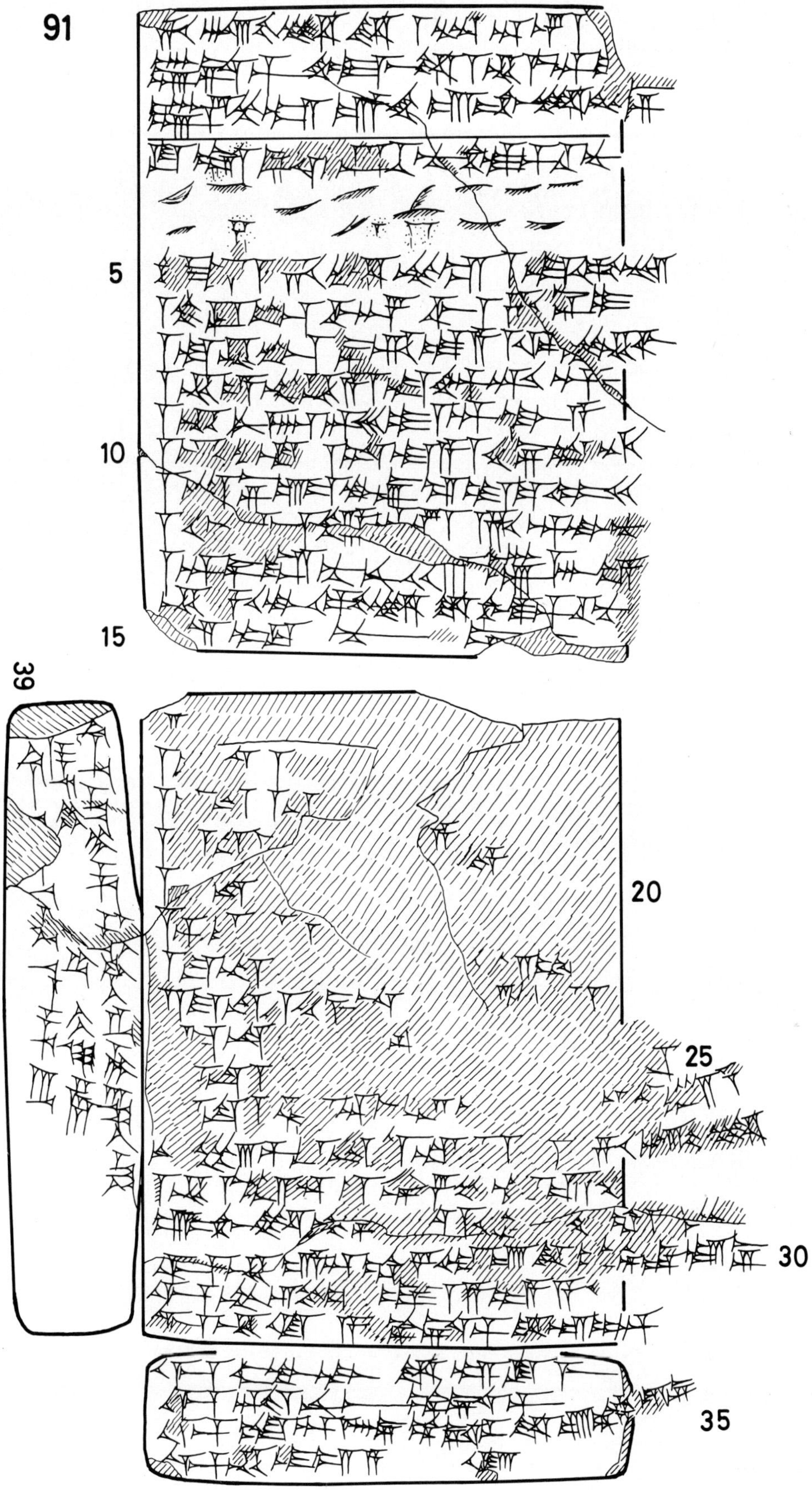

93

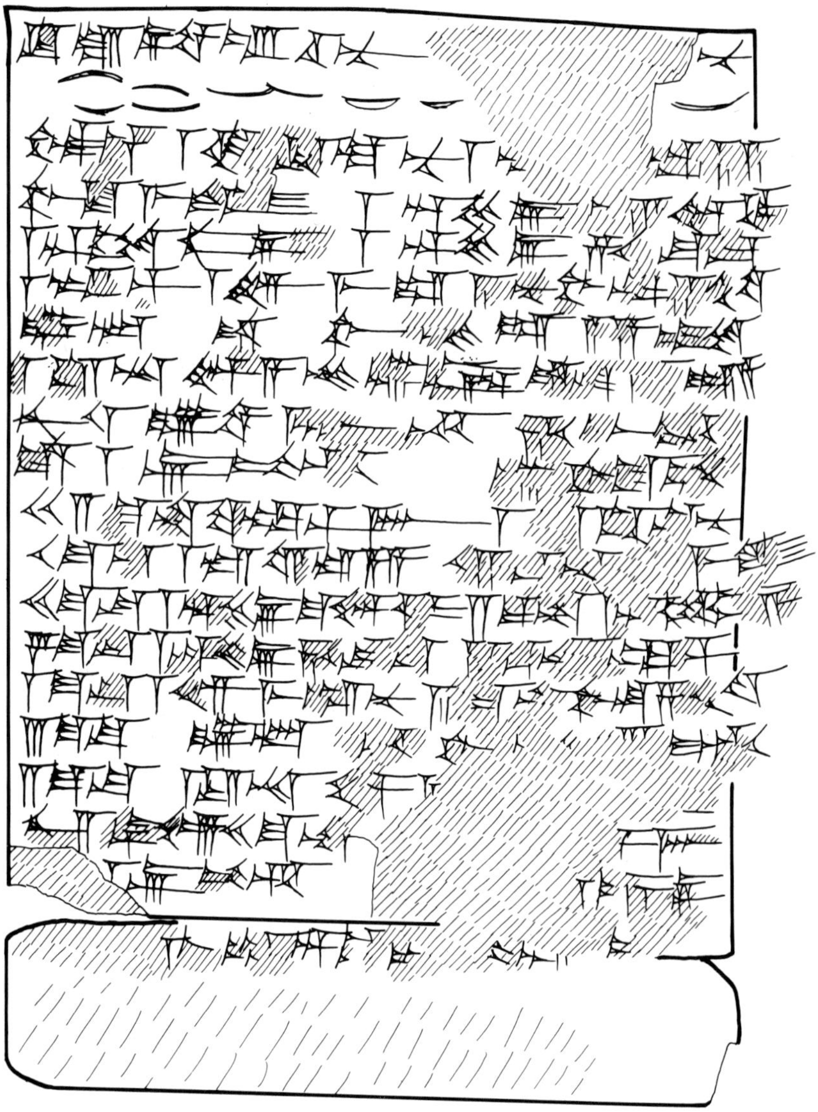

rev

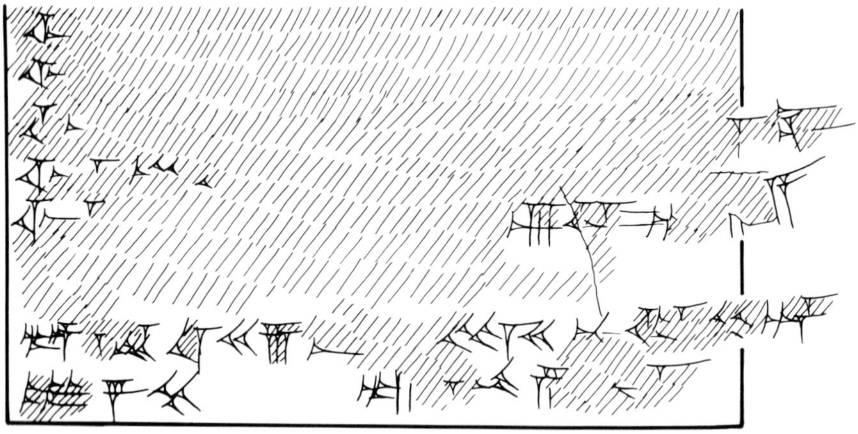

92

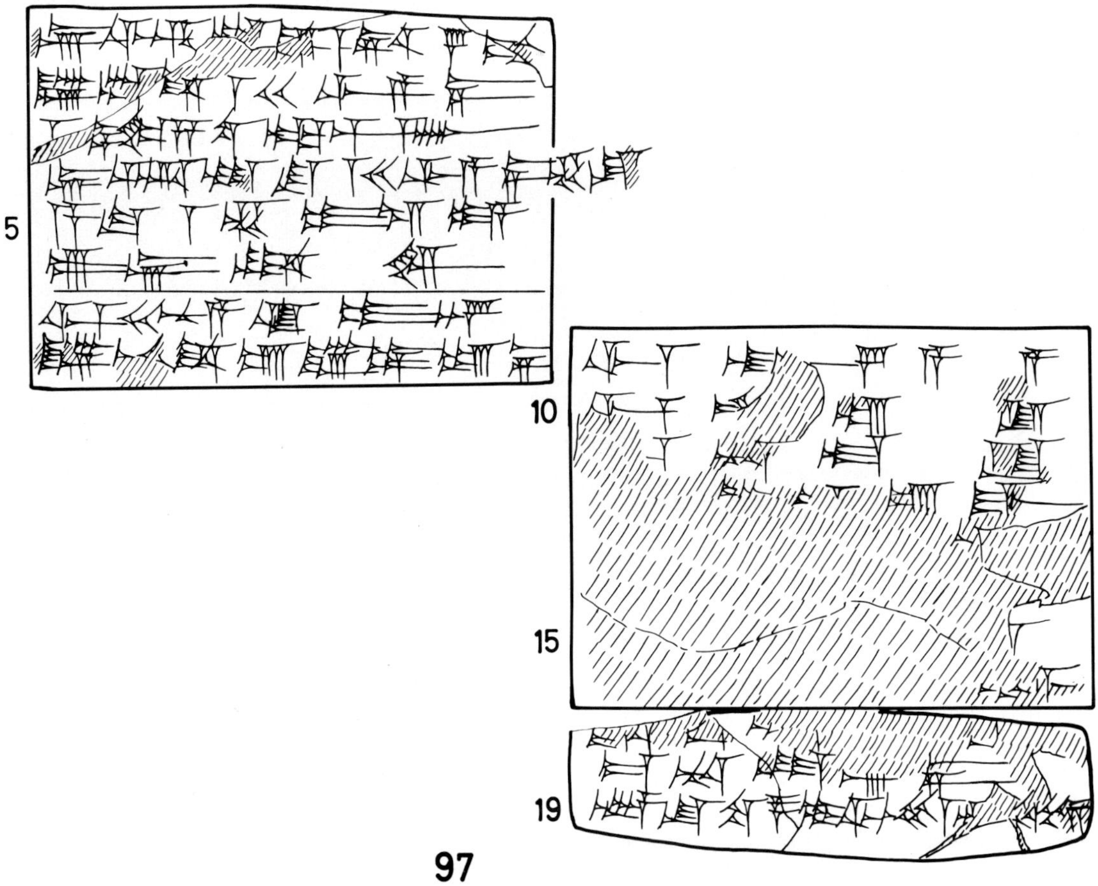

97

rev

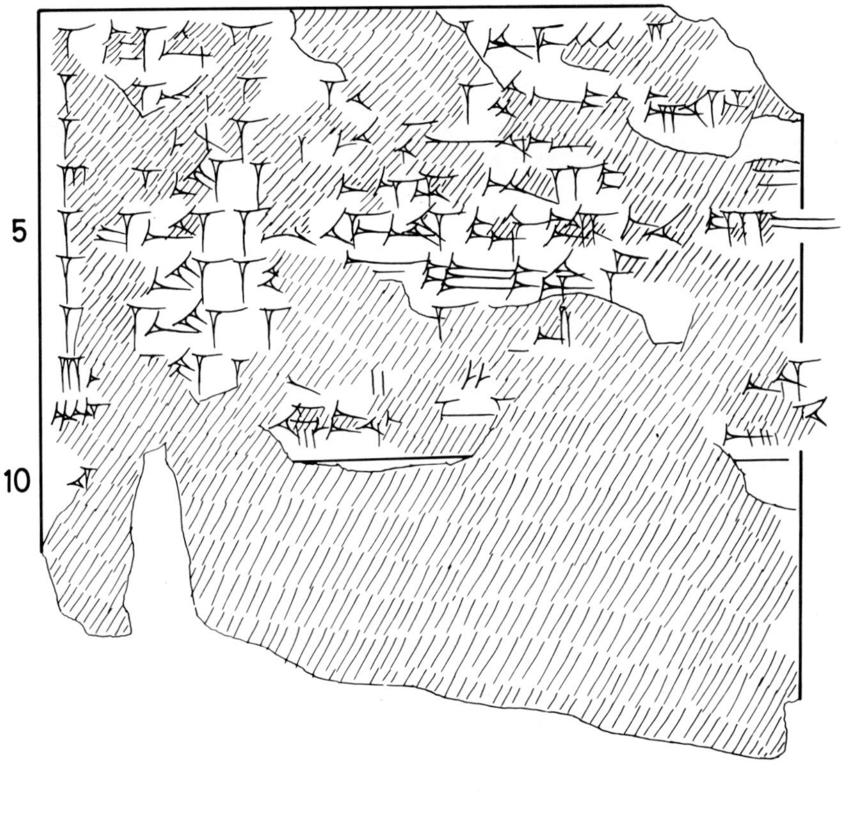

95

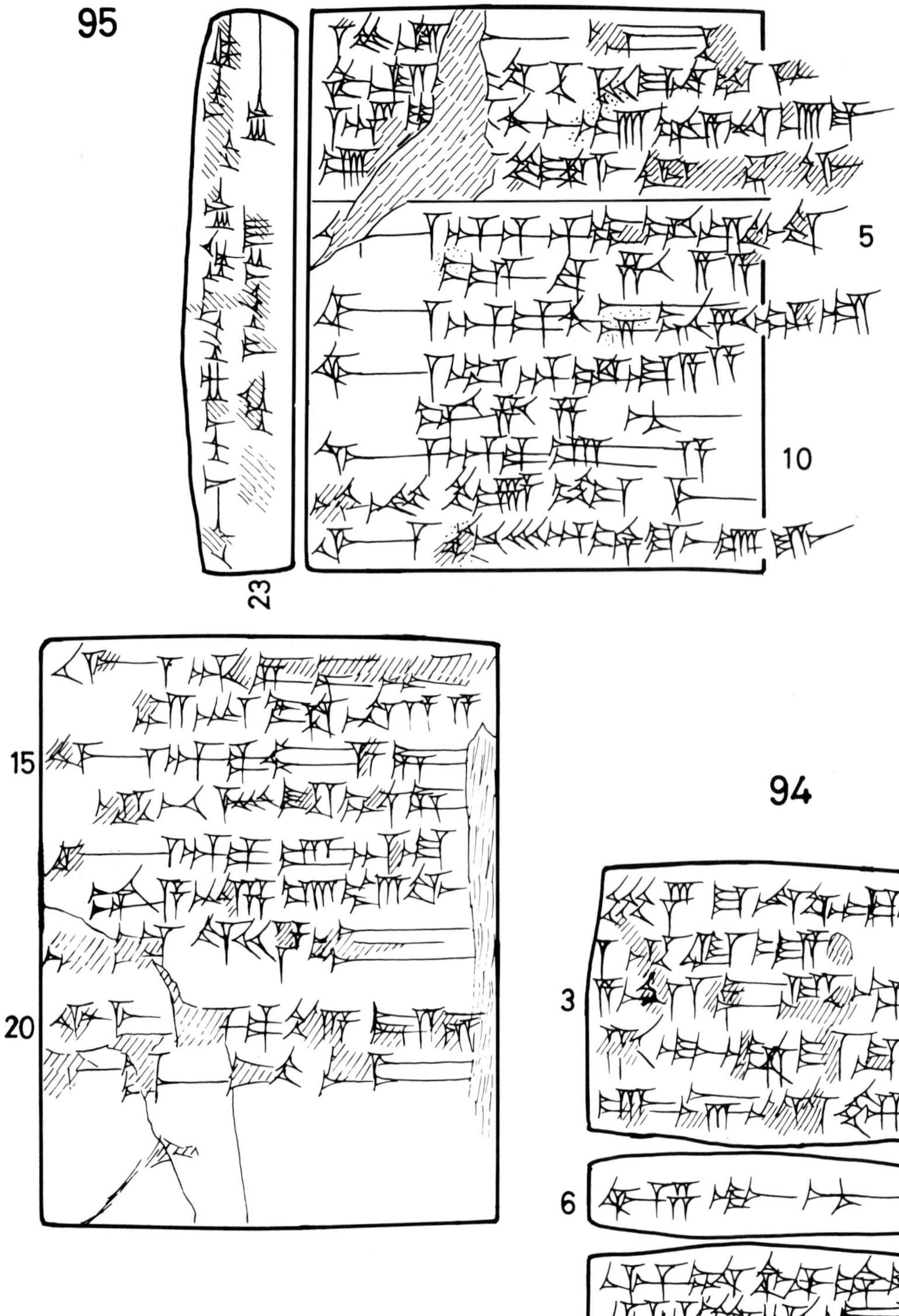

94

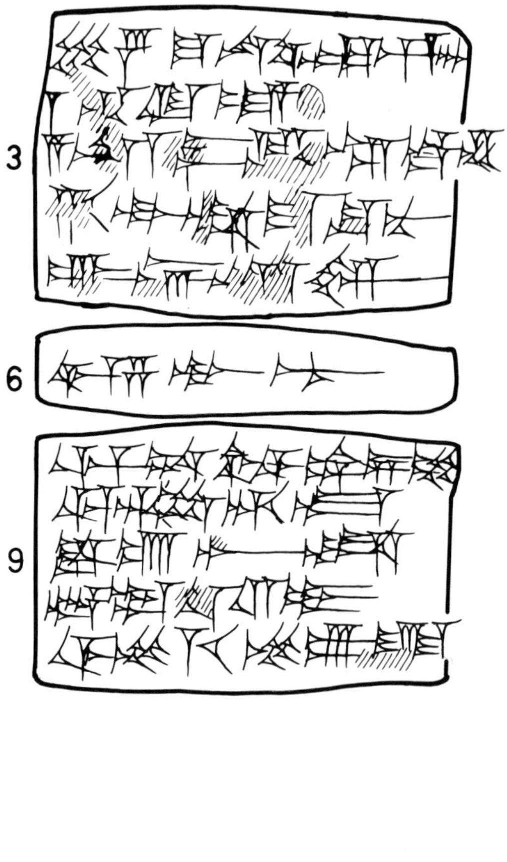

96

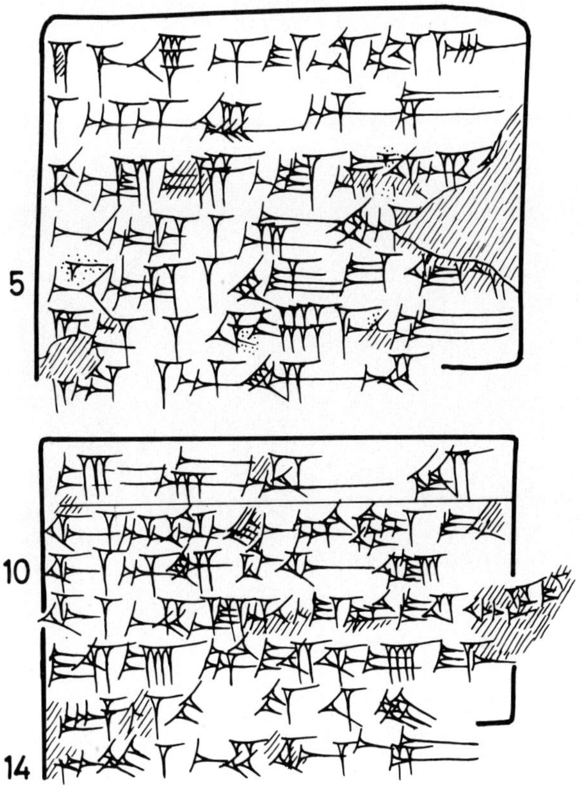

99

env.

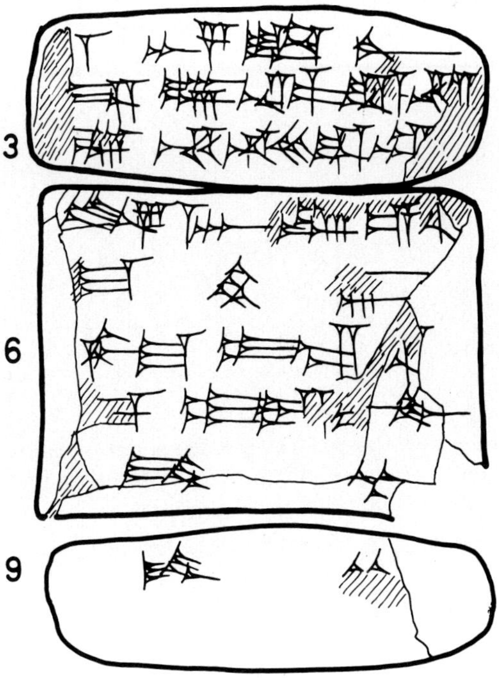

102

rev

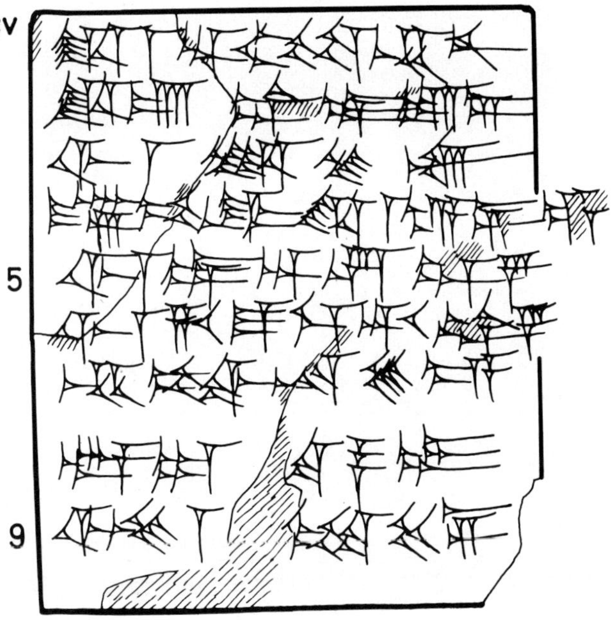

101

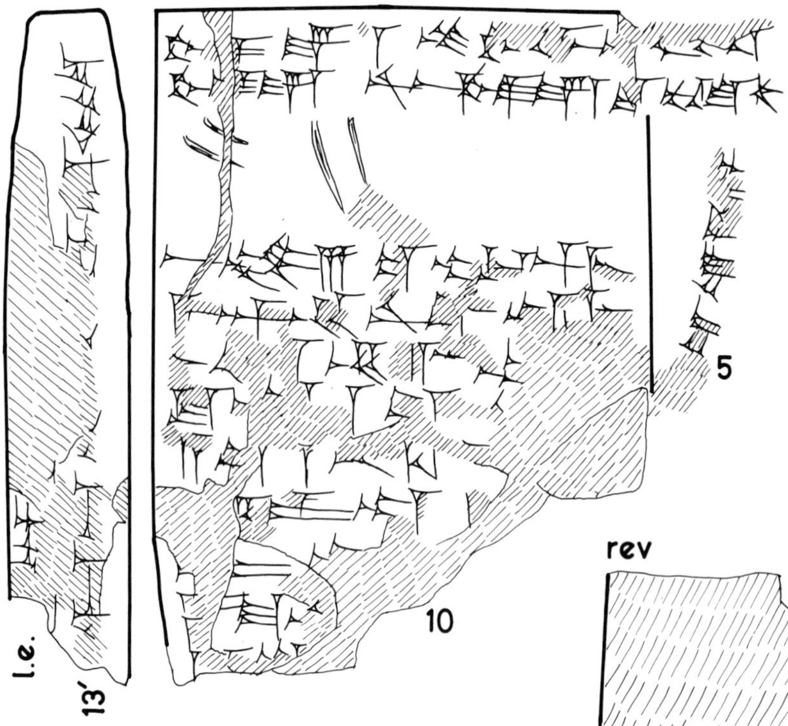

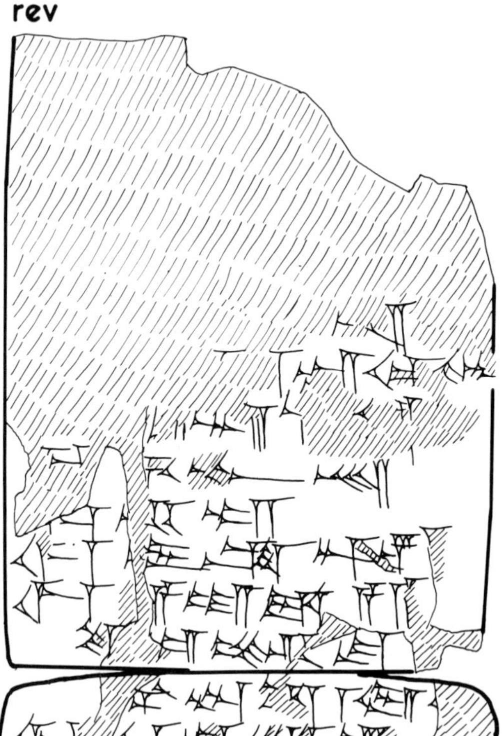

98

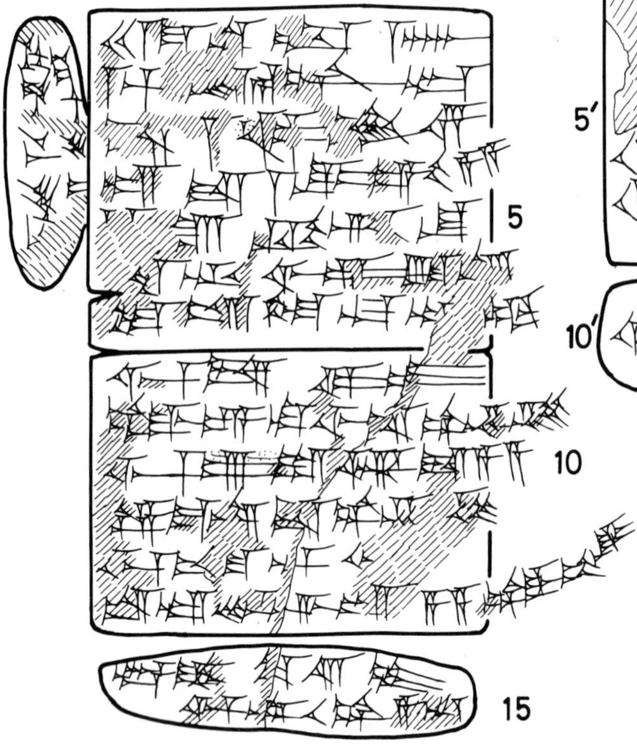

100

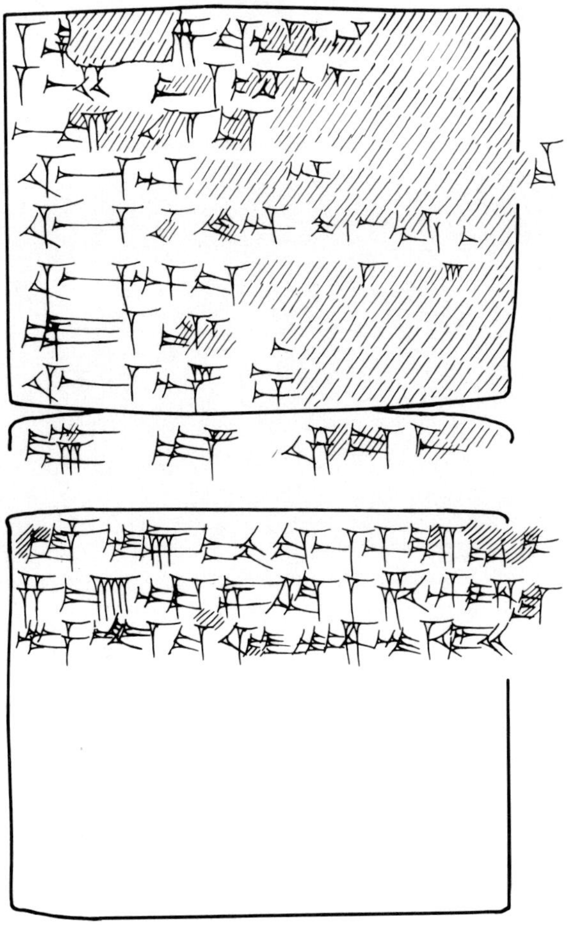

104

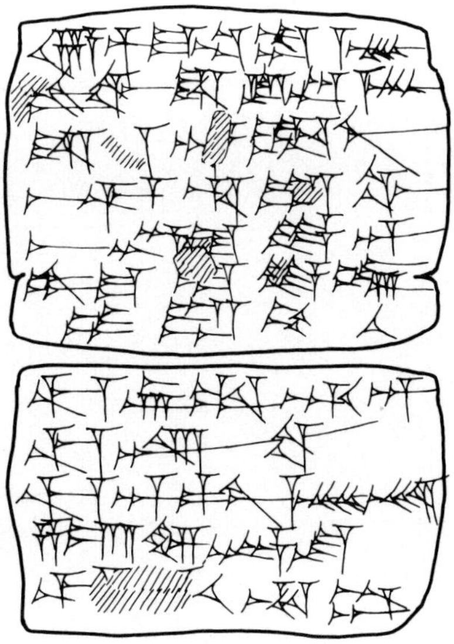

103

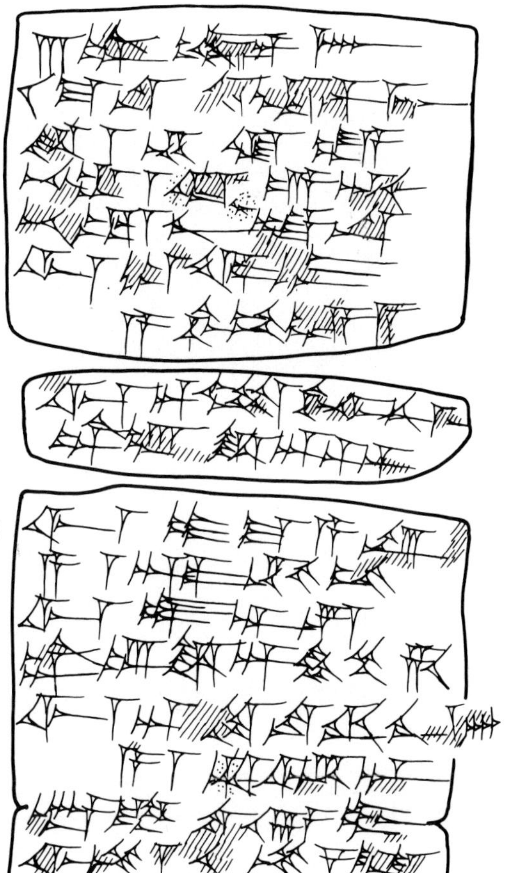

107

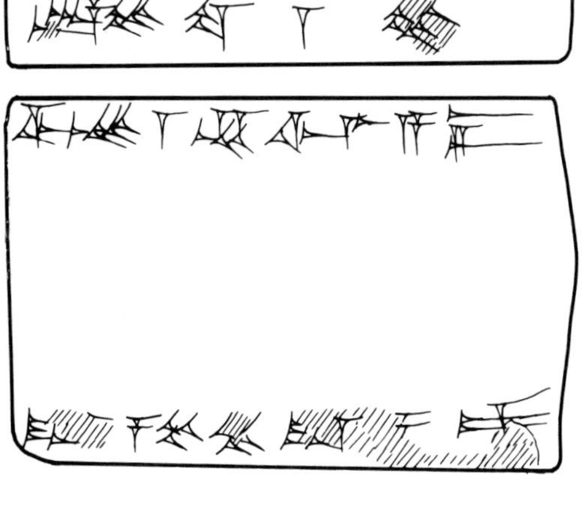

106

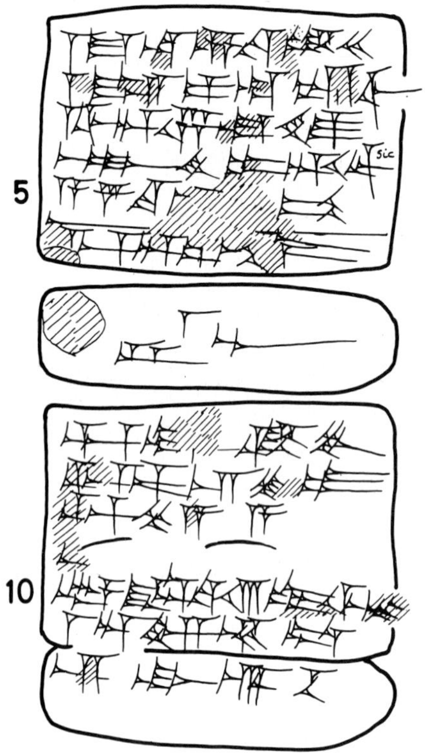

108

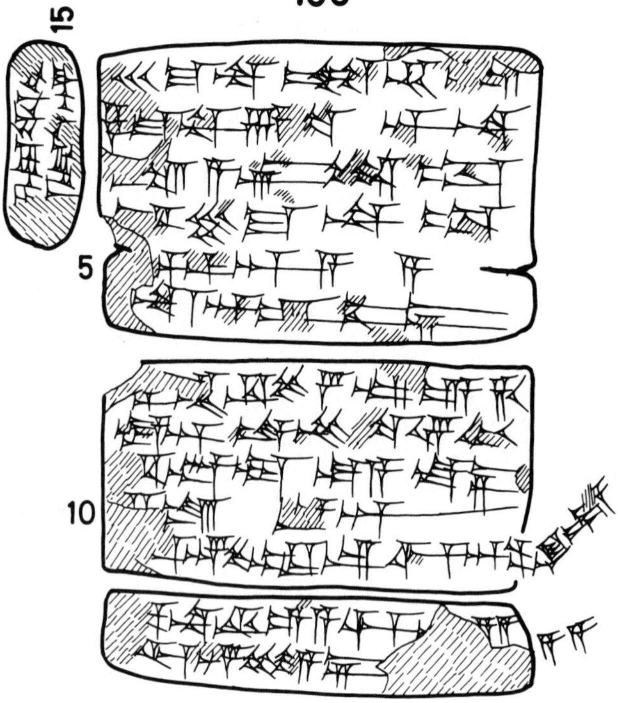

110

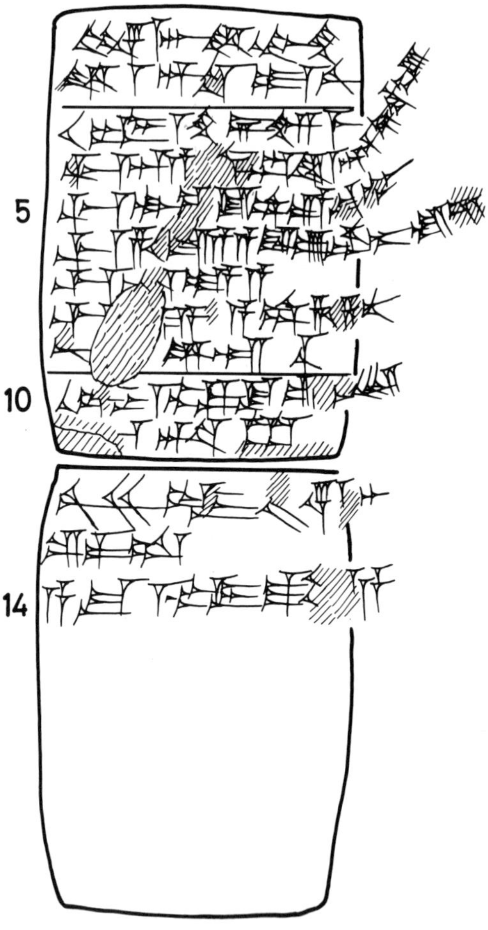

109

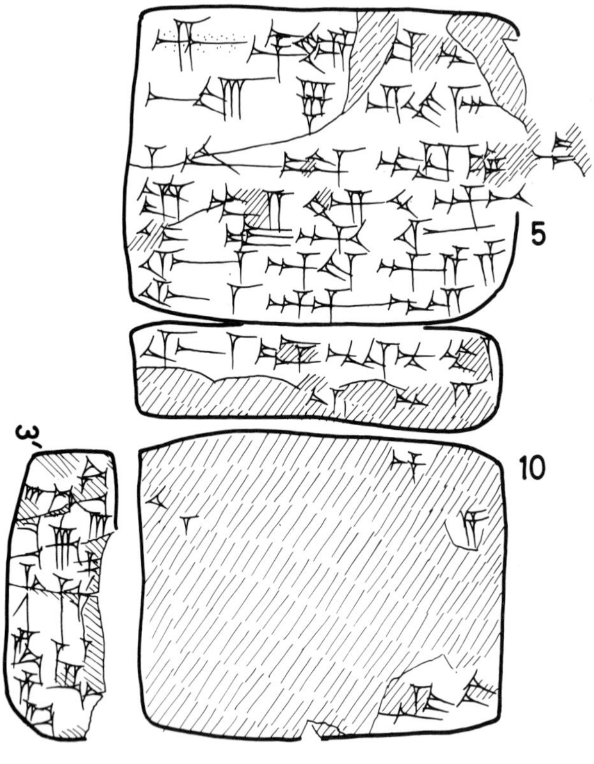

113

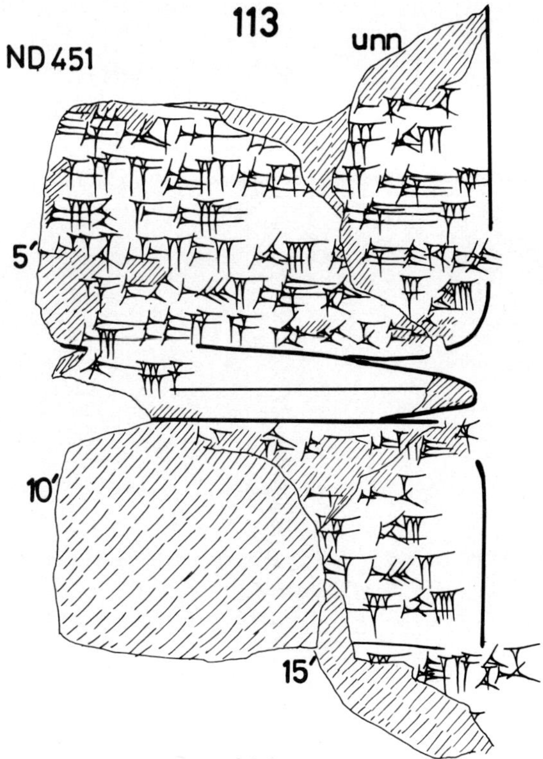

112

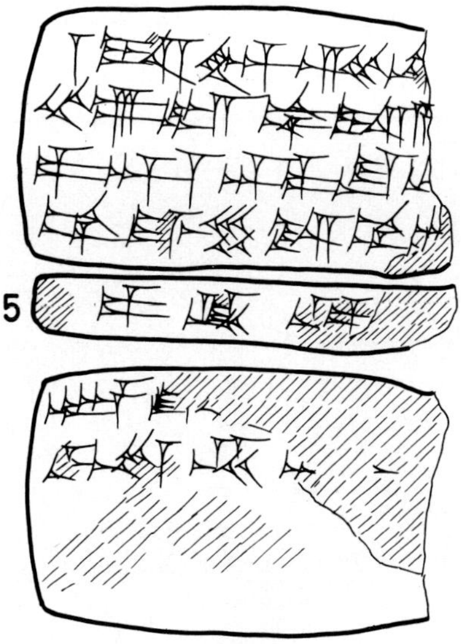

115

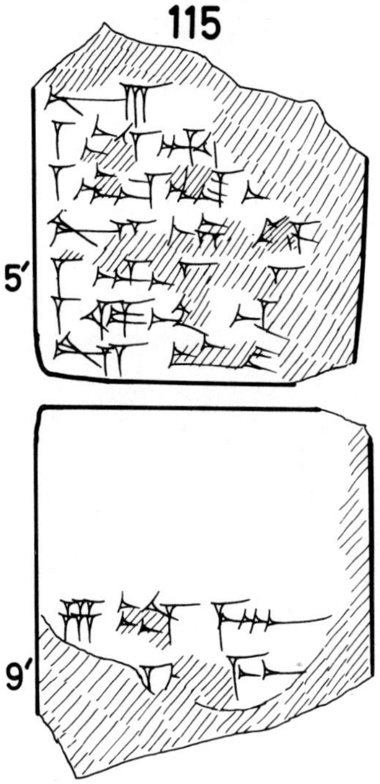

114

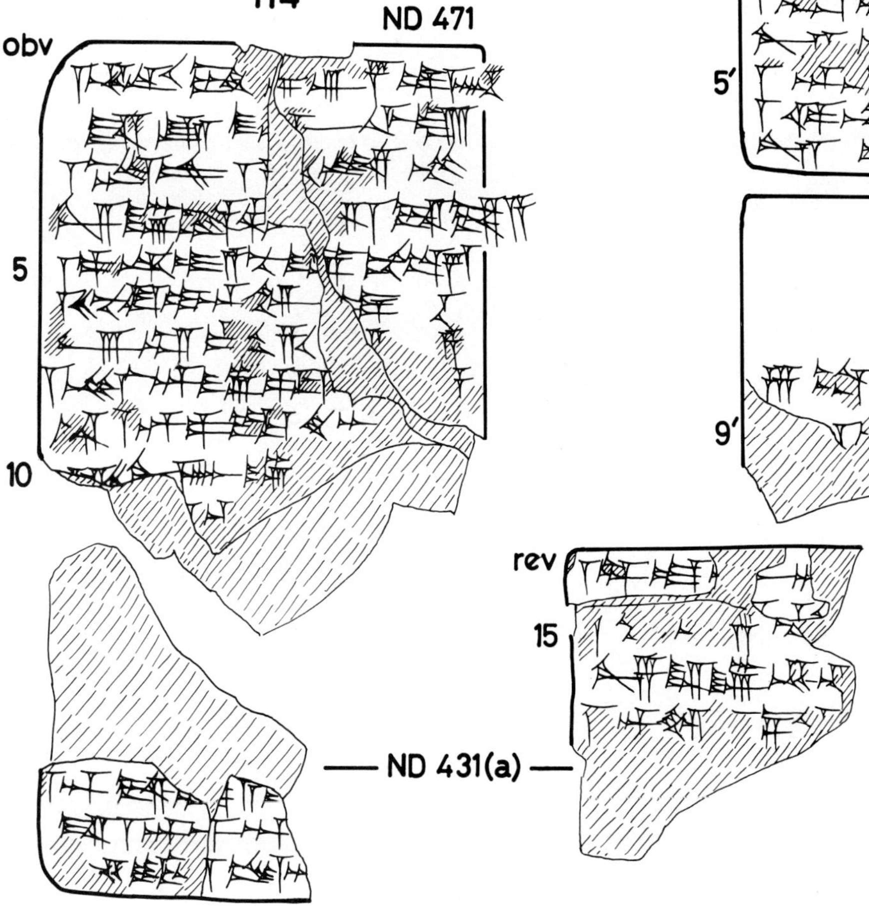

116

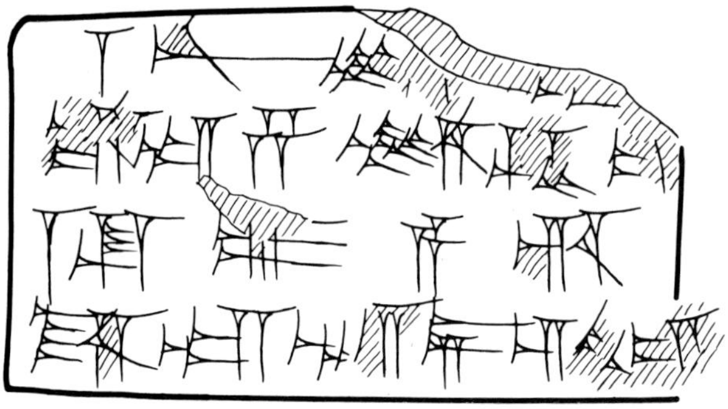

117

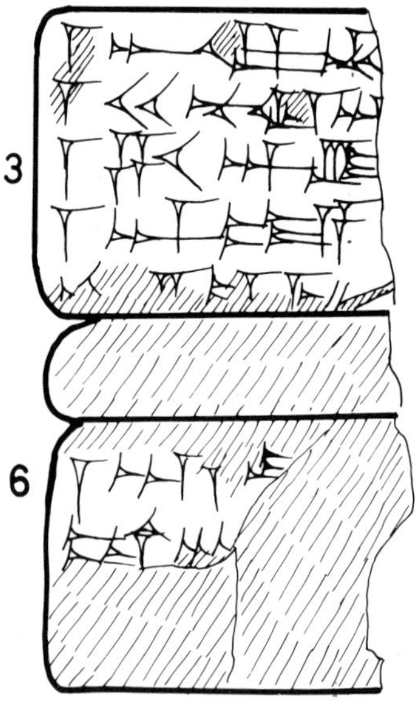

118

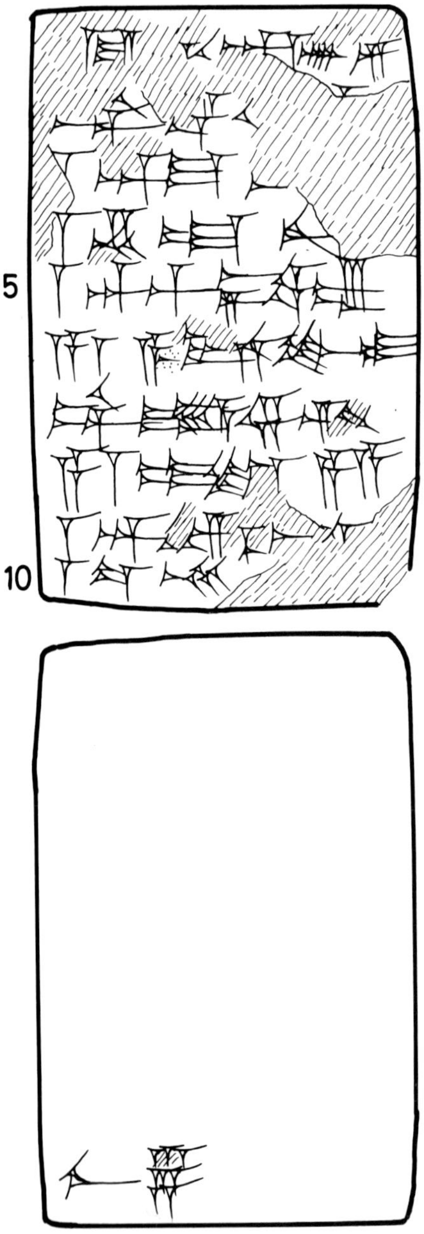

122

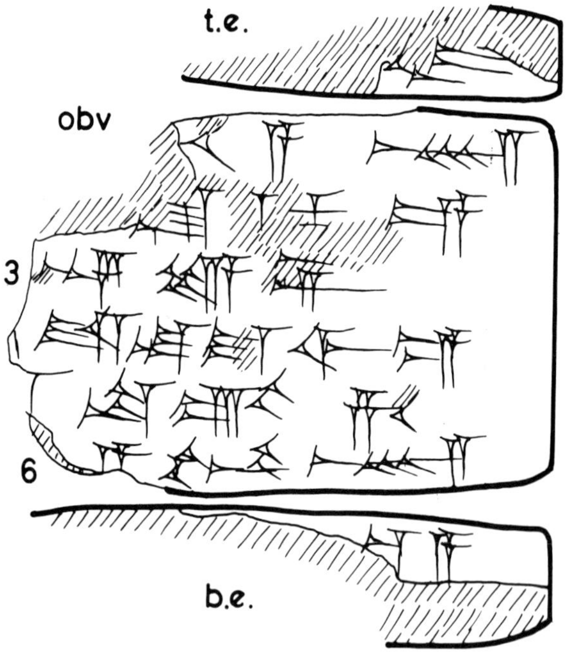

124

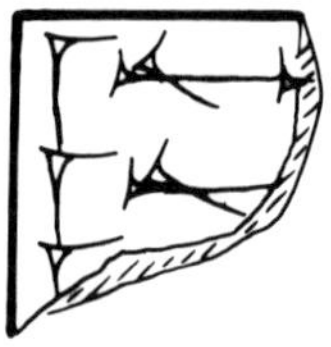

119

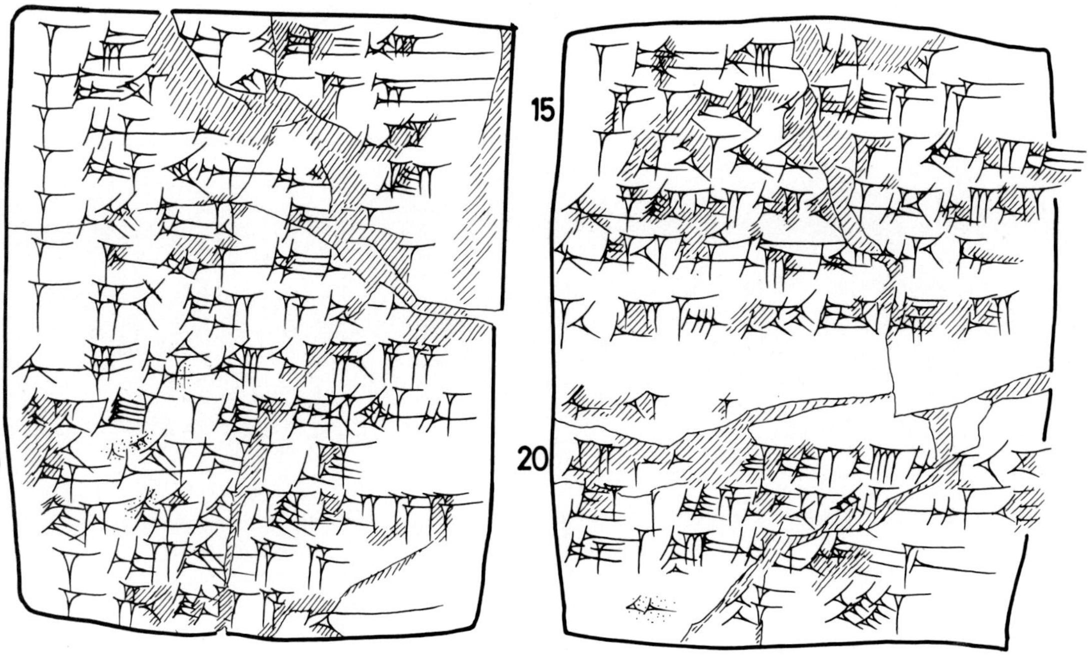

120

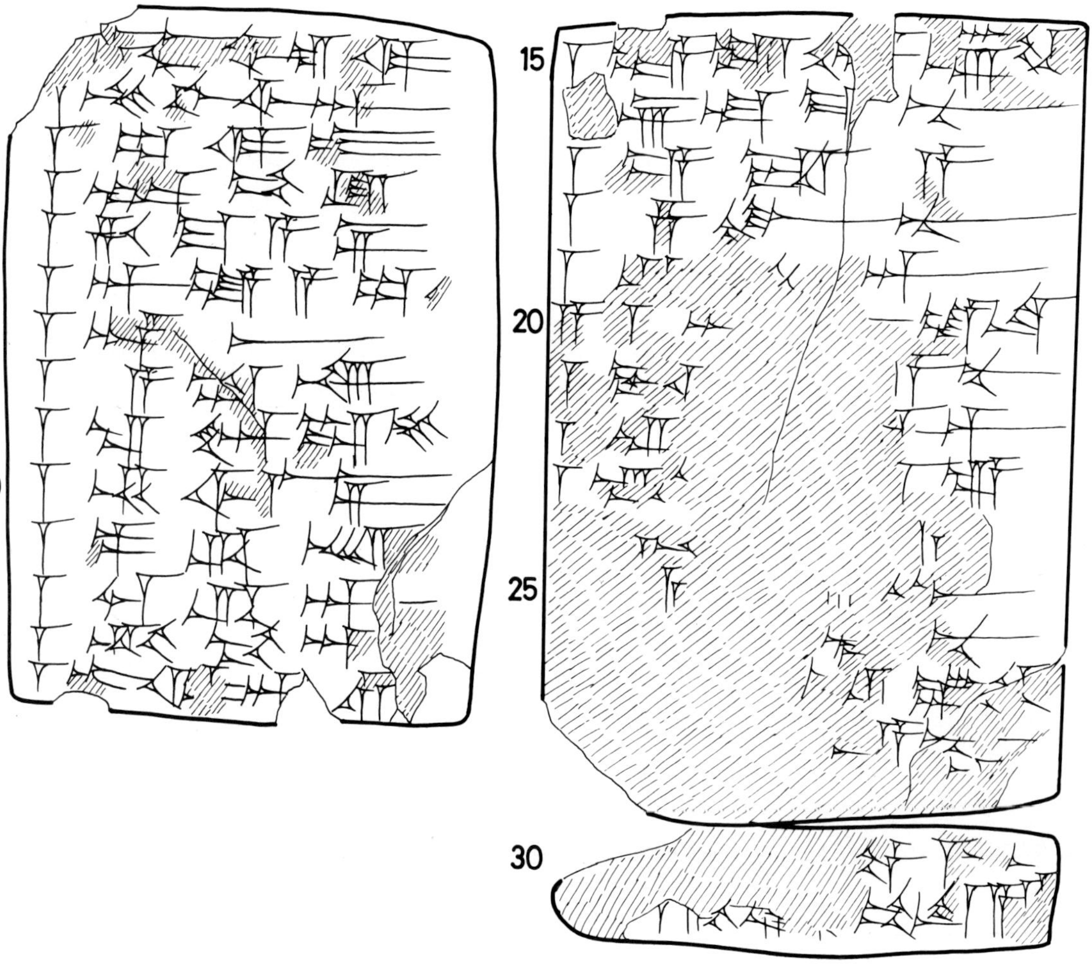

123

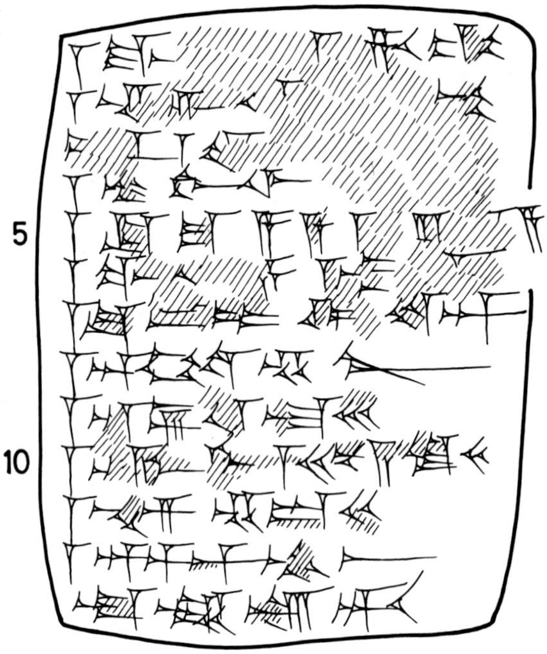

125

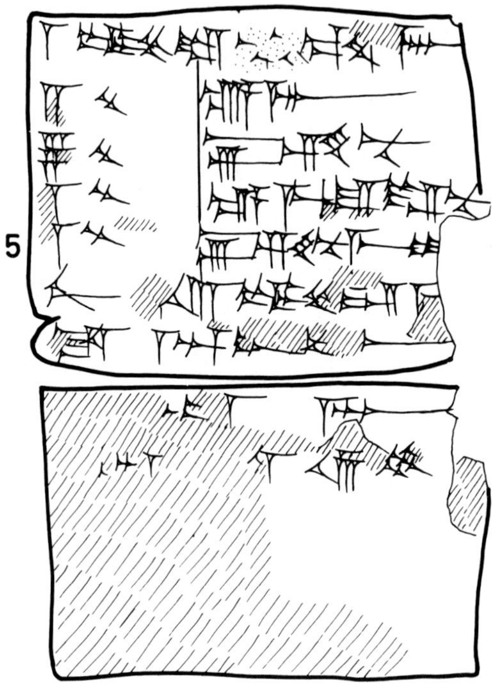

127

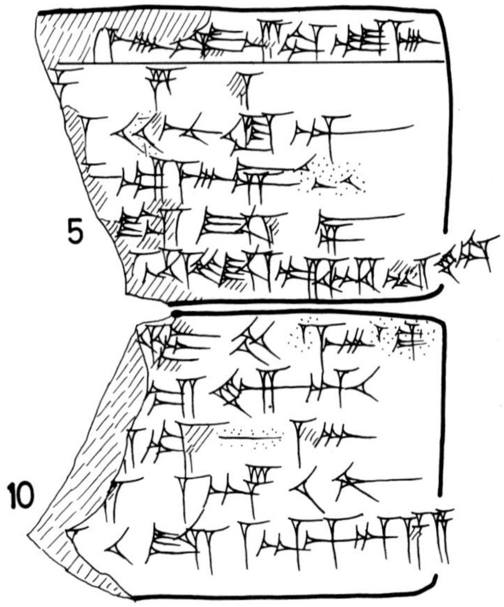

126

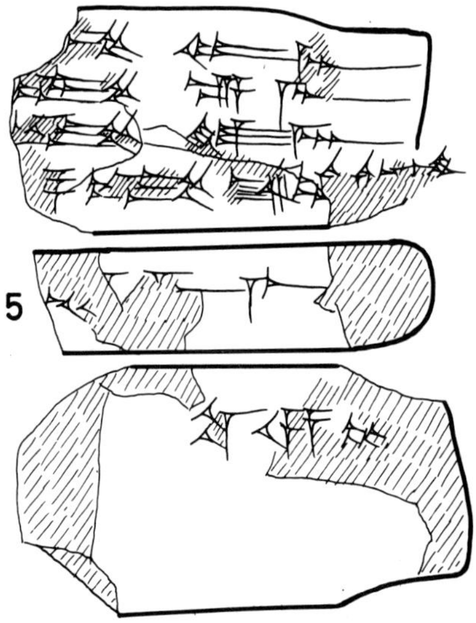

129

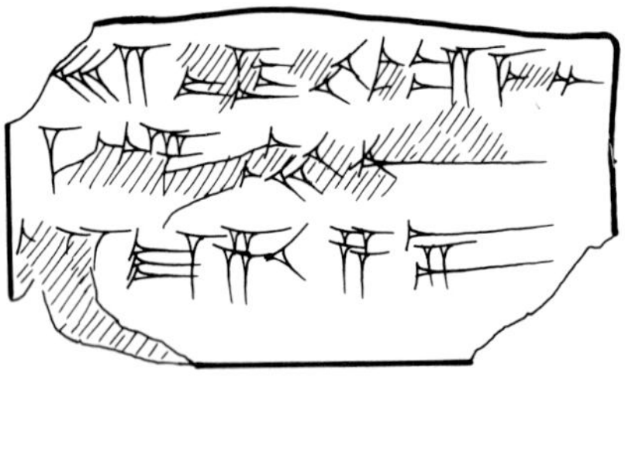

130

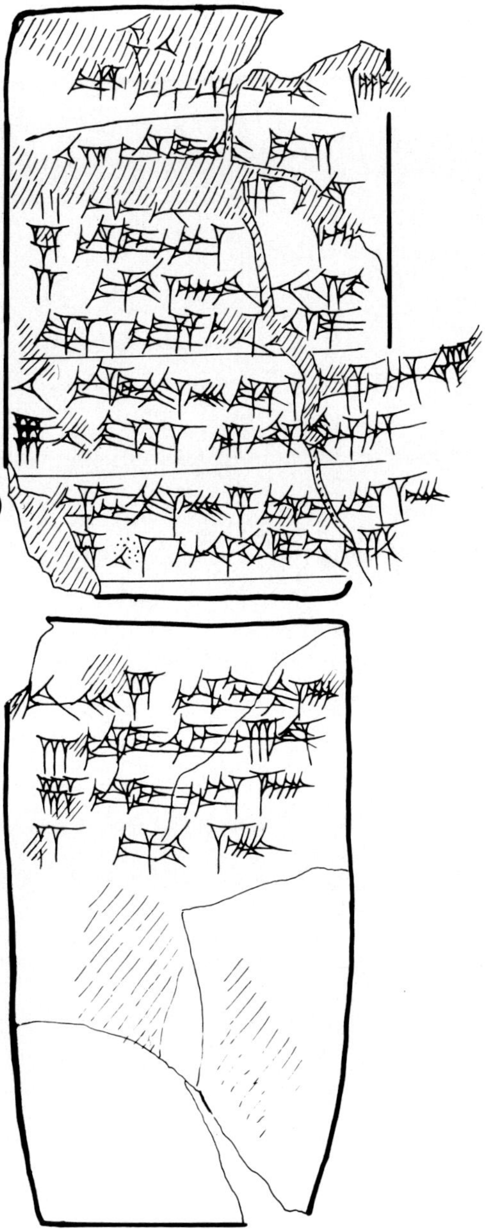

128

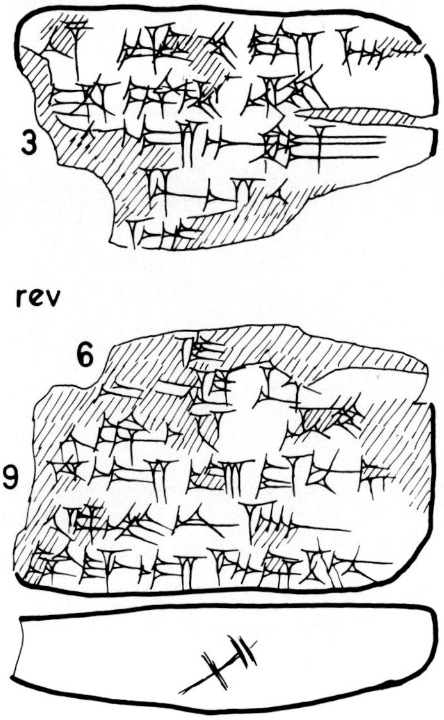

131

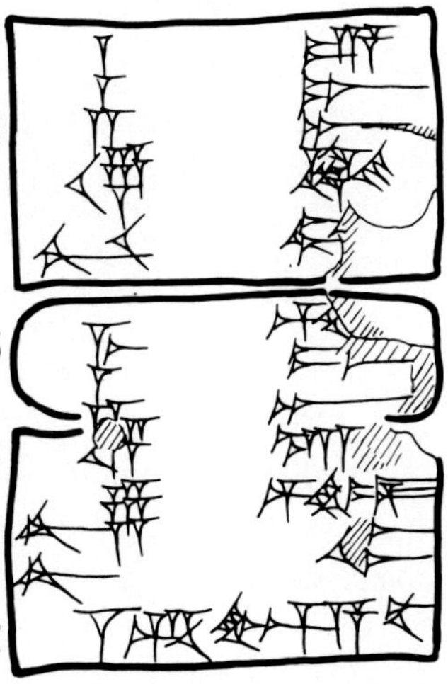

132

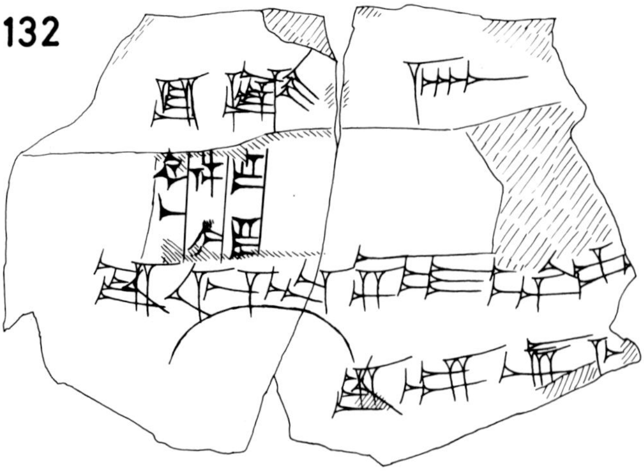

138

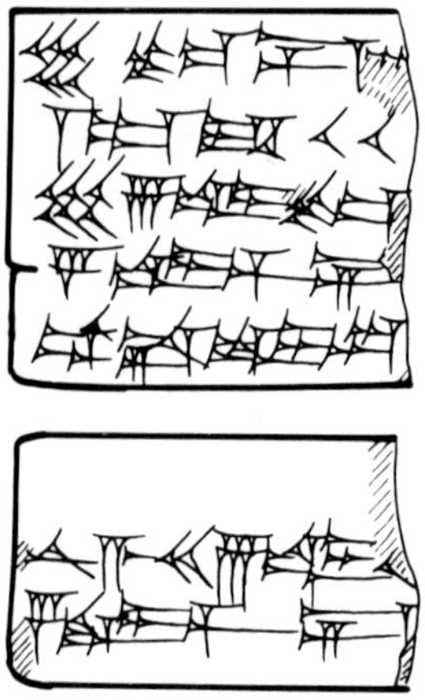

133

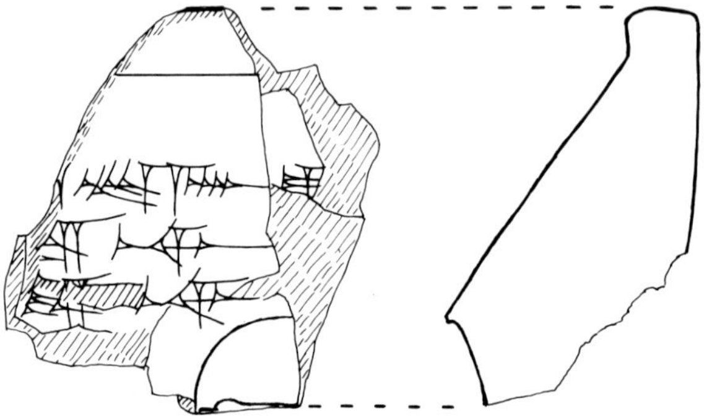

134

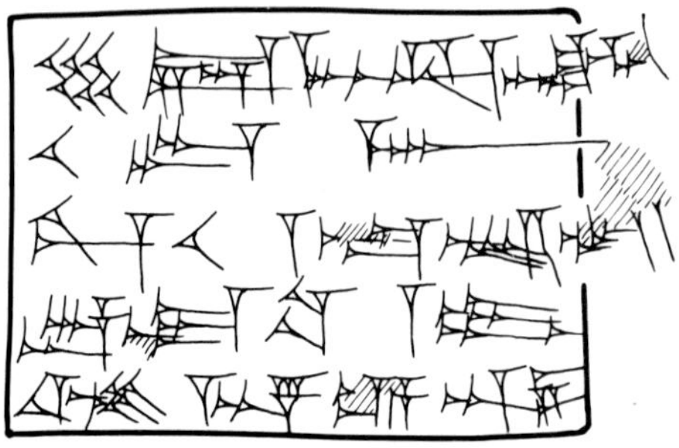

135

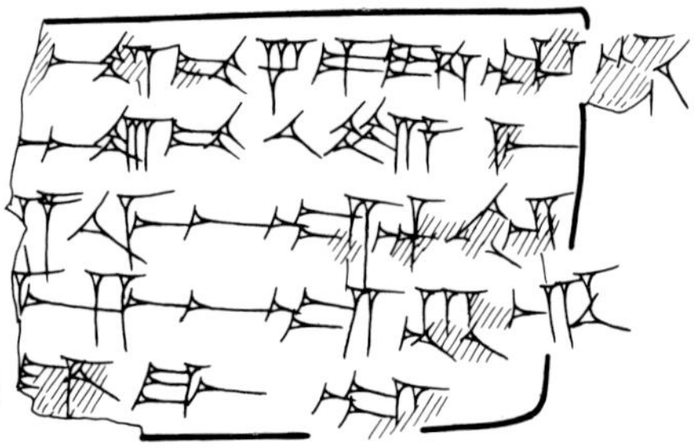

137

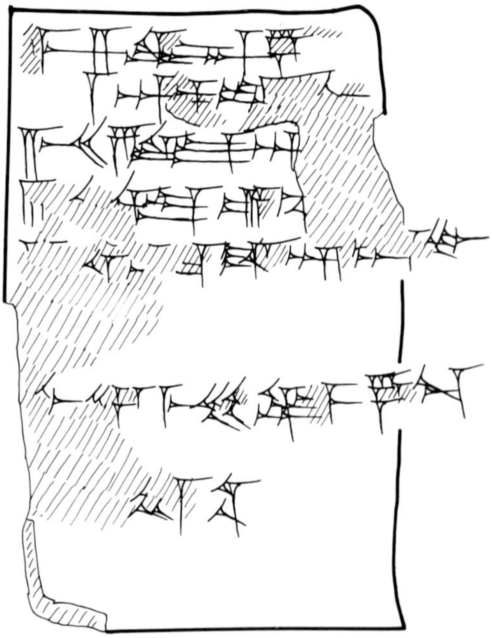

140

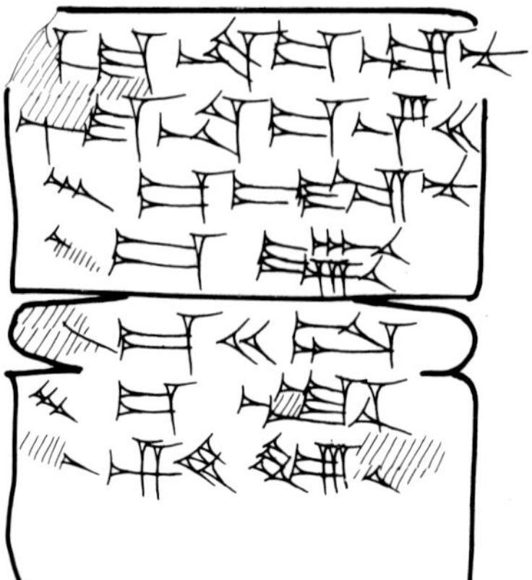

136

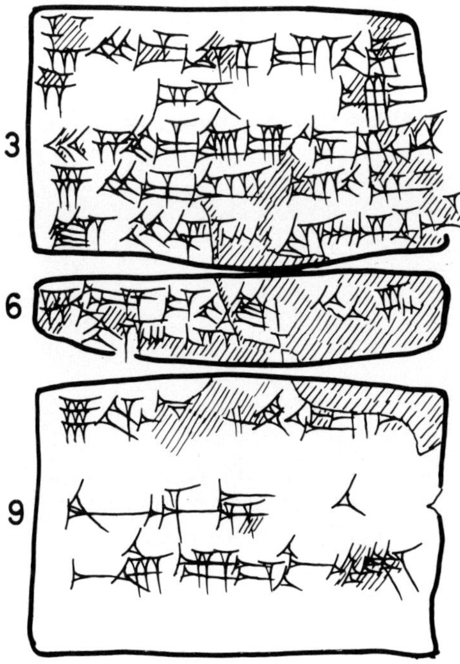

141

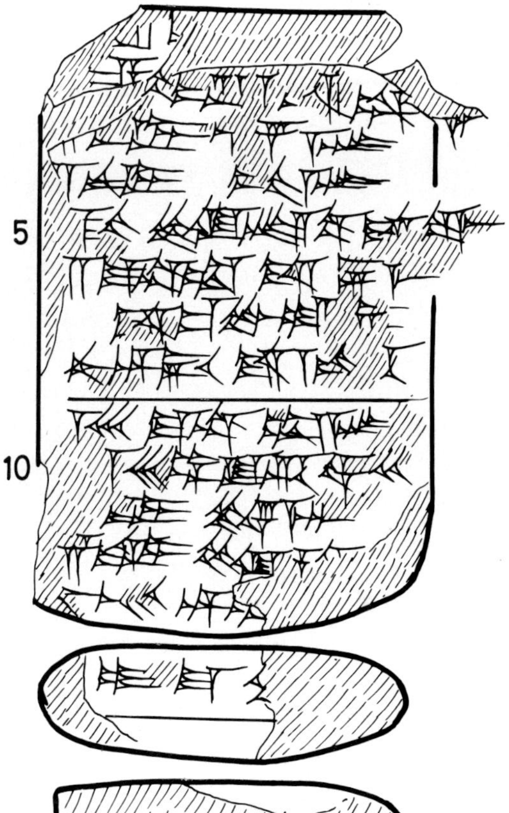

139

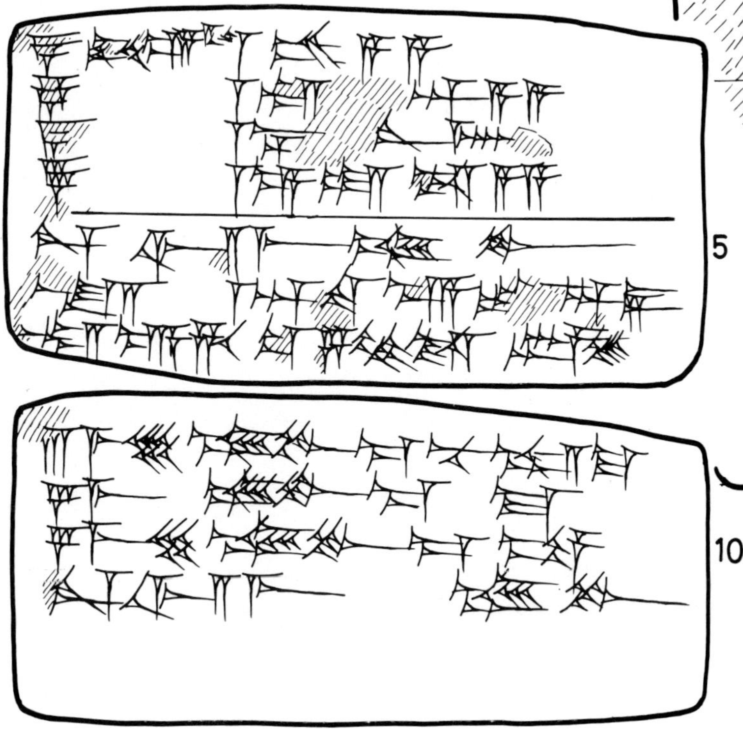

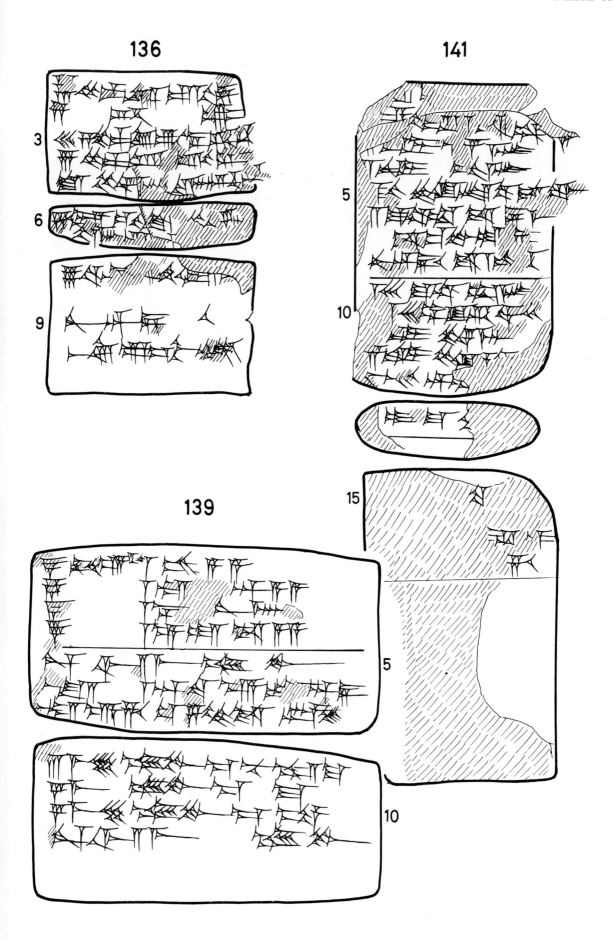

142

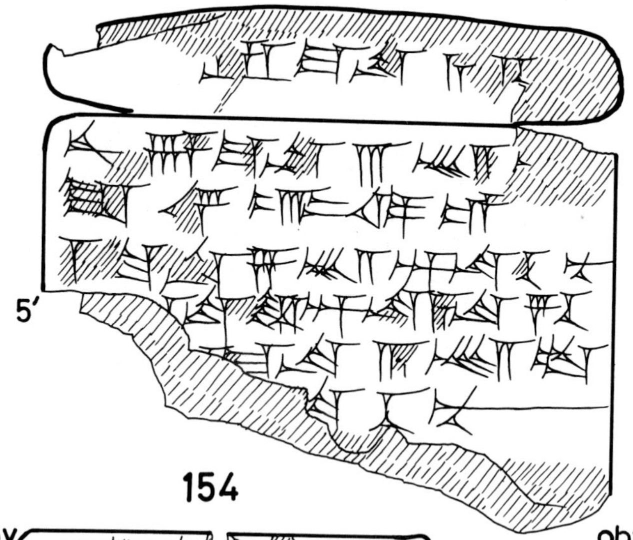

143

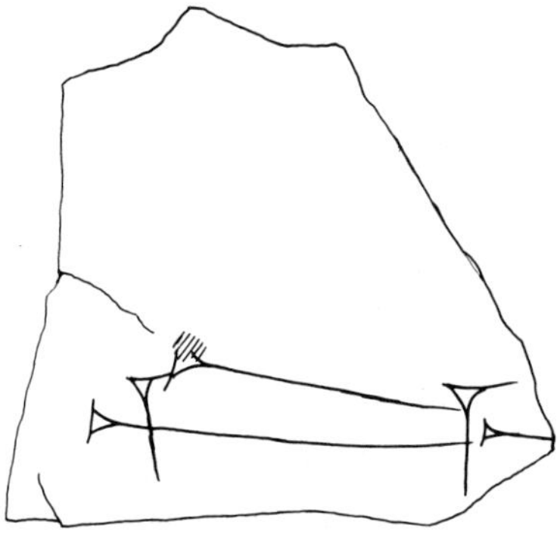

154

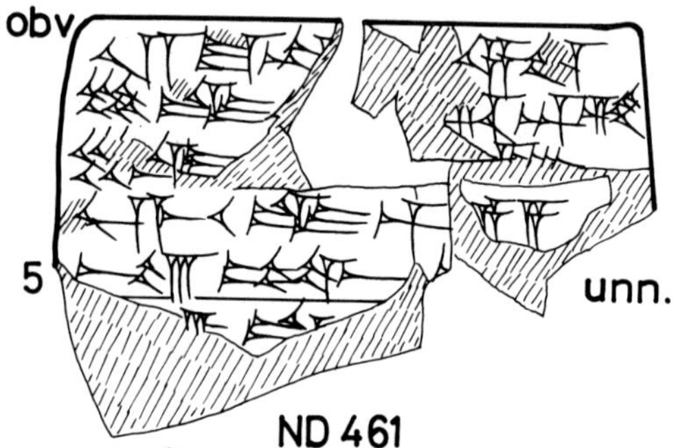

ND 461

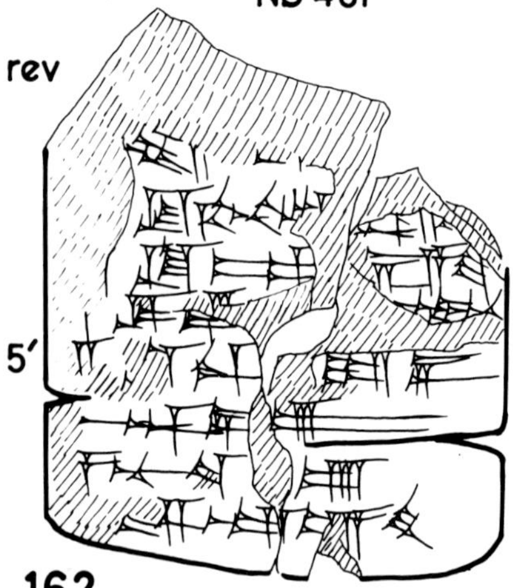

158

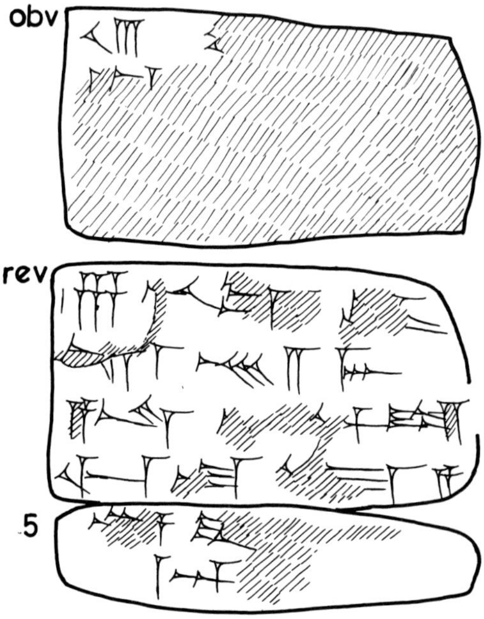

160

162

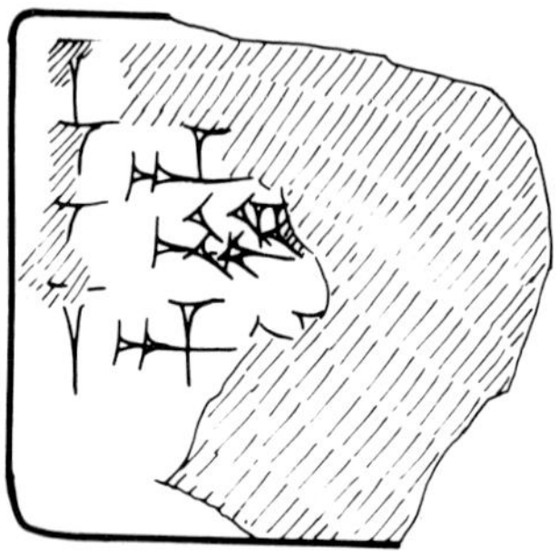

144

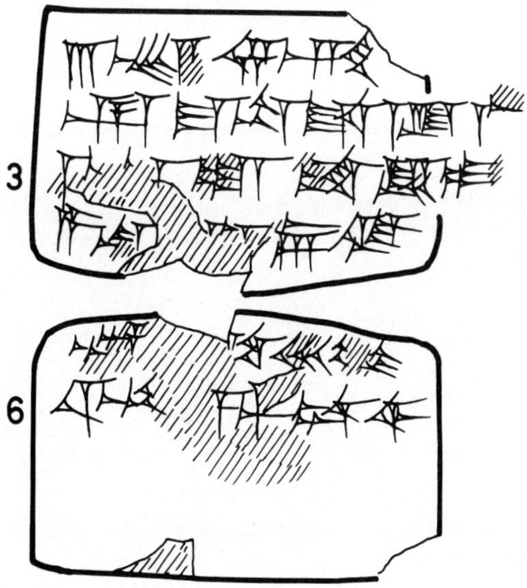

145

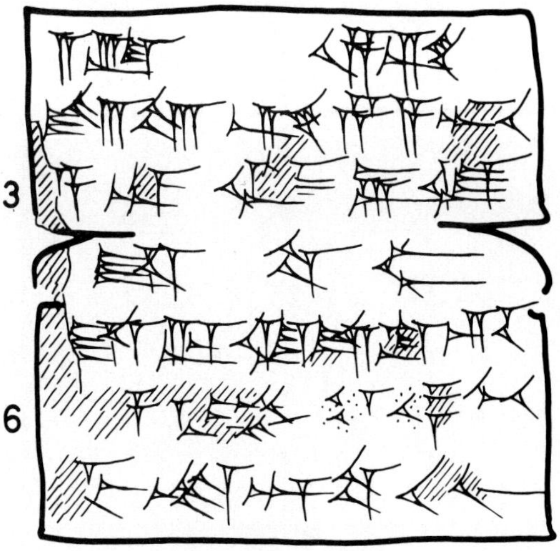

147

148

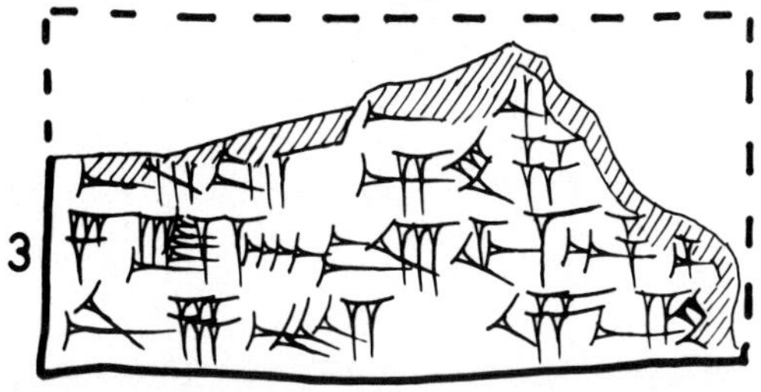

149

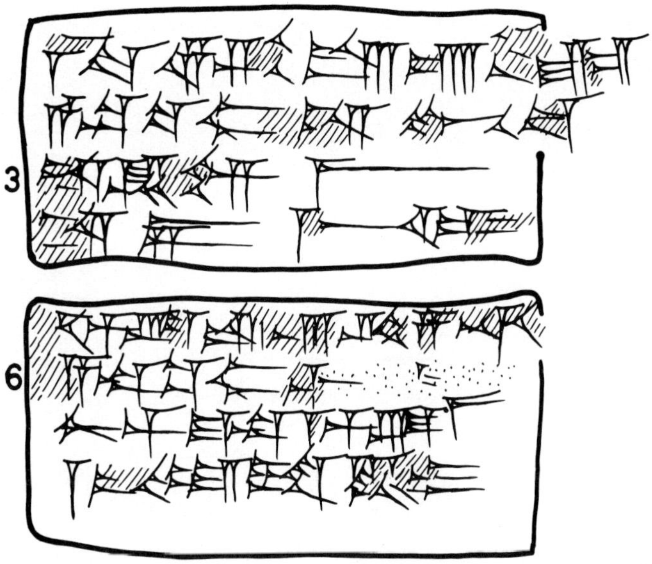

150

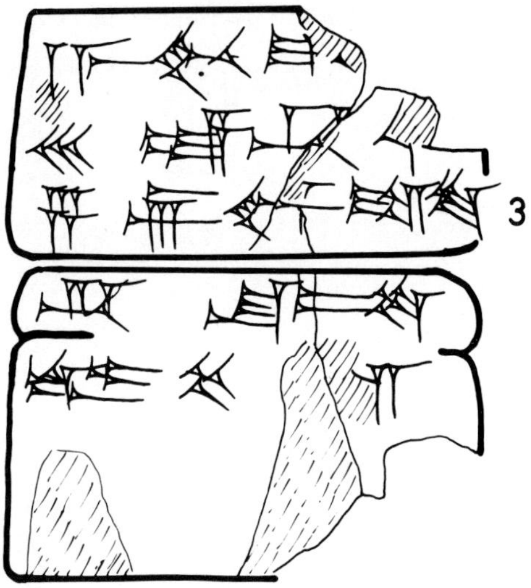

151

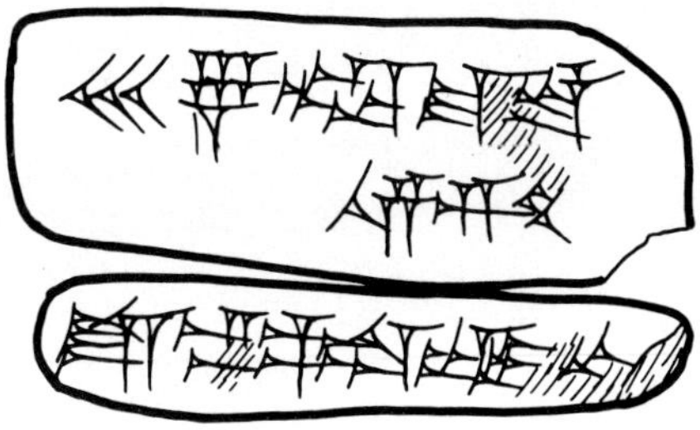

152

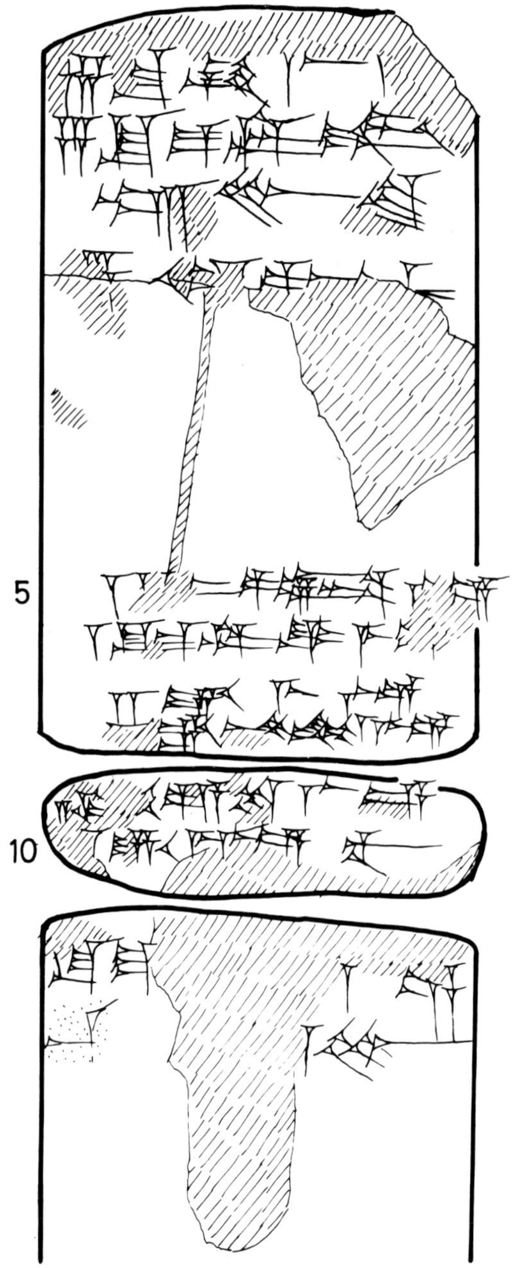

153

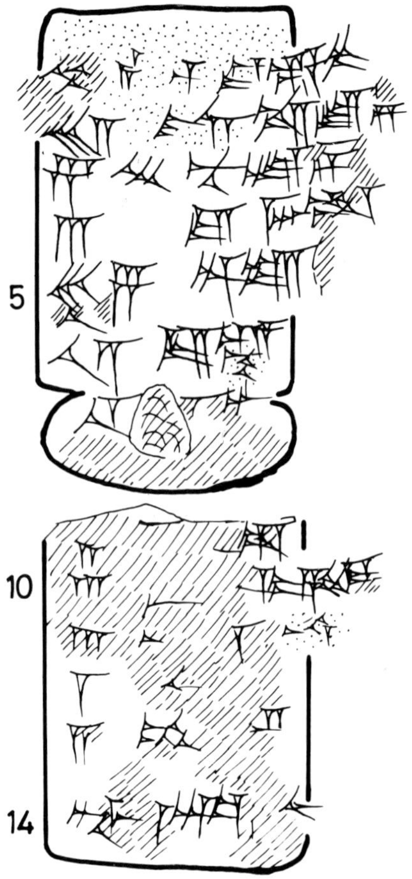

157

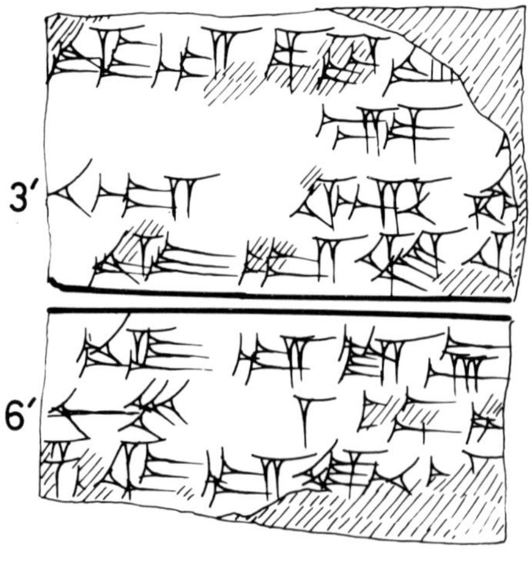

156

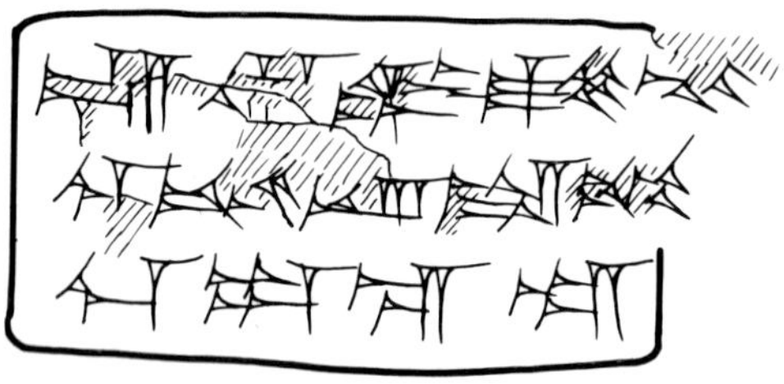

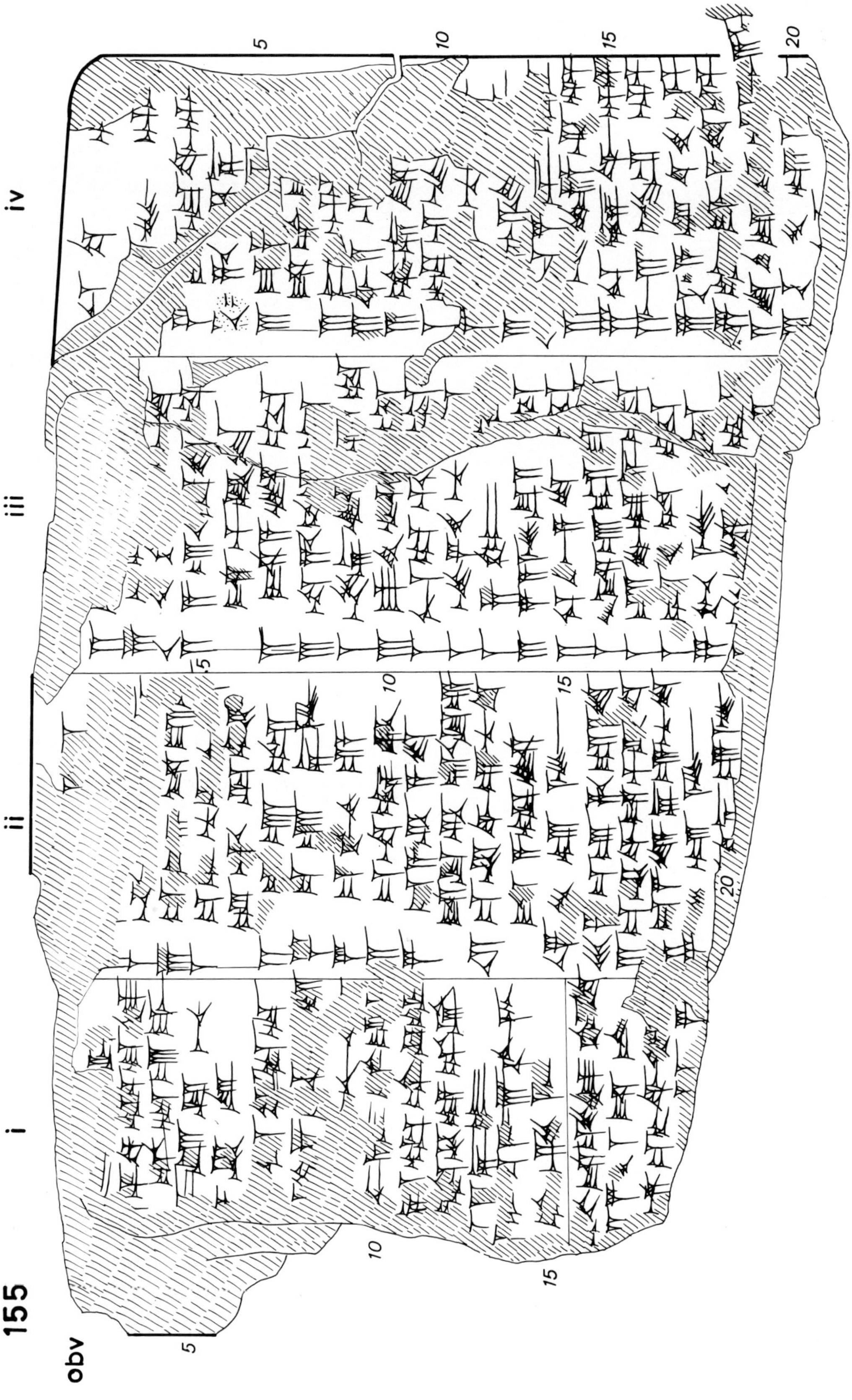
155
obv
i
ii
iii
iv

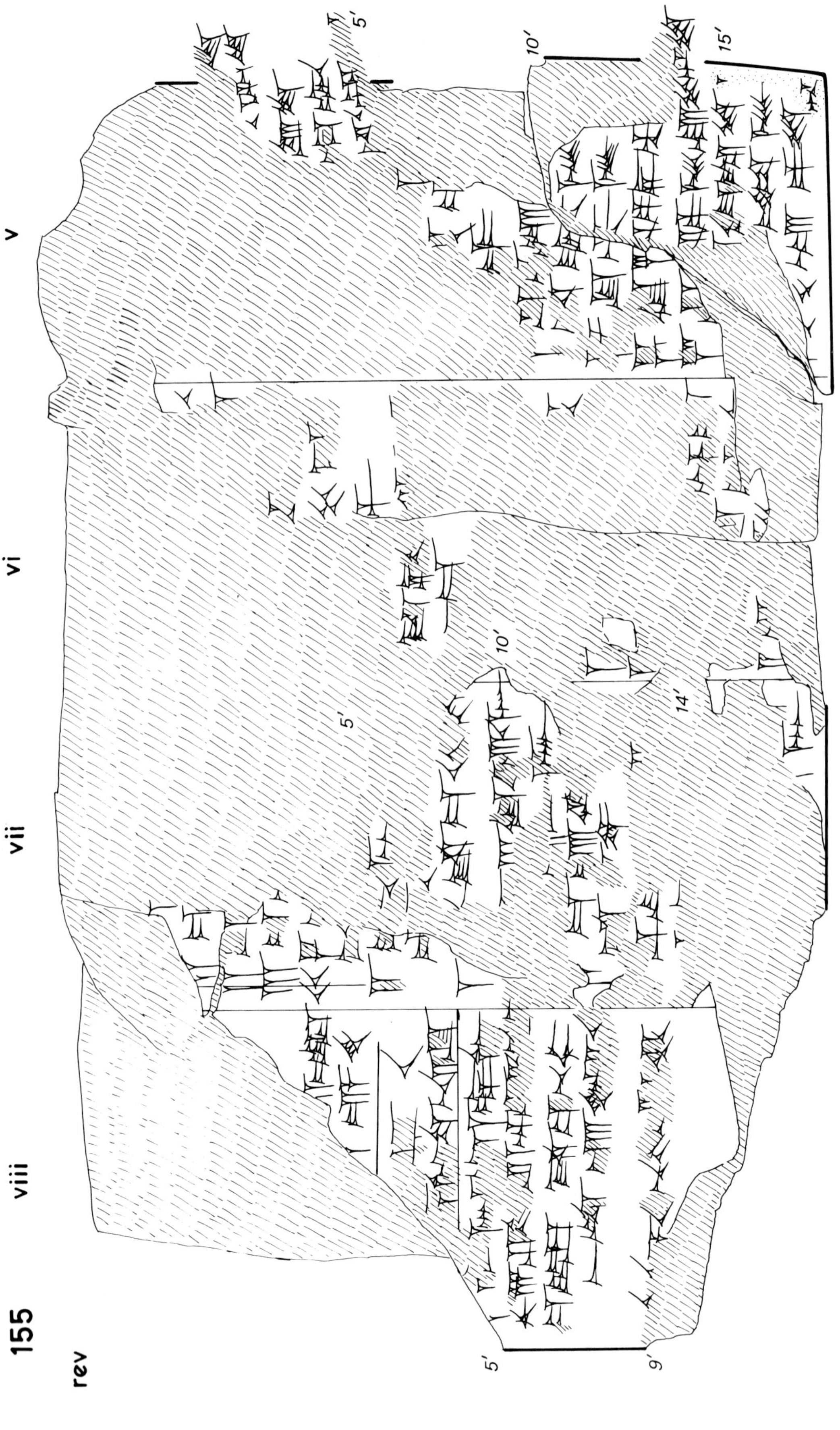

155
rev

161

A

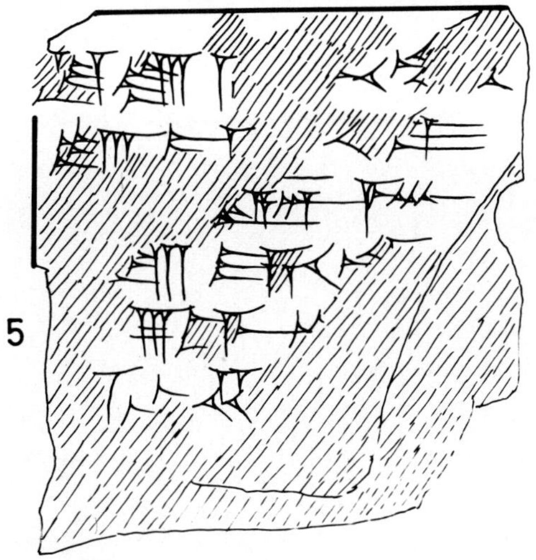

B

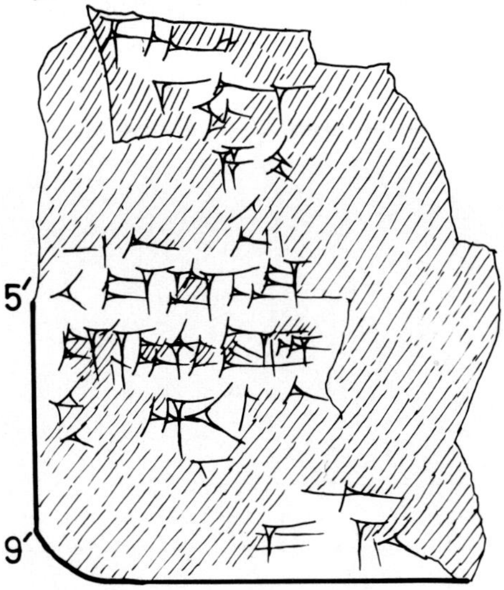

159

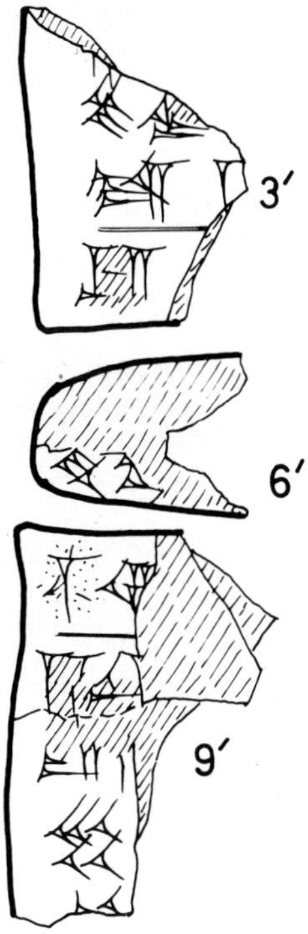

164

166

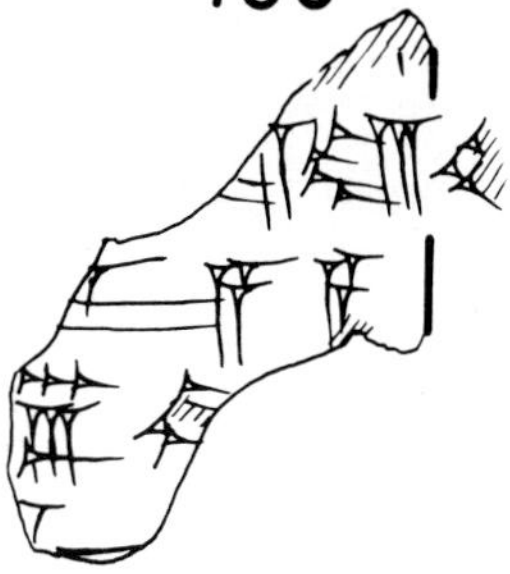

167

168

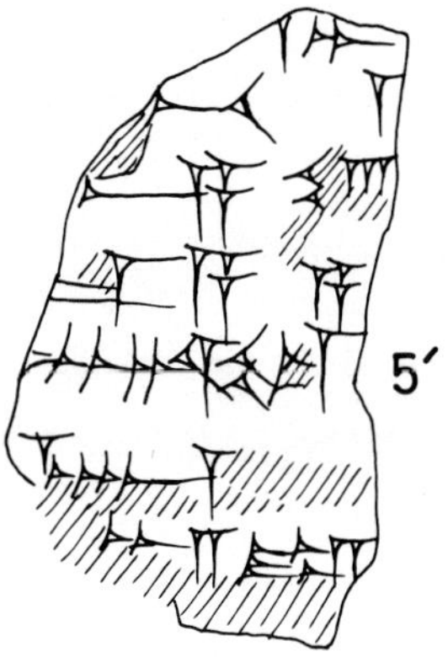

163

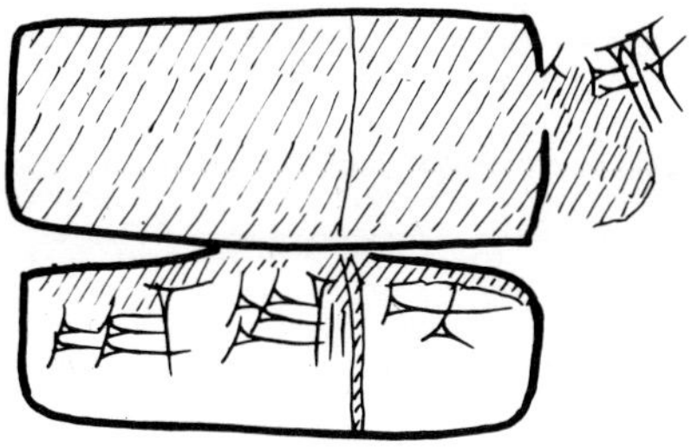

169

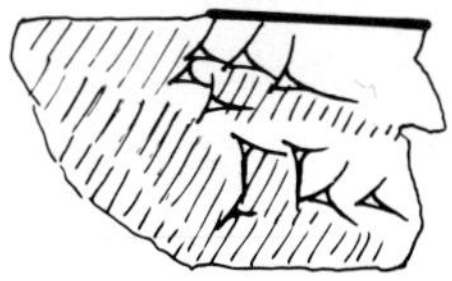

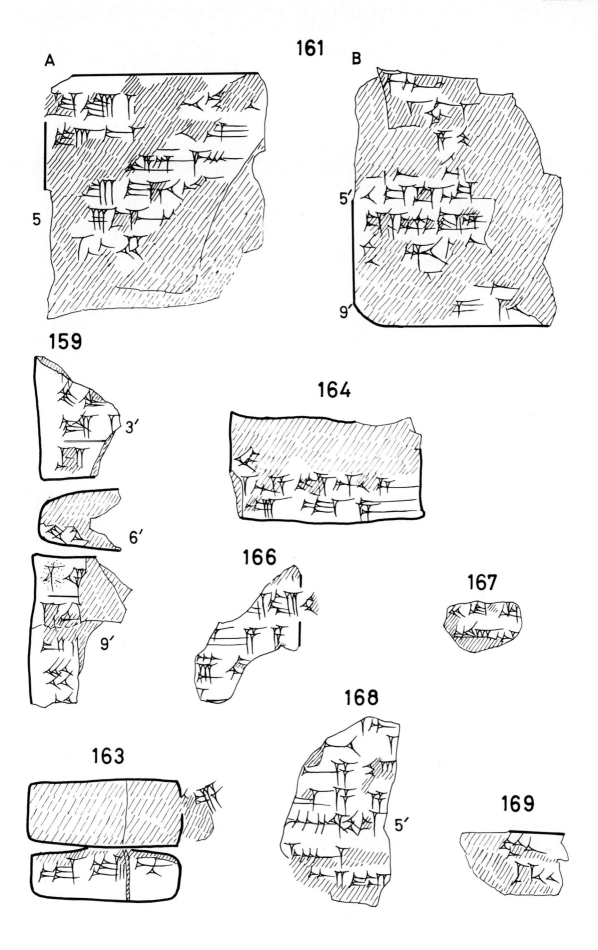

172

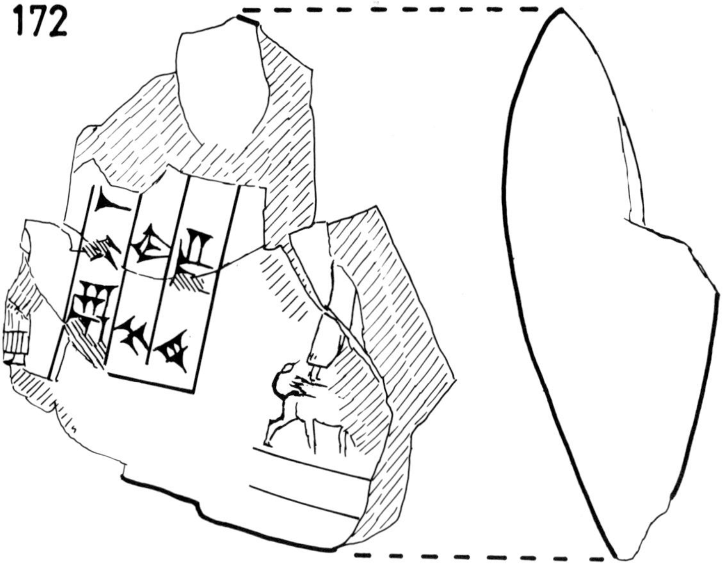

173

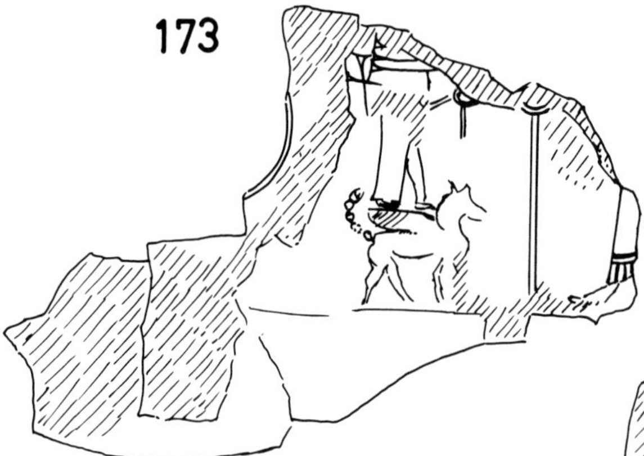

171

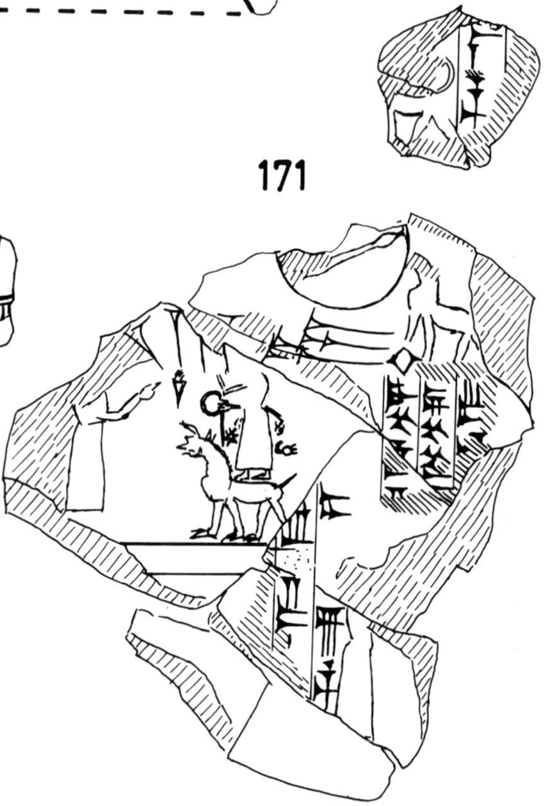

170

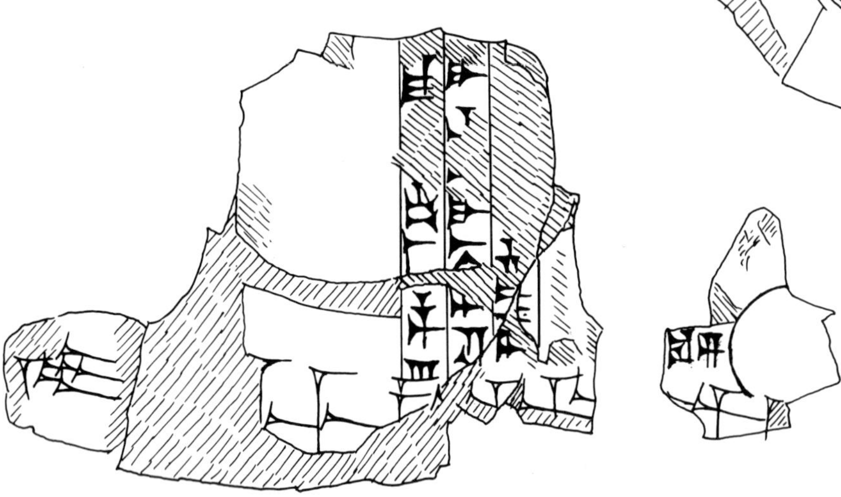

174

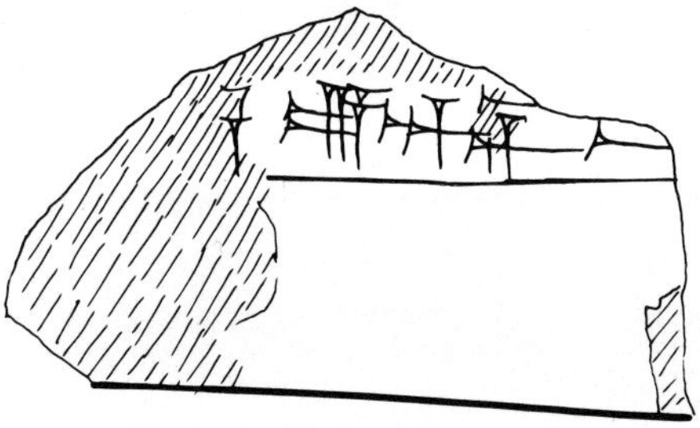

176

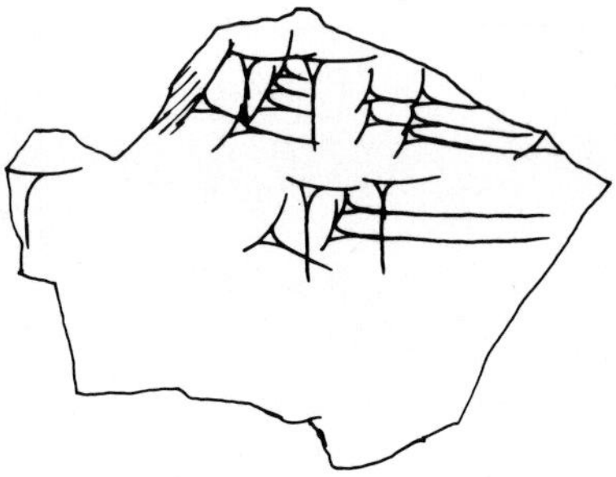

178

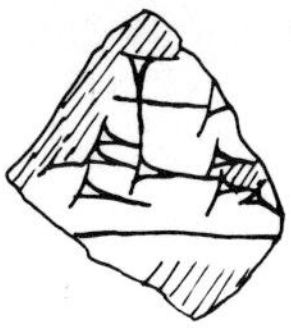

175

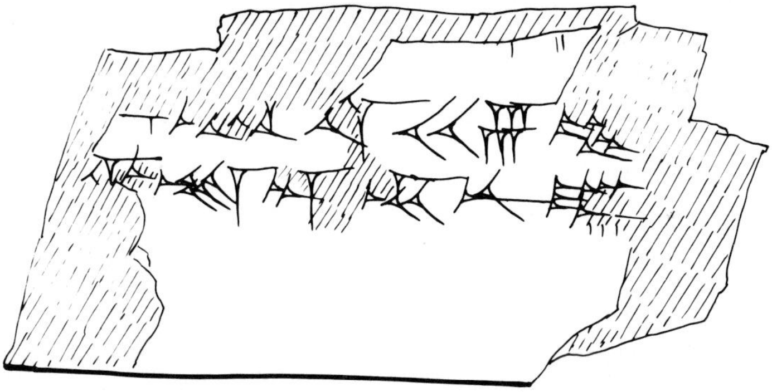

179

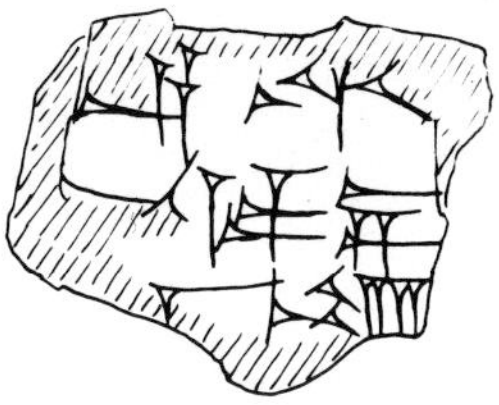

231

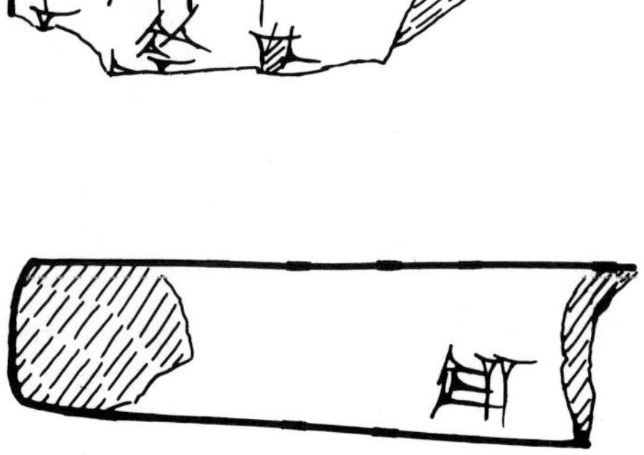

177

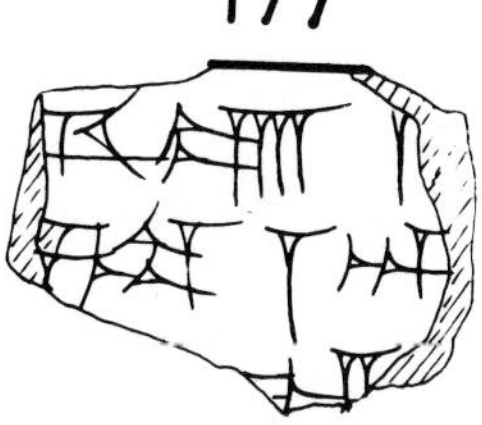

181

obv

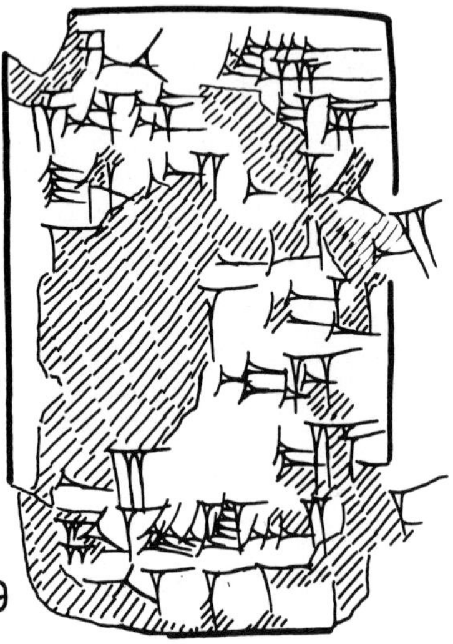

rev

180

obv

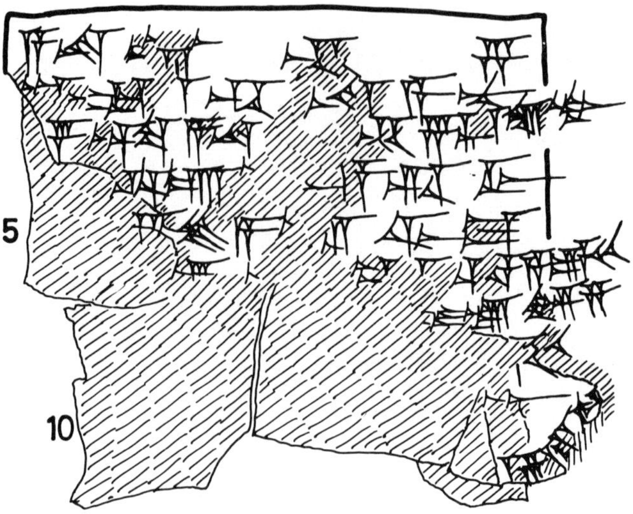

rev

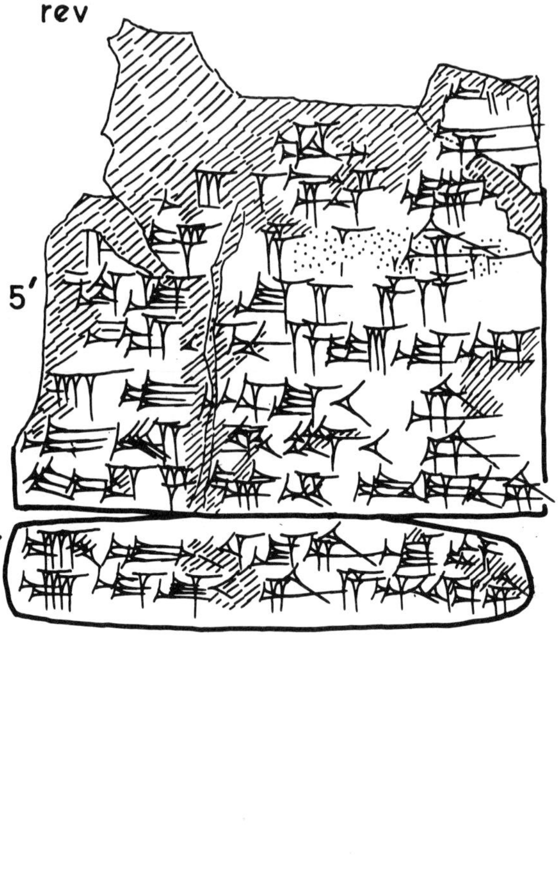

183

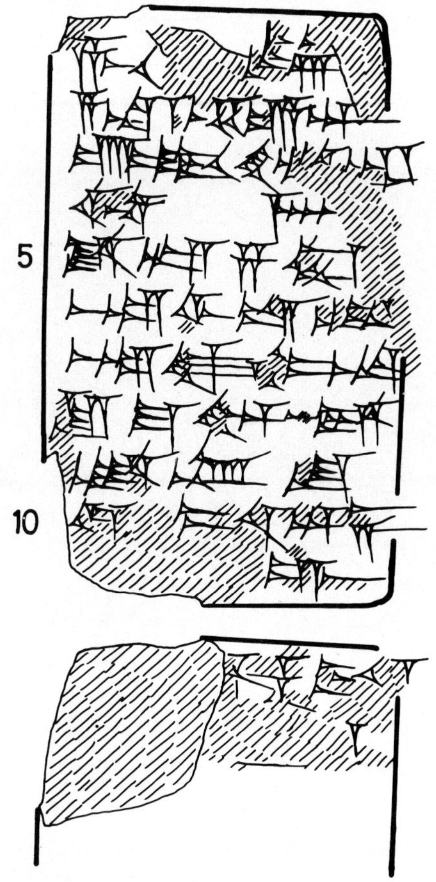

182

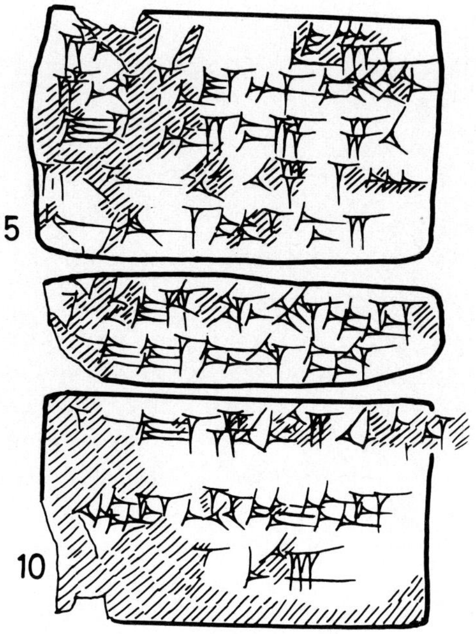

184

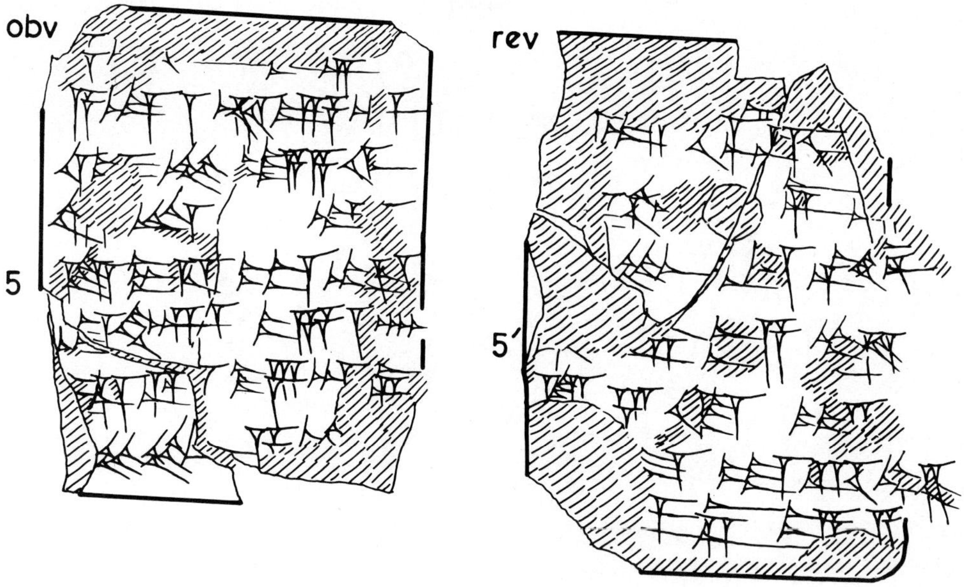

186

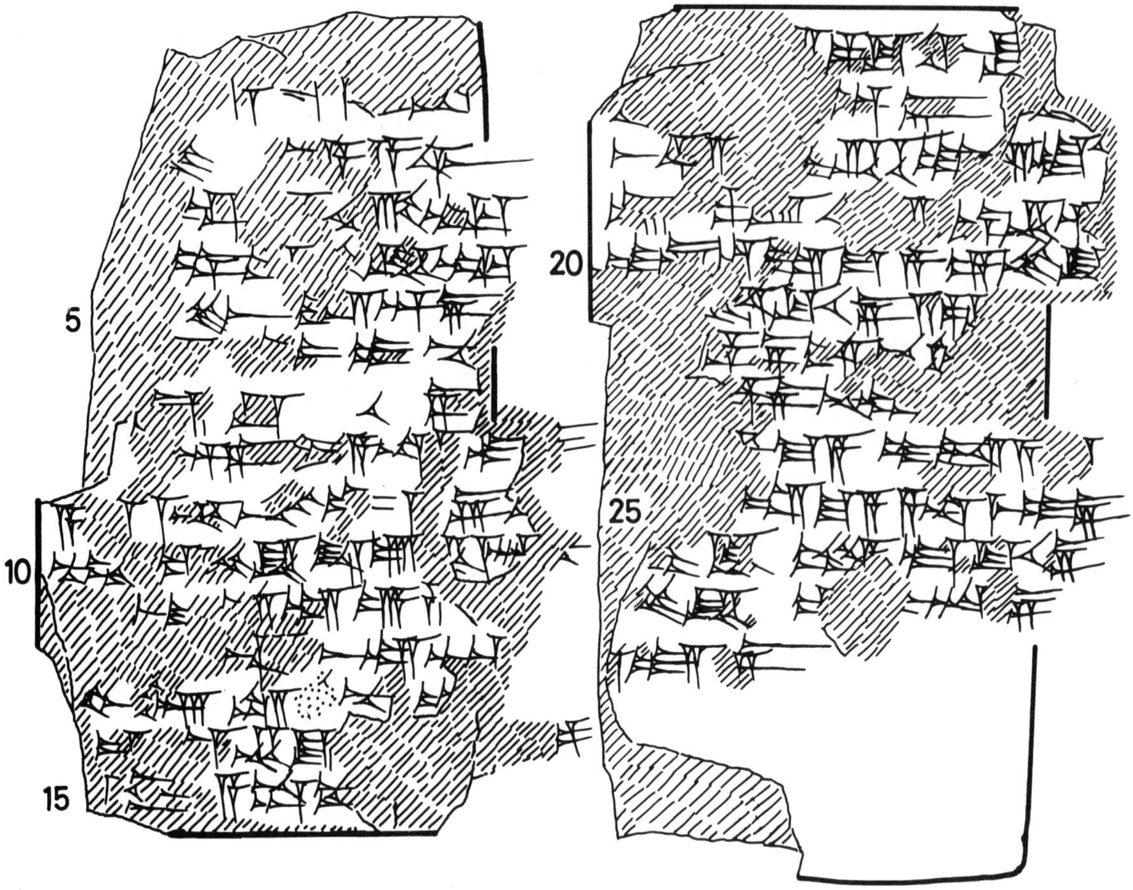

185

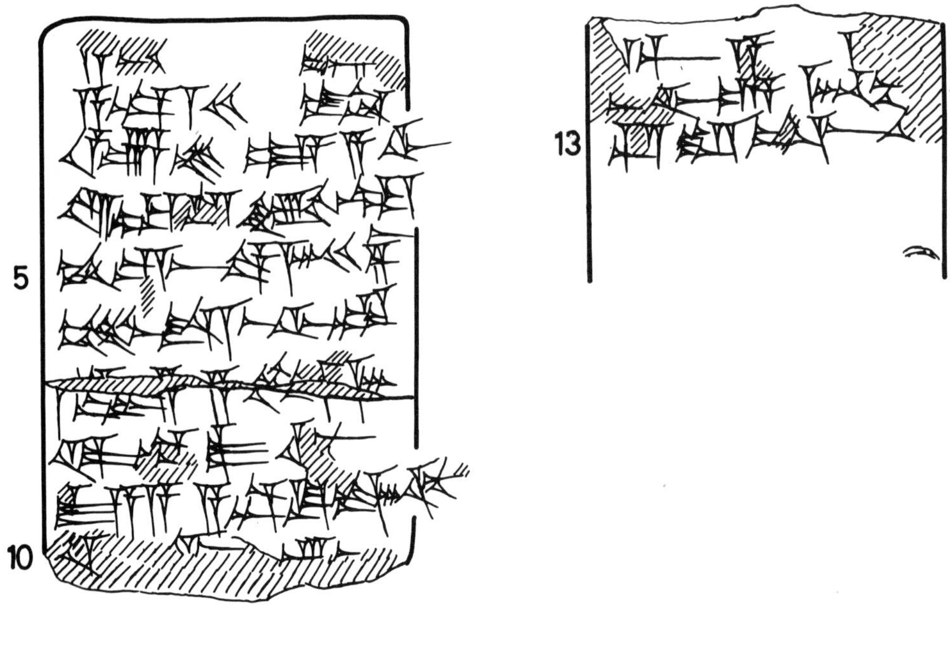

187

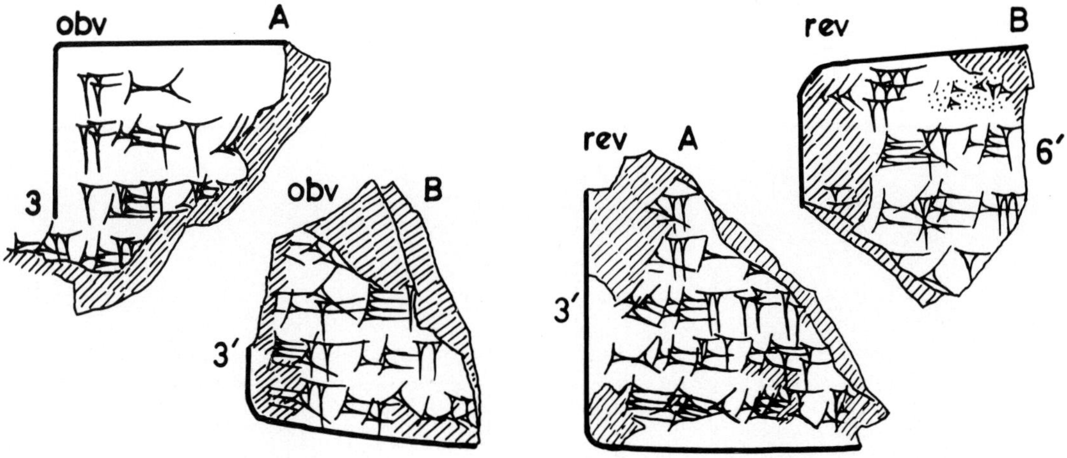

188

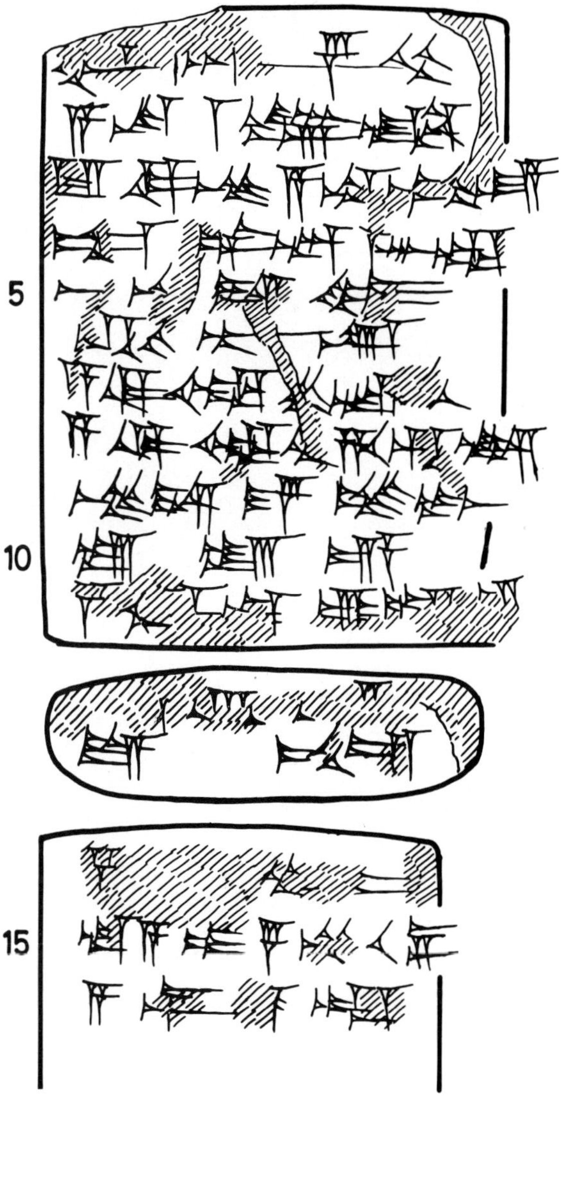

189

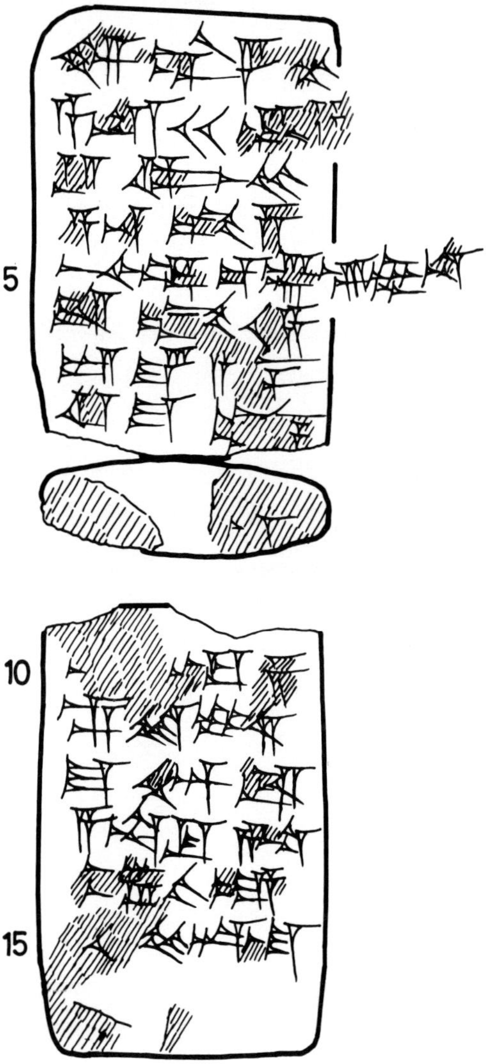

190

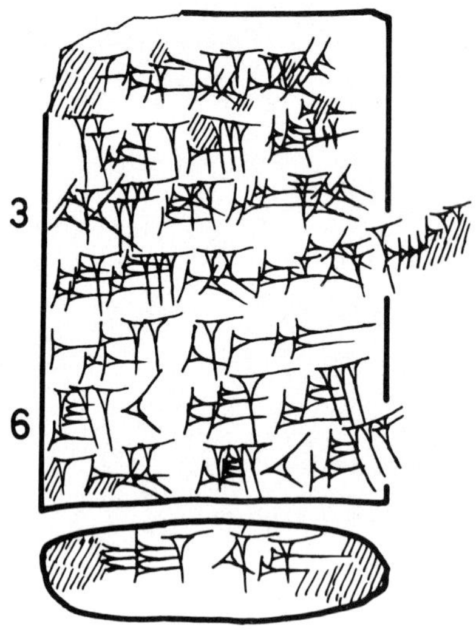

191

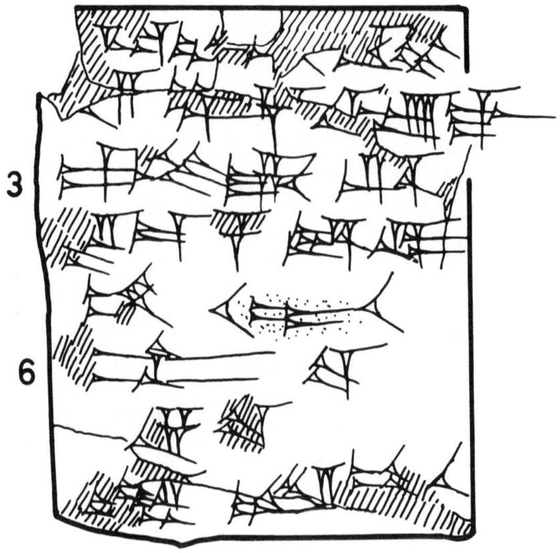

195

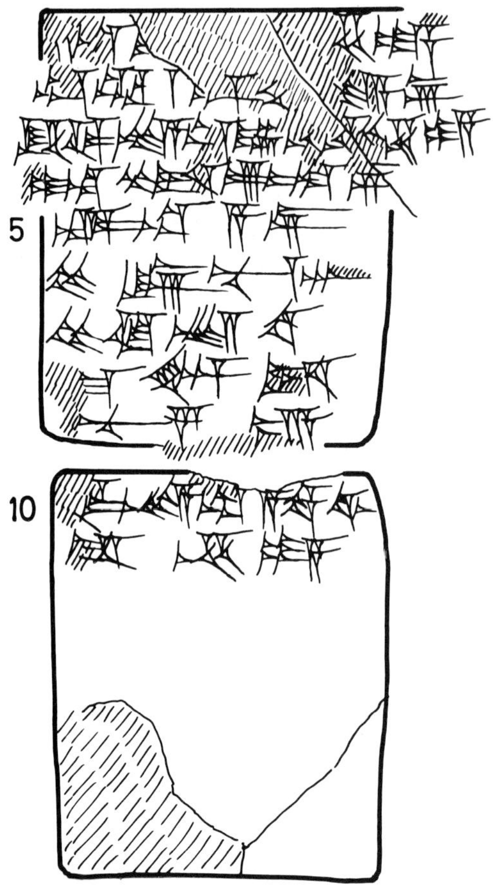

192

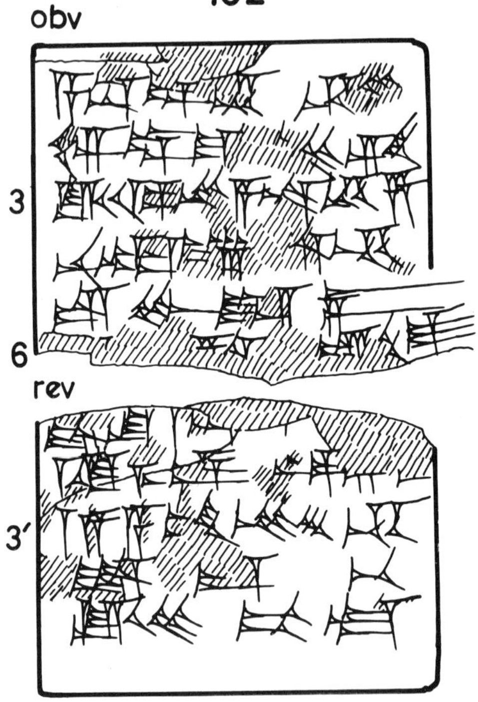

193

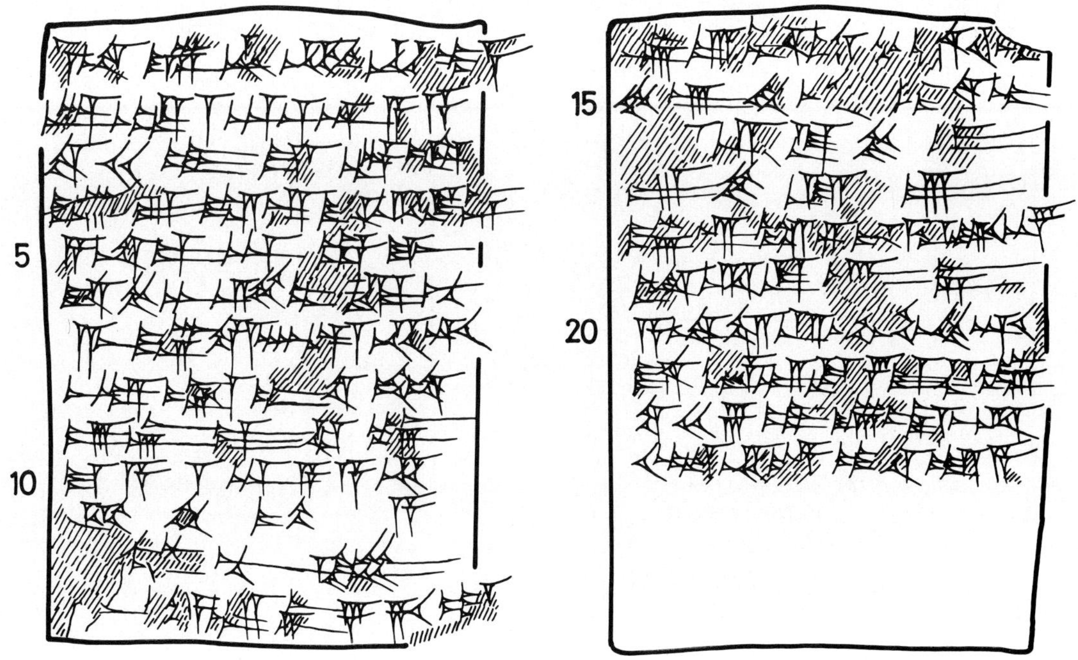

194

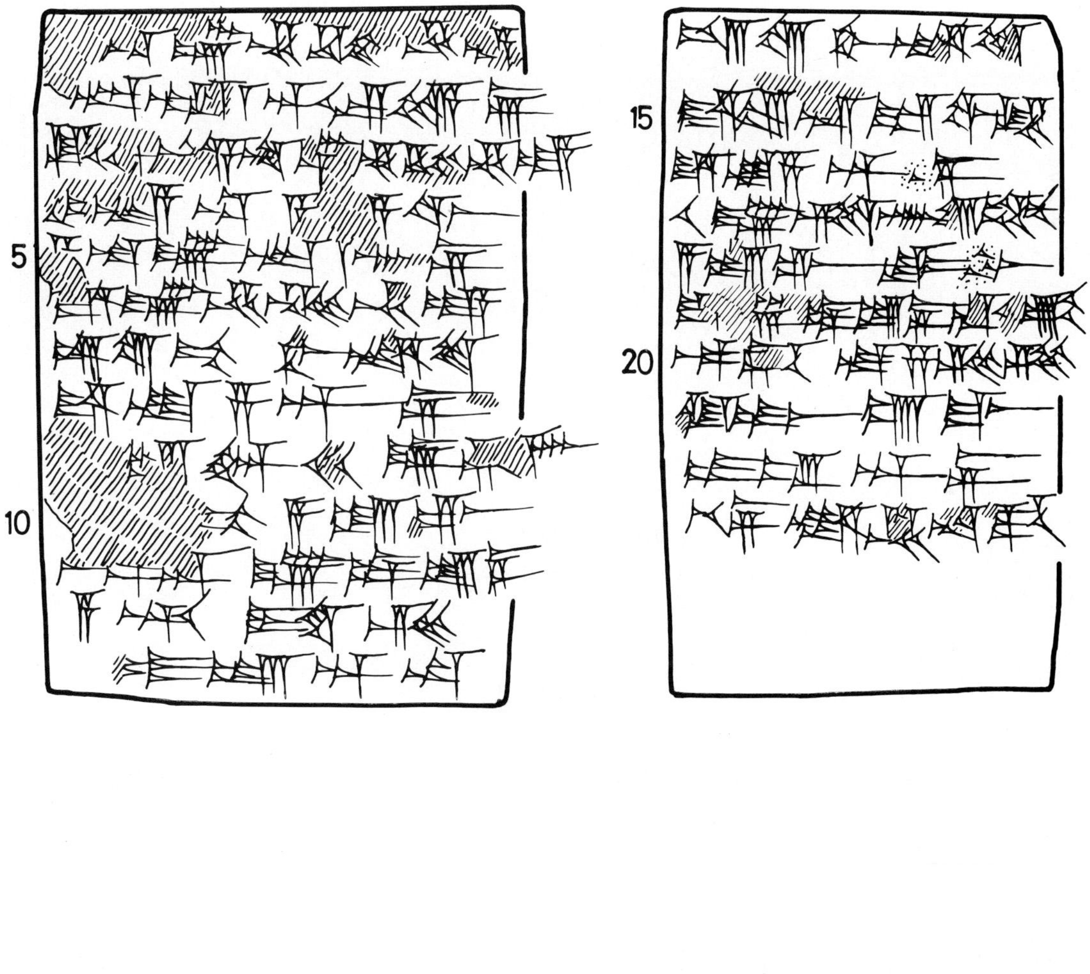

196

197

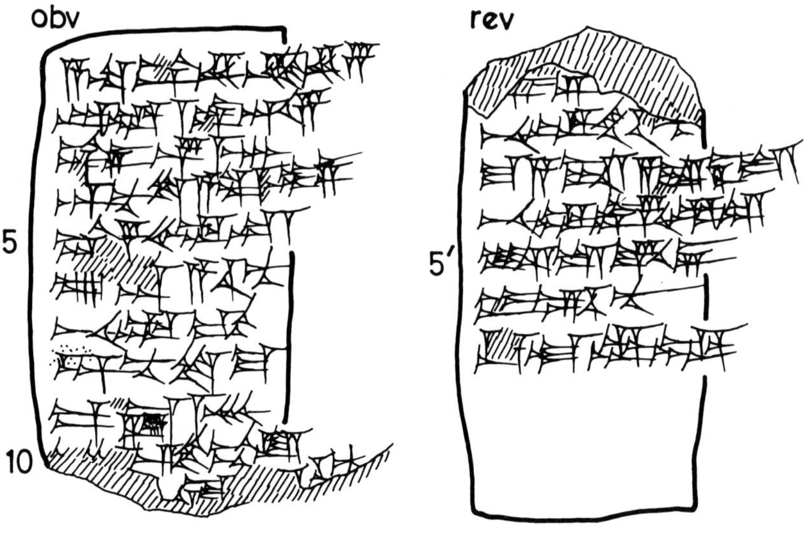

200

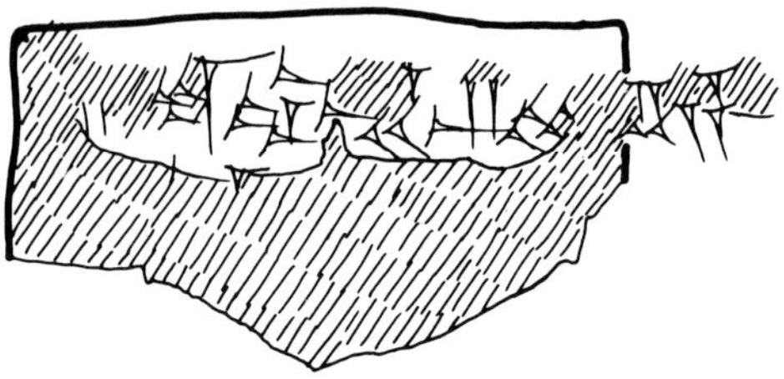

198

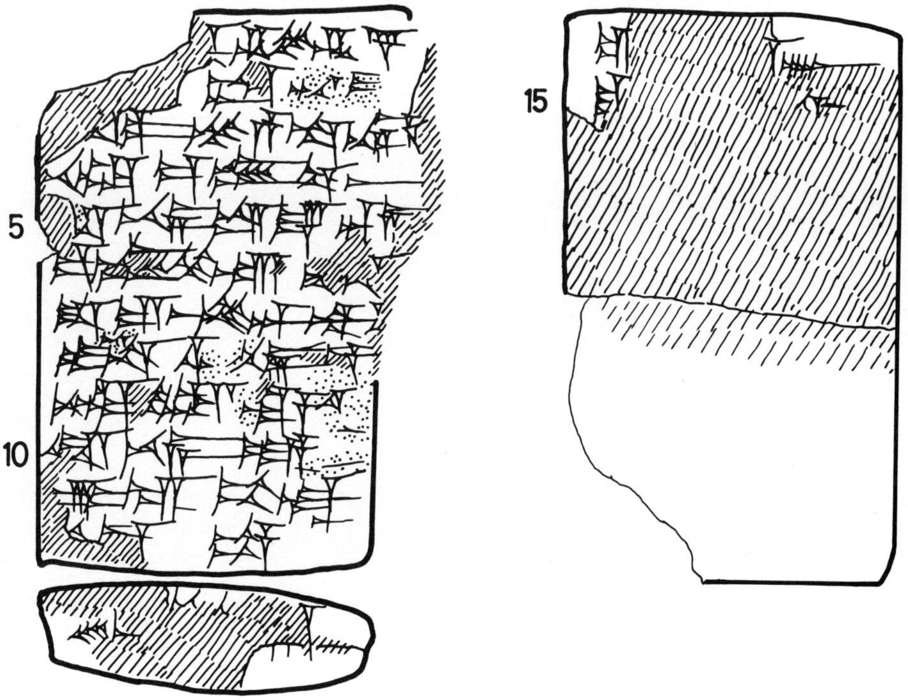

199

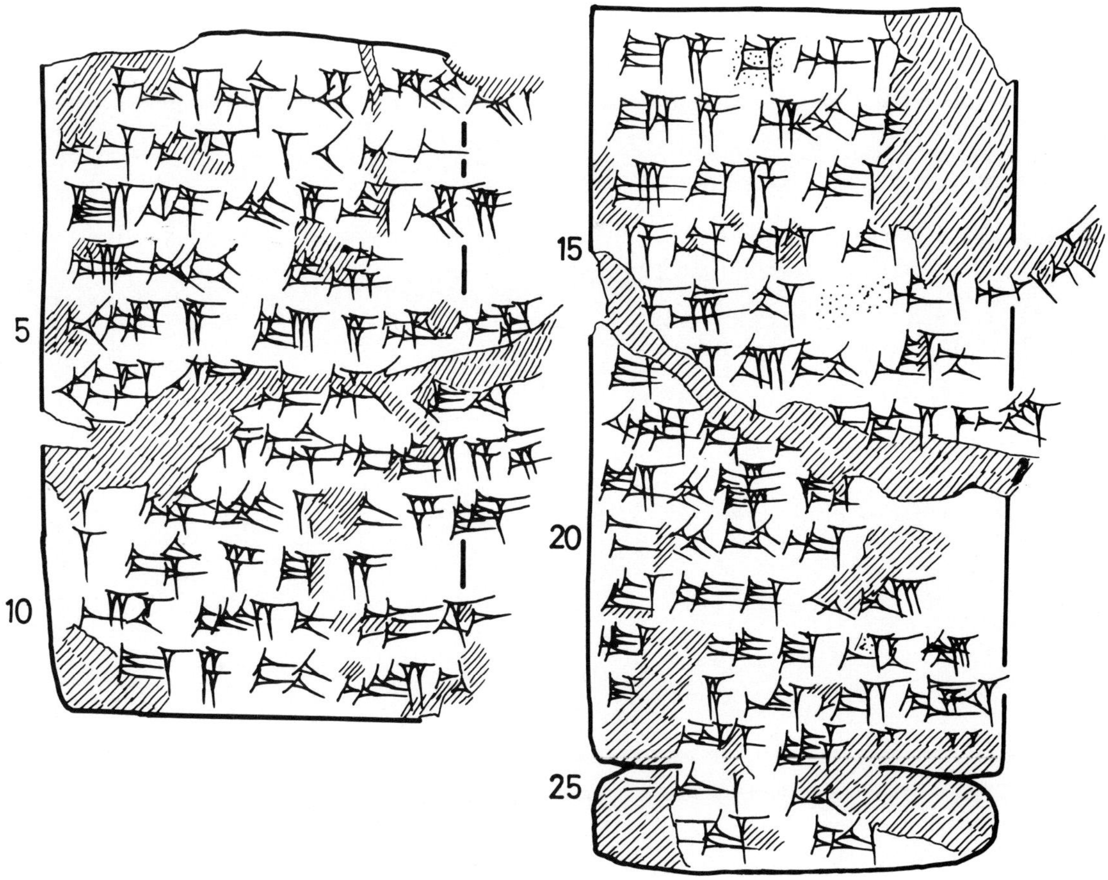

201

202

203

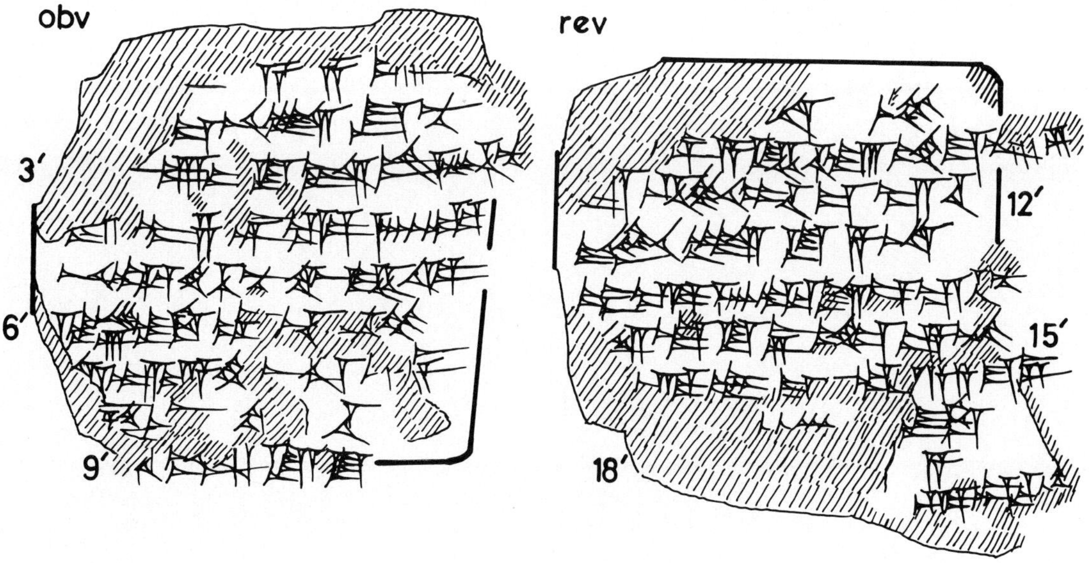

205

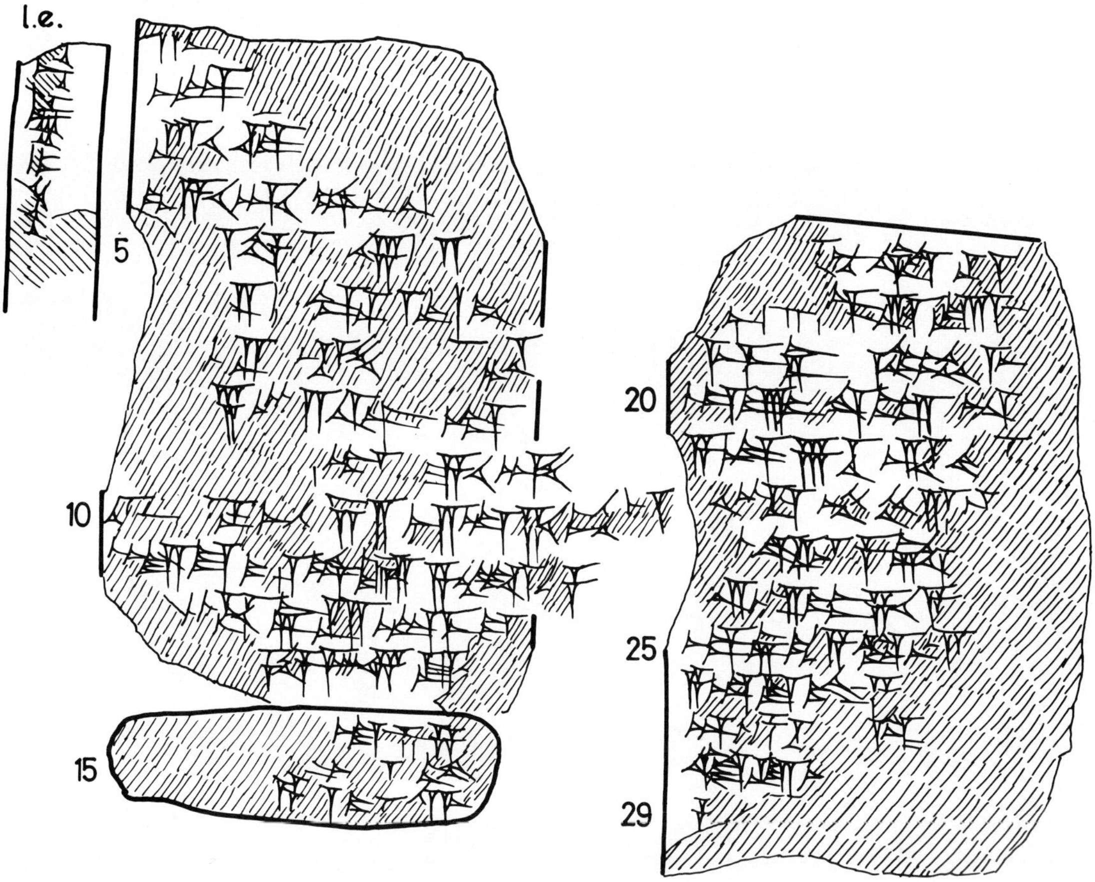

204

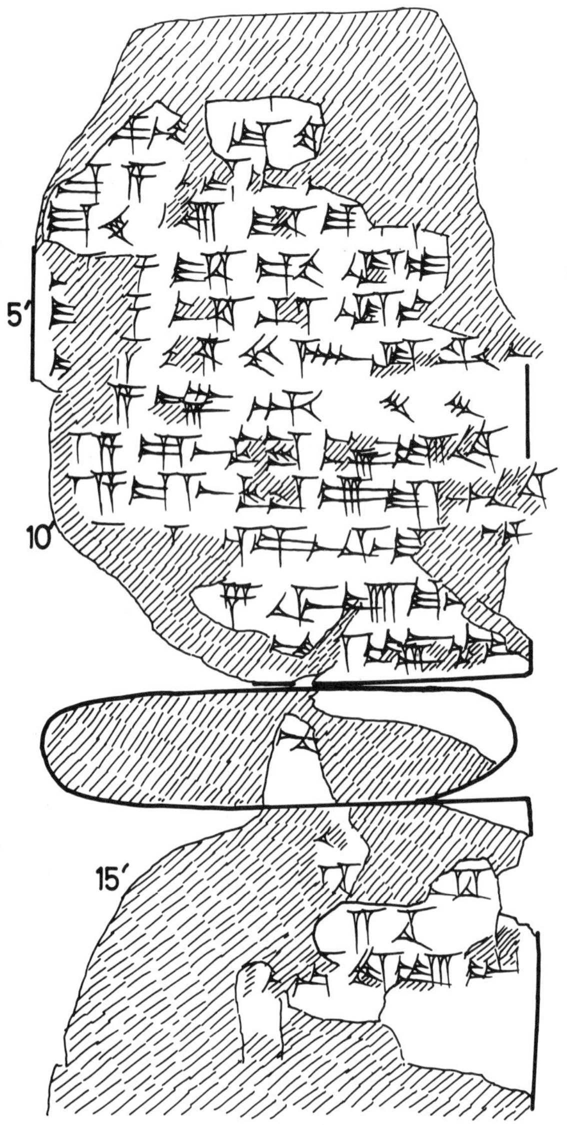

206

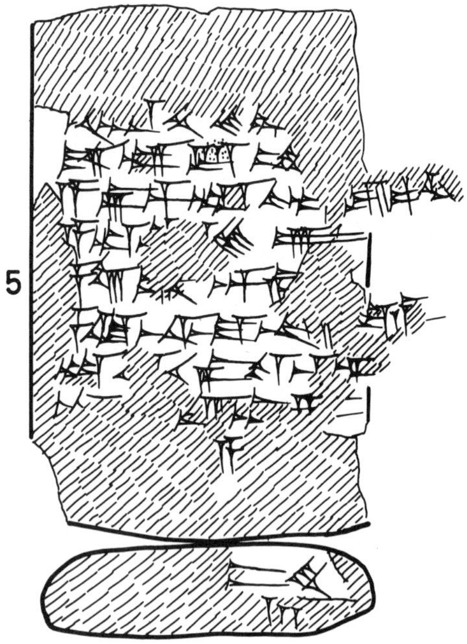

208

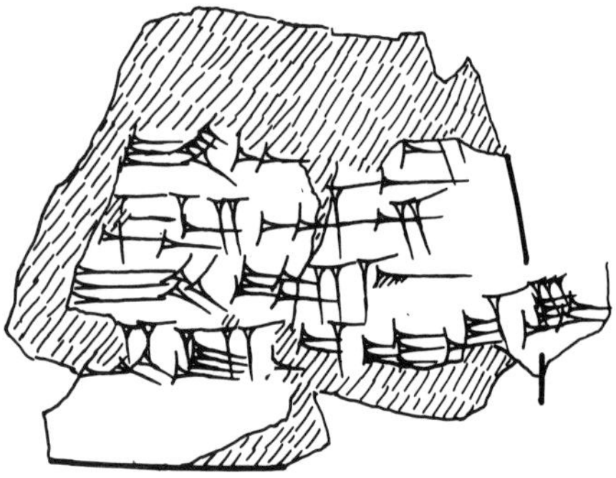

217

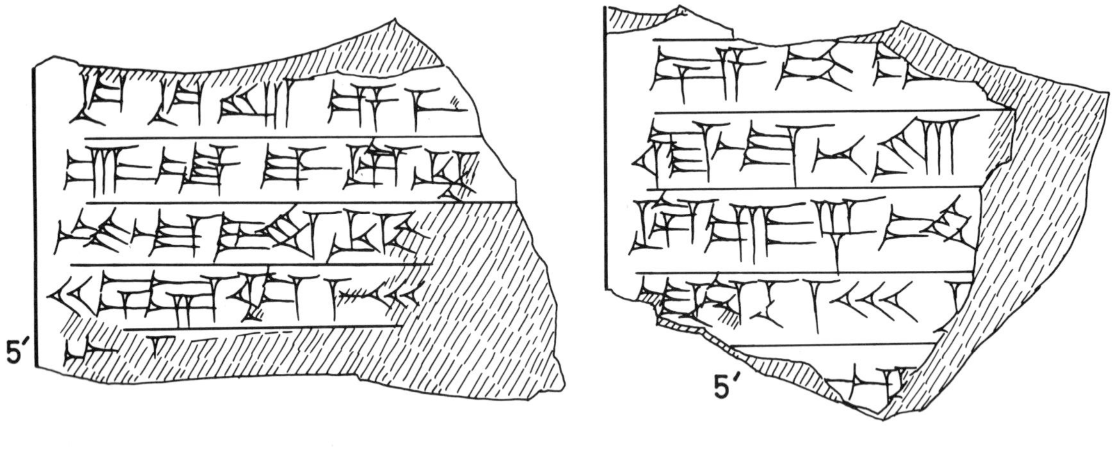

210

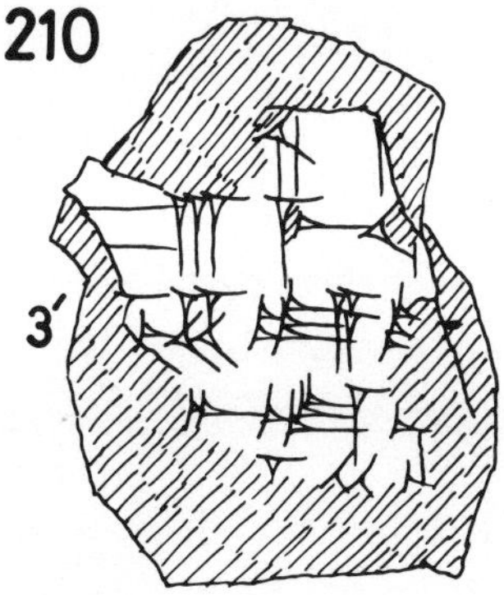

209

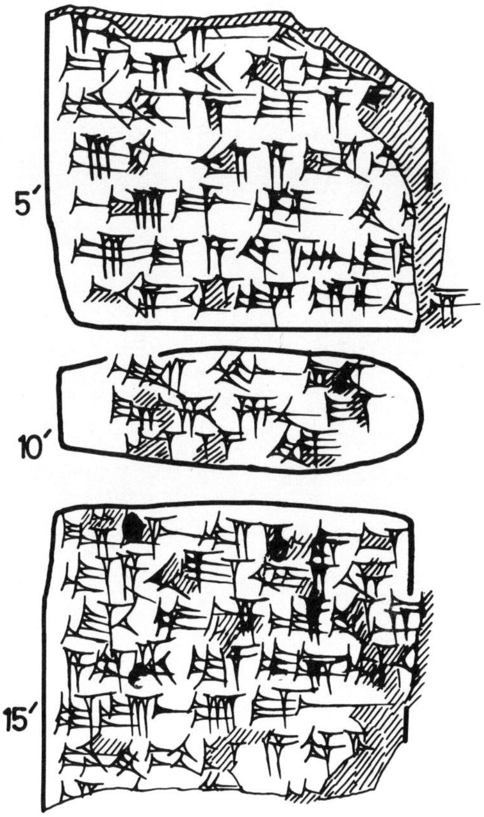

obv

207

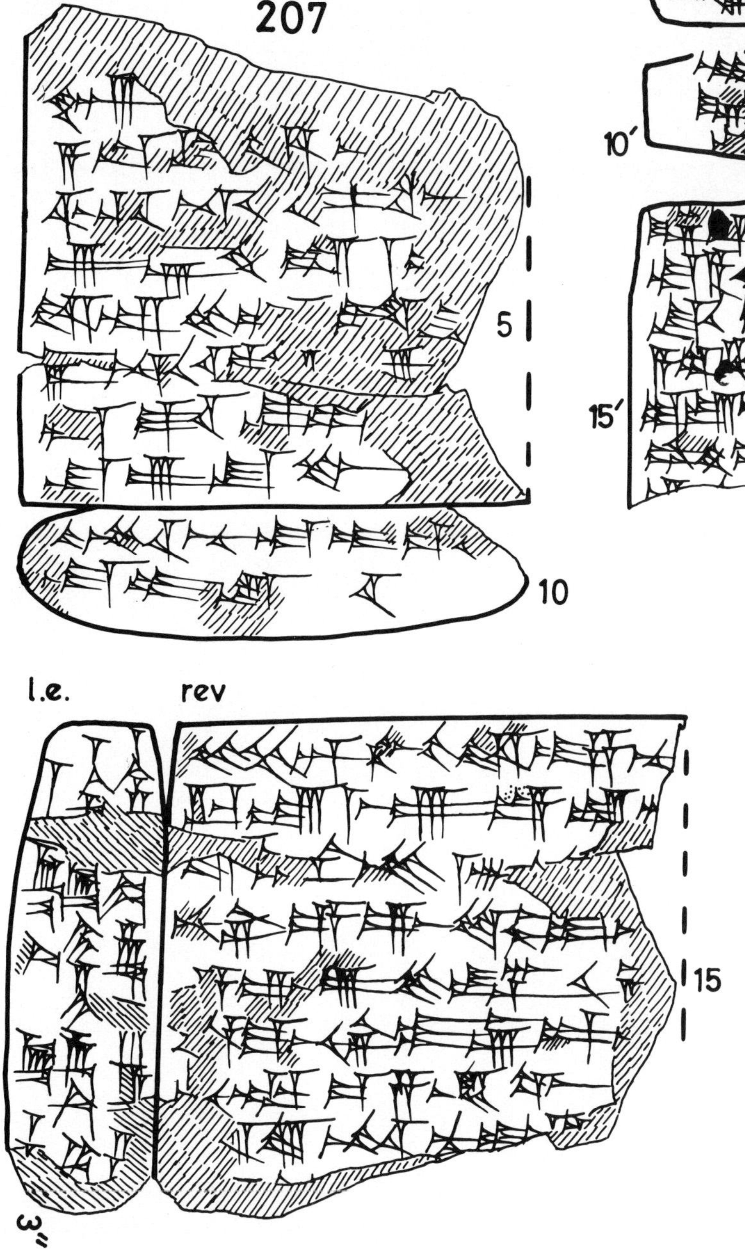

211

214

obv

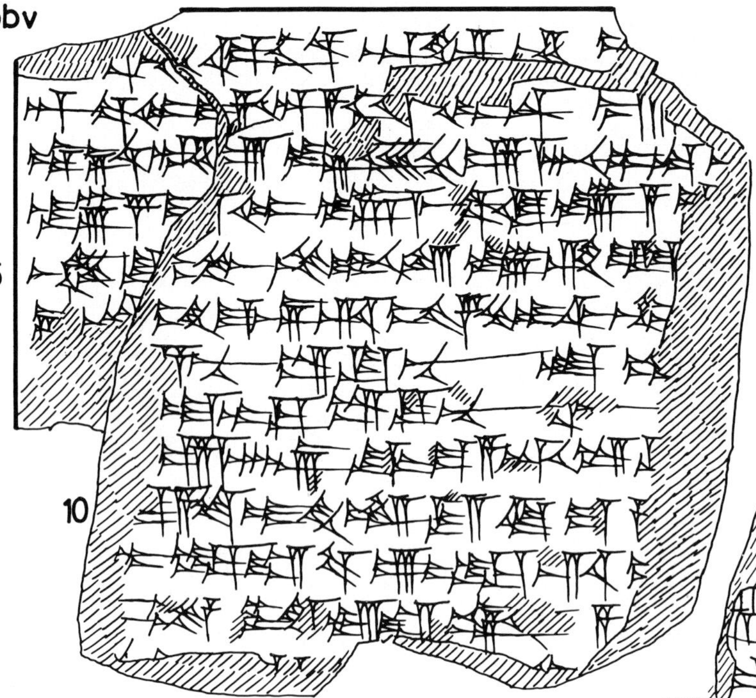

212

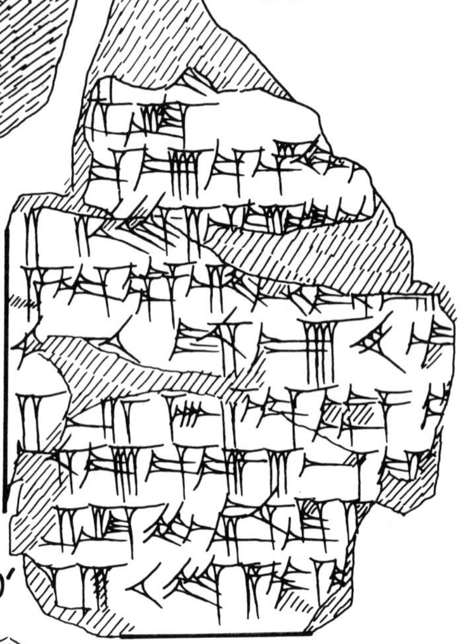

rev

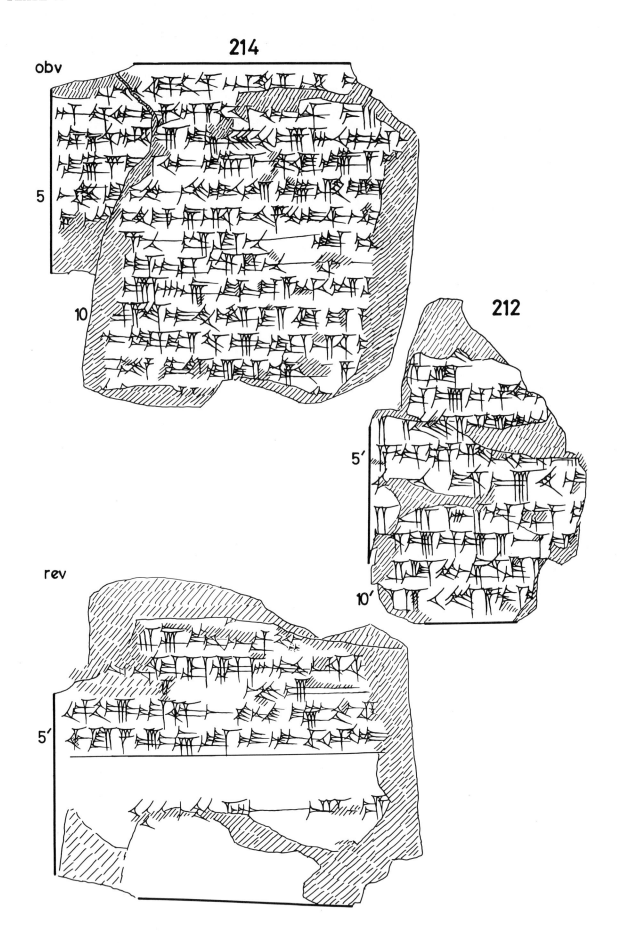

216

A

B

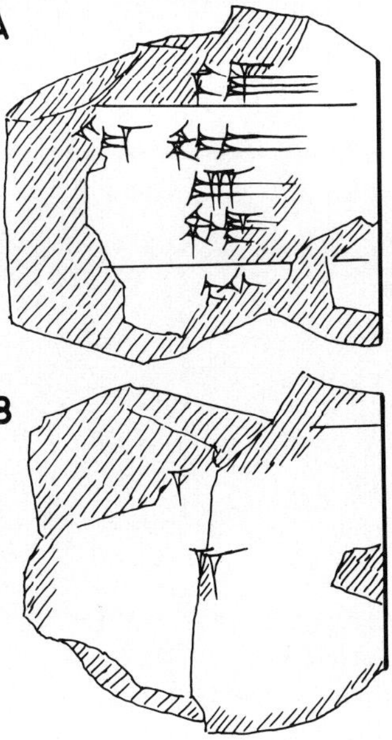

213

215

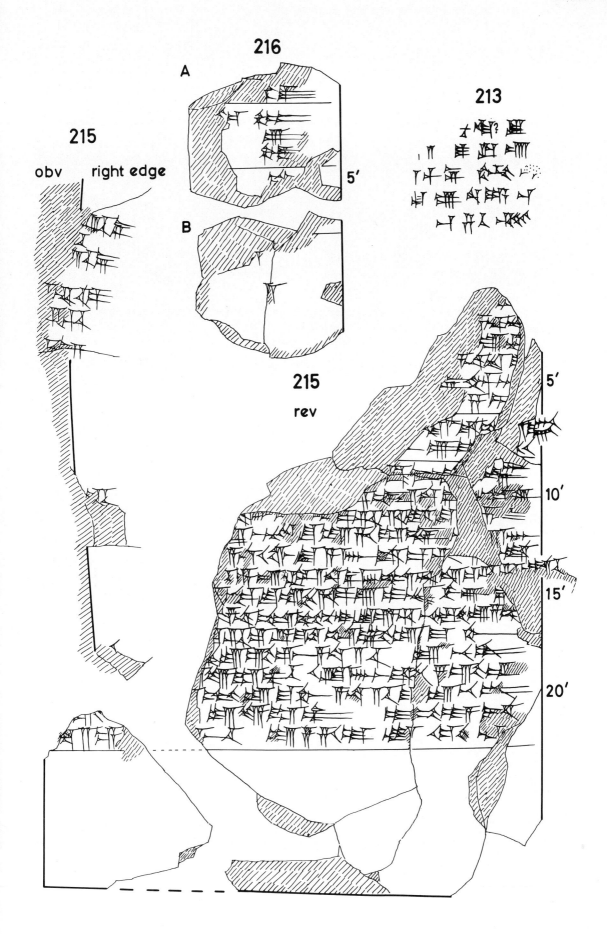

obv right edge

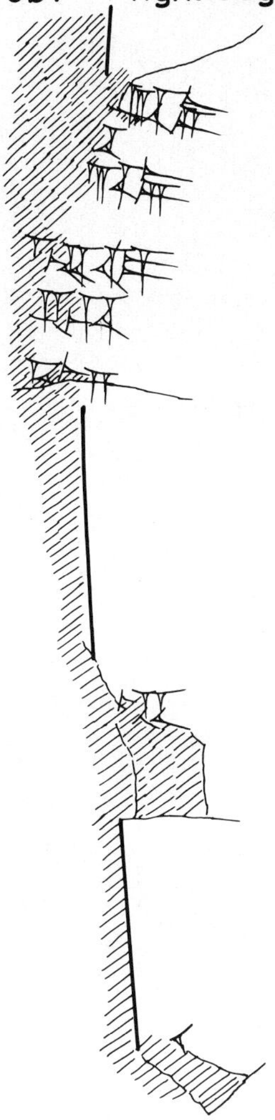

215

rev

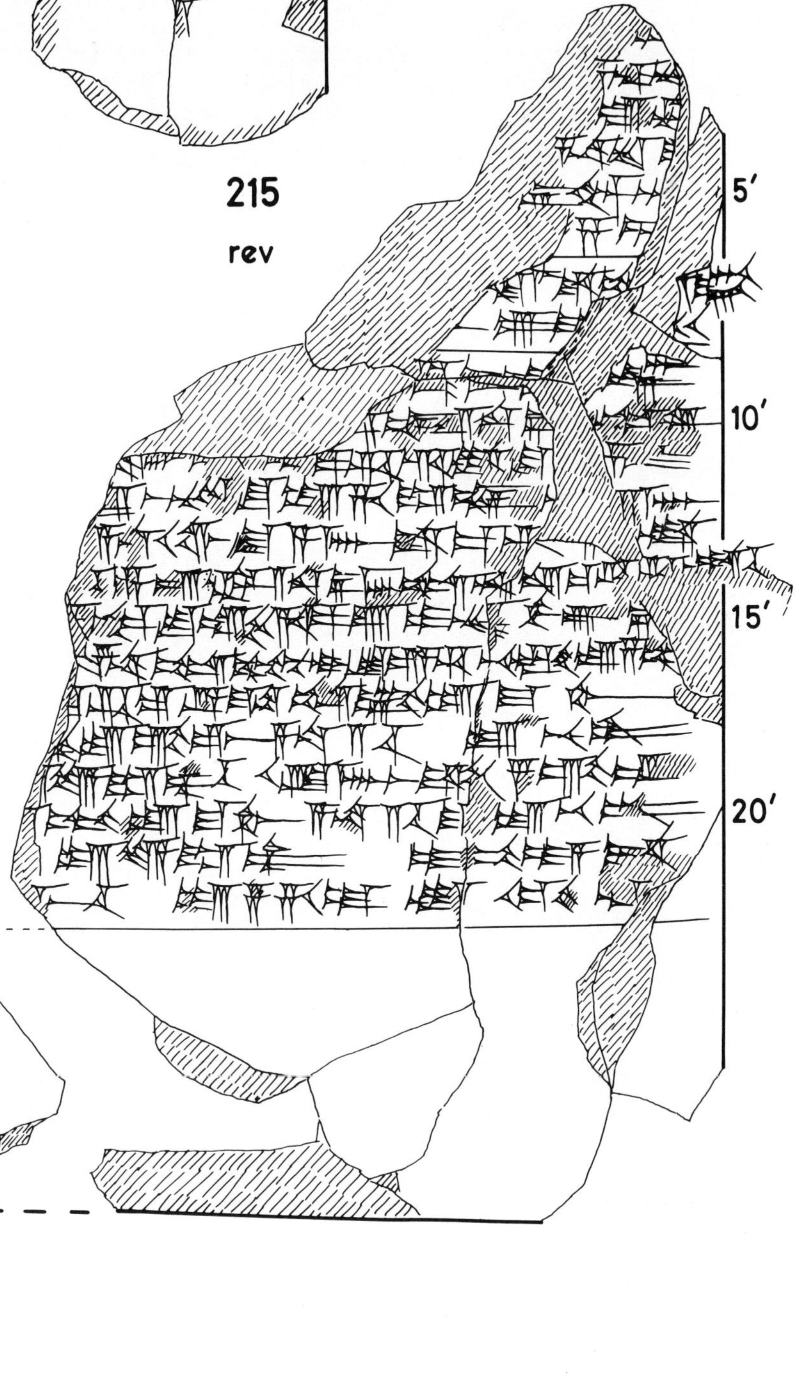

219

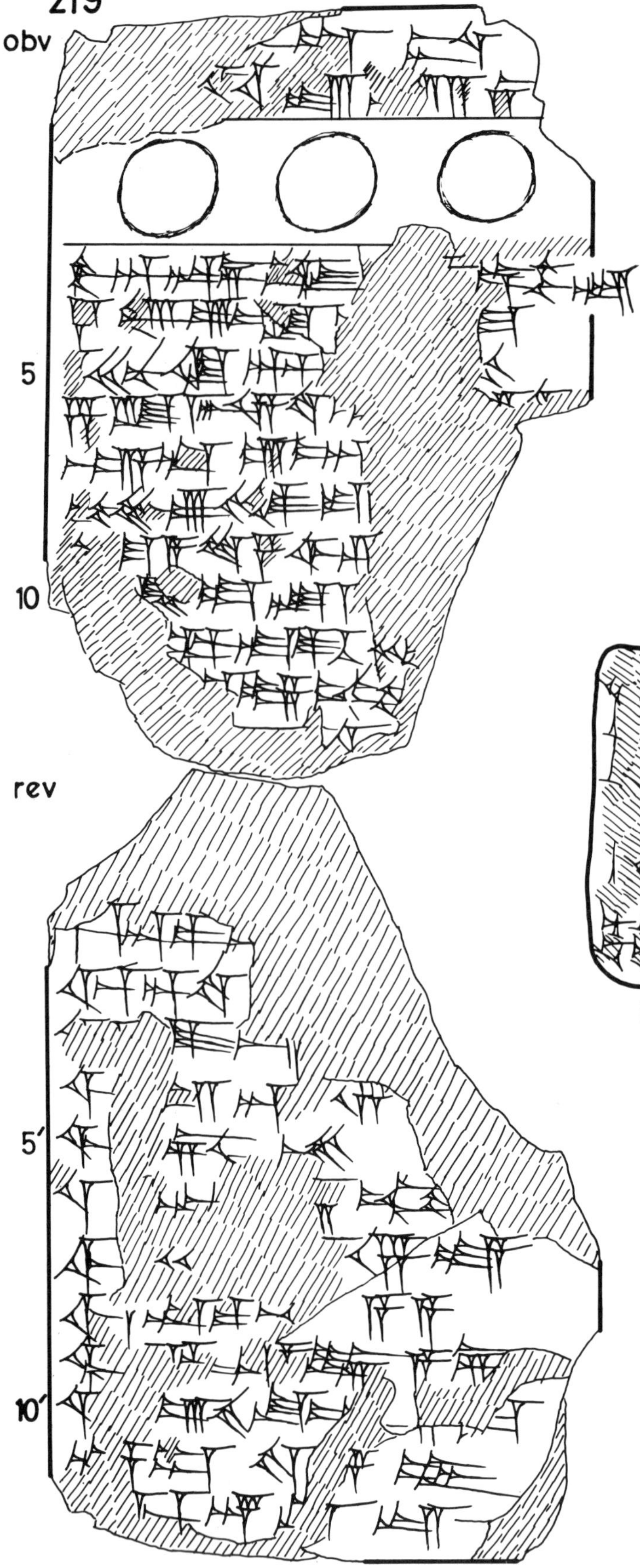

218

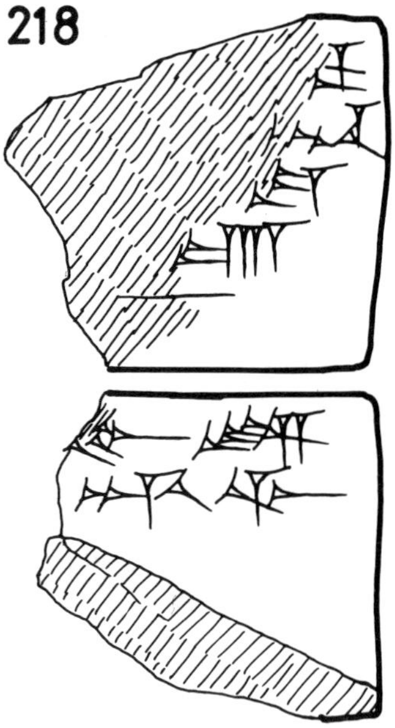

221

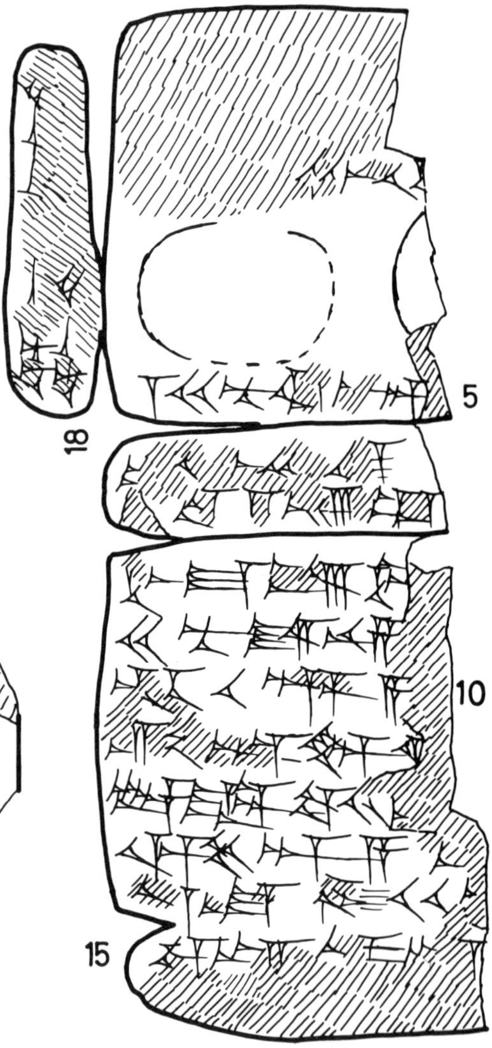

220

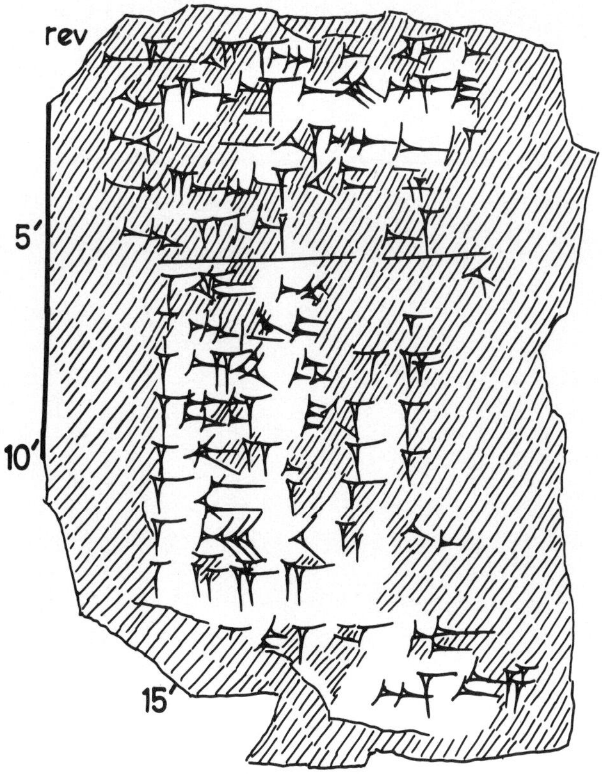

230

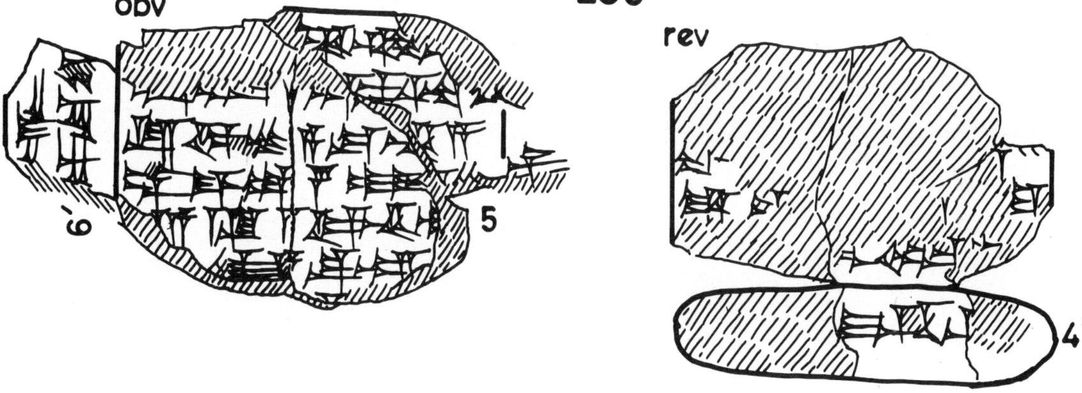

225

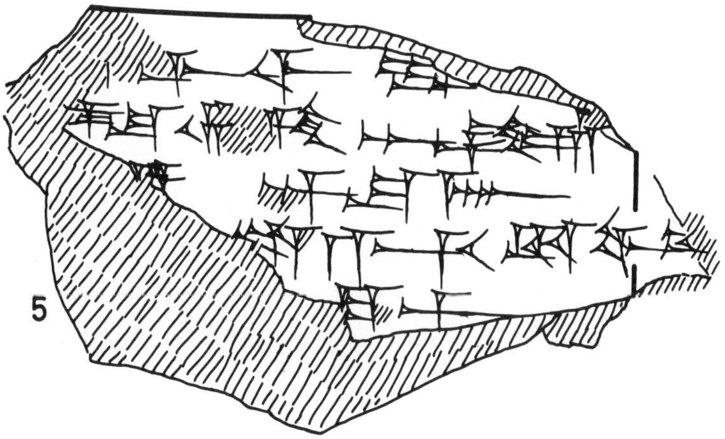

222

A

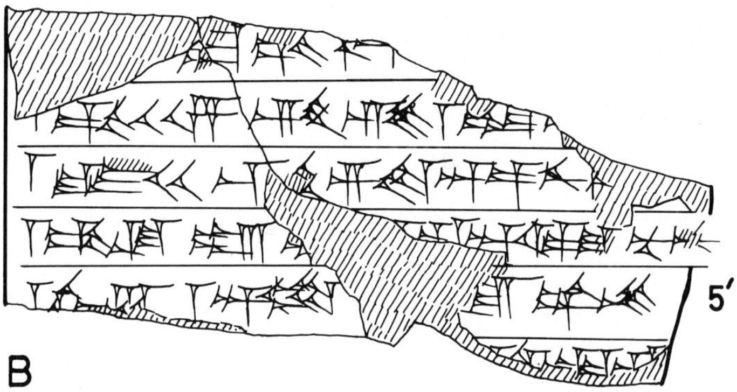

B

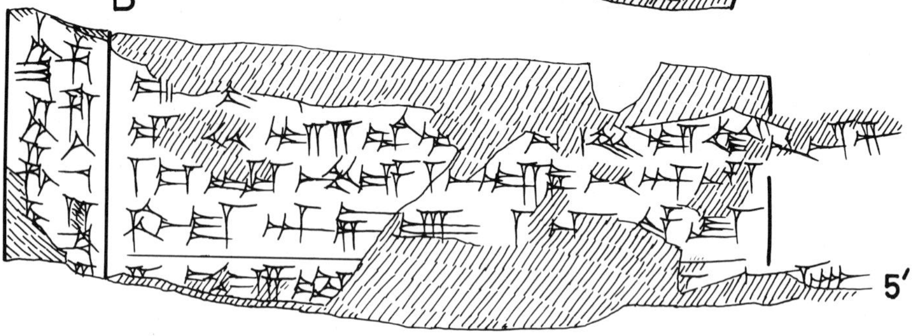

224

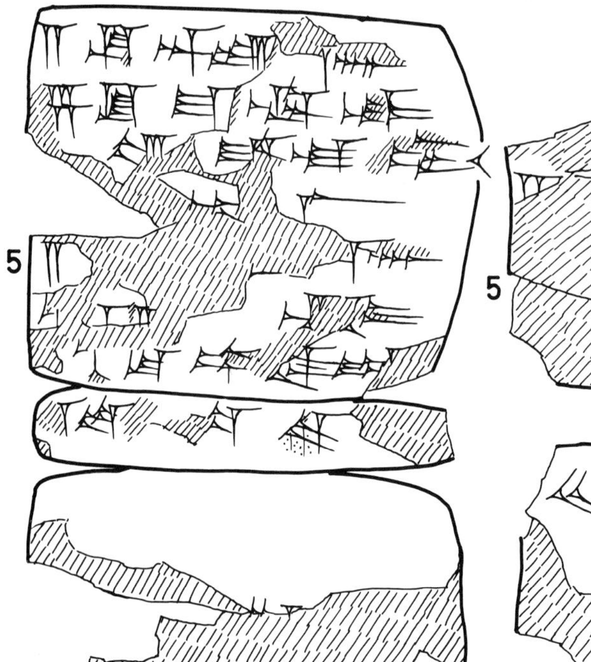

223

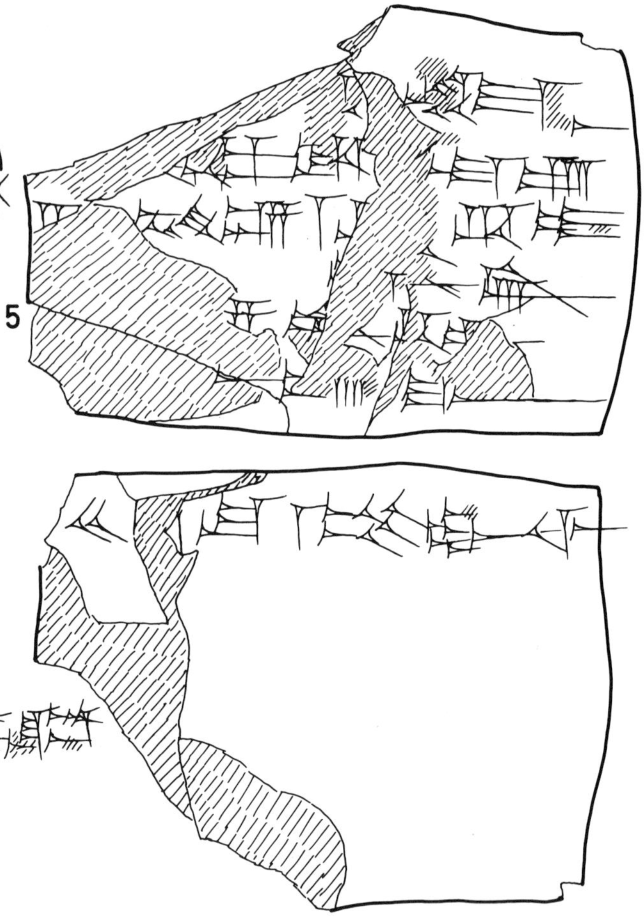

228

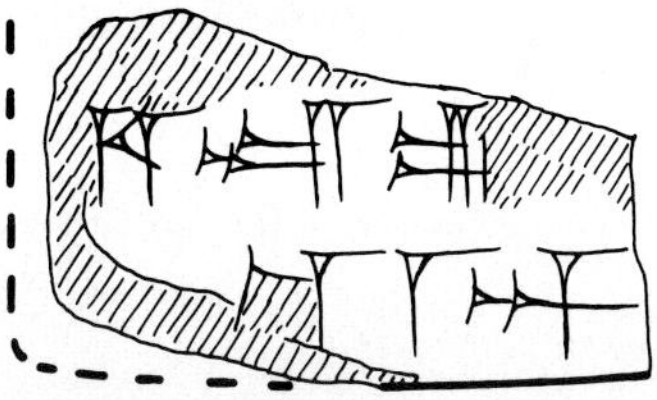

226

A

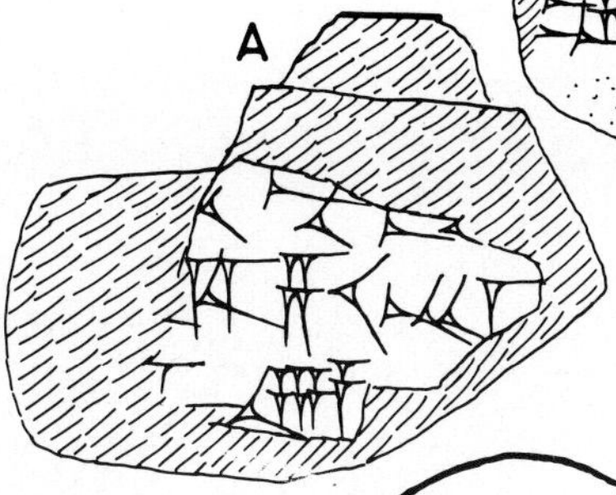

B

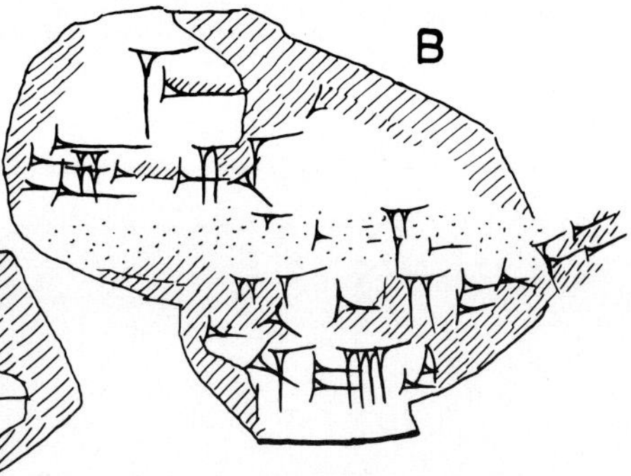

227

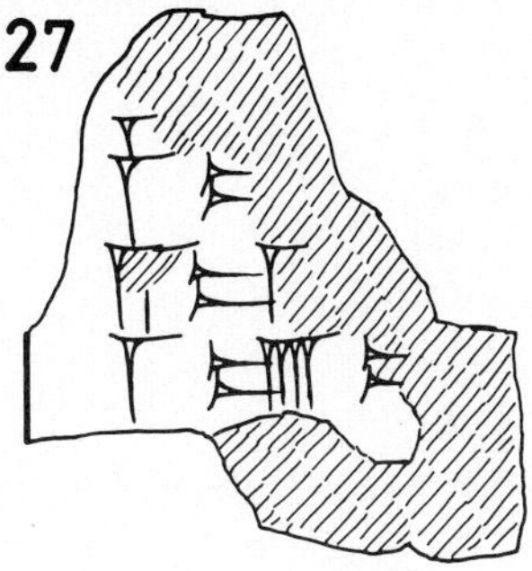

233

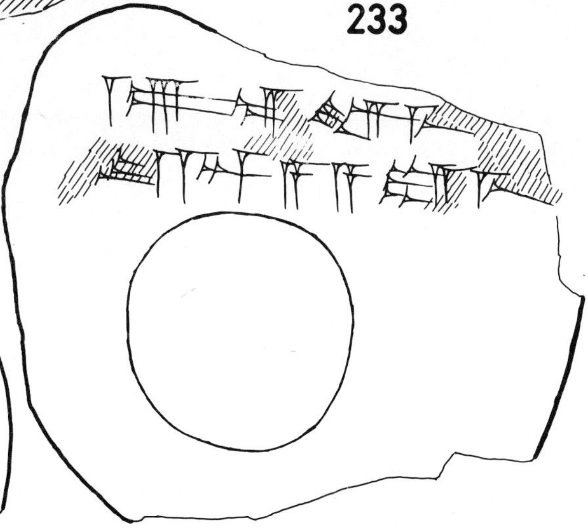

234

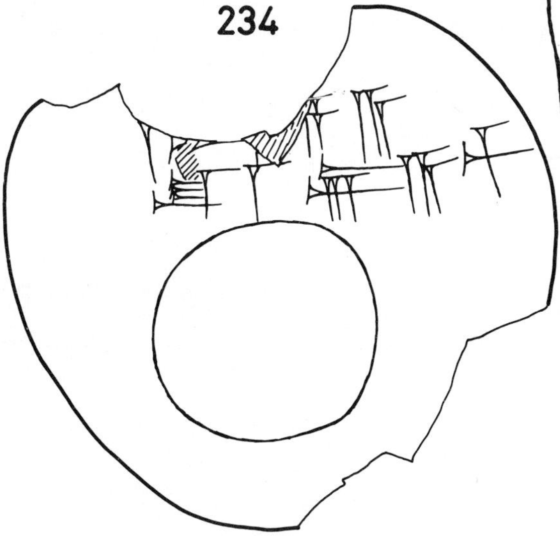

235

236

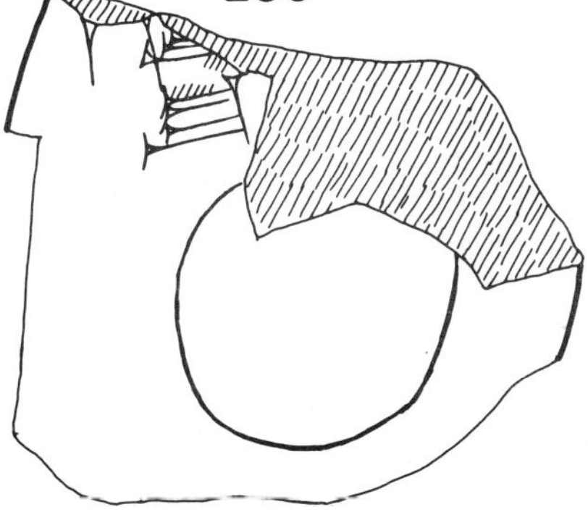

239

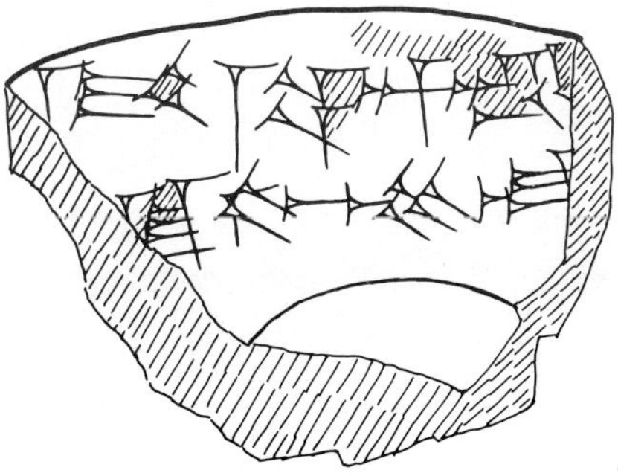

Jar sealing (after no. 233)

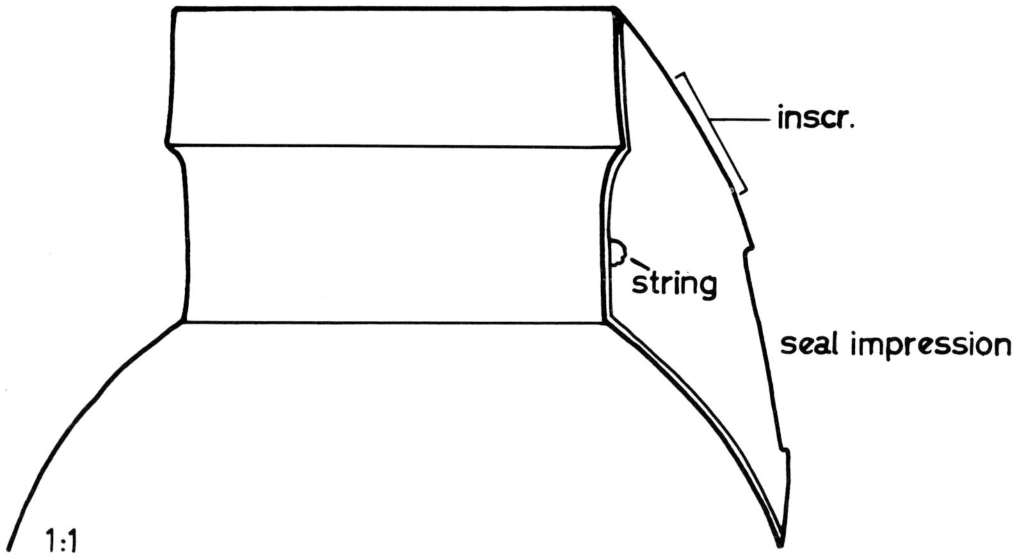

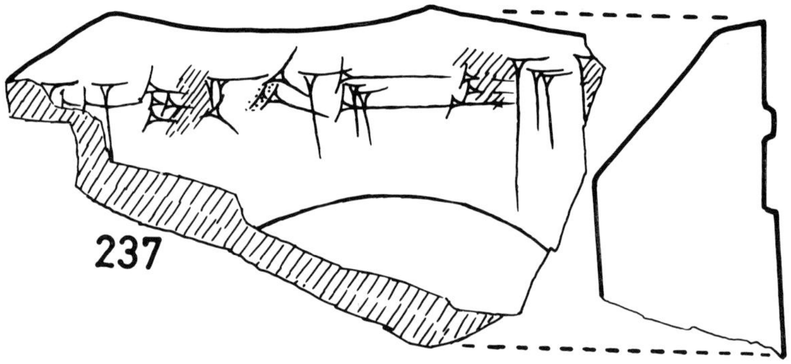

237

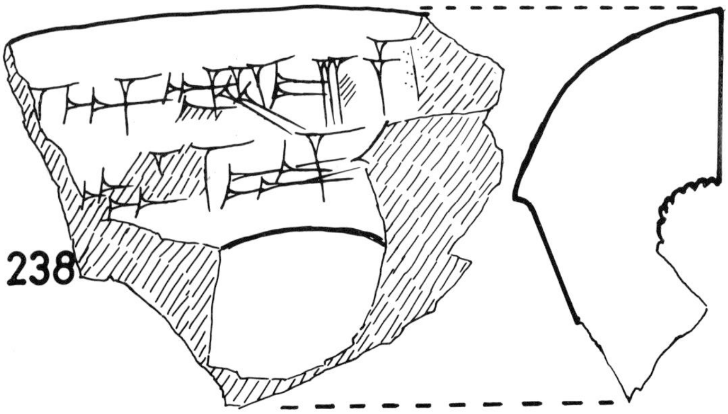

238

232

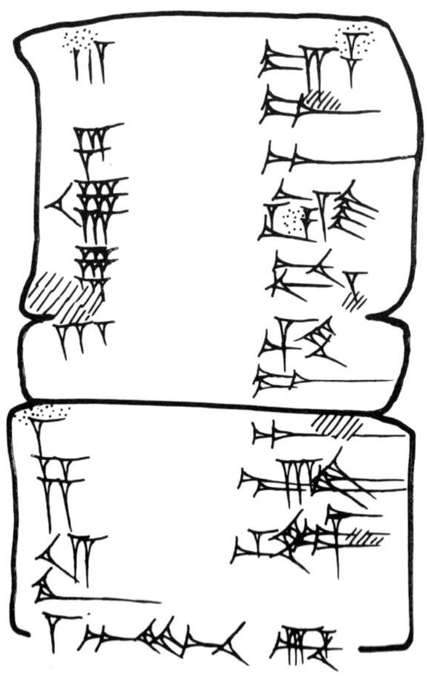

240

obv

5

10

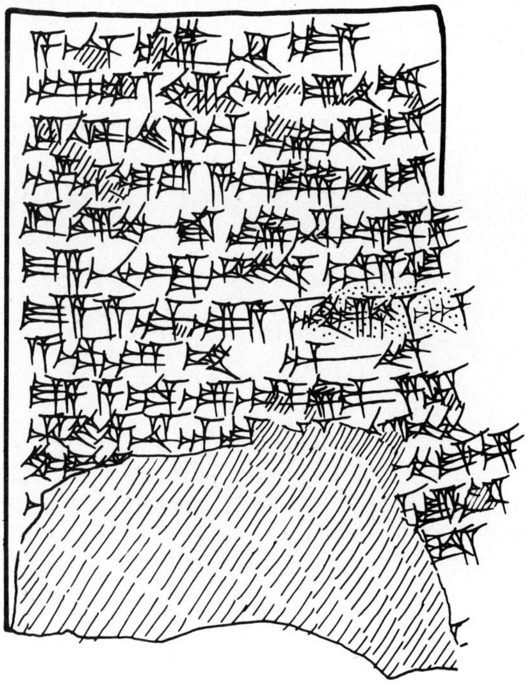

rev

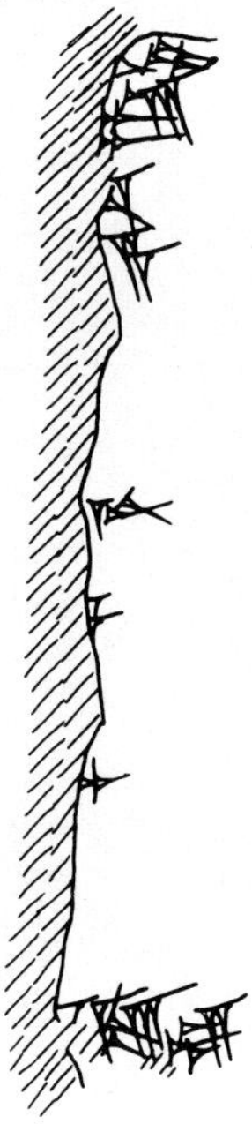

244

5′

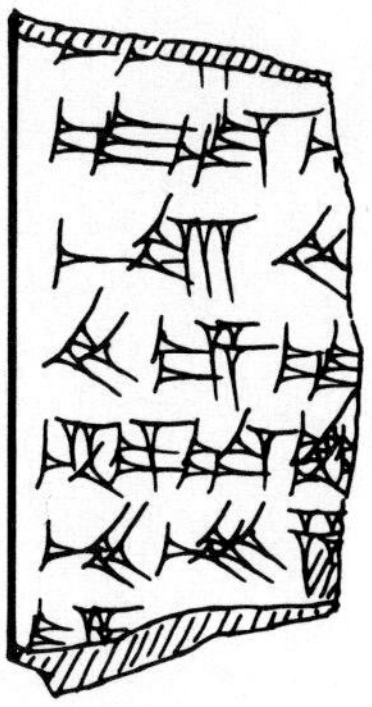

241

obv

5

10

rev

242

obv

5

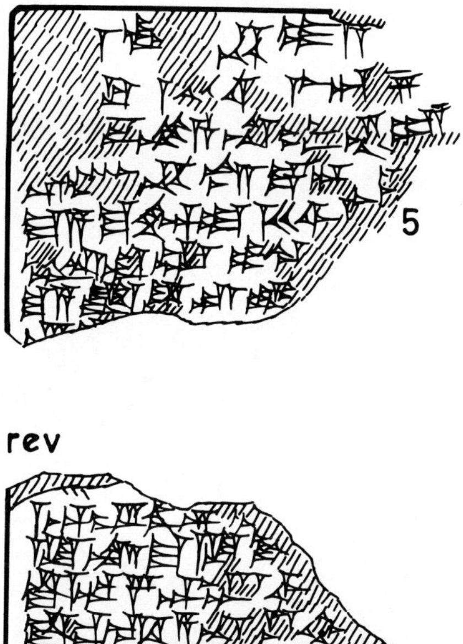

rev

5′

9′

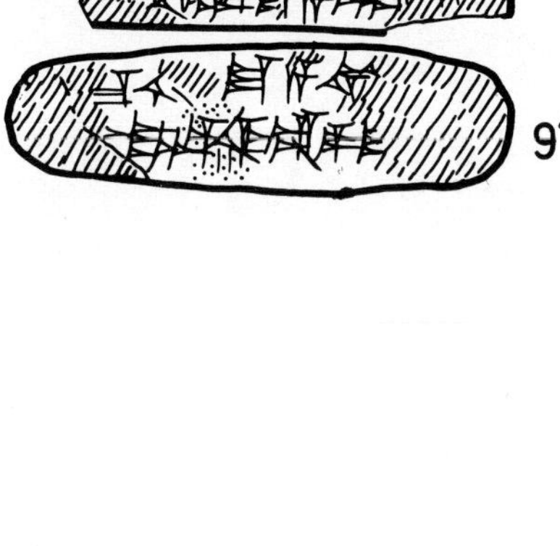

243

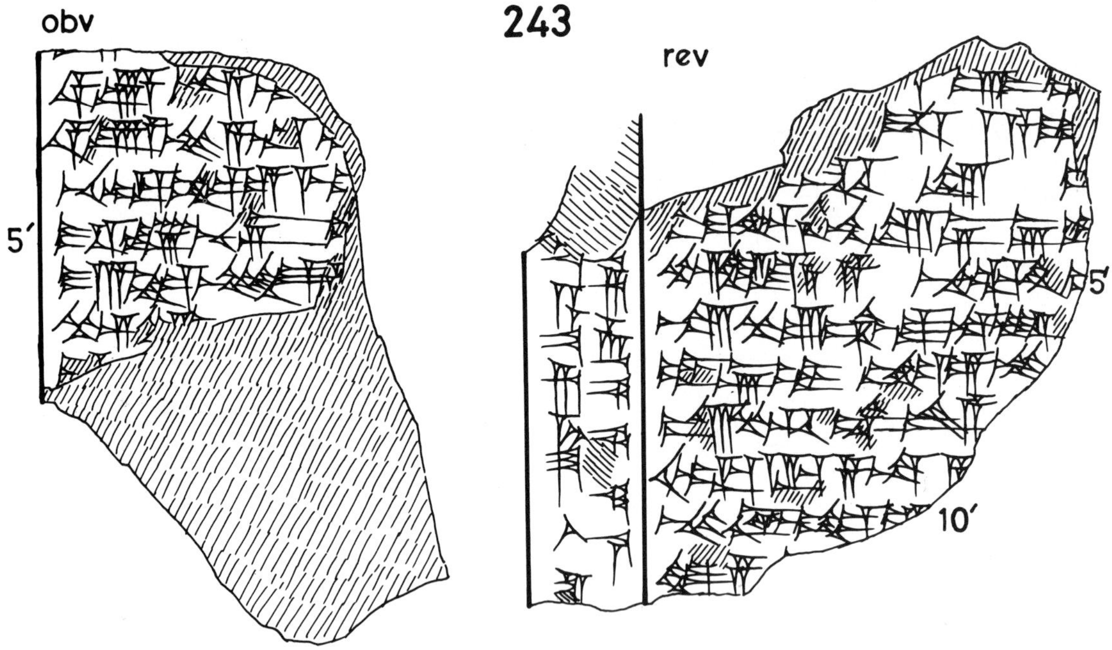

247

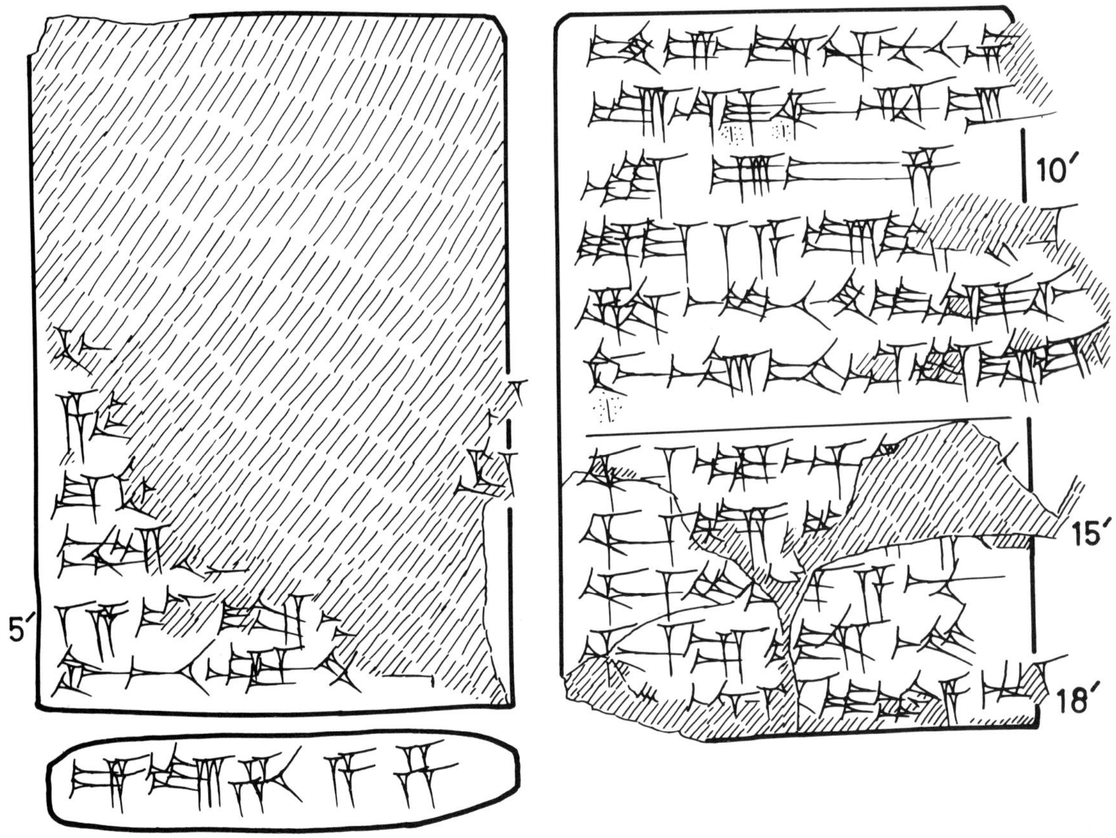

248

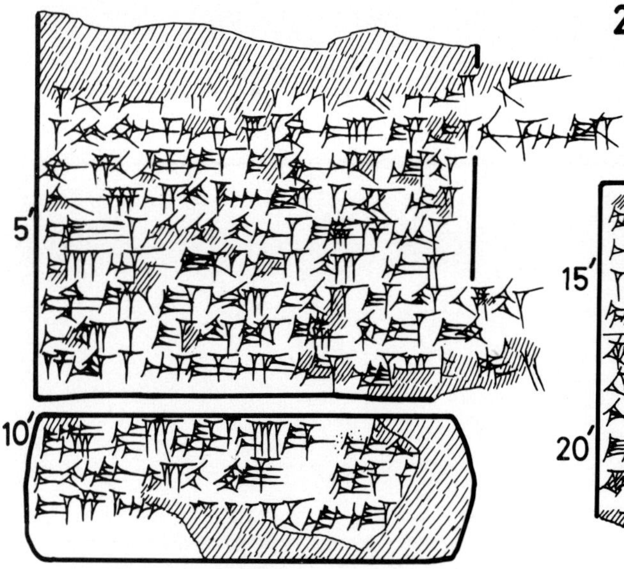

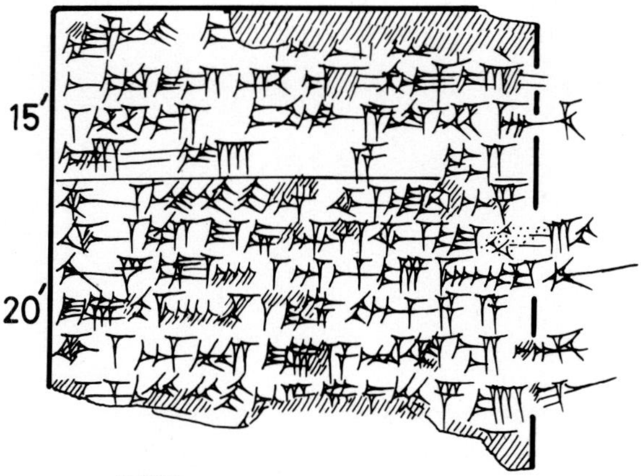

249

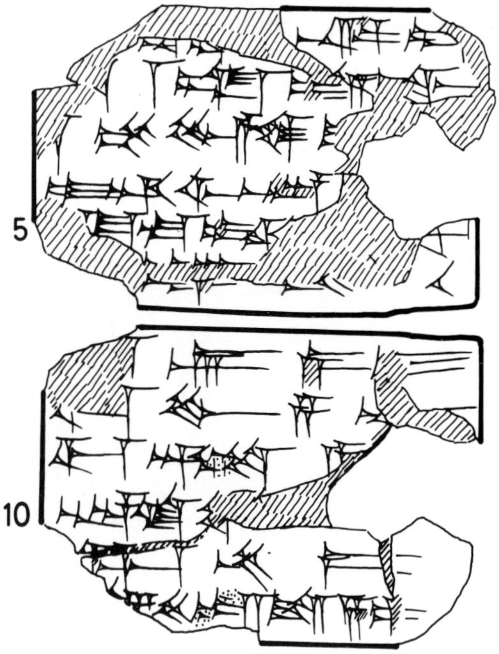

250

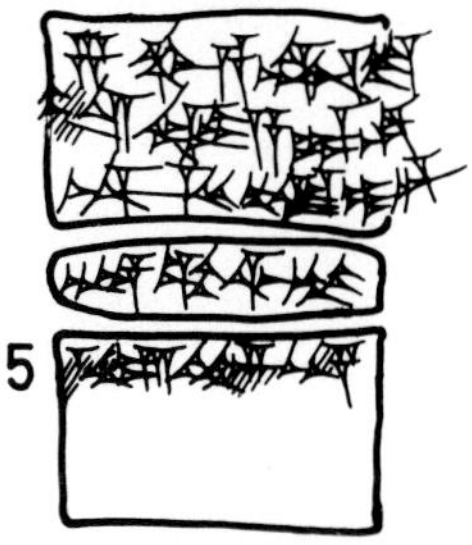

251

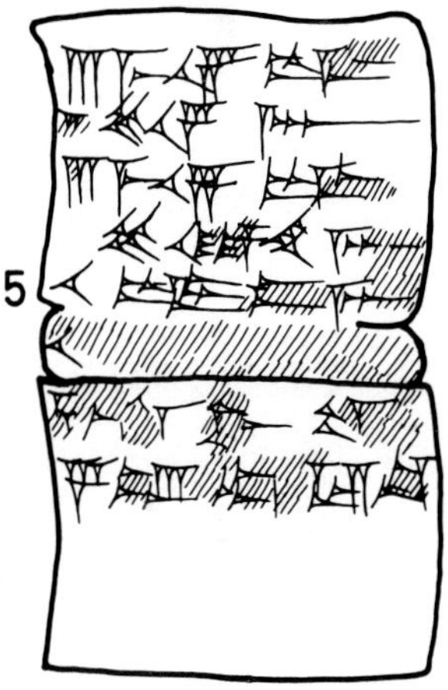

253

252

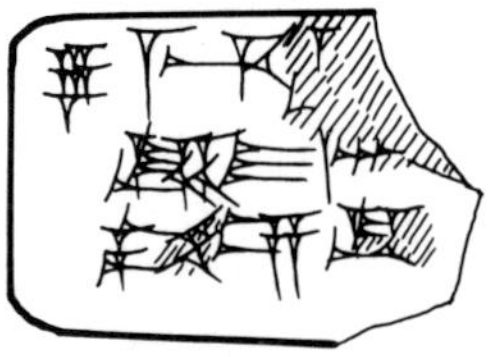

254

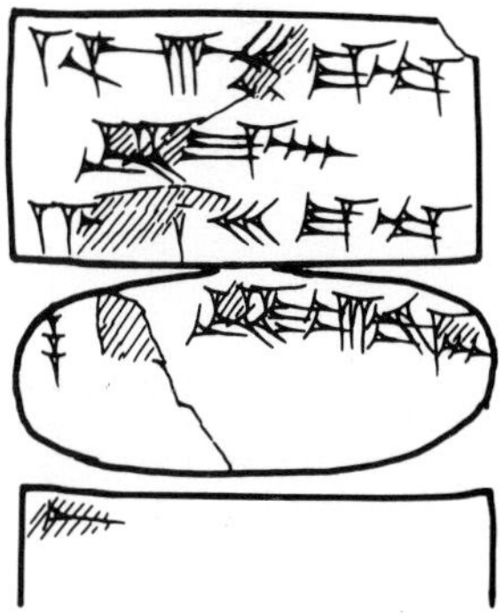

255

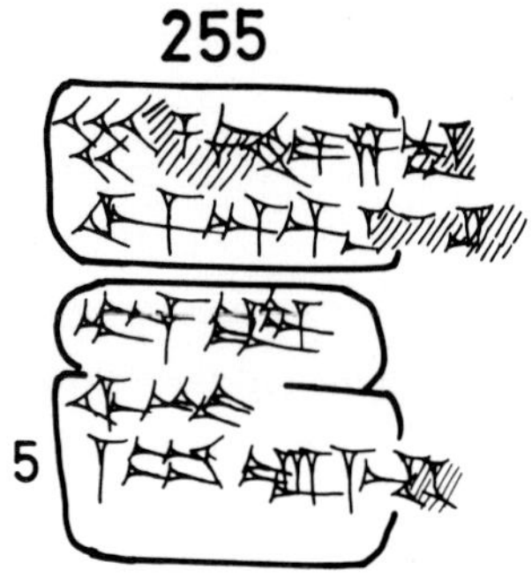

258

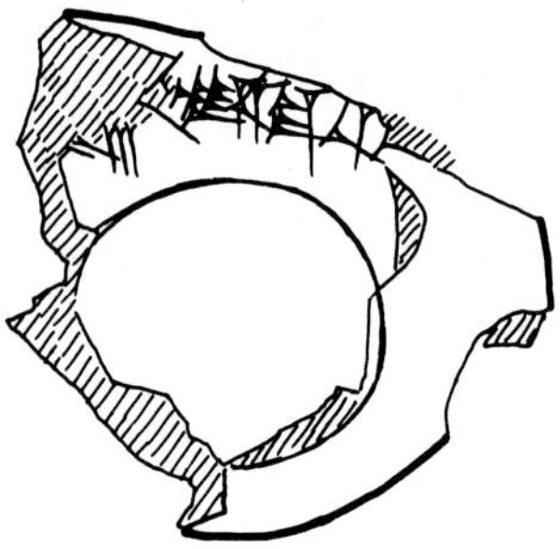

257

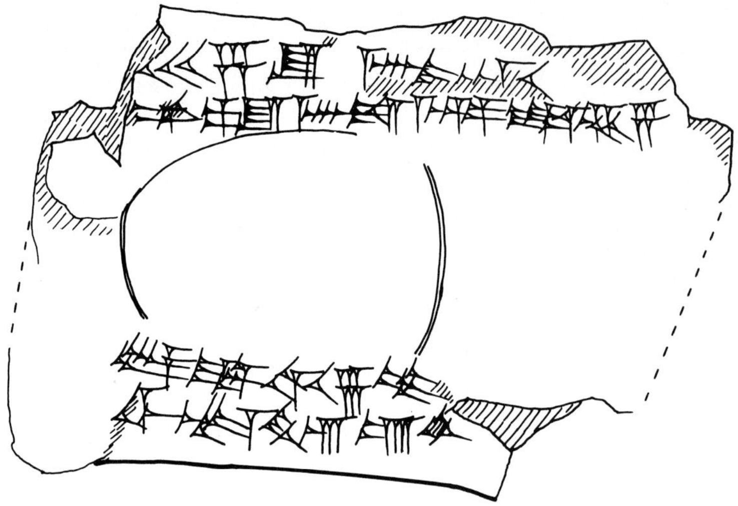

256

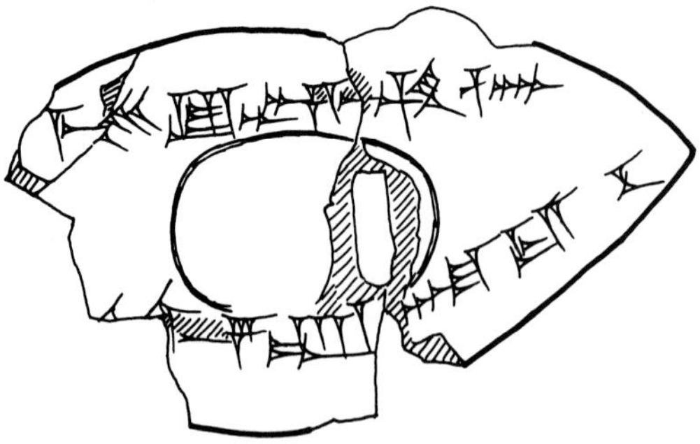

259

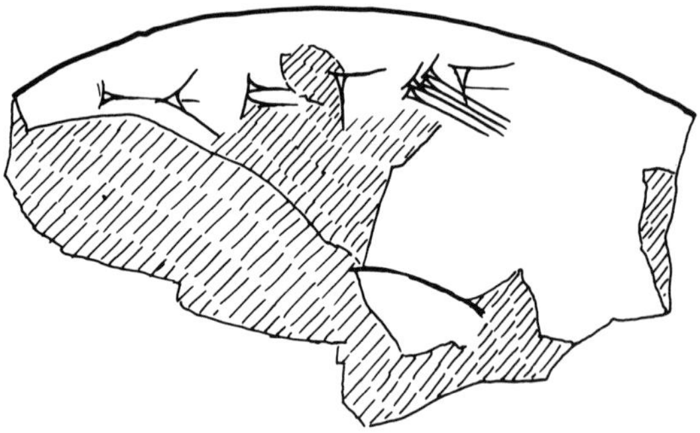

260

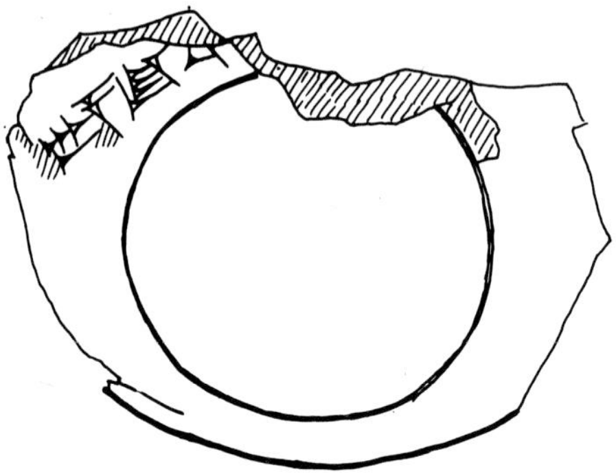

261

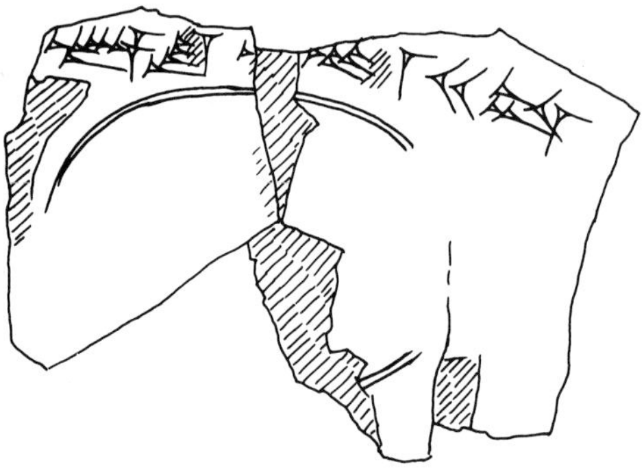

262

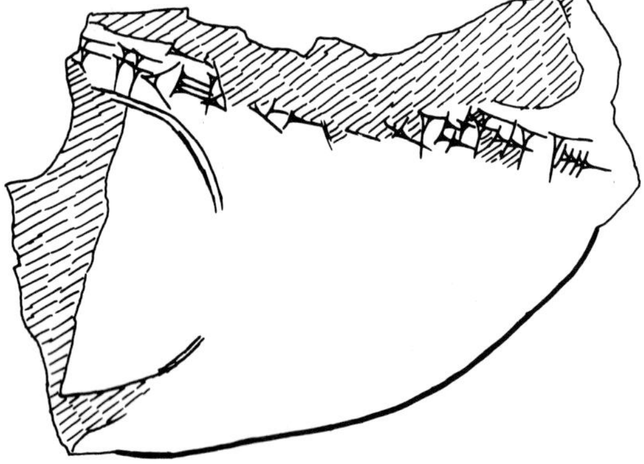

265

obv

rev

268

rev

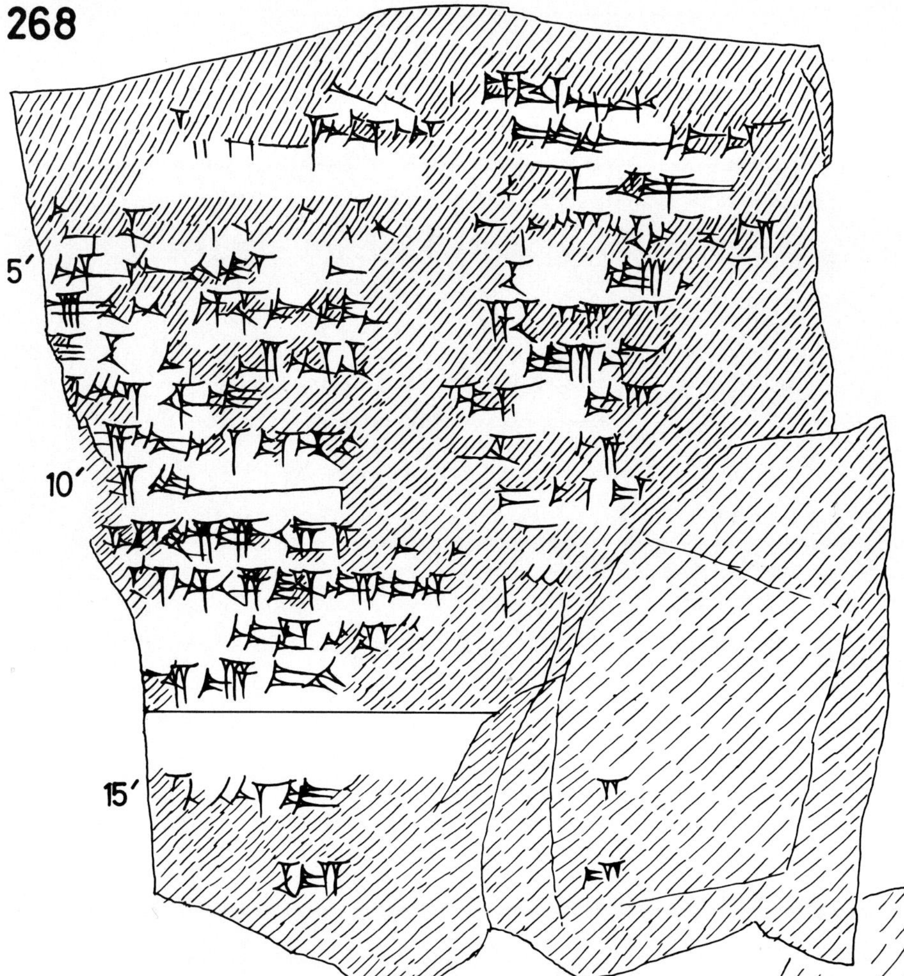

272

271

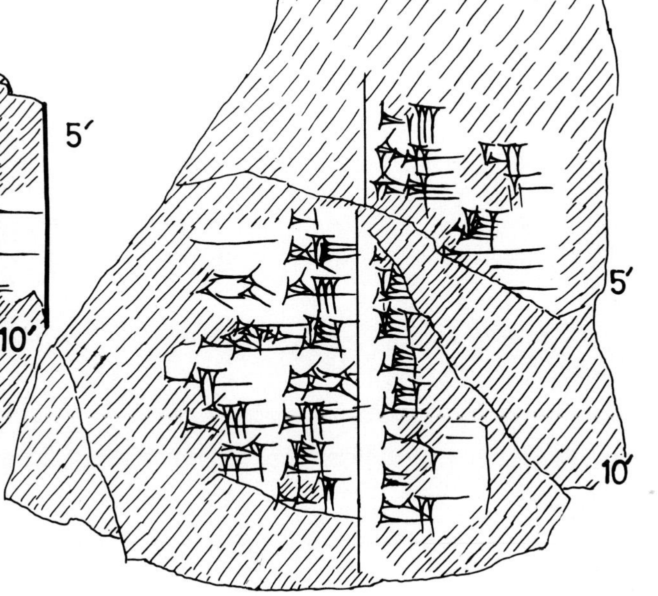

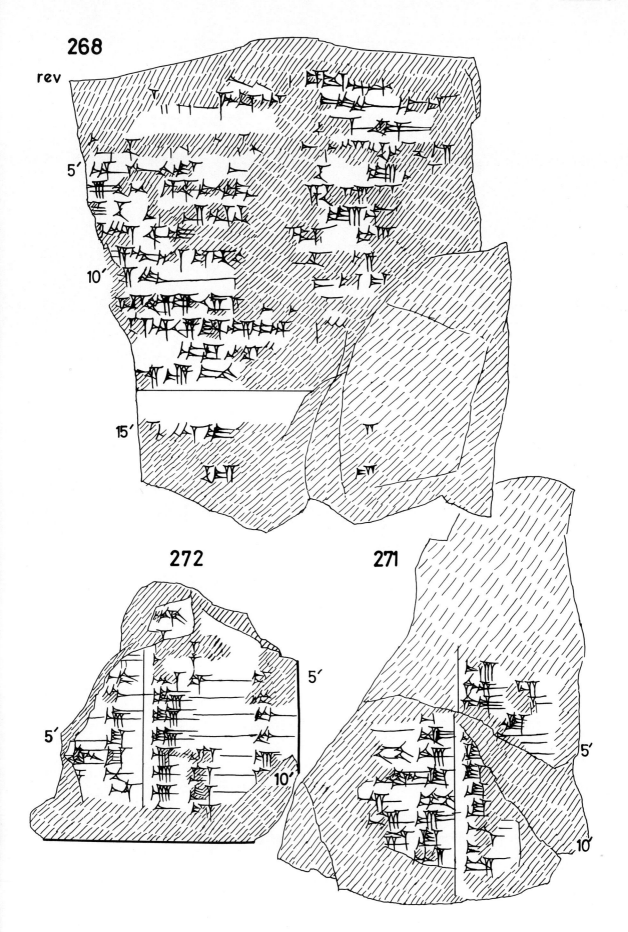

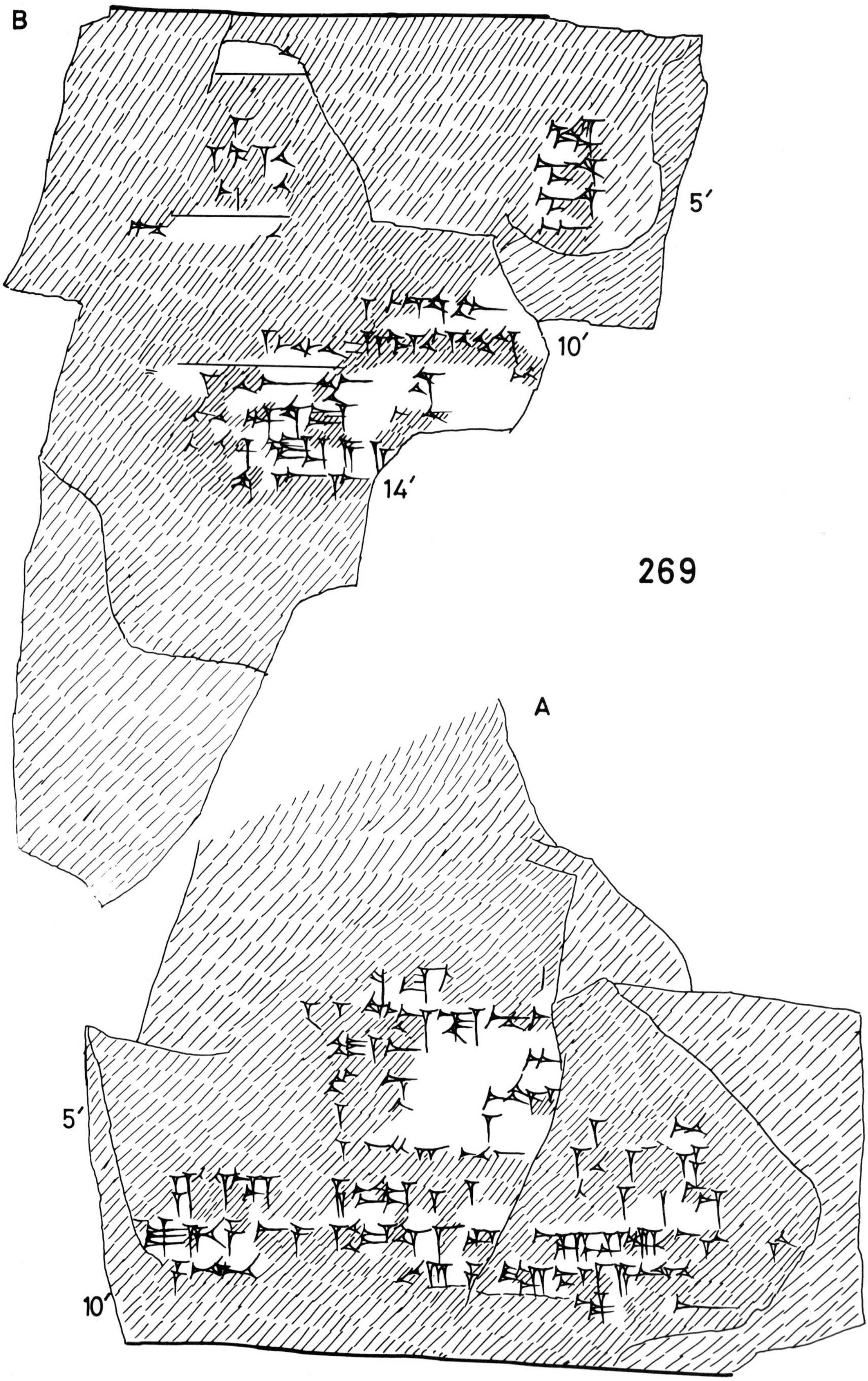

269

270

A

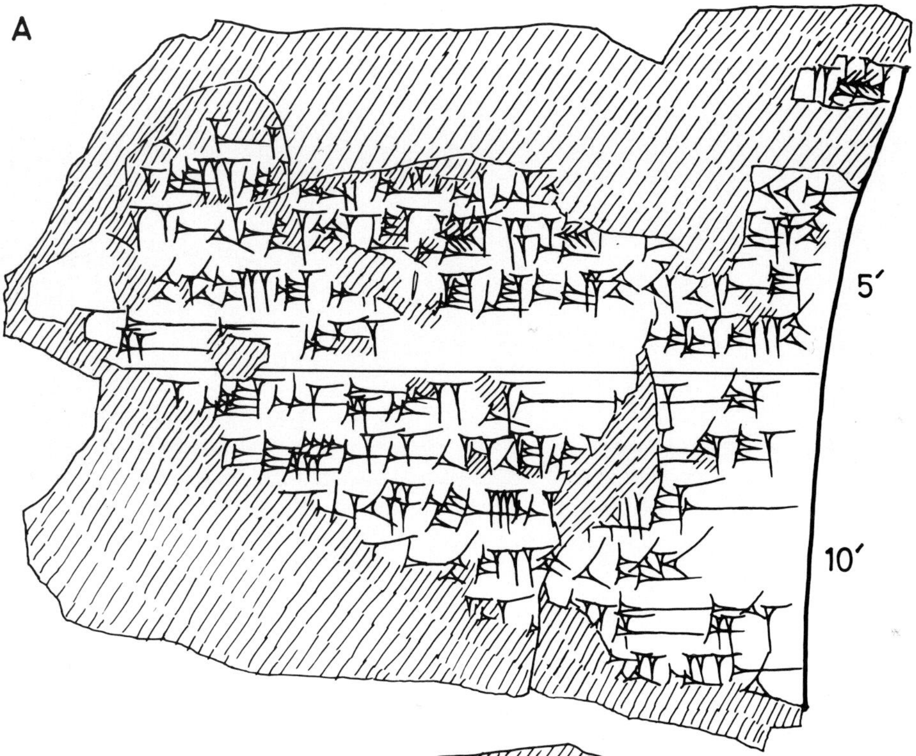

B

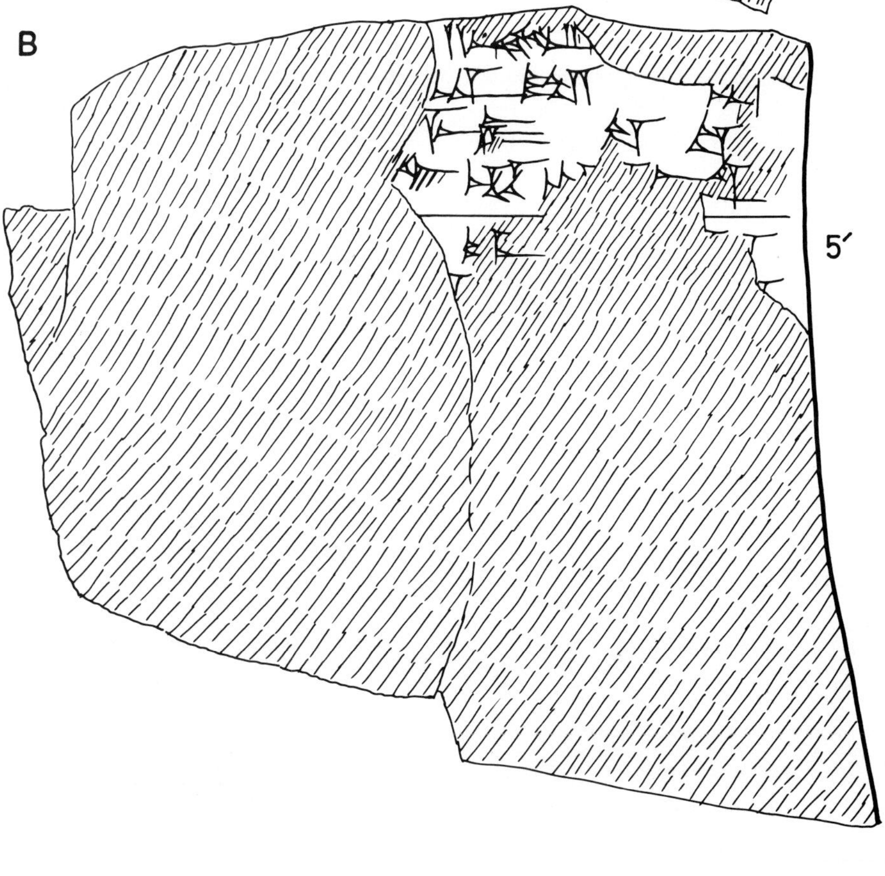

30

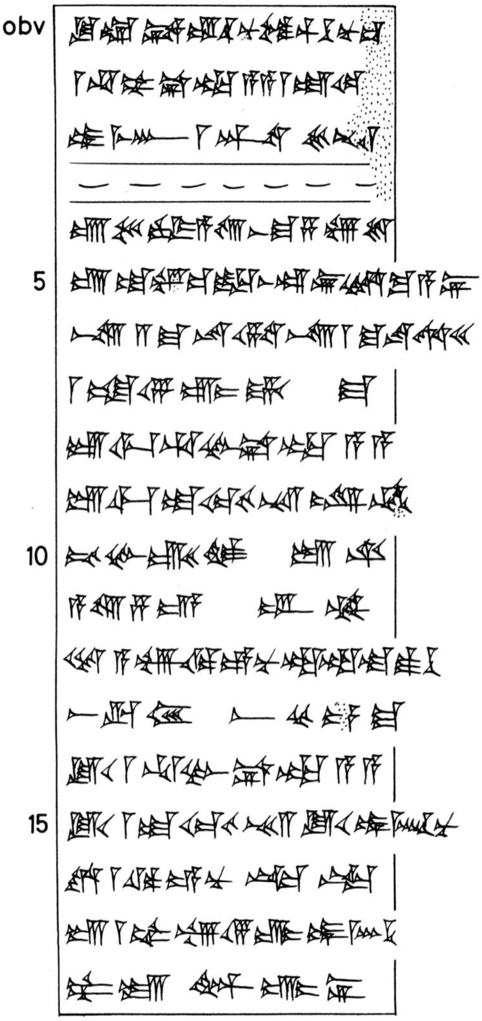

121

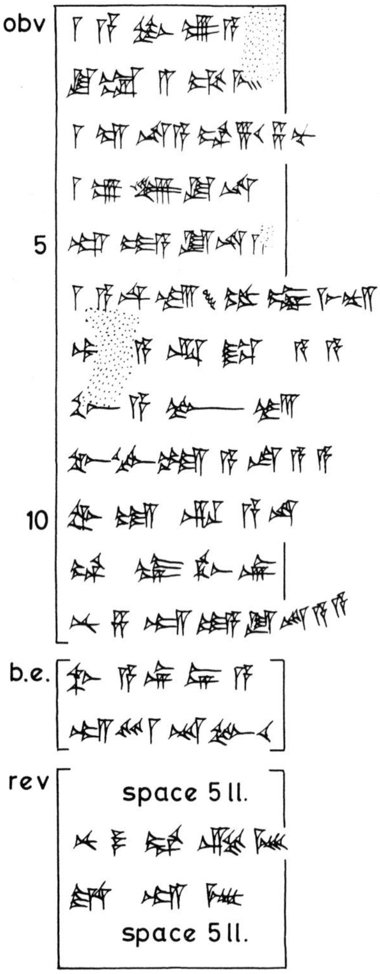

105

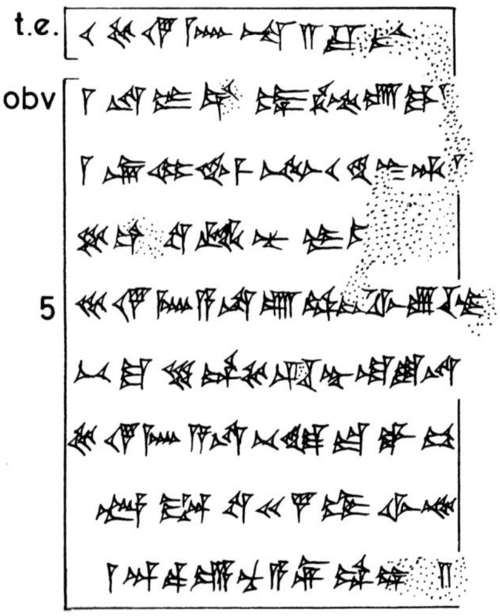

111

245

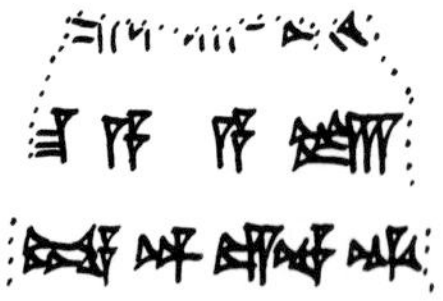

a. No. 155 obv.

b. No. 64

All approx. 1 : 1

a. No. 13

b. No. 9

c. No. 107 rev.

e. No. 183 obv.

d. No. 92 rev.

All approx. 1 : 1

a. No. 44

b. No. 6

c. No. 248 obv.

d. No. 196 obv.

All approx. 1 : 1

a. No. 18

b. No. 99, envelope

c. No. 219

All approx. 1 : 1

a. No. 171, cyl. seal

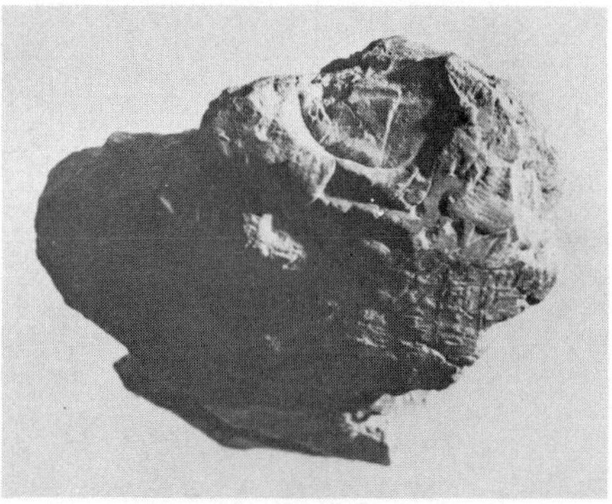

b. No. 171, stamp seal

c. No. 170

d. No. 66

e. No. 264

All approx. 1 : 1

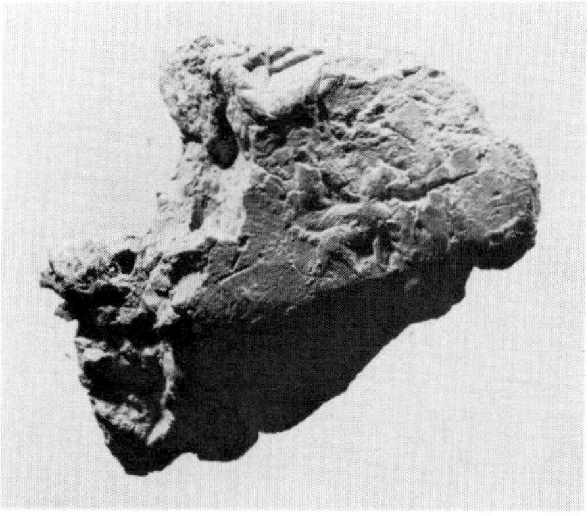

a. No. 173 obv.

b. No. 173 rev.

c. No. 132, cyl. seal (left)

d. No. 132, cyl. seal (right)

e. No. 172

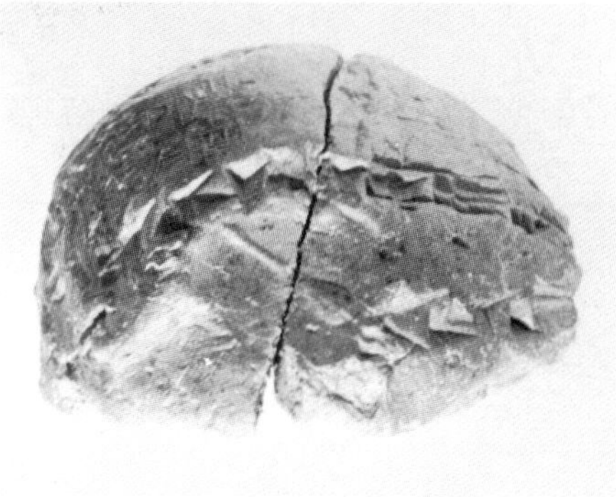

f. No. 132, stamp seal

All approx. 1 : 1

a. No. 237 obv.

b. No. 237 rev.

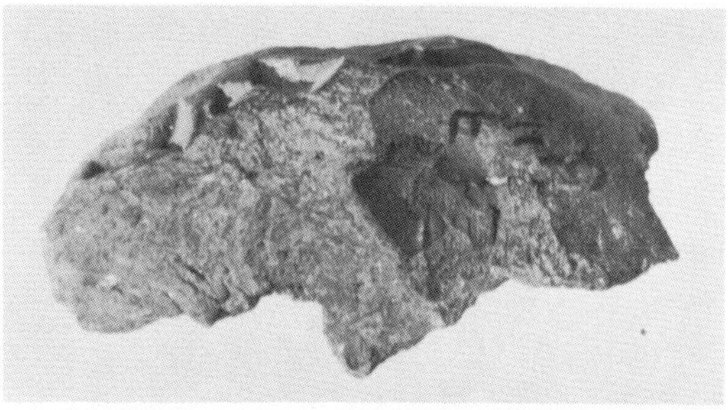

c. No. 259

d. No. 238 obv.

e. No. 238 rev.

f. No. 256

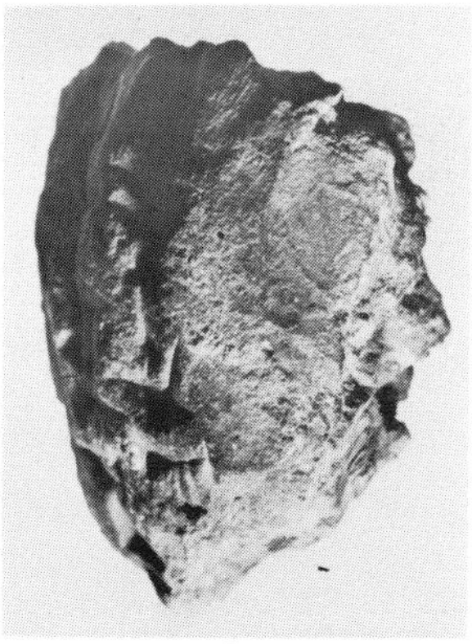

g. No. 239 obv.

h. No. 239 rev.

i. No. 261

j. No. 260

k. No. 257

All approx. 1 : 1

a. No. 234 obv.

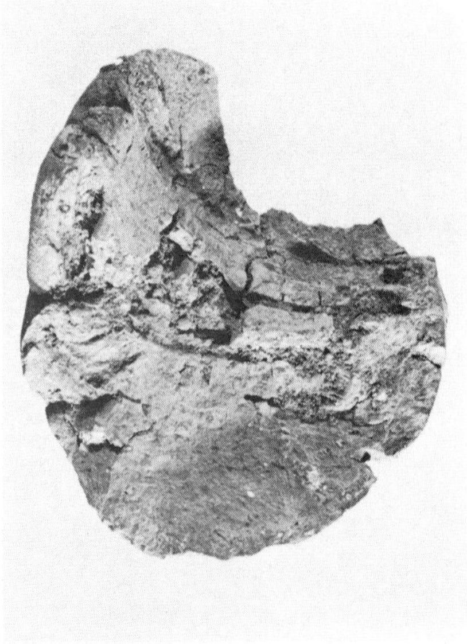

b. No. 234 rev.

c. No. 235 obv.

d. No. 235 rev.

e. No. 236

f, g. No. 229 (two fragments)

All approx. 1 : 1